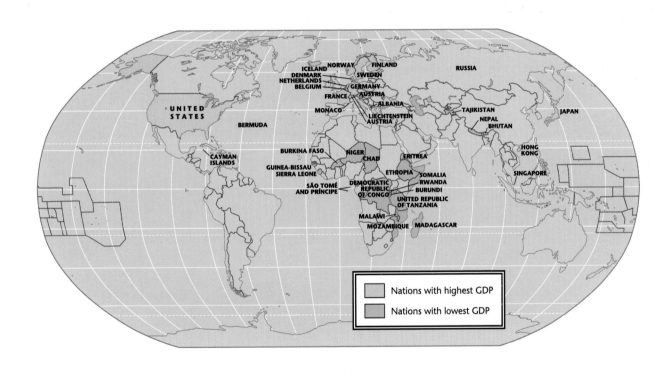

ICELAND NORWAY FINLAND
DENMARK SWEDEN RUSSIA
NETHERLANDS
BELGIUM GERMANY
FRANCE AUSTRIA
MONACO ALBANIA
LIECHTENSTEIN TAJIKISTAN JAPAN
AUSTRIA NEPAL
BHUTAN

UNITED
STATES

BERMUDA

HONG
KONG

CAYMAN BURKINA FASO NIGER ERITREA
ISLANDS CHAD SINGAPORE

GUINEA-BISSAU ETHIOPIA SOMALIA
SIERRA LEONE RWANDA

SÃO TOMÉ DEMOCRATIC BURUNDI
AND PRÍNCIPE REPUBLIC UNITED REPUBLIC
OF CONGO OF TANZANIA

MALAWI

MOZAMBIQUE MADAGASCAR

| | Nations with highest GDP |
| | Nations with lowest GDP |

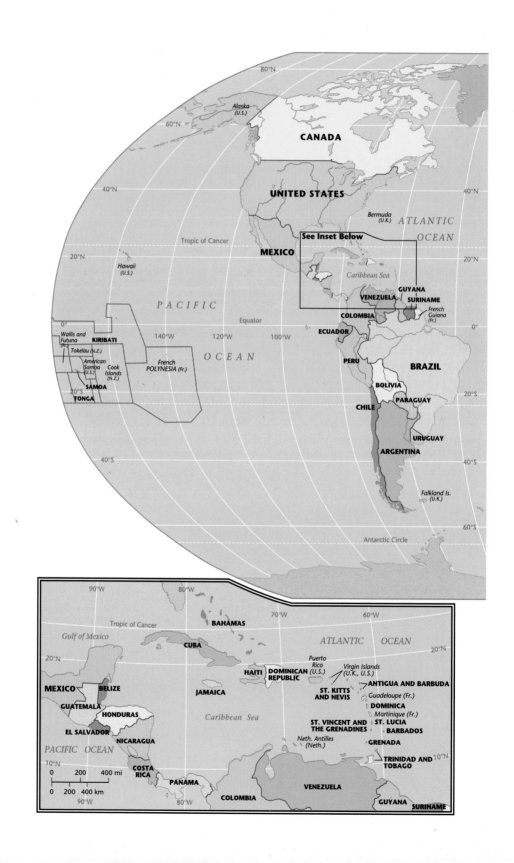

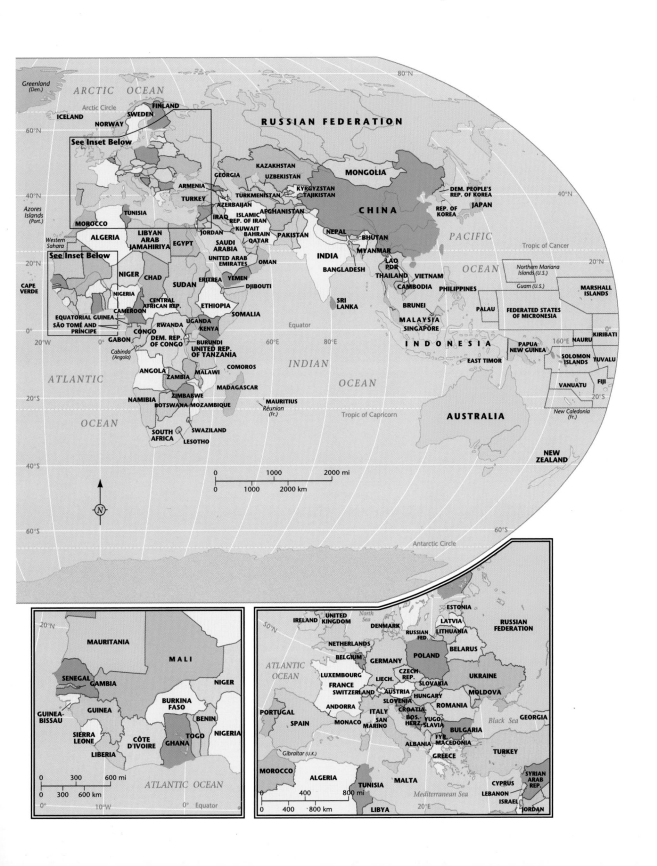

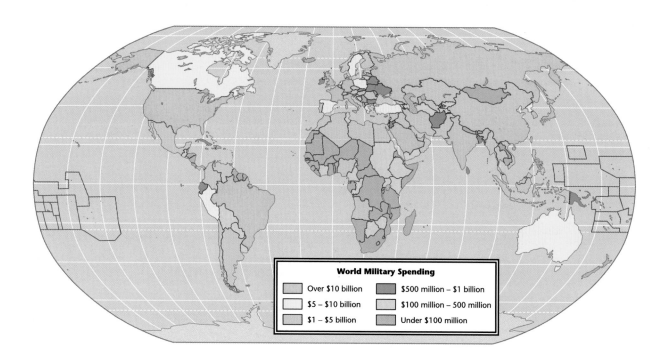

World Military Spending

Over $10 billion		$500 million – $1 billion
$5 – $10 billion		$100 million – 500 million
$1 – $5 billion		Under $100 million

International Relations
Politics and Economics
in the 21st Century

William Nester

St. John's University

WADSWORTH

THOMSON LEARNING   Australia • Canada • Mexico • Singapore • Spain • United Kingdom • United States

WADSWORTH

★

™

THOMSON LEARNING

Political Science Publisher: Clark Baxter
Senior Development Editor: Sharon Adams Poore
Assistant Editor: Jennifer Ellis
Marketing Manager: Diane McOscar
Print Buyer: April Reynolds
Permissions Editor: Joohee Lee
Production Service: Matrix Productions
Text Designer: Ellen Pettengel
Photo Researcher: Sarah Evertson
Copy Editor: Linda Purrington

Illustrators: Asterisk Group, Mapquest
Cover Designer: Qin-Zhong Yu, QYA Design Studio
Cover Photographs: Globe with flags: Bob Anderson/Masterfile;
    24-hour banking: PhotoDisc (PhotoLink); floor traders: Photo-
    Disc (Ryan McVay); handshake: PhotoDisc (Cartesia/ PhotoDisc
    Imaging); cargo ships: PhotoDisc (F. Schussler/ PhotoLink);
    protesters: PhotoDisc (Duncan Smith).
Compositor: ColorType, San Diego
Printer: Courier

Wadsworth/Thomson Learning
10 Davis Drive
Belmont, CA 94002-3098
USA

For information about our products, contact us:
Thomson Learning Academic Resource Center
1-800-423-0563
http://www.wadsworth.com

International Headquarters
Thomson Learning
International Division
290 Harbor Drive, 2nd Floor
Stamford, CT 06902-7477
USA

UK/Europe/Middle East/South Africa
Thomson Learning
Berkshire House
168–173 High Holborn
London WC1V 7AA
United Kingdom

Asia
Thomson Learning
60 Albert Street, #15-01
Albert Complex
Singapore 189969

Canada
Nelson Thomson Learning
1120 Birchmount Road
Toronto, Ontario M1K 5G4
Canada

Library of Congress Cataloging-in-Publication Data
Nester, William R. [date]
    International relations: politics and economics in the
21st century/ William Nester.
        p. cm.
    Includes bibliographical references and index.
    ISBN 0-8304-1552-1
    1. International relations. 2. Geopolitics. 3. War.
    4. International relations—Economic aspects. I. Title.
JZ1242.N47 2001
327—dc21   00-043353

With deepest love to my darling nieces,
Kayde, Sarah, Olivia, and Elizabeth

Brief Contents

Contents

Part 2

The Nation-State *and* International Relations 56
Spy Thriller: The United States versus China?

Part 3

Nonstate Forces *and* Actors *in* International Relations 142

The Great Debate: Sovereignty versus Human Rights

Part 4

Geopolitical Conflict *and* Cooperation 194

Was the Persian Gulf War (1990–1991) the Last Conventional War?

Contents

Part 7 — *The* Fate *of the* Earth 480

List of Tables

List of Maps and Graphs

The New World Order

Revolutionary events have changed the world dramatically in the decade leading up to the millennium 2000. The cold war ended. The Soviet empire collapsed. Communist and other authoritarian regimes are being overthrown around the globe. The White House and Kremlin agreed to deep cuts in nuclear and conventional forces. A comprehensive Middle East peace settlement between Israel and the Arab states is slowly, painfully emerging following the dramatic August 1993 agreement between Israel and the Palestinian Liberation Organization (PLO). The United Nations increasingly manages geopolitical conflicts that were formerly decided by the immediate participants. U.N. peacekeeping forces now patrol 17 countries. In the Persian Gulf War (1990–1991), the United Nations sanctioned an American-led coalition that drove Iraqi forces from Kuwait, and subsequently sent in technicians to dismantle Iraq's chemical, biological, and nuclear weapons program.

More than ever, the reality of international relations is quite different from the traditional emphasis on war and peace. Not only are most states at peace most of

Preface

the time, but only a tiny fraction of the relations between the world's more than 190 states contain even the hint of violence. The diminishing threat or reality of war between states, however, does not mean that international relations are conflict free. Although geopolitical issues dominate the headlines, it is geoeconomic disputes over trade, investments, immigration, pollution, deforestation, foreign aid, drug smuggling, and technology that largely shape international relations. As with geopolitical issues, states cooperate as much as they confront each other in geoeconomic conflicts. But cooperation usually comes only after hard bargaining and the wielding of power by participants. And although nation-states remain the primary actors, their power in different issues is increasingly constrained or enhanced by global economic forces, international laws, regimes, and organizations, multinational corporations, and international mass media and public opinion.

In the post–cold-war world, governments increasingly understand that their prosperity and security depend on working together to address common and worsening economic, environmental, and humanitarian problems. During the summer of 1997, the countries of the Far East collapsed financially, a disaster that threatened to drag down the global economy into a prolonged depression. The United States, leading European economies, the International Monetary Fund (IMF), and the World Bank forged a series of loan agreements with those countries that arrested their free fall, and later with Russia and Brazil in 1998, thus averting a global financial meltdown.

If financial panics immediately imperil the global economy, a range of inter-related, steadily deepening environmental crises such as the population explosion, the greenhouse effect, ozone layer depletion, global warming, deforestation, desertification, and species extinction pose a more distant but much worse threat to humanity. In June 1992, representatives of 178 countries gathered at the Earth Summit in Rio de Janeiro to debate and sign several treaties pledging themselves to alleviate some of those crises. Treaties signed by 154 states at Kyoto in December 1997 and at Buenos Aires in November 1998 commit them to deep cuts in fossil fuel emissions that cause the global greenhouse effect. Whether those states will fill those promises is questionable.

Regional economic alliances at once expand and challenge the global economy. The 15 nations of the European Union (the current name since January 1, 1993, for the former European Community) are struggling to forge tighter economic and political ties. On January 1, 1999, 11 EU members dissolved their currencies and central banks into one. Washington, Ottawa, and Mexico City are developing the North American Free Trade Association (NAFTA), which unites 380 million people. Led by Japan, the newly industrializing countries (NICs), and China, the Pacific basin is surpassing the Atlantic basin as the world's most economically dynamic area. Although the United States, Japan, and the European Union continue to attempt carefully to manage the global economy, they clash frequently over conflicting interests.

Yet all the countries in those regional blocs are among the 135 members of the World Trade Organization, which regulates the global economy under free trade principles. In other international forums, governments implemented agreements to combat terrorism and the illicit drug trade, and regulate the flow of refugees. Although international cooperation has alleviated some problems, countless others fester. Much of humanity remains scourged by disease, poverty, exploitation, and violence. All these forces shape and are shaped by international relations.

Globalization (deepening interdependence among countries) best characterizes these changes in international relations. Computers linked in the worldwide Internet are the essence of globalization. National leaders, corporate executives, scientists, engineers, terrorists, and anyone else plugged in have unprecedented ability to communicate, share information, resolve problems, or create new crises. People respond to that potential power in different ways. Some revel in their ability to shop, chat, or download information from the Internet. Others fear the dangers to personal or national security threatened by Y2K-type meltdowns, terrorist hackers, or spies into our private lives.

Students like to be challenged and stimulated. They want to learn more about the world and themselves. Few subjects are more fascinating or relevant than international relations. But textbooks and lectures that emphasize geopolitics with its overemphasis on issues of war and peace, give students a distorted view of the real world. Many professors recognize this and are searching for an international relations textbook that provides a balanced, in-depth analysis of the way the world really is.

A New Approach *to* Teaching International Relations

Scholars strive to keep up with the changes in their field. Sometimes the cumulative weight of new information and perspectives calls for a new way of analyzing the discipline. In *International Relations: Politics and Economics in the 21st Century,*

I seek to redress the traditional imbalance, which favors geopolitics at the expense of geoeconomics. International relations is not a Hobbesian "war of all against all" in which countries are either preparing for or engaging in war. In reality, most states are at peace most of the time. Unquestionably nation-states still dominate most international relations, and conflict is endemic. Yet most nation-states are primarily motivated by and engaged in geoeconomic rather than geopolitical struggles, and the parameters of those conflicts are shaped by a continually evolving global political economy. State sovereignty itself is increasingly at bay. Although the sovereign state's central role in international relations continues, it is being challenged by increasingly powerful forces such as international law and morality, governmental and private international organizations, multinational corporations, and a thickening web of complex geoeconomic interdependence or globalization.

This is not a traditional international relations textbook, emphasizing war and peace. Although some chapters necessarily emphasize one more than the other, overall this book provides a balanced view of geopolitics and geoeconomics, and their interrelationship.

More specifically, this text will differ from most in the following ways:

1. Most international relations texts follow one of three broad approaches to the subject—theoretical, thematic, or contemporary issues and case studies. This text integrates all three approaches in a balanced, comprehensive presentation.

2. Chapter 1 provides a summary of the major international relations (IR) theories, and each chapter illustrates the applicability or irrelevance of those theories to the real world.

3. This book remedies the traditional neglect of international political economy (IPE) or geoeconomics (a more succinct and increasingly popular term that balances the concept of geopolitics) by weaving the theme throughout each chapter as appropriate.

4. The book provides a balanced analysis of geopolitics and geoeconomics, and their interrelationship, rather than emphasizing one or the other.

5. Altogether nine chapters emphasize the interrelationship of geopolitics and geoeconomics, four of which emphasize the former and five, the latter.

6. This text opens with a succinct chapter on the global political economy's evolution through 1945, giving students a broad overview of the interrelated economic, political, technological, military, social, cultural, and power changes and continuities over the past five centuries, within which to understand the more specific concepts, subjects, and case studies of the following 17 chapters.

7. The book analyzes the "interdependent" relations among the industrialized countries in two chapters, and the "dependent" relations between industrialized and less developed countries in three other chapters.

8. An important theme in all the geoeconomic chapters is the relationship between internal and external forces in shaping a nation-state's development or underdevelopment, and the subsequent impact on national interests, policies, power, and international relations.

9. This text offers important sections on political and economic regionalism, with an emphasis on the European Union and North American Free Trade Association (NAFTA).

10. One chapter is devoted to global environmental crises and international attempts to manage them.

11. Throughout, this book analyzes the role of perceptions and misperceptions (image and reality) in shaping conflicts, interests, policies, and power.

12. Each section starts with a case study that illuminates key themes, trends, concepts, and problems.

13. Each chapter includes at least three short case studies, and about 100 graphs, maps, and photographs through the text vividly enhance the student's understanding.

14. A glossary at the back of the book clearly defines all key words introduced in the text.

15. The prevailing teaching methodology is socratic. Rhetorical questions are posed throughout the text and at each chapter's conclusion.

Elaboration *of the* Text's Themes

This text explores geopolitics with rigor and depth, with a particular focus on the balance of power, crisis management, imperialism, arms races, arms control, the cold war, conventional and nuclear warfare, regional conflicts, terrorism, ideology, and counterinsurgency. I also deal with more recent geopolitical issues and questions: Did ideological conflict really end with the cold war? Has nationalism replaced ideology as a driving force in international relations? Although the emphasis is on the cold war and international wars, an important section discusses the role of civil wars and independence struggles in international relations.

Most textbooks concentrate on geopolitics and generally present this subject very well. Yet geopolitical struggles occur within a global economy, a complex relationship that most textbooks do not explain. Politics and economics are inseparable. Economic alliances such as the European Union, NAFTA, and the Organization of Petroleum Exporting Countries (OPEC) can shape international relations as profoundly as do military alliances such as the North Atlantic Treaty Organization (NATO) and the former Warsaw Pact. Although the global economy is supposed to be based on principles of free trade, governments continually hurl accusation of unfair trade, investment, technology, financial, or industrial policy practices against each other. Democratic industrial countries joust not only with each other but also individually or collectively against less developed countries.

This book addresses liberal and neomercantilist theories and policies and offers clear explanations. One chapter focuses on macroeconomic, industrial, trade, and technology policy. Another evaluates the General Agreement on Trade and Tariffs (GATT), World Trade Organization (WTO), International Monetary Fund (IMF), World Bank, Organization for Economic Cooperation and Development (OECD), and other international economic organizations. Two others analyze, respectively, the conflicts and cooperation among the industrialized states, and between them and the less developed states.

Another important related theme explored is regionalism. Whereas nationalism is tearing some states apart, internationalism is uniting others. In just 40 years, the European Union has evolved into a highly unified economic and political system encompassing 340 million people. Meanwhile the United States is attempting to forge a North American common market. Starting in 1993, the 15 heads of state of the Asia Pacific Economic Cooperation (APEC) have met annually to work toward turning their organization into a free trade zone spanning the Pacific basin.

Major themes of this book are interdependence or globalization and the international efforts to create formal political and economic integration and cooperation. The world is knit together by an increasingly dense network of international organizations and law. According to the U.N. Charter, international politics and individual states should be governed by the ideals of human rights and morality. International relations will be increasingly bound by the formal channels of international organizations, regimes, and law, as well as a range of informal economic, social, political, cultural, moral, psychological, and environmental ties.

Whether the issue is geopolitical or geoeconomic, how do states determine their national interests in conflicts? How is foreign policy made and implemented? This book carefully examines all levels of policymaking, including the roles of individual psychology, group decision-making processes, bureaucratic politics, perceptions, interest groups, formal political systems, public opinion, culture, history, and the international system itself.

Some nations have developed rapidly, whereas others have stagnated. What accounts for a nation's ability to develop? Are development and underdevelopment explained primarily by internal or international forces? What links are there between economic and political development? Many of the world's authoritarian regimes are being swept away or challenged by a wave of popular democratic revolutions. How enduring will these changes be? How do the recent democratic revolutions compare to the communist revolutions of the earlier 20th century? What causes revolutions? This book explores the relationship between political and economic development. It takes a fresh look at questions of modernization, development, and dependence with a particular emphasis on the Third World.

We cannot understand the present unless we understand the past. One problem with many texts is that they give the student slices of history without showing how they all connect. Nor can we study—let alone understand—any subject in a vacuum; politics pervades all human pursuits. To remedy this deficiency, I have provided an analysis (in the first chapter) of the global political economy's development from the late Middle Ages through 1945. Elsewhere throughout the text the emphasis is on the world from 1945 to today. All along, politics is the core concept for exploring the dynamic interrelationship among such international forces as trade, war, technology, the nature and policies of government, development, underdevelopment, ideology, culture, ecology, and psychology. Succinct case studies, many from the last few years, illuminate these related themes.

Approaching an old subject from a new and more comprehensive perspective is a challenge. Yet I believe this exploration of geopolitics and geoeconomics is not only workable, but will help both professors and students gain an deeper understanding of international relations well into the 21st century.

ACKNOWLEDGMENTS

Four individuals provided me with outstanding help in preparing this textbook. I am forever grateful to Clark Baxter for his strategic vision, good humor, and faith; Merrill Peterson for his care in assembling the book's many elements; Linda Purrington for her meticulous copy editing; and St. John's University student George Zaharatos, who found all the URLs and patiently guided me through the bewildering Internet maze. I would also like to thank the following readers of my book who offered interesting and valuable suggestions: Kathy L. Powers, University of Arizona; John P. Willerton, University of Arizona; Renee G. Scherlen, Appalachian State University; and Vincent Wei-cheng Wang, University of Richmond.

International Relations

W hy did violence explode at the WTO Seattle Summit? What issues did the protestors believe were vital enough to risk their own lives or commit destruction to uphold? Was this a human rights protest that was brutally crushed by the secret police of some dictatorship?

The riots broke out in the usually tranquil city of Seattle around a World Trade Organization (WTO)[1] meeting attended by representatives of its 134 members. A spectrum of over 500 groups opposed to WTO policies rallied

Why would anyone protest, let alone riot, over trade? Don't we all benefit from the cheaper prices and more abundant and diverse goods that freer trade provides?

Not necessarily. Labor and environmental groups maintain that the costs of trade under the current WTO rules may exceed the benefits. The labor groups oppose the loss of their jobs to poorer countries with lower wages, standards, and benefits. Environmentalists argue that more trade means more production, which leads to more

Part One Development *of the* Global Political Economy: Swimming Against *the* Globalization Tide: Rioting *at the* WTO Seattle Summit, 1999

in Seattle. Most were environmental and labor groups, and nearly all were committed to peaceful protest. During a march of 30,000 demonstrators, a small number of self-proclaimed anarchists provoked the riots in which over 600 people were arrested, scores injured, and several million dollars worth of property was damaged.

pollution, which hurts everyone through deepening world crises such as global warming, the greenhouse effect, ozone and water depletion, desertification, deforestation, species extinction, and the population explosion. Third World countries tend not to limit the pollution spewing from their factories, fields, automobiles, and homes. The labor and environmental groups, however, are not against trade. They actually support a stronger WTO that requires its members to impose strict regulations to protect labor and the environment.

But the protests were not just in the streets. The WTO itself was split among various factions that opposed each other's proposals. Countries such as Japan, whose firms are accused of dumping goods below cost in the United States to bankrupt their American rivals, tried to get Washington to dismantle its antidumping laws. The United States, Australia, Canada, and Argentina sought the elimination of agricultural trade barriers in Japan and Europe. India, Egypt, and Brazil led a coalition of Third World countries opposed to American efforts to get them to enact labor and environmental regulations.

In all, the WTO meeting was a disaster. The conference dissolved without even issuing a final communiqué, let alone an agreement. The WTO and the constructive labor and environmental groups alike were discredited by the violence and breakdown in talks, both within and outside the conference hall.

Globalization hit a large road bump in Seattle. The riots and deadlock remind us that although interdependence among the world's peoples will steadily grow for the foreseeable future, globalization spawns losers as well as winners.

Yet dramatic as those events were, the WTO Seattle conference's most important results were not the protests and deadlock, but the way in which the issues were confronted. A swarm of nongovernmental organizations (NGOs)

Sion Touhig/Corbis Sygma

lobbied an international intergovernmental organization (IGO), the World Trade Organization. Globalization both promotes and is promoted by IGOs and NGOs. The world's proliferating economic, social, cultural, technological, environmental, and thus political ties provide IGOs and NGOs alike with an increasingly potent role in shaping international relations. The interrelated Internet and global news revolutions have especially empowered NGOs. With email, web sites, and the CNN news channel on television, NGOs can gather information, members, and allies; mobilize "NGO swarms" to lobby governments, IGOs, corporations, and each other; and create news stories beamed instantly by CNN and other 24-hour broadcasters to television viewers around the world. And all this can occur with a few taps on globally linked computer keyboards.

Thus the WTO Seattle conference represents new forces that complement and compete with more traditional forces of international relations. Although nation-states remain, for now, the core of international relations, globalization complicates the ways they promote their interests, in exciting and at times exasperating new ways. Globalization provides new opportunities and raises new problems for nation-states, regions, groups, and individuals all around the world.

What has changed and what has stayed the same in international relations over time? How do conflict and cooperation shape international relations? What role do traditional issues of war and peace (geopolitics) play in an increasingly globalized world run by geoeconomics? Stay linked—or tuned, as once was said.

Contents

Chapter 1 Theories *and* Realities *of the* Changing Nature *of* International Relations

Key Concepts and Terms

Order *or* Anarchy?

During his 1991 State of the Union address, President George Bush argued that international relations were fundamentally changing into a "new world order" in which "diverse nations are drawn together in common cause to achieve the universal aspirations of mankind: peace and security, freedom and the rule of law." Is a *new world order* emerging, as the president declared, and does a new world order imply the existence of an old world order? Or is the international system inherently anarchic, with all states engaged in a perpetual war against each other? Are international politics characterized by order or anarchy?

Clearly, there is no world government that issues laws, regulates behavior, and punishes violators. International relations are shaped by the countless actions of over 190 *nation-states* which, by definition, enjoy *sovereignty*—the freedom to answer to no higher authority than themselves and to act in no other interest than their own.

Is Sovereignty *at* Bay?

Yet sovereignty is more a concept than a reality; international relations is more than a Hobbesian "war of all against all"; and the world is more than a Tower of Babel with everyone speaking and acting at cross-purposes. There is a world system or world order. Governments, corporations, international organizations, and individuals act within the parameters of the global political economy's rules and power distribution. Most states behave and clash within relatively orderly channels that are shaped formally with thousands of international organizations, regimes, and laws, and informally through international customs and morality. All states obey the global system's rules most of the time—some states, of course, much more consistently than others. The strands of that world order in which states act are constantly being knit into an increasingly elaborate web of economic, political, military, nuclear, legal, organizational, ecological, social, psychological, and cultural ties. Complex *interdependence* or *globalization* has dramatically changed the traditional manifestations of global power and relations.

Although most would agree that the world is becoming increasingly interdependent, do these increased ties between countries and people represent a completely new world order? Not necessarily. A world political economy or order has been evolving since the first Portuguese and Spanish adventurers set sail for the world's far corners over 500 years ago. Until recently, the development of that world order was slow. Although countries increasingly traded, allied, and negotiated with each other, the divisions between them far outweighed the ties, and nations often settled their conflicts with war or the threat of war. Since 1945, however, despite—or more likely because of—the cold war, the interdependent world order has developed rapidly and profoundly. Today every human lives under the shadow of potential nuclear and ecological extinction. Nearly all humans are tied together through their country's membership in the United Nations, through numerous political and economic international organizations, and through the benefits of global trade, telecommunications, travel, and the Internet.

Why is interdependence important to us? Globalization means that any major international event can affect us one way or another, and likewise, every major American public issue is, to varying degrees, an international issue. When the

sovereignty authority and self-rule in an independent political system, as in a sovereign **nation-state.** During the early modern era, many political philosophers argued that sovereignty, or the locus of supreme power, should rest in monarchs. During the middle and late modern eras, many political philosophers maintained that sovereignty should lie in all of a state's citizens.

globalization the ever more complex interdependence embracing all nations and individuals in the world.

WTO talks break down, when *OPEC (the Organization of Petroleum Exporting Countries)* raises oil prices, when tropical forests are destroyed, when the ozone layer is eaten away, when the Tokyo stock market plunges, we all, in tiny and usually unobservable ways, are affected. Likewise, when Washington imposes tariffs or fails to reduce the budget deficit, when pollution drifts across to Canada, when the U.S. Defense Department builds new weapons systems, when the economy expands or contracts, we affect the world. The differences between international and domestic issues are increasingly blurred.

Geopolitics *and* Geoeconomics

Yet are relations between states today fundamentally different from the way they were half a century ago? International politics spans conflict in the geopolitical and geoeconomic realms (or the IPE—*international political economy*—as it is sometimes known). *Geopolitics* includes disputes over territory, beliefs, behaviors, or some other issue in which those involved might well consider using some sort of violence to resolve that conflict. Territorial expansion, struggles for independence and human rights, arms races, drug smuggling, refugees, and ideological strife are a few prominent geopolitical conflicts. *Geoeconomics* includes those issues that can be managed by any means short of violence. Disputes over trade, intellectual property, economic development, *multinational corporations (MNCs), industrial policy,* and the environment are several important geoeconomic issues.

Geopolitical conflicts almost invariably have some geoeconomic basis. Sometimes geoeconomic conflicts are the primary reasons states either threaten to or actually do go to war. The *trade wars* of the early 1930s, for example, plunged the world into a severe depression that fueled the rise of *fascism* and *imperialism* in Japan, Germany, and Italy. Each of those states sought security in creating a largely autarchic empire. When participants in a geoeconomic conflict consider using violence, it stops being geoeconomic and becomes geopolitical.

Undoubtedly, the life-and-death issues of geopolitics are more dramatic and pressing than geoeconomics. In geopolitics, a nation's security is sometimes decided through war. In geoeconomics, a nation's security is determined by the sum of countless economic policies and negotiations: Prosperity and deprivation for individuals, industries, and national economies are shaped by thousands of cuts and parries rather than one decisive blow.

In many geopolitical and geoeconomic conflicts, there are distinct aggressors and defenders. Military assaults by one state on another are easily chronicled. On August 2, 1990, Iraq clearly violated international law when it invaded and conquered Kuwait. The United States received U.N. approval to organize and lead a military alliance against Iraq if it did not withdraw from Kuwait by a January 15, 1991, deadline. The deadline passed with Iraq still in Kuwait. The alliance then attacked and expelled Iraq's army from Kuwait.

Clear aggressors and defenders in geoeconomic struggles are less easy to determine, although there are some cases. For example, Japanese corporations have been particularly notorious for *dumping,* or selling their goods, below production cost, in other countries to capture market share from their foreign rivals. International law prohibits dumping and allows governments to retaliate against the aggressive firms. The United States, the European Union, and other countries have imposed penalties against Japanese and other foreign firms found guilty of dumping.

But in most geopolitical and geoeconomic conflicts, it is difficult and sometimes impossible to determine which side is the aggressor and which is the aggrieved. Take the geopolitical conflict over four tiny islands north of Japan, occupied by Russia and claimed by both Russia and Japan. Both Moscow and Tokyo provide in-depth legal and moral arguments for ownership of the disputed islands and the issue remains deadlocked. And what about the geoeconomic question of whether multinational corporations give more than they take from a poor nation's development? Again, there are compelling arguments either way.

The Primacy of Geoeconomics in International Relations

Is geopolitics or geoeconomics more prevalent in international relations? Geopolitical issues certainly make the headlines. During the 1990s, the Persian Gulf, Bosnian, and Kosovo Wars; the fighting between India and Pakistan, Yugoslavia and Bosnia, Azerbaijan and Armenia; civil wars in Peru, Angola, and Sudan; North Korea's nuclear weapons program; conflict between Israelis and Palestinians; and coups in Haiti, Guatemala, and Sierra Leone were all distinctly geopolitical conflicts in which some potential and often actual use of violence was present within and/or between states.

Yet although geoeconomic issues are relegated more often to a newspaper's back pages, if reported at all, they are much more common than geopolitical crises. Most states are at peace most of the time. States rarely have their vital interests threatened or threaten the vital interests of others. Every day the world's 190-plus states conduct thousands of negotiations over thousands of issues in either bilateral or multilateral forums. The vast majority of these issues, however, directly involve the security of influential interest groups rather than the entire nation. In June 1991, after tough and often bitter negotiations, the United States and Japan signed an agreement whereby Tokyo promised to allow greater access for American semiconductor makers in Japan's markets. In April 1992, the United States and Chile began discussing the possibility of forming a *free trade* agreement. In May 1992, the *European Community* (now the European Union) agreed to cut back its agricultural subsidies if the United States and Japan would do the same. In November 1992, Washington threatened to launch a trade war against the European Community if it did not agree to cut back its farm subsidies. These four examples were typical geoeconomic issues whose impact beyond the interest groups immediately involved was unnoticeable. Nonetheless, these issues involve vital questions over power, wealth, employment, income, technology, and national security.

Some geoeconomic issues, however, are potentially as devastating as war. The *greenhouse effect,* in which industrial pollution traps heat in the atmosphere and may cause global temperatures to rise as much as 9 degrees Fahrenheit over the next century, could lead to widespread crop failures, desertification, and the flooding of sea-level land. The result could be starvation, malnutrition, and misery for most people on the planet.

Was *the* Cold War *the* War *to* End All Wars?

Like World War I, World War II ended with the great promise that it had been the war to end all wars. By September 1945, attempts by the totalitarian governments of Japan, Germany, and Italy to conquer the world were decisively defeated. Henceforth, it was hoped, all the world's nations would settle all conflicts peacefully and justly through the *United Nations*. Never again would the world's economy break down into trade wars and depression as it did in the 1930s. Instead, a global free trade system would be created and carefully managed by networks of international trade and finance organizations such as the *General Agreement for Trade and Tariffs (GATT,* later the *World Trade Organization, WTO*), the *International Monetary Fund (IMF)*, and the *World Bank.* All the world's peoples would realize their national and human rights to be free as promised by the Atlantic and U.N. charters.

These dreams proved short-lived. The wartime alliance between the United States and Soviet Union broke down into nearly five decades of geopolitical conflict known as the cold war, fueled by diametrically opposed ideologies, security needs, and threat perceptions between American and Soviet-led blocs. The cold war is now over, with the Soviet empire dismembered and communism renounced almost everywhere except in China, Cuba, Vietnam, and North Korea. The cold war was ended partly by four decades of an American-led *containment* of the Soviet Union, and partly by communism's inability to satisfy even the most basic economic, let alone political, needs of the people under its grip.

Some argue that the world is converging politically. During the 1980s and 1990s, outright *liberal democracies* or quasi-democracies replaced *authoritarian* governments around the world, not just in the former Soviet empire but from Taiwan to Nicaragua, and Nepal to South Korea. Today in the year 2000, according to the human rights organization Freedom House, around 60 percent of the world's countries have liberal democratic constitutions. However, another human rights organization, Amnesty International, pointed out that in the year 2000 nearly 60 percent of the governments of all countries systematically abused human rights. What explains this contradiction? Although Freedom House emphasizes the progress toward human rights and Amnesty International the continuing abuses, both note a steady improvement. Monthly, it seems, another country or two sheds the more outrageous forms of political oppression and adopts the trappings and sometimes the institutions and values of liberal democracy. There is clearly a correlation between economic and political development. The demands for political representation and rights grow along with a middle class.

Assuming that this general trend toward democratization will continue, what impact will it have on international relations? War, many argue, is history's engine. Liberal democracies have never fought each other. The more liberal or quasi-liberal the countries, the fewer the international wars.

Yet war will continue to plague humanity. Liberal democratic states will continue to fight authoritarian states, and authoritarian states will continue to fight each other. But the number of international wars will likely diminish as all countries become so bound by the matrix of global economic and cultural ties that using force to settle international conflicts becomes increasingly costly, if not unthinkable. Complex interdependence and the slow spread of liberal democracy have reduced the relative number of geopolitical conflicts and increased the relative number of geoeconomic conflicts.

Increasingly, war will be within rather than between sovereign states. Although the world is uniting in many ways, parts of it are rapidly disintegrating into civil war and anarchy. *Nationalism* rather than *internationalism* is the driving force behind the independence struggles of scores of suppressed peoples around the world. Although the eastern European states and the former Soviet republics won a largely bloodless independence from the Soviet Union, Kurds and Shiites still struggle for independence from Iraq, Tibetans from China, Tamils from Sri Lanka, Sikhs from India, Palestinians from Israel, and Chechens from Russia, to name a few.

There is more hope, however, for demobilizing most of the vast arsenals and military forces facing each other across international borders. The cold war's nuclear and conventional arms races created weapons stockpiles capable of destroying the planet. Global military spending in 1990 alone was a mind-boggling $950 billion, of which the United States and Soviet Union accounted for half. The planet groaned under the weight of over 50,000 nuclear bombs, many of them resting atop *intercontinental ballistic missiles* (*ICBMs*).

Yet even during the cold war's height, Washington and Moscow tried to rein in the arms race and did succeed in signing several agreements capping the deployment of certain nuclear weapons types. In 1987, Washington and Moscow signed the first treaty, *Intermediate Range Forces* (INF), to actually eliminate a class of nuclear weapons. With the cold war's end, the superpowers and their allies have announced treaties and unilateral promises to pare their nuclear and conventional forces even more sharply. The *Warsaw Pact*, through which Moscow simultaneously threatened western Europe and subjugated eastern Europe, was dismantled in June 1991, and the troops were sent home. Although the *North Atlantic Treaty Organization* (*NATO*) remains intact, the organization is trying to find a *raison d'être* in the new world order. Meanwhile, Washington halved the number of American troops stationed in Europe to 100,000 and pared its military budget by 25 percent during the 1990s. The United States, Russia, and other nations will undoubtedly continue to reduce their nuclear and conventional forces until they reach minimal levels of *deterrence*. Similar arms control agreements are possible in regional geopolitical conflicts elsewhere.

nationalism a feeling of intense emotional identity with one's nation.

internationalism an individual's primary identification with humanity as a whole rather than the nation into which he or she was born.

The Rise *and* Fall *of* Great Powers

During the 1980s and into the 1990s, there were tremendous shifts in the global military and economic power balances. The costs of winning the cold war for the United States were exorbitant. In the late 1940s, the United States was wealthy enough to single-handedly finance the reconstruction of western Europe and Japan, a bill that surpassed $20 billion, or $225 billion in today's dollars, between 1947 and 1952. However, in 1985 the United States was transformed from the world's greatest creditor to the worst debtor nation. Japan inherited America's position as the world's banker as well as that of the leading technological and manufacturing power. Today, although the United States is the world's unchallenged military power, it cannot afford all its foreign or even domestic commitments.

During the Persian Gulf War (1990–1991), for example, Washington had to pass the financial hat to its allies to pay for the war.

What led to America's rapid decline from the world's financier to penny pincher? What accounts for the rise of Japan and the European Union into global economic superpowers? Many argue that by concentrating most of its human, material, and technological resources in its global geopolitical struggle against the Soviet Union, the United States lost a geoeconomic struggle against Japan, and, to a lesser extent, the European Union. If anything, the new world order is shaped largely by economic rather than military competition—a reality most Americans are only slowly understanding.

Regardless of whether Washington can arrest America's relative decline, it is unlikely that either Japan or the European Union will emerge as the economic *hegemon* of the 21st century. There will most likely be a stable geoeconomic power balance among Tokyo, Brussels, and Washington. In an increasingly interdependent world, the prosperity of one great power depends on that of the others. None of the three great geoeconomic powers will jeopardize its own prosperity by going over the brink of a trade war. Conflicts will remain numerous and bitter, but they will continue to be managed so that the global economy continues steadily to develop.

Global Relations *and the* Wretched *of the* Earth

What about the world's real economic losers? Four of five people in the world are poor; one of five in the world exists in abject poverty. What can or should be done about the world's poor? Can every country in the world successfully develop? Are economic winners and losers inevitable? Is the success of some actually built on the exploitation, dependence, and continued poverty of others? Is the failure of a country to develop largely a result of internal or external forces? Will these issues become more or less prominent in the post–cold-war era?

International Relations *and* Global Environmental Catastrophes

As the nuclear shadow hanging over the world's fate wanes, another menacing shadow of global environmental catastrophe thickens, born of the deepening and interrelated greenhouse effect, *ozone layer depletion, population explosion, desertification, deforestation,* mass extinction of species, and air and water pollution. Governments increasingly recognize these threats to humanity and have begun working together to overcome them. The most impressive effort to date occurred in June 1992, when the representatives of 178 nations gathered at the *Rio de Janeiro Summit* to sign two treaties, one in which participants agreed to impose limits on greenhouse gas emissions and the other to protect biodiversity. Even stricter treaties limiting greenhouse gas emissions were signed at Kyoto, Japan, in December 1997 and at Buenos Aires, Argentina, in November 1998.

Remarkable as these achievements seem, political differences watered down the original versions of all three treaties. Protesting what the Bush administration claimed were the treaties' antigrowth measures, the White House succeeded in blocking any timetables or pollution reduction standards, thereby rendering the greenhouse gas emissions treaty's importance symbolic at best. Citing similar concerns, President Bush pointedly refused even to sign the biodiversity treaty. A proposed treaty limiting tropical deforestation was scuttled by Brazil and others, who argued that the countries in temperate climates should impose similar restrictions on their own logging. Meanwhile, India led the poorer countries in demanding that the richer countries transfer technology and funds so the *Third World* can comply with the treaties; no agreement was reached on any burden sharing. Despite the disappointments of the Rio de Janeiro conference, increasing numbers of governments recognize the vital necessity of dismantling the environmental time bomb before it is too late and are actively taking steps to alleviate those problems. But many fear that national and special interest groups will derail any systematic international attempts to address the world's environmental crises. As for the Kyoto and Buenos Aires treaties, the Clinton administration has withheld them from the Senate for fear that antienvironmental senators would kill their ratification. Thus even the most tentative steps toward addressing the global environmental crises have been stymied.

Theories *and* Realities *of* International Relations

So how are we to make sense of all this? Do any patterns or common behaviors unify all the international stories that appear in just one daily issue of the *New York Times*? Many experts on international relations use theories to guide their understanding.[1]

Why are theories important? Theories can help us understand any subject in a more analytical, deep, and meaningful way. Any *theory* includes sets of assumptions and analytical methods about how the world works. A good theory is clear, concise, coherent, unbiased, and both deep and broad in its application. Yet any theory, at best, only simplifies reality. Many theories are so abstract they distort rather than deepen our understanding of the subject. But even the most simplistic or inaccurate theories can provoke us into thinking of more accurate ways of seeing the world. Social scientists are always debating these questions and frequently develop better theories as the flaws in older ones are exposed.

Theories about *international relations* (IR) and its most important subfield, international political economy (IPE), fall into two major categories, *realism* and *liberalism*, and one broad minor category, *Marxism*. Each broad theory has many versions.

Until the 20th century most of those who had written about international relations reflected a school of thought known as *realist theory*. In Western civilization, "classic" realism emerged at least as far back as Thucydides' 5th century B.C.E. study of the Peloponnesian War (431–404 B.C.E.), with Niccolò Machiavelli (1469–1527), Thomas Hobbes (1588–1679), and Hans Morgenthau (1904–   ) making the most powerful contributions since then.[2]

Although they differ in details, realists share basic assumptions about the world. Humans are naturally greedy, fearful, and competitive. States, like the humans who compose them, are driven constantly to seek more power at the expense of others. Thus anarchy, or a *Hobbesian struggle* of all against all, characterizes international relations. Those struggles frequently result in war. History, culture, geography, and

liberalism a political philosophy that emphasizes the importance of human and civil rights and duties and of representative government.

Marxism the philosophy named after Karl Marx, who believed that class struggle and the exploitation of the many by the few could only be resolved by a revolution of the workers, or proletariat, which would usher in a communist utopia of perfect equality and justice.

realist theory argues that humans making foreign policy are essentially "rational" in the sense that they will choose what is best for their state, that states are largely monolithic actors in the world system, and that international relations are largely shaped by the responses of rational leaders to the actions of other states rather than by domestic politics or the state's ideology.

the psychology of leaders are unimportant in shaping international relations. All that matters is the distribution of power among states, and the constant conflict among states to increase their power. Sovereignty, or the freedom of states to do as they please, is a central realist concept.

Critics pounce on so-called realism, arguing that the theory's greatest flaw is that it is unrealistic. They say that realism is ahistorical, deterministic, amoral, abstract, and completely one-sided in its image of human nature. Humans and states do not only compete; they also cooperate with each other. Human (and state) behavior is shaped by the unique history, culture, and geography of each person (or nation). Not only that, but realism's central concern, war, is increasingly rare. Most states are at peace most of the time; geoeconomics rather than geopolitics shapes most international relations. International anarchy, paradoxically, is quite orderly. Nearly all states obey international rules and laws nearly all the time. In all, when measured against history or the real world, realism falls short.

That criticism provoked new versions of realism known as *neorealism*. But rather than alleviating realism's flaws, *neorealist theory* exacerbated them, especially in its determinism. Kenneth Waltz, for example, argued that the international system's structure channeled states into predictable patterns. Thomas Schelling went even further. Through his *game theory,* which highlights notions of rational choice and the *prisoner's dilemma,* Schelling reduced international relations to abstractions of human and state behavior.[3]

Realism's flaws spawned alternative theories about international relations. Early prominent thinkers such as Hugo Grotius, John Locke, William Penn, Immanuel Kant, Jeremy Bentham, and Adam Smith, to name a few, had promoted *liberal theory,* although it did not begin to rival realism until the 20th century. Appalled by World War I's carnage, humanists like President Woodrow Wilson rejected the realist assumption that nation-states and war had to be the most important forces shaping international relations. Instead, humanists urged a new approach to global politics that emphasized the cooperation of states within an international organization dedicated to the peaceful resolution of conflicts, the League of Nations. Wilson hoped to convert the "jungle" of international anarchy into the "zoo" of global cooperation. But that strong normative or ethical stance and the League of Nations' failure discredited what became derisively known as utopian liberalism.

Like neorealism, *neoliberalism* emerged as a more sophisticated version of the original theory. Neoliberalism offers a much more complex view of humans and international relations than does realism in large part because liberals use history rather than abstractions as their guide. They understand that human nature is ambiguous, that individuals can be at once a mix of competitive and cooperative, emotional and rational, materialistic and humanistic, and good and evil drives. Liberals look at history and see that humans have progressed in their living standards and cooperation with each other. Nation-states are still central to international relations, but their power is diminishing in more and more areas as geoeconomic issues proliferate, and international organizations and law, multinational corporations, and sometimes ambitious individuals take precedence. *Anarchy* may be the absence of government, but it is not in their view the absence of order. If realists have a *billiard ball model* of international relations in which states are like balls that strike and propel others in predictably violent ways, liberals have a *cobweb model* in which states are like spiders spinning ever more elaborate webs of relations with other each to their mutual advantage, and only occasionally eating one another.

Neoliberalism's interdependent school emphasizes the global political economy. Robert Keohane and Joseph Nye were among the first to argue that increasingly complex interdependence, or the rise of multinational corporations, global finance, computers, satellite technology, the travel industry, migration, and the Internet are tying the world together in dense webs of relations and thus are fundamentally changing the nature of international politics. Richard Rosecrance has argued that "trading states" such as Japan and Germany have superior means of amassing power and wealth that are superior to "warring states" such as the United States and Soviet Union. Ernst Haas showed how the cooperation of states on one issue "spills over" into progress on other issues. Hedley Bull sees international relations as characterized by an *anarchic society* in which a formal global government may not yet exist but state behavior is constrained and channeled by a social order. In an increasingly interdependent world in which issues proliferate, conflict will actually increase as war diminishes.[4]

Four theories attempt to explain international political economy. Here realism offers a realistic account, whereas liberalism is idealistic. Marxism presents an interesting but narrow critique and explanation of the global political economy. *Hegemonic stability theory* seeks to combine the best elements and discard the worst of the other three theories. All four theories are merely introduced here, and explained and critiqued in much greater depth in later chapters.

Mercantilism is realism applied to international political economy. It asserts that states and markets shape one another. Traditional mercantilism was a strategy whereby states amassed wealth and power by maximizing exports, minimizing imports, and investing the trade surplus in industries and arms with which to capture foreign markets and resources, and further aggrandize state power and wealth. *Neomercantilism* rejects imperialism and concentrates on states achieving a trade surplus and developing with the private sector an ever wider, more technologically sophisticated range of industries with which to acquire more wealth and power in the global political economy. Alexander Hamilton and Friedrich List were leading proponents of mercantilism in the late 18th and mid-19th centuries, respectively, while more recently Chalmers Johnson and William Nester have explored neomercantilist strategies in depth, with an emphasis on Japan.[5]

Liberalism, in contrast, claims that states and markets are and should be separate realms. It assumes that individuals are perfectly rational and enjoy perfect knowledge, whereas markets are shaped only by the laws of comparative advantage and supply and demand. To paraphrase Thomas Jefferson, the economy in which the government governs least, prospers best. Liberal or *modernization theory* asserts that countries that open their markets will develop through various stages, whereas those that do not will not develop. Thomas Jefferson and Adam Smith in the late 18th century, John Stuart Mill and David Ricardo in the early 19th century, and more recently Milton Friedman and Walter Rostow have been leading liberals.[6]

Dependency theory and *world systems theory* are Marxism's contributions to the contemporary debate over the nature of the global political economy. Western imperialism created the global political economy, which continues to be dominated by *neocolonialism* even after the formal empires have broken up. Multinational corporations corrupt Third World governments into exploiting cheap labor and resources. Thus do the *core* or advanced industrial countries exploit the *semiperiphery* or partially industrialized countries and *periphery* or poorest countries, perpetuating the *development of underdevelopment*. Vladimir Lenin fathered those theories, which have been elaborated most prominently by Immanuel Wallerstein, Fernando Cardoso, and Andre Gunter Frank.[7]

Hegemonic stability theory combines the mercantilist and dependence focus on states and multinational corporations competing for global markets. This theory's innovation is the concept of a *hegemon* or dominant state creating and managing the global political economy to advance its own power and wealth. Britain was the hegemon during the late 19th century through 1914, and the United States has been the hegemon since the *Bretton Woods Conference* of 1944. Hegemons justify their policies by citing liberal theory. Hegemons can and have declined when they contribute too much to, and extract too little wealth from, the global political economy. But after a hegemon declines, states still share an interest in maintaining the global economy, so they do so through various international organizations, regimes, laws, and other arrangements. Although hegemonic stability theorists note the global system's hierarchy, they argue that sensible policies can elevate just as irrational policies can erode a state's relative power and wealth. Charles Kindleberger, Robert Gilpin, Susan Strange, Robert Keohane, and Stephen Krasner are among the leading advocates of hegemonic stability theory.[8]

After World War II all theories were challenged by a new analytical method known as *behaviorism*, a variant of *positivism*, which emphasizes scientific ways of studying the world. Behaviorism focuses on data and sees human beings with their political conflicts as so many laboratory rats in different mazes. As such it rejects the study of anything that cannot be measured. It also asserts the belief that laws can be discovered that underlie international relations and can render the future predictable. Behaviorism took the realist belief that the structure of international relations determined its outcome to an extreme abstract level. Among behaviorism's leading champions are David Easton, Morton Kaplan, and Kenneth Waltz.[9]

Traditionalism objects that the real world is too complex to be reduced to such simplistic equations and graphs. History, which encompasses everything humans do including international relations, is messy and can only be understood by an interdisciplinary approach or *humanism* that explores all its many dimensions. Even then, there are limits to what can be truly known; all interpretations fall short to varying degrees of absolute understanding. Although behaviorists claim they are empiricists, they are really idealists. It is the traditionalists who practice *empiricism*, or the study of the real world.

Postpositivist theories blast both the behaviorists *and* the traditionalists. Robert Cox and Andrew Linklater are leading proponents of *critical theory*, which asserts that objective reality does not exist, that all claims about the world, no matter how analytical, merely reflect the observer's biases and drive for power. A related postmodern theory is *deconstructivism*, best articulated by Jean-François Lyotard and John Vasquez, which tries to unravel the meta-narratives or stories that scholars weave about their subjects; "facts" are mere myths employed to assert one's interests. These theories founder on the shoals of nihilism, the belief that all perceptions are equally invalid. If those theories are correct, they are just as wrong as the ones they critique. By contrast, *constructivists* such as John Ruggie and Alexander Wendt do believe in an objective reality but without any law other than that change is constant.[10]

Not all theories are created equal in their applicability to the real world. But even the best theories fall short of conveying the world's complexity. Theories, for example, are supposed to predict the future. Most theories about the natural world are predictive. The theory of gravity predicts, for example, that if someone

behaviorism the psychological theory that humans are shaped by their environment rather than by inner drives; thus human aggression is learned rather than innate.

traditionalism a humanist theory that emphasizes the complexity of human relations.

humanism a philosophy that celebrates humans and their reasoning, creativity, and potential.

jumps off a high place he or she will fall. But can we predict human behavior? Although some make that claim, most would acknowledge that humans and the states they occupy are too complex to allow their futures to be foretold.

So which theory best explains international relations? The realists have clearly won the rhetorical war. They call themselves "realists" who explore the drama of *high politics* or geopolitics and disparage "liberals" mired in *low politics* or geoeconomics. But realism was the best theory of the premodern age. As the global political economy has developed over the past five hundred years, *interdependent neoliberalism* has increasingly provided an ever more sophisticated understanding of international relations, not just geoeconomics but also the geopolitics that erupt from it. Yet realist theory is not completely worthless in analyzing the real world. When it comes to showing how states compete in the global political economy, the realist offshoot mercantilism provides far greater insights than do dependence or liberal theory.

A New Approach *to* International Relations

Clearly the world and the relations that govern it have changed greatly over the past five centuries, with wrenching revolutions occurring with the nuclear age's dawn in 1945 and the cold war's end in 1990. Although conflict remains endemic to international relations, the nature of those conflicts and the means to manage them have changed profoundly. The global interdependence of problems and organized attempts to overcome those problems are steadily increasing, and the global agenda today contains issues such as the environment, economic competition, and human rights, which were not priorities a generation ago. The world is converging politically, economically, and culturally, and that integration is abetted by the proliferation of international organizations and laws. Yet all this represents not a truly new world order but the latest stage in global development.

This book analyzes the changes and continuities in international relations over the past 500 years, with an emphasis on the geopolitical and geoeconomic struggles since 1945. The book's central theme is that international relations take place in a global political economy that has been developing since the 15th century. In a sense, the "world order" is synonymous with the structure and most pressing conflicts and issues of the global political economy—the characteristics of which have changed dramatically over the last five centuries. The global system's structure is shaped by and shapes the distribution of geopolitical and geoeconomic power, the relationship between geopolitical and geoeconomic power and conflicts, and the growing impact of international organizations, law, and other non-state forces.

Part One explores the development of the global political economy and how the manifestation of political and economic power in international relations has changed over time.

Part Two focuses on the nation-state, revealing how governments create and implement policies, and on the types of power they can brandish to promote their national interests in a competitive and often outright hostile world.

Part Three explores other increasingly important forces and actors shaping international relations, including international law, organizations, and morality.

Part Four concentrates on geopolitical issues of war and peace: the cold war; arms races and disarmament; and nuclear, conventional, and unconventional warfare.

Part Five analyzes economic strategies, conflict, and cooperation among the nations of the industrialized world.

Part Six analyzes the same relationships between the industrialized world and the Third World.

Part Seven explores the interrelated global environmental crises that all humans ultimately face and the attempts by nation-states and international organizations to address them.

Study Questions

1. What is the "new world order"?
2. Are international relations characterized by order or anarchy? Explain.
3. Define globalization or interdependence, and explain how it shapes international relations.
4. How are relations among states today fundamentally different from the way they were a half century ago?
5. How do geopolitical and geoeconomic international issues differ?
6. Why have environmental issues become increasingly prominent in international relations?
7. Why are wars between states less frequent in international relations?
8. In this era of unprecedented economic growth, why are four of five people in the world still poor?
9. Explain the strengths and weaknesses of using theories to make sense of the world.
10. What are the strengths and weaknesses of realist and neorealist theory?
11. Describe the strengths and weaknesses of liberal and neoliberal theory.
12. What are the strengths and weaknesses of mercantilist, liberal, and dependence or world system theories?
13. Explain the conflict, and evaluate the strengths and weaknesses of the arguments, between behaviorism and traditionalism.
14. What are the strengths and weaknesses of the postpositivist theories?

☝ InfoTrac College Edition Sources

Using the Subject Guide, enter the search terms *international relations, cold war,* and/or *humanism.* Using Keywords, enter the search terms *fascist* or *fascism, totalitarian* or *totalitarianism.*

Beck, Nathaniel, Gary King, Langche Zeng. "Improving Quantitative Studies of International Conflict: A Conjecture."
Berejekian, Jeffrey. "The Gains Debate: Framing State Choice."
Brown, Lester R. "We Can Build a Sustainable Economy."

Christensen, Thomas J. "Perceptions and Alliances in Europe, 1865–1940."

Chua, Beng-Huat. "World Cities, Globalisation and the Spread of Consumerism: A View from Singapore."

Elliott, Michael et al. "A World of Trouble."

Howell, Llewellyn D. "The Age of Sovereignty Has Come to an End."

Hurd, Ian. "Legitimacy and Authority in International Politics."

Ikenberry, G. John. "Why Export Democracy? The 'Hidden Grand Strategy' of American Foreign Policy Is Reemerging into Plain View After a Long Cold War Hibernation."

Mastanduno, Michael. "Preserving the Unipolar Movement: Realist Theories and U.S. Grand Strategy After the Cold War."

Reilly, John E. "Americans and the World: A Survey at Century's End."

Sally, Razeen. "David Hume, Adam Smith, and the Scottish Enlightenment."

Tschirgi, Dan. "Marginalized Violent Internal Conflict in the Age of Globalization: Mexico and Egypt."

Wohlforth, William C. "The Stability of a Unipolar World."

On *the* Web

http://www.polsci.ucsb.edu/faculty/cohen/working/international.html
Hegemonic stability theory

http://www.etown.edu/vl/
Extensive directory of international relations websites

http://www.marxists.org/
Original writings of Marx, Lenin, Trotsky, and other Marxists.

Contents

Chapter 2 Development *of the* Modern World: From Florence *to* Washington

Key Concepts and Terms

International relations take place in the modern world, and cannot be understood apart from the matrix of modern forces that shape them. *Modernization,* an umbrella term for a series of interrelated and endless intellectual, political, economic, technological, religious, sociological, and psychological revolutions, began in Europe over 500 years ago. These revolutions originated in small corners of Europe, spreading over the continent and eventually, via Western imperialism, the world. Today, either superficially or pervasively all the world's countries are *modern societies* and most of its individuals are modern and modernizing. Recently the term *globalization* has become popular for explaining these changes.

Modernization, however, is a relative rather than an absolute concept. The standards by which we judge an individual's or nation's degree of modernization are continually changing. What was considered modern yesterday is often dismissed as obsolete today. Indeed, modernization's essence is revolutionary change—for the better, although that may not be apparent to those experiencing its effects.

Modernization entails revolutionary changes in outlook, technology, and organization that transform every aspect of a society. The countries that have modernized most successfully have experienced those changes slowly over centuries rather than generations; the revolution of modernization is best achieved through evolution. Yet there is no one modernization pattern; every country must find its own path.

It is in western Europe and North America that modernization has seemingly triumphed. The West had experienced waves of revolutionary progressive changes since the Renaissance, and by the early 20th century its inhabitants enjoyed unprecedented wealth and opportunities. Then twice during the 20th century world wars shattered that progress. From the smoking ruins and rotting dead arose political, economic, technological, and ideological forces that have shaped international relations throughout this century and into the next.

What is modernity?[1] Why did modernity begin in Europe? How did Europe impose itself and sow modernization's seeds in virtually every corner of the globe? This chapter will analyze the development of the modern global political economic system, first by examining further the concept of modernization, and then by detailing the interplay of those revolutionary changes over the past five centuries up through the end of World War II.

What *Is* Modernity?

Modernization is first of all a state of mind—only modern minds can create modern worlds. Modernity thus began with the intellectual revolution of the Renaissance, which in turn eventually spawned a range of other revolutions—political, economic, industrial, technological, sociological, psychological, and cultural. Modernity is conveyed through mass institutions—corporations, schools, bureaucracies, transportation, media, communications, laboratories, and metropolises. But without a modern outlook the vast complex bundle of modern techniques and institutions is unworkable.

Although the modern mind has evolved from the Renaissance through today, its essence is a belief that human reason rather than a transcendent god is the master of humanity's fate, and that individuals should freely pursue their material, emotional, and spiritual needs. *Modern societies* are politically, economically, and socially mobile, and modernity empowers individuals to transform themselves, to satisfy their craving to do, know, and become. More recently, modernity allows

modernization an umbrella term for a series of interrelated and endless intellectual, political, economic, technological, religious, sociological, and psychological changes based on the idea that human reason rather than a transcendent god is the master of humanity's fate, and that individuals should freely pursue their material, emotional, and spiritual needs.

individuals to simply be. Self-transformation and changing the world are inter-related, one cannot exist without the other. Modern individuals change, in usually minute ways, the world and thus themselves, through both thoughts and actions, and can remake themselves in their own images or those of others. An individual's power, position, and opportunities in a modern society thus depends less on ancestry and more on personal abilities and ambitions. Freedom, however, is not absolute. Choices are ultimately limited, and modern individuals must take responsibility for the choices they make and do not make. Authentic choices are made rationally, skeptically, scientifically. The U.S. Marine challenge to recruits to "Be all that you can be" could be the motto for the modern age.

Modernity's essence is rapid change. "All is flux, nothing stays still," Heraclitus said of reality, and his words particularly characterize the world during the past five centuries. Modernity is an endless, accelerating process of creative destruction in which traditions, institutions, buildings, communities, and even people are retained only as long as they can be justified, usually in monetary terms. The obsolete, the functionless are discarded and replaced with something more appropriate, more modern. Modernization never ends. Modernization's only constant is change.

There is some continuity amidst the change. Although we are all modernizing to different degrees and in different ways, traces of tradition are embedded in virtually all individuals even in the most modern societies, and we are all torn, to greatly varying extents, between modern and traditional urges.

Modernity has had its discontents. Modernity's mad pace and bewildering array of choices can be profoundly distressing and alienating for many. In the 19th century, even the transcendentalist Henry David Thoreau admitted that "the mass of men lead lives of quiet desperation."[2] Karl Marx and Max Weber provided more in-depth analyses of modernity, with Marx decrying the alienation of

Part 1 Development of the Global Political Economy

human beings from their community, work, and self, and Weber asserting that modernity imprisons humanity within complexes of omnipotent and unyielding bureaucracies he called "iron cages."[3] In the early 20th century, Sigmund Freud and his followers argued that civilization itself springs not from noble dreams but from the sublimation of humanity's most base hungers.[4] Franz Kafka provided the same bleak vision more poetically in his short stories and the novels *The Castle* and *The Trial.*[5] More recent poets and philosophers have continued exploring modern humanity's fate. In his most famous poem T. S. Eliot declared, "We are the hollow men," and Herbert Marcuse maintained that we are "one-dimensional men."[6] Michel Foucault wholeheartedly agreed, and explored the notion that humanity is trapped in "total institutions."[7] Alvin Toffler described our alienation as "future shock."[8]

Few individuals are more modern than modernity's critics. Modern minds question everything, examine everything under a microscope, and in so doing strip most things of their aura, their remoteness, and in the case of religions, their claims solely to represent truth and salvation. "God is dead," Fredrich Nietzsche triumphantly declared.[9] Or as Marx put it, the

> constant revolutionizing of production, uninterrupted disturbance of all social relations, everlasting uncertainty and agitation, distinguish the bourgeois epoch from earlier times. All fixed, fast-frozen relations, with their train of ancient and venerable prejudices and opinions, are swept away, all new-formed ones become antiquated before they can ossify. All that is solid melts into air, all that is holy is profaned, and men at last are free to face . . . the real conditions of their lives and their relations with their fellow men.[10]

Modern literature is filled with metaphors for the perils and paradoxes of modernization. Mary Shelley's 1818 novel, *Frankenstein,* and Walt Disney's 1940 Mickey Mouse cartoon, "The Sorcerer's Apprentice" explore the consequences of technologies originally created for humanity's sake that eventually mastered and imperiled humanity. As Marx put it, "Modern bourgeois society, a society that has conjured up such gigantic means of production and exchange, is like the sorcerer who is no longer able to control the powers of the underworld that he has called up by his spells."[11] Johann Wolfgang Goethe, in his play *Faust,* portrayed the quintessential modern man. Faust sells his soul to Mephistopheles for the power to modernize the world, but in so doing destroys as much as he creates.

How do people achieve meaning or salvation in a godless universe? Some search for meaning amidst a world of constant chaos and upheaval, but most individuals in advanced industrial societies simply hunker down deep in the routine of office and television. From the Romantic movement of the late 18th and early 19th centuries to the New Age movement of the 1980s, many others have sought refuge from modernity's excesses in the spiritual serenity of temples or wilderness or creativity. The responsibilities that accompany freedom, particularly the imperative to strip away one's illusions and see the world as it really is, overwhelm many people. Confronted with this negation of their basic beliefs, many find salvation in totalitarian political or religious movements. The fascism of Japan, Germany, and Italy during the 1930s, the communist fervor that gripped hundreds of millions throughout the 20th century until recently, and the Islamic fundamentalism that has engulfed Iran since 1979 and Muslim Brotherhoods elsewhere were all built on a popular rejection of the turmoil, uncertainty, and duties of modern life. Adherents immersed themselves in a sea of humanity led by charismatic leaders such as Hitler, Castro, or the Ayatollah Khomeini, and totemic symbols such as the swastika, sickle and hammer, or crescent.

The Rise *and* Fall *of* Civilizations

Although modernity is relatively new, international relations are as old as *civiliza-tion*. Although human beings have existed for almost 200 thousand years, until the last 10,000 years they all wandered the earth in small groups hunting, gathering edible plants, and attempting to survive threats from other humans, beasts, and vile weather. Although they warred, traded, allied with, or avoided other groups, and thus all had relations, whether or not these groups can be described as "nations" and their relations "international" is problematic, and will not be addressed here.

Eventually some groups settled down in river valleys and began sowing and reaping crops. Over centuries some of these settlements developed into complex civilizations that included most of the following components: the mastery of agriculture; domestication of animals; complex and hierarchical political, social, economic, and religious institutions; the use of metals, the wheel, and writing systems; clearly defined territories; and trade with other peoples. The first civilization emerged in Mesopotamia around 5000 B.C.E., and for the next six thousand years great civilizations there and elsewhere have risen, extended their rule over vast areas, and then collapsed, for a variety of interrelated political, technological, economic, military, and ecological reasons.

During the 15th century, beyond Christian Europe, advanced and powerful civilizations sprawled across vast stretches of the globe: Ming China, Aztec Mexico, Inca Peru, Benin Africa, Mogul India, Ashikaga Japan, and Ottoman Asia Minor. In Southeast Asia alone, there was a patchwork of smaller civilizations such as the Khmer, Thai, Vietnamese, Burmese, and Javanese. All these non-European civilizations were ruled by centralized bureaucracies and achieved enormous advances in technology, the arts, philosophy, and wealth. However, despite their dazzling achievements, none of the non-European civilizations developed the intellectual, organizational, and technological prerequisites for modernity and global conquest.[12] Elsewhere humans were largely organized in small hunter-gatherer groups or primitive farm communities.

Ironically, the western European states set sail for the western hemisphere at a time when Europe was threatened with an invasion from the East. Seven centuries after Islamic Arab armies had overrun the southern Mediterranean and Iberia, new Muslim armies, led by several Turkish and Persian nations, overran all of the Middle East and Southeast Europe, and much of South and Central Asia.

Of these imperial nations, the Ottoman Turks directly threatened Europe, and seemingly possessed enormous potential for becoming a global power. The Ottomans captured Constantinople in 1453, carved out an empire in the Balkans and eastern Mediterranean, and seriously threatened Europe for the next 300 years, twice marching to the gates of Vienna itself (1529, 1683). Like the previous Arab empire, the Ottoman empire had well-run cities, universities and libraries, a vigorous intellectual class, excelled in advanced science and such technologies as cannon and musket production, and possessed a well-organized bureaucracy; well-trained, tough, and loyal armies; and vast fleets of fast, maneuverable galleys. The capital, Constantinople, had a population of half a million, far larger than any European city, and the empire included 14 million people.

What limited the Ottomans' expansion and prevented their modernization? Imperial overstretch and a succession of incompetent rulers eventually brought the Ottomans' expansion to a halt and long decline. The Ottomans failed to keep

Among those countries with the most potential to develop in the 15th century was China. The huge Chinese empire was economically and technologically rich. It had dynamic cities; extensive trade throughout East, Southeast, and West Asia; rich agriculture; a highly developed port; communications, and transportation infrastructure; a large, literate merchant class; advanced technology such as gunpowder, cannon, ocean-going ships, and printing; and highly refined products such as steel, porcelain, and the use of credit and paper money. The Ming dynasty ruled China's 100–130 million inhabitants through a professional bureaucracy and a unifying political philosophy, Confucianism. Militarily, the Chinese had over a million men under arms and a 1,350-ship navy. Between 1405 and 1433, Admiral Cheng Ho led seven naval, trade, and exploration expeditions that reached as far as the Persian Gulf and East Africa. The Chinese could have "discovered" Europe rather than the Europeans, China.

Yet the Ming dynasty retreated from the brink of becoming a global power. Not only were the naval expeditions discontinued but the emperor also forbade any further construction of ocean-going ships. Geopolitics partly explains this withdrawal. Ming China shifted from an offensive to defensive stance in response to a failed attempt to defeat Annan Vietnam and to the aggression of Mongols along China's vulnerable northern frontier and Japanese pirates along the coast. Philosophical and political reasons reinforced the geopolitical imperative for withdrawal. Confucianism celebrated the scholar-bureaucrats who ran China and denigrated both merchants and soldiers. The court may have feared that its military and merchant classes were gaining too much wealth and power from their naval expeditions, and those very expeditions may have drained China's wealth with no real return at a time of northern and eastern military threats. Not only did the Ming retreat from the world, but they also failed even to maintain China's canals, ports, and industries. In 1644, the Manchurians conquered the Ming and ruled China until 1911.

up with advances in weapons, ships, and arms developed in western Europe. Essentially, the Ottoman empire failed to generate the wealth and innovations necessary to fulfill its ambitions and commitments. Islam, like Confucianism, tended to inhibit individual initiative. Similar problems plagued Muslim empires elsewhere, particularly the Mogul empire of northern India and Pakistan.

Of the great civilizations patching the world during the 15th century, all but Europe's failed to develop into modern civilizations and project their power worldwide.

The Transition *from* Feudal *to* Modern Europe

We cannot understand the emergence of modernity in Europe without exploring what preceded it. For over five centuries, the Roman Empire had cloaked most of Europe and the Mediterranean basin with a common government, law, and market. Long before the last western Roman emperor was deposed in C.E. 476, the empire itself had collapsed under the weight of political corruption and inefficiency, economic decline, and waves of foreign invasions. A united market from England to Syria and Gibraltar to the Rhine disappeared with the Roman Empire.

What followed was a millennium of European history from around 450 to 1450 called the Middle Ages. The loss of Roman law and administration meant that everyone had to fend for themselves. At first the population declined from pestilence and the sword. The survivors fled into the countryside and even the greatest cities dwindled into towns and most towns reverted to nature. Although slavery disappeared with Rome's fall, few peasants retained their own land. Eventually most peasants sold out to the local strongman and his warriors, who protected them, often in return for half of their production.

Thus during this time Europe was fragmented politically into hundreds of small fiefdoms, a political system known as *feudalism*. The local strongmen became lords, and their followers knights. Few lords remained completely independent. Most allied with other lords under the distant authority of the greatest lord of all, the king. There were no nations. The identity of most serfs centered on their village. Languages such as French, German, Italian, or Spanish were so fractured into dialects that often people from nearby valleys or even villages had trouble understanding each other. Latin was Europe's lingua franca.

Feudal Europe came to be composed of four interdependent classes—priests, nobles, serfs, and merchants. There was virtually no movement among classes. With *primogeniture*, a noble's eldest son inherited the property, forcing other sons to look for employment elsewhere. The vast majority of people—80 to 90 percent—were serfs who tilled the land of nobles. The clergy was the most open class, with peasants as well as nobles often entering monasteries.

The least populous were the merchants and artisans, who organized themselves into craft guilds for protection and promotion. The guilds were monopolies that determined the producers, production, and price of a particular good, as well as the civic duties of the guild members. Each profession—mason, silversmith, armorer, shipwright, weaver, and so on—had its own exclusive guild. Prices were fixed, and the primary goal was order rather than profit.

For most of the Middle Ages, most kings were weak and controlled little more than the lands immediately surrounding their castles. Lords supplied their kings with no more than 30 days of military service a year and a cut of the production seized from their serfs. By the 15th century, however, the kings of England, France, Portugal, Castile, and Catalonia had amassed considerable power over their lords. Elsewhere in central and eastern Europe, kings remained weak or nonexistent and local lords were largely independent.

The foundation of European civilization was Christianity, and Europe's political as well as spiritual leader was the pope, who ruled from Rome. Only the pope possessed sovereignty, which, according to the great medieval theologian Thomas Aquinas, was the complete power to determine one's fate. As God's earthly emissary, the pope's sovereignty extended over all within Christendom. All Christian lords ultimately bowed to Rome. The power to excommunicate and thus deny the sacraments allowed popes to keep recalcitrant kings and lords in line. Faced with being condemned to an eternity in hell, more than one medieval king found himself crawling literally on his hands and knees to the pope to seek forgiveness.

Rome's powers were economic as well. The Catholic Church inhibited trade by imposing the notion of a just price, which meant selling something only for what it cost. Thomas Aquinas called it "wholly sinful to practice fraud for the purpose

feudalism a system that organizes people into rigid political, social, and economic classes in which land ownership and power reside with a small elite.

of selling a thing for more than its just price."[13] The Church also condemned lending money for interest (usury) as a mortal sin. Usurers were excommunicated and sometimes even tried as heretics. Jews thus became the medieval world's chief moneylenders, although some Christian institutions such as the Knights Templars also lent money at interest to medieval kings and lords. With most people forbidden to enjoy a profit motive, trade expanded slowly.

What, then, enabled Europe to break free of the massive bonds of religious, economic, political, and social feudalism?

Ironically, the Church's attempts to free the Holy Land (Palestine) from the "infidel" Muslims unleashed forces that eventually cracked open the medieval world and allowed the seeds of modernity to be planted in its crevices. For almost two hundred years (1095–1291), Rome issued papal bulls or orders calling on all knights to gather in crusades to retake the Middle East and the Iberian peninsula. Although the Crusades failed dismally in their mission, they proved to be a vital boost to Europe's development. Crusades took enormous resources to organize, launch, and sustain, and stimulated enormous strides in production, trade, and finance. The Crusades also exposed the medieval world to the philosophical, technological, artistic, and sybaritic world of the Arab and Byzantine empires. The primary beneficiaries were Venice and the northern Italian city-states, which prospered enormously as the middlemen between the eastern Mediterranean and northern Europe.

Despite the Crusades' stimulus, trade revived slowly. Although the fiefs were self-sufficient in producing food and clothing, most had to obtain armor, tools, and weapons elsewhere. But with little money in circulation, most trade was conducted through the barter of one fief's surplus production for that of another and occurred in local villages or annual country fairs. Each fief imposed its own taxes on merchants, creating virtually insurmountable trade barriers. For example, there were 60 toll stations on the Rhine River alone.[14]

Despite these constraints, each kingdom and all of Europe were slowly knit together into a slowly expanding network of trade routes and small cities. Europe's diverse climate and natural resources allowed the creation of a range of products. Many navigable rivers and proximity to the sea further enhanced trade. The exchange of such bulk items as grain, lumber, wool, and wine made regions interdependent, and large numbers of people prosperous. The invention of double-entry bookkeeping in 1494 was in many ways as revolutionary a development as Columbus's discovery of America two years earlier. Trade was increasingly conducted with money and even credit rather than barter. More people became free to rise or fall in the world largely according to their own ambitions and skills. The guilds were unable to control the expansion of trade, and the prices of increasing amounts and types of goods were shaped by supply and demand. A society of law and contract began to replace a society of status. Huge banking houses emerged to finance kings and merchants alike. The Fuggers of Augsburg and the Medicis of Florence had financial empires with bank branches across Europe. Genoese bankers financed both the Middle East and Atlantic trades. The Hanseatic League was a trading alliance of city-states bordering the North and Baltic seas.

Medieval kings and the growing merchant or bourgeois class shared a common interest. The kings needed the bourgeoisie for money and goods, and the bourgeoisie needed the king for trade protection and promotion. Only the king could cut through the web of local trade restrictions, and his patronage stimulated the mass production of tapestries, armor, furniture, paintings, and the like. The wealthier the king and his nobles, the greater the patronage, which encouraged the further creation of production and wealth. Increasingly dependent on merchants for loans and luxury goods, kings and princes competed fiercely with each other to promote trade. In return for a percentage of the profits, kings and queens licensed huge trading companies to explore and exploit foreign lands and negotiate with foreign powers.

Closely related to the expansion of trade was the expansion of cities. Modernity is an urban phenomenon. The growth in the size and number of cities during the Middle Ages was extremely slow. Cambridge, for example, expanded at the rate of one house a year between 1086 and 1279, and all together about 1,000 towns or only one a year emerged during the Middle Ages.[15] Crossroads hamlets, castles, and monasteries gradually became trade centers and towns. As towns grew in population, status, and economic vitality, they gradually obtained more freedom from the local lord, and began minting their own money and establishing laws. As cities grew in wealth and population, they demanded more goods and services, which in turn created more wealth and population. Countryside and city were increasingly linked economically, socially, and politically, with cities leading development.

Despite the revival of trade and cities, Europe remained largely agrarian. Ninety percent of the population were peasants who toiled endlessly in the fields and lived from one day to the next on what little that was not confiscated by their lords. Production was hand-crafted rather than mass produced. Most people continued to be paid in kind rather than wages for their labor.

Ultimately, modernity began in the minds of a few men. During the late Middle Ages, universities emerged in the cities to replace the monasteries as the centers of learning. At the universities, one could study not just the Christian Scriptures but ancient Greek, Roman, Arab, and Byzantine texts as well, many of which were filled with startling new and often heretical ideas. Europe's intellectual revolution, however, did not truly begin until movable type was perfected in the 1440s, inaugurating an explosion in the amount and types of books, literacy, and knowledge. According to historian Kirkpatrick Sales, "by 1500 there were over 110 places on the subcontinent, from Toledo to Stockholm, with at least one printing press and some with three or four. Within the relatively short period of half a century—from 1454 to 1501 . . . there were, by one estimate, 20 million books printed, in at least 40,000 separate editions."[16] For the first time in human history, learning and knowledge were no longer the privilege of a few but available to anyone with the ability to read.

The dynamic interplay between these intellectual, commercial, and political revolutions led to what became known as the *Renaissance* or rebirth of rational learning, and new ideas in philosophy, the arts, and technology. The Renaissance emerged from two clusters of city-states. Starting in the late 14th century, the Italian states of Florence, Venice, Genoa, Milan, Urbino, and Modena (to name some of the more prominent) became powerful centers of trade, philosophy, and the arts. This northern Italian Renaissance was further stimulated in 1453 when the fall of Constantinople to the Turks unleashed a flood of merchants, nobles, and intellectuals fleeing to those city states. During the 15th century, similar forces stimulated trade and learning in the northern European cities of Amsterdam, Antwerp, and Delft.

Modernity's central pillar rests on the shift from a God-centered universe in which individuals devoted themselves to fulfilling their class roles to a human-centered universe in which people were largely free to fulfill their individual creative

Renaissance a rebirth of learning around new ideas in philosophy, the arts, and technology. The Renaissance's central pillar rested on the shift from a God-centered universe, in which individuals devoted themselves to fulfilling their class roles, to a human-centered universe, in which individuals were largely free to fulfill their creative and economic potentials. Man, most importantly the rational mind, became the measure of all things. The *uomo universale* was skilled in all the fine arts, philosophy, etiquette, languages, history, science, and music. The Renaissance saw not just a toleration but a celebration of new ideas and ways of seeing the world.

and economic potential. Man, or most importantly his rational mind, became the measure of all things. An *uomo universale* (universal man) was skilled in all the fine arts, philosophy, etiquette, languages, history, science, and music. There was not just a toleration but a celebration of new ideas and ways of seeing the world.

Artists increasingly explored secular as well as religious themes. Portraits of smug, well-fed and -clothed financiers and merchants replaced Christ on the cross and the Madonna and child as dominant artistic themes. And the religious themes of artists such as Michelangelo, Leonardo Da Vinci, or Botticelli, to name a few, were explored through distinct styles and perspectives that made the anonymous medieval paintings seem wooden and shallow in comparison.

The shift from a god-centered to a human-centered world was symbolized by the gradual replacement of Latin by the local language as the language of discourse and literature. Dante's *Divine Comedy* and Machiavelli's *The Prince* were written in Italian rather than Latin. The Age of Reason emerged alongside, competed with, and eventually overwhelmed the Age of Faith.

Western Imperialism's First Wave

Imperialism, or the conquest of one people by another, is as old as humankind. Yet even the greatest past conquerors never dreamed of subduing the entire world. How did Europe succeed in spreading its power and influence around the globe?

imperialism the conquest of one people by another.

There were two waves of European imperialism, the Age of Sail (1450–1850) and the Age of Steam (1850–1950). Each wave was stimulated by a dynamic mix of technological, political, economic, and intellectual changes. During the first phase, the same forces that began to transform Europe from feudalism to modernity also stimulated a global quest among Europeans for wealth, power, and discovery. The immediate catalyst for European imperialism was the Ottoman conquest of the Middle East, which disrupted the flow of Southeast Asian spices to Europe. During the 1450s, the first Portuguese caravels sailed south along the African coast trying to find a direct route to the Spice Islands.

Europe's division into a half-dozen large centralized kingdoms and hundreds of smaller fiefdoms, and the incessant warfare and rivalry between them, was perhaps the ultimate reason for Europe's eventual domination of the world. The rivalry bred new innovations in technology, in particular gunpowder-based military technology, which in turn spawned new military tactics, better ship designs, and the creation of wealth. Kings understood the relationship between wealth and power. With money, kings could build up armies and navies with which to seize more wealth. Kings followed a strategy of mercantilism in which they tried to maximize exports and minimize imports, thus increasing the amount of available money. Trade was seen as a zero-sum war in which one nation's gains were losses for all the other nations.

Europeans could never have sailed to the world's far ends without new navigational devices such as the compass and sextant, and new ship and rigging designs. The need to navigate tempestuous waters such as the North Sea, Bay of Biscay, and even the Atlantic Ocean (for hardy fishermen bound for the Newfoundland fishing banks) required tough, well-built ocean-going ships that could carry large loads. The invention of new metal alloys allowed for the development of lighter-weight yet powerful cannon and muskets. These revolutionary technological advances launched an arms race among the European states that gave them virtually

The Cost of Modernization for Mexico

At times modernization's survivors may envy the dead. There were an estimated 25 million people in Mexico before the Spanish conquest in 1521; within a century, disease and exploitation had cut down the population to less than 2 million. The Spanish soldiers had conquered for gold and the priests, for converts. Neither group understood that forces we now label modernization were insidiously eating away the medieval world in which they thought and acted, and they would have been terrified if they had known. Nonetheless, the unforeseen and unwanted long-term result of the conquest was modernization. Today Mexico's population is soaring past 90 million and is expected to double within a generation. Although most Mexicans remain poor, virtually all lead more comfortable and longer lives than their pre-Cortez ancestors. Most important, they perceive themselves and the world largely through modern rather than traditional minds. Yet Mexico may be successfully modernizing only by early rather than late 20th-century standards: Countries with unbridled population and pollution growth are now considered modernization laggards rather than leaders. To varying degrees, nearly all countries have experienced similar modernization triumphs, tragedies, and dilemmas.

uncontested sea power against non-European states. In contrast, the slender-oared Ottoman and Venetian galleys may have been swifter and more maneuverable but were fragile on the open ocean and held limited cannon, freight, and supplies. The western European three-masted ships evolved into floating, ocean-going gun platforms that could blast any Ottoman galley, Arab dhow, or Chinese junk out of the water, and if necessary sail for months without replenishment of supplies.

The perennial insecurity that bred strength among European states contrasted with the security of other great civilizations, which bred complacency. Without the constant threat of war, the Chinese, Turks, Moguls, and other great empires had no compelling reason to innovate technologically, organizationally, or economically. Thus despite enormous advantages in manpower, the other great civilizations were inevitably beaten by superior European military technology and tactics.

Europe's first wave of imperialism also depended on the revival of trade and emergence of huge merchant and banking corporations that financed most of the voyages of discovery and conquest. Private corporations were given royal charters that entitled them to conquer and colonize foreign lands in the king's name. The conquistadors were more entrepreneurs than royal servants and were driven by visions of gold, spices, silver, and slaves. After the colonies were established, other commodities such as sugar, indigo, rice, tobacco, timber, furs, hides, and cotton became the most important products.

How did the Europeans justify their conquest of other peoples and lands? Essentially, Europeans considered the non-Christian world *terra nullius*, which meant that it belonged to no one and thus could be taken by anyone. Whether it was the king of a civilization thousands of years old or the headman of a wandering band of hunter-gatherers, a non-European leader could gain legitimacy in European eyes only if he were formally recognized by Europeans as the rightful ruler. In this way, Europeans completely remade the world in their own image. It was this outlook that allowed the pope to issue a bull in 1494 dividing the entire world beyond Europe between Spain and Portugal!

Within 100 years of the first Portuguese expeditions, the globe was clearly being integrated into one vast trade system. In 1522, the remnants of the Magellan expedition sailed back to Cadiz after circumnavigating the globe. By the mid-1550s the Spanish and Portuguese had conquered virtually all of Central and South America, while the British, French, and Dutch had launched their own exploration and trade expeditions across the Atlantic and around Africa. The transatlantic trade grew eightfold between 1510 and 1550, and a further three-fold between 1550 and 1610.[17]

The influx of silver from the mines of Peru and Mexico vastly stimulated Europe's economic development and shifted the power balance, but ironically, it was the northern Europeans rather than the Iberians that gained the most. Rather than investing their wealth into productive enterprises that would create yet more wealth, the Spanish simply bought luxury items produced elsewhere in Europe. Between 1520 and 1650, prices rose 200 to 400 percent throughout Europe as American gold and silver flooded local markets, and eventually found its way into the coffers of French, Dutch, and English merchants and manufacturers. Europe was enriched by more than silver. New crops such as maize, potatoes, and tomatoes expanded diets, and the incessant international rivalries stimulated rapid scientific and technological advances in all fields.

The Emergence of Sovereign Nation-States

Meanwhile, the intellectual revolution that sparked the Renaissance reached a new stage called the *Reformation* (1517–1648). Few acts in history were as revolutionary as when Martin Luther nailed his "95 Theses" to the door of Wittenburg Cathedral in 1517, condemning a corrupt papacy that sold indulgences and usury. Luther's act tapped a deep well of resentment against the Church's corruption and hypocrisy and, in so doing, launched the Reformation. Other religious revolutionaries emerged to found the different sects of what became known as Protestantism, named for their adherents' "protests" against Catholicism. The Protestants' central message was that individuals could reach God directly by their own faith rather than through "good works" sold to them by a corrupt church or the priest's transformation of the "host"—the bread and wine of the Church's communion ritual.

One of the most prominent Protestants, John Calvin (1509–1564), preached a harsh doctrine in which most people were predestined for hell. Slender as the chance was, some might be saved by single-mindedly focusing their lives on fulfilling their calling or profession. Calvinists exalted rather than condemned the merchant or moneylender. Profit, interest, and wealth were created for God's glory as well as one's earthly comfort. The Calvinist work ethic may not have had as major a role in Europe's development as is commonly believed. Calvinism's theological justification for making money reflected attitudes that had been developing within Europe's cities and trade routes over hundreds of preceding years. Thus Calvinism did not create a new value system so much as it legitimized an existing one.

The Protestant revolution could not have survived had it not been championed by kings and princes. In 1534, Henry VIII became the first king to declare his independence from Rome and others followed suit. For the next 120 years until

Reformation an attempt to reform the Catholic Church in Europe and the occasion for a century of religious and political upheaval. Started in 1517 when Martin Luther nailed his 95 Theses to the door of Wittenburg Cathedral and condemned a corrupt papacy for usury and selling indulgences. Other religious revolutionaries (1517–1648) emerged to found the different sects of what became known as Protestantism, named for the various "protests" against Catholicism. The Protestants' central message was that individuals could reach God directly by their own faith rather than through "good works" sold to them by a corrupt church.

1648, Europe was torn apart by religious warfare with a largely Catholic southern Europe attempting to conquer a largely Protestant northern Europe. These religious wars were aimed at either converting or killing the enemy's population, and culminated with the Thirty Years War (1618–1648), in which Catholic and Protestant lords and kings devastated most of central Europe in their struggle for supremacy.

The religious wars finally ended with the Treaty of Westphalia in 1648. As early as 1586, the French legal philosopher Jean Bodin, in his "Six Books on the State" had rejected the notion of papal sovereignty and instead argued that every king was sovereign, although his powers were restricted by his kingdom's laws. Bodin's principle formed the treaty's basis. Henceforth, every lord could decide for himself his realm's religion, each state would be considered independent from and equal to all others, and no state had the right to interfere in the internal affairs of others. Westphalia thus marked the end of papal and beginning of national sovereignty.

The period from 1648 to 1789 was known as the age of absolute monarchs, epitomized by Louis XIV's remark *"L'état, c'est moi"* ("I am the state"). During the 16th and 17th centuries, the balance of power between kings and lords shifted decisively in favor of the former. The king's power flowed from several sources. Kings and bankers formed alliances in which the kings would grant protection and privileges to the bankers in return for huge loans that augmented the royal tax receipts. This financial power allowed kings to build professional armies and bureaucracies with which to subjugate the lords and protect the state. Despite this vast accumulation of power, the king's rule was never truly absolute; there were always some administrative and cultural constraints on royal power.

Technology aided this transition from medieval feudalism to absolute monarchy. Gunpowder enabled kings to batter down the thin castle walls of rebellious princes and unify the realm. The nature of warfare changed markedly after 1648 as the waging and goals of warfare became more limited. Untrained, undisciplined feudal levies were abandoned, and armies were composed of highly professional mercenaries. Bayoneted muskets replaced pikes as the dominant infantry weapon. Campaigns and battles were fought with chessboardlike strategies in which casualties were relatively limited and most of the population was untouched.

The nobility became increasingly superfluous in a world of professional armies and bureaucracies. They produced nothing and leeched off of society rather than protecting it as they had during the Middle Ages. The income from their fiefs was steadily eroded by the inflation that swept Europe after the colonization of the Americas. Louis XIV constructed elaborate court rituals and ranks just to give the nobles something to do and keep them quiescent and obedient. Louis XIV's court became the model for the other European monarchies of Prussia, Austria, Russia, and Spain, and the scores of smaller ones in central Europe and Italy.

Meanwhile, the money-making bourgeois class surpassed the nobility in numbers, income, and, increasingly, status. By the 17th century, Europe's economy ran predominantly on cash or credit and most urban dwellers labored for wages rather than in kind or tenancy. The interrelated processes of increased trade, urbanization, and monetarization in Britain, and to a lesser extent elsewhere, were boosted by the enclosure movement, in which lords enclosed pastures that had previously been common land for all. By the early 19th century nearly half of Britain had been enclosed. Unable to graze their flocks, the peasants drifted off to the towns to find new livelihoods. This population movement eroded the feudal society and economy of countryside and town alike. Not only did the lords find fewer peasants under their sway, but the guilds could not control the influx of emigrants to the cities, as newcomers refused to join. The result was a rationalization of agriculture, increased competition among craft producers, greater social mobility, and a growing bourgeois class.

Political Revolution

The age of absolute monarchy was short-lived. Europe's intellectual revolution, which had passed through its Renaissance and Reformation phases, now entered the *Enlightenment* (1648–1789) period, which, among other things, marked the

Enlightenment the name for a period of European philosophy (1648–1789) that emphasized the concepts of representative government and political freedom.

transcendence of northern Europe, particularly France, Great Britain, and Holland, as Europe's dynamic intellectual core. Britain's Hobbes, Hume, Locke, and Newton; France's Descartes, Rousseau, and Voltaire; and Holland's Leibnitz, Erasmus, and Spinoza created a vast range of seminal works in science and political philosophy. Whereas the major issues of the Renaissance were intellectual and artistic freedom, and of the Reformation, religious freedom, the Enlightenment's central focus was political freedom. Although a few philosophers such as Thomas Hobbes reinforced the notion of absolute monarchy, most championed the concept of popular *sovereignty* better known as *democracy.*

This notion of popular sovereignty fueled revolutions in Britain (1642–1688), the United States (1775–1791), and France (1789–1804), exemplified by the words of America's Declaration of Independence from Britain in 1776:

> We hold these truths to be self-evident: That all men are created equal; that they are endowed by their Creator with certain unalienable rights, and among these are the rights of life, liberty, and the pursuit of happiness; that, to secure these rights, governments are instituted among men, deriving their just powers from the consent of the governed; that whenever any government becomes destructive of these ends, it is the right of the people to alter or to abolish it, and to institute new government.

Nationalism and *liberalism* marched hand in hand. During the independence struggles of Holland and the United States, most people transferred their predominant loyalty and identity from their village to their nation-state. Although America's independence struggle against England is the most famous, Holland's war of liberation from Spanish Habsburg rule lasted eighty years, from the 1560s to 1648!

The period from the storming of the Bastille (1789) to Napoleon's defeat at Waterloo (1815) dramatically changed both national and international politics. From the French Revolution emerged the idea of a radical "left" striving to overthrow the status quo and a conservative "right" attempting to maintain it. Anticipating the Bolsheviks by over a century, the French leaders attempted to export revolution and overthrow monarchs across Europe. Robespierre and the other revolutionary leaders also created Europe's most elaborate police state to date, using terror and mass executions as a means of destroying their opponents. With its *levée en masse,* Paris mobilized all of its citizens against the counterrevolutionary armies of Austria, Prussia, Russia, and England. Wars were once again fought over ideas rather than just territory. Warfare changed as French conscripts and Spanish guerrillas presented organizational and tactical innovations.

France's revolution was short-lived. In 1794, Robespierre and 21 other leaders were deposed and executed by a conservative coalition that ruled France for the rest of the decade until it yielded power to Napoleon in 1800. Napoleon assumed dictatorial powers and in 1804 had himself crowned emperor. The coalition of European powers that eventually defeated and exiled Napoleon, met at the Congress of Vienna in 1815 and attempted to return Europe to its pre-1789 status quo. In 1817, Austria, Prussia, and Russia formed the "Holy Alliance," a year later joined by France, to put down any revolutions that challenged the divine right of kings. From 1815 through 1848, attempts at revolution flared across Europe and were invariably crushed by one or more of the great powers.

Yet the revolutionary ideals of "liberty, equality, and fraternity," along with nationalism, lived on, eventually swept the world, and remain perhaps the most powerful force in international relations. This process "began in Europe itself, as the advanced ways of western Europe descended, irresistibly and at a fast clip down the cultural slope into central, southern, southeastern, and eastern Europe, into the fringe lands of the continent, as it also spilled overseas into the non-European world."[18] In Europe, Napoleon's armies marched from Lisbon to Moscow and left the seeds of liberty and nationalism in their footsteps. In the early 19th century, precocious Germans, Italians, Poles, and Hungarians were among the first to conceive their respective nations, although the cultural boundaries were often hazy. Pan-Germanism and pan-Slavism preceded pan-Africanism and pan-Asianism by a century. After long struggles, Italy was unified in 1861 and Germany in 1871 but the nationalist aspirations of the Poles, Serbs, Hungarians, Czechs, and others would remain suppressed until 1919.

Elsewhere, liberalism and nationalism were conveyed from America, England, France, and Holland by example as well as conquest. Political exiles in London, Amsterdam, New York, or Paris carried back to their subjugated lands the ideals of the American Declaration of Independence and the French Declaration of the Rights of Man. But the largely unwitting global champions of these ideals were England and France, whose troops, gunboats, and colonial administrators carried with them the flames of liberty and nationalism. Intellectuals throughout Latin America increasingly rallied around the liberal and nationalist ideals expressed by the American and French revolutions. In 1804, Haiti became the second country in the western hemisphere to win its independence. By 1824 virtually all Latin America had been liberated and divided into a score of nation-states. Although most of these states started out with liberal constitutions often modeled after America's, the new regimes usually collapsed and were replaced by authoritarian governments. From 1775 through 1825 alone, 95 colonial relationships were severed, mostly in Europe and the western hemisphere.[19]

Economic Revolution

In the late 18th century, the notion of popular economic sovereignty arose to reinforce that of popular political sovereignty. Throughout the early modern era, governments followed *mercantilist* policies in which they attempted to maximize exports and minimize imports to garner as much wealth in their own realm as possible. Trade was seen as a zero-sum rivalry in which one nation's gain was the others' loss. Although Louis XIV's finance minister, Jean-Baptiste Colbert, most systematically formulated and implemented mercantilist policies, his predecessors—most notably Henry IV's minister, Maximilien Bethune, the Duke of Sully—had adopted similar measures.

Adam Smith (1723–1790) developed a philosophy of economics diametrically opposed to mercantilism.[20] In some respects, the publication of Smith's *Wealth of Nations* in England in 1776 was as revolutionary as the Declaration of Independence that year on the other side of the Atlantic. Smith called for *economic liberalism* in which everyone could produce and consume what they wanted, and celebrated the laws of supply and demand, the division of labor, and mass production. If everyone did what they did best and traded their production or wages for everything else, everyone would be better off. Prosperity springs from everyone's being free to fulfill his or her respective self-interest.

Other thinkers expanded on Smith's thesis. In 1817, David Ricardo argued that every nation, like every individual, had certain natural or comparative advantages in production. Ricardo illustrated this concept by comparing Britain and Portugal, in which Britain had a natural advantage in raising sheep and Portugal

mercantilism the policy by which governments created wealth and strengthened security by maximizing the nation's exports through state-licensed monopolies and subsidies, and minimizing imports through high trade barriers. The idea was to gain a continual trade surplus and thus a steady influx of gold into the coffers of the state and domestic businesses. Overseas colonies enlarged the state's raw materials and market resource base, and enabled entrepreneurs to enjoy large-scale production and profits. The goal was autarchy or self-sufficiency within a large empire.

economic liberalism an economic theory under which government plays a minimal role in the economy, and the laws of supply and demand shape production and consumption. Individuals produce and trade what they can best produce and trade. Prosperity springs from all being free to fulfill their respective self-interests. Trade should be free not just within but *between* states, allowing each to specialize in those products it is best suited to produce and then to trade those products for foreign products.

World Industrial Production and Trade: Early Industrial Revolution
Source: W. W. Rostow, *Getting from Here to There* (New York: McGraw-Hill, 1978). Reproduced with permission from the publisher.

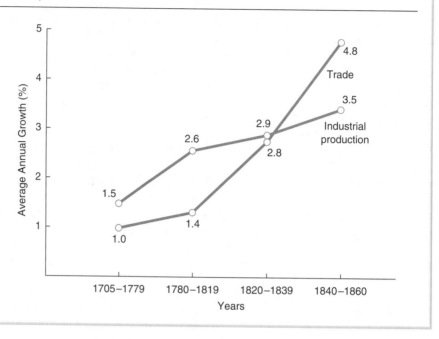

in producing grapes. Wool can be developed into textiles and grapes into wine. Although Britain could try to grow grapes and Portugal raise sheep, the costs would be high. It thus makes much more sense for Britain and Portugal to produce what they naturally excel at and trade for everything else.

In the mid-19th century, Great Britain championed the concept of free trade and began negotiating market-opening agreements with other countries. Trade, however, was never completely free. Although there was a significant series of trade agreements and reductions of trade barriers between the leading European states during the late 19th century, significant barriers remained and most imperial states prevented others from trading with their colonies.

These new concepts of economic liberty coincided with what has been perhaps the most important revolution of all—the *industrial revolution*. The industrial revolution marked the shift from small-scale handcraft production to large-scale assembly-line factory production that used inanimate energy sources such as coal. The industrialization revolution represented "the transformation of an essentially commercial and agricultural society into one in which industrial manufacture became the dominant mode of organizing economic life. After 1850, the factory was not only the key economic institution of England, it was also the institution that shaped its politics, its social problems, and the character of its daily life just as decisively as the manor or guild had done a few centuries earlier."[21] Marx vividly captured industrialization's vast changes and impact:

> The bourgeoisie, in its reign of barely a hundred years, has created more massive and more colossal productive power than have all previous generations put together. Subjection of nature's forces to man and machinery, the application of chemistry to agriculture and industry, steam navigation, railways, electric telegraphs, the clearing of whole continents for cultivation, canalization of rivers, whole populations conjured out of the

ground—what earlier century had even an intimation that such productive power slept in the womb of social labor?[22]

Why did Britain lead the industrial revolution?[23] In Britain as elsewhere, an agricultural revolution preceded the industrial revolution. The "enclosure movement" rationalized livestock production by squeezing out the small producers and allowing the landowners to engage in large-scale production. Then, inspired by the theories of Jethro Tull and Lord Townsend, landowners applied such scientific methods as crop rotation, fertilizers, and improved seeds to agriculture. The increased farm production fed the increased population manning the shops and factories of the cities.

The industrial revolution was also preceded by a trade revolution, and here again Britain led the way. Mass industrial production could never have emerged without an existing network of national and international trade. British war and merchant ships dominated the global trade system. No country was better organized than Great Britain, with its centralized administration and well-developed transportation and communications systems. It also held considerable amounts of coal and iron ore, which would form the basis of iron and steel industries, shipbuilding, railroads, bridges, and military weapons manufacture.

Finally, an intellectual revolution must precede an industrial revolution. No Europeans had a more positive attitude toward linking science, inventions, and business than the British. Journals such as the *Gentlemen's Magazine* and groups such as the Royal Society and the Society for the Encouragement of the Arts and Manufacture, whose members were a dynamic mix of England's leading intellectuals, merchants, and inventors, aided industrialization through the constant promotion and exchange of ideas and business. The government developed the patent system to promote and protect inventors.

Thus Britain had all the prerequisites for successful industrialization: an enterprising, inventive, entrepreneurial class; a mobile population; an expanding middle class; ample resources; a relatively efficient administration; a well-developed transportation and communications infrastructure; and naval and trade supremacy. And Great Britain was the world's wealthiest country.

In this very favorable setting, a number of entrepreneurs and tinkerers invented machines that were essential to industrialization. In 1769, Richard Arkwright invented the spinning jenny, which revolutionized textile production; throughout the late 18th century, James Watt invented a series of increasingly efficient steam engines; Benjamin Huntsman, more efficient methods of steel production; Josiah Wedgwood, mass production techniques for china; John Wilkinson, new methods for creating iron; James Maudslay, the automatic screw machine. With mass production, goods were created more quickly, cheaply, and uniformly, and often included more interchangeable parts, which gave the manufacturer an enormous advantage over those who still relied on handcrafted production.

The increase in production was extraordinary. Between 1701 and 1781 raw cotton imports increased from 1 million to 5 million pounds, then skyrocketed to 60 million pounds by 1802! Pig iron production increased from 68,000 tons in 1788 to 1,347,000 tons in 1839![24] By 1830, with only 10 percent of Europe's population and 2 percent of the world's population Britain accounted for two-thirds of European industrial output, and 9.5 percent of global output, including 53 percent of the world's iron, 50 percent of its coal and lignite, and 50 percent of cotton consumption.[25] The second industrializing nation, France, was at least two generations behind Britain. Yet between 1815 and 1845, France's pig iron production grew fivefold, its coal production, sevenfold, and imported goods ten-fold! Britain remained the largest industrial power for most of the 19th century, with its share of global manufacturing rising from 1.9 percent in 1750 to 18.5 percent in 1900, while France's rose from 4.0 percent to 6.8 percent, Germany's from 2.9 percent to 13.2 percent, Japan's from 3.8 percent to 2.4 percent, and the United States from 0.1 percent to 23.6 percent.[26]

In the late 19th century, the United States surpassed Great Britain and became the world's dominant industrial power. America's Civil War revolutionized industry as the Union side's demand for mass quantities of steel, ships, weapons, textiles, railroads, canned foods, to name a few, transformed relatively small industries into vast mass production complexes. New wealth and economic dynamism were created amid four years of destruction.

As in Britain, America's mass industrialization was led by entrepreneurs who combined revolutionary production techniques with ruthless business tactics; for example, Andrew Carnegie in steel, Cornelius Vanderbilt in railroads, John D. Rockefeller in oil, Henry Ford in automobiles, Gustavus Swift in meat packing, Cyrus McCormick in farm machinery, and J. P. Morgan in banking.[27] America's millionaires numbered 100 in 1880; 40,000 in 1916.[28] American industry was transformed from a collection of hundreds of small factories employing dozens to vast industrial complexes employing thousands. By the late 19th century, the so-called captains of industry had become virtual industrial dictators with monopoly power over their respective sectors. Enormous political as well as economic power was concentrated in the hands of a few.

How did this political economic concentration occur? The winner of price wars would buy out the opposition, acquiring more economic power with which to undercut the remaining competitors. Meanwhile he would pour money into the pockets of elected and appointed officials to tip the rules in his industry's favor. When there was a balance of power between two or more huge corporations in the same industry, they usually agreed to form an *oligopoly* and maintain high price levels. Mergers were organized into vast "trusts" in which the corporation and its stocks were controlled by a board of directors. For example, J. P. Morgan's banking empire included 341 directorships in 112 corporations whose total wealth was three times greater than the value of New England's total wealth![29] Although Washington attempted to rein in these monopolies by passing the 1890 Sherman and 1914 Clayton Antitrust Acts, they largely failed to check, let alone reverse, corporate concentration and power. Although the government used the Sherman Antitrust Act to break up the Standard Oil Trust in 1911, between 1909 and 1928 it stood by as the largest 200 corporations increased their gross assets 40 percent more rapidly than all other corporations, to the point where they owned 85 percent of all corporate wealth.[30]

The result was the opposite of Adam Smith's free competition ideal. As Adolf Berle and Gardiner Means say, "A society in which production is governed by blind market forces is being replaced by one in which production is carried on under the ultimate control of a handful of individuals."[31] President Woodrow Wilson clearly addressed the problem: "If monopoly persists, monopoly will always sit at the helm of government. I do not expect to see monopoly restrain itself. If there are men in this country big enough to own the government of the United States, they are going to own it."[32]

The agricultural and industrial revolutions had both positive and negative effects on the world. On the one hand, they allowed production to rise faster than population, raising the living standards of most people, and better hygiene, diet,

Birth *of the* Welfare State

The industrial revolution created enormous wealth for the factory owners, abundant goods for those who could afford them—and mind-numbing drudgery and often gruesome injuries or even death for those who operated the whirling machines for 14 or more hours a day. Among those that early industrialization both appalled and fascinated were Charles Dickens and Karl Marx, who exposed the machine age's horrors and promises; the former advocated reform, and the latter demanded revolution to curb industrialization's excesses and harness its potential. Other powerful writers and activists took up those cries. By the 19th century's end, ever more workers defied the law and organized into unions that demanded better pay and safety, and fewer hours. Socialist parties mushroomed and united in an international movement that lobbied governments and protested in the street. Public opinion slowly shifted in favor of state regulations on business and a safety net for the aged, sick, and infirm. Eventually one government after another gave in to one demand after another. A century of laws, regulations, and institutions developed into the modern welfare state, which in some countries offers its citizens "cradle-to-grave" protection.

So which country initiated the welfare state? Was it Great Britain, which started the industrial revolution? Was it the United States or France, whose own revolutions began a generation or so later?

Germany's Chancellor Otto Von Bismarck introduced the world's first state pension in 1889; laws granting health insurance, limiting work hours and requiring safe conditions, and relief for the poor soon followed. Politics rather than morality motivated those policies. Germany's socialist movement was growing ever more powerful. Bismarck realized he could splinter and weaken the movement by granting some of its demands, thus co-opting the moderates and marginalizing the radicals. Faced with similar threats, other leaders elsewhere at later times adopted the same strategy.

Today variations of the welfare state are central to every democratic industrial country. But in alleviating some problems, have governments inadvertently created others? Does cradle-to-grave protection crimp the work ethic, inventiveness, and entrepreneurship, as some argue? What are the strengths and weaknesses of the various forms of welfare? What would Bismarck think if he were alive today? Or Dickens or Marx, for that matter?

medicine, and safety allowed people to enjoy longer and more productive lives. The high living standards and quality of life in the democratic industrial countries would not have been possible without the industrial revolution. Many other countries around the globe are currently passing through the different industrial revolution stages.

On the other hand, the horrors of early industrialization seemed to outweigh the benefits. The new manufacturing techniques and products created as much poverty as wealth by bankrupting obsolete industries and often underpaying the workers of new industries. And while industrialization brought tremendous wealth to the factory, mine, and shop owners, it imposed mass misery on the armies of men, women, and children who worked as much as 16 hours a day, six days a week, for subsistence wages. The machines claimed countless limbs and lives of the operators. Even Adam Smith had mixed feelings about the industrialists with their "mean rapacity, the monopolizing spirit . . . they neither are, nor ought to be, the rulers of mankind."[33]

Industrialization resulted in the alienation of many from their workplaces, communities, and even selves. Under industrialization, virtually no one is an artisan producing an entire product through idea, design, and manufacture; almost everyone produces just one tiny part of the final product. People themselves become machinelike, repeating the same simple task hundreds or thousands of times daily alongside hundreds and sometimes thousands of workers performing similar functions. The final product to which they have contributed becomes an abstraction, a source of imprisonment rather than pride. Smith deplored the effects of mass production in which the worker repeating the same motions "becomes as stupid and ignorant as it is possible for a human being to become."[34]

Finally, the industrial, technological, and medical revolutions resulted in a *population explosion,* as the birth rate exceeded the death rate. In the century from 1750 to 1850, Europe's population rose from 140 million to 266 million, and Asia's from 400 million to 700 million. Most of this new population was born into or migrated to cities. The world's population skyrocketed throughout the 20th century, reaching 6 billion in 1999 and is expected to reach 10 billion by 2020! This population explosion is increasingly straining the earth's carrying capacity and has unleashed a range of global environmental problems that may eventually devastate the earth.

Industrialization's horrors caused many to seek economic reform or even revolution. As early as 1813, mobs of unemployed craftsmen or Luddites marched into factories and destroyed the machines that had taken their jobs. The pressure for reform rather than revolution was more common and came mostly from the workers themselves who organized into unions that lobbied both the factory owners and the government. In 1848, Karl Marx issued his *Communist Manifesto,* calling for revolution: "Workers of the world, unite! You have nothing to lose but your chains!" Inspired by the words of Marx and other radicals, socialist parties organized to overthrow governments across Europe.

The governments of most industrializing countries attempted to undercut these revolutionary forces by enacting reforms and co-opting the more moderate opposition. Starting in 1802, London enacted a series of child labor laws that gradually eased work hours and conditions in factories and mines and enacted similar laws for women and men. Other industrial countries experienced the same cycle of industrialization, political backlash, and reform. At first, the unions were outlawed and their leaders imprisoned. But after decades of struggle, unions were legalized in the democratic industrial countries, which then spawned political parties based largely on union membership and finance. Gradually, most workers rose from a subsistence existence to relatively comfortable lives, and labor unions and socialist parties became accepted players in the political system.

Western Imperialism's Second Wave

Like its first wave, Western imperialism's second wave was stimulated by a mix of political rivalries, ideological excuses, economic imperatives, and technological advances. Economic reasons were perhaps the most important—the need for cheap and secure sources of food, raw materials, and minerals, captive markets, and the imperative to offset the expanding power of rivals. Nationalist rivalries and the prestige of empire were also important. British Prime Minister Benjamin Disraeli captured the *Zeitgeist* when he asked publicly in 1872, "whether you will be content to be a comfortable England, modeled on continental principles . . . , or whether you will be a great country—an imperial country—a country where your sons, when they rise, rise to paramount positions, and obtain not merely the respect of their countrymen, but command the respect of the world."[35]

Britain was hardly alone in its quest for global power. New powers such as Germany, the United States, Japan, Italy, and Belgium joined the ranks of such older imperialists as Britain, France, and Russia. Not all states with the potential to conquer did so. Spain, Holland, and Portugal clung to old conquests rather than attempt new ones. Some states, such as Sweden and Austria, spurned any overseas expansion.

Europe's great powers sublimated their ancient animosities and ambitions on the continent by conquering distant lands around the globe. Yet in doing so, Europe's conflicts were globalized and a final reckoning simply postponed. Benjamin Cohen writes,

> The imperial powers typically pursued their various interests overseas in a blatantly aggressive fashion. Bloody, one-sided wars with local inhabitants of contested territories were commonplace: 'sporting wars,' German Chancellor Otto Von Bismarck once called them. The powers themselves rarely came into direct military conflict, but competition among them was keen, and they were perpetually involved in various diplomatic crises.[36]

Europe's power imbalance shifted in 1870 when Prussia defeated France, seized the provinces of Alsace and Lorraine, and united Germany under its leadership. But having achieved his aims in Europe, Bismarck wanted peace in Europe while Germany pursued an empire overseas. Thus the great powers cooperated in dividing much of humanity among them. At the Congress of Berlin in 1885, Great Britain, France, Germany, Portugal, Italy, and Belgium simply drew carefully negotiated lines across a map of West Africa and what became the Congo, carving it into separate empires. Likewise in China, the great powers negotiated different spheres of influence along the Chinese coast for their exclusive exploitation. During this second imperial wave, most of Africa and Asia came under foreign rule. In 1800, Europeans controlled 35 percent of the earth's land surface. During Western imperialism's second wave, the Europeans doubled their control to 67 percent of the world in 1878 and 84 percent by 1914![37]

Why were the Europeans, Americans, and Japanese so successful?

The industrial revolution gave Great Britain in particular, and the other great powers as well, a decisive advantage over the rest of the world. In 1750, the world's great civilizations may well have had roughly similar levels of industrialization. Britain's industrial revolution gave its manufacturers an enormous comparative advantage that, when combined with imperialism masquerading as free trade, wiped out vigorous industries in India, Turkey, China, Egypt, and elsewhere, impoverishing millions. The British East India Company's export of cotton fabrics to India alone rose from 1 million yards in 1814 to 995 million in 1870. Europe's share of global manufacturing rose steadily from a mere 23.2 percent in 1750 to 62.0 percent in 1900, while the rest of the world's share plunged from 73.0 percent to 11.0 percent.[38]

Advances in military technology and tactics gave Europeans and their cultural descendants in the United States an invincible edge over other peoples. Modern warfare blossomed to its full horrors during the American Civil War. Technology supplied railroads, the telegraph, rifles, long-range cannons, and steam-fired iron-clad warships, allowing armies and navies unprecedented mobility and firepower. Thus handfuls of well-trained and -equipped troops or gunboats could humble vast civilizations. With only six gunboats in 1854, America's Commodore

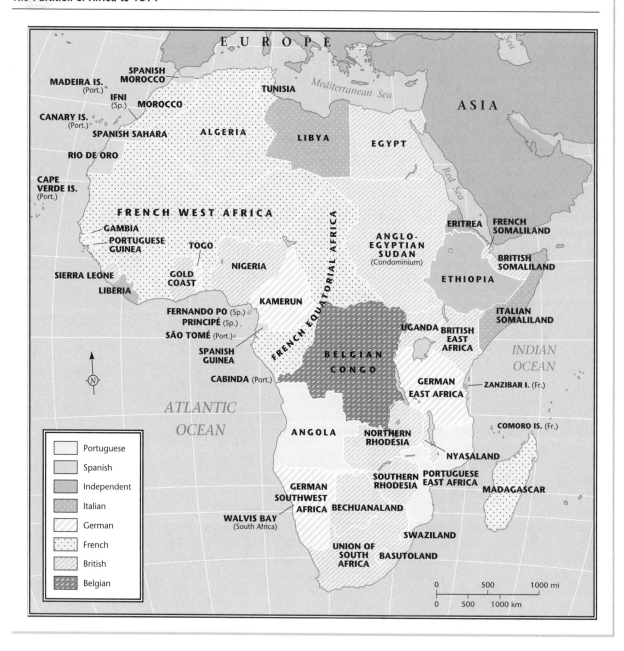

Matthew Perry forced Japan to open itself to the global trade system. At the Battle of Omdurman in 1898, British troops killed over 11,000 Sudanese dervishes and lost only 48 of their own men.

Meanwhile major advances in medicine, nutrition, mass production, national and international credit, and sanitation enabled governments to supply and maintain armies in jungle, desert, or mountains around the world. The conquest of Africa, for example, would not have been possible without medicines that safeguarded soldiers and officials from the ravages of tropical diseases. The pen and sword were equally vital to the war effort. War was waged as much by armies of bureaucrats setting production quotas and moving supplies as it was by the soldiers in the field. Increasingly, war was fought not just against the uniformed enemy army, but against the entire enemy population.

These industrial, technological, and organizational advances allowed the Western powers and later Japan not only to conquer but rule other peoples at a relatively small cost. By the late 19th century, Great Britain ruled a vast global empire on a shoestring budget. From 1815 to 1880, Britain expended only 2–3 percent of its GNP on defense. The British army actually decreased from 255,000 in 1816 to 248,000 in 1880.[39] Although London's expenditures on imperialism were relatively cheap, however, Britain did experience continual balance-of-payments problems as its foreign investments exceeded its profits.

Japan and the United States were the two newest great powers. Less than a generation after being forced by gunboats to open to the world economy, Japan embarked on an ambitious imperial drive. In 1868, a coup overthrew the decadent Tokugawa regime, which had ruled Japan since 1600. The new regime embarked on a comprehensive attempt to create modern political, economic, industrial, educational, military, and social institutions. Japan's leadership understood that the Western imperial powers only respected strength, and so Japan embarked on a step-by-step conquest of northeast Asia. Japan took over the Ryukyu Islands in 1872, sent gunboats to Pusan in 1876 to force the Korean king to open his realm to Japanese trade, acquired Taiwan and the Pescadore Islands after a successful war with China (1894–1895), and acquired Korea after a winning a war with Russia (1904–1905).

Although the United States expanded across the continent through a series of successful wars against and negotiations with the Native American nations, Mexico, Spain, and Britain, it did not become an overseas power until it defeated Spain in 1899 and acquired the Philippines, Puerto Rico, and several other Pacific and Caribbean islands. Despite their original promise to aid the Philippines' struggle against its colonial master Spain, after defeating the Spanish, the Americans reneged on their promise and fought a bloody three-year war to conquer the Philippines.

Imperialists justified their conquests by citing the "white man's burden" or civilizing mission. Such thinkers as Britain's Herbert Spencer and Karl Pearson and America's Josiah Strong championed imperialism as a natural struggle among nations in which the fittest survive and subjugate the others by right of their natural superiority. According to *social Darwinism*, as the biologist Pearson put it in 1901, "History shows . . . one way, and only one way in which the high state of civilization has been produced, namely, the struggle of race with race, and the survival of the physically and mentally fitter race."[40] Even Marx was ambivalent about Western imperialism, recognizing that it brought revolutionary advances as well as destruction in its wake: "England has to fulfill a double mission in India, one destructive, the other regenerative—the annihilation of the Asiatic society, and the laying of the material foundations of Western society in Asia."[41]

What impact did colonization have on its subjects? Colonization unleashed the same modernization processes among the oppressed peoples that had earlier occurred in Europe, but much more rapidly. Money replaced barter as the medium of exchange, and labor was paid with wages rather than kind. Communal land became privatized in the hands of the few while the many became tenants, and most people survived on a hand-to-mouth basis. Agriculture was organized into

social Darwinism argues that nations, like animal species, are engaged in a perpetual war for survival, from the simplest hunter-gatherer groups of a 100,000 years ago to the complex **nation-states** of today. Progress comes from competition as the strong and more advanced vanquish the weak. Thus **imperialism** is natural and even moral because it allows superior peoples to subdue and civilize the inferior ones.

huge plantations producing cash crops such as cotton, rubber, or coconuts, and these products were tied to the economy of the metropolis. New cities arose as trade or administrative centers, and even the most remote regions were linked to centers with telegraph, railroads, steamships, and later airplanes and telephones. Modern medicine allowed people to lead longer, healthier lives, causing rapid population growth. Mass school systems encouraged an increasingly high literacy rate and an awareness of the world and one's place within it. Individuals began to transfer their identities and loyalties from their village to their nation. Western liberal democratic concepts of freedom, equality, and representation mingled with Marxist notions of class struggle and national liberation in an increasing number of minds within the indigenous populations.[42] But all these changes were enormously costly in lost lives and traditional ways of life.

World War I

By 1914, nearly all humanity had either achieved liberation from or remained directly ruled by Western imperialism, and even the world's most remote regions bore some imprint of Western culture. All the easy conquests were gone. In August 1914 Europe's great powers turned against each other and fought a four-year war that destroyed virtually everything—the empires, ideologies, and economic order—that had been so carefully constructed since 1815.

Why did they do it? Although the imperial nations had largely cooperated in dividing much of the world between themselves, tensions had several times almost led to war. The imperial race was both stimulated by and fostered an arms race. Germany in particular expended enormous quantities of financial and human resources in efforts to build a fleet that could rival Britain's. By the early 20th century, Europe's great powers had divided into two rigid alliance systems reinforced by a web of secret agreements concerning the division of spoils. Germany, Austro-Hungary, and Italy formed the Triple Alliance in 1882, which was balanced by the Dual Alliance of France and Russia in 1894. Britain continued to play its role as "balancer" and remained aloof from any entangling alliance until it signed a defense treaty with Japan in 1902, ententes with France in 1904 and Russia in 1907, and a naval agreement with France in 1912. The two alliances went to the brink of war over Morocco (1901, 1911, 1912) and the Balkans (1908–1909, and 1912–1913).

These alliances were balanced on a hair-trigger. As the American Civil and Franco-Prussian wars had shown, wars were won by speed, maneuver, and the attack of huge forces at the enemy's critical points. The general staff of each European army had devised elaborate railway schedules to mobilize and send their soldiers to the front. Because of vast differences in their respective territories and railway systems, the mobilization time varied considerably from power to power. Germany's mobilization only took two weeks, whereas Russia's lumbered along over six weeks. Thus time was essential to victory. One nation's mobilization was as good as a war declaration.

The European powder keg was fused; all that was needed was a spark to ignite it. The assassination of Austria's crown prince, the Archduke Ferdinand, in Sarajevo, Bosnia, in June 1914 sparked World War I. Austria used the assassination as an excuse to attack Serbia, Russia's ally. Austria had long feared that Serbian nationalism could serve as a model for national groups within its own polyglot empire. Russia then declared war on Austria, Germany's ally, and Berlin then declared war on Russia and France. Germany felt compelled to move first, to avoid fighting a two-front war against France and Russia. But its invasion of Belgium in August 1914 to flank French forces massed along the Rhine, prompted Britain to enter the war. Without British troops at Mons and the Marne, the French army would have been overwhelmed, as it had been during the Franco-Prussian War of 1870, and Germany would have become Europe's unchallenged hegemon.

The anticipated quick war of maneuver and mass attacks that had characterized most conflicts for 400 years gave way under the concentrated fire of massed machine guns and artillery, to trench warfare in which gains were measured in yards at the expense of hundreds of thousands dead. Other powers entered the bloodbath. Turkey joined the Central Powers in November 1914; Japan and Italy, the Allies in 1915; Bulgaria, the Central Powers; and China and Siam, the Allies in 1917. The stalemate was not broken until the United States joined the Allies in 1917. The weight of over a million American troops tipped the balance on the western front. On November 11, 1918, the guns finally fell silent.

World War I *and the* Versailles System

World War I and its settlement caused tidal waves of changes to sweep the world—changes whose effects we are still experiencing. The war left 20 million dead and Europe physically and psychologically devastated. It immediately destroyed four empires—the Austro-Hungarian Habsburg, German Hohenzollern, Russian Romanov, and Turkish Ottoman—and eventually all others as each colonial power proved impotent against the growing nationalism in its possessions.

World War I marked the end of Europe's domination of the world, although this did not become apparent until later. The United States had become the world's largest economic power in the late 19th century and its entry into World War I tipped the balance in favor of the Allies. Yet, despite a promising beginning, the war did not mark the start of American hegemony. On January 8, 1918, President Wilson announced his *Fourteen Points,* the ideals for which the United States was fighting, whose most important points were the creation of a League of Nations that would attempt to settle disputes peacefully, self-determination for all peoples, the end of secret negotiations and treaties, freedom of the seas, free trade, and arms reduction. Although the *Treaty of Versailles,* signed on June 28, 1919, rejected Wilson's notion of self-determination for all peoples, it did include the *League of Nations.* The U.S. Senate, however, refused to approve America's membership in the League of Nations, and the United States retreated into political isolationism.

To the victors went the spoils. The Versailles peace settlement conferred on Britain and France the former Ottoman provinces in the Middle East as "mandates" to be prepared for eventual self-rule. Elsewhere, the German possessions in Africa were mandated to Britain and South Africa, and those in the Pacific to Japan. The French won control over the German industrial Saarland until Germany paid its reparations. The fallen eastern European empires were carved and then remolded into nine new states: Austria, Hungary, Czechoslovakia, Yugoslavia, Poland, Finland, Estonia, Latvia, and Lithuania.

Although World War I had been declared the "war to end all wars," like many preceding peace settlements, the Versailles treaty sowed the seeds of future conflicts. New totalitarian and expansionist ideologies such as communism and fascism

Treaty of Versailles signed on June 28, 1919, by the participants in World War I and ending that conflict. The settlement imposed a harsh peace on Germany by requiring payments of huge reparations to its former enemies. It also created the **League of Nations.**

League of Nations (1920–1945) charter established by the Treaty of Versailles at the peace conference in 1919; organized the following year into an assembly that included representatives of all members and met for about one month once a year; a 10-member council in which the four great powers were permanently represented while the other seats rotated, and which met four times annually; and a secretariat that administered the organization. Decisions passed in both the Council and Assembly only with unanimous approval. Forty-five countries were members at the first session in 1920; at the league's peak it had 59 members. The league's headquarters were in Geneva. The United States was not a member.

emerged, which led to a range of new rivalries, wars, and changes. But this new scene would not be evident for another generation. At first, the world did appear to have abandoned old power-balance norms and embraced internationalism as the guiding principle of international relations. The Washington Treaty of 1922 and the London Treaty of 1930 led to great power agreements capping the naval arms race, while the 1928 Kellogg-Briand Pact outlawed wars of aggression.

The world economy grew rapidly during the 1920s. Few countries grew faster than the United States, which had been the world's leading economic power since the late 19th century, and its expansion stimulated the global boom. World War I enormously accelerated America's economic development as American firms sold to both sides of the conflict and captured foreign markets from the hard-pressed European firms. But that wartime stimulus only contributed to a growth that had persisted for decades. America's economy grew about 1.5 percent to 2 percent annually between 1874 and 1929, allowing a doubling of per capita income every 20 years. In 1911, America's per capita annual income was $368 compared to Britain's $250, Germany's $178, France's $161, and Italy's $108. In 1928, a year before the stock market crash, America's $541 per capita income overshadowed Britain's $293, Germany's $199, France's $188, and Italy's $96. America's per capita income had increased by 46 percent, while that of Britain and France by one-third, Germany by one-quarter, and Italy's actually declined.[43]

Although by refusing to join the League of Nations, it seemed to relinquish its international political obligations, Washington did in fact take over London's role as global banker. In 1919, America's GNP (gross national product) surpassed that of all Europe, and New York replaced London as the world's financial capital. The United States lent Germany the money to hand over to France and Britain as reparations, keeping all three great powers, and thus the world, afloat financially.

After leading the industrial revolution, why had Europe fallen behind the United States? Europe remained divided into a half dozen large nation-states and a dozen or more smaller ones, each competing fiercely with the others. With the populations of Europe's largest countries—Germany, France, Great Britain, Italy, and Austria—each one-third to one-quarter that of the United States, the industries of these states lacked the markets within which to achieve large-scale production and profits. Traditionally, the Europeans attempted to alleviate their own limited markets by capturing others through colonialism and trade. But colonialism not only failed to create large-enough markets, it imposed enormous financial costs on the imperial state as well. Rather than risk losing their industries to international competition, each state allowed their industries to organize into huge cartels that maintained high prices and low production. Thus each European state was trapped in a vicious development cycle in which low growth crimped consumer spending, which further lowered growth.

The 1920s economic boom was fueled partly by a steadily expanding New York stock market. Between 1920 and 1929, the market expanded 4000 percent in value and over 10 million in new investors, whereas industrial production itself grew only 45 percent. Canny investors grew increasingly nervous as the gap widened between stock prices and corporate earnings. The bubble burst on "Black Tuesday," October 29, 1929, when investors dumped over 16 million shares and the market free fell, losing $30 billion in value over the next two weeks.

The stock market collapse deeply depressed an economy that was already in recession. Production dropped from $104 billion in 1929 to $56 billion in 1933, with 25 percent of the working population unemployed. The Depression seemed to wipe out all the gains America had made during World War I and the 1920s. America's GNP was cut in half, its industrial output by two-thirds, and its trade, by three-quarters. The United States's share of global manufacturing plunged from 43.3 percent in 1929 to 28.7 percent in 1938![44]

Why did the New York stock market and global economy crash? The stock market skyrocketed from speculation and a "get rich quick" psychology to the point where it no longer reflected any genuine production value. There were no government restraints on the speculative bubble. Stocks and bonds of dubious value were traded to enormous heights, and often traded on credit. The stock market rise hid severe problems in America's economy, with the farm sector in particular lagging far behind. Four out of ten farmers were tenants by 1929, and the average farmer made only 30 percent of the average urban wages. Perhaps the major reason for the farm depression was low productivity brought about by exhausting the soil with obsolete plowing, fertilizer, and seed technology. So the farm economy was already depressed when the stock market collapsed.

With the world's most productive economy and wealthiest population, and because of global economic interdependence, when America's economy collapsed it pulled the rest of the world down with it. American bankers recalled their foreign loans, which caused widespread foreign bankruptcies. Although other states struck first by erecting huge trade barriers and sparking a global trade war, Washington exacerbated these problems with its Smoot-Hawley legislation in 1930 mandating tariff hikes of 50 percent. Other countries boosted their tariff barriers and engaged in competitive currency devaluations to expand exports and repel imports. The result was a global depression with world trade and production cut to half its peak, and the armies of unemployed and impoverished people threatening all countries with political instability.

Totalitarianism: *The* Rise *of* Communism *and* Fascism

The most disturbing development of the interwar era was the emergence of totalitarian communist and fascist governments. Mussolini coined the word *totalitarian* to express the state's role of personifying the "immanent spirit of the nation," but the word has come to mean the state's total control of politics, economics, and society. In this sense, *totalitarianism* has been more nearly a communist than fascist phenomenon. Fascist Italy, Germany, and Japan all allowed some economic and social freedoms, and perhaps only in Japan was political rule "total" in the sense that there was no opposition and virtually all Japanese were prepared to sacrifice themselves for the state.

Totalitarianism is modernity's stepchild, fueled by the mass reaction to the economic and political failures of many democratic regimes, and made technically possible on a national scale through modern mass communications and transportation that allow mass mobilization, surveillance, and repression. Mussolini's minister of justice, Alfredo Rocco, could have been describing communism or fascism when he called for the necessity "of sacrifice, even up to the total immolation of individuals, in behalf of society. . . . For Fascism, society is the end, individuals the means, and its whole life consists in using individuals as instruments for its social ends."[45] Adherents of totalitarian creeds believed they possessed a transcendent truth whose pursuit and fulfillment justified any action. *Communism* and *fascism* are secular religions whose disciples must blindly follow and sacrifice everything to their dictates. Marx, Lenin, Hitler, Mussolini, and Hirohito became messiahs who sought to liberate the masses from the evils of contrary beliefs and practices and lift them above all other nations.

Perhaps the most important result of World War I was the Russian Revolution. Vladimir Lenin, the Bolshevik party (later renamed the Communist party) leader, differed with Marx in several key areas. Whereas Marx thought revolution would break out in the most advanced industrial states, Lenin argued that the late industrializing states such as Russia were the ripest for revolution because

totalitarianism a system of government under which the state has total control of politics, economics, and society. Totalitarianism is made technically possible on a national scale through modern mass communications and transportation, which allow mass mobilization, surveillance and repression.

fascism an ideology that proclaims a **nation** superior to all others and promotes the devotion of all individuals to the state. Individuals achieve their identity and meaning, and fulfill national culture by serving the state and basking in its glories. Conquest and empire are considered to be the state's most sublime achievements. Sometimes known as state socialism. During the 1930s and through the end of World War II, Japan, Germany, and Italy had fascist governments.

industrialization's worst excesses had not yet been softened by reform. Marx organized mass socialist movements: in contrast, Lenin advocated a "dictatorship of the proletariat" that would seize power and then mobilize the masses.

In 1917, Russia certainly teetered on the brink of revolution. Over the previous two decades, the Russian Imperial government had been thoroughly discredited. First, in 1905, after massacring over a thousand war protesters in front of the imperial palace in St. Petersburg, Moscow lost the Russo-Japanese War. Then it refused to enact anything more than cosmetic political or economic reforms, which failed completely to address the rising pressure for a constitutional monarchy and popular representation and for alleviation of wretched factory and field work conditions and of the vast gap between the small rich class and the masses of poor. Finally, the imperial government sent millions of Russians to their deaths and suffered repeated defeats during World War I. On February 28, 1917, the Tsar finally abdicated and allowed the creation of a popularly elected national assembly. But Alexander Kerensky's progressive government, which then took power, upheld its pledge to its allies to remain in the vastly unpopular war. Meanwhile it refused to redistribute land, and thus soon lost legitimacy as well.

Contrary to popular image, the Bolsheviks took power via a carefully planned and executed *coup d'etat* rather than the mass protests that toppled eastern Europe's communist dictatorships in the late 1980s. When Bolshevik "Red Army" units seized key administrative posts in St. Petersburg and Moscow on October 24, 1917, they encountered little opposition. With the cry of "bread and peace," the Bolsheviks gained support and consolidated power by distributing food and land, thus satisfying the basic needs of most peasants and workers, and by promising to hold elections and sign a peace treaty with the Germans. But the Bolsheviks received only 9 million of 36 million votes cast during the election of November 25, so on January 19, 1918, the Red Army dissolved the National Assembly, arrested the representatives, and formed a dictatorship. The result was civil war. To gain popular support and concentrate on defeating their opponents, the Bolsheviks signed the Brest-Litovsk Treaty with Germany on March 3, 1918, in which they surrendered the western part of the Russian empire. It took three more years of brutal civil war before the Communists were able to defeat the counterrevolutionary forces, which were aided by British, French, American, and Japanese troops and supplies.

Like most revolutionaries, the Bolsheviks were brilliant conspirators but administrative neophytes. Leninism, like Marxism, critiqued the old society and devised a means of overthrowing it, but failed to provide a blueprint for the new society. When once asked the revolution's guiding principles, Lenin replied, "Soviets (popular councils) plus electricity." In 1921, after the civil war had been largely won and with the need for reconstruction increasingly pressing, Lenin announced his New Economic Policy (NEP), under which the state nationalized the major industries but allowed smaller-scale private enterprise to flourish.

Whether the Soviet Union might have eventually become a mixed economic system presided over by the Communist party will never be known. Lenin died in 1924. Over the next four years Joseph Stalin succeeded in eliminating all the other Communist leaders and emerging as the Soviet Union's totalitarian dictator. How did Stalin do it? After becoming the party's general secretary in 1922, Stalin used his position to fill the party's ranks with his own followers. Then, by using his majority in the party congresses, he adroitly played off the more moderate "right wing" Communists against the radical "left wing" led by Trotsky. By 1927, Stalin succeeded in eliminating both groups of opponents and asserting total

How *to* Make *a* Modern Soviet Omelet

The modernization paths advocated by some prophets led to dead ends. In the Soviet Union, Vladimir Lenin asserted confidently that his modernization vision entailed taking one step back for every two forward; Joseph Stalin argued just as confidently that you have to break eggs to make omelets. Many governments attempted to follow the Soviet modernization model of central planning, state ownership of production, and political oppression. Although the Soviet model did achieve some gains in mass education, industrialization, and science, it largely failed to develop a complex modern economy and proved devastating by most human, material, and ecological measures. Indeed, at least 20 million people may have died from state oppression and starvation during the transition to communism. In the late 1980s and into the 1990s, anticommunist revolutions destroyed one Leninist regime after another, culminating with the collapse of the Soviet empire and communism. Liberal political economic systems are emerging from the ruins.

power over the Soviet Union. In 1928, he embarked on a massive collectivization campaign to nationalize all private businesses and farms and control all aspects of the Soviet economy. To achieve total power, Stalin had an estimated 20 million people murdered either directly through execution or indirectly through starvation or being worked to death. Von Laue captures Stalin's total power: "He was the state; his security was state security; his will constituted sovereignty; his power created the distinction between right and wrong; his personality set the style for the heroic Soviet experiment that was to complete Lenin's vision."[46] Communist parties that have seized power since the Russian Revolution have carefully emulated Stalin's "democratic centralist" model.

While Stalin was methodically destroying his opponents and creating a totalitarian political, economic, and social system, an extreme form of nationalism and authoritarianism was emerging in Italy, Japan, and Germany. There were significant variations among these three national socialist or fascist states in the government's ability to mobilize the nation's human and material forces, with Japanese fascism clearly exerting the most powerful grip over the population, followed by Germany, and then Italy. All three governments promoted an ideology that proclaimed their nation superior to all others, and demanded the devotion of all individuals to the state. Fascism exalted the nation, the state, and war; the state was the instrument that expressed national culture and waged war. Individuals achieved their identity and meaning, and fulfilled national culture, by serving the state and basking in its glories. Conquest and empire were the state's most sublime achievements.

Benito Mussolini originally was a radical socialist who became an ardent nationalist during World War I. He founded his own party in March 1919 based on demands for social justice and national vigor, and for the next three years the Fascist party developed a national following. In November 1922 Mussolini threatened to march on Rome with his small army of Blackshirts. Rather than arrest Mussolini, the king, army generals, and leading power brokers agreed to offer him the prime ministership. As prime minister Mussolini suspended many civil liberties and forged a government–business alliance that succeeded in rapidly expanding Italy's industrial power and middle class. Mussolini's "totalitarianism" was actually an authoritarian state that actively developed the economy and maintained political stability.

Adolf Hitler, like Mussolini, fought in World War I and, after the war founded his own party, the National Socialist (Nazi) party, which combined ideas of socialism and nationalism. The Nazi party's popularity rose slowly over the next decade from its founding in 1922. But in 1932, the Nazis won 40 percent of the Reichstag's (parliament's) seats, the largest share for any party. President Hindenburg named Hitler the prime minister of a coalition government. The Nazis won 44 percent of the vote in 1933. The Nazi-led coalition passed an Enabling Act that granted Hitler dictatorial powers. Like Mussolini, Hitler retained his popularity through his boundless charisma, appeals to German nationalism, and ability successfully to develop the economy. Unlike Italian or Japanese fascism, however, Hitler's fascism also scapegoated Jews and other "undesirable" minorities as the cause of all Germany's problems, rounded them up into huge concentration camps, and eventually murdered over 6 million of them.

Japanese fascism grew not from one individual but from many, and its imperialism during the 1930s was simply the second stage of an expansion that began in the 1870s and continued through World War I. Prime Minister Tanaka expressed his nation's grand strategy for expansion clearly in 1927: "The way to gain actual rights in Manchuria and Mongolia is to use this region as a base and under the pretense of trade and commerce penetrate the rest of China. Armed by the rights already secured we shall seize the resources all over the country. Having China's entire resources at our disposal we shall proceed to conquer India, the Archipelago, Asia Minor, Central Asia, and even Europe."[47]

Like Italy and Germany, during the 1920s Japan had a liberal democracy that was badly discredited by corruption, inefficiency, and an indifference to mass poverty and other social problems. Small ultranationalist groups began assassinating Japan's political and economic elite and advocating the system's overthrow and replacement with an imperial state in which the emperor would enjoy total power. During the 1930s, the government gradually co-opted many ultranationalist ideas and in 1940 dissolved all political parties, unions, and all other organizations and merged them into the Imperial Rule Assistance Association (IRAA), whose power to mobilize the Japanese population into sacrificing themselves for the state far exceeded that of the fascist governments of Germany and Italy and even Stalin's Soviet Union.

Communist totalitarianism differs from fascist totalitarianism in two important ways. First, communist power is far more "total." Under the concept of "democratic centralism," the Communist party controlled not just all political relationships, but all economic, social, religious, and cultural ones as well; fascist totalitarianism tolerated no political opposition but did allow some limited economic, social, religious, and cultural freedoms. Secondly, communism is theoretically a universalistic ideology that applies to all humanity; fascism is a nationalistic creed.

The Anticolonial Struggle

World War I, Wilson's plea for self-determination, and the global depression greatly encouraged existing anti-imperial movements. As early as 1885, Western-educated Indian nationalists founded the Indian National Congress to lobby

Britain for home rule and later independence. The first Pan-African Conference was held in 1900, and in 1914, responding to the outbreak of World War I, a Pan-African Congress leader wrote with incredible foresight that "We can only watch and pray. Unarmed, undisciplined, disunited we cannot strike a blow, we can only wait the event. But whatever that may be, all the combatants, the conquerors and conquered alike, will be exhausted by the struggle, and will require years for their recovery, and during that time much may be done. Watch and wait! It may be that the non-European races will profit by the European disaster."[48] Black activist W. E. B. Du Bois offered a bleaker vision in 1915: "The colored peoples will not always submit to foreign domination. . . . These nations and races, composing as they do the vast majority of humanity, are going to endure this treatment as long as they must and not a moment longer. Then they are going to fight and the War of the Color Line will outdo in savagery any war this world has yet seen. For colored folk have much to remember and they will never forget."[49]

The most important independence agents were the imperial countries themselves. Nationalist leaders in the colonies took up President Woodrow Wilson's call for self-determination for all nations. France and Britain had used colonial laborpower and taxes to help fight the war, and the hundreds of thousands of Africans, Chinese, Vietnamese, and Indians who served behind the lines in Europe took home liberal and socialist ideas. During the interwar years, what had been mostly small conspiratorial independence groups in Asia and Africa became mass movements. Britain responded positively to the more organized of these movements, granting colonial assemblies for India in 1917, and for West Africa in 1919, while in 1935 America's Tydings-McDuffy Act promised the Philippines' independence in 1945. However, elsewhere the colonial powers brutally suppressed these movements and arrested the leaders.

The most successful anti-imperial struggle of the interwar era was in China. The Western powers and Japan had carved spheres of influence from its coastal regions during the late 19th century. In 1905, Sun Yat-sen founded the Nationalist Party (or Kuomingtang, KMT) based on the "Three Principles" of national independence, democracy, and socialism. In 1911, the KMT and other forces rebelled openly against the Manchurian Ching dynasty, which abdicated the following year. But a rival to Sun, Yuan Shikai, became president of the new republic. Neither Yuan at Beijing nor Sun's KMT at Canton was powerful enough to reunite China, which broke up into autonomous states lead by warlords after the Ching dynasty fell. In 1915 Tokyo took advantage of the war among the Western powers and anarchy in China by imposing its infamous "21 Demands," which allowed Japan the premier imperial position in China. Yuan's government in Nanjing was powerless to resist the Japanese demands. China's chaos and weakness worsened in 1916 when Yuan died. Chinese resentment at Japanese imperialism grew, culminating with the 1919 "May Fourth Movement," in which there were mass Chinese protests against Tokyo's imperialism and boycotts of Japanese goods.

China's internal divisions were complicated further by the founding of the Chinese Communist Party (CCP) in 1921, which formed a shaky alliance with the KMT in 1924. The Soviets supplied advisers and aid to the two parties and helped forge a united front between them against the warlords during the mid-1920s. When Sun Yat-sen died in 1925, Chiang Kaishek succeeded him. Fearing the steadily growing CCP, Chiang launched a sneak attack against the communists in 1927 and wiped out the cadres in most of the cities. The remnants fled into the countryside, rallied, and continued to fight against the KMT. In 1934, Chiang began a new offensive against the communist stronghold in Jiangxi and eventually drove the communists on an 8,000-mile retreat. The communist remnants of the "Long March" took refuge around Yenan in the vast, arid lands of northern China. Here Mao Zedong took undisputed leadership of the CCP and imposed a new revolutionary philosophy based on peasant rather than proletariat power. With the Japanese invasion of China in 1937, the KMT and CCP once again formed a united front. Although foreign powers were finally freed from China in 1945, the KMT and CCP fought bitterly for another four years before the communists' victory.

World War II *and* American Hegemony

World War II was caused by Japanese, German, and Italian imperialism. By 1941, all the world's great powers and many of its smaller states were at war. The League of Nations, which was inaugurated with so much hope that collective security would keep the peace, failed utterly to live up to its mission. The league's two major powers, Great Britain and France, along with the nonmember United States, failed to provide the leadership that might have nipped fascist imperialism in the bud. All three great powers were hobbled by the political and economic isolationism of their electorates during the 1930s.

Japan conquered Manchuria in 1931. The League of Nations dispatched the Lytton Commission to investigate and, acting on the findings, condemned Japan's aggression in 1933. The league, however, failed to threaten Japan with economic or military sanctions. Tokyo responded by withdrawing from the league, and continued to penetrate north China economically and politically. The League of Nations did condemn Italy in 1935 for its attack on Ethiopia, but failed to halt the German army's march into the demilitarized Rhineland the following year. In 1937, the Japanese attacked China and overran most of its northern and eastern regions. The league turned a blind eye to Japan's attack. Germany's merger with Austria in 1938 likewise elicited not even a league protest. In 1938, Britain and France actually acquiesced to Germany's takeover of Czechoslovakia's Sudetenland.

Only when Germany and the Soviet Union conquered Poland in September 1939 did France and Britain declare war on Germany. A German blitzkrieg in May 1940 conquered the Netherlands, Belgium, and France. The Japanese took advantage of the puppet Vichy government the Germans imposed on France to demand and receive permission to occupy northern Indochina in 1940 and southern Indochina in 1941.

The war became global on December 7, 1941, when the Japanese attacked American forces in Hawaii and the Philippines and British forces throughout Southeast Asia. As in World War I, the mobilization of America's vast economic and military power proved the deciding factor in World War II. After three years of devastating warfare, the American-led Allies finally crushed Germany in May 1945 and Japan in August 1945.

In many ways, World War II was as cataclysmic a watershed in American history as was the Civil War. For 170 years the United States had prospered in relative geographic and political isolation, its leaders obeying President Washington's admonition to avoid entangling alliances while its merchants gathered wealth from the world's markets. America's diplomacy and its wars with England (1812–1815), Mexico (1846–1848), and the Indian nations, were almost solely to

Although less well known, Japanese imperialism was just as vicious and genocidal if not as systematic as that of the Nazis. Estimates of the number of Asian victims of Japan from 1931 to 1945 are as high as 30 million. In December 1937, Japanese troops captured China's capital of Nanjing and engaged in a month-long orgy of murder, rape, torture, and destruction that Chinese historians estimate may have led to the deaths of up to 300,000 people.

On August 6 and 9, 1945, the United States dropped atomic bombs on Hiroshima and Nagasaki, Japan, while on August 8 the Soviet Union attacked Japan's army in Manchuria. Japan's imperial government surrendered on August 14, finally ending the Asian holocaust.

A Chinese orphan amid Japan's rape of Nanjing, December 1937.

The atomic bombing of Nagasaki, August 9, 1945.

promote the nation's expansion to the Pacific Ocean. America's global power increased with its territorial, industrial, and population growth. Victory over Spain in 1899 won America a small overseas empire encompassing the Philippines, Puerto Rico, and a scattering of small Pacific Islands, and thus made the United States a minor "great power"; intervention in World War I made the United States one of the Big Three powers at the Versailles peace conference. Yet the United

States turned its back on the responsibility that accompanies power; it rejected membership in the League of Nations and returned to political isolation. The "business of America is business," President Coolidge dourly declared, and America's foreign policy remained mercantilist. In the early 1930s, America's isolation became economic as well when the Smoot-Hawley Act helped topple the global trade system.

All this began to change with Franklin Roosevelt's election to the presidency in 1932. Roosevelt understood that the United States could no longer afford to turn its political or economic back on the world. In an increasingly interdependent global economy, America's prosperity depended on global prosperity. As the world's largest economy, the United States had both a national interest and an international duty to revive and nurture that global economy. The Roosevelt administration first began to fulfill this mission after Congress passed the 1934 *Reciprocal Trade Act,* which authorized the president to conduct trade negotiations with other countries. Although Roosevelt signed several trade agreements up through the early 1940s, these had a relatively limited effect on alleviating the global depression and trade wars. The Japanese attack on Pearl Harbor and across Southeast Asia in December 1941 gave Roosevelt the national emergency he needed to justify the mobilization of America's vast potential economic and military power toward defeating the fascist powers and reviving the global economy.

Roosevelt sought to succeed where his predecessor Wilson had failed in creating a lasting and just global peace and prosperity. This vision would rest on two pillars: an improved version of the League of Nations—the United Nations—which would keep the peace, and a network of international organizations to rebuild the global economy. In 1944 at the Bretton Woods resort in New Hampshire, representatives from 44 countries joined to create the International Monetary Fund (IMF) and International Bank for Reconstruction and Development (IBRD, nicknamed the World Bank), which were designed to reconstruct those countries devastated by war, revive their economies and trade, and fix all currencies to the dollar and gold. In 1945, 50 nations met in Washington to sign the U.N. Charter, which embodied the ideals of a new world order, calling for all nations to work toward achieving peace, human rights, gender equality, national self-determination, political liberty, and economic development.

By 1945, the United States had clearly accepted the gavel of global leadership, and the policies it pursued in that role reflected its liberal democratic values and institutions, sense of cultural superiority, and belief in progress. The world would be a far better place, so the American outlook went, if its countries would just discard their corrupt and inefficient institutions and practices and adopt those of America. From now on the United States would lead, not as in the past by providing a distant model, but by plunging into the complex world of international politics and convincing others to follow. Former President Wilson perhaps captured this vision best when he declared, "Sometimes people call me an idealist. Well, that is the way I know I am an American. America is the only idealistic country in the world."[50]

Study Questions

1. What are modernization's central and interrelated characteristics? What has modernization changed and what has stayed the same? What have modernization's positive and negative effects been?

2. Explain the political, social, economic, religious, and psychological characteristics of European feudalism.

3. What technological, economic, social, political, intellectual, and religious forces contributed to the breakdown of European feudalism and the rise of modernization?

4. Why did modernity begin in Europe? Why did modernization not emerge in other advanced non-Western civilizations of the 15th and 16th centuries?

5. Analyze the major characteristics of the Renaissance, Reformation, and Enlightenment, and their role in Europe's early modernization.

6. Analyze the technological, political, religious, economic, and social reasons for Europe's first wave of imperialism. What were the positive and negative effects of European imperialism for Europe and the conquered lands?

7. Define sovereignty. How has the focus of sovereignty shifted throughout the modern era?

8. Explain the characteristics of and differences between a feudal and absolute monarchy. What political, religious, economic, technological, social, and intellectual forces led to the transition from feudal to absolute monarchy in Europe?

9. What political, economic, intellectual, religious, technological, and social forces led to the political revolutions in the United States and France in the late 18th century? What were the consequences of those revolutions for those two countries and the world?

10. Define nationalism. How is nationalism both stimulated by and a stimulant of modernization?

11. Define liberalism. Why did not liberalism take root in other countries experiencing revolutions or independence struggles?

12. What are major tenets of economic liberalism? Who were its major philosophers? Why and how did Britain champion economic liberalism in the 19th century?

13. What social, technological, political, agricultural, intellectual, and economic forces led to the industrial revolution? Why did it begin in Britain? How did industrialization spread elsewhere? What were the positive and negative consequences of the industrial revolution in the 19th century?

14. Analyze the technological, political, religious, economic, intellectual, and social reasons for the second wave of European (along with American and Japanese) imperialism in the 19th and early 20th century. What were the positive and negative effects of this second imperial wave on both the conquerors and conquered?

15. What were the political, economic, balance of power, and psychological consequences of World War I and the Versailles treaty?

16. Why did the global economy collapse into depression and trade wars during the 1930s, and what were the political consequences of that collapse?

17. What is totalitarianism? What accounted for the rise of totalitarian fascist and communist systems during the early 20th century?

18. Why did a communist revolution occur in Russia in 1917? What were the major political, economic, and social characteristics of the communist system?

19. Compare and contrast the origins, development of fascism in Italy, Japan, and Germany.
20. What were the origins and political, economic, and balance of power consequences of World War II?

⚲ InfoTrac College Edition Sources

Using the Subject Guide, enter the search terms *Middle Ages, Enlightenment, Renaissance,* and/or *Industrial Revolution.* Using Keywords, enter the search terms *feudalism* or *feudal.*

Barthelemy, Dominique, and Stephen D. White. "The 'Feudal Revolution.'"
Beissinger, Mark R. "How Nationalisms Spread: Eastern Europe Adrift the Tides and Cycles of Nationalist Contention."
Berdell, John F. "Adam Smith and the Ambiguity of Nations."
Berger, Mark T. "Specters of Colonialism: Building Postcolonial States and Making Modern Nations in the Americas."
Chernus, Ira. "Eisenhower's Ideology in World War II."
Clements, Peter. "Legacies of Empire."
Darwin, John. "Imperialism and the Victorians: The Dynamics of Territorial Expansion."
Errante, Antoinette. "Education and National Personae in Portugal's Colonial and Postcolonial Transition."
Fisher, John R. "Commerce and Imperial Decline: Spanish Trade with Spanish America."
Gould, Eliga H. "American Independence and Britain's Counter-Revolution."
Greenfeld, Liah. "Nationalism and Modernity."
Henderson, Martha L. "Geography, First Peoples, and Social Justice."
Mazower, Mark. "Two Cheers for Versailles."
Muthu, Sankar. "Enlightenment Anti-imperialism."
"The Peace to End War."
Pearce, Robert. "The Origins of the First World War."
Petras, James. "NGOs: In the Service of Imperialism."
Robinson, R. A. H. "The Birth of Fascist Ideology: From Cultural Rebellion to Political Revolution."
Reid, Richard. "The Ganda on Lake Victoria: A Nineteenth-Century East African Imperialism."
Singer, Barnett, and John Langdon. "France's Imperial Legacy."
Zakaria, Fareed. "The Birth of Modernity."

🌐 On *the* Web

http://www.acs.ucalgary.ca/HIST/tutor/eurvoya/index.html
European Voyages of Exploration

http://members.aol.com/mhirotsu/kevin/trip2.html
The Industrial Revolution

http://www.geocities.com/CapeCanaveral/Launchpad/9983/renaissance.html
Major Renaissance Figures

Depending on the issue, countries can be either partners or adversaries. Take the relationship between the United States and China, for example. These two countries share such geoeconomic interests as expanding trade and investment between them, developing China's modernization, and curbing pollution and the population explosion. But are they or will they become geopolitical rivals? That debate currently rages in the United States.

tiple warheads on their missiles. The Cox Report blasted two American firms, Hughes and Loral, for transferring missile launch technology to China in return for launching their commercial satellites into space. The report concluded with 38 recommendations to protect American nuclear weapons and missile technology from further leaks.

If the Chinese did it, how did they do it? Chinese agents posing as scientists enjoyed access to American nuclear laboratories at Livermore, Sandia,

Part Two *The* Nation-State *and* International Relations
Spy Thriller: *The* United States *versus* China?

In May 1999, the Cox Committee of the House of Representatives issued an 872–page report that accused China of stealing American nuclear weapons secrets over a 20-year period. In all, the Chinese may have received information on five types of nuclear weapons. That technology would boost China's development of three mobile ICBM programs, two land-based and one submarine-based, along with mul-

Oak Ridge, and Los Alamos. Those agents are the elite of a vast army. China's spy network is woven through 3,000 companies and tens of thousands of employees operating in the United States.

Assuming that the accusations are true, should China be criticized for spying on the United States? Certainly the United States is not innocent of spying on China. And after all, it was American policy that allowed the Chinese access. In 1988, the Reagan administration allowed American firms to use Chinese rockets to launch their satellites. The Energy Department never tightened the lax security standards at its nuclear laboratories and allowed Chinese and other foreign scientists to visit. Loose campaign finance laws allow American politicians to raise hundreds of millions of dollars from any source, including foreign interests. Chinese agents gave money to both political parties, most notoriously the Democratic. Does that money buy influence in American politics and policies?

The Cox report bluntly accuses the Chinese of spying but offers no direct proof. Beijing predictably rejected the accusations as groundless. Who is correct?

The Central Intelligence Agency's assessment was much more sober. According to published CIA reports, no direct evidence links China and American nuclear secrets. If the Chinese did steal secrets, they have not yet incorporated them into their nuclear forces. In all, the CIA dismissed the Cox Report as peddling worst-case scenarios unsupported by evidence.

But is the CIA assessment accurate? It cost the United States $400 billion and a half-century of effort to develop its nuclear weapons technology. How much if any of that technology did the Chinese get? How much will it improve their own nuclear forces? Will those nuclear weapons

threaten the United States? Only the Chinese know for sure.

The Chinese nuclear spy case reveals much about international relations, especially the nature of power and the relative merits of geoeconomic versus geopolitical interests in a bilateral relationship, the importance of international organizations and laws, and the impact of ever more complex global interdependence.

How has the Cox Report affected the relationship? The two countries were poised to sign a treaty whereby nearly all of China's economy would be opened to American trade and investments in return for U.S. agreement to allow China into the World Trade Organization (WTO). Tens of billions of dollars of potential additional sales and profits to American businesses are lost as long as that bilateral economic treaty is not signed. The agreement was eventually signed later that year, but currently has no chance of gaining the necessary two-thirds ratification vote in the Republican-dominated Senate.

Existing economic ties could also be harmed. Congress annually votes on whether or not to renew China's most-favored-nation status, originally granted under a 1979 commercial treaty. Bilateral trade and investments will likely drop if Congress refuses to renew that privilege.

The spy scandal affects yet another treaty. The Comprehensive Test Ban Treaty was signed by 151 countries, including China and the United States, in 1996. Signatories promised not to field-test nuclear weapons. The

effectiveness of nuclear weapons can be tested in two ways, by exploding them or by simulating the explosions through supercomputers. By forbidding explosions the treaty ideally freezes nuclear development for those countries including China that lack supercomputers powerful enough to simulate such tests. Did the Chinese sidestep those restrictions by stealing America's nuclear secrets? If so the Comprehensive Test Ban Treaty would have forbidden China from testing the technology. But the Republican Senate rejected that treaty in 1999. So the Chinese now are free to test what they might have stolen.

If Beijing did get all that technology, the real threat might come not from improved Chinese missiles and warheads but from that information reaching other aggressive countries. Until 1998, when it agreed to stop, Beijing transferred missile and conventional weapons technology to America's enemies Iraq and Iran as well as to its erstwhile allies Pakistan and Saudi Arabia.

Does China pose a geopolitical threat to the United States? What is the relative distribution of power between the two countries? Power equals capacity plus will. China has 24 single-warhead ICBMs, whereas the United States has over 7,000 warheads capable of reaching Chinese targets. America's overwhelming advantage most likely would deter Beijing from launching a nuclear attack against the United States, even if conventional war broke out. But why would China and the United States go to war?

China does not now pose a geopolitical threat to the United States. Alienating China, however, could create an animosity that otherwise would not exist. Would that animosity lead to a future geopolitical nuclear or conventional threat? China has 3 million troops, but lacks the logistic ability to mount a serious invasion of the United States.

But what about China's neighbors? China actually attacked Vietnam in 1979. But the Vietnamese repelled the Chinese with heavy losses, and Beijing has not committed a similar attack since then. Why would China attack a neighbor today or in the future? The only realistic scenario would be for China to invade its breakaway island province of Taiwan if it formally declared independence. China does not now have the conventional power for a successful invasion. Assuming that it could achieve that in the future, the costs of doing so would soar and any benefits plummet as China's geoeconomic integration with the global economy steadily deepens. China's economic partners would sever or restrict ties, plunging China into depression and chaos. That alone should deter a Chinese attack on Taiwan. Thus geoeconomic interests swallow geopolitical ambitions.

But much more seriously, does China pose a geoeconomic threat to the United States? America's GNP in 1998 was $7,921.3 trillion, more than eight times China's GNP of $928.9 billion. China's economy grew an annual average of 10.2 percent

from 1980 to 1990 and 11.1 percent from 1990 to 1998, compared with America's rates of 3.0 percent and 2.9 percent. America's per capita income in purchasing power parity for 1998 was $29,340, dwarfing China's $3,220. If those trends continue, China's economy will steadily catch up with America's within a generation. Although China's trade surplus with the United States was $60 billion in 1999, the composition of that trade was mostly toys and textiles. American firms have invested $21 billion in China. Over 700,000 Americans travel to China annually, pumping millions of more dollars into the country.

China's prosperity and the continued legitimacy and power of its ruling Communist party depend on the United States. The wealthier the Chinese people become, the greater the Communist party's legitimacy and more likely that its rule will remain largely unchallenged. The Communists do not want to jeopardize their rule by risking an economic war with the United States.

But the geoeconomic dependence of China and the Communist party on America goes far beyond trade. Over 50,000 Chinese students are currently studying in America, and over 500,000 have done so since 1979. Among those are the children of China's elite, including the current president, vice president, and prime minister. President Jiang Zemin's son, Mianheng, earned a doctorate in electrical engineering from Drexel University and currently is a busi-

ness executive who makes frequent trips to the United States. Xiaolin, the daughter of the unofficial vice president, Li Peng, studied at M.I.T. and now works for a company with strong business ties to the United States. Prime Minister Zhu Rongji's son, Yunlai, studied and worked for 10 years in the United States and is now a senior executive in a joint venture between the two countries. If you were a Chinese leader and had children with similar ties, how would that affect your perceptions of and policies toward the United States?

Although China does not now pose a geoeconomic threat to the United States, what about a generation or so in the future? China is emulating Japan's neomercantilist policies of targeting industries for development, dumping exports, and restricting imports. That neomercantilist strategy allowed many Japanese industries and technologies to catch up with and sometimes surpass their American rivals. Will it do the same for China? Or will the United States maintain its lead? Will the geoeconomic partners of today become future rivals?

How Not to Catch a Spy: The Saga of Wen Ho Lee

The Federal Bureau of Investigation (FBI) is in charge of counterintelligence, or spy catching, within the United States. In 1996, the FBI began an investigation into the apparent loss of American nuclear weapons technology secrets to China. The investigation centered on the Los Alamos

National Weapons Laboratory in New Mexico. In early 1999, the FBI announced they had a prime suspect.

Taiwan-born Wen Ho Lee is a naturalized American citizen. Now 60 years old, Lee worked at Los Alamos for twenty years, much of that time in the top secret "X Division." Lee was investigated, along with seventy others who had access to top secret weapons information, through the FBI's "matrix" suspect computer program. The suspect list was soon cut to twelve people, and the FBI finally focused on Lee. Why? The most important reason was the discovery that Lee had downloaded 806 megabytes of classified information onto his computer.

In March 1999, the Los Alamos laboratory fired Lee for violating security measures. In December 1999, the FBI arrested him on charges of spying for China. The FBI assumed that the Chinese recruited him as a spy during one of Lee's visits to China. Lee was held in solitary confinement without bail.

Then on September 20, 2000, the FBI dramatically dropped its spy charges against Lee under the agreement that he plead guilty to improperly downloading classified information and explain why he had done so. Why did the FBI suddenly about-face? One reason may be that an over zealous investigator committed perjury when he testified against Lee. Another, that the federal government was afraid of

Is this man a spy? The United States government charged Wen Ho Lee with giving nuclear weapons technology secrets to China, then later dropped the charges against him.

AP/Wide World Photos

revealing nuclear weapons information as evidence in court.

If Lee did not pass the secrets on to China, who, if anyone, did? In all the time that the FBI has concentrated its suspicions on Lee, the real spy—if he, she, or they actually exists—has remained free and likely has continued to pass information. Clearly Los Alamos has a grave security problem. Two computer hard drives filled with sensitive information disappeared while Lee was in prison then mysteriously reappeared. No other suspects have been identified. The Wen Ho Lee saga may become a classic case of how not to catch a spy.

Contents

Chapter 3 Nations, Nation-States, *and* Nationalism

Key Concepts and Terms

A Nation Without *a* State: *The* Kurds

The homeland of 20 million Kurds sprawls across southeastern Turkey and northern Iran, Iraq, and Syria. For decades the Kurds have been fighting for autonomy or outright independence in all four countries. To date all have been either crushed or contained. The Kurdistan Workers Party (PKK) was founded in 1978 and began an armed revolt lin 1984 for liberation from Turkey.

That 15-year war has cost Turkey $100 billion to fight and 30,000 dead, mostly Kurds.

The war turned in 1999 when the Turks captured Abdullah Occalan, the PKK's leader, and put him on trial for treason, a capital offense. To the surprise of Kurds and Turks alike, Occalan denounced the PKK's violence and asked for mere cultural and linguistic autonomy for the Kurds

within Turkey. Was this a deathbed or sincere conversion? Regardless, the PKK's Leadership Council rejected Occalan's plea and vowed to fight on. To date Turkey's bloody civil war has no end in sight. Unlikely as it currently seems, a generation from now the Middle East might well include a new Kurdish nation-state, which could have a profound effect on the regional power balance.

Nations, nation-states, and nationalism are largely modern concepts that have evolved in importance over the last several hundred years. Despite growing interdependence and the proliferation and power of international organizations, regimes, law, world opinion, and multinational corporations, the nation-state remains central to international relations. In 1945, there were 51 nation-states. In the year 2000 there were 191, along with 61 related and disputed territories! In the decades ahead, how many of those 61 other territories may achieve independence?

Nationalism, nation building, and multinationalism may well be the heart of geopolitical issues in the post–cold-war world. More established and newly independent states alike are faced with the problem of making real the slogan "Out of many, one" (*e pluribus unum*). A study found that in only 9.2 percent of all the world's countries had populations 100 percent of one nationality. In 18.9 percent, the largest nationality accounted for 90–99 percent of the population; in 18.9 percent, 75–89 percent; in 23.5 percent, 50–74 percent; and in 29.5 percent, less than 50 percent.[1] Of 166 nation-states in the mid-1980s, only one-third were considered homogenous (90 percent of the population was of one *ethnic group*). Of the multinational states, the dominant nation accounted for less than 70 percent of the total population in about half of those countries, and less than 50 percent in one-quarter.[2]

Governments from Nigeria to Malaysia and from Canada to Belgium are trying to promote new cultural identities that sometimes span dozens of distinct cultural identities. In many of these nation-states, people are forced to choose between loyalty to one's government and loyalty to one's culture, whether that culture is predominantly ethnic, racial, religious, or some combination. These unification efforts often fail. Sometimes, as in Yugoslavia, northern Ireland, Nigeria, Sri Lanka, Chad, Iraq, Lebanon, or Angola, to name a few, the nation-state dissolves into civil war as long-suppressed and exploited minority cultures seek independence.

Thus civil rather than international wars increasingly make the headlines as minorities sharing a common culture and heritage demand their own autonomous or independent state. One study identified over 260 ethnic groups that could qualify for sovereignty, of which more than 50 had separatist movements and 20 were fighting for independence.[3]

The number of potential international conflicts relates in part to the number of nation-states, especially if newly independent nation-states carry deep animosities toward the nation-states that formerly suppressed them. If so, in the future we could return full circle to an era of international wars. To understand the forces of nationalism and multinationalism, we must understand the vessels that give them meaning—culture, ideology, nation, state, and nation-state. Although we tend to use the words interchangeably, the concepts differ. A state is any political entity, a nation-state is a political entity with sovereignty, and a nation is primarily a population with a common culture, language, history, and ideals. Ideologies are systems of beliefs, behavior, and institutions that can span nations. This chapter explores these concepts and their impact on international relations.

Culture

culture any group's distinct collective means of interpreting and interacting with the world and each other within a given environment. More specifically, culture is a group's integrated and distinct system of values, ethics, behavior patterns, history, and language, which are in turn reflected in that group's social, economic, and political institutions.

The word *culture* conjures up a host of images. The popular view of culture is one of symphony orchestras and art museums attended by wealthy, snobbish patrons. In that sense, "culture" in every society is the privilege of the few. In reality, we are all constantly immersed in a culture, whether we are aware of it or not. Everyone is part of a predominant culture and is often partly influenced by many others as well. Culture shapes everything we see, do, think, feel, and even dream. Historian Theodore Von Laue asserts that "culture, like the individual mind, is a complex universe of which the major part is hidden in the vast recesses of the subconscious."[4]

Culture is any group's distinct collective means of interpreting and interacting with the world and each other within a given environment. More specifically, culture is a group's integrated, distinct system of values, ethics, behavior patterns, history, arts, and language, which are in turn reflected in that group's social, economic, and political institutions. Cultures are not isolated. Every culture borrows from and lends to others; generally, the more dynamic and successful a culture, the more it exchanges with other cultures. Yet despite this exchange, a culture must retain its essential values largely unchanged in order to survive.

People are born into a culture and from birth are constantly socialized into that culture's values, ethics, behavior, and so on. The family provides the individual's most important socialization experience. Babies join families with a certain socioeconomic level, composition (single- or two-parent, number of children, extended or nuclear), ethnicity, religion, and set of values. Usually the family's belief system reflects society's prevailing culture. Other forces are important in deepening the individual's socialization, including the school, neighborhood, workplace, mass media, peers, and government.

socialization the means by which an individual is indoctrinated into the values and behaviors of a **culture.**

Ideally, all these *socialization* forces work together to socialize the individual with the same or similar cultural values. Sometimes these socializing institutions represent different cultures. Then the individual may be torn between conflicting values and expectations. People born into an immigrant family might receive both the culture of their parents' ancestry and that of the new country. Sometimes

Tibetan Buddhism and an independent kingdom dates back to the seventh century and developed in relative isolation until the 1300s, when the Mongols asserted control. The Mongol emperor granted Tibet autonomy and designated the Dalai Lama as its leader in 1577. It was not until 1751 that China invaded Tibet and incorporated that remote theocracy into its empire. Tibet declared independence in 1911 when a revolution toppled China's imperial dynasty and the country dissolved into civil war. Not until 1950, the year after the communists took power, did they reinvade Tibet and assert control. Tensions between Tibetans and the Chinese colonizers grew. In 1959, the Chinese crushed a Tibetan revolt. The Dalai Lama and eventually a million followers reached Dharamsala in northern India and there formed a government and nation in exile.

In the four decades since then Beijing has engaged in a systematic policy of cultural genocide, murdering 1.2 million Tibetans, razing 6,000 monasteries, destroying ancient writings and works of art, and flooding the country with millions of Chinese settlers who now outnumber the 2.4 million Tibetans. The Chinese deny having committed these atrocities and claim that they have modernized Tibet with schools and health clinics, replacing a repressive regime in which 90 percent of the people were illiterate. The current 14th Dalai Lama, the equivalent of a pope, wants autonomy rather than independence for Tibet. He won the Nobel Peace prize in 1989. But the Chinese government refuses to negotiate with him and continues to destroy Tibet's culture.

What international principle should prevail in this conflict, sovereignty or human rights? What will be the likely fate of Tibetan culture if the Chinese persist in their policies? If you believe that China should be forced to stop its policies, how would you do so?

there is a discrepancy between a society's ideals and the behavior of its institutions and individuals. A culture's socializing forces can be offset by an individual's exposure to violence, injustice, corruption, socioeconomic exploitation, and unfulfilled expectations, or by defeat in war that could discredit the institutions or even values of the dominant culture.

There are no truly monocultural nations. Even nation-states such as Iceland, Portugal, Bangladesh, Korea, and Japan have some *subcultures*. For example, although Japan is considered a "homogeneous" culture, there are ethnic subcultures such as the Okinawans, Koreans, Chinese, and Ainu, which speak Japanese yet whose ancestry represents a different national culture, and social subcultures such as the untouchable class (*burakumin*), atomic bomb victims (*hibakusha*), and mixed-race people (*konketsujin*), whom the dominant culture has set aside and often discriminates against.

Although culture is most commonly used to distinguish between nations, we can talk about cultures that embrace several nations or are national subcultures. Examples of such *supranational cultures* are "Western culture" or "Far Eastern culture" in which various nationalities share some basic values, ethics, institutions, and history, if not language. Likewise, a nation can have many subcultures that are variations of the national culture.

Table 3.1 **Government Types by World Regions in 2000**

	Free	Partly Free	Not Free	Electoral Democracy
Africa	9 (17%)	21 (40%)	23 (43%)	17 (32%)
Asia	19 (50%)	9 (24%)	10 (26%)	24 (63%)
Eastern Europe, former USSR	10 (37%)	11 (40%)	6 (23%)	19 (70%)
Americas	25 (70%)	9 (27%)	1 (3%)	31 (88%)
Middle East	1 (7%)	3 (23%)	10 (70%)	2
Western Europe	24 (100%)			

Source: Freedom House 2000 Report.

Ideology

Human behavior is shaped by ideals. We believe or do not believe certain things, and we then act accordingly. We are all, to varying degrees, prisoners of the belief systems that permeate, inspire, and constrain our societies. As we have seen, cultures are, in part, belief systems.

Ideologies are more systematic belief systems that can transcend a given culture. Ideologies include political philosophies such as liberal democracy, communism, or fascism, religions, and even nations and cultures with very explicit, systematic world views. The essence of every ideology is a value system that determines that society's prevailing patterns of behavior, organization, goals, and policies. Some ideologies proscribe relatively strict sets of ideals and behavior, such as communism and fascism, whereas others, such as liberal democracy, are more permissive. Religions also vary to the degrees they restrict human behavior.

Individuals are not born with ideologies; as with cultures, individuals are socialized into an ideology. Individuals socialized the same way in the same ideology may vary considerably in how strong a hold that ideology has on them. Some individuals rigidly adhere to their world view and reject any information that runs counter to their beliefs. However, this resistance, sometimes referred to as "cognitive dissonance,"[5] can also lead to widened consciousness. Some individuals are relatively open-minded and can empathize with the situations and perspectives of others. Each individual is a unique mix of natural intelligence, aptitude, interests, humor, personality, ambitions, and experiences, all of which shape that individual's own version of his or her society's ideology and sometimes result in the individual adopting a completely different world view.

Why do ideologies, or any belief system, have such a strong hold on us? Our minds are not open enough to see the world, let alone understand it as it really is. Instead, our minds are selective—they grab bits of reality and give us the illusion that we are seeing the complex whole rather than fragments. Ideologies help our minds make those selections. As a system of related values, attitudes, beliefs, and behavior, an ideology gives the individual a systematic way to make sense of the world and find a place in it. Ideologies bring order to a chaotic world in which we are bombarded with thousands of bits of often conflicting information every second.

Yet ideologies have their drawbacks. Although they provide us with systematic beliefs, ideologies can also limit our ability to see the world in different ways or

ideology a system of beliefs, behaviors, and institutions that can span national boundaries.

Part 2   The Nation-State and International Relations

Democracy, Dictatorships, *and* Religion

Religion and freedom are clearly linked. According to the human rights watchdog group Freedom House, of the 88 free countries, 79 are Christian, two have large Christian minorities, four are mostly Buddhist, one is Jewish (Israel), one Hindu (India), and only one largely Muslim (Mali). Only 11 of the 67 countries with the worst civil and human rights records are mostly Christian. In all, Christian countries are five and a half times more likely to be free than repressive. Catholic and Protestant versions of Christianity have traditionally varied sharply in their relative compatibility to democracy. Until the late 1970s, dictatorships ruled most Catholic countries. Democracy and Islam are clearly incompatible. Of 43 countries with Muslim majorities, 28 are not free, 14 are partly free, and only one (Mali) is free. Six largely Muslim countries have electoral democracies. Why might Christian, especially Protestant, countries be compatible with democracy and Muslim countries be opposed to it?

Table 3.2 **Nationalities in the Former Soviet Republics (by population)**

Former Republic	Nationality or Ethnic Group (percentage)	Population (millions)
Russia	83% Russian, 4% Tatar, 3% Ukrainian	148.9
Ukraine	74% Ukrainian, 21% Russian	52.0
Uzbekistan	69% Uzbek, 11% Russian, 4% Kazskh, 4% Tajik, 4% Tatar, 2% Karakalpal	21.0
Kazakhstan	40% Kazakh, 38% Russian, 6% German, 6% Ukrainian, 2% Tatar	17.0
Belarus (Byelorussia)	79% Belarussian, 12% Russian, 4% Polish, 2% Ukrainian	10.4
Azerbaijan	78% Azeri, 8% Russian, 8% Armenian	7.3
Tajikistan (Tadzhikistan)	59% Tajik, 23% Uzbek, 10% Russian, 2% Tatar	5.5
Georgia	69% Georgian, 9% Armenian, 9% Russian, 5% Azeri, 3% Ossetian, 2% Abkhazian	5.5
Kyrgyzstan (Kirghizia)	52% Kyrgyz, 22% Russian, 13% Uzbek, 3% Ukrainian, 2% German, 2% Tatar	4.5
Moldova (Moldavia)	64% Moldovan, 14% Ukrainian, 13% Russian, 4% Gagauzi, 2% Bulgarian	4.4
Turkmenistan	68% Turkmeni, 13% Russian, 9% Uzbek, 3% Kazakh	3.8
Lithuania	80% Lithuanian, 9% Russian, 8% Polish	3.8
Armenia	90% Armenian, 5% Azeri, 2% Russian, 2% Kurdish	3.3
Latvia	54% Latvian, 33% Russian, 5% Belarussian	2.7
Estonia	62% Estonian, 30% Russian	1.6

Figures are approximate because of postindependence migrations.

Sources: Based on *Journal of Soviet Nationalities* (Spring 1990), pp. 150–53. *New York Times,* August 29, 1991, p. A19, and September 1, 1991, Section 4, p. 2; *Time,* September 9, 1991, pp. 18–19. Charles Kegley and Eugene Wittkopf, *World Politics: Trend and Transformation* (New York: Bedford Books, 1998).

The World's 13 Worst Dictatorships

In 1998, the world's 13 most repressive countries were Afghanistan, Burma, Cuba, Equatorial Guinea, Iraq, Libya, North Korea, Saudi Arabia, Somalia, Sudan, Syria, Turkmenistan, and Vietnam, along with the worst-rated subjected territories, Tibet and Kosovo. What do these countries share besides brutal dictatorships? Three were one-party Marxist-Leninist regimes and eight were predominantly Islamic.

understand it as it really is. Individuals raised in a liberal democratic society, for example, have trouble understanding the world through a communist's eyes, and vice versa. Agreements between those with different ideologies would usually be more difficult to forge than between those sharing the same ideology. Ideologies such as communism and fascism, whose values demand the subjugation of the individual to the state, are especially susceptible to the abuse of power and sometimes even genocide by their adherents.

A comprehensive ideology asks and then answers a set of important, interrelated questions.[6]

1. *Human nature:* What is the nature of humans? Basically good, basically bad, or mixed? Are we shaped mostly by nature or by nurture? How does human nature affect politics?

2. *Roles:* What are the respective roles and duties of government, society, and the individual? Which needs should take precedence—society's or the individual's?

3. *Law:* What is the nature and role of law in society? Are some laws—such as the Constitution—fixed, or is everything open to question and change?

4. *Human rights:* What rights do individuals enjoy? How much liberty? How much equality? What duties? What limits if any should be placed on human rights?

5. *Power:* How is power organized? How is the power distribution justified? How powerful are the power holders? How are leaders selected? What restrains their power? How do those holding power make decisions?

6. *Justice:* What is it? How does the system guarantee it?

7. *Goals:* What is the purpose of society? Of government? What are the society's ideals? How are those ideals best achieved?

8. *Institutions:* What are the best political, economic, and social institutions for fulfilling society's ideals?

Nations

nation primarily a population with a common culture, language, history, traditions, ideals, and sense of common destiny.

What is a nation? A *nation* is a people with a common culture, ideology, language, traditions, and history, or, as John Stoessinger put it, "a people's sense of collective destiny through a common past and the vision of a common future."[7] The most important distinction between a nation and a culture is that a nation must

Middle Kingdom *of* Babel: China's Linguistic Stew

Nearly one of every five people on earth lives in China. The official language of those 1.2 billion people is Putonghua or Mandarin Chinese. But only about 800 million people speak Putonghua, which is the largest of eight main and hundreds of lesser languages spoken across that huge country. What is popularly known as Chinese is actually a group of related languages, much as the Germanic language groups embrace such mutually unintelligible tongues as English, Dutch, German, and Swedish, to name a few. Putonghua has become the international language for Chinese much as English has for the world, including speakers of other Germanic languages. Among the other Chinese languages are the 90 million Wu speakers in the lower Yangtse valley with most in Shanghai and the 70 million Yue or Cantonese speakers in the south. Those Chinese languages share a written form with 40,000 different characters, each of which is pronounced differently in each language. But because the meaning is the same, speakers of different Chinese languages can communicate through the written word even though they do not understand what comes from each other's mouths. Thus written Chinese characters provide a common ground for communication much as Latin did for medieval Europe, although Latin was spoken as well as written the same way by those who knew it.

be believed in to be realized. One can be part of a culture and not be aware of it. To be part of a nation, the individual must recognize that relationship. People cannot be nationalistic if they do not know they are part of a nation. Self-identity depends on context. We define ourselves by what we are not and identify with those who share similar characteristics. In traditional societies, the primary loyalty was to the village. In the modern world, advanced communications and transportation allow individuals to identify with those sharing a similar culture over large areas. Thus *nationalism*, the political assertion of one's national identity, independence, and interests, is a modern phenomenon, a result of a people with a common culture, language, ideology, tradition, and history becoming aware of that reality, and acting on that awareness. National identity can only occur after a people has achieved certain levels of socioeconomic, technological, and political development. Nations need not necessarily be included within the same territory or legally defined—in fact most are not. Where was the nation of Israel before the sovereign state was created in 1948? Where does the Palestinian nation exist today? The answer is, In the minds of those two peoples.

nationalism a feeling of intense emotional identity with one's nation.

The first *nation-states* that achieved mass national identity were Great Britain, Holland, the United States, and France. During the 1820s, nationalism swept away Spanish and later Portuguese rule from most of Latin America. During the mid-19th century, political unification for Germany and Italy, and revolution in Japan succeeded in creating modern mass national states, while nationalism fermented in dozens of other nation-states in Europe and elsewhere. The 1919 Versailles Peace Conference and President Wilson's call for "national self-determination" stimulated nationalism among colonial peoples. The imperial powers were able to suppress these independence movements until after World War II, when one by one new countries emerged from the ruins of former empires.

nation-state a sovereign state or system of government over a clearly defined territory whose legitimacy is recognized by other nation-states.

Nationalism can be either a powerfully constructive or destructive force in international relations. Nationalism by definition means a unified, mobilized, loyal population that governments can deploy for development or aggression. Nationalism can be expressed either through liberal democracy in which the state's purpose is to guarantee individual rights and democratic processes, or statism in which the state personifies the nation's glories and all citizens are mobilized by the state for the state. Nationalists are committed toward putting national interests ahead of all others—individual, group, or international. In identifying so powerfully with one's own national interests, individuals can be indifferent to the needs of other peoples. Nationalism often promotes feelings of superiority over or fear of others, which can damage international relations. At worst, nationalism can lead to the frenzied expansionism of fascist Japan, Germany, and Italy, which resulted in the deaths of over 50 million people between 1931 and 1945.

States, Nation-States, *and* Sovereignty

States are almost as old as humankind and its cultures. The first states emerged from the first attempts of small groups of people to divide political duties, establish formal rules, and designate leaders among themselves. Since then, as cultures became more complex and often encompassed other cultures, states have come in all shapes and sizes, from the city-states of the ancient Greeks and Renaissance Italy; to the huge empires of Rome, China, and Persia; to the democracy of Athens or many Native American (Indian) tribes; to the despotism of Tzarist Russia or Tokugawa Japan; to the religious and political responsibilities shared by the Roman Catholic Church and the Holy Roman Empire; to the emerging multinational state, the European Union.

Nation-states are products of the modern world; any political entity can be a state, but nation-states must by definition be sovereign. The first nation-states emerged with the Treaty of Westphalia of 1648, which ended the Thirty Years War between Protestant and Catholic princes and kings. The Thirty Years War was the culmination of 130 years of religious warfare sparked by Martin Luther's rebellion against the Pope in 1517. Henceforth, according to the Westphalia Treaty, each prince had the sovereign right to decide his state's religious preferences (*cuius regio eius religio*), a principle that had first been articulated with the Peace of Augsburg in 1555, but was now made irrevocable. The 1,200-year religious and secular power of Rome was destroyed, along with the feudal world of decentralized power beholden to a faraway ruler with limited but ultimate secular power (suzerainty). Through imperialism, diplomacy, and decolonization, Europe's nation-state system eventually spread around the world.

Sovereignty thus depends on a government having the highest authority within a clearly defined territory encompassing a population, and that authority is recognized as legitimate by both its inhabitants and other sovereign governments. Sovereign states are considered equal in status according to international law, and have basic rights and duties. One basic right according to international law is that every nation-state should be free to run its internal affairs as its government sees fit. This right is also a duty in that no nation-state can interfere in the internal affairs of others. Regardless of whether a nation-state's inhabitants are citizens or residents they must all follow that government's laws. As Hedley Bull put it, sovereignty includes both "internal sovereignty, which means supremacy over all

The Newest Independent State: East Timor

Imperialism and colonialism are not only committed by the West against the rest of the world. The European great powers, the United States, and Japan gave up their empires. Portugal was one of the last remaining colonial holdouts. The Portuguese colonized the spice island of East Timor in the 16th century and ruled it for the next three centuries. Indonesia invaded East Timor in 1975 and named it the 27th province in 1976.

A quarter-century of violence followed. The East Timorese revolted, and war has plagued the island ever since. Of a population of 800,000, perhaps 200,000 have died from fighting, disease, and starvation. The struggle ensured that the costs for Indonesia to colonize East Timor far exceeded any benefits. That war finally exhausted Indonesia politically and economically. President Suharto called East Timor a "pebble" in his shoe that he longed to cast off. Setting aside the fear that freeing one oppressed people would encourage liberation groups elsewhere, Suharto

and his successor President J. B. Habibie opened negotiations with the United Nations. On May 5, 1999, U.N. and Indonesian envoys agreed to a referendum that offered a choice between autonomy and independence. On August 8, 1999, the population of East Timor voted overwhelmingly for independence in a referendum monitored by the United Nations. In 2000 a U.N. peacekeeping force arrived to quell violence and assist independence.

other authorities within that territory and population . . . and external sovereignty, by which is meant not supremacy but independence of outside authorities."[8]

Throughout the modern era, political philosophers, rulers, and politically active people have agreed that sovereignty is the right to assert supreme authority over a realm. Where that sovereignty lies, however, has been hotly debated. A succession of political philosophers—Jean Boudin (1530–1596), Hugo Grotius (1583–1645), and Thomas Hobbes (1588–1679), among others—explored the concept of sovereignty and argued that sovereignty, or the highest authority, should reside in the king. In 1571, Jean Boudin defined sovereignty as "supreme power over citizens and subjects, unrestrained by law."[9] Later political philosophers—John Locke (1632–1704), Charles-Louis Montesquieu (1689–1755), Jean-Jacques Rousseau (1712–1778), Thomas Paine (1737–1809), and Thomas Jefferson (1743–1826), among others—rejected the concept of a monarchy with absolute sovereign powers and instead argued that sovereignty should be based in the people. Despite their differences, starting with Hobbes's *Leviathan* (1651) all these political philosophers shared the idea that the state resulted from a "social contract" between ruler and ruled, in which the latter granted authority to the former in return for security and justice. Thus the state is a legal abstraction, like a corporation, in which its citizens or subjects are shareholders, as well as a concrete reality. The concept of popular sovereignty has become universal. Today, in virtually every country, sovereignty theoretically lies with the people who are "citizens" rather than "subjects." Nearly every nation-state has a constitution that articulates the political system's sovereign purpose, values, and organization.

Once recognized, however, sovereignty is not absolute. Traditionally, a state was considered sovereign only if it could defend itself. Thus imperialism—the conquest of one state by another—was considered just. Sovereign Poland was conquered and divided among Russia, Prussia, and Austria in 1796. The European powers, later joined by the United States and Japan, used this principle to justify conquering hundreds of nations around the world over the past 500 years.

States could gain as well as lose their sovereignty through armed struggle. Starting with America's war of independence against Britain in 1776, increasing numbers of states achieved freedom through revolt. After 1945, although some colonies continued to win their freedom through bloodshed, most have achieved it by the imperial power voluntarily granting it in the face of mass political movements within the colony, international pressure, and the growing liability of maintaining an empire. Between 1989 and 1991, the sovereign states of Yugoslavia and the Soviet Union disintegrated into many.

Just because a state is recognized as sovereign by some does not mean it is recognized by all. For example, a state's membership in the United Nations depends on the U.N. Security Council and a majority in the General Assembly recognizing that state's sovereignty. Some states appear to have the prerequisites for sovereignty yet are not recognized by other nation-states. For instance, although the Soviet Union and the Union of South Africa created "republics" within their respective countries, virtually no other countries recognized them as such. The governments of the 15 Soviet "republics" and six South African "homelands" were clearly not the highest sovereign authority—real power resided in Moscow and Pretoria, respectively.

Revolutionary change in which a government is overthrown and a new regime installed sometimes poses problems of international recognition. Many countries may favor waiting for the dust to settle before they extend diplomatic recognition to the new regime. For example, after the 1949 communist revolution in China, the United States continued to recognize the government in exile in Taiwan rather than the communist government that ruled the mainland (excluding Hong Kong). In 1971, the United States established informal relations (*de facto*) with China, and in 1979 granted full legal recognition (*de jure*) to the Beijing regime. In contrast to the United States, Britain follows a policy of recognizing whatever regime is in power, regardless of whether or not it is politically or morally compatible. Thus London officially recognized the Communist party as China's legitimate government in January 1950.

In a world of sovereign states, international relations are by definition anarchic. If not a constant "war of all against all," international relations are certainly shaped by constant conflict as each state pursues its own interests, often to the detriment of other nation-states. Each nation-state is solely responsible for its own protection, often leading to a "security dilemma" in which the military and other preparations a nation-state takes to protect itself from potential aggressors in turn potentially threatens the security of other states, thus leading them to take similar precautions and exacerbating the arms race. Steps taken to ensure the security of one nation-state may lead to the insecurity of others.

Theoretically all nation-states enjoy independence and equality. In reality, no nation-states are equal in status, power, or even rights, and the sovereign power of nation-states to act as they will within their borders, to varying extents, is severely eroded. Sovereign power is not enough. Although nation-states are theoretically equal, they differ profoundly in power and its territorial, population, economic, technological, financial, cultural, and military components. The more powerful a country, and the more skillfully a government wields its nation's power,

Not only are ever more nation-states joining the ranks of the world's countries, but a greater percentage are liberal democracies. That is great news for freedom-loving people everywhere. Of the world's 191 countries in 1998, 88 (46 percent) were "free," 52 were "partly free," and 50 were "not free" (26 percent), according to Freedom House, a human rights research organization. "Free" countries were those whose people enjoyed the full spectrum of human and civil rights within political systems with elected legislatures, independent courts, and two or more competitive parties. A country is considered "not free" if it has none of those characteristics and "partly free" if it has some.

How Much Freedom?

Just because a country has competitive elections does not make it free. In 1998, 117 countries (61 percent of all countries and 55 percent of the world's population) were "electoral democracies" that had fair, free, competitive elections to legislatures, although 29 of those governments deprived the populations of full civil rights. That is up sharply from 69 countries in 1987 but has held steady at 117 since 1995.

Fareed Zakaria, the editor of the influential journal *Foreign Affairs,* wrote a 1997 article entitled "The Rise of Illiberal Democracies" in which he lamented that half-way political house between free and not free. But for now such pessimism is unwarranted. The practice of electoral democracy often leads gradually or abruptly to civil rights democracy. In just three years the number of those 117 electoral democracies rated "free" jumped from 76 (64 percent) to 88 (75 percent), whereas the 40 "partly free" and one "not free" (war-torn Bosnia-Herzegovina) dropped to 29 "partly free" countries.

Liberal democracy is spreading to ever more countries. The percentage of the world's population living in free countries increased from 35 percent in 1981 to 39 percent in 1998, while the percentage living in not free countries plummeted from 42 percent to 33 per-cent. Seven new countries became free in 1998 alone. But will that trend continue? What determines whether a country is free, partly free, or not free?

Liberal democracies tend to thrive in middle-class societies where at least three of four people share the same nationality. Nonetheless democracy has flourished in such multinational countries as Belgium, Canada, and Switzerland. Partly and not free countries often share mass poverty and multinational tensions or outright violence. A handful of countries, such as Estonia, Latvia, Mali, Namibia, and South Africa, have established electoral democracies despite the obstacles of poverty and multinationalism. Religion is also important. Christian states are five and a half times more likely to be free as to be repressive, but no Arab state and only one non-Arab Muslim state is free. The record for other religions is mixed.

Table 3.3 **Freedom, by Number and World Percentage of 191 Nation-States and 61 Territories**

	Free	Partly Free	Not Free
Nation-States	88	53	50
Territories	44	4	13
Percentage of the World's Population	39.84%	26.59%	33.58%

Source: Freedom House 2000 Report.

Table 3.4 **Freedom, by Number and Percentage of World Population**

	Free	Partly Free	Not Free	World
January 1981	1,613.0 (35.90%)	970.9 (21.60%)	1,911.9 (42.50%)	4,495.8
January 1998	2,354.0 (39.84%)	1,570.6 (26.59%)	1,984.1 (33.58%)	5908.7

Populations are in millions.

Source: Freedom House 2000 Report.

the more easily it can safeguard and expand its national interests. Likewise, although the international norm of sovereignty theoretically empowers states with independence, in an anarchic world states must ultimately defend themselves. Without a "world policeman," the stronger nation-states can often get away with exploiting the weaker nation-states.

Nation-states vary in population size from such behemoths as China and India with 1,239 billion and 980 million people, respectively, to such microstates as Nauru with 7,000. They vary in territory from continent-sized powers such as Russia, the United States, and Canada to tiny states such as Monaco, Vanuatu, or the Cook Islands. Thirty-eight nation-states, or one-fifth of the world's total, have a combined population of only 10,668,000. Many of these "microstates" have given up some of their sovereignty in return for economic and political security. For example, the Republic of the Marshall Islands and the Federated States of Micronesia have signed a Compact of Association with the United States, giving Washington responsibility for their defense and foreign affairs. Monaco and Liechtenstein have granted to France and Switzerland, respectively, the rights to manage their defense and diplomacy.

Sovereignty means one country cannot interfere in another's internal affairs. In reality, despite the conceptual persistence of sovereignty and the lack of a world government, there are numerous and expanding webs of constraints on a state's foreign and domestic policies. The growing body of international law imposes clear restraints on a government's action not only toward other nation-states but even within its own borders. International law condemns both a government's aggression against other nation-states and its own people. Iraqi President Saddam Hussein was cited not just for ordering his armies to invade neighboring Kuwait, but for his brutal repression of Kurdish and Shiite separatists within Iraq itself. The United Nations sanctioned international forces led by the United States to expel Iraq from Kuwait, and later to extend security and humanitarian aid to the Kurds and Shiites. That mission is not an exception. The United Nations now has peacekeeping troops in over a score of countries to deter the organized violence of some people toward others.

Multinationalism

Although the United States is often seen as a vast mosaic of diverse ethnic, racial, and cultural groups, it is actually one of the world's most unified nations. More than 90 percent of those living in the United States identify themselves primarily as Americans rather than as their distant ancestry. Like the United States, all of the five largest European countries—France, Great Britain, Germany, Italy, and Spain—have distinct racial, linguistic, ethnic, and religious minorities. London, Berlin, and Paris are just as much a mosaic of different subcultures as New York City. Which country is more ethnically divided—the United States or France with its large Breton and Corsican minorities; Britain with its Welsh, Scots, and Irish as well as English; or Spain with its Basques and Catalonians? The American South, Southwest, even New England and California, have distinct regional identities, although none today is separatist and all mesh within a common American culture. Contrast America's relative regional unity with the immense regional, linguistic, and cultural differences between northern and southern Italy and Germany, or between Catalonia and the rest of Spain. Countries such as Britain, the United States, Spain, Germany, or France are considered multiethnic rather than multinational.

Corbis/Sygma

The Face of Terror?

Osama Bin Laden. Is this the face of terror or liberation? In scores of countries around the world armed groups are trying either to overthrow and replace a hated government or free their nation from control by another. How do those independence or revolutionary struggles affect international relations? Should all those nationalities who want their own country be granted one?

These nations have a range of distinct subcultures, some of which originated in another nation but have largely assimilated or blended into the values, language, behavior, and so on of the dominant culture.

multinationalism two or more distinct nations, each with a large population, existing within one **nation-state.**

However, about 90 percent of existing nation-states actually are *multinational* states, including such advanced industrial states as Canada, Belgium, and Switzerland and less developed states as Nigeria, India, Mexico, and Fiji, to name a few. Many believe that ideally every nation should have its own sovereign state. The United Nations enshrines the ideal of "self-determination for all peoples" whether its members choose to recognize a particular people or not. In 1992, the U.N. General Assembly passed a "Declaration of Rights of Indigenous Peoples" to help protect the estimated 300 million indigenous peoples living in more than 70 countries.

Indigenous peoples are the original inhabitants of a land that was invaded and conquered by others. Self-determination does not necessarily mean separation, but the right of those peoples to pursue their traditional way of life without interference from the dominant culture.

Some multinational nation-states have stayed together, and others have been torn apart by civil war. Switzerland, Belgium, and Canada are examples of multinational nation-states that have so far remained intact despite resentments and conflicts in those nations. The glue that holds diverse peoples together consists of many ingredients. The same ingredients that form a cohesive nation can shape a cohesive multination—a shared history, culture, economy, language, ideals, government, laws, and goals.

Governments attempt to "*nation-build*" or create a common identity out of many different nationalities. In multinational nation-states people's loyalties often become divided between their national identity and the supranational identity promoted by the nation-state. For example, with what culture does a French Canadian identify more—Quebecois, French, or Canadian? The answer would vary considerably from one French Canadian to the next. Support for a separate Quebec is steadily rising, with 41 percent voting in favor in a 1990 referendum, 45 percent in 1992, and 49.4 percent in 1994. Will a majority vote *oui* in the next referendum? If so, will Canada grant autonomy to Quebec?

How do you create a new identity without destroying old ones? One way is to stress a common purpose and values. There is a close relationship between policy, stability, and prosperity. The more politically stable a country, the more prosperous, and vice versa. Countries cannot enjoy political economic development without constructive, far-sighted government policies designed to create and

Table 3.5 **Correlation of Mononationality and Multinationality with Freedom, 2000**

	Mononationality Number Percentage		Multinationality Number Percentage	
Free	66	(58%)	22	(29%)
Partly Free	22	(19%)	31	(40%)
Not Free	26	(23%)	24	(31%)
Total	114	(100%)	77	(100%)

Countries with a dominant nationality, defined as 75 percent or more of a population, tend to be more democratic than multinational states.

Source: Freedom House 2000 Report.

Part 2   The Nation-State and International Relations

distribute wealth and power as equitably as possible both between and within the nations it rules.

Since the early 1950s, western Europeans have attempted to create an ever more integrated economic and political union with a capital at Brussels. There are now 15 nation-states and 375 million people in the European Union. In addition to deepening these political and economic institutions, Brussels is attempting to build a European "nation." These efforts have brought a mixed success. Although surveys indicated that over the past 40 years increasing numbers of Europeans are identifying with the concept of being European, few seem willing to abandon their national identity. Most Europeans favor ever greater economic and even political unity; few are willing to exchange their primary loyalty to the nation in which they were born for the more abstract identity of Europe. At best, Europeans will increasingly accept an European identity as secondary to their real nation.

Nation-building problems of newly independent countries are often much more severe than those of Europe. European identity is shaped by widespread literacy, high living standards, extensive trade and travel, and mass media that help different nationalities empathize with each other and search for a common identity. Newly independent underdeveloped countries lack those forces that are essential to forging a new identity.

Language is one of the more important sources of common identity and purpose, and is a divisive force in multinations. English or French remains the official language for several score of countries around the world long after they have achieved independence. Why don't those countries adopt one of their native languages as their official language rather than retain the colonial master's tongue? The answer is the neutrality of English or French.

Both Nigeria and India have chosen to retain English as their official language. With 121 million people, Nigeria is Africa's most populous country. Although over 260 dialects are spoken, Nigeria's different cultures can be grouped into Yoruba, Hausa, and Ibo. Seven years after Nigeria achieved independence in 1960, the Ibo nation tried to gain independence and form the Republic of Biafra. Over the next three years of civil war, 1.5 million people died from fighting and starvation. The Biafran independence movement was finally crushed in 1970.

India has 14 major language groups and 1,600 dialects! Although 85 percent of the population is Hindu, large, concentrated Muslim (12 percent of the population) and Sikh (1 percent) populations have demanded either outright separation, as in Muslim Kashmir and Assam, or increased autonomy, as in Sikh Punjab. If India adopted 1 of the 14 languages spoken in the country as official, that would offend the hundreds of millions of speakers of the other 13 unofficial languages. Those who spoke the official language would have a political, economic, and social edge over those who did not. Large parts of India are already torn by religious and ethnic strife. To make one native language official could well tear India apart.

Independence movements gain adherents when minority national groups feel they are being discriminated against or exploited by the majority. Like communism's collapse, the Soviet Union's breakup in 1990 and 1991 was inevitable—the only question was when. The Soviet Union was simply another name for the Russian empire; the 14 non-Russian Soviet "republics" were in effect Moscow's colonies. Russians were exactly half the Soviet population, with another 20 percent Slavic Ukranians and Belorussians, 20 percent Muslim Kazakhs, Azerbaijanis, Kirghiz, Turkmen, Uzbeks, Tadjiks, and others, about 3 percent Christian minorities such as the Baltic Estonians, Latvians, and Lithuanians, and Caucasus

The Changing Face of Europe? Europe's Population Crisis and Immigration

Both the existing EU nationalities and the common identity of being European may be challenged by immigration early in the next century. Europeans are aging rapidly, and the birth rate is plummeting to the point where most native populations are actually diminishing. By the year 2025, the European Union will be short 135 million workers to replace and support those which have retired. Those workers will mostly come from Africa, Asia, and Latin America. Europe's population will become as physically diverse as that of the United States. Since colonial times, America has been a land of immigrants, but the concept is new for Europeans. Will they welcome or reject that human tide? Will those immigrants be assimilated through socialization, marriage, and socioeconomic mobility, or will they mostly cling to their own communities? Or will they be ghettoized? How will the immigrants change the culture of each EU country and Europe as a whole? These questions will become increasingly central to European politics and its foreign relations.

Georgians and Armenians, and 1 percent Romanian Moldavians. In addition, there were hundreds of much smaller cultures.

A vast totalitarian state apparatus and communist ideology allowed the Russian empire (as the USSR) to remain intact generations after other great empires—the Austro-Hungarian, Ottoman, British, French, and others—had crumbled. Moscow's totalitarian political, economic, and social controls had steadily loosened and its communist ideology had become increasingly discredited over the 40 years following Stalin's death in 1953. It took President Mikhail Gorbachev's policies of openness (*glasnost*), restructuring (*perestroika*), and democracy to finally topple the tottering empire. But unlike the breakup of other empires, Moscow's received its death blow when Russian President Boris Yeltsin declared his republic's independence from the Soviet empire in 1991, and the other republics followed suit.

Nationalism has replaced communism as the *raison d'être* of the new nation-states. Yet independence has not solved a range of political, economic, ethnic, and environmental problems. Like other fallen empires, the broken pieces of the Soviet Union remain economically interdependent, the products of seven decades of centralized economic planning. Of the former 15 republics, 12 remain loosely tied through the Commonwealth of Independent States (CIS). Another problem is the Russian diaspora. Over 60 million Russians are scattered across the other former republics, and the newly independent states are debating how to fit the Russians into their political, economic, and social life. Estonia arrived at a harsh solution. With nearly half of its population Russian, Estonia's government has ruled that only Estonians or those of other cultures who settled in the country before 1940 are allowed to be citizens. The law disenfranchises most of Estonia's Russian population. Russia and Ukraine are squabbling over who owns the Crimean peninsula. Stalin handed over the Crimea from Russia to Ukraine in 1946, and now the Russians want it back from independent Ukraine.

Irredentism occurs when nations scattered among two or more nation-states want to reunite. There are three types of irredentism. One pattern is when the government of one united nation claims that its compatriots in another state should be joined to it. For example, during the 1930s, Hitler followed an irredentist policy of uniting into Germany those Germans living in surrounding countries such as Austria, Czechoslovakia, and Poland. The result of Hitler's ambitions, of course, was World War II.

More commonly, a nation divided among several nation-states desires its own sovereign state. The Palestinians are divided across Israel, Lebanon, Syria, Jordan, and Egypt, and there are exiles in a dozen other countries. The Palestinian Liberation Organization (PLO) was founded in 1964 and dedicated to Palestinian independence. Originally the PLO favored the destruction of Israel and creation of a Palestinian state on its ruins. More recently, it has settled for a Palestine encompassing the West Bank of the Jordan River and the Gaza Strip of lands occupied by Israel since the 1967 War. Israel's Likud party, which ruled from 1975 to 1991, was adamantly opposed to any Palestinian autonomy, let alone independence. When the Labor party was elected in June 1991, it favored some Palestinian autonomy as part of its "land for peace" policy. Under treaties at Oslo in 1993 and Wye in 1998, Israel granted increased autonomy to the PLO to rule the West Bank and Gaza Strip under a state known as the Palestinian Authority. Now autonomous under Israeli sovereignty, the Palestinian Authority will most likely achieve independence.

Finally, there is the cold war problem where one previously united nation has been divided between communist and noncommunist halves, and the halves want to become whole again, as in East and West Germany, East and West Austria, North and South Korea, and North and South Vietnam. The allies agreed to temporarily divide Germany, Austria, and Korea into occupation zones after the defeat of Germany and Japan. These divisions solidified with the cold war and the fears of Moscow and Washington that reunification could lead to a government that would join the other side. Vietnam was divided at the 17th parallel between a communist North and non-communist South at the Geneva Convention of 1954, when France granted the country independence.

After tough negotiations between the occupying powers, East and West Austria were rejoined in 1955, with the stipulation that the nation-state be neutral. Following advice from Washington, which feared a communist takeover, South Vietnam's government rejected holding elections as stipulated by the Geneva Convention. For two decades, South Vietnam battled a growing communist insurgency backed by North Vietnam. The country was reunified in 1975 after the Saigon regime was conquered by North Vietnam. In 1986, Gorbachev renounced the Brezhnev Doctrine, which justified Soviet military intervention in communist countries experiencing a democratic revolution. In 1989, he allowed the Berlin Wall to be destroyed, and in 1990 he nodded as East Germany was reunited with West Germany. Starting in the late 1980s, the South and North Korean governments began negotiating their nation's reunification but to date have made no progress. Reunification is unlikely unless one of the two Koreas experiences a revolution that brings to power a government similar to that in the other half. Most analysts say a revolution in either Seoul or Pyongyang is unlikely.

In no region are irredentist claims more possible than in Africa, in which only one of the 64 countries, Somalia, is not multinational. Tanzanian President Julius Nyerere recognized this problem when he said that "African boundaries are so absurd that they need to be recognized as sacrosanct." He meant of course that Western imperialism had so arbitrarily and thoroughly divided African nations that any attempt to reorganize the continent along the "one-state, one-nation" principle would only result in chaos and war. The Organization of African Unity (OAU) has attempted to defuse any potential irredentist claims by declaring that Africa's present boundaries are inviolable. Somalia's claim to being one nation is no guarantee of order. In 1992, the country was torn apart by civil war and famine as rival groups fought for spoils and supremacy. It took the intervention of a 20,000-person U.N. peacekeeping force to restore order and prevent genocide from starvation and murder.

Nationalism *and* Internationalism

Since the 17th century, nation-states have been the central players in international relations. In a world knit by thousands of international organizations and multinational corporations, is the nation-state becoming obsolete? Will nation-states become just one player among many on the global stage?

As we saw with Europeans, just because peoples are becoming more interdependent does not mean they are becoming more international. Individuals identify primarily with their respective nations rather than with humanity, and governments continue to put their perceived national interests before international interests, even though as the world becomes ever more interdependent it is increasingly difficult to distinguish between the two.

In the contemporary world, nationalism and *internationalism* both powerfully affect the world system. On the one hand, such regions as Europe, North America, and Southeast Asia are attempting to forge closer international ties. People of different nationalities are increasingly entwined through trade, travel, television and radio, and the deepening global environmental crises that adversely affect us all.

Elsewhere, on the other hand, nationalism is growing. Although there are many nations in the world, few are synonymous with the nation-states in which they reside. Most of the world's nation-states are multinational. Nation building has become the modern world's version of the philosopher's stone. The world's last great empire, the Russian, crumbled as much from growing nationalism as communism's failures. Yugoslavia was torn apart as Croats, Slovenes, Albanians, and Bosnians won independence from the Serb majority.

Interdependence will continue, although it is clear that nationalism will add more independent nation-states to the global system. The nation-state will remain the world system's most important unit. World government is unlikely for the foreseeable future.

Study Questions

1. What is culture?
2. What is an ideology? Give an example.
3. Define the term *nation,* and give an example.
4. What is a nation-state?
5. How does socialization occur?

6. What is sovereignty, and how has the concept changed throughout the modern era? Why is sovereignty more an ideal than a reality?

7. How have nation-states coped with the problems of multinationalism?

8. What are the types of irredentism, and what are examples of irredentist conflicts?

9. In an increasingly interdependent world, is the nation-state becoming obsolete? Are there any viable alternatives?

∮ InfoTrac College Edition Sources

Using the Subject Guide, enter the search terms *Reformation, nationalism, sovereignty,* and/or *ethnicity.* Using Keywords, enter the search term *Thirty Years War.*

Bolton, Patrick, and Gerard Roland. "The Breakup of Nations: A Political Economy Analysis."
Buckley, William F., Jr. "'Ideology' on Our Mind."
Drucker, Peter F. "The Global Economy and the Nation-State."
Enriquez, Juan. "Too Many Flags?"
Freeze, Gregory L. "Subversive Piety: Religion and the Political Crisis in Late Imperial Russia."
Lammi, Walter. "The Hermeneutics of Ideological Indoctrination."
Medoff, Marshall H. "The Political Implications of State Political Ideology: A Measure Tested."
Meyer, John, et al. "World Society and the Nation-State."
Minogue, Kenneth. "Does National Sovereignty Have a Future?"
Shlapentokh, Dmitry. "The Russian Identity Crisis."
Singer, Brian C. J. "Cultural versus Contractual Nations: Rethinking Their Opposition."
Talbott, Strobe. "Self-Determination in an Interdependent World."
Van den Berghe, Pierre. "Denationalizing the State."
Wiebe, Robert H. "Humanizing Nationalism."

On *the* Web

http://www.uni-potsdam.de/u/geschichte/mdk/hle.htm
Important aspects of the Thirty Years War

http://www.wisc.edu/nationalism/
Website focused on the study of nationalism

http://www.inter.nl.net/users/Paul.Treanor/plana.html
Site that contains many links to specific studies of nationalism

Contents

Chapter 4 *The* Power *and* Wealth *of* Nations

Key Concepts and Terms

During five centuries of modernization, the manifestations of power have changed dramatically with new technologies, ideologies, political economic development and strategies, and various interdependencies. What aspects of power have changed, and what have remained the same?

Hans Morgenthau maintained that "international politics, like all politics, is a struggle for power. Whatever the ultimate aims of international politics, power is always the immediate aim."[1] Is Morgenthau right? Are all global politics essentially power struggles? Is the nature of power and international relations eternally fixed, or are their manifestations and patterns much more complex, subtle, and varied? Just what is politics? What is power? And what is the relationship between the two?

Politics and power are inseparable, but they are not synonymous. The essence of *politics* is conflict and the ways in which participants assert their respective interests in that conflict. Politics exists wherever the interests of two or more people or groups clash. *Power,* its distribution, and the skill with which each side wields it determine whether a conflict is resolved, managed, or deadlocked. Tradeoffs, compromises, and cooperation are inevitable even in the most acrimonious or imbalanced of power relationships. Politics and power thus decide "who gets what, why, when, and how."[2] Political systems, whether on a local, national, or international level, are devised to manage politics and power.

Every political scientist seems to have his or her own definition of power. According to Morgenthau, power "may comprise anything that establishes and maintains control of man over man."[3] Robert Dahl calls power simply "the ability to shift the probability of outcomes."[4] Kenneth Waltz agrees partly with Dahl but adds that "politics is preeminently the realm of unintended and unexpected consequences . . . one is powerful to the extent that he affects others more than they affect him."[5] Karl Deutsch analyzes power in terms of its domain, range, and scope, in which a state's power domain includes both internal tangible and intangible resources as well as international constraints and opportunities on those power resources; its power range includes the spectrum and severity of coercion and persuasion a state could employ against its opponent; and power scope just what the state wishes to achieve, and the domain and range of power which it wields to achieve those goals.[6]

Essentially, power can be two things: (1) the ability of an individual or group to mobilize appropriate resources to get others to do things that they otherwise would not do or refrain from doing things they intended to do (Morgenthau, Dahl, Deutsch); and (2) the inadvertent impact of individuals or groups on others (Waltz).

Power is often described as a type of currency. States want something, which can simply be more power, and they use power to "buy" it. Some countries spend their power wisely, investing it in ways that enhance their abilities and goals; others fritter it away in wasteful consumption or projects; and yet others hoard power and rarely use it.

Power is relative. The power of one individual, group, nation, or alliance depends on that of others with which it has conflicting interests. Mexico is economically and militarily weak, compared to the United States, and economically and militarily strong compared to Guatemala. National power varies widely from one issue to the next. Every state faces a different distribution of power and interests for every different issue with which it is involved. The distribution of power is ever changing. The United States has continued to grow economically, but at a much slower rate than its rivals, and thus America's power has declined accordingly. Finally, power is relative to a government's perception of and ability to achieve its nation's interests. If a government is too ambitious and wants, for

politics conflict and the ways in which participants assert their respective interests in that conflict. Politics exists wherever the interests of two or more people or groups clash.

power the ability of an individual or group to get others to do things that they otherwise would not do, or, refrain from doing things they intended to do.

Power is not always what it seems. In 1979, Iranians captured the American embassy in Teheran and held 54 personnel hostage for 444 days. In addition to diplomacy, President Jimmy Carter used economic sanctions and a military raid to free them, but those means failed. He did not consider an all-out war against Iran, reasoning that the costs would far surpass any conceivable benefits, and the hostages would most likely be killed by their captors. The Iranians released the Americans only after the Carter administration left office. The United States was powerless to gain the release of its hostages. What would you have done if you had been president? What could anyone have done?

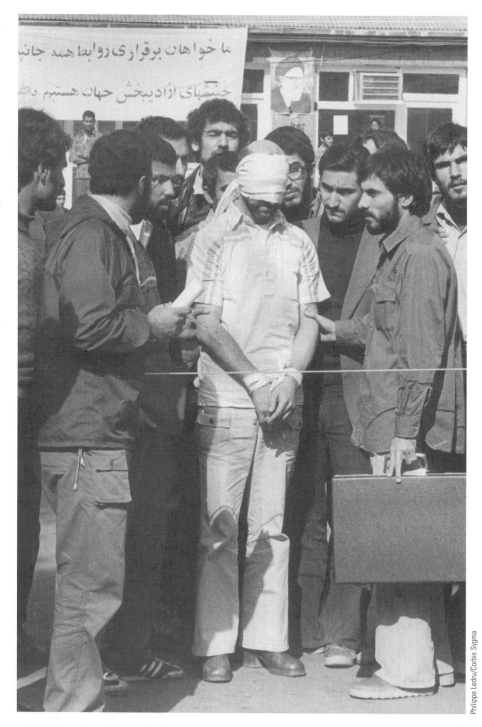

example, a massive expansion of territory or economic growth and cannot get it, then it is relatively powerless. States with far less ambitious but more easily attainable goals can be considered relatively powerful. Even the smallest of states in territory, population, wealth, natural resources, or military forces can be considered powerful if it protects and enhances its national interests.

Part 2   The Nation-State and International Relations

How is power asserted? Many people consider power's bottom line as simply the ability to hurt others worse than they can hurt you or, in international terms, the ability to successfully wage war. Yet the most obvious assertions of power—holding a gun to another's head and demanding money or marching an army to another's frontier and demanding territory—are the least common. Power is manifested in many ways of which military force is perhaps the least cost effective in advancing national interests. Most power is wielded much more subtly. Power spans everything from rational or emotional persuasion to the most brutal forms of coercion and violence. Power is the ability to give as well as take away. States can offer others incentives—alliances, open markets, economic aid, technology, and so on—to change their behavior.

And sometimes the assertion of power is unintended, as when an economic "cold" (recession) in the United States causes "pneumonia" (depression) in poorer countries economically dependent on the United States. In this chapter I concentrate on power consciously deployed by states to achieve goals.

Logic, bribes, and threats are the three ways in which power can be wielded.[7] Logic involves persuading the other side to concede through the force of argument or emotion. Bribes are given to the other side to change their behavior. Threats are made and sometimes acted on to force the opponent to yield. The more of these means a state employs in a conflict, the greater its chance of prevailing. For example, Washington's efforts to rebuild the global political economy during and after World War II involved logic, bribes, and threats. Washington used the logic of liberal economic theory to convince the Western Europeans that it was in everyone's interest for them to slowly liberalize and integrate their economies and sweetened that logic with the bribe of the Marshall Plan, which dispensed over $14 billion in economic aid to help rebuild the continent. Finally, the United States used military threats to deter the Soviet Union from disrupting or possibly invading Western Europe.

States can use threats to defend, deter, or compel others, in which

> *compellence* is an attempt to force someone to give up something he or she values. *Deterrence* is designed to convince someone not even to try to engage in compellence owing to the adverse consequences that such an effort would create. Defense is an action taken to protect oneself when an opponent ignores or fails to understand one's deterrent efforts and initiates the act of compellence anyway. Under such circumstances, defense usually centers on the ability to defeat the opponent in a trial of strength.[8]

Thus, in a conflict in which threats are made, one side attempts to compel and the other side attempts to deter, and if that fails, defend against that compellence.

It is relatively easy to tell when *defense* or compellence succeeds, but it is not so easy to tell about deterrence that demands that the status quo be maintained. Thus the claims for its success "must rest on assertions about why something did not happen."[9] For example, the United States created NATO and built up its conventional and nuclear forces to deter a possible Soviet attack on Western Europe. Did America's deterrent strategy against the Soviet Union succeed? Certainly the Soviets never attacked Western Europe. But maybe Moscow never intended to do so even if Western Europe were defenseless. In that case, the United States and NATO deterred nothing.

Every assertion of power must include several ingredients to increase the chance of success. A state must clearly communicate what it wants in a conflict, and the means by which it intends to get what it wants, whether by logic, bribes, and/or threats. A state has a greater chance of success if its demands require its opponent to make relatively minor rather than major changes. To be taken

Table 4.1 Military Spending in 1999: The United States and Its Allies, Friends, and Foes

Which countries are allies of the United States, which are friendly, and which are avowed enemies? Add up the defense spending in each category. Do America and its allies face any significant threat from any of its foes? Of course military spending can only give an impression of potential power. Much depends on whether that country's military has any ability to project destruction beyond its borders. Even more important is whether or not its leadership is committed to aggression. Capability plus will equals power. The amounts are in billions of dollars. An asterisk (*) denotes 1998 funding.

Country	1999 Amount of Military Spending	Country	1999 Amount of Military Spending
United States	288.8	Greece	3.8
Russia*	55.0	Poland	3.2
Japan	41.1	Norway	3.2
China*	37.5	Kuwait	3.0
Britain	34.6	Syria	2.9
France	29.5	Pakistan	2.7
Germany	24.7	Denmark	2.6
Saudi Arabia	18.4	Belgium	2.5
Italy	16.2	Egypt	2.2
South Korea	11.6	Portugal	1.6
Taiwan	10.7	Iraq	1.4
India	10.7	Libya	1.3
Brazil	10.3	North Korea	1.3
Turkey	8.9	Yugoslavia	1.3
Australia	7.2	Czech Republic	1.2
Netherlands	7.0	Vietnam	0.9
Israel	6.7	Cuba*	0.8
Canada	6.7	Hungary	0.7
Spain	6.0	Sudan	0.4
Iran	5.7		

Source: Center for Defense Information, 1999. Adapted with permission.

seriously, a state must demonstrate both the capacity and will to employ the power it claims to possess. Obviously, the greater a state's relative capacity to punish another state, and the more determined it seems willing to use that capacity, the more credible its potential power. Finally, the credibility of a state's capacity and will must be communicated in a way that weakens rather than strengthens the opponent's resolve on the issue.

For example, in July 1990 Iraq threatened to invade Kuwait. The United States warned Iraq not to do so. On August 2, Iraqi armies invaded and quickly conquered Kuwait. Why did Baghdad disregard Washington's warning? The reasons are complex but essentially, although Baghdad surely understood Washington's military capacity to defeat Iraq, it judged that President George Bush lacked the will to back up his warning. The U.S. ambassador to Iraq, April Glaspie, made a vague, ambiguous last-minute statement to President Hussein that was interpreted as

Part 2   The Nation-State and International Relations

meaning that the United States valued its relationship with Iraq over anything Iraq did to Kuwait. Thus the White House's attempts to deter an Iraqi attack were undermined by poor communication, which in turn damaged the credibility of America's threat. After deterrence failed, the Bush administration then had to attempt to compel Iraq to withdraw from Kuwait. Even then, after a six-month buildup of American-led Coalition forces that eventually numbered over half a million troops, Hussein believed that Bush was bluffing. He refused to give in until after the Coalition destroyed or captured most of his army in Kuwait.

Power is both a means and an end. Ideally, participants in a conflict marshal all the means at their disposal to protect or augment their respective interests. The winners often have their power enhanced so that they have a better chance of realizing their interests in future conflicts. Thus states use power to win a struggle and attempt to enhance their power by their victory. The increased power might include a legal precedent, territorial gain, reparation, or reduction of the other sides' power resources.

How is power measured? Power is rarely absolute; it is almost always offset by other powers. There is often a wide gap between a state's human and material resources and its ability to achieve its goals. States rarely mobilize all the resources at their disposal in any one conflict. A state's potential power may differ greatly from the power it actually employs in a conflict. Power cannot be truly measured until it is used.

Despite these difficulties, many analysts have tried to measure power.[10] Most equate economic and military size with potential power. Some analysts have devised more sophisticated comparative methods. James Lee Ray, for example, combined total population, urban population, steel production, energy consumption, military personnel, and military budget to rank the eight leading countries every five years from 1900 to 1985.[11] Jack Sawyer measured 236 variables among 82 countries to determine whether a country was developed or developing, had an open or closed political economy, and was a large or small country, all of which helped determine that country's power.[12] The significance of such number crunching may be as difficult to determine as power itself. And it only attempts to measure a state's potential power; it tells nothing about how governments wield their resources to protect or enhance national interests.

What are *the* Prerequisites *of* National Power?

Power can be both tangible or easily measured or intangible and difficult to measure.

TANGIBLE SOURCES OF POWER

National power is based on a range of tangible or "hard" resources such as relative GNPs, military forces, or technology, and intangible or "soft" factors such as leadership, national cohesion, and political will. It is the *intangible power* sources that often decide the winner in a conflict between forces with relatively evenly matched *tangible power*. Yet when many people think of power, they often think of tangible sources of power and believe bigger or more is better. Take population, for example. If all other power factors are equal (which of course they never are), then one could argue that the most populous state is the most potentially powerful. The quality of

intangible power less easily measured or *soft* sources of power such as leadership, national cohesion, and political will. Intangible power sources often decide the winner in a conflict between forces with relatively evenly matched tangible power.

tangible power assets or resources that are relatively easy to quantify, such as relative GNP, military force, or technology.

a population, however, is more important than its quantity. China and India have the world's first and second largest populations, respectively, but their vast, poverty-stricken, poorly educated peoples are a liability rather than an asset. There are simply too many people for the available land and resources, and both countries would be better off with half the number of people.

One of every 5 people in the world is Chinese, but only 1 in 20 is American. Yet which country more consistently and decisively shapes the world's fate? The great powers have not necessarily been the most populous states. Portugal, Holland, and Great Britain became leading European powers despite having populations well below those of their rivals France or Spain. However, for those nation-states with educated, prosperous, skilled populations, the larger the better. With 270 million and 126 million people respectively, the United States and Japan enjoy huge markets within which their industries can achieve large-scale production, profits, and wealth.

One might also think that the more natural resources a nation has, the better. But as with anything else, it depends. Fertile land bountiful enough to support one's population is always an important pillar of power. Both traditionally and throughout the early modern era, nations with more natural resources usually had at least that advantage over those with less. Imperialism has often been motivated by the attempt of one state to seize the resources of another.

interdependence the drawing together in varying degrees of all the world's countries and individuals into an ever more complex economic, political, technological, ethical, communication, transportation, and cultural, global political economic web.

But the importance of directly owning vast realms of natural resources diminishes as the world becomes more *interdependent*. Many richly endowed countries concentrate on extracting rather than refining their resources. Often, as in Zaire, Indonesia, or Papua New Guinea, to name a few, the result is a capital-intensive mining sector that brings great wealth to a few while much of the population remains mired in poverty. In the short run, the mining, logging, or energy wealth can be used to prop up the rest of the economy. But over the long term those non-renewable resources will inevitably run dry. And even in more advanced countries such as Germany and Belgium, coal or iron ore mining corporations can use their political clout to suck in huge government subsidies long after their mines' viability has ended. As a result the nation's competitiveness is weakened because its industries are required to buy that more expensive domestic resource rather than find the cheapest international source. For example, although Japanese complain frequently of their country's dearth of natural resources, Japanese industries actually benefit because they can search the world for the cheapest possible sources, which helps bring down their product's final costs. Armed with this enormous comparative advantage, Japanese firms can undercut their foreign rivals and reap enormous wealth for their country. Wolfram Hanrieder captured very concisely the shift in how states view territory and resources: "Access rather than acquisition, presence rather than rule, penetration rather than possession have become the important issues."[13]

A nation-state's location, topography, and climate can all enhance or detract from power. Size is important. A small state such as Kuwait is easily overrun by enemies, whereas the vast lands of Russia and China have swallowed up most foreign invaders. Size, however, does not matter geoeconomically. Hong Kong and Singapore are small city-states with populations of only 5.5 million and 2.5 million, respectively. Yet both have prospered while China and Russia have remained economic cripples. A country's terrain can affect a nation's power as well. Vast deserts or mountains, or extremes of heat and cold, or humidity or dryness can simultaneously impede potential invaders and national development. Simple accidents of topography can help seal the fate of nations. The shallow seas on the Netherlands coast prevented the Dutch navy from adopting the huge warships that might have enabled it to win its naval wars against England in the mid-17th century.

A state's location is clearly important but there is no consensus on what location is the most advantageous. Historian Sir Halford Mackinder asserted that "he who rules Eastern Europe commands the Heartland of Eurasia; who commands the Heartland rules the World Island of Europe, Asia, and Africa; and who rules the World Island commands the World."[14] The naval historian Alfred Mahan argued the opposite, that naval supremacy was the key to global power: "If a nation be so situated that it is neither forced to defend itself by land nor induced to seek extension of its territory by way of land, it has, by the very unity of its aim directed on the sea, an advantage as compared with a people whose boundaries are continental."[15] Another historian, Nicholas Spykman, agreed with Mahan and argued that the industrialized rimland of Europe, the Middle East, and South and East Asia were the world's most important regions.[16] Spykman's theory, in turn, greatly influenced George Kennan's containment policy (see Chapter 9). History supports the Mahan rather than Mackinder thesis.

Geography has often protected the most powerful states. The power of England, Japan, the United States, Portugal, Spain, and Russia has clearly been enhanced by their existence on the fringe of power systems, either outright protected by an ocean or enjoying mountain ranges or vast steppes on which to defend themselves or launch an attack. As island nations, Great Britain and Japan have natural moats protecting them from foreign invaders. With oceans east and west and weak neighbors north and south of a vast territory, the United States has been blessed both geopolitically and geoeconomically. To even contemplate invading the United States, an aggressor would need complete naval and air superiority; to march inland and occupy the United States would require millions of troops. Geoeconomically, the United States benefits greatly from being the centerpiece of both the Atlantic and Pacific basin trade systems.

INTANGIBLE SOURCES OF POWER

"Soft" or intangible power such as national cohesion and determination, culture, institutions, and worldview can be as important as the "hard power" of tanks and missiles in achieving goals. Population, resources, and geography are power's raw materials, but leadership and political economic systems give them shape and purpose, and strategy and will deploy and unleash them. History is filled with examples of states disadvantaged in population, resources, or geography besting much larger states. Israel, for example, with only a fraction of the land, people, and resources of its neighbors, has defeated alliances of surrounding Arab states in five wars.

Does humanity make history, or does history make humanity? When many people think about history, the faces, words, and actions of famous leaders first come to mind. What would have been the world's fate if Churchill rather than Chamberlain had been prime minister when Hitler marched into the demilitarized Rhineland in 1936 or when he demanded Czechoslovakia's Sudetenland in 1938? Leadership clearly can be a decisive factor. Yet even the greatest leaders are prisoners of their time and place, shaped and limited by historic forces far beyond their control.

In any struggle, the balance of will may be more important than the balance of tangible resources. All other things being equal, a contest will go to the side

The powers of states vary with their differing means and ends. Sometimes power is not wielded for any positive end, but is simply the ability to destroy. Iraq's attempts to conquer Kuwait were defeated by a United States-led 37 state alliance in 1991. Rather than gracefully accept defeat, Iraqi President Saddam Hussein ordered his troops to ignite Kuwait's oil fields, destroying billions of dollars of that country's wealth and creating an environmental disaster in the weeks before firefighters could extinguish all the flames.

that has more to lose and is more willing to sacrifice to prevent that loss.[17] The Venetian Republic was 14th-century Europe's most dynamic power. But Venice's power declined rapidly after its access to Southeast Asian spices disappeared when the Ottoman Turks closed the land route through the Middle East. Why did Venice not emulate the Portuguese, Spanish, and other powers that built and dispatched ocean-going ships to Southeast Asia via the route around Africa?

Part 2   The Nation-State and International Relations

Certainly Venice possessed the economic and technological skills to do so. What was missing was Venice's recognition of the threat to its wealth, and the political will to marshal all its power to overcome that threat.

Power begins in the mind; its essence is psychological rather than material. Thus power is best wielded through psychological rather than physical manipulation. The most effective use of power is the ability to get others to obey one's dictates unquestioningly. In national crises, people tend to set aside their internal conflicts and rally around the flag against the external threat. Governments have been known to provoke international conflicts just to divert internal conflicts. Why do most people tend to march off to war without wondering whether their government's position was right or wrong? Governments wield enormous school, mass media, and other resources to socialize a deep and unquestioning loyalty in their population toward the country and leadership.

However, the loyalty of populations to their government and country varies considerably. During World War II, when faced with imminent defeat Japanese soldiers charged in vast human wave attacks and were often cut down by the defenders to a man, while at home Japanese women, old men, and children were armed with bamboo spears and grenades and trained to charge any American invaders. Only the atom bomb forced the Japanese to surrender rather than fight to the death. During the Persian Gulf War (1990–1991), also faced with imminent defeat, the Iraqi army deserted or surrendered by the thousands while large segments of the population rose in revolt against the Hussein government. In retrospect, however, the willingness of Japanese soldiers and civilians to toss away their lives without any chance of victory did not prevent Japan's defeat any more than Iraq's disloyal soldiers and civilians caused Iraq's defeat. Other power factors in both wars were much more important.

Prestige is having something that few or no others have but many want. Prestige involves both symbols and concrete accomplishments, and is both a sign and a source of power. It is a reputation for success, for doing things most others cannot do. Prestige can come to countries that win wars, negotiate peace agreements, build nuclear bombs, put an astronaut on the moon, enjoy high economic growth, productivity, literacy, and longevity, and low crime, inflation, and unemployment, or develop new technologies and products, to name a few.

Prestige is clearly a sign of power, but how is it a source? Prestige breeds prestige. States with less prestige are more likely to give in or not challenge states with more. The power to deter is also the power of prestige. The perception by some states that another is powerful can become a self-fulfilling prophecy. The more powerful a state is perceived to be, the less likely others will challenge it and more likely they will bow before it. It is often said that military power need not be used to be useful. Threatening a country with war can be enough to force concessions.

Yet prestige can also constrain power. The more prestige a state has to lose, the more careful a government will be to avoid sticky situations where prestige can be easily lost. The United States lost enormous prestige as well as 58,000 lives and $200 billion in Vietnam. Resolved to avoid any further loss of prestige, the Pentagon has pressured presidents to avoid any wars in which the United States might be defeated militarily or politically.

Power ultimately may lie in the ability to affect how others see and act in the world. Setting the agenda and terms of the debate can be as important in helping achieving one's goals as any other "power" one brings to the table. In 1920, historian J. F. C. Fuller predicted that as mass communications improve, warfare

Bombs Alone?

How much has high technology affected warfare? Can bombing alone win a conflict? Not always. Three wars during the 1990s offer different results.

In 1991, two months of bombing failed to force Iraqi President Saddam Hussein to withdraw his army from Kuwait. It took a massive invasion by a coalition of 28 nations supplying over 500,000 troops to defeat Iraq.

Nor did bombing alone force Slobodan Milosevic to sign the Dayton Accord ending a three-year, three-way war among Serbs, Croatians, and ethnic Albanians over Bosnia-Herzegovina in 1995. NATO bombing simply tipped the scales of a war against the allied Yugoslav and Serbian armies that they were already losing against 100,000 Croatian and ethnic Albanian forces, while 35,000 French and British troops deployed nearby added more pressure on Milosevic.

But NATO bombing alone did win the war with Yugoslavia over Kosovo in 1999. During the 78-day air war, NATO flew 35,000 missions, including 12,500 combat flights that released 23,000 bombs or missiles, of which 99.6 percent hit their targets, and inflicted $40 billion worth of damage to Yugoslavia. During that time no NATO pilots were killed in combat and only two planes, a Stealth F-117 and an F-16 were shot down. Faced with such overwhelming power that was systematically destroying Yugoslavia's military and economy, Milosevic had no choice but to surrender.

As missile and bomb technology becomes ever more accurate, air power will increasingly be the decisive if not sole element in waging war. Ground and in some cases naval forces will remain important auxiliaries to threaten invasion, or supply and defend the air forces. The jets themselves will fly either from carriers or land bases. And skillful diplomacy, of course, can advance either a nation's or an alliance's interests without war or once the fighting begins.

characterized by mass violence and death may eventually give way to "a purely psychological warfare, wherein weapons are not even used or battlefields sought . . . but rather the corruption of the human reason, and dimming of the human intellect, and the disintegration of the moral and spiritual life of one nation by the influence of the will of another is accomplished."[18] Fuller's vision has yet to be fulfilled. Totalitarian states have succeeded in destroying the will of others and replacing it with their own, but only against their own people, not against foreigners.

Education presents all sides of an issue; *propaganda* presents only one side. The most effective propaganda should not seem to be propaganda. Propaganda based on facts is obviously more effective in the long-run than that based on falsehood, because outright lies can be exposed. The ability of governments to use powerful radio and television stations to beam propaganda to any spot on the globe is not a source of power if the message is rejected. To be effective, a message must appeal to an individual's identity, beliefs, and conscience. During the 1950s, Egyptian President Nasser achieved ascendancy in the Arab world, in part by skillful use of the "transistor revolution" to beam the message of Arab nationalism and unity under his leadership to surrounding states.

Traditionally, diplomats and government leaders met and negotiated only with their counterparts. Today and into the future they can use the electronic and print media to directly address not only their foreign counterparts but their own populations as well. Government propaganda or public relations, is a vital part of international relations. Virtually all governments try to promote a favorable image of themselves and an unfavorable one of their foes. Much of the cold war was a propaganda war. The U.S. Information Agency (USIA) was created in 1953 to help Washington win on the public relations front of the cold war. Washington has spent billions of dollars transmitting news and commentaries to communist countries through the Voice of America, Radio Liberty, and Radio Free Europe. To promote its own views and undermine those of the United States, the Soviet Union not only had Radio Moscow but bankrolled innumerable scholarly and news conferences, demonstrations, publications, advertisements, labor unions, student groups, and peace movements, to name the more prominent. Mass media include not only the obvious, such as newspapers, television, radio, journals, and magazines, but also posters, films, flyers, billboards, murals, monuments, museums, postage stamps, street names, and even rumors.[19]

Every government must have some means of gathering and analyzing information vital to understanding the capabilities and intentions of other states. Ideally, the better the intelligence or understanding of what one's foes are doing, the better the policies can be designed to deal with those foes. By knowing another state's plans, a government can take measures to counteract those plans. Whereas popular films and novels tend to focus on the real and imagined paramilitary activities of such intelligence organizations as the CIA or KGB, the primary function of any intelligence organization is gathering *intelligence*. Information, however, must often be obtained by illegal or unethical means, which often includes getting foreigners to betray their respective countries. Intelligence gathering and assessment is a difficult and risky business. Even the best funded and

Table 4.2 **Economic Comparison of World Regions**

Region	Population (Millions)	Gross Domestic Product (GDP)	
		Total (Trillion $)	Per Capita (Dollars)
The North			
North America	300	$8.5	$29,000
Western Europe	400	7.5	19,000
Japan/Pacific	200	4.1	18,000
Russia and Eastern Europe	400	2.0	5,000
The South			
China	1,200	4.5	3,700
Middle East	400	1.9	5,300
Latin America	500	3.1	6,400
South Asia	1,800	4.1	2,300
Africa	600	0.9	1,400
Total North	1,300 (23%)	22.1 (60%)	71,000
Total South	4,500 (77%)	14.5 (40%)	19,000
World Total	5,800	$36.6	$90,100

Note: Data adjusted for purchasing power parity. 1996 GDP estimates (in 1997 dollars) are from the World Bank. Those for Russia and eastern Europe and for China should be treated especially cautiously.

Source: World Bank 2000, Entering the 21st Century (New York: Oxford University Press, 2000), pp 22–49.

trained intelligence organizations equipped with the latest satellites and computers have trouble gathering and assessing all the important information. And it is much easier to count weapons and military units than assess motivations and plans. In the last two decades, the CIA was criticized for failing to predict such important international events as the Iranian revolution in 1979, Eastern European and Soviet revolutions starting in 1989, or Iraqi invasion of Kuwait in 1990, or Indian and Pakistani nuclear tests in 1997. Intelligence organizations must address all the important threats and challenges a country faces. During the 1990s, the CIA began to shift from its almost total emphasis on geopolitics to an increasing attention on geoeconomic and environmental conflicts.

Religious or political ideals can be a vital power resource. Joseph Stalin once scornfully dismissed the Catholic Church by asking how many army divisions the pope had. Yet spiritual power can play an important role in international politics. In 1979, fundamentalist Muslims dramatically shifted the power balance in the Persian Gulf when they overthrew Iran's shah and erected an Islamic theocracy. To varying extents, fundamentalist Muslim forces threaten every state in the Middle East and southwest and central Asia. The fundamentalists are fiercely anti-Western, and their possession of oil-rich Persian Gulf states may dramatically affect the global economy.

Although many around the world do so, the French are particularly fond of condemning what they call "American cultural imperialism." Although there is no evidence of a secret Washington agency that forces peoples around the world to listen to Madonna or Michael Jackson, drink Coca-Cola, watch *Raiders of the Lost Ark*, or ingest other icons of American pop culture, their popularity can subtly aid the United States's pursuit of its overseas interests. Von Laue argues that "cultural understanding is a matter of raw power; who has the power to make his own understanding prevail? Similarly, in all cross-cultural comparison, the question is: who compares himself to whom on whose terms? Who has the power to impose their own terms in the comparison? Who provides the premises of comparison?"[20]

In other words, when one state accepts willingly, unwittingly, or by force another state's cultural values and symbols, it makes itself vulnerable to the culturally more powerful state. For over 500 years, international relations have been shaped by Western culture and power. The West has imposed its values and institutions on the rest of humanity largely by military or economic force, but often by sheer example. Since 1945, American mass culture has penetrated virtually every society around the world, providing a common language with which states interpret and negotiate their respective interests.

America's most potent source of cultural power, however, has not been its pop culture, let alone its rich high culture of literature, painting, architecture, sculpture, music, theater, or dance, but its political philosophy. "Liberty," wrote former State Department official Paul Nitze, "is the most contagious idea in history."[21] No country has more deeply explored or attempted to fulfill the concept of liberty than the United States. Washington was largely responsible for ensuring that the Western conception of human rights was enshrined in the U.N. Charter and the 1948 Declaration of Human Rights, which every U.N. member is pledged to uphold. Traditionally, however, despite the United Nations's clear human rights standard, most countries scorned it. Recently, the elite and mass acceptance of human rights is growing and serves as an increasingly powerful check on state behavior. In response to international moral pressure, countries as diverse as Nicaragua, the Philippines, and Kampuchea have held United Nations-sponsored elections; South Africa eased apartheid and the Soviet Union allowed more Jewish

Table 4.3 **Shares of Exports of High-Technology Products, 1980 and 1989**

Microelectronics		Computers	
1980	1989	1980	1989
1. United States (18.3%)	1. Japan (22.1%)	1. United States (38.6%)	1. United States (24%)
2. Japan (13.2%)	2. United States (21.9%)	2. West Germany (11.5%)	2. Japan (17.5%)
3. Singapore (10.1%)	3. Malaysia (8.9%)	3. Great Britain (10.4%)	3. Great Britain (9%)
4. Malaysia (8.9%)	4. South Korea (7.4%)	4. France (8.6%)	4. West Germany (6.9%)
5. West Germany (8.4%)	5. West Germany (5.8%)	5. Italy (6.6%)	5. Taiwan (5.8%)

Aerospace		Telecommunications Equipment	
1980			
1. United States (47.6%)	1. United States (45.8%)	1. West Germany (16.7%)	1. Japan (24.7%)
2. Great Britain (19.7%)	2. West Germany (12.5%)	2. Sweden (15.3%)	2. West Germany (9.5%)
3. West Germany (9.1%)	3. Great Britain (10.9%)	3. United States (10.9%)	3. United States (8.8%)
4. France (6.0%)	4. France (10.2%)	4. Japan (10.3%)	4. Sweden (8.1%)
5. Canada (4.4%)	5. Canada (4.4%)	5. Netherlands (9.3%)	5. Hong Kong (6.3%)

Machine Tools and Robotics		Scientific/Precision Equipment	
1980			
1. West Germany (25.8%)	1. Japan (23.3%)	1. United States (28.3%)	1. United States (25.2%)
2. United States (14.1%)	2. West Germany (20.8%)	2. West Germany (18.1%)	2. West Germany (18.5%)
3. Japan (11.3%)	3. United States (12.1%)	3. Great Britain (9.4%)	3. Japan (12.9%)
4. Sweden (9.1%)	4. Italy (10%)	4. France (8.0%)	4. Great Britain (9.6%)
5. Italy (8.7%)	5. Switzerland (8.4%)	5. Japan (7.1%)	5. France (5.6%)

Medicine and Biologicals		Organic Chemical	
1980			
1. West Germany (16.7%)	1. West Germany (15.6%)	1. West Germany (19.1%)	1. West Germany (17%)
2. Switzerland (12.5%)	2. Switzerland (12.2%)	2. United States (13.9%)	2. United States (15.5%)
3. Great Britain (12.0%)	3. United States (12.2%)	3. Netherlands (10.9%)	3. France (8.7%)
4. France (11.9%)	4. Great Britain (11.8%)	4. France (10.7%)	4. Netherlands (8.1%)
5. United States (11.4%)	5. France (10.3%)	5. Great Britain (8.4%)	5. Great Britain (8.4%)

Numerals 1–5 indicate rankings.

Source: Paul Kennedy, *Preparing for the Twenty-First Century* (New York: Random House, 1993), p. 153.

emigration. The power balance between liberal democratic and authoritarian states is tipping decisively in favor of the former, and with it will come increased international cooperation, peace, and more subtle ways of wielding power.

Global Wealth *and* Power

Power and wealth are virtually inseparable. Wealth is power's bottom line. The great powers have always been the great economic powers, although the distribution and source of that economic power has varied greatly. The wealthier a state, the more easily it can achieve its geopolitical and geoeconomic interests.

Imperial overstretch ultimately defeated one great power after another. There are interesting parallels between the respective declines of Spain and the United States. Between the 1560s and 1648, Spain fought continually to crush Holland's independence, an effort that proved as debilitating to Madrid as Washington's much shorter venture in Vietnam. By the early 1600s, Spain had exhausted itself financially and psychologically from the costs of conquering and holding its American empire and defending its European territories. With the 1648 Treaty of Westphalia, Spain not only signed away its claims to European territory beyond the Pyrenees but largely withdrew from European affairs and concentrated its efforts on administering and exploiting the Americas.

Why did Spain cling to its possessions long after it was clear that they were economic liabilities rather than benefits? Spain's Philip IV argued in 1648 that "although the war which we have fought in the Netherlands has exhausted our treasury and forced us into debts that we have incurred, it has also diverted our enemies in those parts so that, had we not done so, it is certain that we would have had war in Spain or somewhere nearer."[23] Madrid feared at that time that if it lost Flanders it would inevitably lose its German, Italian, and even American possessions. For decades, Spain's Army of Flanders cost one-quarter of Madrid's budget.[24] Yet, the costs did not seem exorbitant because Spain could always

pay them with American silver—at least until the mines began to peter out in the 1630s. This outlook differed little from the domino theory that led the United States into the quagmire of Vietnam. President Johnson succinctly captured the theory's "logic": "If we don't stop the Reds in South Vietnam, tomorrow they will be in Hawaii, and next they will be in San Francisco."[25]

Paul Kennedy argues that, debilitating as these endless wars were, "at the center of Spanish decline . . . was the failure to recognize the importance of preserving the economic underpinnings of a powerful military machine."[26] Ironically, in 1492, the same year it financed Columbus's voyage, Spain expelled the Jews from its kingdom. Through their financial and commercial ventures, the Jews had contributed enormous wealth to Spain. Exiling them crippled Spain's economic vitality.[27] Spain failed to reinvest the great wealth it extracted from its American empire into productive industries within Spain that would create new wealth long after the American mines played out.

American silver paid only one-quarter of Spain's budget; the rest had to be extracted from the peasants and merchants. Lacking and not interested in nurturing skilled artisans and entrepreneurs that could establish viable industries, Spain imported virtually all its finished goods, and thus suffered perennial and severe trade deficits. What little production occurred in Spain was further inhibited by internal customs barriers that drove up prices

and quelled initiative. Agriculture remained backward, and Spain increasingly had to import grain. Although its vast sheep herds did produce wool, Spain imposed heavy taxes on wool exports for the revenues and thus ended up importing woolen goods from Britain and elsewhere. Madrid even allowed its once vast merchant fleet to rot away. By 1640, three-quarters of Spain's trade was carried in Dutch ships. Spain's international debt and the percentage of its national budget which paid interest on that debt steadily increased. Madrid attempted to service the debt by raising taxes, but that only further stifled individual initiative and wealth. Spain's bureaucracy was inefficient, corrupt, and incapable of understanding, let alone addressing, the range of severe, interrelated national problems. Most Spanish kings after Charles V and Philip II were weak leaders.

Does any of this sound familiar? Although the particulars differ, the United States, like Spain in the 16th and 17th centuries, has diverted far too many resources into building and maintaining the world's greatest military machine and deploying it in far-flung commitments while failing to reinvest in commercial technology and production. Meanwhile, Japan has leapfrogged the United States to become the world's most dynamic economic superpower in one industry after another. In 1999, America's trade deficit with Japan soared to $75 billion!

Modern history records a parade of great military powers whose reach was, for a while, global: Portugal, Spain, Holland, France, Great Britain, the United States. What caused the rise, dominance, and fall of these great powers?

Historian Paul Kennedy argues that national power is rooted ultimately in economic, technological, and organizational prowess:

> There exists a dynamic for change, driven chiefly by economic and technological developments, which then impact on social structures, political systems, military power, and the position of individual states and empires. The speed of this global economic change has not been a uniform one, simply because the pace of technological innovation and economic growth is itself irregular . . . different regions and societies across the globe have experienced a faster or slower rate of growth, depending not only on the shifting patterns of technology, production, and trade, but also on their receptivity to the new modes of increasing output and wealth . . . military power rests on adequate supplies of wealth, which in turn derive from a flourishing productive base, from healthy finances, and from superior technology . . . major shifts in the world's military-power balances have followed alterations in the productive balances.[22]

Thus, military victory, more often than not, rests ultimately on which side can devise, build, and sell a better mousetrap.

Although all nations ultimately benefit from technological advances, most benefits accrue to the state that best capitalizes on those advances. Generally, the state that benefits is the state in which the new technology was invented and commercially applied. There are, of course, exceptions. Japan's rise into an economic superpower has been based in part on its ability to commercialize the research efforts of others. And then there are states that invent but fail fully to use their technology and thus decline relative to more dynamic states. Ming China had the technology to become a global power—gunpowder and ocean-going ships—but failed to exploit it. Among other things, the United States has failed to mobilize all its vast technologies and science laboratories into production and thus has fallen behind in many industries it might otherwise have dominated.

States that face geopolitical challenges must walk a tightrope between spending too much and too little wealth on the military. The diversion of too much wealth into military power will ultimately sap a nation's economic vitality and power; the diversion of too little wealth into military power in a world filled with militarily powerful rival states can leave that nation vulnerable to foreign aggression. As Kennedy warns, "A large military establishment may, like a great monument, look imposing to the impressionable observer; but if it is not resting on a firm foundation (in this case a productive economy), it runs the risk of future collapse."[28]

Great powers decline because, according to Kennedy, their reach has exceeded their grasp. In other words, they lack the economic capacity to fulfill their defense commitments. Not enough human and material resources are reinvested in the creation of wealth, the state's economy eventually breaks down under the defense burden, and its economic position in the world is overtaken by others.

Geopolitical Power

THE REAL HIERARCHY

We can distinguish among military superpowers, great powers, middle-ranking powers, and small powers. The distinction concerns each state's ability to project military power beyond its borders. During the cold war, the two *superpowers*, the

United States and the Soviet Union, had enough nuclear and conventional power to fight virtually anywhere. The *great powers*—Britain, France, China, and Israel—have nuclear and conventional forces but have a limited power to fight overseas. Regional or *middle-ranking powers* have large conventional military forces but lack the power to project it outside the region. Two middle-ranking powers—Germany and Japan—have relatively large conventional militaries, but are constitutionally limited in projecting that power abroad. Some mid-rank powers dominate their regions such as Vietnam, India, Nigeria, and South Africa. Other mid-rank powers are offset by others within a region. North and South Korea balance each other and are overshadowed by the United States, Russia, China, and Japan. In the Persian Gulf, Pakistan, Iran, Iraq, and Saudi Arabia balance each other and are dominated by the United States. In the Middle East, Syria, Egypt, Israel, and Libya balance each other beneath America's shadow. In southern Latin America, Argentina, Brazil, and Chile balance each other without the immediate presence of the United States or another great power. Nearly all countries are *small powers* whose militaries maintain internal order and a minimum deterrent against foreign invasion and even less of a threat to others.

The military power of the countries within each of these categories can be ranked by comparing the size of their national military budgets and personnel. Those which spend the most do not necessarily have the largest militaries. In 1989, the last year of the cold war, in terms of sheer expenditure, the United States spent $307.7 billion on the military, followed by the Soviet Union with $299.8 billion, France with $36.0 billion, West Germany with $35.1 billion, Britain with $34.7 billion, Japan with $28.9 billion, and China with $21.3 billion. Measured by the number of people in military uniforms, China was first with 3.90 million, followed by the Soviet Union with 3.78 million, the United States with 2.25 million, India with 1.36 million, Vietnam with 1.10 million, and Iraq with 1.00 million. Of the other great powers, France ranked 11th with 560,000, West Germany 12th with 500,000, Britain 19th with 320,000, and Japan 25th with 180,000. Fortunately, the cold war's end did provide a "peace dividend." Eight years later in 1997, global spending on the military had dropped by 25 percent to $740 billion from $1 trillion.[29]

But these categories and rankings are inadequate; they merely measure a state's potential military power. Military power, like all power, can only be ultimately measured according to whether or not it is successfully used. Factors other than military budget and personnel size are often decisive. For example, after 1945, despite America's vast military expenditures and soldiers, the United States suffered a series of humiliations by countries with much smaller forces. American and other allied forces were fought to a standstill in Korea; the United States lost the Vietnam War; a communist government seized and continued to maintain power in Cuba despite enormous American efforts to overthrow it; in 1968 the North Koreans seized the U.S. spy ship *Pueblo* and held it for nearly a year; and in 1979 Iranians overran the American embassy and held its 56 employees hostage for 444 days. Why did the United States lose these geopolitical conflicts? Essentially, Washington did not have the political will to use the overwhelming force that might have allowed the United States to prevail in these conflicts. There may have been good reasons for that prudence. The escalation of any of those conflicts could well have started World War III.

Other countries thought to be more powerful have been humbled by their lessers. Soviet military superpower failed to subject Afghanistan; after nearly a decade of bitter guerrilla fighting, Moscow was forced into a humiliating retreat in 1989. The Chinese army invaded northern Vietnam in 1979 to retaliate for Vietnam's invasion of Cambodia. China's supposedly crack divisions were repulsed by supposedly second-rate Vietnamese units. In 1982, Britain had difficulty mustering enough troops and ships to fight Argentina after it invaded Britain's Falkland Islands (the Malvinas), and might have lost had not Washington shared important intelligence over Argentina's fleet movement with London, along with essential logistic support. Thus raw power—the number of troops, tanks, and bombs a state holds—tells nothing about how skilled a government is in brandishing that power.

Can we in fact identify a decisive factor in a military struggle? Scholars differ over whether the side with the larger military usually prevails or not. One study compared 32 wars between 1816 and 1965 and found that the side with the largest forces won only 21 times.[30] In contrast, a much more comprehensive study of 164 conflicts between 1816 to 1976, most of which were resolved peacefully, found no correlation between military size and victory.[31]

Other factors are often much more decisive. History is filled with instances of armies with smaller numbers defeating far larger forces. With less than 35,000 men, Alexander the Great conquered most of the Middle East and defeated armies many times superior in numbers all the way to the Indus River. The United States, despite its vast material advantage, lost its war with Vietnam because it lacked the political will to win by either invading the north or using nuclear weapons. The United States was inhibited both by international and domestic moral constraints on the use of nuclear weapons, and the fear that it could provoke a nuclear war with Vietnam's allies, the Soviet Union and China. Likewise, Washington feared that an invasion of the North would bring China into the war, and ultimately force the United States to use nuclear weapons to win. Washington even failed to mobilize all its forces available for defending South Vietnam; at most, only 0.25 percent of America's population fought at any one time, whereas North Vietnam seemed prepared to sacrifice an endless number of its population in the struggle.[32]

In the 19th century, the great powers could humble large but backward states by dispatching a few gunboats to bombard or blockade coastal cities, and well-trained, armed, and equipped infantry to defeat native armies many times larger. Those days of *gunboat diplomacy* are long past. The transfer of advanced weapons to the Third World has undermined the ability of the superpowers and other great powers to win militarily, and has even led to their defeat, such as North Vietnam over the United States or the Afghan rebels over the Soviet Union. Recently, for example, French Exocet antiship missiles supplied to Argentina made Britain's victory much more costly. The Argentineans used Exocets to sink two British warships. American shoulder-fired Stinger antiaircraft missiles supplied to Afghani guerrillas broke the Soviet command of the air and were probably the most important reason that Moscow eventually decided to withdraw from that country.

Some weapons in Third World hands are overrated. The SCUD missiles that Iraq lobbed in the Persian Gulf War (1990–1991) against Saudi Arabia and Israel did minor damage and may have actually been inferior to the German V-2 bombs launched fifty years earlier. However, the mere Iraqi threat to place chemical weapons on their SCUD missiles caused the Coalition enormous political problems. Israel threatened to retaliate if Iraq launched chemical SCUDS, and an Israeli retaliation might have caused the Coalition's Arab members to withdraw or even change sides. To prevent this possibility, the Coalition diverted tens of thousands of air force sorties in a largely unsuccessful effort to search and destroy the SCUDS rather than other far more dangerous targets.

In addition to advanced weapons, the effective use of nationalism, modern arms, the mass media, and international organizations such as the United Nations has empowered Third World countries to successfully resist "great power" intervention. The diffusion of military technology to the Third World and the ability to mobilize entire populations behind *"people's liberation wars"* makes the costs of great power intervention excruciatingly painful and ultimately fruitless. For example, Washington stood largely impotent in the 444 days following the seizing of the American embassy in Iran in 1979. The rescue attempt resulted in disaster. Joseph Nye points out that in 1953 Washington used covert means to restore the shah to power in Iran, then asks, "How many troops would have been needed to restore the shah in the socially mobilized and nationalistic Iran of 1979?"[33]

BALANCE OF POWER

Regardless of the reasons for victory or defeat, just what is the basis for most geopolitical struggles? The Morgenthau school of scholars argues that such conflicts result from states attempting to assert their interests at the expense of others within the prevailing international balance of power.

The classic *balance-of-power* system operates on the rather simple notion that "The enemy of my enemy is my friend." Few concepts of international relations have been as thoroughly explored. In the premodern era, Thucydides, Kautilya, Lord Shang, Polybius, and Machiavelli all analyzed the concept in depth and urged their governments to apply it to policy.[34] The classic system requires a half dozen or more states of relatively similar size and capabilities; limited geographical area; a shared political culture among national elites; no fixed alliances; the tendency for most states to combine to offset any aggressor state or coalitions of states; the absence of ideology as a motivation for expansion; the preservation of defeated states in the system; the recognition that it is in all their interests to maintain the system; relatively slow means of transportation and communication that inhibit rapid mobilization and attacks; relatively limited means of mass destruction; the absence of international organizations that inhibit the actions of states; and a consensus among the governments of each state as to the system's rules. Power is not balanced for all states. The great powers ally and fight with and preside over more numerous intermediate and small states.

Although there is a consensus over the classic model's attributes, there is considerable disagreement over what the balance of power actually is, let alone which periods of international relations it characterized.[35] Some, such as A. F. K. Organski, argue that a balance can only exist with a half dozen states with relatively equal power (*multipolarity*); others, such as Morgenthau, argue that the balance refers to alliances of states (*bipolarity*).[36]

Did the classic balance of power ever exist? Although the period of European history from 1648 through 1792 did exemplify the classic balance of power, analysts argue endlessly over whether the system characterized any period after 1792. The French Revolution of 1789 dramatically changed the stakes of Europe's geopolitical system. The revolution's beheading of Louis XVI and declaration of a republic challenged every European monarchy. In 1792, the first coalition of counterrevolutionary states attacked and was defeated by France. That same year, Austria, Prussia, and Russia departed from the classic rule that no states would be destroyed when they agreed to divide Poland among themselves. From then until 1815, the other European powers allied repeatedly to first destroy the revolutionary French government and later Napoleon's imperial rule.

From 1815 to 1890, there was a condominium (coalition) rather than a balance of European power. Unlike during the classic period, no general European war broke out each generation, and great powers fought each other on only three occasions—the Crimean War (1853–1854), the Austro-Prussian War (1866), and the Franco-Prussian War (1870). The major conflicts were not between the great powers but between the great powers and lesser states experiencing democratic revolution. Russia, Austria, Prussia, and France cooperated to squash any revolutionary threats to monarchs anywhere in Europe, and all the great powers colonized overseas conquests. As Organski put it, during "the nineteenth century, after the Napoleonic Wars, there was almost continuous peace. The balance of power is given a good share of the credit for this peaceful century, but . . . there was no balance at all, but rather a vast preponderance of power in the hands of England and France."[37]

The condominium of power ended with German Kaiser Wilhelm II's forced resignation of his prime minister, Otto von Bismarck in 1890. Wilhelm abandoned Bismarck's policy of retaining Europe's status quo after achieving German unification in 1871 and instead embarked on a naval and army buildup designed to win for Germany hegemony over Europe. Until then the great powers had sublimated their own conflicts into a largely cooperative effort in divvying up much of Africa and Asia among themselves. Afterward Europe became divided into two rigid alliances that before 1914 went to the brink of war several times over disputes in the colonies and Balkans.

Was the 1890–1914 system a bipolar or multipolar system? Those who measure power on an individual state basis would argue that the pre-1914 system was multipolar, because there was a relatively equal distribution among the great powers. Those who measure power among alliances as well as among states would argue the opposite, that the pre-1914 system was bipolar, because the great powers were locked into two diametrically opposed alliances of relatively equal power.

At the Versailles peace conference in 1919, France, Great Britain, and the United States attempted to reassert a condominium of power over Europe and the world system. But the condominium unraveled as the United States immediately returned to political, (and, in 1930, economic) isolation, and as France and Great Britain failed to check the imperialist ambitions of fascist Japan, Italy, and Germany during the 1930s. In 1941, a global balance of two alliances emerged but with ideological differences at its core it bore no resemblance to the classic system.

Likewise, the cold war has represented a global power balance between two diametrically opposed ideologies, each represented by a military superpower with enough nuclear power to destroy the world several times. Analysts are divided over just what to call the post-1945 system. The dispute centers over determining whether a system is multipolar or bipolar, and here we return to the question of whether the power distribution should be determined by states or alliances.

One way to finesse this problem is to distinguish between polarity, which refers to the distribution of power among states, and polarization, which refers to the alliances among states.[38] Thus the system can be bipolar in structure, but multipolar in the power distribution among states, a framework that can be applied to both world wars and the cold war. Although the post-1945 system remained bipolar in polarization, the system's polarity became increasingly multipolar.[39] States ally against threats rather than power per se. For example, the United States continued to hold predominant power throughout the postwar era, but the Western European states chose to ally themselves with Washington rather than offset America's power by allying with Moscow because the Soviet Union rather than United States posed the genuine threat.

MILITARY ASSETS, LIABILITIES, AND SECURITY

Militaries must not only be financed, but they also need a purpose. Governments often divert enormous wealth and human resources preparing for threats that do not exist, or overspend for those that do, and thus ultimately undermine their total power. For example, what is the United States going to do with 250,000 *cruise missiles* or 4,000 battle tanks? Military budgets are often shaped by political rather than strategic demands. Politicians lobby for a military base or armaments factory because it brings jobs and money to their district, even though those resources might have been better invested elsewhere. The result is that a nation's potential power sources are squandered rather than invested.

security dilemma a situation in which the military buildup that one state undertakes to feel more secure makes other states feel more insecure so they in turn build up their own forces. The original state then feels threatened so it further builds its force to deter a perceived foreign threat. Other states do the same, and the result is an arms race that may lead to a war that all sides would have preferred to avoid.

mutually assured destruction (MAD) the likelihood that a full nuclear exchange between Russia and the United States would destroy both countries. Thus both sides have been more cautious in nearing the brink of war with each other.

And then there is the *security dilemma*. Ironically, the military buildup that one state undertakes to feel more secure often makes other states feel more insecure, so they in turn build up their own forces. The original state then feels even more threatened so it accelerates its buildup. The other state reciprocates. The result is an arms race, which may lead to a war that all sides would have preferred to avoid. The United States and Soviet Union were caught in just such an arms race from 1945 to 1991, a race that ultimately undermined the economic and thus total power of both countries.

How does nuclear power enhance or detract from a nation's total power? Theoretically, nuclear weapons deter foreign attack, although we can never know if potential enemies would have attacked had there been no nuclear weapons. The knowledge that they would destroy each other in a nuclear war, a situation known as "*mutually assured destruction*" (*MAD*), may well have deterred a war between the United States and Soviet Union. Washington's rattling of its nuclear saber during the Korean War (1953) and the Quemoy and Matsu crises (1958) may have enhanced its bargaining power with its opponents during those conflicts. Certainly nuclear power confers a dark prestige on countries that possess it.

Weighed against these factors, however, are the enormous financial, human, and technological resources that must be marshaled to build up and maintain a nuclear force, resources that could be invested much more profitably elsewhere. Like other forms of military power, nuclear weapons drain a nation's economy. Unlike other military weapons, nuclear bombs that are accidentally or purposely exploded can kill millions and render land uninhabitable. The constraints on the use of nuclear power largely eliminate its military function. International morality and an absence of vital interests at stake may well have prevented the two superpowers and other nuclear powers such as China, France, Great Britain, or Israel from using their weapons in wars with smaller states. America's tens of thousands of nuclear weapons did not prevent OPEC from nationalizing its oil fields and quadrupling oil prices in 1973, North Vietnam from conquering South

Vietnam in 1975, or the Soviets from invading Afghanistan in 1979. Even more than other forms of destruction, nuclear weapons are a double-edged sword.

MILITARY ALLIANCES

The greater a nation's military spending, the greater the sacrifices made in forgone investments and opportunities in more economically and socially productive pursuits. Alliances would seem to be a way to share defense burdens. But not always. Whether alliances help or hurt their members varies considerably from one to the next. There can be weakness as well as strength in numbers.

There are many kinds of alliances. States balance or counter threats, not power. What is important is not how powerful another state or group of states is, but whether it is threatening. Some alliances are between countries of a similar ideology facing a common ideological threat, such as the American-led North Atlantic Treaty Organization (NATO), which successfully helped contain the Soviet Union for over four decades. Most alliances are based on the principle that "The enemy of my enemy is my friend." These are marriages of convenience between countries of quite different ideologies facing the same threat, such as when the democratic powers, the United States, Britain, and France teamed up with the communist Soviet Union to defeat the fascist powers Germany, Japan, and Italy. Since its creation in 1948, Israel has maintained its security in part by playing off the various intra-Arab, Sunni Muslim, and Arab-Iranian rivalries through secret diplomacy in which it would favor one side against the other. India formed an alliance with the Soviet Union and Pakistan with China to strengthen themselves against each other.

How do governments decide whether or not to join an alliance? An imminent or actual attack is an obvious reason. But when these conditions are not present William Riker theorizes that alliance "participants create coalitions just as large as they believe will ensure winning and no larger."[40] The reason is that although the larger the coalition, the greater the chance for victory, the share of the spoils diminishes accordingly. This may have been true of coalitions before the mid-20th century when the victors often took territory and wealth from the losers. The benefits of contemporary alliances are more intangible than in the past—security, community, and prestige rather than the spoils of war.

When faced with a threat, it sometimes pays to not join an alliance if it is clear the alliance will defeat or deter that threat. France dropped out of NATO in 1964, thus regaining its independence and shedding its duties while continuing to shelter under that alliance's conventional and nuclear umbrella. The United States sat on the sidelines of both world wars until it was directly attacked. One can argue, however, that the United States would have gained more by joining an alliance with Great Britain and France in the late 1930s, because it possibly could have led to a negotiated settlement or bolstered allied forces in France. That would have made a German victory there in 1940 much less likely and perhaps deterred an attack altogether. The human and material costs of waiting may have been greater for the United States in the long run. The trouble with this scenario is that, given America's deep isolationist sentiment before Pearl Harbor, it would have been politically impossible for President Roosevelt to formally enter an alliance with Great Britain and France unless the United States was directly attacked.

The benefits of being in an alliance seem obvious. A nation's security tends to strengthen with its alliances' troops, weapons, geographical expanse, coordination, and will. Alliances can deter aggression. States with smaller populations, economies, and militaries can particularly benefit by joining an alliance. A study of alliances between 1815 and 1965 found that, if attacked, states with allies received help 76 percent of the time; without allies, only 17 percent of the time.[41]

The balance-of-power theory holds that weakness invites aggression, whereas in numbers there is strength and a greater chance for peace. In a world of sovereign states, each struggles to enhance its interests, often at the expense of others. When one state grows too powerful and aggressive, other states tend to ally to offset that power and potential threat. Being in an alliance, however, does not guarantee victory. The key to victory in war from 1816 to 1976 was who initiated, not whether there was an alliance.[42]

At times an alliance's costs exceed its benefits. For very sound reasons, George Washington in his farewell address warned his fellow Americans against entanglements in foreign alliances: "It must be unwise . . . to implicate ourselves by artificial ties in the ordinary vicissitudes of her [Europe's] politics, or the ordinary combinations and collisions of her friendships or enmities."[43] Or, as Thomas Jefferson put it even more succinctly: "Commerce with all nations, alliance with none, should be our motto."[44]

American diplomat George Kennan eloquently explored the reason for the caution with which most states approach alliances:

> The relations among nations, in this imperfect world, constitute a fluid substance, always in motion, changing subtly from day to day in ways that are difficult to detect from the myopia of the passing moment, and even difficult to discern from the perspective of the future one. The situation at one particular time is never quite the same as the situation of five years later—indeed, it is sometimes very significantly different, even though the stages by which this change came about are seldom visible at the given moment. This is why wise and experienced statesmen usually shy away from commitments likely to constitute limitations on a government's behavior at unknown dates in the future in the face of unpredictable situations.[45]

Great powers sometimes force minor powers into alliances in order to more easily dominate and extract benefits from them. For example, most would agree that the Soviet Union created the Warsaw Pact simply to justify subjugating and exploiting eastern Europe.[46] Far less convincingly, some have made the same claim for the American creation of NATO and the Organization of American States (OAS).

If change is constant, the longer an alliance exists, the more likely it is oriented toward past rather than present challenges and opportunities. Alliances themselves can prevent positive change by freezing rivalries and conflicts. Although alliances provide states with greater potential military resources, they take away their members' diplomatic flexibility. Alliance building is a type of arms race, with a similar escalation of perceived threats and tensions. One alliance's creation is likely to spark the creation of an opposing alliance, thus possibly exacerbating the threat that the first alliance was originally created to deter. If war breaks out, the destruction and death can become as widespread as the alliance itself.

Napoleon once said, "I'd rather fight than join a coalition." The difficulty in coordinating the strategy and tactics of an alliance at war are vast and often unmanageable. The more states in an alliance, the weaker the influence of any one state on the alliance's policies and the greater the difficulty in reaching decisions. Napoleon and many other leaders have found that the advantages of fighting alone with a unified and decisive command outweigh the added troops and resources that alliances can provide.

Historically, alliances have been ephemeral, arising and dissolving with perceived threats. Most governments recognize that in a constantly changing world they have no permanent friends or enemies, just national interests that must be preserved. Today's friend can be tomorrow's enemy. One of ever four wars between 1815 and 1965 was fought between allies![47]

Geoeconomic Power

Military rather than economic power was traditionally considered the more important component of national power. As Machiavelli put it, "The sinews of war are not gold, but good soldiers; for gold alone will not procure good soldiers, but good soldiers will always procure gold."[48]

No longer. As the United States and former Soviet Union discovered to the former's tripling of its national debt during the Reagan 1980s and the latter's self-destruction, overinvesting heavily in a huge *military-industrial complex* may actually diminish rather than enhance national power in an increasingly interdependent world. Military power was traditionally used to seize wealth; today, most countries create wealth and then divert no more than a token fraction to the military, investing most of it in industries that can create more wealth. In his book *The Rise of the Trading State,* Richard Rosecrance argued that today economic rather than military means are the primary source of national power. He contrasted military states such as the United States and Soviet Union with trading states such as Japan, and concluded, "Since 1945, a few nations have borne the crushing weight of military expenditure while others have gained a relative advantage by becoming military free-riders who primarily rely on the security provided by others. While the United States spent nearly 50 percent of its research and development budget on arms, Japan devoted 99 percent to civilian production."[49]

Military power becomes increasingly irrelevant to most conflicts in an increasingly interdependent global political economy in which all states are ever more tightly bound as both the system's beneficiaries and prisoners. As Rosecrance points out, autarchy is impossible for a modern country:

> In the world economy of the 1990s, however, it would be much more difficult to conquer territories containing sufficient oil, natural resources, and grain supplies to emancipate their holder from the restraints of the interdependent economic system. . . . Such an aggressor would need the oil of the Middle East, the resources of Southern Africa, and the grain and iron of Australia, Canada, and the American Middle West. Too much dependence and too little strength make that list unachievable."[50]

Most states are at peace most of the time. Of the over 20,000 possible bilateral relations among the over 190 states in the world, only a handful actually contain the possibility of war. Virtually all the bilateral relations are friendly and a military clash unthinkable.

But a war-free relationship is not necessarily conflict free. States bicker continually over a wide range of economic and other issues. And as in geopolitical conflicts, that side prevails that can best mobilize and assert all available power resources. In an interdependent world, nations still struggle to defend and expand

Oil, Wealth, *and* Power

The dozen Organization for Petroleum Exporting Countries (OPEC) accounted for nearly two-thirds of world oil exports and sat on nearly 75 percent of global oil reserves in 1973. That gave OPEC enormous potential power. By cutting back their own production, cutting off oil shipments to such countries as the United States and others who supported Israel, and nationalizing the foreign-owned oil industries in their land, OPEC engineered a quadrupling of oil prices by 1974 and further doubled them between 1979 and 1980. In all, the price of a barrel of oil rose from $2.75 in 1973 to $34 by 1981.

What impact did that have on the OPEC members and rest of the world? OPEC's policies powerfully shifted the global geoeconomic distribution of power. Hundreds of billions of dollars in wealth poured from those who needed the oil to those who had it. The industrial world suffered a decade of low economic growth, and high inflation and unemployment known as "stagflation." The Third World's debt soared as its countries had to borrow ever more money to pay for ever more expensive oil vital for fueling their own industrialization ambitions.

But OPEC's geoeconomic power was fleeting. The higher prices pressured the rest of the world to enact strict conservation measures, develop alternative energy sources, and exploit remote oil fields such as the North Sea and Alaska's north slope that previously were too expensive to reach. OPEC's share of global oil exports dropped to one-third of the total. By the mid-1980s the price of an oil barrel had plunged to $12.

Will OPEC rise again? From 1999 to 2000 OPEC manipulated supply and demand to triple the price of an oil barrel back to $30. So will stagflation's bad old days return? That is unlikely. Governments and consumers will respond even more rapidly to higher prices by conservation, tapping new oil fields, and using alternative forms of energy. The current price is unlikely to remain high long. As long as globalization's market forces, energy alternatives, conservation, and technological revolutions continue, OPEC will never recover the geoeconomic heights to which it once soared.

national security and prosperity. Power flows, not out of gun barrels, but from bank vaults, laboratories, boardrooms, factory floors, classrooms, and the Internet. Nations tip the balance of power in their favor, not with vast military forces, but with vast trade surpluses. Armies are equipped with business suits, laptops, and flowcharts rather than khaki, rifles, and tanks. Superpower rests on corporate rather than nuclear power.

Until recently, most of those who studied power thought of it largely in geopolitical rather than geoeconomic terms. But events over the last several decades have resulted in increased attention to geoeconomic power and conflicts in international relations. OPEC's quadrupling of oil prices in 1973 and further doubling in 1979; the relative decline of the United States, and rapid rise of Japan, and to a lesser extent the European Union, and the incessant trade, investment, and technology conflicts among all three; the rise of the newly industrializing countries (NICs) of eastern Asia; the collapse of communism and the Soviet empire; and the fleeting fear that the financial meltdown of first eastern Asia, then Russia, and Brazil in the late 1990s might drag down the global economy all reinforced the realization that in an increasingly interdependent world geoeconomic conflicts and power were the most important.

GEOECONOMIC POWER AND ITS CREATION

So how then is geoeconomic power amassed and wielded? Robert Isaak asserts that geoeconomic power or the

> structural position (and relative independence or dependence) of states and multinational corporations in the world political economy is made up of at least five primary structures:
>
> 1. *Security structure:* the maintenance of order both within the organization or state and outside—within the international system at large.
>
> 2. *Money and credit system:* the stability and relative value of the currency and the sources and flexibility of short- and long-term finance.
>
> 3. *Knowledge structure:* literacy rates, technological competitiveness, training systems, and the distribution of critical economic information and skills throughout the population.
>
> 4. *Production structure:* the way resources are organized and the knowledge structure is utilized to determine what is produced.
>
> 5. *Value structure:* a cluster of psychocultural beliefs and ideological preferences that transcend and color "the rational"—what the people predominantly choose to learn.[51]

Each state follows its own policies for maximizing its geoeconomic power. Not every means of acquiring geoeconomic power is successful. But there has been a convergence in understanding how best to go about pursuing that quest. Throughout the modern era, the democratic industrial states have increasingly assumed a greater responsibility for regulating their economies to create and distribute wealth. In so doing, they have marched steadily away from the free market ideals that economists Adam Smith and David Ricardo formulated in the late 18th and early 19th centuries. In the last few years, most of those states that suffered communist revolutions or had communism imposed on them by Soviet imperialism, have thrown off the shackles of state ownership of all production and property for a more market-oriented system. States are trying to find a sensible middle way between the extreme, unachievable, and flawed "liberal" (free market) and "Marxist-Leninist" (state ownership) models. But ultimately there is no one formula for success. Geoeconomic power is achieved by adapting to circumstances.

How does a state become the world's leading and most dynamic geoeconomic superpower? In their book *Politics and Productivity: The Real Story of Why Japan's Economy Works,* Chalmers Johnson, John Zysman, and Laura Tyson argue that first the United States and then Japan became political economic superpowers by mastering a new means of production and innovation, or a "technoeconomic paradigm."[52] America's economic supremacy throughout most of the 20th century resulted from its ability to create and then master two dynamic innovations: mass production and the hierarchical, multidivisional corporation. America led the world in manufacturing high-quality, inexpensive products, and other industrial nations scrambled to emulate its system. Since 1950, Japan has mastered a technoeconomic paradigm that represents a fundamentally different, superior way of production and technological innovation and thus is leading a third industrial revolution that may guarantee its economic supremacy for the foreseeable future as thoroughly as Britain's mastery of steam power did throughout the 19th century and America's mass production did throughout much of the 20th century.

Until recently no country has been more successful in creating, distributing, and securing wealth than Japan. By carefully nurturing strategic industries into global champions by cartels, technology infusions, various subsidies, import barriers, and export offensives, Tokyo achieved growth rates as much as four times higher and an income distribution more equitable than that of the United States.[53] Although the collapse of Japan's stock and real estate markets in the 1990s took some luster from its accomplishments, many other countries, including the United States, are trying to emulate Japan's success by adopting some of its strategies. The Clinton administration policies of balancing the budget, reducing the national debt, cutting back military spending, and investing in high-technology industries created an economic renaissance for the United States in the 1990s. America's growth, productivity, employment, and inflation rates were the healthiest in the country's history. The Clinton boom reversed America's relative decline of the 1980s and developed the economy into a dynamic growth engine for the world. But problems linger—most ominously, huge trade deficits that are approaching the heights of the 1980s.

IMBALANCES IN POTENTIAL GEOECONOMIC POWER

Potential economic power, like military power, can be measured, although such measurements give an even less reliable idea of the outcome of a power struggle. Evaluating the power of states by their economic power provides a pyramid ranking similar to that of military power. *Gross national product (GNP)* per capita income, finance, technology, manufacturing, productivity, savings, investments, and income distribution, to name a few, are all aspects of raw economic power, which reveal nothing about how skilled governments are in using their economic power.

There are two great patterns of relationships in the global political economy. Interdependent relations are generally between countries of roughly equal development levels and/or economic size. Dependent relations are generally between countries of roughly unequal development levels and/or economic size. The difference between an interdependent and a dependent relationship is one of power. In interdependent relationships there is generally a power balance; in dependent relationships, a power imbalance.

In *dependent* relationships, the poorer or economically smaller nation is more vulnerable to an economic slowdown or erection of trade barriers in the richer or larger nation. Both Canada and Mexico are trade-dependent on the United States, importing and exporting a far greater percentage of their GNP with the United States than vice versa. Although the living standards of Canadians and Americans are similar, Canada's economy is only one-tenth the size of the United States', and thus would suffer far more if trade relations ended. Mexico's per capita income is about one-sixth that of the United States.

There are three economic superpowers, the United States, Japan, and the 15-nation European Union.[54] In bulk consumption power, the European Union's 375 million population far surpasses America's 271 million or Japan's 126 million, while the European Union's combined GNPs account for about 22 percent of global GNP, slightly larger than America's 19 percent and much larger than Japan's 14 percent. The Big Four—Germany, France, Italy, and Great Britain—account for about 75 percent of the European Union's population and 85 percent of its GNP. With 80 million people, Germany by far is the largest, followed by about 60 million for the other three. The other members vary in size from Spain with 39 million to tiny Luxembourg with 370,000.

Beached Behemoths: Japan's Banking Crisis

D oes size matter? Japanese banks prove that old adage "It ain't the meat, it's the motion." In 1989, Japan's banks were 8 of the 10 and 13 of the 25 largest in the world. How did Japanese banks amass so much money? Decades of Japanese neomercantilism, which conquered one foreign industry after another by maximizing exports and minimizing imports, left Japan's bank vaults bulging with cash. It seemed then that Japan's banking industry would dominate world financial mar-

kets like their partners in microelectronics, automobiles, and so on. But that did not happen. What when wrong?

Wealth and power wisely invested beget yet more wealth and power. Japan's bankers failed to invest wisely that mountain of cash so that it would get even larger. Lacking the sophisticated financial instruments of their American and European rivals, Japanese banks instead went on a buying and lending spree both at home and abroad. Many of those were speculative gambles rather than sound investments.

After soaring in previous years, Japan's "bubble" stock and real estate markets burst in 1989. The stock market's value dropped to 40 percent of its height and dragged down the entire economy to a decade of low growth. By 1999 Japan's entire banking system was plagued by at least $1 trillion of bad debt.

Will Japanese power ever revive and match or exceed its heights in the late 1980s? What means would Tokyo have to pursue to achieve that end? What keeps Tokyo from successfully implementing those policies?

The United States remains by far the greatest country in sheer economy size and the average wealth of its people. In 1998, America's $7,922.6 trillion GNP and $29,340 in *purchasing power parity (PPP)* per capita dwarfed that of the second largest economy, Japan, with $2.928.4 trillion and $23,180. Of the four leading European countries, Germany's rates were $1,708.5 trillion and $20,810, France's $1,312.0 trillion and $22,320, Britain's $1,218.6 trillion and $20,640, and Italy's $1,163.4 trillion and $20,200.

There is a dynamic relationship between savings and investment—generally, the more a nation saves, the higher its investment rate. Nations can augment their savings and investments by borrowing foreign capital or contribute to foreign savings and investments by investing overseas. In 1997, Japan's gross domestic savings rate was 30 percent, nearly double America's 16 percent and well above Germany's 22 percent, France's 20 percent, Britain's 15 percent, and Italy's 22 percent.

What is important, however, is not the savings but the investment rate. By virtually any measurement, EU investments have lagged far behind those of Japan and even the United States. Japan's growth in gross capital formation has continually outstripped that of both the European Union and the United States. From 1969 to 1979, Japan's gross capital formation grew an annual average 4.9 percent compared to Europe's 1.9 percent and America's 2.7 percent, and from 1979 to 1987, Japan's grew an average 3.8 percent compared to the European Union's dismal 0.5 percent and America's 2.4 percent. From 1985 to 1988, Japan's gross capital formation rate of 23.7 percent was more than double the European Union's 11.0 percent or America's 11.3 percent. Japan's net government investment in infrastructure as a percentage of GDP from 1980–1989 also outstripped its rivals,

Per Capita Income *versus* Purchasing Power Parity

Per capita income, which is GNP divided by population, is not considered an accurate guide to living standards because it does not account for living costs. Purchasing power parity (PPP) is a more accurate measure of relative living standards because it compares the costs of the same "basket" of goods such as food, housing, transportation, clothing, and so on in different countries and thus determines the relative purchasing power. The different results of the two methods are striking. For example, Japan's GNP and per capita income under the old method were $4,089.0 trillion and $32,380, compared with America's $7,921.3 trillion and $29,340.

averaging 5.7 percent compared to Germany's 3.7 percent, France's 2.7 percent, Britain's 2.0 percent, and Italy's 4.8 percent. During this "Reagan era," America's was a mere 0.3 percent! One major reason for Japan's extraordinarily high investment rate has been its extremely low prime lending rate, which in 1988 was 4.88 percent compared to America's 10 percent, Germany's 10.50 percent, France's 11 percent, Great Britain's 16 percent, and Italy's 14 percent.[55] Japan's gross domestic investment rate remains very high, 30 percent in 1997 compared to America's 18 percent, Germany's 21 percent, France's 17 percent, Britain's 16 percent, and Italy's 17 percent.

Productivity and investment rates are closely linked. Generally the more money a firm invests the greater its productivity. An essential portion of investment goes into research and development (R&D) of new product and technologies. During the 1980s, the Americans lagged far behind the Japanese but have recently regained the lead. From 1994 to 1999, American spending on R&D increased from $97.1 billion to $166 billion, a 71 percent increase, whereas Japan's rose to $95 billion.

The advanced industrial countries are racing to master new technologies and adopt them to new products—a process at which the Japanese excel. How do countries acquire advanced technologies? They can either invent, buy, or steal them. Japan's rapid technological development depended on acquiring high technologies, mostly through licensing but also through invention and copying. Between 1950 and 1980, Japanese firms signed about 30,000 licensing agreements for foreign technology worth about $10 billion, which originally cost between $500 billion and $1 trillion to develop.[56] The Japanese continue to vacuum the world's laboratories for all potentially profitable technologies as American rivals caught up in the 1990s after their nadir in the 1980s. By the late 1990s, the Japanese and the Americans were neck and neck in the high-technology race, while the Europeans lagged behind in most areas.

The world economy runs on money. National and corporate success in the global economy depends on those which have the greatest financial power. Over the past two decades, the shift in the global balance of banking power has been extraordinary. In 1998, of the world's ten largest banks, the first, third, seventh, and eight largest were Japanese, the sixth largest was American, and the rest were European. The largest Japanese bank had $1,320.5 trillion in assets, more than

Table 4.4 **The Imbalance of Trade Power, 1998**

	Imports	Exports	Balance
United States	$944.580	$682.977	–$261.603
Japan	$280.531	$387.965	$107.434
Germany	$466.619	$539.689	$73.070
France	$287.210	$307.031	$19.821
Great Britain	$316.077	$272.692	–$43.385
Italy	$213.995	$240.869	$26.821

Figures are in billions of dollars.

Source: U.S. Department of Commerce, 2000.

Table 4.5 **Bilateral U.S. Trade Deficits, 1997**

	U.S. Imports	U.S. Exports	U.S. Deficit
Japan	$121,663.2	$65,548.5	–$56,114.8
European Union	$157,527.8	$140,773.4	–$16,754.5
China	$62,557.6	$12,862.3	–$49,695.3
Pacific Rim	$315,367.7	$193,740.4	–$121,627.4
Europe	$172,956.8	$155,383.9	–$17,572.9
South/Central America	$53,696.9	$63,021.1	$9,324.2
OPEC	$44,025.3	$25,525.6	–$18,499.8
World	$870,670.7	$689,382.4	–$181,488.2

Figures are in billions of dollars.

Source: U.S. Department of Commerce, 2000.

twice CitiGroup's $668.6 billion assets. Yet Japan's position has slipped since 1989, when it owned eight of the world's ten largest banks; the other two were European.

Trade prowess is yet another indicator of a nation's global political economic power. In 1998, the United States suffered a trade deficit of $260 billion, whereas four of the next five largest economic powers enjoyed trade surpluses, much of which was with the vast open American market. The other mostly liberal economy of the group, that of Great Britain, also suffered a deficit.

Another measure of national power is the percentage of exports and imports in relation to GNP. For the economic great powers, the smaller the percentage of trade to GNP the less vulnerable that country is to cutoffs and the more potential power it has to trade access to its own markets for foreign concessions from more vulnerable countries. There is a clear relationship between the population size of an industrial country and its trade dependence. The larger the population, the lower its dependence on trade as a percentage of GNP, while the smaller the population the greater the trade dependence. In 1997, America's exports were 12 percent and imports 13 percent of GNP compared to Japan's 10 percent and 9 percent, Germany's 24 percent and 23 percent, France's 24 percent and 21 percent, Britain's 30 percent and 30 percent, and Italy's 27 percent and 21 percent.

Why Trade Deficits Matter: Japan Against *the* United States

Economists (theorists) assert that a trade deficit is a strength rather than a weakness because it reflects that country's buying power. Political economists (empiricists) dismiss economic theories as inadequate to explain the ever more complex and changing real world. A deficit helps a country if it is composed of goods that cannot be produced at home and hurts if those imports destroy domestic industries, companies, and jobs.

If economists are correct and 20,000 jobs are lost for every $1 billion of a trade deficit between industrial countries, then Japan's $56 billion surplus in 1997 destroyed 1,120 million American jobs that year alone! Nearly all those jobs were in manufacturing.

Why is Japan so successful in its trade war with the United States? Although the United States follows a liberal philosophy of open markets, Japan single-mindedly pursues a

neomercantilist strategy of *dumping* goods below their costs in the United States while maintaining high trade barriers to keep competitive American goods from entering or capturing more than slivers of market share in Japan. American exports to Japan were mostly raw natural resources that Japanese companies make into sophisticated goods to sell back to the United States.

A bilateral trade account reveals much about the relative strength of the two partners. The United States suffers huge annual deficits with most countries, most painfully with Japan and the European Union. The composition of bilateral trade is decisive. America's trade deficits with Japan and the European Union destroyed more jobs and bankrupted more companies than its deficits with China and OPEC. Why? China exports mostly low-value toys and textiles, whereas OPEC exports mostly oil in return for American manufactured goods. It is quite possible that the United States actually gained jobs and wealth despite its trade deficits with China and OPEC. In contrast, Japan and the European Union sell high-value manufactured goods such as automobiles, consumer electronics, steel, and other products that provide high salaries to workers and high profits to companies. So America's trade deficits with those rivals clearly cost the United States jobs and wealth. Another interesting phenomenon revealed by the trade statistics is that America's trade with Asia is far greater than with Europe. That shift from Europe to Asia occurred in the early 1980s and has been widening ever since.

How does all this translate into power? Robert Gilpin clearly understands the expanded criteria for great power status and national security in an interdependent world:

> Today Great Power status accrues only to those nations which are leaders in all phases of basic-research and which possess the financial and managerial means to convert new knowledge into advanced technologies. In the case of the two superpowers, eminence in science and technology go hand-in-hand, and it appears unlikely that any nation or group of nations can ever again aspire to a dominant role in international politics without possessing a strong, indigenous scientific and technological capability. International politics has passed from the era of traditional industrial nation states to one dominated by the scientific nation state.[57]

Although Gilpin was referring to the United States and Soviet Union as the two superpowers of the 1960s, today he would certainly replace the Soviet Union with Japan.

HOW IS GEOECONOMIC POWER USED?

How is economic power wielded? Klaus Knorr reminds us "just as army divisions per se are not military power, so GNP or national wealth per se is not economic power."[58] Geoeconomic power is the ability of a state to enrich itself while harming others. National economic power is actualized when wealth and economic policy are used deliberately to modify the behavior or capabilities of other states. The ability to shut off valuable markets, to preempt sources of supply, to stop investments, or reduce economic aid would constitute elements of national economic strength comparable to military strength. Knorr points out that geoeconomic power can be actualized in three ways: (1) A applies economic power directly; (2) A threatens B with economic attack; (3) B anticipates the threat and adjusts according to A's wishes.[59]

In an interdependent world, states often use "co-optive" rather than coercive power to achieve their foreign policy goals. According to Nye, co-optive power "is the ability of a nation to structure a situation so that other nations develop preferences or define their interests in ways consistent with one's own nation. . . . The international institutions that the United States helped to establish have not merely affected the way in which other states pursue their interests but also how they understand their own behavior and define their national interests."[60] For example, by opening the American market to foreign competition, extending economic aid, and persistently touting the theoretical virtues of free trade, Washington has succeeded in persuading many other countries to lower their trade and investment barriers.

The coercive use of geoeconomic power is more common than its co-optive use. The power to give is also the power to deny. *Economic sanctions* are the most obvious way in which states employ geoeconomic power. Sanctions were rare in international relations before the mid-20th century. Napoleon tried to force Britain to accept his European conquests by organizing an international trade boycott against Britain known as the "continental system." The sanctions failed because many European states and merchants cheated, while Britain itself depended more on its trade with the empire than Europe. And like many economic sanctions, the continental system hurt its perpetrators as bad and perhaps worse than its object.

Between 1914 and 1990, there were 142 international economic sanctions, of which 129 have occurred since 1940.[61] By far the most common situation has been for developed states to impose sanctions on developing states, which accounted for 66 cases since 1940. During the same period, while democratic industrial states imposed sanctions on communist states 18 times, the reverse occurred only 5 times.

The trouble with economic sanctions is that they rarely work. A state can buy all it needs through third parties, albeit at higher prices. Although inflation may rise and shortages occur, but overall few countries suffer grievously from economic sanctions. Perhaps no country has faced more systematic international sanctions than Iraq, and yet that country continues to defy the United Nations. The value of economic sanctions lies chiefly in that they offer states a face-saving alternative to war. States can act tough and pretend to punish others without resorting to mass destruction.

Often the economic sanctions hurt the country that imposes them worse than the target. The Kennedy administration imposed an embargo on Cuba after it embraced communism and the Soviet Union; the Carter administration, a grain embargo on the Soviet Union after it invaded Moscow; the Reagan administration, an embargo on machine tools and earth-moving equipment to western Europe and the Soviet Union when the Europeans and Soviets agreed to build a gas pipeline across the continent; the Bush administration, an embargo on trade with Panama to force out dictator Manuel Noriega. In all these examples, the United States suffered more because American businesses lost out to their foreign rivals as the targeted country simply switched suppliers and markets.

The longest-lasting economic sanctions have been imposed by the *Coordinating Committee on Export Controls (COCOM)*, which was founded in 1948, includes nearly all the democratic industrial countries, and is organized to impede the export of high technology to communist countries. COCOM's efforts have had only a limited success. Moscow and the other communist states were usually able to find a Western firm willing to cheat on the restrictions, and redoubled their own research and development efforts to catch up to the West.

Sanctions aside, states can assert geoeconomic power in a variety of ways. *Neomercantilism* is the strategy whereby a state targets its most important industries with subsidies, import protection, and export incentives in order to capture wealth that otherwise would have flowed to more efficient overseas producers. A particularly effective neomercantilist strategy is for an industry to dump or sell below price its products in foreign markets in order to drive competitors out of business. After taking over the market, the industry will then raise prices to recoup earlier loses. But sometimes a government will attempt to protect its industry against a foreign dumping attack. For example, in 1986, the United States and Japan signed an agreement in which Tokyo pledged to stop the dumping by Japanese semiconductor firms in the United States and elsewhere and guarantee American producers a 20 percent market share in Japan.

Another neomercantilist strategy is to refuse to sell or license technology to other countries. In his book *The Japan That Can Say No,* one of Japan's most prominent political leaders, Shintaro Ishihara, bluntly advocated using America's growing high-technology dependence on Japan to extract political concessions: If Japan sold "microprocessor chips to the Soviet Union and stopped selling them to the United States, this would upset the entire military balance. . . . The more technology advances the more the U.S. and Soviet Union will become dependent on the initiative of the Japanese people."[62] Charles Ferguson concisely captures the dangers inherent in America's loss of technological leadership to Japan:

> technological revolutions often contribute to shifts in wealth and geopolitical influence by changing the sources of industrial and military success. . . . As this transformation progresses, the United States is being gradually but pervasively eclipsed by Japan . . . [a development that could lead to American] decline and dependence on Japan . . . [and] major economic and geopolitical consequences. . . . (W)hile Japan is a military ally . . . American policy must recognize that Japan is also a closed, highly controlled, and systematically predatory actor in the international economy . . . [and] a statist, strategically cohesive free rider in the world technological system. . . . The simultaneous need to preserve the military-diplomatic alliance while responding to Japan's technoeconomic Prussianism will therefore prove a critical challenge for U.S. policy . . . the United States must learn that the . . . issue of high technology and Japanese industrial policy, not just Soviet warheads, will determine the future national security of the United States.[63]

Any nation that dominates the technology food chain's base—the components and manufacturing equipment industry—has the power to dominate all the other links up the chain. With Japan's takeover of these segments, American industries are increasingly dependent on Japanese corporations for their components. Japan's most blatant use of its technology power has been to withhold or delay selling key equipment to American manufacturers. For example, America's remaining supercomputer producer, Cray, is dependent on Japanese suppliers for most of its key components, and the Japanese have not hesitated to exploit this dependency: In 1986, Hitachi delayed shipping a key component that Cray had actually designed, giving Hitachi's computer group a one-year lead time designing it into its own supercomputers.[64] American firms have been complaining about the practice for years, but quietly, for fear that the Japanese firms will withhold even more equipment. On May 6, 1991, Sematech, an American consortium of 14 chip and computer makers publicly denounced Japan's hoarding of essential equipment for as long as 6 to 18 months and then selling it at prices 20 to 30 percent higher than Japanese firms pay, in an attempt to damage the American firms as much as possible.

There is a reciprocal relationship between economic power—the ability to capture markets, play off raw material, capital, and component suppliers against each other to extract the lowest possible price, and technologically leapfrog, financially outspend, undersell, and eventually bankrupt rivals—and political power. Money buys access to political power, which can then be used to promote policies favoring the buyer, which allows even greater resources with which to buy more political power. In his book *Agents of Influence*, Pat Choate reveals that the Japanese spend over $400 million annually in the United States lobbying politicians at the national, state, and local levels for favorable policies, a sum greater than what American business lobby groups spend![65] The result, according to Choate, is that America's political and policy process is increasingly distorted to conform to Japanese rather than American interests.

Conclusion

Throughout history, thousands of analysts and practitioners have grappled with the concept of power. About the only thing that most agree on is that power is the ability to get others to do things they otherwise would not do. Power permeates all human relations and, as Morgenthau pointed out, can be asserted by any means "from physical violence to the most subtle of psychological ties by which one mind controls another."[66]

Stalin once allegedly said of Yugoslavia's independent communist president, "I shall shake my little finger and there will be no more Tito." Achieving one's desires with a mere gesture is ultimate power, but one that does not exist in international relations or even within the most totalitarian of countries. There are always some constraints on power whether the wielder be an individual, group, country, alliance, corporation, or international organization.

International relations have not fundamentally changed throughout history: states still use power to assert their interests with some and against other states. However, the means by which states assert power and interests has changed dramatically in just the last half-century. A state was once deemed powerful or weak by the size and prowess of its military relative to those of other states. No longer. States increasingly defend and enhance their interests through geoeconomic rather than geopolitical means.

Study Questions

1. Define politics. What is power? How are the two related?
2. How is power relative?
3. List ways in which power can be asserted.
4. What are the differences and relationships among compellence, deterrence, and defense?
5. What is the relationship between power and wealth?
6. How is power measured? Give examples.
7. What are the tangible sources of national power? How has the relative importance of different tangible power sources changed throughout history?
8. What are the intangible sources of national power? How has the relative importance of different intangible power sources changed throughout history?
9. Are all global politics essentially power struggles? Is the nature of power and international relations eternally fixed, or are their manifestations and patterns much more complex, subtle, and varied? Explain.
10. Describe the role of public relations or propaganda in power.
11. How can culture be a source of power?
12. According to Paul Kennedy, why do nations rise and fall in relative power?
13. List the different ways of categorizing and ranking the military power of states.
14. What is gunboat diplomacy, and why is it increasingly ineffective in the contemporary world?
15. What are the various ways of understanding the "balance of power"?
16. Describe the security dilemma.
17. How does nuclear power enhance or detract from a nation's total power?
18. Why is military power increasingly unimportant in an evermore interdependent global economy?
19. List the different ways of categorizing and ranking the economic power of states.
20. In what ways can geoeconomic power be wielded?
21. How effective are economic sanctions as a form of geoeconomic power?
22. What is a neomercantilist strategy to amass and wield geoeconomic power? Give an example.

ⓖ *InfoTrac College Edition* Sources

Using the Subject Guide, enter the search terms *economic sanctions* and/or *international economic relations*. Using Keywords, enter the search terms *security dilemma, deterrence,* and/or *mercantilism*.

Boutros-Ghali, Boutros. "Global Leadership After the Cold War."

Catley, Bob. "Hegemonic America: The Benign Superpower?"

DeMarrais, Elizabeth, Luis Jaime Castillo, and Timothy Earle. "Ideology, Materialization, and Power Strategies."

Kupchan, Charles A. "After Pax Americana: Benign Power, Regional Integration, and the Sources of a Stable Multipolarity."

Luttwak, Edward N. "A Post-Heroic Military Policy."

McNicoll, Geoffrey. "Population Weights in the International Order."

O'Loughlin, John, and Luc Anselin. "Geo-Economic Competition and Trade Bloc Formation: United States, German and Japanese Exports, 1968–1992."

Saxe-Fernandez, John. "NAFTA: The Intersection of the Geopolitics and Geoeconomics of Capital."

Shlapentokh, Dmitry. "The Permanent Russian Crisis."

Soderberg, Nancy E. "U.S. Intervention in the Post–Cold War Era."

White, Robert. "Climate Science and National Interests."

Zhao, Suisheng. "Asia-Pacific Regional Multipolarity: From Alliance to Alignment in the Post–Cold War Era."

On *the* Web

http://www.freetrade.org/
Cato Institute site extolling the virtues of free trade

http://csf.colorado.edu/ipe/
International political economy

http://cs.muohio.edu/
Economic History Web Sites

Contents

Chapter 5 Foreign Policy Making *and* Implementing

Key Concepts and Terms

Foreign policy is as old as the first states and their conflicts with other states. Throughout the modern era, the issues, means, and ends of foreign policymaking for nation-states have proliferated and changed significantly.

The popular image of foreign policymaking is a council of wise men carefully and rationally choosing among alternatives until they find the one best able to fulfill *national interests*. In reality, policymaking is a messy, imprecise process that varies considerably from one issue, time, and government to the next. There are as many different policymaking processes as there are issues.

Policymaking is thus a multistranded tug of war between different and often diametrically opposed experts, interest groups, and public emotions. There are as many policymakers as there are individuals and groups interested in that particular issue. However, some individuals and groups are obviously much more influential in shaping foreign policy than others.

Although it is perhaps more accurate to speak of a nation's foreign "policies" than "*policy*," most nations do have a broad set of national goals and strategies that guide the formulation of specific policies affecting specific issues. For example, America's foreign policies from 1947 through 1990 generally operated under the rubric of "containment." The foreign policy ends of many Third World states are development and nonalignment, although the means to attain those ends vary considerably.

A nation's foreign policy includes the specific goals that leaders pursue in the global system, the values that shape those goals, and the means by which those goals are achieved. This chapter explores the concept of national interests on which governments base their policies; some flawed foreign policy models; the "level-of-analysis matrix," which enables analysts to gain an in-depth understanding of why countries do what they do; and, finally, several policy types.[1]

foreign policy a broad set of national goals and strategies that guide the formulation of specific policies affecting specific issues. A nation's foreign policy includes the specific goals that leaders pursue in the global system, the values that shape those goals, and the means by which those goals are achieved.

national interests both the broad goals that all states share—political independence, economic growth, cultural preservation, and peace—and the distinct goals each state pursues on specific issues.

policymaking the means by which policies are decided and acted on.

How Do National Interests Shape Foreign Policy?

Why do governments do the things they do, and not the things they seemingly *could* do? The answer is usually national interests. Governments follow policies that they believe protect or enhance their nation's interests. When Winston Churchill was asked for an explanation of Soviet behavior, he replied, "I cannot forecast to you the action of Russia. It is a riddle wrapped in a mystery inside an enigma; but perhaps there is a key. That key is Russian national interests."

National interests are evoked to justify virtually every act of state, from generosity to genocide. And, of course, some states follow policies that in retrospect undermined rather than enhanced national interests. The imperialism of Germany, Japan, and Italy during the 1930s and 1940s and Iraq's invasion of Kuwait in August 1990 were justified by the leaders of those countries as being in their nations' interests. But imperialism left those nations in ruins. Virtually all analysts agree that the United States was weakened economically, politically, militarily, and morally by its war in Vietnam. Yet the various administrations continually attempted to justify America's long involvement in Vietnam in terms of national interests. In evaluating a nation's policies, the first rule is that they should be achievable. Paul Kennedy's *Rise and Fall of the Great Powers* shows how great powers eventually declined because their ambitions—their declared national interests—exceeded their abilities.[2]

American Policy Toward Iran: Containment *or* Engagement?

Iran was once the linchpin of America policy toward the Persian Gulf. From 1953 when the Americans helped him gain power in a coup until his overthrow by an Islamic revolution in 1979, Shah Reza Pahlavi aligned Iran with the United States. His regime's economic and military dependence on Washington, systematic corruption, and brutal repression of dissenters, including radical Muslims, provoked the fundamentalist Islamic regime to retaliate by capturing the American embassy and holding its 54 employees hostage for 444 days.

With the revolution and embassy takeover, American policy toward Iran shifted from alliance to containment. For the last two decades the United States has severed diplomatic relations with Iran and imposed an economic embargo on it. What has that policy gained and lost the United States? The economic loss has been severe, as its economic rivals took over markets and investments once dominated by American corporations. But could and should Washington have responded

differently to a radical regime with ambitions to become a nuclear power and spread an Islamic revolution across the Middle East through terrorism, a regime that continues to call the United States "the Great Satan"?

Recent changes in Iran have stimulated an American policy debate. In 1997 the moderate Mohammed Khatami won the presidency. Iranian politics split between Khatami, who favors better relations with the United States and the country's spiritual leader Ayatollah Ali Khameni, who remains bitterly anti-American. Despite Khameni's opposition, Khatami has made some significant steps toward reconciliation with the United States. In December 1997, he publicly announced that Iran now embraced peace between Israel and the Palestinians. In January 1998, he declared that Iran had renounced terrorism. In May 1998, U.S. Secretary of State Madeleine Albright responded by declaring it was time for both countries to draw "a road map leading to a normal relation."

But to date Washington and Teheran have yet to draw that map, let alone journey down it. Should American policy toward Iran change or remain the same? What are American national interests with Iran? Would a containment or engagement policy better advance the American interests of ending Iran's nuclear weapons program and support of terrorist groups? Do America's economic interests in expanding trade and investments with Iran inhibit, encourage, or have no affect on Teheran's policy of promoting Islamic revolutions against moderate Arab countries in the Persian Gulf and across the Middle East? Have Iran's national interests shifted? Does Teheran's interest in economic development replace or reinforce its revolutionary and nuclear ambitions? Should Iran resist or embrace the United States? What interest groups, ideologies, and political factions shape policy toward each other in both countries?

All states share some common interests—political independence, economic development, cultural preservation, environmental safety, and peace. The most obvious national interest is self-preservation, and the greatest threat to that basic interest is an enemy invasion. That threat, however, is increasingly rare in international relations. Four other core national values vary in their degree of importance with promoting economic development and environmentalism more challenging than independence from the interference of foreigners in one's domestic affairs and the preservation of one's "way of life" or culture.

Other national interests are less concrete. Governments often pursue policies that enhance national prestige, or the acknowledgment by other states of one's economic, social, political, technological, military, or cultural achievements. This "interest" is particularly difficult to measure, and achieving it may well conflict with other more concrete national interests. For example, in the interests of national prestige many developing and smaller nations have their own national airlines, even though they cost an enormous amount to create and often run at a loss. The U.S. space station currently being assembled may cost as much as $180 billion, a sum that will never pay off economically. Many analysts argue that the same experiments designed for the space station could be conducted at a fraction of the cost on earth. Yet its advocates continually justify the project for national prestige reasons. Is the prestige generated by the space station worth that cost?

For almost 50 years, American policymakers and the public agreed that the nation's interests were best served by the interrelated goals of containing the Soviet Union and developing and defending the global political economy. These policies were enormously successful. The Soviet empire and *communism* were contained and eventually crumbled. The world economy is increasingly prosperous and dynamic. In achieving these national interests, other interests were neglected. The Soviet Union's demise and a secure, prosperous world economy does not automatically mean a secure, prosperous American economy. Different policies have different results. Although Washington mobilized vast intellectual, scientific, financial resources to contain the Soviet Union, and opened its markets and aided the world, economic rivals caught up to, often surpassed, and diminished one American industry after another.

Foreign policy debate is usually over means rather than ends. Although there was a national consensus on the perceived need to contain the Soviet Union and communism, there were considerable differences over just how to do so. Some, such as analyst George Kennan, advocated a *selective containment* in which only those areas with vital geopolitical and geoeconomic importance (such as Europe, Japan, and the Middle East) would be defended, and economic rather than military means would be used. Others, including former secretaries of state Dean Acheson and John Foster Dulles, pushed for "global containment" in which every government facing a communist rebellion must be supported for fear that its loss would result in a "domino effect" in which neighboring governments would also be overthrown by communists; military means were emphasized. The tug-of-war between advocates of selective and global containment continued through the cold war. Selective containment prevailed from 1947 to 1950 and from 1969 to 1979; global containment dominated American policies from 1950 to 1969 and from 1979 to 1991.

The debate over America's war in Vietnam was essentially a debate over the best containment strategy. Advocates of selective containment maintained that Vietnam had no geopolitical or geoeconomic importance to the United States and thus should be avoided. Advocates of global containment countered that if Vietnam fell, so would the rest of Southeast Asia, and then the entire global power balance would shift against the United States. The global containers won the debate, and the United States became deeply involved in a war it eventually lost.

Global containment was exorbitantly expensive and eventually undercut American interests. In expending enormous amounts of wealth, expertise, and blood confronting every communist or anti-American government around the world, the United States neglected to maintain its own economic vitality and security. This was glaringly evident from 1981 to 1993, when Reaganomic policies of tax cuts for the rich and spending hikes for the military quadrupled America's national debt, and transformed the United States into the world's greatest debtor nation, with the lowest growth rates of any industrial democracy and huge trade deficits. The United States fell behind Japan as a manufacturing, technological, and financial power. Socioeconomic ills such as poverty, crime, homelessness, drug addiction, crumbling infrastructure, and racism worsened. Since 1993, White House policies of spending cuts, tax hikes for the rich, subsidies for high-tech industries, and market-opening agreements with foreign countries reversed America's startling decline and restored its position as the world's geoeconomic superpower. How much stronger would America be today if different policies had been pursued before 1993?

There can sometimes be tradeoffs between a nation's short- and long-term interests. For example, the United States has an interest in political stability and open markets in all foreign countries. The question is, how best to achieve this national interest? In the case of Nicaragua, Washington sent in the Marines on five occasions earlier in the 20th century to maintain order and protect American investments. After 1930, Washington helped the Somoza dictatorship take and maintain power. Yet American support for the increasingly corrupt and brutal Somoza regime contributed to anti-Americanism and revolutionary conditions that eventually resulted in the regime's overthrow in 1979 and establishment of the communist Sandinista government. The United States continued to intervene in Nicaragua by arming and training the Contras or anticommunist guerrillas. In 1989, the Sandinistas lost power in an election to a coalition of forces that re-opened the country to foreign trade and investment.

Were America's economic interests in Nicaragua worth the billions of dollars the United States spent over the past century in maintaining or reinstating friendly governments? It can be argued that Washington's interventionist policy served not the American public, but only that tiny number of businesses that traded or invested with Nicaragua. And even then, the interventionist policy may have protected those American business interests over the short term while failing to do so over the long term, because it contributed to the Sandinista revolution. However, those who advocated an interventionist policy throughout the past century justified it not in dollars and cents but in its balance-of-power and domino effects. A communist victory in Nicaragua, it was argued, might not be important in itself, but could lead to communist victories throughout Central America, which would threaten the Panama Canal and the regional power balance.

Who defines the nation's interests? The answer varies from one country and time to the next. National interests may be articulated by a dictator, a council of experts, or by the give and take of countless interest groups and public opinion.

In democratic countries, one political party's definition of national interests may differ markedly from other parties, and thus foreign policy may shift with each change in leadership. In Israel, the conservative Likud party opposes and the liberal Labor party supports trading land for peace with the Palestinians. Both parties claim that their policies best safeguard Israel's interests. Various circumstances may allow a political party in power to fulfill or force it to turn its back on its principles. The Labor party signed the 1993 Oslo Accord with the Palestinians, which granted the latter increased autonomy in the West Bank and Gaza Strip. When the Likud party returned to power, it was legally bound to fulfill the accord that it had fiercely denounced. Although it threatened to tear up the Oslo accord, the pressure of Israeli public opinion and the White House eventually forced the

Relations between states can change quickly, as these photos reveal. In 1998 China's President Jiang Zemin journeyed to Washington to meet with President Bill Clinton. They toasted and vowed to strengthen the "strategic partnership" between the United States and China. A year later Ambassador Jim Sasser stares from the shattered windows of the embassy in Beijing. Government-controlled mobs attacked the embassy after NATO missiles mistakenly destroyed the Chinese embassy in Belgrade. The attack symbolized for Chinese the deteriorating relations that ranged over such issues as trade, Taiwan, spying, campaign contributions, missile proliferation, and human rights.

Ellis/Corbis Sygma

AP/Wide World Photos

Likud government to sign the 1998 Wye Accord, which granted even more autonomy to the Palestinians.

National interests are often defined by special interest groups, and the policies followed to achieve those special interests often largely benefit those groups. In the United States it was once said that "as GM goes, so goes the nation," meaning that as long as GM was prosperous so, too, would be the country. During the 1980s and into the 1990s, America's automobile industry was severely battered by cheaper, better-quality Japanese imports that captured 30 percent of the market. Although consumers benefited from the wider choices and cheaper prices that Japanese imports presented, America's automobile industry succeeded in pressuring the Reagan and Bush administrations to convince Tokyo to "voluntarily" restrict exports to 2.1 million vehicles a year starting in 1982 (since dropped to 1.6 million), and to build automobile factories in the United States to help employment here. Although these policies saved America's automobile industry, Japan's market share continues to rise, and American consumers pay higher prices than if free markets existed. Some argue, however, that if the Japanese succeeded in bankrupting America's industry, America's economy would suffer severely because of the loss of millions of high-paying jobs and profits to Japan, while the Japanese automobile makers would take advantage of their oligopoly power and raise prices. Which policy better serves American interests?

A vital national interest is preserving national ideals and culture, or ideology. How important is ideology in shaping a nation's foreign policy? Ideology often takes a back seat to other national concerns. During the cold war the United

States and Soviet Union frequently proclaimed that their policies were based on their nations' ideals—liberal democracy and communism, respectively. However, neither country allowed its national ideals to interfere when other more concrete national interests were thought to be threatened. Despite its democratic ideals, the United States supported dozens of brutal anti-Communist dictators around the world, and some administrations even suppressed political groups and information in the United States. Despite its ideal of Communist party solidarity and self-proclaimed leadership of the global communist movement, the Soviet Union maintained close relations with such governments as Iran, Egypt, and Iraq, which purged the local Communist parties.

Nonetheless, ideology is often used to justify a particular policy. The Bush administration argued that its wars against Panama's President Manuel Noriega and Iraq's President Saddam Hussein were democratic crusades against vicious dictators. Opponents countered that much less idealistic interests were at stake—Bush's virility in the Panama War, and oil in the Persian Gulf War. If fact, American troops were committed in both countries for far more complex reasons than either its advocates or opponents argued.

Often what is important is not whether ideology guides policy in an objective sense. Instead, the belief that one's actions are based on the highest principles can be an enormous source of power. Idealism can allow a leader and his or her followers to cast aside the moral ambiguities and compromises that accompany most political decisions. Decisive action is more likely when a leader believes that he or she is acting on principle, and more importantly, is able to convince the political establishment and public that together they are embarked on a crusade to protect or expand their national ideals. Of course, ideological fervor can be a double-edged sword; it can lead to defeat and sometimes outright ruin—as the Germans and Japanese, for example, discovered in 1945.

Raymond Aron explained the difficulties of defining national interests:

> The plurality of concrete interests and ultimate objectives forbids a rational definition of 'national interest,' even if the latter did involve, in itself, the ambiguity that attaches to collective interest in economic science. [Nation-states] are composed of individuals and groups, each of which seeks to maximize its resources, its share of the national income, or its position within the social hierarchy. The interests of those individuals and groups . . . added together . . . do not constitute a general interest.[3]

The debate over national interests is unresolved. Some argue that national interests are ultimately subjective, defined by the specific interests, prejudices, and perceptions of each individual or group with a stake in the issue, and policy results from the struggle among these different parochial interests. Others believe that although perceptions of national interests may vary according to narrow interest groups, all countries share an objective set of general national interests such as political economic development and security from military or political invasion, along with a set of specific interests for each country. If every nation has a set of interests, then there should be a clear set of policies that best protect those interests. The first view simply says that politics shapes policy, and thus national interests are whatever the power balance or imbalance of parochial interests say they are; the second view acknowledges that although this reality may currently be true, there are genuine national interests, and we can evaluate the relative success or failure of a nation's policies by how it addresses those national interests. Which view do you support?

Hans Morgenthau tried to bridge the gap between these two views by proposing that foreign policy makers evaluate an international issue by three criteria. First, policymakers should determine just what kind of issue was at stake—whether it involved the nation's physical safety, material well-being, political independence, and/or national cohesion. Second, they should distinguish between that issue's relative importance over the short and the long term, in which the latter should take precedence. Finally, they should figure out whether the issue is of primary or secondary importance to the country over both the short and long term in relation to all other current issues. In this way, the nation's interests could be objectively determined.

Flawed Models *of* Foreign Policy

How and why do governments follow certain policies and reject or not even consider others?[4] Analysts are deeply divided over this basic question, and have presented different models or theories to explain foreign policy behavior. Each model is provocative, but all fall short of providing an adequate understanding of the diversity and complexity of foreign policy making.

The "power balance" or "realist" explanation sees foreign policy as essentially shaped by one's relative power within the international system.[5] States are monolithic actors that simply react to shifts in the regional or global power balance. Domestic politics play no significant role in shaping foreign policy. Democratic or authoritarian, communist or capitalist, the state's internal organization and ideology are unimportant in explaining why states do the things they do. The only important factor is power. States constantly try to increase their own power and offset the rising power of others in the international system. The behavior or policies of states thus change with shifts in the international power balance. The human beings who make foreign policy decisions are assumed to be "rational," to have access to enough information to make rational decisions, and then to choose the option that best advances their nation's interests within the prevailing power balance. The realist perspective is both an explanation and a strategy for state behavior.

This *realist theory* of global politics is not as realistic as it may appear. Although policymakers do consciously try to make decisions rationally, they can rarely do so. Real policymaking is not a rational process. States are not unitary actors. They are composed of very human individuals and institutions that are incapable of flawlessly gathering and processing the information vital for every decision, and then rationally making and implementing the best decision for a given situation. Policymakers and institutions are forced daily to make dozens of important and routine decisions, and rarely have the time, information, or ability to rationally evaluate the options. And even when policymakers make a rational decision, they often lack the power to implement that policy as they wish. As former secretary of state Henry Kissinger put it, policymakers "are locked in an endless battle in which the urgent constantly gains on the important. The public life of every political figure is a continual struggle to rescue an element of choice from the pressure of circumstances."[6] A Kennedy adviser, Ted Sorensen, commented, "Each step cannot be taken in order. The facts may be in doubt or dispute. Several policies, all good, may conflict. Stated goals may be imprecise. There may be many interpretations of what is right, what is possible, and what is in the national interest."[7]

Strange Bedfellows? Israel *and* Turkey

Can Jews and Muslims be allies? Israel and Turkey certainly can. Operating on the classic diplomatic maxim "The enemy of my enemy is my friend," Tel Aviv and Ankara signed a military cooperation pact in 1996 and have since staged joint maneuvers, traded weapons, and shared intelligence. The Israelis and Turks are trying to reinforce their military ties with ever greater economic ties. Bilateral trade reached $2 billion in 1999. They eventually hope to entice Jordan into their pact.

What drives them together? Despite peace treaties with Egypt and Jordan, Israel remains a small island in a Muslim Arab sea where attitudes toward it vary from resentful tolerance to outright hostility. Until December 1999, when it received an invitation, Turkey's attempts to join the European Union were repeatedly rebuffed. The Turks are fighting a bloody and seemingly endless civil war with the Kurds in the country's southern region. Beyond are the hostile Arab states Syria and Iraq and the fundamentalist Muslim state Iran. To Turkey's west are its traditional enemies Greece and Cyprus. Thus the two isolated states of Turkey and Israel seek security with each other.

Does the partnership strengthen their mutual security by deterring potential enemies? Does it weaken their security by provoking potential enemies? Or does their pact cause only a diplomatic ripple in a tumultuous regional sea?

Although realist theory offers a strategy for governments, it cannot explain why states do not always or even usually follow the dictates of power politics. For example, according to realist theory Britain and France should have intervened against Hitler in 1936 when German troops marched into the demilitarized Rhineland rather than wait until Poland was attacked in 1939. Realist theory can only point out that Britain and France *should* have intervened, it cannot explain why they did not.

Another explanation of foreign policy is that states hold either a "status quo" or "revisionist" orientation toward the world, and act accordingly. Although all states strive to protect their national interests, most are content with the international status quo and their place in it. War is caused by a few troublemakers who try to revise the power balance in their favor. During the 1930s, for example, ambitious, authoritarian governments in Japan, Germany, and Italy sought to expand their power and carve out huge empires in Europe, the Middle East, and Asia. At first, hobbled by an isolationist public, the status quo powers watched helplessly as Japanese, Italian, and German armies conquered one state after another. Eventually, however, the *status quo states* went to war—France and Britain after Germany attacked Poland, and the Soviet Union and the United States after they were directly attacked by Germany and Japan, respectively.

What causes a nation to be revisionist or status quo? Some argue that a nation's ideology is the most important factor, that democratic states are naturally peaceloving, whereas authoritarian or revolutionary states are inherently aggressive. George Kennan argued that

A democracy is peace-loving. It does not like to go to war. It is slow to rise to provocation. When it has once been provoked to the point where it must grasp the sword, it does not easily forgive its adversary for having produced this situation. The fact of the provocation then becomes itself the issue. Democracy fights in anger—it fights for the very reason that it was forced to go to war. It fights to punish the power that was rash enough and hostile enough to provoke it—to teach that power a lesson it will not forget, to prevent the thing from happening again. Such a war must be carried to the bitter end.[8]

But democracy did not prevent Britain and the United States from pursuing imperialist policies.

Revolutionary states are naturally aggressive—they seek a "revolution without borders" in which their ideology is imposed everywhere. Revolutionary France, the Soviet Union, and Iran all dispatched their agents to foment turmoil elsewhere. The classic expression of a revolutionary ideology affecting a nation's foreign policy was the 1793 declaration by France's government that

> The French nation declares that it will treat as enemies every people who, refusing liberty and equality or renouncing them, may wish to maintain, recall, or treat with the prince and the privileged classes; on the other hand, it engages not to subscribe to any treaty and not to lay down its arms until the sovereignty and independence of the people whose territory the troops of the Republic shall have entered shall be established, and until the people shall have adopted the principles of equality and founded a free and democratic government.[9]

Eventually, though, the fires of revolutionary ardor burn out and the *revisionist state* becomes a status quo state. For example, Lenin had argued that in order for a revolution to succeed in Russia, it had to succeed everywhere. To that end he created the Communist International (Comintern) in 1918 as a secret organization that attempted to provoke revolutions abroad. By the late 1920s the failure of communist revolutions elsewhere and growing problems at home caused Stalin to shift to a "socialism in one state" policy. In 1956, Moscow adopted a policy of "peaceful coexistence" in which war between communist and capitalist countries was not inevitable, and in fact both systems could exist peacefully alongside each other as the capitalist countries slowly crumbled and were transformed by communism. Other revolutions have experienced similar transformations. The French were exhausted by a decade of revolution and eagerly accepted Napoleon's dictatorship in 1800, although that did not inhibit the emperor from attempting to conquer Europe. Similarly in Iran, two decades of revolution and foreign war sapped the government and people's revolutionary fire. Following the death of the Ayatollah Khomeini, the new leader, President Rafsanjani reined in his revolutionary agents and attempted to re-establish normal relations with other states. In 1997 the moderate Mohammed Khatami won the presidency with two-thirds of the vote and has called for détente with the United States and Western world. The fundamentalists may be down but by no means completely out. To date they have blocked any thaw in Iran's ties with the United States.

Like the realist model, the "revisionist/status quo" foreign policy model is limited. Few states in history have been revisionist in the revolutionary sense of trying to overthrow and change the entire world order. Virtually all states are revisionist in the sense that they want things from each other—territory, open markets, less pollution, and so on. At times governments believe their interests in a conflict are worth going to war to protect or enhance. Some wars lead to sweeping changes in the power relations among states.

Do individuals make history, or does history make individuals? Is history simply the sum of countless decisions made by unique, ambitious, powerful characters, or do leaders, even the mightiest, operate under enormous political constraints? Some argue that the character of those in power is decisive in shaping a nation's foreign policy. Leaders constantly face choices. Their decisions reflect a complex mix of their personality, intelligence, knowledge, view of history, fears, and ambitions. Because all individuals are different, each will make different decisions. Contrast the conflicting positions of British Prime Minister Neville Chamberlain and Winston Churchill to Hitler's rise. During the Czechoslovakian crisis of 1938, while Churchill advocated a strong British response, Chamberlain remarked, "How horrible, fantastic, incredible it is that we should be digging trenches and trying on gas-masks here because of a quarrel in a faraway country between people of which we know nothing!"[10] And what would have been the fate of Germany and the world had Hitler been killed rather than spared in World War I?

The "great man explanation" is flawed as well. Clearly, great leaders do at times matter. Try to imagine the 20th century without the birth of Lenin, Mao, or Hitler. Yet of all the countless decisions made by a succession of national leaders, few dramatically change that nation's direction. We will, of course, never know how different leaders would have responded to the same situation. But every leader, even those with the most sweeping dictatorial powers, faces both domestic and international constraints. A leader is only as powerful in international relations as his nation. For example, since coming to power in 1969, Libya's President Mu'ammar Gadhafi has attempted to create a North Africa empire with himself at its head. His ambitions have been derailed repeatedly because his country lacks the labor power, military prowess, finance, technology, and allies to take over the region. Other Arab states, the United States, and France have intervened to thwart his attempts to intimidate surrounding governments.

The "interdependence explanation" combines elements of international and national perspectives, and maintains that growing ties among states and democracy within states will bind them to the point where power politics becomes impossible. International relations will increasingly be shaped by shared interests and negotiation rather than force. Secretary of State Cordell Hull succinctly captured this internationalist perspective, although ironically he was writing during the cold war's early years: "There will no longer be need for spheres of influence, for alliances, balance of power, or any other of the special arrangements through which, in the unhappy past, the nations strove to safeguard their security or promote their interests."[11]

Clearly the world is becoming more economically interdependent, and more and more states within the global system are becoming democratic. Yet these trends do not erase the reality that every state has different power and interests in the system. Conflicts between states may well increase with interdependence, even if they are settled with diplomacy rather than force. The interdependence explanation cannot explain why states follow such different policies.

It is easy to reveal any model's shortcomings. One of the most sophisticated attempts to analyze policymaking was Graham Allison's *Essence of Decision*. Through three decision-making models, Allison explored the Kennedy administration's handling of the Cuban missile crisis.[12] The "rational model" assumed that the decision maker sat down and carefully analyzed all the information and options affecting that issue, and then chose that which best advanced national interests. The "organizational process model" examines how different organizations with different missions filter information and options to decision makers that advance their own interests rather than provide an objective overview of the situation and national interests. The "bureaucratic politics model" focuses on how each adviser to the president represents his or her respective bureaucracy's interests. Allison reveals the flaws in each of these models. None of them alone provides an accurate understanding of what actually occurred.

The Level-*of*-Analysis Matrix

So how then is foreign policy made? Is it possible to find a model that works? Indeed, social scientists have found a theory of foreign policy elusive—the real world is too complex to be reduced to a few simple axioms or patterns. Yet there are some similarities among countries in foreign policymaking, and thus a basis for comparison.

In every sovereign state, there is a head of government who is responsible for making decisions. Yet the popular belief that a president or premier makes decisions after carefully and rationally weighing the alternatives is inaccurate. A leader's decision depends on and is shaped by five complex interrelated systems: (1) *leader's psychological system*—personality, character, intelligence, knowledge, experiences, aptitudes, interests, and world view; (2) *decision-making system*—the leader's core group of advisers, and their respective psychological systems; (3) *political system*—impact of relevant ministries, political parties, interest groups, mass media, and public opinion; (4) *national system*—the nation's history, traditions, ideology, and culture related to the immediate issue and similar issues; and (5) *international system*—the effects of the first four systems in all states involved in that issue and the subsequent power distribution.

These different levels all interact with each other as parts of the country's policymaking system, although their relative importance differs from one policy to the next. To examine a simple decision from each different perspective would result in five different answers to the basic question of why the government acted as it did.

LEADER'S PSYCHOLOGICAL SYSTEM

Many studies have examined how a leader's personality, character, and world-view affect his policies.[13] How does a leader's psychology affect foreign policy?

Every second we are bombarded with thousands of bits of sensory and cognitive information, of which we must somehow make sense. It is impossible to understand this shifting world directly in its infinite complexity and ambiguity. Instead, we use mental maps or belief systems to screen out most of this flood of incoming information while clinging to key elements. What *actually* happens is often not as important as what we think has, is, and will happen. Kenneth Boulding wrote that we do not "respond to the 'objective' facts of the situation . . . but to [our] image of the situation. It is what we think the world is like, not what it is really like, that determines our behavior . . . we act according to the way the world appears to us, not necessarily according to the way it 'is.'"[14] In other words, facts do not exist until we create them.

What is important is not the real world but how it is perceived by those with the most power to shape it. Policymakers are no less prisoners of their respective mental maps of reality than anyone else. Every leader has an *operational code* or system of "general beliefs about fundamental issues of history and central questions of politics."[15] A leader's operational code gives him or her a means of evaluating information and problems, and making choices about them.

Some people are open to new ways of understanding the world. All too many others reject information that conflicts with their belief system, causing mental discomfort known as *cognitive dissonance*. A classic decision-making study showed that Eisenhower's Secretary of State John Foster Dulles interpreted and acted on all Soviet actions through his passionate belief that communism was a ruthless, godless system single-mindedly dedicated to world conquest and thus communists could never be trusted and no deals could be negotiated with them.[16]

Mental maps are formed by many forces. From birth, an individual's world view is shaped by a succession of interrelated environments, of which the family is the first and most important. Key events in a person's life also shape his or her outlook. Generals and politicians alike often prepare psychologically and militarily for the most *recent* war, rather than carefully analyzing and preparing for current and future challenges.

Throughout the cold war, American presidents continually compared Soviet with previous German and Japanese expansion. They were particularly sensitive to being accused of "appeasing" the Soviets as British Prime Minister Chamberlain had appeased Hitler during their meeting at Munich in 1938 by granting him the Sudetenland region of Czechoslovakia. For example, President Lyndon Johnson justified his escalation of America's involvement in Vietnam by arguing, "Everything I knew about history told me that if I got out of Vietnam . . . then I'd be doing exactly what Chamberlain did in World War II. I'd be giving a big fat reward to aggression. . . . And so would begin World War III."[17]

Actors in conflicts are often trapped in a vicious cycle of misperceptions and corresponding actions. Although both sides may have originally intended to remain defensive, they interpret the other side's action as aggressive and thus respond similarly. *Mirror images* occur when opponents view the other's actions as malevolent and aggressive and their own actions as innocent, just, and defensive. Throughout the cold war, the United States and Soviet Union held mirror images of each other, thus making agreements difficult and reconciliation virtually impossible. President Jimmy Carter once said, "The hardest thing for Americans to understand is that they are not better than other people."[18] He might have added that it was equally difficult for Americans during the cold war to perceive the Soviet Union as anything less than an "evil empire" bent on world conquest.

There is a tendency to believe that the opponent is united behind a master plan in which the immediate issue is just one stage toward ultimate victory, while seeing ones' own country as largely divided, weak, and defensive. As Kissinger put it, "The superpowers often behave like two heavily armed blind men feeling their way around a room, each believing himself in mortal peril from the other whom he assumes to have perfect vision. . . . Each tends to ascribe to the other a consistency, foresight, and coherence that its own experience belies."[19]

A leader's physical and mental health, and ego and ambition all shape the ways in which he or she evaluates and decides policies. President Wilson suffered a stroke during the Versailles Peace Conference, which may have strongly affected his negotiating abilities with the other leaders at the time, and later to get the Senate to approve the treaty. President Roosevelt was only two months away from his death at the Yalta Conference with Stalin and Churchill in February 1945, and many argue that with his weakness he made unnecessary concessions to the Soviet Union in Eastern Europe. A superinflated ego and ambition may be as self-defeating as a weak body and mind. Megalomaniac leaders such as Hitler or Hussein are inclined to embark their countries on aggressive wars against their neighbors, even when a rational analysis might show a significant chance of ultimate failure.

DECISION-MAKING SYSTEM

The leader's psychology alone does not explain foreign policy. The mix of a leader's immediate advisers and ministry heads have a profound impact on policy. Leaders vary considerably in the advisers they choose. Some leaders, such as John F. Kennedy, Jr. chose advisers who are foreign policy experts who challenge the leader's views and provide alternatives. Others, such as Lyndon Johnson, prefer advisers who are loyalists rather than experts and who are willing to mirror rather than confront the leader's assumptions and perspectives.

Groups can become just as mired in a narrow view of reality as individuals, a phenomenon known as *groupthink*.[20] Individuals are pressured to be team players and not rock the boat with options or information that counter the prevailing assessment. Those who do dissent are often left out of the policy loop by the other policymakers, as Defense Secretary Robert McNamara was during the Vietnam War when he began to express doubts over the Johnson administration's policies, or Secretary of State Cyrus Vance was during the Iranian hostage crisis when he objected to Carter's plans for a rescue attempt. This pattern is particularly common in a crisis situation where information and time are limited and the stakes are crucial. Leaders and advisers collectively fall back on stereotypes to evaluate the situation and *standard operating procedures (SOPs)* or pre-existing plans to deal with it. For example, the Carter administration decided to attempt the rescue of American hostages held by Iran despite the mission commander's belief that the chance of success was virtually nil, and the CIA's assessment that at least 60 percent of the hostages would be killed.

Groupthink does not affect most policies. Whether the adviser was chosen to be a "yes man" or a "devil's advocate," his positions often reflect the ministry or agency he represents, thus following the maxim "Where you stand depends on where you sit." There are, of course, always exceptions to this bureaucratic politics rule.[21] Advisers quickly learn how to best pitch an idea to their leader. Some leaders are known for following the advice of the last person they talked to, so advisers scramble to be last in line. With his limited attention span, knowledge, and intelligence, President Ronald Reagan was particularly susceptible to colorful one-page synopses or even short films on complex issues, so his advisers tried to make their presentations as Hollywoodish as possible.

POLITICAL SYSTEM

To truly understand a government's decisions, the analyst must explore the endless maze of a state's domestic politics. Governments interpret and act on international threats and opportunities within the context of a complex domestic political situation. Every state has its own distinct policymaking system. Generally speaking, democracies and dictatorships do have significantly different policymaking processes. But policymaking systems also clearly differ among democratic countries, and among authoritarian countries. The number of groups that affect policy is obviously vastly more numerous in a liberal democracy than in a communist dictatorship. Yet even in totalitarian systems such as the Soviet Union under Stalin, there were distinct interest groups involving heavy industry, light industry, agriculture, technology and science, and military industry that battled each other, albeit it subtly, for a greater share of the budget and other resources. Each issue in each system elicits a different constellation of bureaucracies, interest groups, public opinion, and, in democratic countries, political parties.

Although the leader hand-picks decision makers, he or she inherits an army of career bureaucrats whose primary loyalty is to themselves and then to their organization. Although each bureaucracy has its own mission, they share the imperative of expanding their respective power, responsibilities, and personnel, often at the expense of their rivals. Each organization in the bureaucracy is a distinct *interest group* with its own values and priorities. Like any other interest group, it confuses its interests with national interests, and presents its narrow view to the leadership. The result in every political system is a constant, behind-the-scenes struggle among different bureaucracies over their different interests on different issues. When a bureaucracy presents options, it may package a reasonable option—the one it wants chosen—along with several unreasonable ones, while leaving out other viable alternatives.

A vital role of bureaucrats is to collect information with which to evaluate old policies and to propose new ones. As information is collected and passed up through the system, some is highlighted and much discarded. Information is often provided by inferiors according to what they believe their superiors want to hear. The result of this filtering process for decision makers is often a narrow set of options and a distorted view of the issue. For example, for years intelligence reports on Vietnam presented a rosy view that victory was just around the corner, that with more troops, firepower, and bombing the communists would be defeated. The reality was just the opposite. How did this intelligence distortion develop? President Lyndon Johnson made it clear through his statements and actions that this was the result he wanted, and thus key officials at different levels in the intelligence community filtered out any information that ran counter to what the administration wanted to hear. The Navy and the Air Force in particular deliberately exaggerated the effectiveness of their respective bombing campaigns, with each hoping the president would favor one branch of the military over the other. But the chief effect of these exaggerations may have been to convince President Johnson that he could win the war through bombing.[22]

A similar corruption of intelligence occurred during the Reagan years when CIA analysts complained that their director William Casey "does not ask us for a review of an issue or a situation. He wants material he can use to persuade his colleagues, justify controversial policy, or expand the agency's involvement in covert action." Former CIA chief Robert Gates admitted that "during the 1980s our projections of Soviet strategic forces were clearly too high" along with assessments of Soviet economic power and how destructive high military spending was on the economy. When analysts reported that Soviet military spending was actually flat in the early 1980s, the Reagan White House furiously ordered the assessment rewritten to justify is own military buildup. The result was that the United States nearly tripled its defense spending and its national debt with no discernible effect on the Soviet Union, which did not try to raise its own military budget. When the Reagan administration distorted intelligence analysis with ideological fantasies, its policies damaged the United States rather than the Soviets.[23]

Finally, bureaucracies shape decisions when they are responsible for implementing them. Ronald Reagan once lamented that "one of the hardest things [about being president] is to know that down there is a permanent structure that's resisting everything you're doing." Or, as Harry Truman put it just before he handed the White House over to Dwight Eisenhower, "Poor Ike, he's used to having orders carried out and he'll sit in the Oval Office and no one will do what he wants."

Graham Allison's analysis of the Cuban missile crisis provides many cases of bureaucracies continuing to pursue their own narrow interests while the nation's interests hung in the balance. For example, the missiles could have been revealed sooner had the Defense Department and CIA not squabbled for five days over who should be responsible for flying over Cuba. The Defense Department won, but its overflight failed to provide the necessary intelligence. Negotiations resumed and it was finally decided to allow Air Force pilots to fly the CIA U-2 spy planes. Another five days were then squandered training the Air Force pilots for the mission. During the crisis itself, adhering to its standard operating procedures, the Navy refused to obey President Kennedy's order that they move their blockade from 800 to 500 miles from Cuban shores to give the Soviets more time to consider the consequences. Fortunately, Premier Khrushchev ordered his ships carrying missiles to reverse course before they reached the American blockade. In addition, the Navy forced Russian submarines to the surface without presidential authorization. The Air Force also acted contrary to instructions, sending a U-2 spy plane over Soviet territory after Kennedy's order not to commit any provocative acts. The Cuban missile crisis provides one of countless examples of how bureaucratic politics shape foreign policy.

Although bureaucracies play an important role in policymaking everywhere, the role of political parties varies greatly from one political system to the next depending on the relative importance of a state's legislature in the system. Obviously, parties play no role in those countries in which they are outlawed, and their importance varies from each one-party state to the next. In Communist party states, the party and government are synonymous, and thus the party plays the central role in policymaking. Political struggles occur within the party in a tug-of-war among a range of ideological and personal factions. The communist parties of the Soviet Union and China are particularly known for their divisions between ideological hard-liners who wanted to maintain the confrontation with the West and pragmatists who sought détente and economic development. In noncommunist one-party states, the party's role may be purely symbolic. The legislature's purpose is simply to rubber-stamp the executive's decisions without dissent, while elsewhere the party is used to mobilize the population behind government decisions.

The role of political parties in foreign policy is often constrained even in liberal democracies. In parliamentary systems, the prime minister is chosen by the majority party or coalition of parties in the legislature. Although the majority party may be divided on issues and harshly debates them, once a decision is reached the party generally votes as a bloc.

In contrast, there is no party discipline in the U.S. Congress; every representative and senator votes his or her own interests regardless of the position the party leaders try desperately to encourage. Groups of like-minded legislators representing powerful interests can have an enormous impact on policy. Because of its constitutional powers involving trade and the declaration of war, Congress leads as much as it follows in foreign policy. Frequently a Republican president confronts a Democratic Congress, and the result can be either consensus or deadlock, depending on the issue and the president's skills.

Interest groups actively lobby government for decisions favoring themselves. Although bureaucracies and political parties can both be considered interest groups in the broad sense of the term, lobbyists are generally thought to be private citizens rather than public officials. Interest groups for business, labor, or the environment tend to be more broad based, with opinions on a range of issues, whereas ethnic groups such as Jewish Americans or Cuban Americans tend to focus on relations with their ancestral country.

Perhaps no country has more formal interest groups than the United States—in 1998, there were over 50,000 lobbyists registered in Washington. In America's open political system, foreign interest groups often play an important role in policy. Pat Choate's book *Agents of Influence* reveals that Japan's government and business spend over $400 million annually in the United States trying to influence laws and policies in Japan's interests.[24] In the 1970s, the "Koreagate scandal" revealed huge bribes paid by South Korean agents to politicians to swing their votes on issues affecting South Korea. In the late 1990s, Chinese agents supplied ample cash to both the Republican and Democratic parties, although how those contributions affected voting is unclear. Many American bureaucrats resign their positions and go to work for foreign interest groups, using their understanding of and access to America's political system to great advantage for their foreign employers.

To greatly varying extents, public opinion plays a role in every state's foreign policy making process. Clearly, the more democratic the country, the more leaders make decisions with one eye glued to public opinion polls. Public opinion's influence on policy, in turn, varies from one democratic country to the next. A study of four liberal democracies found that public opinion had the greatest impact on foreign policy in the United States, followed by Germany, Japan, and France.[25]

Public opinion is not a monolithic bloc, but reflects all the divisions of that nation's political spectrum. One study identified four major public opinion groups in the United States and Western Europe, with the relative strength of each bloc varying considerably among Europeans and Americans. A slightly greater percentage of Americans (24 percent) than Europeans (21 percent) were "cold warriors" who took a hard line against the Soviet Union and favored higher military spending. Conversely, more Europeans (34 percent) than Americans (28 percent) were "internationalists" who favored open markets and increased social and cultural ties. More Americans (26 percent) than Europeans (20 percent) were "accommodationists" who favored international economic and social ties but little military activity. Almost exactly a quarter of the populations on each side of the Atlantic were "isolationists"—Europeans (25 percent) and Americans (24 percent).

There is a dynamic relationship between governments and public opinion, in which each shapes the other's view. For example, America's opinion of the Soviet Union shifted markedly between 1989 and 1990. In April 1989, half of Americans believed the Soviets sought to dominate the world, a percentage that fell to 29 percent by May 1990. This view undoubtedly reflected Gorbachev's revolutionary policies, which liberated Eastern Europe and democratized the Soviet Union. But how much did this public opinion shift to reflect the Bush administration's increasingly conciliatory policies toward the Soviet Union, and how much did it encourage the Bush administration to become more conciliatory?

American public opinion is usually important only on such emotional issues as American involvement in wars, famine relief, or trade disputes that result in lost American jobs. Although, like people elsewhere, Americans tend to rally around the flag in a *crisis*, throughout the 20th century—but particularly since Vietnam—American presidents have become increasingly careful about how and when they commit American troops to combat. For example, President Bush

A single image can profoundly shift public opinion and thus policy. In the first photograph a Yugoslav boy gleefully poses atop a downed American jet. Did that image broadcasted on Yugoslavia's television stiffen that nation's will to continue the fight against NATO in 1999? In the second photo a Somali mob drags a dead U.S. Ranger through the streets of Mogadishu in 1993. Public support for America's participation in a peacekeeping mission to Somalia plummeted after that photograph was widely broadcasted and printed.

Ilkka Uimonen/Corbis Sygma

Phil Watson/The Toronto Star/Corbis Sygma

spent six months carefully building American support for the Persian Gulf coalition as well as nurturing international opinion, and actually won U.N. backing of his plans before he sought congressional approval.

Public opinion can be both contradictory and fickle. All along, the public gave President Bush mixed messages about what it considered the proper policy in the Persian Gulf. Between August 1990 when Iraq's invasion occurred and the beginning of fighting in January 1991, 66 to 75 percent of the public consistently favored sending troops to the region, even though 80 percent thought that the result would be war. Yet a majority were against sending any troops to the Persian Gulf if it cost any American lives or was done simply to keep oil prices low. Fearing to inflame public opinion, President Bush did not explain to the American people that America's interest in the Persian Gulf was to keep oil flowing at low prices and that the best means of achieving that goal was to prevent any one country from dominating the region. He also did not explain that to satisfy American interests, the United States had to protect Kuwait and Saudi Arabia, which had highly authoritarian political systems. Instead, he justified America's involvement by describing Iraqi President Saddam Hussein as another Hitler bent on regional conquest and was committing genocide with his invasion of Kuwait, and that the United States had a moral mission to protect "democracy and freedom" in the region. Before the Coalition forces went to war against Iraq in January 1991, the American people were almost evenly divided over whether or not war in the Persian Gulf was justified. However, as soon as the bombs began to drop, those who approved of the war shot up to nearly 80 percent!

Often coalitions of bureaucrats, representatives, and interest groups form to promote their collective interests on specific issues. An example of one of these *iron triangles* is the *military-industrial complex* composed of the Defense Department, congressional representatives from districts with military bases or factories, and military contractors, who together wring more money, programs, and power from the political system, regardless of whether those bases or weapons can be justified strategically. President Eisenhower coined the term "military-industrial complex" in his farewell speech in 1960, and warned Americans that its continued growth imperiled democracy itself.

Iron triangles with opposing interests often check each other's power. Perhaps a more accurate way to understand policymaking is to think of *"policy clusters,"* which, along with either iron or loose triangles, include prominent journalists and academics, public opinion, and foreign groups that share an interest in the policy.

NATIONAL SYSTEM

A nation's heritage can profoundly affect its foreign policy. Culture and ideology provide a value system for evaluating present conflicts, dilemmas, and choices. History offers lessons from similar past situations to apply to contemporary ones. A nation's geographic position, development level, and natural and human resources all affect national interests and policies.

For example, many scholars have argued that Soviet foreign policy is simply a continuation of traditional Russian foreign policy, which sought to expand national territory to defensible natural borders, dominate (either directly or indirectly) eastern Europe, and achieve great power status and equality with the West. That policy of territorial, military, and political expansion, in turn, was shaped by the vulnerability to foreign invasion of the Russian people on the vast steppes. During Russia's 1,000-year history, it suffered over 250 invasions of various magnitudes. Different leaders have advocated different strategies for achieving those goals. *Slavophiles* from Ivan the Terrible to Stalin have emphasized the importance for Russia of carving out a vast empire and acting as the political and cultural leader of the Slavic peoples while shunning the West. *Westernizers* from Peter the Great to Gorbachev have argued that Russia can best achieve its security by adopting advanced Western technology and organization and maintaining good relations with the West.

History, however, is often an unreliable guide to present circumstances. American leaders learned from the 1930s policy toward Japan, Germany, and Italy that appeasement only whets the appetite of dictators for more conquests. Hence after 1945, vowing "no more Munichs," the United States refused to compromise on virtually every conflict with the Soviet Union and assumed that every Moscow move was part of some grand design to conquer the world. This uncompromising stance may have wrecked any possibility of reconciliation and deepened cold war animosities. In 1949, the communists overthrew the American-backed Chiang Kaishek regime. The question "Who lost China?" soon reverberated accusingly through America's political system, a cry that may have influenced Presidents Eisenhower, Kennedy, and Johnson to do anything to avoid losing Vietnam.

People often judge others by their past rather than present behavior. For example, in the 50 years since World War II ended, Japan has developed not only into a dynamic economic superpower but also into a highly democratic nation

Policy, Power, *and* Pride: Gadhafi's Dreams *and* Realities

Every nation's foreign policy making system differs, just as every policy that comes from any system may be shaped and implemented in different ways. The policy-making systems of liberal democracies are far more complex and varied than in dictatorships. Although a dictator certainly has a greater impact on his system's policies than a liberal democratic leader, he still faces various constraints from the country's bureaucracy, interest groups, political factions, and relative international power, to name the more common. But sometimes a dictator can largely determine his nation's foreign policy goals, if not outcomes.

Libya's dictator Mu'ammar Gadhafi is such an example. He seized power in a 1969 coup and has held it ever since. Despite numerous setbacks, Gadhafi has never shaken his dreams of heading a pan-Arab or pan-African union of states that defies and surpasses the democratic industrial countries led by the United States and destroys Israel. With only 5.3 million people to feed and earnings of $5 billion from oil exports in 1998 alone, Gadhafi has a lot of money with which to pursue those dreams, however chimerical they may be. And Libya's

30 billion barrels of reserves, which cost only a dollar per barrel to produce, ensure Gadhafi and any ambitious successors a steady income for decades to come.

What means has he wielded to his ends? Terror is the most common. He sheltered a variety of groups that used terror to advance their interests. He has also used his own agents to sow terror elsewhere, most prominently at a Berlin disco in 1985, which provoked an American bombing attack on Libya, and the destruction of an airliner over Lockerbie, Scotland, in 1988, whose suspects he finally agreed to hand over to an international court in 1999. Gadhafi also used his military to advance his ambitions. In the mid-1980s, the French thwarted his attempt to hack off Chad's northern half and attach it to Libya; French troops routed a Libyan army that invaded the region. Gadhafi also massed troops on Egypt's borders several times in attempts to pressure Cairo into making concessions on various disputes; although war never broke out, the Egyptians rebuffed Gadhafi. In all Gadhafi's various schemes failed miserably, although hundreds of innocent people died in the process.

More recently Gadhafi fancies himself Africa's peacemaker. Here he has been more successful. In April 1999 alone, nine African leaders journeyed to Tripoli and met with him. He succeeded in brokering a cease-fire in the war between Uganda's President Yoweri Museveni and the Congo's Laurent Kabila. He has also acted as a diplomatic go-between in the fighting between Sierra Leone and Togo, and Sudan's civil war. Meanwhile he has funded rebel groups in several countries, including Charles Taylor, who seized power in Liberia; Foday Sankoh, the leader of the Revolutionary United Front who was finally captured after trying to take over Sierra Leone, and antigovernment movements in Guinea, Gambia, and Burkina Faso.

Why do so many government and rebel leaders pay attention to Gadhafi? In a word, money—Gadhafi buys their friendship. And what do those "friendships" bring Libya? Those diversions of Libyan wealth economically undermine the country while boosting the diplomatic prestige and ego of its dictator. Is it worth it? Gadhafi certainly believes so.

with an excellent human rights record and mass antiwar sentiment. For East and Southeast Asians, however, memories of Japan's brutal aggression and occupation of their nations remain vivid and shape their perceptions of Japan's policies toward them and the world. Because of this fear of Japanese domination and exploitation, a formal East and Southeast Asian Community, patterned after the

European Community (or Union) or the North America Free Trade Association, is unlikely to emerge soon if at all.

Ideology is important in helping define the ends and means of a nation's interests. A liberal democratic state emphasizes the importance of preserving civil rights and the democratic political process. Marxist-Leninist states strive to achieve a centrally planned economy that promotes relative income equality and universal health, education, and retirement benefits. Countries with a revolutionary ideology such as communism or fundamentalist Islam often try to promote revolution elsewhere.

INTERNATIONAL SYSTEM

Ideally, foreign policy is a grand plan to effectively overcome foreign challenges and create or take advantage of opportunities to advance national interests. But even in the most powerful states, policymakers spend more time and energy reacting to rather than shaping international issues. Ultimately, a government's decisions on an international issue depend on the decisions of other states involved directly and indirectly on that issue. Policy is obviously shaped by a nation's power relative to that of other states involved in that international conflict. Depending on the issue, the global or regional geopolitical or geoeconomic power balance profoundly affects the options a government can pursue to serve its national interests.

Kenneth Waltz pointed out that the "international structure emerges from the interactions of states and then constrains them from taking certain actions while propelling them toward others."[26] There is thus a dynamic relationship between the actions of states and the system of which they are a part. The system's parameters are determined by the power balance and the values of the most powerful states. The system's parameters change through the countless actions of states, and the more powerful the state, the more it shapes the system. Yet the system itself constrains the range of a state's policy options, and the less powerful the state the more the system constrains it. As John Ruggie argued, the international system "becomes a force that the units may not be able to control; it constrains their behavior and interposes itself between their intentions and the outcomes of their actions."[27]

Geography can also impose both policy opportunities and constraints. The most important issues for most countries are with those across the border. Dealing with adjacent enemies becomes the central focus of a state's foreign policy. For example, Israel's foreign policy is largely shaped by the question of what to do about being a small country surrounded by hostile neighbors. Different Israeli governments have dealt with that reality by pursuing dramatically different policies of either confrontation or reconciliation, or some combination of the two. To explain these differences, we must consider the other levels of analysis.

Economic interdependence or outright dependence also constrains a nation's foreign policy. For example, because America's economy is so economically intertwined with Japan's, Washington would probably never seriously retaliate against Japan's neomercantilist policies for fear that both countries would be plunged into a deep depression. Developing countries that depend on world currency markets or the IMF for finance must often promise to cut back spending, devalue their currency, and free markets in return for loans.

Perfect freedom is impossible for states in an international system, just as it is for individuals within a state. Those very constraints motivate many states to try

Slobodan Milosevic and Jesse Jackson.
Many forces shape the making and implementation of a nation's foreign policy. Diplomacy does not always follow official channels. In 1999 Reverend Jesse Jackson brushed aside criticisms that he would complicate White House and NATO policy toward Yugoslavia if he traveled to Belgrade to convince President Slobodan Milosevic to release three captured American soldiers. Jackson, shown here with Milosevic, succeeded in winning the soldiers' freedom. Did Jackson help or hurt American and NATO strategy? What are the potential advantages and disadvantages when private citizens conduct their own foreign policy?

John W. White/Corbis Sygma

to maximize their independence within an existing state system and shift the system's rules in their favor. According to Waltz, "states seek to control what they depend on or to lessen the extent of their dependency. This . . . explains quite a bit of the behavior of states: their imperial thrusts to widen the scope of their control and their autarchic strivings toward greater self-sufficiency."[28]

What Types *of* Policies Govern Foreign Relations?

The more powerful a country, the more complex its international relations and the more extensive its range of policies. In their analysis of 63 types of foreign policy behavior among major states, Charles McClelland and Gary Hoggard found three predominant behavior patterns—conflictual (crisis), cooperative, and routine—and that the five most active states were involved in 40 percent of all recorded behavior.[29]

CRISIS POLICYMAKING

Daily the newspapers and televisions blare accounts of crises at home and abroad. A *crisis* is any unanticipated situation in which one's vital interests are threatened and there is little time in which to decide what to do. There are many types of crisis—the driver of a car faces a crisis when he fishtails on a patch of ice. He did not anticipate the situation, his life is at stake, and he has a limited time in which to decide what to do.

International crises occur when a nation's vital interests are at stake, there is the threat of violence, and a limited time in which to respond. The time constraints and high stakes limit those involved in decision making to a small group of advisers around the leader. Natural or human disasters such as earthquakes or famines require those in a position to help to decide quickly whether or not to intervene and if so how. The most common international crises, however, involve two or more states threatening war over a conflict. The problem may have been long-lasting but becomes a crisis when either one side or the situation itself demands a dramatic change in the status quo, as during the two times Moscow attempted to squeeze the Allies out of Berlin (1948–1949, 1958–1961), or when Argentina invaded Britain's Falkland Islands in 1982.

Usually neither side wants war or to give in to the other's demands. Most crises are contained through diplomacy and reason; sometimes they escalate into war. Usually neither side wants a war but they are willing to go to war's brink in order to win their particular interest or just not lose. States in a crisis play a game of "*chicken*" or "*brinkmanship*" in which they escalate the conflict and the chance of violence until the other side gives way. Both sides try to manage the crisis so that they can wrest concessions from the other side without violence. *Crisis management* involves the belief by all sides of a conflict that war should be avoided and a compromise reached. Of course, each side wants the other to make the major concessions. The result is a poker game in which each side raises the stakes until the other side folds. Sometimes they carefully manage the crisis so that it is resolved short of war. At other times they mismanage the crisis and war results. Since 1945, 19 of 25 crises have exploded into war.[30] Through skilled diplomacy and luck, the superpowers successfully managed all crises between themselves.

Crisis management is very difficult. Given the time constraints, it is impossible to have all the information necessary to make a clear, rational choice among alternative policies. Thus decision makers make the best decision based on what information they can collect and process within what time the crisis allows. Unable to gain access to all the information they need and unable to make sense of what information they have received, crisis decision makers often fall back on pre-existing

crisis management the attempts by both sides in a serious dispute to manage events so that the crisis does not escalate into an unwanted war.

stereotypes about their opponent's characteristics and behavior and the outcome of previous similar situations. They tend to believe the worst about their opponents and judge any action in that light. Henry Kissinger explained the psychology of crisis decision making: "During fast-moving events those at the center of decision are overwhelmed by floods of reports compounded of conjecture, knowledge, hope, and worry. These must then be sieved through the [decision makers'] preconceptions. Only rarely does a coherent picture emerge."[31]

Decision makers tend to fall back on standard operating procedures and to "*satisfice*" or make the decision that seems to make the most sense at the time rather than examine alternative views of the situation.[32] The result is often a serious misjudgment or misperception about what is actually happening, and thus the crisis is escalated rather than defused.

The events leading to the outbreak of World War I provide a classic example of misperceptions leading to tragedy. World War I broke out largely because the participants were unable to successfully manage the crisis that preceded it. All the great powers had very rigid timetables for mobilizing their forces for war. Time was essential for all, particularly Germany, which faced the possibility of fighting a two-front war against France and Russia. When one country began its mobilization, all others had to begin theirs or face being overrun. Because mobilizations were based on highly intricate railroad schedules, any delay or cancelation would create mass havoc. The great powers were also locked into two rigid alliance systems. Thus when Austria declared war on Serbia when the visiting Austrian Archduke Ferdinand was assassinated by anarchists in Sarajevo (Bosnia), Russia went to Serbia's defense, Germany to Austria's, and France and eventually Britain to Russia's. At no point did anyone attempt to determine whether the assassination of the archduke was the work of Serbia (it wasn't), and even if it was whether it was worth risking a European-wide war.[33]

Perhaps the most essential aspect of crisis management is allowing the opponent a face-saving way to back down, which often requires both sides to compromise. Kissinger writes that if "crisis management requires cold and even brutal measures to show determination, it also imposes the need to show opponents a way out. Grandstanding is good for the ego but bad for foreign policy. Many wars have been started because no good line of retreat was left open. Superpowers have a special obligation not to humiliate each other."[34]

During the Cuban missile crisis, Kennedy offered Khrushchev a face-saving opportunity by promising to withdraw American missiles from Turkey if Moscow withdrew its missiles from Cuba, and further softened Khrushchev's defeat by describing the crisis resolution as a "victory for peace" rather than an American victory. Rather than backing Khrushchev against the wall with humiliating terms, Kennedy allowed him a way out and in so doing probably avoided World War III.

ROUTINE POLICYMAKING

Noncrisis decisions and policies are reached after the issue has been debated by all relevant actors. Most policies are "incremental" and simply involve small policy adjustments to reflect new realities. For example, President Nixon's *Vietnamization* policy of gradually handing over the fighting to the South Vietnamese army did not represent a dramatic change from America's Indochina policy. Others are "innovative" and are characterized by a significant shift in policy. For example, President Nixon's decisions to establish relations with mainland China and take the United States off the gold standard were two highly innovative policies.

INTERMESTIC POLICIES

intermestic policies those policies that involve both foreign and domestic issues.

As the world becomes ever more interdependent, policies become increasingly *intermestic* or involve both foreign and domestic issues. For example, the United States's 1992 military budget remained an enormous $274 billion despite the cold war's end, not so much because there were clear and present military dangers abroad—there were none that justified that spending level or force structure—but because a rapid reduction in spending would exacerbate the recession at home and worsen George Bush's chances for re-election. During September 1992, George Bush promised to sell 150 F-15 fighter planes to Saudi Arabia and 50 F-16 fighters to Taiwan despite the complications both sales would cause American relations with Israel and China, respectively. The reasons for these sales again were jobs and the president's re-election. Similarly, during his 1992 campaign then-governor Clinton promised that he would build two Seawolf submarines that the Pentagon had canceled.

Conclusion

President Kennedy once said, "Domestic policy can only defeat us, foreign policy can kill us."[35] Certainly the foreign policy stakes for a superpower in the nuclear age are high. Yet despite the preponderant weight of the great powers in international relations, each country's foreign policy is vital to protecting and enhancing its own respective national interests. Virtually all countries share the goals of military security, economic development, political independence, and cultural preservation. Each state varies considerably, however, in how they define these broad interests, and the means they use to achieve them.

To try to understand foreign policy is to try to understand history.

Why did things happen as they did? What alternatives existed, and why were they not followed? The answer varies from one policy and one government to the next. In every country, each policy is shaped by an often vastly different constellations of internal and external forces. The process by which national interests are defined is also largely the process by which they are promoted. As Waltz put it, the policies of countries "fluctuate with the changing currents of domestics, are prey to the vagaries of a shifting cast of political leaders, and are influenced by the outcome of bureaucratic struggles."[36] Invariably we come back to the level-of-analysis matrix to make sense of it all.

Study Questions

1. Define foreign policy and give examples.
2. What are national interests, and why are they often so difficult to define?
3. When does ideology play an important role shaping foreign policy?
4. Describe some models by which analysts attempt to understand how foreign policies are made. What are the flaws in these models?
5. Does history make humanity, or does humanity make history?
6. What are the five components of the level-of-analysis matrix?
7. In what ways can a leader's psychology and character affect foreign policy? Give examples.

Part 2   The Nation-State and International Relations

8. Describe the psychological phenomena groupthink, mirror image, and cognitive dissonance, and how they can affect foreign policy.

9. How can a leader's immediate system of advisers, bureaucracy, political parties, interest groups, public opinion, and the mass media affect foreign policy?

10. Explain how a nation's history, culture, and power can affect foreign policy. Give examples.

11. How can the international system provide opportunities, constraints, and challenges for a nation's foreign policy?

12. Define *crisis decision making*. What are the ingredients of successful crisis management?

InfoTrac College Edition Sources

Using the Subject Guide, enter the search terms *Sandinista* and/or *cognitive dissonance*. Using Keywords, enter the search term *military industrial complex*.

Albright, Madeleine. "Challenges Facing U.S. National Interests at Home and Abroad."
Clover, Charles. "Dreams of the Eurasian Heartland."
Denning, Brannon P., and Jack H. McCall. "States' Rights and Foreign Policy: Some Things Should Be Left to Washington."
Dessler, David. "National Interests in International Society."
Dobrianski, Paula J. "Russian Foreign Policy: Promise or Peril?"
"Domestic Sources of Foreign Policy."
"Foreign Policy: The 'Isolationist' Slur."
Huntington, Samuel P. "The Erosion of American National Interests."
Kubicek, Paul. "Russian Foreign Policy and the West."
Legvold, Robert. "National Identity and Foreign Policy."
Ming, Yuan. "On Analysis of China's National Interests."
Paul, Joel R. "The Geopolitical Constitution: Executive Expediency and Geoeconomics of Capital."
Raymond, Gregory A. "Necessity in Foreign Policy."
Roy, Denny. "The Foreign Policy of Great-Power China."
Scott, James M. "Organizing for Foreign Policy Crises: Presidents, Advisers, and the Management of Decision Making."

On *the* Web

http://www.state.gov/
Official site of the United States State Department

http://www.mtholyoke.edu/acad/intrel/morg6.htm
Hans Morgenthau's six principles of realism

http://www.foreignpolicy-infocus.org/
Foreign policy of the U.S. and other countries

The concept of sovereignty, or the right of a nation-state's government to be free from foreign interference, is enshrined in international law, including the U.N. Charter. But so too is the concept of human rights, which are accorded universal legal validity by the U.N. Charter, the U.N. Declaration of Human Rights, and a range of international treaties. What happens when these two great principles, each rooted in international law and practice, clash?

"crimes against humanity," better known as genocide.

Was Pinochet guilty as charged? Assuming the charges were valid, how did Spain or any other country (France, Germany, Italy, Luxembourg, Sweden, Belgium, and Switzerland also filed or pursued extradition warrants) have jurisdiction over crimes that were alleged to have been committed in Chile?

Pinochet's crimes are well documented. He seized power over Chile in a 1973 coup against a popularly

Part Three Nonstate Forces *and* Actors *in* International Relations: *The* Great Debate: Sovereignty *versus* Human Rights

That issue provoked an international debate on October 16, 1998, when Great Britain's Home Secretary Jack Straw ordered the arrest of Augusto Pinochet, then 82 years old, who was visiting London for medical treatment, to serve an extradition warrant issued by a Spanish National Court, prompted by Judge Baltasar Garzon and submitted via Interpol, the international police organization. The charges against Pinochet were

elected government led by the socialist Salvador Allende. During the next 15 years, until he handed his power to a democratic government, 2,095 people died under "extralegal" circumstances and 1,102 disappeared and are presumed murdered. The real death toll is undoubtedly much higher but will probably never be known. The crimes were documented by several U.N. commissions, the Inter-American Commission on Human Rights,

Amnesty International, and other interested watchdog groups. In 1978 Pinochet's government issued a blanket amnesty for any human rights crimes committed by any of its officials.

Pinochet's defense largely rested on his argument that he was immune from arrest and prosecution on several grounds. While he was head of state, he enjoyed sovereign immunity under international law from prosecution under any other international laws. Chile's constitution specifically grants him immunity as a former head of state and as a senator for life. Thus he was immune from arrest as a former head of state and senator for life traveling on a diplomatic passport. When a lower court upheld Pinochet's argument, Jack Straw appealed to Britain's highest court, the Law Lords of the House of Lords.

So what happened? A judicial committee of five Law Lords in the House of Lords, issued a three-to-two decision on November 25, 1999, arguing that mass murder, torture, and imprisonment without trial are not the normal functions of a head of state and thus Pinochet could be arrested and extradited for trial to Spain. In reaching its split decision, the Law Lords listened to evidence and arguments submitted by 55 different lawyers, including not only the legal teams of Pinochet and the prosecutor, but also Amnesty International and other international human rights groups. The Law Lords did not rule on Pinochet's guilt or innocence, but only whether he could be extradited. As for the argument that Chile's constitution granted Pinochet immunity, the Law

Agents of Augusto Pinochet's autocratic government of Chile murdered thousands of people who opposed his regime. He was arrested on charges of genocide when he visited London, though later released. Protesters for and against Pinochet filled streets in London and elsewhere.

AP/Wide World Photos

Lords ruled that Britain is bound by international law and not Chile's laws. The Law Lords also rejected Pinochet's claim of diplomatic immunity, arguing that it was not valid because the former dictator was not accredited to the British government. Pinochet remained under house arrest in London until March 2000 when the Law Lords, Great Britain's highest court, ordered him released for health reasons.

What international legal principles are invoked by the Pinochet case? "Sovereign immunity" once was an universally accepted legal principal. In the second half of the 20th century, however, international law through treaties and customs steadily diluted and finally eliminated the principal that sovereign states and the people who run them could legally commit any crime, including genocide. Thus no government can issue a legally binding amnesty for human rights crimes, especially massive, systematic "crimes against humanity." This principle was first clearly evoked in both the 1945 Tokyo and Nuremberg charters, which articulated the legal grounds for prosecuting Japanese and German war criminals. The 1948 Genocide Convention and U.N. Declaration on Human Rights, the four 1949 Geneva Conventions on War, the 1979 Convention Against the Taking of Hostages, and the 1984 Torture Convention all reinforced that principle. Additionally, the more recent U.N. Security Council statutes authorizing international tribunals to prosecute Rwandan and Yugoslav war criminals in 1993 and 1994, and a 1998 treaty, which will create a permanent Human Rights Court when enough countries ratify it, further weaken the legality of sovereign immunity.

Other legal principles raised by the Pinochet case are more debatable. What country has "jurisdiction" in a human rights case? When should "extradition" occur? States vary in their interpretations of these two essential international legal principals. German and Spanish courts, for example, will accept the jurisdiction for cases that arise overseas if either or both the accused and victims are of their nationality. Thus they could demand that the accused be extradited. This provided Spain's legal justification for demanding Pinochet's extradition; although the crimes were committed in a foreign land by a foreigner, some were committed against Spanish citizens. British courts have a more limited jurisdiction; they will only try cases of murders committed overseas if the accused is British; victims must seek justice where the crime is committed. France, Canada, and Belgium uphold the principle of "universal jurisdiction" for human rights crimes, whereby all states have the legal right and duty to either try or extradite any so accused.

Pinochet's extradition inspired those concerned with human rights. In March 1999, the Human Rights Watch group presented the U.N. Human Rights Commission with a long list of exiled dictators accused of crimes against humanity. Few if any of the accused now enjoying luxurious retirements will ever stand trial. What deterrent effect the Pinochet case has on current or future dictators is impossible to say. Nonetheless, the Pinochet case does represent an important step in the development and application of international human rights law.

So what do you think of the Pinochet case? If you were a judge, would you have ordered his release or extradition? More broadly, which international principle do you believe should take precedence, sovereignty or human rights? Should there be restrictions on jurisdiction and extradition in human rights cases, or should universal jurisdiction and extradition prevail whereby all countries should have the right and duty to try or extradite anyone accused of those crimes? Should a permanent international court on war crimes and crimes against humanity be established, should international tribunals be established for specific crimes, or should sovereign immunity prevail?

Contents

Chapter 6 International Law *and* Morality

Key Concepts and Terms

Does international law truly exist, and if so how does it govern international relations? Some argue that despite the plethora of legally binding treaties, customs, and principles, international law is more a moral and theoretical than legal framework for international behavior. They feel that without a global legislature that creates laws, an international police force that can bring violators to trial, a comprehensive global court system, and a means of enforcing legal decisions, international law is almost meaningless. At best, they suggest, the world is governed by frontier and often vigilante justice. International relations are shaped by a Darwinian survival-of-the-fittest mentality in which the strong battle the strong and subject the weak. Adherence to international law is purely voluntary, not coerced. Although states may comply with most international laws most of the time, they do so because compliance serves national interests rather than international concepts of right and wrong. Whenever national interest and international law conflict, most states will serve the former. Israeli diplomat Abba Eban summed up this perspective by arguing that "international law is that which the wicked do not obey and the righteous do not enforce."

All this may be true, but it still does not mean that international law is nonexistent. Every legal system has those who follow and those who break the law. Of the criminals, some are caught and punished, whereas others escape. In any legal system, individuals and groups choose to obey the law because it is in their interest to do so, which may include the fear of the consequences of not doing so. National legal systems have often proved no more effective than international law in preventing crime and sometimes total breakdown of law. After all, civil wars are more common than international wars.

In reality, states are just as law-abiding in the global system as individuals and groups are in most national legal systems. International lawbreakers make the news, but most states follow international law. As in national legal systems, international law may be vague or nonexistent in some disputes. Right and wrong may be blurred or ambiguous. Yet international law does indeed exist.[1]

This chapter analyzes the role of law in international relations, examining first its development, sources, and subjects, and then such issues as jurisdiction and immunity, sovereignty and recognition, the acquisition of territory, enforcement, and human rights.

How Has International Law Developed?

Order, not anarchy, rules the world, and international law is a vital component of that order. International law has evolved with the global political economy and is inseparable from it. The first international laws, however, are nearly as old as international relations. Treaties are a form of international law, and were signed by ancient Egyptians, Assyrians, and Hindus, among others. In time, international law evolved beyond the legal obligations of treaty signers to the Roman Empire's *corpus juris gentium*, or "body of international law among nations."

Modern international law evolved with the modern state system. The 1648 Treaty of Westphalia, which ended the Thirty Years War, began the modern era of sovereign nation-states, whose relations were increasingly governed by a steadily expanding body of international customs, treaties, and principles, known then as the "law of nations." It has expanded rapidly over the centuries in response to the challenges the continual changes in the global political economy

Terrorism, Sanctions, *and* Justice: Gadhafi Surrenders Suspects

In December 1988, a bomb exploded aboard a Pan American flight over Lockerbie, Scotland, killing 270 passengers and people below. In September 1989, a bomb destroyed a French UTA flight from Brazzaville, killing 170 people. Who committed those mass murders?

It took four years before enough evidence was amassed to identify suspects and the country that sponsored them. In 1992, the United States convinced the U.N. Security Council to impose economic sanctions on Libya for harboring those accused of the Lockerbie bombing. Washington also imposed its own sanctions that penalized any country whose firms invested more than $40 million in Libya's oil industry. Libya's dictator Mu'ammar Gadhafi denied the charges. Those sanctions took their toll on Libya's development, wealth, and power, $18 billion according to a World Bank study. A high birth rate, 30 percent unemployment, a 40 percent drop in oil revenues in 1998, and a compromise eventually led Gadhafi to surrender two of eight accused terrorists.

In March 1999, after two years of negotiations, Gadhafi agreed to turn over the two Lockerbie suspects if the United Nations would suspend economic sanctions and the trial would be conducted at the International Court of Justice at The Hague. U.N. Secretary-General Kofi Annan and South African President Nelson Mandela, along with lower-ranking Egyptian and Saudi Arabian officials, were instrumental in securing the compromise that cinched the deal. The Americans and British agreed to allow the jurisdiction moved from Scotland to the Netherlands, although Scottish judges would still preside over the trial, while the sanctions would be suspended rather than outright canceled. When Gadhafi turned over the suspects, the Security Council voted to suspend the sanctions on Libya on April 5. The trial of the two suspects began February 2000.

Meanwhile, that same month, a French court trying six Libyan suspects *in absentia* for the UTA bombing found them guilty. The French ordered Gadhafi to turn them over to serve sentences of life imprisonment. Gadhafi refused to extract them.

Why did Gadhafi chose to hand over one set of suspects and not the others? The case against the Lockerbie suspects is actually quite circumstantial and most likely will lead to a dismissal. He may score both a propaganda coup if that occurs along with the lifting of the sanctions. The case against the other suspects apparently includes hard evidence that could convict them. He would gain nothing and lose much by extraditing those suspects. Thus Gadhafi used international law to advance his own interests.

posed to international relations. There is a dynamic relationship between politics and law, in which laws emerge from attempts to resolve political issues and then in turn shape the context in which politics take place. Although international law primarily governs relations among states, (public international law), it has expanded to include international organizations, multinational corporations, and individuals (private international law).

Although few disputed international law's reality, there were fierce debates over its inherent nature and applicability. The first legal scholars argued that international law was rooted in natural law. Although three Spanish legal scholars—Francisco de Victoria (1486–1546), Alberico Gentili (1552–1608), and Francisco Suarez (1548–1617)—laid the groundwork, the Dutchman Hugo

Grotius (1583–1645) is regarded as the "founder" of international law and the *naturalist school*. Although Grotius agreed with the Spaniards that international law had a divine origin, in his *On the Law of War and Peace* (1625), he argued that it would exist even without God. Some laws are natural to all human beings despite the various cultures to which they belong. Human reason can break free of any culture's values and customs to discover the underlying natural laws. Samuel von Pufendorf (1632–1694) went beyond Grotius to argue that the only true laws were from nature and denied the validity of any laws originating from treaties or custom.

A reaction to this view emerged during the 18th century as ever more theorists argued that law's origins are human rather than divine or natural, and involve consent and self-interest. The most prominent of this *positivist school* was the Dutchman Cornelis van Bynkershoek (1673–1743). The *eclectic school* attempted to bridge the gap between naturalists and positivists. The Swiss theorist, Emmerich von Vattel (1714–1767) maintained that although states did indeed have natural rights and duties, they were only obliged to fulfill them if those laws were codified. According to Vattel, "the Law of Nations is the science of the rights which exist between Nations or States, and the obligations corresponding to those rights."[2]

The *neorealist school* of international law argues that power and policy shape the rules or laws of the international system. International law changes and develops with shifts in the power distribution and the proliferation of issues in an increasingly interdependent global economy. Just as the most powerful states make the system's laws to protect and promote their own rather than international interests, they use the same criteria when choosing to obey or disregard international law.[3] In the late 20th century, the neorealist school was reinforced by the statements of many Third World leaders who argued that international law is rooted in Western civilization's values, and thus discriminates against nonwestern peoples.

What Are *the* Sources *of* International Law?

sources of international law the **International Court of Justice** bases its decisions on three primary sources of international law (treaties, customs, and general principles) and two secondary sources (judicial opinions, and legal theorists).

Although scholars and statesmen may bicker over the nature of international law, there is a near universal consensus on its sources. Article 38 of the Statute of the *International Court of Justice* (ICJ) identifies three primary *sources of international law*—treaties, customs, and general principles, and two secondary sources—judicial opinions and legal theorists.

Sometimes the sources of international law conflict on a given subject. Treaties generally override custom and form the basis for new customs. The more signatories to a treaty, the more easily it can sweep away existing customs. Yet if countries follow old practices rather than the proscriptions of a new treaty, then customs clearly are more important. Legal principles are considered more important than treaties. According to the 1969 Vienna Convention of Treaties, "a treaty is void if . . . it conflicts with a peremptory norm [principle] of general international law [*jus cogens*]." Judicial decisions and scholarship are generally subordinate to treaties, customs, and principles because judges and scholars use those sources as the basis for their own legal interpretations.

TREATIES

Treaties are the most explicit sources of international law and are signed with the universal understanding that they are legally binding (*pacta sunt servanda*). The number of international treaties has soared over the modern era: Between 1648 and 1919, the treaties filled 226 thick volumes; between 1920 and 1946, 205 volumes; and between 1946 and 1978, 1,115 volumes.[4] There is probably no aspect of international relations, no matter how obscure, that has not been regulated by treaty. There is even an international treaty— the 1969 Vienna Convention on the Law of Treaties—regulating the writing and signing of international treaties. The convention was the culmination of two decades of work begun in 1949 by the International Law Commission, set up by the United Nations as an advisory group to draft a treaty codifying several hundred years of customary law regarding treaties. The Law of Treaties came into force on January 27, 1980, when the 35th state ratified it.

The convention states that treaties "are an international agreement concluded by states in written form and governed by international law," which are "binding upon the parties to it and must be performed by them in good faith." Most treaties carefully explain the duties of participants and the consequences if those duties are violated. Not included are oral agreements between states, or any agreements between states and international organizations, or between international organizations. Every sovereign state has the right to negotiate and sign treaties—or to refuse to do so.

A state may ratify a treaty with written *reservations* in which the state unilaterally declares itself not bound by certain aspects of that treaty. The Vienna Convention allows states to do so as long as the specific reservation is not prohibited by the treaty or is incompatible with the treaty's purpose. The other parties then may or may not agree to those reservations. If the reservation is compatible with the treaty's purpose and obligations, it is legally acceptable even if other signatories disagree. If not, the treaty must be renegotiated. Treaties are obviously weakened in proportion to the number and type of reservations imposed by signatories.

The Vienna Convention allows states to suspend or terminate a treaty (1) if all parties agree to do so; (2) if one or more parties seriously violate a treaty; (3) if it is impossible for one or more parties to discharge their duties; (4) if there is a fundamental change in circumstances (*rebus sic stantibus*); (5) if the state's own diplomats were corrupted or coerced into agreements at odds with their instructions; (6) if the treaty was imposed by force; or (7) if it conflicts with international law. Many treaties include provisions that terminate the signatories' obligations after a certain period, if its objectives have been fulfilled, or the parties give notice— usually six months—that they are withdrawing from the treaty.

The Vienna Convention is not retroactive—any treaties that were negotiated by force before the convention went into effect remain valid. Any party that challenges a treaty's validity can take the dispute to the International Court of Justice if the issue has not been resolved among the signatories within one year of the official protest.

A treaty comes into force when all parties have ratified it, or provisions in the treaty allow it to do so after a certain number (often two-thirds) of parties have ratified it, or by a certain date after it has been ratified, to allow states to adjust to the new obligations, or by any other arrangements the parties to it deem appropriate.

The more states that are party to a treaty, the more usually it comes into force after a certain number ratify it. Treaties usually apply only to those states that have ratified it. However, fulfilling treaty obligations can imply tacit ratification. States can also become parties to a treaty by accession or signing it after it has been negotiated by others.

CUSTOMS

Customs may be the ultimate source of international law. Vattel defined them as "certain maxims and customs consecrated by long use, and observed by nations in their mutual intercourse with each other as a kind of law."[5] Whereas treaties express explicit rules of international law, customs represent an implicit understanding. Customs must generally be practiced by most states before they are considered the basis of law. Often a custom will be codified by treaty. Contemporary sources of customs include U.N. General Assembly recommendations. Although not legally binding in themselves, they often identify international customs that can be important legal sources. Custom need not have been of long duration as long as it is, in the words of the International Court of Justice in the North Sea Continental Shelf case, "both extensive and virtually uniform."[6]

How do customs bind states? States need not practice a custom to be considered as following it. If states do not protest a generally followed custom, that implies their consent to it. This affects newly independent states as well. The Soviet legal theorist G. I. Tunkin argued that new states "are legally entitled not to recognize particular customary rules of general international law. However, entry into official relations with other countries without reservations means that the new state accepts a certain body of principles and rules of existing international law which form the basis of relations between states."[7]

A classic example of the use of custom in international law occurred in 1898 when the U.S. Supreme Court ruled in the *Paquete Habana* (1900) case that the U.S. Navy had illegally seized and sold at auction two Cuban fishing boats during the Spanish-American War. Although there was no explicit international treaty governing the situation, the Court reasoned that "by ancient usage among civilized nations, beginning centuries ago, and gradually ripening into a rule of international law, coast fishing vessels, pursuing their vocation of catching and bringing in fresh fish, have been recognized as exempt, with their cargoes and crews, from capture as prize of war."[8]

PRINCIPLES

As a source of international law, principles are those considered so basic that they are found in most legal systems. Although specific laws vary considerably between countries, they may well be related by the same principles. Principles fill the theoretical gap between custom and treaty, especially in new areas of international law. For example, in the 19th century the arbitration of international disputes became common. The trouble was there were no existing customs or treaties regulating *arbitration*. Identifying general principles allowed diplomats to close that gap. Sovereignty and human rights are general principles of international law.

Many scholars argue that no greater principle guides international law than the "golden rule." In his *Commentaries on the Laws of England* Sir William Blackstone

Part 3   Nonstate Forces and Actors in International Relations

International law enshrines the principles of both sovereignty and human rights. Those concepts sometimes conflict. Usually citing the need to maintain law and order, the sovereign governments of two-thirds of the world's 190 nation-states systematically violate the human rights of the people under their rule. Perhaps no photograph better expresses the courage it takes for freedom-loving individuals to confront tyranny. On June 4, 1989, the Chinese government crushed a democracy movement led by students that had demonstrated for two months in Beijing's Tiananmen Square. One of those protesters is blocking a column of tanks heading toward the thousands of young protestors. What was his fate? He was arrested and later executed for treason. How should democratic countries react to oppression in other countries? What explains their usual reactions? What should take precedence in international law, sovereignty or human rights?

Reuters/Stringer/Archive Photos

(1723–1780) wrote, "The law of nations is a system of rules, deducible by human reason, and established by universal consent among the civilized inhabitants of the world. . . . This general law is founded upon this principle, that different nations ought in time of peace to do one another all the good they can, and in time of war as little harm as possible, without prejudice to their real interests."

COURT DECISIONS AND SCHOLARLY OPINIONS

The decisions of both international and national courts can also shape international law. Legally, the statutes governing the International Court of Justice do not obligate it to take legal precedents (*stare decisis*) into account when making decisions. In practice, however, the ICJ uses previous decisions in similar cases to help decide new cases. Judicial decision can also be signs of customary law. The U.S. Supreme Court has been especially sensitive to international law in its decisions. Yet judicial decisions can create law where none previously existed.

Scholars originated the study of international law and have continued to shape its evolution throughout the modern era. They explore the vast and expanding body of international treaties, practices, and principles, and help codify and expand international law.

SUBJECTS OF INTERNATIONAL LAW

A *subject of the law* or *legal person* has legal rights and duties. Before the 20th century, only states were legal persons in international law. Since then corporations, organizations, and individuals have also become subjects of international law. Yet even today, only states can be parties before the International Court of Justice. Because sovereign states, not governments, are the subjects of international law, each new government of a state assumes the same legal rights and duties of the previous governments—even revolutionary regimes.

Whether or not individuals are proper subjects of international law has been highly controversial. When the natural law perspective held sway, individuals were considered legal personalities. This view was rejected during the 19th century when positivists argued that no international laws could affect individuals or corporations, because they were bound by the national laws in which they reside. Behind this reasoning is the fear that accepting international personality for individuals would undermine national laws over citizens.

However, starting with the Nuremberg and Tokyo war crime trials in the 1940s and continuing through the Serbian war crime trials of the late 1990s, the notion of individual duties and rights has grown in importance, thus eroding the positivist contention that only states are the proper subjects. The Nuremberg Tribunal contended that "crimes against international law are committed by men, not by abstract entities, and only by punishing individuals who commit such crimes can the provisions of international law be enforced."[9]

JURISDICTION

comity a legal principle in which one state allows the intrusion of another state's laws into its territory.

When a dispute occurs, the parties must determine which country or international court has *jurisdiction. Comity* is a legal principle in which one state allows the intrusion of another state's laws into its territory. Extradition is an example of comity. (See the box on page 153.)

At times jurisdiction over a crime can be shared and disputed by two or more countries. Under the territorial principle, a state has jurisdiction over crimes committed in its territory. The only exception is if a crime occurs in two states—for example, a murder or robbery spree—in which case both states have jurisdiction. The nationality principle allows states to persecute their own citizens for crimes committed anywhere in the world. The protective principle permits a state to persecute foreigners who commit crimes within its borders if those crimes—plots to overthrow the government, drug running, spying, and so on—jeopardize the first state's national security. Finally, the universality principle allows a state to persecute foreigners who commit crimes within its borders even if they do not directly harm the persecuting state's security, if the crime threatens the international community as a whole. War crimes and aggression are examples.

When a criminal seeks refuge in another country, he or she can be extradited back to the country where the crime was committed. Without an extradition treaty, states are neither required to nor prevented from handing over criminals. Extradition treaties are usually bilateral and list the specific crimes under which

Part 3   Nonstate Forces and Actors in International Relations

The Long U.N. Struggle *for* Human Rights: *The* Commission *and the* Tribunals

All 185 current U.N. members must sign the 1945 Charter, which, among many other principles, requires them to "reaffirm faith in fundamental human rights . . . and for fundamental freedoms for all without distinction as to race, sex, language, or religion." In 1946 the U.N. set up the Commission on Human Rights to help fulfill that solemn commitment. The cold war and differing interpretations of just what human rights mean delayed the commission's implementation of its duties. It drafted the Universal Declaration on Human Rights, which was signed in 1948. But then it took two decades before it was able to draft and gain the mandatory signatories and ratification in 1966 for the International Covenant on Civil and Political Rights and the International Covenant on Economic, Social, and Cultural Rights, which help implement the Universal Declaration on Human Rights. The

commission was not authorized to investigate accusations of human rights abuses until 1970 and received only 2 percent of the U.N. budget. Even today politics stymie the commission's work. The General Assembly, which votes on the commission's proposals to condemn countries for human rights violations, tends to single out Israel and South Africa before apartheid ended and turn a blind eye to communist countries such as China and Cuba. Will politics rather than strict rule of law forever prevent the U.N. Commission on Human Rights from fulfilling its mandate?

Two recent institutions reveal that the United Nations can set politics aside in specific situations. The U.N. Security Council established an International Criminal Tribunal for Yugoslavia in 1993 and for Rwanda in 1994. To date the Yugoslavian tribunal has issued 21 public indictments against 56 war crimes suspects from

all three Bosnian factions, and an undisclosed number of secret indictments. Twenty-five of the suspects are in custody, of which five have been convicted and sentenced. The Rwandan tribunal has issued 28 indictments on 45 people, nabbed 32 of the suspects, and has so far sentenced two of them. Countless others who committed atrocities in Yugoslavia and Rwanda will evade justice, either because they cannot be apprehended or, more commonly, no formal charges have been filed.

Yet the punishment of some war criminals is better than none. How much if at all will the existence of such tribunals deter any future atrocities elsewhere? In 1998, 120 countries signed a treaty in Rome creating a permanent International Criminal Court. Presumably that court will deter and bring to justice more criminals than do the tribunals set up after the atrocities were committed.

extradition would occur, which must also be considered crimes by both states. If there is no extradition treaty between two states, one state may use its municipal law of deportation to get rid of criminals who committed crimes in the other states.

IMMUNITY

Sovereign states and their diplomats are generally immune from the jurisdiction of national laws. *Sovereignty,* by definition, means no state and its laws have power over another. Thus, when one state accuses another of having committed a crime, the accused state only appears in the other's courts voluntarily. *Immunity* is granted only to the actions and property of states, not to those of its private firms, organizations, or individuals, unless the state has a proprietary interest in them.

Princess Diana is comforting children who lost their legs when they stepped on land mines. Land mines kill or maim thousands of people each year. Most of those victims are civilians rather than soldiers. In the mid-1990s, a human rights group began lobbying the world's governments to negotiate a treaty banning land mines. That lobbying was successful. In 1997, a treaty banning land mines was signed by almost all of the world's countries. The United States was among half a dozen that spurned the treaty, arguing that its military would be more vulnerable to attack if it could not use land mines. International law declares aggression illegal and defense legal. What weapons are appropriate for defense, and which, if any, should be outlawed? Do the means always justify the ends?

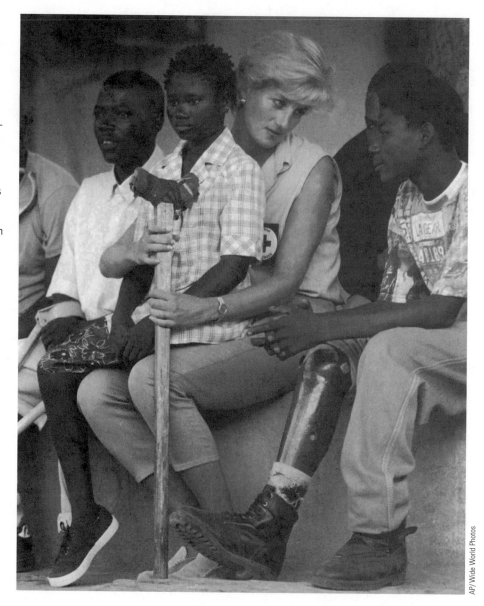

AP/ Wide World Photos

Diplomatic immunity is one of the oldest, most developed, and universal areas of international law. The 1961 Vienna Convention on Diplomatic Relations codified centuries-old customs on diplomatic exchange and immunity. Article 29 states that "the person of a diplomatic agent shall be inviolable. He shall not be liable to any form of arrest or detention. The receiving State shall treat him with due respect and shall take all appropriate steps to prevent any attack on his person, freedom, or dignity."

Diplomats have several important functions. Their overall duty is to protect their country's national and private interests vis-à-vis that foreign country. This involves negotiations on important issues, gathering information about and proposing policies for that state, promoting a positive image of one's country and policies, and protecting the rights of national firms, organizations, and individuals operating in that country.

Diplomatic relations between two or more states occur by mutual consent. The receiving state has the power to approve any members and the size of the foreign mission, and can at any time declare a foreign diplomat *persona non grata* (unacceptable) and expel him or her from the country. States can unilaterally break off their relations with others, which usually involves withdrawing its own embassy and expelling the other state's embassy from its own territory.

Diplomats and their families (unless they are nationals of the receiving states) are immune from all criminal and most civil prosecution, and from any arrest or detention. The only civil law exceptions involve nonofficial commercial transactions. In cases where a diplomat commits a serious crime, the receiving state can always ask the other state to withhold immunity, a request that is often granted to preserve good relations. The embassies, residences, archives, documents, communications, and property of diplomatic missions are also inviolable and may only be entered by permission. Embassies, however, are not extraterritorial and may neither harbor criminals who take refuge there nor imprison people. The exception is when someone seeks political asylum. Embassies and diplomats are exempt from all taxes, and must be allowed to import duty free any items for official or personal use. The receiving state is obligated to protect foreign embassies and their personnel from attack.

All states with overseas embassies have a clear interest in supporting diplomatic immunity. Major violations of diplomatic immunity such as when Iranians invaded the American embassy in Teheran in 1979 and held the diplomats hostage for 444 days, are extremely rare. The International Court of Justice ruled in that case "there is no more fundamental prerequisite for the conduct of relations between States than the inviolability of diplomatic envoys and diplomats."[10]

Consulates and consuls differ from embassies and diplomats. Their primary duty is not diplomacy but such apolitical functions as issuing visas and passports, and promoting their country's commercial interests. The 1986 Vienna Convention on Consular Relations grants consuls a more limited protection than diplomats, holding them liable for both criminal and civil offenses that were not official acts.

The United Nations also enjoys immunity from all legal processes, its premises, archives, documents, and property are inviolable, and it is exempt from taxes and import duties. The Secretary-General and assistant secretaries-general enjoy complete diplomatic immunity, whereas staff members and foreign diplomats have consular immunity.

SOVEREIGNTY

Political philosophers originally conceived sovereignty as the distribution of power and location of supreme power within a state. Jean Bodin, in his *Republic* (1576), defined sovereignty as the supreme lawmaking and law-enforcing authority in a territory. Eventually, it came to mean the recognition and relationship of states with each other. According to the 1933 Montevideo Convention on the Rights and Duties of States, a sovereign state has a clearly defined territory, permanent population, government with ultimate power over that territory and people, and recognition of independence by other sovereign states.

Sovereign states are legal equals. Vattel made the classic natural law case for equality among sovereign states:

> Since men are naturally equal, and a perfect equality prevails in their rights and obligations, as equally proceeding from nature, nations composed of men, and considered

as so many free persons living together in the state of nature, are naturally equal, and inherit from nature the same obligations and rights. Power or weakness does not in this respect produce any difference. A dwarf is as much a man as a giant; a small republic is no less a sovereign state than the most powerful kingdom.[11]

A sovereign state is independent but not above the law. A change in government does not affect the state's sovereignty, or that state's obligations incurred by the previous governments. For example, although denying it, the Soviet government that came to power after the November 1917 revolution was still responsible for the foreign debts owed by the Russian government. Likewise, the Russian government that broke from and dissolved the Soviet Union in December 1991 is still required to fulfill its predecessor's duties.

RECOGNITION

recognition the right of every sovereign state to accept—recognize—or deny the sovereignty of another state.

Governments are free to recognize or withhold *recognition* of each other. Some states distinguish between recognizing the sovereignty of a state (*de facto* recognition) and having diplomatic relations with it (*de jure* recognition). Or a government may not formally recognize another through the exchange of embassies yet carry on full economic, diplomatic, and other relations. Most governments recognize others when they have achieved control over their population and territory. Some, such as the United States, have based recognition on whether or not they agree with another government's political ideology and practices. The United States did not formally recognize as legitimate the communist government that took over China in 1949 until 1979! Most states, including the United States, now recognize states rather than governments.

There are two perspectives on recognition. The *constitutive theory* argues that states can only be legitimate if they receive international recognition. The *declarative theory* argues that recognition has no legal effect; states either exist or they do not, and recognition simply acknowledges that fact. For example, at first the Western states refused to recognize the German Democratic Republic (East Germany) because it was created by the Soviet Union in violation of treaties. By the 1970s, however, most of the Western states had abandoned their constitutive position for a declarative position and recognized East Germany as a state regardless of its origins.

The 1923 *Tinoco* case illustrates both the international recognition and sovereign responsibilities issues. Frederico Tinoco was a dictator of Costa Rica who made concessions to British companies, some of which were payments in special banknotes. The government that came to power after Tinoco's overthrow repudiated his actions and promises. Britain sued Costa Rica. The arbitration court ruled that the Tinoco government clearly controlled Costa Rica, and the new government was responsible for the obligations of the old, even though the Tinoco regime was considered unconstitutional and was not recognized by several states, including Britain. Thus the declarative principle was weighed more important than the constitutive principle.

There is a body of international law that obligates states not to recognize territorial changes caused by aggression. After Japan took over Manchuria in 1931, Secretary of State Henry Stimson announced what became known as the "Stimson Doctrine," whereby the United States would not recognize any changes brought by Japanese imperialism. In 1932, the League of Nations adopted the same principle when it resolved that "it is incumbent upon the members of the League of Nations not to recognize any situation, treaty or agreement which may be brought about by means contrary to the Covenant of the League of Nations or to the Pact of Paris." The U.N. General Assembly passed a similar resolution in 1970 when it declared that "no territorial acquisition resulting from the threat or use of force shall be recognized as legal."

International law has a Janus face regarding whether or not states are free from external interference in their internal affairs. (Janus was the two-faced Roman god of the new and old year—hence, January.) On the one hand, states are legally considered sovereign powers accountable to no higher authority, and free to rule their inhabitants and war against their neighbors as they see fit. Yet on the other hand, states can also be condemned and sanctioned for their human rights abuses, are prohibited from launching aggressive wars, and have eroded their own sovereignty by signing countless treaties and the U.N. Charter that expand their international duties and limit their behavior.

THE ACQUISITION OF TERRITORY

States can acquire territory by several means. One state can cede land to another. States can claim unoccupied territory (*terra nullius*). By controlling another country's territory without dispute, states can acquire "squatters' rights" to it. Nature can give land through volcanoes or changes in river courses. Land disputes can be adjudicated by a third party, which can decide to grant the land to one or more of the interested states. States can lease their land to others, as China did with Hong Kong's New Territories to Britain, or Cuba, Guantanamo Bay to the United States. States can also acquire rights over the resources of other states, such as water for irrigation or transportation. The 1888 Convention of Constantinople declared the Suez Canal open to ships of all nations. International authorities can redraw boundaries and award mandates. For example, the Treaty of Versailles created Yugoslavia, Poland, Czechoslovakia, Hungary, Austria, Latvia, Estonia, and Lithuania, and mandated that the defeated powers give their colonies to the victors. At times two or more states have jointly occupied a territory (*condominium*). For example, the New Hebrides Islands were a condominium of Britain and France before it received independence in 1980.

Traditionally, states could incorporate conquered territory into their own land if acknowledged by treaty and the international community. Today, given the United Nations and international law proscriptions against aggressive wars, land acquired by conquest is considered illegal even if it is taken by the victim of aggression. For example, a large majority in the United Nations opposes any Israeli attempts to incorporate land it conquered in the 1967 War.

If conquest is no longer a valid means of acquiring territory, who is entitled to land that was conquered in the past? In 1961, India invaded the Portuguese colony of Goa, even though Portugal had originally acquired the territory in the sixteenth century, its inhabitants wished to remain Portuguese, and, following its independence in 1947, India itself had recognized Portugal's title. The Nehru government justified its takeover by claiming the land was traditionally Indian. The United Nations did not protest the conquest. China used India's rationale as an excuse for invading part of northern India that had traditionally been Chinese but had been taken by the British in the 19th century. India shrilly protested China's action.

UPHOLDING THE LAW

Compliance with international law is largely voluntary. Virtually all states obey the law virtually all the time. Why?

Self-interest is obviously an important reason for compliance. International laws are created to regulate behavior and thus provide a degree of security for all if they are obeyed. If a state regularly violates the law, other states will avoid relations with it or retaliate, thus hurting that state. States realize that although the law may work against them in one situation, it may work for them in other situations. When states break the law, they create a precedent that can be used against them; other states can justify breaking that law in a different situation that harms the original lawbreaker. Finally other states can impose economic and even military sanction against international lawbreakers. All these consequences tend to deter states from violating the law.

Sanctions work best, when they work at all, if they are imposed by a large group of states on the international lawbreaker. In 1990, the United Nations imposed sanctions against Iraq for its invasion of Kuwait. All international trade with Iraq except humanitarian and food shipments was forbidden until Baghdad compensated Kuwait for the damage it caused during the invasion and surrendered all its nuclear, chemical, and biological weapons. Despite a decade of economic boycott following a devastating war sanctioned by the United Nations, Iraq remains defiant.

Reprisals against lawbreakers are legal as long as they are proportional to the original crime. For example, in 1986 the United States bombed Libya in reprisal for an earlier Libya terrorist attack that killed two American servicemen. But 37 people were killed in the American bombing raid, sparking a controversy over whether the action was a legitimate reprisal or a crime.

Governments, like individuals, do not obey the law primarily because they fear sanctions. States also obey the law because they have deeply internalized concepts of right and wrong and they believe the law is just. International laws are often based on long-standing international customs. In other words, states have already followed a particular behavior long before it was codified into law. International law expert Michael Akehurst argues that, paradoxically, the absence of an international legislature is one reason why most states comply with international law. States make law for themselves and thus are more apt to comply with it than if it were imposed by a higher authority.[12]

International laws provide clear rules of behavior that, when followed, reduce international conflict. States recognize that they all lose if any state breaks the rules. Governments, however, sometimes weigh the short-term concrete advantages of breaking a law as greater than the long-term abstract advantages of obeying it. This is particularly common when the law is vague or ambiguous. Then any behavior can be justified, and states will try to get away with what they can. International tensions, however, increase. One sign of international law's growing importance is that states often claim they are obeying the law even as they break it, or justify actions by pointing to possible loopholes in that law.

Most of the time, states settle their differences through negotiations, which are often decided by international law. There are several ways to negotiate conflicts that do not involve going to court but include a third neutral party. In international conflicts, interested third parties can offer their *good offices*, in which they provide a neutral location but refrain from moderating the actual negotiations,

Part 3 Nonstate Forces and Actors in International Relations

A Court *That* Works:
The European Court *of* Justice

Can an international court truly promote justice in an age when sovereign nation-states continue to reign supreme? The International Court of Justice (ICJ) at The Hague disappoints those who want a world court with global reach to indict, convict, and punish. For a powerful international court, one must journey about 300 miles south of The Hague to Strasbourg, France.

The European Court of Human Rights is based on the 1953 European Convention on Human Rights, eventually signed by the 40 members of the Council of Europe. All members accept its jurisdiction as their highest appeals court for individuals. States not only comply with its decisions, but they also sometimes adjust their laws accordingly. For example, after receiving adverse rulings, Britain and France revised their wiretapping laws, Ireland legalized homosexuality, Germany's courts provided interpreters for defendants who did not speak German, and Austria dropped its state satellite and cable television cartel. The successful transition of Spain, Portugal, and Greece to democracy in the 1970s was in part guided by European Court of Justice standards.

But the European Court of Justice's reputation for fair, powerful decisions is not without cost. It is so popular that supplicants must queue for a long five-year wait before their case is heard. Of course, the court's success is hardly surprising. After all human rights are an integral part of liberal democracy, which all those European countries have embraced if not fully realized. Still the European Court of Human Rights can be a beacon for regions of the world still darkened by governments that systematically violate the rights of the people under their rule.

as when the United States hosted the Middle East Peace negotiations in 1992. Or it can *conciliate* a conflict by giving advice to both sides while not offering a resolution. States can also *mediate* conflict, in which they propose nonbinding solutions to the participants, as in the Camp David negotiations of 1977 when President Carter mediated between Egyptian President Anwar Sadat and Israeli Prime Minister Menachem Begin, or the Wye, Maryland, bargaining between the Israeli Prime Minister Benjamin Netanyahu and Palestinian President Yasser Arafat in 1998. Finally, arbitration involves a neutral state or body giving a binding decision through a specially convened court for that particular issue.

International arbitration of property disputes dates to the Jay Treaty of 1794 between the United States and Great Britain, which set up the machinery to settle cases involving national boundaries, seizures of ships at sea, and other expropriation of property. The Jay Treaty became the model for dozens of other bilateral and multilateral treaties on the subject. Between 1795 and 1914, over 200 arbitration panels were instituted among states. The 1874 *Alabama* case was an important step in international arbitration. The case concerned whether Britain had violated international law of neutrality during America's Civil War by allowing the Confederacy to build warships in Britain with which to attack Union shipping. A panel of five judges from the United States, Britain, Italy, Switzerland, and Brazil ruled that Britain had violated neutrality laws and was ordered to pay the United States $15,500,000 in damages. President Grant was so pleased by the decision and Britain's compliance that he predicted "an epoch when a court recognized by all nations will settle international differences instead of keeping large standing armies."[13] That epoch has not yet arrived.

In 1899, representatives at an international conference at The Hague signed the Convention for the Pacific Settlement of International Disputes in which they promised to submit conflicts to arbitration panels. The *Permanent Court of Arbitration (PCA)* was set up to hear and decide on grievances. Between then and 1914, the PCA settled over 120 conflicts. The court, however, had no powers to either require disputants to appear or comply with its decisions. It has been rarely used since 1914, deciding only ten cases through today.

Although the PCA has dwindled, other, more specialized international arbitration courts are increasingly important forums in which conflicts can be resolved. In 1922, the International Chamber of Commerce (ICC) established a *Court of Arbitration* in Paris, which since then has heard over 5,000 cases, recently more than 250 a year. Parties in a dispute can elect to take their case to the Court of Arbitration. The cases are decided according to international law. The American Arbitration Association is second only to the ICC in the number of international conflicts it has settled. The World Bank has its International Center for Settlement of Investment Disputes.

In 1919, at the Versailles Peace Conference ending World War I, President Wilson lobbied the other delegates for the creation of a world court for the League of Nations. On February 15, 1922, the League of Nations established the *Permanent Court of International Justice (PCIJ)*. Between 1921 and 1945, the court issued 31 judgments, 25 substantive orders, and 27 advisory opinions—about three or four decisions annually. However, the World Court, like the League of Nations, did nothing to prevent World War II and sat for the last time on December 4, 1939.

Like President Wilson, President Roosevelt was determined to create a global assembly and court that would help preserve peace. Throughout World War II Roosevelt pressured America's allies to create a new set of institutions that would, it was hoped, succeed where the League and PCIJ had failed. In August and September 1944, the United States, Britain, and the Soviet Union agreed at Dumbarton Oaks to establish the International Court of Justice (ICJ). In March 1945, a Committee of Jurists made up of representatives from 44 countries met to draft the agreement for a new court, and submitted its proposal before the San Francisco Conference, which created the United Nations. The new court was formally established on April 18, 1946.

In form, function, and location, the ICJ is largely the continuation of the PCIJ. Located at The Hague, the ICJ hears cases and then rules. The court has 15 judges, 5 of whom are elected every three years to hold office for nine years. The U.N. Security Council and General Assembly vote to elect the judges. International organizations, including the Security Council, General Assembly, and any other institutions, can ask the court for advisory opinions. Every signatory to the U.N. Charter agrees to comply with ICJ decisions. Between 1946 and 1988, the ICJ heard only 55 cases, rendered judgments on 30, and handed down 19 advisory opinions.[14] The ICJ or a party to a dispute can call on the U.N. Security Council to act against recalcitrant states. The Security Council can vote on the measures necessary to implement a court decision.

Although the ICJ's decisions are binding, its jurisdiction is not. Although 162 of the U.N. members have agreed to accept the court's jurisdiction, 155 have included reservations that allow them to determine the cases under which it would accept jurisdiction. For example, in 1984, the Reagan administration simply announced that it would not accept the ICJ's jurisdiction in a suit filed by Nicaragua that alleged the United States had mined its harbors, supplied rebels, and tried to overthrow the government.

There are two other important international courts: the European Court of Justice (ECJ) at Luxembourg and the European Court of Human Rights at Strasbourg, both institutions of the 15-nation European Union (EU). Unlike the ICJ, the ECJ has compulsory jurisdiction over member states that have broken the rules. The ECJ has 13 judges—one from each member and one rotated from different members. They are advised by six advocates-general. The ECJ can hear cases brought by states, organizations, or private litigants, including firms, interest groups, and individuals, which involve a breach of European Union law. The ECJ has the power to overturn decisions by the executive commission and council. The ECJ caseload is far greater than that of the ICJ.

There is disagreement over whether or not the ECJ is a true international court. Some argue that European Union law differs so significantly from international law that they are different species. Furthermore, the European Union is seen as increasingly a federal state and its laws thus as national rather than international. Others argue that because members retain their sovereignty and can withdraw from the European Union, the laws uniting them are by definition international, and in most cases do not differ substantially from those international laws with a global dimension.

HUMAN RIGHTS

Which are more important, the sovereign rights of governments to do what they will within their country or the rights of all humans to be free of repression, ill treatment, and genocide? Sovereign rights are increasingly giving way to human rights.

In 1815, Great Britain launched perhaps the first human rights effort when it unsuccessfully attempted to forge an international treaty suppressing the slave trade. Throughout the 19th century and into the 20th century, a number of multilateral treaties were signed which protected civilians in warfare. At the Versailles Conference, there were agreements protecting the rights of certain minorities in eastern Europe, and the International Labor Organization was created to protect the rights of workers.

However, despite these efforts, no systematic attempts to address human rights occurred until the United Nations was created in 1945. The Preamble of the U.N. Charter required signatories to "reaffirm faith in fundamental human rights, in the dignity and worth of the human person, in the equal rights of men and women and of nations large and small." Article 55 states that the United Nations will "promote . . . universal respect for, and observance of, human rights and fundamental freedoms for all without distinction as to race, sex, language or religion." Article 56 then requires that "all members pledge themselves to take joint and separate action in cooperation with the organization for the achievement of the purposes set forth in Article 55." Although the word *pledge* implies a legal duty, it leaves states the freedom to decide in what ways and to what degree to implement the duty of respecting human rights. Thus, only states that regress in fulfilling human rights are liable to criticism. The U.N. Commission on Human

Rights was established in 1946 to monitor the progress of states in fulfilling their pledge. The commission has only the power of publicizing human rights abuses, in the hope it will pressure states to curtail their violations.

On December 10, 1948, the U.N. General Assembly passed the Universal Declaration of Human Rights with 48 votes in favor, none against, and 10 abstentions—the eight communist countries, South Africa, and Saudi Arabia. The declaration proclaims itself "as a common standard of achievement for all peoples and all nations, to the end that every individual and every organ of society . . . shall strive by teaching and education to promote respect for these rights and freedoms and by progressive measures, national and international, to secure their universal and effective recognition and observance." More specifically, the declaration lists dozens of civil, political, social, economic, and cultural rights. In 1966 after 12 years of negotiations, the United Nations offered two treaties for signature, the Covenant on Civil and Political Rights and the Covenant on Economic, Social, and Cultural Rights. Although both treaties came into force in 1976, the United States has yet to sign either. States are bound by those treaties whether or not they signed them. The 1968 U.N. Conference on Human Rights asserted that "the Universal Declaration on Human Rights . . . constitutes an obligation for the members of the international community."

These U.N. efforts were paralleled in Europe on November 4, 1950, when representatives signed the European Convention for the Protection of Human Rights and Fundamental Freedoms. The convention came into force on September 3, 1953 after the tenth state ratified the treaty. All European Union members are legally bound by the treaty except in case of war.

Two institutions serve the convention. The European Commission on Human Rights investigates possible violations of human rights. Groups and individuals as well as states can petition the commission for a hearing. If the commission finds that a violation has occurred, it then offers to serve as an intermediary for a friendly settlement of the violation. If a settlement is not reached, the commission can refer the case to the European Court of Human Rights in Strasbourg for a binding legal decision. Expulsion from the organization is the ultimate penalty. Or, if three months have elapsed since the investigation began, the case goes to the Committee of Ministers of the Council of Europe, which can decide by a two-thirds vote that there has been a violation. Individuals can only petition the commission, not the court.

Human rights in the western hemisphere are shaped by the 1948 Charter of the Organization of American States (OAS). In 1960, the OAS created the Inter-American Commission on Human Rights, which investigates human rights violations. The 1967 Buenos Aires Protocol and 1969 American Convention on Human Rights strengthened the Inter-American Commission's powers and created the Inter-American Court, both modeled on Europe's human rights institutions. Only 18 of the 31 OAS members have ratified the convention; the United States has refused to sign. Although the commission and the court do render decisions, they have no means to enforce their decisions.

Human rights extend to foreign nationals as well as citizens residing in a country. States cannot prosecute foreigners for crimes they have committed elsewhere, although they can extract them to the country where the crime was committed. States, however, do not have to extract their own citizens unless required by treaty. Foreigners cannot be drafted into the army unless they are permanent residents in that country. When a state expels foreign citizens back to their own country,

We're *for* Human Rights!—*to a* Point: America *and the* Human Rights Court

In July 1998, an international treaty setting up a permanent International Criminal Court was signed by envoys of 120 countries. Seven countries who attended the conference adamantly refused to sign. Presumably the idea of an international court dedicated to prosecuting war criminals made those holdouts very nervous. Who were the holdouts, and what did they have to hide?

Among those who resisted the court's creation were China, Libya, and Iraq—all systematic human rights abusers—and, oh yes, the United States. Why would a nation that prides itself on its highly developed liberal democracy and human rights protection be opposed to an international court that promotes those very values?

During the prolonged negotiations over the treaty, the United States insisted that its own soldiers and citizens be immune from prosecution on war crimes charges from any but its own courts. Not surprisingly the other countries rejected the notion of a double standard for Americans and all other nationalities. That was not the first human rights treaty that Washington has rejected for itself but insisted on for others. The United States has either not ratified or actively campaigned against the 1948 Declaration on Human Rights, the 1984 Torture Convention, and the 1997 Land Mine Treaty, among others.

Under heavy pressure from the Republican party's right-wing, various administrations have maintained the principle that sovereignty—or at least American sovereignty—should prevail over human rights and war crimes. The fear was that Ronald Reagan or George Bush could be liable for their respective invasions of Grenada and Panama, both of which violated international law.

Some argue that the United States could have attached reservations specially protecting its interests. Indeed, most signatories did so only with reservations of "complementarity" whereby the new court would complement and not supersede their national courts. That would allow those governments to choose whether they would allow their own accused nationals to be tried at home or in the international war crimes courts. But if Washington signed the treaty with a complementarity reservation, it would be legally obliged to choose between trying Reagan and Bush at home or extraditing them to the international court if someone brought charges against them.

Should the United States spurn or sign the International Criminal Court treaty? Under what circumstances should the United States grant a foreign request for an extradition against one of its citizens, including presidents? Should the United States bring charges against former presidents of having violated international human rights and war crimes laws or extract the accused to foreign courts?

that state must receive them unless they are willing to go to another state. International law allows each state to decide its own citizenship requirements.

The 1951 Geneva Convention declared that refugee status depends on "a well-founded fear of persecution for reasons of race, religion, nationality, membership in a particular social group, or political opinion." Recently there has been an attempt to broaden the definition to include those displaced because of environmental catastrophes.

States are not obligated to accept foreign nationals, although when they do those individuals deserve full human rights. If a violation occurs, the government of that individual may sue for compensation on his or her behalf. States may agree to settle the dispute by arbitration or court, and if an injury is found the compensation goes to the victim's government rather than the victim. Of course, after winning compensation the government can and usually does compensate its citizen.

States are only liable for those crimes that its officials commit if they are following clear orders. States are never liable for actions of private citizens. Yet states are liable when they encourage their citizens to attack foreigners, fail to provide enough protection for foreigners in case of an imminent attack, fail to punish crimes committed by their citizens against foreigners, fail to provide foreigners with the legal ability to gain compensation for losses, materially benefit from an attack, or express approval of the attack.

Throughout the 19th and 20th centuries, Western governments argued that states were liable for harm to foreign nationals if they did not meet minimum international standards of human rights. Third World countries counter that they are only required to treat foreign nationals as they do their own citizens. Akehurst suggests that the sensible solution to this impasse is that "if the minimum international standard appears to give aliens a privileged position, the answer is for states to treat their own nationals better, not for them to treat aliens worse; indeed the whole human rights movement may be seen as an attempt to extend the minimum international standard from aliens to nationals."[15]

As in other areas of international law, the upholding of human rights depends largely on the actions of sovereign states. John Rouke juxtaposed two speeches giving very different views of the importance of human rights in foreign policy.[16] In 1978, on the 39th anniversary of the Universal Declaration of Human Rights, President Carter declared himself "proud that our nation stands for more than military might or political might. . . . Our pursuit of human rights is part of a broad effort to use our great power and our tremendous influence in the service of creating a better world in which human beings can live in peace, in freedom, and with their basic needs met. Human rights is the soul of our foreign policy."[17] Former secretary of state to President Carter, Cyrus Vance, later argued that it was a "dangerous illusion" to believe that "pursuing values such as human rights . . . is incompatible with pursuing U.S. national interests. . . . Our own freedom, and that of our allies, could never be secure in a world where freedom was threatened everywhere else."[18]

Secretary of State George Shultz gave a very different view in 1985 when he said, "We Americans have had to accept that our passionate commitment to moral principles could not be a substitute for sound foreign policy in a world of hard realities and complex choice . . . our moral impulse, noble as it might be, could lead either to futile and perhaps dangerous global crusades, on the one hand, or to escapism and isolationism, equally dangerous, on the other."[19]

Which of those two views do you share?

Conclusion

International law is clearly riddled with seeming paradoxes, limitations, and contradictions. Power, not law, rules international relations. Although states are legally equal, there are clear differences in their respective power. Even if it does not make right, might seems to determine when international law is used or neglected in regulating international behavior. Compliance with the existing law is voluntary. States choose whether or not to go before and heed the International Court of Justice and other arbitration courts, and law violators are the least likely to assent to legal rulings against them.

Yet power is always limited. International relations are shaped by order, not anarchy, and international law is a major source of that order. True, states obey or break the law when they perceive it is in their interest to do so, and, given the ambiguity of international law, can use it to justify virtually any action. Yet is this so different from how people act in any society? People violate the law in every legal system.[20]

The U.N. Charter clearly represents shared community values, fulfilling the Roman precept "Where there is society, there is law (*ubi societas, ibi jus*)." States signing the charter agree to those values whether they live up to them or not. International law should be considered important, if only because virtually all states think it is important and adjust their behavior accordingly. In the post–cold-war world, the U.N. Security Council is increasingly serving as a world court, police, and prosecutor.

National prosperity and security depends on a government's ability to promote its country's political economic interests in an increasingly interdependent world. Reputation is important, if only for reasons of self-interest. Virtually all states obey the law most of the time. Law-abiding states generally shun or retaliate against those that regularly violate international law, to the latter's detriment. Iraq is a classic example of what can happen to a state that aggressively violates international law.

The body of international law is expanding. One of the most remarkable milestones of the 20th century is the outlawing of aggressive war. Most states are at peace most of the time, and international law of war has been an important factor creating that reality. Yet international law involves more than questions of war and peace. Law regulates dozens of areas of international relations—trade, investments, debt, currency flows, travel, embassies, and so on. International law, and the institutions for enforcing it, will continue to evolve into the 21st century.

Study Questions

1. Is international law really law?

2. Describe the different schools of international law.

3. Trace the major developments in international law's evolution from its origins through today.

4. What are the primary and secondary sources of international law?

5. Why and how are treaties a basis for international law?

6. Explain why and how customs are a basis for international law.

7. Why and how are principles a basis for international law?

8. How and why are legal decisions and legal opinions a basis for international law?

9. What is the proper "subject" and "jurisdiction" of international law?

10. What is the extent of diplomatic immunity? How did the practice arise?

11. Define sovereignty. What is its significance for international law?

12. Define recognition. What are the "constitutive" and "declarative" schools concerning recognition?

13. Why do most states obey international law most of the time?

14. How is the International Court of Justice organized? What are its strengths and weaknesses?

15. Discuss the development of international law concerning human rights.

 *InfoTrac College Edition* Sources

Using the Subject Guide, enter the search terms *international law, International Court of Justice, human rights, Hugo Grotius,* and/or *Nuremberg trial.*

Chua, Amy L. "Markets, Democracy, and Ethnicity: Toward a New Paradigm for Law and Development."

Esman, Milton J. "International Law and Ethnic Conflict."

Ferrall, Bard R. [Book review of] *The Treatment of Prisoners Under International Law,* 2nd ed.

Forde, Steven. "Hugo Grotius on Ethics and War."

Fromkin, David. "International Law at the Frontiers."

George, William P. "Looking for a Global Ethic? Try International Law."

Jefferson, Kurt W. "The Bosnian War Crimes Trial Simulation: Teaching Students About the Fuzziness of World Politics and International Law."

Kocs, Stephen A. "Anarchy and Order: The Interplay of Politics and Law in International Relations."

Monshipouri, Mahmood. "Human Rights and International Political Economy in Third World Nations: Multinational Corporations, Foreign Aid, and Repression."

Perrez, Franz Xaver. "The Relationship Between 'Permanent Sovereignty' and the Obligation Not to Cause Transboundary Environmental Damage."

Philpot, John. "Colonialism and Injustice: The International Criminal Tribunal for Rwanda."

Rabkin, Jeremy. "International Law vs. the American Constitution."

Ratner, Steven R. "International Law: The Trials of Global Norms."

Reif, Timothy M., and Gary E. Bacher. "Trade Laws, Antitrust Laws, and the Process of Economic Integration."

Scheffer, David J. "The War Against Atrocities: Perspectives on the Enforcement of International Humanitarian Law."

Sheinblatt, Julie S. "International Law and Treaties."

Villalon, Leonardo A. "Sovereigns, Quasi Sovereigns, and Africans: Race and Self-Determination in International Law."

On *the* Web

http://www.etown.edu/vl/intllaw.html
Directory of international law sites

http://www.lawschool.cornell.edu/library/International_Resources/foreign.htm
Cornell University's annotated international law links

http://www.icj-cij.org/
Website covering the International Court of Justice

Contents

Chapter 7 International Organizations

Key Concepts and Issues

As globalization intensifies the interdependence among all nations, ever more international organizations emerge to manage new conflicts and interests.[1] International organizations breed related ones in related fields. Over time, different international organizations merge to form stronger and more comprehensive ones. Organizations binding nations economically or socially eventually bind them politically as people increasingly transfer their loyalties from the nation-state to the international state. These are the major assertions of functionalist theory. Its founder, David Mitrany, wrote in 1943 that functionalism proposed "not to squelch but to utilize national selfishness; it asks governments not to give up sovereignty which belongs to their peoples but to acquire benefits for their peoples which were hitherto unavailable, not to reduce their power to defend their citizens but to expand their competence to serve them."[2]

The *United Nations* and European Union (EU), then called the European Community (EC), were cited as models of functionalism. But it soon became evident that they were not living up to their ideals. The United Nations deadlocked on many vital issues during the cold war and remains unwieldy. The EC suffered periodic stagnation and stalemate especially during the 1960s and 1970s. Although *functionalists* insisted that these international organizations would evolve steadily in purpose and power, a new group of theorists called *neofunctionalists* recognized that conflicts between a nation's sovereign instincts and international needs could limit or derail the development of international organizations.

The European Union provides the best illustration of neofunctionalist theory. Its development from a coal and steel organization through a common market, customs union, and, for 11 of its members, currency and central bank union by January 1, 1999, was slow and uncertain. Periods of EU expansion and optimism were followed by retrenchment and pessimism. Neofunctionalists argue that the EU's unsteady but persistent progress toward economic and eventually political union is inevitable—the question is when and how. But just because it happens in Europe does not mean it will happen elsewhere. Every region is unique and thus has its own natural limits or potential for integration.

Although the European Union and the United Nations are the world's best known international organizations, thousands of others evolved in similar ways. They differ greatly, however, according to their respective purposes, powers, and memberships. One distinction is between the over 300 *intergovernmental organizations (IGOs)* such as the United Nations and the EU, and over 26,000 international *nongovernmental organizations (NGOs)* such as Greenpeace, the Red Cross, or Amnesty International. There is a vast budget and personnel range among international organizations. The United Nations has a $15 billion annual budget and 50,000 personnel, whereas the average IGO has a $10 million budget and 200 personnel. In contrast, the average NGO has a budget of $1 million and 10 staff.[3]

There are four types of IGOs.[4] General-membership and general-purpose organizations, such as the *League of Nations* and United Nations, have global duties and many functions, including collective security, economic development, and human rights. General-membership and limited-purpose organizations, such as the World Health Organization (WHO) and the *World Trade Organization (WTO)*, focus on fulfilling one function, such as health or trade. Limited-membership and general-purpose organizations, such as the EU or the *Arab League*, are usually confined to states that share similar values and culture in the same region yet address a range of issues. Finally, limited-membership and limited-purpose organizations, such as the *North Atlantic Treaty Organization (NATO)* or the *North American Free Trade*

international intergovernmental organizations (IGOs) international organizations of government members.

nongovernmental organizations (NGOs) international organizations of members that are not governments.

Association (NAFTA), are regional organizations dedicated to one specific function such as defense or trade.

These differences aside, nearly all international organizations share some characterics. Most have a *secretariat* or full-time administrative staff in a permanent headquarters to implement decisions, regular meetings for representatives of members, a process to make binding decisions, and an executive council. Although membership in all international organizations is voluntary, compliance with the IGO's treaty is legally binding.

International organizations are created by treaty, which means they are derived from and subsequently can be a source for international law. The *International Court of Justice (ICJ)* ruled that international organizations have international legal standing, which "is not the same thing as saying that it is a State, which it certainly is not, or that its legal personality and rights and duties are the same as those of a State. . . . What it does mean is that it is a subject of international law and capable of possessing international rights and duties, and that it has capacity to maintain its rights by bringing international claims."[5] The extent of an international organization's legal standing, however, depends on the treaty creating it. Members have usually delegated some of their sovereign rights to the organization, and thus any organization is only as strong as the powers granted to it.

Of all the international organizations, the most ambitious are those dedicated to collective security. National interests and security are closely linked. Until the late 20th century, most states were trapped in a security dilemma whereby if one state tried to make itself more secure from foreign attack by building up its military, it correspondingly made its neighbors less secure. They, in turn, boosted their militaries to strengthen national security. The result was an arms race, which often ended in war.

In a world knit ever more closely by nuclear, economic, and environmental interdependence, national and international interests and security are increasingly indistinguishable. Virtually all states share a need for peaceful, prosperous relations with each other. Thus security becomes "collective" or grounded on the idea that "the basic requirement for peace is that states have the wit to cooperate in pursuit of national interests that coincide with those of other states rather than the will to compromise national interests that conflict with those of others."[6] In other words, states work with rather than against each other to achieve common interests and overcome common threats. Like the Three Musketeers, the members of an IGO dedicated to collective security promise "All for one and one for all!"

Collective security was the central reason for the creation of the League of Nations and United Nations. But the hopes on which those two organizations were founded eventually turned to disappointment as they were unable to halt international aggression. Although most member-states shared those organizations' ideals, they differed sharply over how, where, and when those ideals should be implemented, while carefully guarding any erosion of their own sovereignty.

How Was Collective Security Negotiated Before *the* United Nations?

Throughout early modern European history (which includes colonial American history), some intellectuals—such as Dante Alighieri, William Penn, Jean-Jacques Rousseau, Immanuel Kant, and Jeremy Bentham, to name the more famous—

called for the creation of an international organization dedicated to maintaining the peace.[7] The 1648 *Peace of Westphalia* was the first attempt of European states to negotiate restrictions on warfare and reasons to go to war. The treaty was negotiated over a three-year period by representatives who met at Osnabruck and Munster in Westphalia. The peace conference became known as the First European Congress. The Treaty of Westphalia's major tenets were reconfirmed at the 1713 Treaty of Utrecht ending the War of the Spanish Succession. Although neither the Westphalia or Utrecht treaties attempted to create a collective security organization, they were important steps in that direction.

Collective security was not addressed until a century later at the 1815 Congress of Vienna, which concluded a quarter-century of almost constant warfare from the French Revolution's outbreak to Napoleon's defeat at Waterloo (1789–1815). The European states represented at the *Congress of Vienna* attempted to undo the territorial and political changes that transformed the continent over the previous blood-soaked 25 years. Following the Congress, Europe's great powers—Britain, Prussia, Russia, Austria, and later France—formed the *Concert of Europe,* a collective security association in which they mobilized their troops against any forces that threatened Europe's peace. This association was largely successful in maintaining peace among the great powers and squashing most revolutionary and independence movements that challenged the political status quo. Between 1815 and 1914, the great powers fought only three wars among themselves: the Crimean War (1856) in which France and Britain fought Russia, the Prussian-Austrian War (1866), and the Franco-Prussian War (1870–1871).

Meanwhile, the first genuine international organizations were created to deal with shared economic interests—the Rhine River Commission (1815), the Danube River Commission (1857), the International Telegraphic Union (1856), Universal Post Union (1874), International Telecommunications Organization (1875), and International Office of Weights and Measures (1875). As functionalism predicts, the success of these organizations encouraged the creation of an even more ambitious one. During the late 19th century, statesmen signed a series of treaties that attempted to limit war's brutality and promote peace. These efforts culminated with the 26 nations represented at the 1899 *Hague Conference* and 44 at the 1907 Hague Conference. Over a score of treaties were negotiated and signed at these two conferences. Most peace conferences were held after wars, but the Hague conferences were notable for being convened when nations were at peace. Hopes were high among participants for taking even more sweeping measures at the next Hague Conference in 1915. Those plans, of course, were disrupted by World War I!

In January 1918, to justify America's participation in World War I, President Woodrow Wilson presented before Congress his Fourteen Points, one of which was the creation of a League of Nations dedicated to collective security. Wilson was not the only collective security advocate. Groups in all the major powers lobbied their governments for some international peace organization. Wilson's dream was partially realized.

In the *Treaty of Versailles* ending World War I were tenets creating the League of Nations and *Permanent Court of International Justice (PCIJ)* in which participants would settle disputes according to international law. The League was organized into an assembly, which included representatives of all members and met for about a month once a year; a nine-member council in which the four great powers were permanently represented while the other seats rotated, and met four times annually; and a secretariat, which administered the organization. Decisions only passed in both the council and assembly with unanimous approval. Forty-five countries were members at the first session in 1920 at its Geneva headquarters; at the League's peak it had 59 members.

The central purpose of the League of Nation was collective security, and the *Covenant* or constitution creating the organization empowered it to maintain the peace in several ways. Covenant Article 12(1) stated that "if there should arise between them [the members] any dispute likely to lead to a rupture, they will submit the matter either to arbitration or judicial settlement or to inquiry by the Council, and they agree in no case to resort to war until three months after the award by the arbitrators or the judicial decision, or the report by the Council." Article 16 declared that "Should any member of the League resort to war . . . it shall . . . be deemed to have committed an act of war against all other members of the League, which hereby undertake immediately to subject it to the severance of all trade or financial relations, the prohibition of all intercourse between the nationals of the Covenant-breaking State and the State, and the prevention of all financial, commercial, or personal intercourse between the nationals of the Covenant-breaking and the nationals of any other State, whether a Member of the League or not." The League council could then recommend that member states contribute military forces to deter the aggressor state.

These seemingly powerful means of managing conflicts were reinforced by the *Kellogg-Briand Pact*, signed on August 27, 1928, by the great powers, including the United States and many other countries. Signatories renounced "the recourse to war for the solution of international controversies, and . . . as an instrument of national policy in their relations with one another . . . the settlement or solution of all disputes or conflicts of whatever nature or of whatever origin they may be . . . shall never be sought except by pacific means." This principle was reaffirmed in the 1933 Rio de Janeiro Anti-War Treaty.

Contrary to popular views, the League of Nations was actually quite successful. It addressed over 60 international problems, and resolved about half. The Permanent Court of International Justice ruled on an additional 60 conflicts. Of those geopolitical disputes in which the League became directly involved, it failed to keep the peace only four times—Japan's invasion of Manchuria, Italy's invasion of Ethiopia, the Chaco War between Paraguay and Bolivia, and the Soviet Union's attack on Finland. Although the League identified aggression in some of these disputes, it never threatened to use military force to deter that aggression, and the economic sanctions it applied were disregarded by most states. Unfortunately, the League of Nations failed to get involved in the worst cases of aggression, such as Japan's invasions of China in 1937 and across Southeast Asia and into the Pacific starting in 1941, or Germany's attack on Poland in 1939 and across Europe starting in 1940. As a result, the League failed to prevent World War II.

Behind these failures were some important weaknesses. First, the United States refused to join. Although President Wilson was the most important force behind the League's creation, because of his conflict with key Senate leaders and America's traditional political isolationism the Senate voted down the Treaty of Versailles, which would have made the United States a member. Without the world's largest industrial power lending its weight to decisions, the League was hobbled from the start. Secondly, members could decide for themselves when a breach of peace occurred and whether or not to impose sanctions against the aggressor. States almost always put their immediate economic needs before more abstract military threats and thus turned a blind eye to aggressors. By 1941, the League of Nations was thoroughly discredited, but visionaries refused to abandon the collective security dream.

How Does *the* United Nations Affect Collective Security Today?

ORIGINS AND POWERS

During World War II, President Franklin Roosevelt became just as determined to create an international organization dedicated to maintaining the peace as Wilson had during World War I. When the United States and Britain signed the *Atlantic Charter* on August 14, 1941, they pledged themselves to, among other things, the creation of a United Nations. At the Moscow Conference of Foreign Ministers in October 1943, the United States and Britain convinced the Soviet Union and China also to support a future collective security organization. At the *Dumbarton Oaks Conference* in August 1944 and the *Yalta Conference* in February 1945, participants debated and began to forge a consensus on U.N. institutions and functions. Perhaps the most significant addition occurred at Yalta. Fearing that the Soviet Union would continually be outvoted by the Western powers, Stalin insisted on veto power for the permanent members. Roosevelt and Churchill agreed. The finishing touches to the U.N. *Charter* or constitution were negotiated by representatives of 51 countries at the San Francisco Conference in April and May 1945. The Charter was signed on June 26, 1945, and on July 28, the Senate overwhelmingly voted 89 to 2 in favor of joining the United Nations.

The Charter's preamble clearly stated the U.N. ideals: peace, human rights, international law, prosperity, and collective security. The U.N. central purpose was collective security. Article 2(3) maintains that all "members shall settle their international disputes by peaceful means in such a manner that international peace and security, and justice, are not endangered." Article 2(4) prohibits "the threat or use of force against the territorial integrity or political independence of another state." Three articles of Chapter VII empower the *Security Council* to uphold the peace. Under Article 39, the Security Council is authorized to determine whether a breach of peace occurred, under Article 41 it can impose economic, transportation, and communications sanctions on the aggressors, and under Article 42, if sanctions under Article 41 fail, it can "take such action by air, sea, or land forces as may be necessary to maintain or restore international peace and security." National sovereignty is upheld by Article 2(7), which states, "Nothing contained in the present Charter shall authorize the United Nations to intervene in matters which are essentially within the domestic jurisdiction of any state or shall require the members to submit such matters to settlement under the present Charter; but this principle shall not prejudice the application of enforcement under Chapter VII." In addition to these powers, Article 43 gives the United Nations international legal personality by empowering it to make treaties with sovereign states. This was reinforced by the favorable International Court of Justice ruling in the 1948 *Reparations for Injury* case, in which the United Nations asked for an opinion as to whether it had the legal personality to take a sovereign state to court and receive compensation for damages.

Cleaning *the* Augean Stables: Can Kofi Annan Reform *the* United Nations?

The United Nations is besieged by a spectrum of critics who advocate everything from its drastic overhaul to its outright abolition. Which criticisms are the most accurate? Nearly all agree that U.N. actions fall far short of its ideals. But is it a bloated, corrupt, inefficient club whose administration costs devour much of its income, as many assert? Some argue that the United States dominates the proceedings and then free-rides on the budget. Others believe it is simply an expensive forum for Third World countries to blame others for their own faults. Are either, both, or neither views valid? If true what should or can be done about those problems?

Since becoming secretary-general in 1996, Ghanaian Kofi Annan and his right-hand man Joseph Connor have initiated a "quiet revolution" that has alleviated many problems. In four years the personnel was cut by 8,800, or 14 percent, largely by attrition. He organized the administration into five "executive groups" organized around key issues that meet regularly as a "cabinet" that targets problems and coordinates policies. A computer system that will boost productivity and further cut personnel is slowly being installed.

What problems linger? Money woes predominate. Not enough money is generated, and too much of the budget funds administrative costs rather than development or peacekeeping needs. The United Nations has yet to fulfill Annan's goal of trimming its administrative costs from 38 percent to 25 percent of the total budget. Then there are the deadbeats, the worst of which is the United States, which in 1999 owed $1.6 billion in dues and $1 billion for peacekeeping, a bill that kept rising. Among Washington's many excuses is that it is forced to pay 25 percent of the U.N. budget even though America's economy is only 20.8 percent of the world's total; it insists that it will pay no more than 20 percent. Should the United States pay less and other countries more? China, for example, pays only 0.9 percent of the U.N. budget but generates 5.3 percent of the world's economy.

Money disputes reflect deeper problems and debates. Washington also refuses to pay up unless the United Nations achieves thorough financial and administrative reforms. The power distribution within the United Nations rankles nearly all members. Germany and Japan argue that their economies are greater than those of France, Great Britain, China, and Russia, yet the latter are four of the Security Council's five permanent members (the other is the United States) with veto power. Third World countries with huge populations—such as India, Nigeria, Brazil, Pakistan, Indonesia, South Africa, and Mexico, to name a few—insist they should be permanent members. Most Third World countries believe the General Assembly should have genuine legislative powers.

How far can Annan's reforms go before they run into political roadblocks? Can those obstacles be hurdled, and if so, how? What would be the ideal U.N. organization, with the most efficient and just distribution of power and duties? Those concerned will debate these and related questions for the foreseeable future.

MEMBERSHIP

In 1999, there were 185 U.N. members. It is expected that U.N. membership will rise steadily into the 21st century as more states win their independence. Membership is "open to all other peace-loving states which accept the obligations contained in the present Charter, and, in the members' judgement, are able and willing to carry out these duties. Some nongovernmental organizations, such as

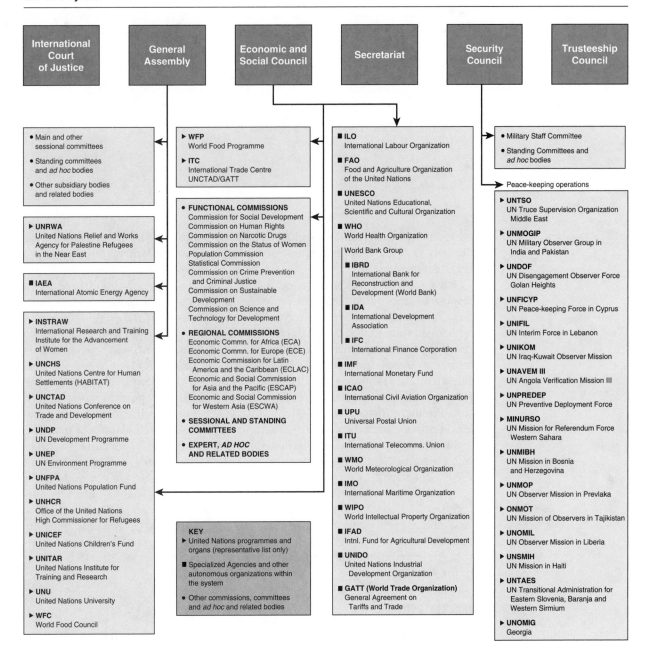

the Palestine Liberation Organization (PLO), enjoy nonvoting observer status. The Security Council and *General Assembly* vote on admission.

The United Nations can vote to suspend the membership of a state that violates the Charter. There are no provisions, however, for voluntary withdrawal from the United Nations, thus avoiding the League of Nations situation where aggressor states such as Japan quit the organization rather than subscribe to its obligations. In 1965, Indonesia announced its withdrawal in protest against Malaysia's (with

Table 7.1 The Distribution of U.N. Dues, 1998–2000

Rank by Contribution	Percentage of Budget	Percentage of World GDP, 1996
1. United States	25.0	20.8
2. Japan	18.0	8.3
3. Germany	9.6	4.8
4. France	6.5	3.5
5. Italy	5.4	3.2
6. Britain	5.1	3.3
7. Russia	2.9	1.7
8. Canada	2.8	1.8

which it had a territorial dispute) election as a nonpermanent member of the Security Council. Indonesia later rejoined the United Nations without having to seek readmission.

For over two decades following the Chinese revolution in 1949, there was a dispute in the United Nations over which government should represent China, the Communist party, which controlled the mainland, or the Nationalist party, which had retreated to the island of Taiwan after losing a civil war. China joined the United Nations under the Nationalist party. The United States vetoed all attempts to unseat Taiwan until 1972, when the United Nations voted to expel Taiwan and seat China. Until that year Washington clung to the position that the Nationalist party was China's legitimate government and thus deserved a U.N. seat. President Richard Nixon changed American policy to the more realistic and legal position that accepted the Communist party as China's actual government.

Members pay dues based on a complicated "ability to pay" formula that takes into account GNP and population. In 1999, the United States paid 25.0 percent of the budget, Japan 15.6 percent, Germany 9.1 percent, France 6.4 percent, Britain 5.3 percent, Italy 5.3 percent, Russia 4.3 percent, and Canada 3.1 percent, or altogether 74.1 percent of the budget while casting only 4.3 percent of the General Assembly. Seventy-nine countries pay the minimum of 0.01 percent, and nine countries 0.02 percent. Those countries that pay the minimum 0.01 percent assessment or less contribute less than 1 percent of the U.N. budget but cast 49.0 percent of the General Assembly votes.

INSTITUTIONS

The Security Council is the U.N. executive branch, with the power to make decisions legally binding on the entire United Nations. Of its 15 members, 5—the United States, Russia, China, Great Britain, and France—are permanent and have veto power on nonprocedural issues, and the other 10 are elected for two-year terms by the General Assembly. In practice there is a quota system for the nonpermanent members—five come from Africa and Asia, two from Latin America, one from eastern Europe, and two from the advanced industrial countries. The post of president of the Security Council is held for a month and rotated among the members.

A measure passes the Security Council with a majority of nine or more votes, unless of course it is vetoed by a permanent member. The pattern of the 264 vetoes cast from 1946 to 1989 changed significantly.[8] The United States did not cast a veto until 1970, the first of 20 during the 1970s, followed by 46 between 1980 and 1989, for a total of 66. In contrast, the Soviet Union cast 92 vetoes between 1945 and 1960, 13 in the 1960s, 9 in the 1970s, and only 4 between 1980 and 1989, for a total of 118. Of the other members, Great Britain cast 26, France 16, and China 3, of which 22 British, 12 French, and 2 Chinese vetoes were after 1971.

There are two significant reasons for this shift in the balance of vetoes. During the first decade, Moscow often used its veto to block the admission of states with pro-Western governments. In 1956, Washington and Moscow agreed not to block each other's allies from membership, so Soviet vetoes fell sharply after that time. The shift in vetoes also reflects changes in the General Assembly's composition. Up through the 1960s, most of the General Assembly members voted with the United States on most issues, and Moscow vetoed many resolutions that seemed to challenge its interests. The proliferation of newly independent states during the 1960s and 1970s, many of them pro-Soviet, anti-Israel, and committed to a *new international economic order (NIEO)* involving a redistribution of global wealth, put the United States on the defensive, leading Washington, London, and Paris to increasingly use their veto power. Since the cold war's end, vetoes have become rare.

new international economic order (NIEO) espoused by the nonaligned movement and based on the idea of new trade, investment, and aid relations between the **First** and **Third Worlds** in order for the latter to accrue more benefit.

Each member has one vote in the General Assembly, which has the power to study, debate, and decide any issue as well as approve the annual budget. Decisions, however, are binding only if they achieve a two-thirds majority and are confined to addressing the administration of the United Nations. The General Assembly can issue "declarations" or broad statements of principle such as its 1948 Universal Declaration on Human Rights, and "resolutions" or policy recommendations for specific issues. It can also convene "special sessions" to address a particular issue such as disarmament or Namibia; "conferences," which deal with broader issues such as women's rights or population; and "conventions," which are treaties among U.N. members or between the United Nations and other states. Despite these limited powers, General Assembly resolutions do often represent global opinion and thus carry heavy political pressure. They may also identify international customs or principles that can be codified as law.

There has been a significant shift in the power balance within the General Assembly between 1945 and 2000. In 1945, of the 51 members, 44 percent were from the Western bloc, 12 percent from the Soviet bloc, 16 percent from Asia and the Pacific, 8 percent from Africa, and 20 percent from Latin America. In 1999, only 14 percent of the U.N. membership was from the Western bloc, 32 percent from Asia and the Pacific, 33 percent from Africa, and 21 percent from Latin America, and the Soviet bloc had disappeared. Today the most important voting bloc is the 132-member Group of 77, composed of the poorer countries, which pressure the wealthier countries on various issues.

The voting records of the United States and the Soviet Union in the General Assembly paralleled their veto record in the Security Council, in which at first it was the United States that favored resolutions and the Soviet Union that voted no until gradually they reversed themselves. In 1986, Washington and Moscow voted no on 81 percent and 8 percent, respectively, of the resolutions. In 1989, the United States voted with the majority on only 16.9 percent of all resolutions, and even with the European Community only 59.5 percent and NATO 57.3 percent of the time, in contrast to the period between 1945 and 1950 when the United States voted with the majority 71 percent of the time. Most American

Kofi Annan, the U.N. secretary-general, has few powers to realize great duties. He not only manages the U.N. administration but often tries to negotiate solutions to geopolitical and humanitarian conflicts around the world. The real power in the United Nations is in the Security Council. Should the secretary-general have more power? Is the U.N. organization, distribution of powers, and budget adequate to realize the goals of the United Nations?

Jason Szenes/Corbis Sygma

vetoes and negative votes involve resolutions that condemn Israeli aggression or human rights abuses.[9]

The Secretariat is the U.N. administration. In 1998, the Secretariat included 8,850 personnel, down from 12,000 in 1985. The Secretariat supervises all the scores of U.N. agencies, whose personnel number 51,484. The U.N. operating and peacekeeping budgets amounted to $2.583 billion in fiscal 1999. The Secretariat is headed by the *secretary-general,* who is nominated by the Security Council and elected by the General Assembly for a five-year renewable term. The secretary-general's role is to administer rather than lead the United Nations, and has only the power to persuade. There have been seven U.N. secretaries-general, all from neutral or nonaligned states: Trygve Lie of Norway (1946–1952), Dag Hammarskjöld of Sweden (1953–1961), U Thant of Burma (1961–1971), Kurt Waldheim of Austria (1972–1982), Javier Perez de Cuellar of Peru (1983–1991), Boutros Boutros-Ghali of Egypt (1992–1997), and Kofi Annan of Ghana (1997–present).

No secretary-general before or since Hammarskjöld has been as active in confronting international problems. Hammarskjöld saw crisis management as his primary role. In 1960, he issued his policy of "preventive diplomacy" for those cases "where the original conflict may be said either to be the result of, or to imply risks for, the creation of a power vacuum between the main blocs. Preventive action . . . must . . . aim at filling the vacuum so that it will not provoke action from any of the major parties . . . [t]he United Nations enters the picture on the basis of its noncommitment to any power bloc . . . to provide . . . a guarantee in relation to all parties against initiatives from others." Hammarskjöld died in a plane crash in 1961, and his successors have largely concerned themselves with administration rather than policy. Kofi Annan, the most recent secretary-general, did play a decisive role in defusing a crisis between the United States, the Security Council, and Iraq in 1998.

There are three other, less prominent U.N. organizations. The 54-member Economic and Social Council (ECOSOC) oversees the dozens of U.N. agencies, organizes conferences, and dispenses funds; members serve for three-year terms. The International Court of Justice (ICJ) includes 15 judges who serve nine years and hear cases referred to the court from any state or U.N. organization. Although the ICJ's decisions are binding, its jurisdiction is not. The five-member Trusteeship Council oversaw those states that were given territories to manage for eventual independence. But with all those territories now independent, this council no longer functions.

These three organizations address a range of issues including decolonization, human rights, the environment, health, poverty, law of the sea, natural disasters, women's equality, trade, investments, agriculture and food, and so on. One important U.N. contribution is simply the gathering of information on the socioeconomic conditions of every country, which helps identify problems and means of alleviating them. Many of these issues boil down to one word—*development*. Here ECOSOC takes the lead by coordinating policies implemented by 16 affiliated organizations and consulting with over 300 NGOs, of which 35 are designated Category I, which can contribute issues to ECOSOC's agenda.

COLLECTIVE SECURITY AND PEACEKEEPING

Collective security and *peacekeeping* differ. Peacekeepers are invited by the warring sides to help keep the peace after a cease-fire has occurred. Collective security is the use of force against an aggressing state or alliance.

The United Nations has no troops of its own. Whenever the Security Council identifies a peacekeeping or collective security mission, it determines the mission's strength and time frame, then calls for volunteers. Interested nations contribute whatever troops and equipment they wish. Although the Security Council remains in operational command, the troops remain in their own national units and uniforms. For a peacekeeping mission, the soldiers wear blue helmets or berets and U.N. patches, are lightly armed, and fire only in self-defense; U.N. observers and police are usually unarmed. In a collective security mission, the security council deputizes a country (the United States in Korea and the Persian Gulf), which forms a "coalition of the willing" or existing alliance (NATO in Yugoslavia), which then musters the resources of its own members. Under an "enforcement" action, the Security Council authorizes the coalition to use "all necessary means" to fulfill its resolutions. In either a peacekeeping or collective security mission, the

collective security the means by which a community of nations attempts to maintain the peace through negotiation or the threat of **sanctions** against international aggressors.

peacekeeping occurs when an international military force helps maintain a peace between two or more belligerents.

When Peacekeeping Becomes War Making: Somalia *and* Bosnia

Not all peacekeeping missions have been peaceful. The effort in Somalia (1992–1993) failed when the peacekeepers abandoned their neutrality and took sides in the conflict by trying to capture the warlord Mohammed Aidid. The result was a disaster as a score of American Rangers and several hundred Somalis were killed in the botched operation. The televised image of a dead, naked, bloating U.S. Ranger being dragged by a jubilant mob through the streets of Mogadishu caused American support for the operation to plummet. Several weeks later the U.N. peacekeeping force in Somalia was withdrawn as the country once again dissolved into civil war.

A peacekeeping mission to Bosnia turned deadly in 1995. When the Serbs violated the demarcation zone, the United States and other NATO members bombed those positions. The Serbs retaliated by kidnapping peacekeeper soldiers and chaining them to the fences of possible bomb sites. The Security Council backed down, withdrew its peacekeepers from Bosnia, and turned the operation over to NATO. President Clinton was able to broker a peace treaty among the Serbs, Muslims, and Croats fighting within Bosnia. U.N. peacekeepers then returned to Bosnia to help uphold the peace treaty.

United States compensates each contributing government for $1,000 a month for each soldier. The government then pays its own troops. Because that salary often far exceeds what the troops would receive in most countries, volunteers are not lacking. By contributing to missions, poorer countries receive compensation and combat conditions that they could not otherwise afford.

U.N. peacekeeping forces can be dispatched only after three conditions have been met: All parties in the conflict agree to accept U.N. forces, the Security Council and General Assembly agree to send them, and members agree to provide troops for the operation. The Charter does not explicitly empower the United Nations to dispatch peacekeeping forces. The practice was inspired by Secretary-General Hammarskjöld's concept of "preventive diplomacy." A mission involves sending military or police into a country or region to separate and cool down enemies to prevent more bloodshed. Other peacekeeping actions can include disarming opponents, clearing landmines, monitoring elections, training military and police training, providing security for the distribution of humanitarian aid, demarcating boundaries, aiding and repatriating refugees, reconstructing a war-shattered country, running a government, promoting human rights, and monitoring the withdrawal of foreign troops.

Through 1999, the United Nations dispatched 39 armed peacekeeping forces and 12 unarmed military observer missions, which deployed more than 750,000 troops or police from 76 countries; by August 1998, 1,581 had died while performing U.N. duties. Cold war politics limited the number of peacekeeping missions to 13 between 1945 and 1988. Since 1988 the United Nations has mounted 36 new missions. During 1994 and 1995, the number of missions and operational costs peaked at 18 and $3 billion, respectively. The number of personnel deployed reached its height at 78,744 in 1993. In the first half of 2000 there were 17 missions, which together annually cost $1 billion.

Table 7.2 U.N. Peacekeeping Missions, to Year 2000

Africa
1. Central African Republic (MIMURCA): April 1998 to present.
2. Sierra Leone (UNAMSIL): July 1998.
3. Western Sahara (MINURSO): April 1991 to present.
4. Democratic Republic of the Congo (MONUC): November 1999 to present.

Americas
5. Haiti (MIPONUH): December 1997 to present.

Asia
6. East Timor (UNTAET): October 1999 to present.
7. India/Pakistan (UNMOGIP): January 1949 to present.
8. Tajikistan (UNMOT): December 1994 to present.

Europe
9. Bosnia and Herzegovina (UNMIBH): December 1995 to present.
10. Croatia (UNMOP): January 1996 to present.
11. Cyprus (UNFICYP): March 1964 to present.
12. Kosovo (UNMIK): June 1999 to present.
13. Georgia (UNOMIG): August 1993 to present.

Middle East
14. Golan Heights (UNDOF): June 1974 to present.
15. Iraq/Kuwait (UNIKOM): April 1991 to present.
16. Lebanon (UNIFIL): March 1978 to present.
17. Middle East (UNTSO): June 1948 to present.

Until Yugoslavia collapsed into civil war during the 1990s, most peacekeeping missions went to the Middle East. As early as 1948, the Security Council created the U.N. Truce Supervision Organization (UNTSO) to monitor the cease-fire between the Arab states and Israel, and in 1958, a U.N. Observer Group was set up in Lebanon. The first formal peacekeeping venture was the creation of the U.N. Emergency Force (UNEF I) in 1956, which separated Egyptian and Israeli forces in the Sinai peninsula for the next decade. UNEF I was set up following the 1956 war, which broke out when Israel, Britain, and France attacked Egypt because President Nasser nationalized the Suez Canal. The 1967 war occurred when Nasser demanded that the UNEF withdraw from the Sinai and threatened to attack Israel. UNEF II was established in the Sinai and the Golan Heights following the 1973 war and remains there today. In 1978, the U.N. Interim Force in Lebanon (UNIFIL) was created to separate Israeli and PLO forces in southern Lebanon and continues to patrol the region. U.N. missions have been active elsewhere in the Middle East. In 1988, the United Nations helped negotiate an end to the Iraq–Iran War and dispatched 350 troops to monitor the cease-fire. That same year, U.N. observer teams were sent to Kabul and Islamabad to observe the Soviet withdrawal from Afghanistan and the return of Afghan refugees. The U.N. peacekeeping missions have been largely successful in managing conflicts that might well have broken into war.

Collective security can occur when peacekeeping fails. Under collective security, the United Nations goes to war against an aggressive state or alliance. By that definition collective security is as rare as peacekeeping has become common. The United Nations has never collectively gone to war. What the U.N. Security Council has done is to authorize others to go to war on its behalf. That has happened three times—Korea (1950–1953), Iraq (1990–1991), and Yugoslavia (1999). When communist North Korea attacked South Korea, the Security Council was only able to intervene because the Soviet Union was boycotting the United Nations in protest that the nationalist government still held China's seat after the communists won their civil war. The Persian Gulf and Kosovo interventions occurred after the cold war ended and only after those who favored it engaged in extensive diplomacy to convince those who were reluctant to do so. As President Bush said before the General Assembly in October 1990, "This is a new and different world. Not since 1945 have we seen the real possibility of using the United Nations as it was designed, as a center for international collective security."[10]

peacemaking occurs when an international military force imposes peace by fighting one or more belligerents.

Peacemaking involves the United Nations acting as an intermediary in negotiations over a conflict. Between 1945 and 1984, 137 of 319 international conflicts were referred to the United Nations for settlement. The United Nations succeeded in alleviating 53 percent and settling 25 percent of these conflicts.[11] The different techniques U.N. diplomats use to help make peace include (1) *inquiry:* investigating a conflict and publishing a neutral account; (2) *good offices:* providing a neutral setting in which opponents can negotiate; (3) *mediation:* actively suggesting ways the opponents can resolve their conflict; (4) *arbitration:* proposing a systematic solution to the conflict; and (5) *adjudication:* having the International Court of Justice rule on the conflict.

The United Nations might have settled more conflicts during that time but for the cold war. After 1945, the United States and Soviet Union manipulated or joined many international and internal conflicts, and thus would veto each others' attempts to secure U.N. intervention. Vetoes were issued in 220 or 35 percent of the 642 Security Council resolutions between 1946 and 1990.[12] Collective security depends on more than an international organization and ideals. The Security Council had to be united ideologically and politically before the United Nations could live up to its ideals. The collapse of communism and the Soviet empire made this unity possible.

A related reason was the existence of the NATO and Warsaw Pact alliances dedicated to defeating the other should war break out. Alliances and collective security are incompatible. Collective security can only work if states agree to resist aggression no matter who commits. If a state's alliance commits aggression, that state would be more likely to fulfill its alliance rather than collective security duties. These problems diminished with the dissolution of the Warsaw Pact in 1991 and NATO's difficulty in justifying its own continued existence in the post–cold-war era.

And then there is the difficulty in defining aggression itself. Although U.N. Charter Article 2 clearly prohibits the use of force, there are some exceptions. Under Article 51, every sovereign state has "the inherent right of individual or collective self-defense if an armed attack occurs." States that attack other states try to justify their actions by claiming "self-defense." For example, was the United States the aggressor when it invaded Grenada in 1983 or Panama in 1990? Many argue that those invasions were clear examples of aggression, but the White House attempted to legally justify them by claiming that the United States was simply responding defensively to aggressive threats by the Grenadan and

The U.N. Security Council has 15 members, 5 of which are permanent with veto powers, and the other 10 are elected by the General Assembly for two-year terms. The permanent members—the United States, Russia, Britain, France, and China—were World War II's victors. The global distribution of power has shifted dramatically since then. The United States is the world's sole superpower. Russia's empire and economy has collapsed. Japan and Germany surpassed Britain and France in economic power decades ago. China's economic power has been expanding for two decades. Countries such as Brazil, Mexico, Argentina, India, Pakistan, Indonesia, and Nigeria are demanding a voice in the United Nations appropriate to the size of their populations and economies, including permanent Security Council seats. What power should the Security Council hold, and how should it be distributed among its members in a way that balances efficiency and fairness?

AP/Wide World Photos

Panamanian governments. Critics scoffed at the notion that Grenada's several hundred troops or Panama's several thousand could pose any threat to anyone, let alone a superpower such as the United States.

The global power imbalance allows the most powerful states to act with impunity. Although most states may well have agreed that the Soviet Union was the aggressor in Hungary in 1956, Czechoslovakia in 1968, and Afghanistan in 1979, they did not attempt to sanction the Soviet Union for its actions, because they lacked the political and military power to do so. However, the power balance between the United States and Soviet Union prevented them from acting decisively against each other. They have tolerated each other's aggression in their respective *spheres of influence* because they knew that to challenge those actions could result in World War III.

sphere of influence a region in which a **great power** declares that it will not tolerate any outside interference while reserving for itself the right to intervene.

The biggest constraint on an expansion of U.N. peacekeeping missions may be financial rather than political. Although most nations agree in principle to the missions, few willingly pay their share. In 1999, U.N. members were $1.1 billion in arrears to the total peacekeeping budget.

Given these constraints, the United Nations successfully managed conflict when (1) the issue did not involve the superpowers or the East–West conflict; (2) Washington, Moscow, and the Security Council agreed on how to resolve the issue; (3) the issue involved fighting and was in danger of spreading beyond the states involved; (4) the issue involved decolonization and small or medium-sized states; and (5) the issue was identified as a threat to peace by the secretary-general, who actively lobbied the United Nations to overcome it.[13]

EVALUATION

How effective has the United Nations been? As John Kennedy once said, the United Nations "is our last hope in an age where the instruments of war have far outpaced the instruments of peace." Any evaluation of U.N. effectiveness must first address its major role—that of keeping the peace. There it was hoped that the United Nations would succeed where the League failed. Since 1945, there has been no third world war and no use of nuclear weapons. What role, if any, the United Nations played in keeping the peace between the superpowers is impossible to say. U.N. efforts have been important and often decisive in hundreds of other conflicts, alleviating about half of all disputes brought before it and outright settling a quarter. Between 1945 and 1999, the United Nations dispatched 27 collective security and peacekeeping forces, using troops or police from 75 countries. Clearly, if the United Nations had never existed, international conflicts would most likely have been much more frequent and bloody.

Although the United Nations was founded on the collective security ideal, it was structured to preserve sovereignty and national interests, particularly that of the great powers. By concentrating power in the Security Council, the architects hoped to avoid the inevitable indecision of a General Assembly of all members. Few if any states would consider threatening the peace if they faced the combined military forces of the five great powers, plus any other forces contributed by other U.N. members. It was not anticipated, however, that given the five great powers' conflicting interests and ideologies, there was just as much chance of stalemate in the Security Council as in the General Assembly. In fact, granting veto power to each of the five not only virtually ensured deadlock, it allowed them even more leeway to act as they wished in the international system. Although the five were empowered to uphold international law, they themselves could follow or break it as they wished. The power balance and spheres of influence, not the law, constrained their behavior.

Even when a consensus emerges, the United Nations is hampered by financial constraints. Virtually everyone favors peace; few willingly pay for it. By 1999, U.N. members owed $3.5 billion, of which $2.4 billion was for regular dues and $1.1 billion for peacekeeping forces. The United States was the biggest deadbeat, owing $1.6 billion in dues and $1 billion for peacekeeping. Many American politicians and citizens justify this debt by arguing that their country's share and U.N. inefficiencies are too great. John Rouke counters by arguing that the 1989 U.N. budget of $1.79 billion was only one-half the cost of building one American aircraft carrier, or .00179 of the world's $1 trillion in military expenditures, an amount that could finance the United Nations for 559 years! Given the limited U.N. resources and the vast array of problems it faces, it has been remarkably successful in many areas.[14] Critics of Washington's refusal to pay charge it with "representation without taxation," a twist on the slogan of the American Revolution.

The United Nations has many critics. During the 1980s the United States led in demanding reforms of many inefficient, wasteful, and anti-Western practices. In 1983, the United States and Britain withdrew their membership and funding

Lender *of* Last Resort: *The* IMF

Most U.N. agencies and their affiliates assist global economic development and integration. The most important affiliated developmental organizations are the *International Monetary Fund (IMF)*, which lends governments money to cover payment deficits and manage currency fluctuations in return for those recipients reforming their economies, and the International Bank for Reconstruction and Development (IBRD, *World Bank*), which funds specific development projects.

Poor countries have a love/hate relationship with the IMF, which will lend them money when no one else will, but for a price. The loans themselves are actually much cheaper than market rates. But the conditions for the loan exact short-term economic and political costs that can be excruciatingly painful. Recipient governments must reform their economies by cutting their bloated budgets, staff, subsidies, and welfare; devaluing their currencies, which raises prices; and opening their markets further to international trade. Although these reforms might strengthen that economy in the long run, they often cause "IMF riots" as people lose their jobs and inflation eats away incomes. Ideally the recipients wisely invest the IMF loan in infrastructure and industries that expand the economy. Perhaps more often than not, they don't do so.

How does the IMF decide the recipient, amount, and condition of its loans? The IMF headquarters are in Washington, D.C. By 1999 182 members had contributed money to the IMF and were entitled to take a loan when their economies faltered. Voting rights are proportionate to the amount of the total a member contributes. The 24-member interim committee, is composed of the finance minister or central bank presidents of those states that contribute the most money and meets twice a year to set the IMF's broad policies. The IMF secretariat or bureaucracy then implements those policies.

from the U.N. Educational, Scientific, and Cultural Organization (UNESCO), charging it with a persistent anti-Western bias and mismanagement of funds. In 1985, Congress passed a law threatening to cut American contributions by 20 percent unless the United Nations undertook reforms and gave Washington a say in budget matters equal to its 25 percent contribution. In 1987, Washington began cutting back its membership dues until it owed over $500 million by 1993. This pressure partially worked. The United Nations agreed to cut its staff by 15 percent, allowed all budgetary decisions to be approved unanimously, toned down some of the anti-Western rhetoric, and revamped UNESCO.

Many criticize the "one state, one vote" U.N. system, which is based on the concept of the sovereign equality of states. There are some obvious flaws in this system. A two-thirds majority in the General Assembly can be assembled by states whose combined population is less than 8 percent of the world's total. Some states argue that it is ridiculous that tiny states such as Nauru (7,000) should have the same voting weight as China (1.2 billion), and advocate that voting power should be proportional to a state's population. The smaller states are naturally opposed to such a change. Some Americans argue that voting power in the United

Nations should be based on one's financial contributions. The combined contributions of over 80 members make up less than 1 percent of the total budget. Because the United States contributes 25 percent of the U.N. budget, it should enjoy 25 percent of the votes. Virtually all other U.N. members, however, object to basing voting on budget contributions.

The five permanent Security Council members are criticized for their monopoly of power. Some propose abolishing not just the veto power but the entire notion of "permanent members." All Security Council members would be elected by the General Assembly. Other proposals would make Japan, Germany, Nigeria, India, and Brazil permanent members with veto power, which would only make stalemates more likely. To these proposals, some counter that although the veto has created deadlock on hundreds of issues, it has also preserved the Security Council—without veto power, any of the permanent members, particularly the Soviet Union, might well have walked out if a vote had severely affected its national interests.

U.N. politics have always mirrored global politics. The cold war and north–south standoffs limited U.N. ability to deal decisively with international problems for much of the first 45 years. The cold war is now over and the emergence of newly industrializing countries has diluted the rancor between the world's rich and poor countries. Cooperation among the permanent Security Council members allows the United Nations to embark decisively on peacekeeping and humanitarian missions that formerly would have been unlikely.

The United Nations provides the world's poorest and least populated states with a forum in which to cite their grievances and proposals. The Third World has attempted to use the U.N. General Assembly as a lawmaking body. Although General Assembly resolutions are not binding, they can create new customs that eventually become the basis of treaties. The Third World attempts during the 1970s to create a NIEO and during the 1980s and 1990s to implement a new world information order (NWIO) involved a vastly different legal view of property and the mass media from the dominant western one. Many Third World states believe a double standard governs the application of international law, in which the more powerful states can literally get away with murder and other violations while weaker states are forced to comply. Even if many governments believe their interests are not being met, the United Nations allows communication and debate of issues sometimes not possible elsewhere. For example, although the United States does not have diplomatic relations with the Palestine Liberation Organization (PLO), it can meet with its representatives at the United Nations.

The United Nations will continue to expand its duties and power. A consensus is building within the United Nations that sovereignty is no longer sacrosanct, and can be set aside when a government violates human rights and self-determination. For example, in December 1992 alone, the U.N. General Assembly voted overwhelmingly to rebuke Cuba, Sudan, Serbia, Iraq, Iran, and Myanmar for widespread human rights abuses. U.N. intervention is also justified when a government dissolves into anarchy and civil war, as in Cambodia, Somalia, and Bosnia. There is increasing support in favor of reviving the old U.N. trusteeship system in which unstable countries are administered until they become capable of self-rule. Many Third World countries, however, insist that U.N. calls for human rights, self-determination, and trusteeship are neocolonial attacks on their rights as sovereign states.

In all, the United Nations has aided peacekeeping and development in many countries and regions around the world. The cold war's end freed the United Nations from some of the shackles that restrained its peacekeeping. Nonetheless the United Nations continues to play largely a secondary role in international relations. Will the United Nations expand its duties and powers in the coming decades? Could it ever become the world government that inspires hope in some people and provokes dread in others? That is unlikely, given the interrelated forces of political opposition and financial restrictions.

International Intergovernmental Organizations (IGOs)

The number and type of international intergovernmental organizations (IGOs) expanded steadily during the 20th century, from about 50 in 1914 to 90 in 1935 and over 300 with over 100,000 employees today. Interdependence is the most important reason. New issues demand new international organizations to manage them. The failure of the nation-state system to keep the peace and the devastation of the two world wars stimulated the rapid expansion of international organizations to help resolve conflicts. After World War II, the emergence of low-cost jet travel and instantaneous communications further developed the global political economy and the organizations that manage it.

Although the *European Union (EU)* has been by far the most successful regional international organization, several others have also recorded achievements. The *Organization of Petroleum Exporting Countries (OPEC)* nationalized oil production and increased prices in the 1970s and more recently in 1999 was able to double oil prices. Several regional organizations including the *Organization of American States (OAS)*, the *Organization for African Unity (OAU)*, the Council for Europe, the Association of Southeast Asian Nations (ASEAN), and the Arab League are dedicated to regional collective security and development. However, they were no more successful than the United Nations in fulfilling their mission. Between 1945 and 1984, these organizations addressed 86 of 317 international conflicts, alleviated 56 percent, and settled 26 percent.[15]

Although the successes were relatively few, they were notable. In 1979, the Arab League negotiated the end of fighting between North and South Yemen, and in May 1990 their unification into one country. In 1988, the OAU negotiated a peace agreement between Chad and Libya, and in 1992 helped end a 15-year civil war in Angola. In 1996, the Economic Community of West African States (ECOWAS) deployed an 8,000-man peacekeeping force composed of troops from Nigeria, Ghana, Guinea, and Sierra Leone to quell a civil war in Liberia. Throughout the 1980s and into the 1990s, the United Nations and ASEAN worked diligently to first negotiate the withdrawal of Vietnamese troops from Cambodia and the end of Cambodia's civil war.

Alliances differ from collective security. Although everyone is encouraged to become a member of a global or regional collective security organization, alliances are exclusive organizations that mobilize against an enemy country or alliance. The North Atlantic Treaty Organization (NATO) remains the world's most powerful regional security organization, having seen the collapse of its rival, the Warsaw Pact nations in 1992.

Who's Heard *of* SADC?

The European Union is a household word, but how many people have heard of the Southern African Development Community (SADC)? It was created in 1980 not to promote integration but independence. What did the founders want to escape? South Africa's relatively prosperous, advanced economy dominated the continent's southern cone. Although the region's countries gained desperately needed wealth by trading with South Africa, they objected to Pretoria's apartheid system by which the white minority discriminated against blacks and others.

But SADC foundered. Those poverty-stricken countries could not forge with one another the natural ties with South Africa they tried to sever. When South Africa abandoned apartheid in 1994, SADC welcomed it as its newest member. The following year SADC added geopolitical to developmental goals when it began trying to mediate African international and civil wars. But here too, the 14-member SADC faltered. South Africa's President Nelson Mandela and Zimbabwe's President Robert Mugabe were bitter rivals for SADC's leadership. Mandela opposed and Mugabe favored intervention in Congo's war.

That split between two ambitious leaders threatened to break up SADC. However, Mugabe has since agreed to consult South Africa's new president Thabo Mbeki and other SADC leaders to restrain his aggressive regional foreign policy.

Table 7.3 **Southern African Development Community, 1996**

	Population in Millions	GNP in Billions
South Africa	37.20	$127.10
Angola	11.10	$10.67
Zimbabwe	11.80	$8.63
Tanzania	30.60	$5.17
Botswana	1.48	$4.40
Mauritius	1.14	$4.02
Zambia	9.65	$3.30
Namibia	1.62	$3.23
Malawi	10.14	$2.20
Congo	45.40	$1.73
Mozambique	18.10	$1.71
Swaziland	0.94	$1.21
Lesotho	2.11	$0.82
Seychelles	0.08	$0.51

Source: World Bank 2000.

Inspired by the European Union's success, countries in several regions have tried to reduce economic barriers among themselves, including most notably the North American Free Trade Association (NAFTA) of the United States, Canada, and Mexico; the Andean Group of Venezuela, Columbia, Ecuador, Peru, and Bolivia; the Southern Common Market (Mercosur) of Brazil, Argentina, Uruguay, and Paraguay; the Central American Common Market (CACM) of Guatemala, Honduras, El Salvador, Costa Rica, and Nicaragua; the Economic Community of West Africa (ECOWAS); the Southern African Development Community (SADC); the Association of Southeast Asian Nations (ASEAN); the South Pacific Forum

(CARICOB); and the Asia-Pacific Economic Cooperation (APEC). All those regional economic organizations except NAFTA have fallen short of creating true common markets.

The regional NGOs play varying roles in the duties they have accepted. It is not surprising that the two organizations that have scored the greatest economic accomplishments—the EU and, to a far lesser extent, NAFTA—are largely composed of the wealthiest states. With more diversified economies, those members could afford to take a chance on economic union. With their much less diversified and poorer economies, the members of other regional organizations have much more to lose from freer trade. With its members from around the world united by export of one product—oil—OPEC is an anomaly among the international economic organizations. OPEC's ability to realize its goals has risen and fallen sharply over time. Ultimately its success rests on how far its members use their oil wealth to diversify their economies and develop a mass middle class. So far none have achieved that. As for peacekeeping, the regional organizations also have very mixed records, with ECOWAS achieving the most. As for the standoff between NATO and the Warsaw Pact, both succeeded in the sense that World War III did not explode. What role they played in deterring war is difficult to say. In all, international regional organizations play a constructive, largely secondary, but growing role in international relations.

International Nongovernmental Organizations (NGOs)

Nongovernmental organizations (NGOs) are all those groups with international interests. There are over 26,000 NGOs in the world today, up from 6,000 a decade earlier in 1990, with more being created daily, and include a vast range of political, economic, social, health, business, humanitarian, environmental, religious, and other concerns. The membership of many NGOs has expanded just as quickly. The Sierra Club's membership, for example, soared from 181,000 in 1980 to 570,000 today, the Worldwide Fund for Nature even faster—from 575,000 in 1985 to 5 million by 2000. NGOs operate in the global political system just like interest groups in a national political system, lobbying the powerful to advance their interests, rallying supporters and appealing to others via mass communications and the news media, and gathering and releasing information that promotes their cause.

Why have NGOs proliferated so quickly and have become so powerful in influencing international relations? Globalization both shapes and is shaped by NGOs. The Internet revolution allows like-minded individuals and groups to communicate instantly with one another. Countless more people join or form groups every day and promote their interests with web pages and email. In controversies an *NGO swarm* can assemble: Like a disturbed nest of angry bees, NGOs can swarm around the governments, corporations, or IGOs involved in a controversy, stinging their opponents with protests and adverse information while rallying the mass media to expose the situation to the general public. These swarms have no central leadership but can be initiated by a few taps on the keyboard by a concerned individual or group with inflammatory information and ideas.

The WTO's November 1999 Seattle meeting was disrupted by just such an NGO swarm. For months before the meeting, concerned labor, environmental, human rights, and other groups had exchanged information and plotted strategy. When the meeting opened, representatives of those groups were in Seattle lobbying and protesting those delegates, and appealing to the world via CNN and other 24-hour-a-day global news organizations. That swarm exacerbated existing sharp differences among countries within the WTO. The result was the deadlock and breakup of the WTO meeting. In 2000 another NGO swarm mobilized to resist China's proposed membership in the WTO.

As within countries, international economic interest groups have the greatest intrinsic power among NGOs to assert their interests. The International Chamber of Commerce lobbies governments to ensure favorable business environments. The International Federation of Airline Pilots (IFAP) boycotts flights to those countries that harbor skyjackers. In 1968, an IFAP boycott pressured Algeria to quickly end the detention of an El Al plane that had been skyjacked. The International Council of Scientific Unions (ICSU) is the world's foremost group lobbying for greater scientific cooperation and openness.

International groups focusing on nuclear proliferation issues have been vocal in lobbying for their goals. The Committee for Nuclear Disarmament (CND) and Greenpeace played a significant role in mobilizing antinuclear support throughout the 1980s. In 1985, French government agents exploded a bomb on Greenpeace's ship, the *Rainbow Warrior,* which was about to monitor French nuclear testing in the Pacific. The *Rainbow Warrior* sank, and a Greenpeace volunteer was killed. When the agents were caught and their plot revealed, French atmospheric nuclear testing policies became thoroughly discredited and Paris eventually agreed to hold the tests underground.

Human rights, humanitarian, and environmental organizations have become increasingly potent in pressing their interests. By lobbying and disseminating information, Amnesty International, Freedom House, America's Watch, Asia Watch, and other international organizations have been effective in alleviating human rights abuses in many countries. The International Red Cross, Oxfam, CARE, Medicins Sans Frontieres, the Ford Foundation, and the Rockefeller Foundation are some leading humanitarian groups committed to helping the victims of wars, natural disasters, plagues, and famines. International environmental organizations such as Greenpeace, Friends of the Earth, the Sierra Club, and others have become increasingly powerful in their ability to pressure countries to address worsening national and international environmental crises.

International conflict and politics are inescapable, even for groups that are not ostensibly political. An organization such as the International Olympic Committee, for instance, is heavily involved in politics if only because the members have so frequently disrupted the Olympics for political purposes. In 1980, the United States and many other states boycotted the Moscow Olympics because of the Soviet invasion of Afghanistan. In 1984, the Soviet bloc retaliated by boycotting the Los Angeles Olympics. So far the Olympics has escaped such political grandstanding in the post–cold-war era.

Some NGOs have been quite successful. Jody Williams founded and led the Campaign to Ban Land Mines, which eventually persuaded 122 governments to sign a treaty doing just that; Williams and her NGO jointly won the Nobel peace prize for their efforts. Friends of the Earth spearheaded the campaign to convene a global environmental conference at Rio de Janeiro in 1992 and has been a persistent voice in the environmentalist community at subsequent international conferences. The humanitarian organization Oxfam International channeled more than $10 billion to the world's poor in 1997 alone and has worked with U.N. agencies to alleviate poverty. The Italian organization Comunità di Sant'Egidio helped broker peace between the government and rebels in Mozambique. The Ford Foundation underwrote peace between the government and rebels in El Salvador in 1991.

Religious groups can play an important role in certain international issues. The Catholic Church is perhaps the world's largest NGO. Although Vatican City is only a few acres large, the pope commands the loyalty of one out of eight humans and an international organization with a significant presence in most countries. The Catholic Church has not hesitated to involve itself in a nation's politics on issues it deems important. For example, the Church was instrumental in helping to forge the popular revolution that toppled Poland's communist regime.

Such dazzling NGO successes were once the exception. With globalization, NGOs grow ever more numerous and powerful in shaping international relations. Although NGOs differ markedly in their aims and orientation, nearly all seek change, and nearly all, change for the better.

Conclusion

International government organizations are perhaps the most visible manifestation of interdependence. They serve many functions, the most important of which may well be to provide a forum in which states can debate and act on issues. Even when they cannot reach consensus, an IGO can provide states a face-saving means to blow off steam rather than use more violent means of advancing their interests. Generally speaking, the more narrow an international organization's focus—mail, shipping, railroads, telecommunications, and so on—the more successful its performance. But one general-membership and general-purpose IGO, the European Union, has surpassed all others in achieving its goals of economic and political integration. Nongovernmental organizations, meanwhile, proliferate in numbers, membership, and power to promote their interests in an increasingly globalized world.

What does the future hold for international organizations and their role in shaping international relations? Many believe that ever greater interdependence, the erosion of sovereignty, and the proliferation of IGOs and NGOs may eventually lead to some type of world government, in which nation-states abandon their sovereignty to a supreme authority. The amount of power a world government holds could vary from a relatively weak arrangement in a decentralized confederal, to a more centralized federal, or highly centralized unitary system. If a world government ever does emerge, international relations will have been fundamentally changed. But given the tenacity of state sovereignty and popular nationalism, that day is not yet foreseeable.

Study Questions

1. Discuss the functionalist and neofunctionalist theories of international organization.

2. What is the legal status of international organizations established by treaty?

3. Define collective security. How have states attempted to achieve it throughout history?

4. Describe the League of Nations' strengths and weaknesses, successes and failures.

5. What have been the United Nations' strengths and weaknesses, successes and failures?

6. List the major U.N. institutions and their responsibilities?

7. Discuss U.N. collective security and peacekeeping operations.

8. Discuss the ways in which secular and religious NGOs affect international relations.

$\mathscr{G}$ InfoTrac College Edition Sources

Using the Subject Guide, enter the search terms *United Nations, League of Nations, European Union, international agencies,* and/or *non-governmental organizations.*

Arias, Inocencio F. "The United Nations Information System and the World Citizen."

Barnett, Michael N., and Martha Finnemore. "The Politics, Power, and Pathologies of International Organizations."

Ewig, Christina. "The Strengths and Limits of the NGO Women's Movement Model: Shaping Nicaragua's Democratic Institutions."

Harriss, John. "Government-NGO Relations in Asia: Prospects and Challenges for People-Centered Development."

Howes, Mick. "NGOs and the Institutional Development of Membership Organisations: A Kenyan Case."

"International Governmental Organizations."

Keith, Suter. "Reforming the United Nations."

Kent, Ann. "China, International Organizations and Regimes: The ILO as a Case Study in Organizational Learning."

Lauren, Paul Gordon. "Between Pandemonium and Order."

Luong, Pauline Jones, and Erika Weinthal. "The NGO Paradox: Democratic Goals and Non-Democratic Outcomes in Kazakhstan."

March, James G., and Johan P. Olsen. "The Institutional Dynamics of International Political Orders."

Marlay, Ross. "Organizing for Democracy: NGOs, Civil Society, and the Philippine State."

Maynes, Charles William. "America's Fading Commitments."

Midlarsky, Manus L. "International Organizations and Ethnic Conflict."

"NGO: Friend or Foe?"

Paris, Roland. "Peacebuilding and the Limits of Liberal Internationalism."

Quinn, Mary Ellen. [Book review of] *Historical Dictionary of International Relations.*

Reus-Smit, Christian. "The Constitutional Structure of International Society and the Nature of Fundamental Institutions."

Russett, Bruce, John R. Oneal, and David R. Davis, "The Third Leg of the Kantian Tripod for Peace: International Organizations and Militarized Disputes, 1950–1985."

Shanks, Cheryl, Harold K. Jacobson, and Jeffrey H. Kaplan. "Inertia and Change in the Constellation of International Governmental Organizations, 1981–1992."

"Unreported: News on the United Nations System at Work."

On *the* Web

http://www.undcp.org/unlinks.html
Comprehensive website covering the UN

http://www.euroguide.org/euroguide/subject-listing/
An excellent guide to the European Union

http://www.tufts.edu/departments/fletcher/multi/www/league-covenant.html
Covenant of the League of Nations

During the past decade only one major war has broken out, the Persian Gulf War, in early 1991. That war provides an excellent case study in which to explore a range of related geopolitical problems, including the problem of identifying a growing threat in a crowded and demanding policy agenda, policy debate over containing versus appeasing an aggressor, the diplomatic challenge of building and leading an alliance, the role of high technology in fighting wars, the policy debate over Iraq out of Kuwait. The question was, How? Over the next six months the White House forged and led a coalition of armed forces that began a massive air assault on Iraq on January 17, 1991, and a ground attack on February 23 that destroyed Iraq's forces in Kuwait and liberated that country. The war cost $61 billion dollars, and the lives of hundreds of Coalition members, thousands of Kuwait citizens, and hundreds of thousands of Iraqi soldiers and civilians. Why did Iraq invade Kuwait? Why did

Part Four Geopolitical Conflict *and* Cooperation: Was *the* Persian Gulf War (1990–1991) *the* Last Conventional War?

whether to fight a limited or total war, and the challenge of containing an aggressive leader who remains in power despite having been defeated.

On August 2, 1990, Iraqi military forces invaded and conquered Kuwait. In the months leading up to the invasion, President Saddam Hussein had repeatedly asserted his intention to make Kuwait Iraq's 19th province. Within days of the invasion, the Bush administration had decided to force

the United States lead the Coalition against Iraq? Could both Hussein's invasion of Kuwait and the war against him have been avoided?

Ironically, the Reagan and Bush administrations' policies during the 1980s built up Iraq's military power and inadvertently encouraged its aggression. They did so believing they could use Iraq to contain Iran's Islamic revolution, which threatened other pro-Western regimes in the region and beyond. In 1982, the Reagan White House removed Iraq from the list of states that sponsor terrorism, allowing the United States to resume trade with that country. In 1984, the Reagan administration abandoned its official neutrality and tilted toward Iraq. For the next six years until Iraq invaded Kuwait, the United States supplied Iraq with billions of dollars worth of weapons and aid while overlooking its support for international terrorist groups and gross abuse of human rights. Throughout the 1980s, the White House did not have a uniform policy toward states that promoted terrorism. Although Libya, Iran, and Iraq all supported terrorism, the Reagan White House cut its trade and diplomatic relations with Libya, ransomed hostages from Iran, and plied Iraq with advanced technology, weapons, aid, and intelligence on Iran. Congressional voices demanded that the United States sever its relations with Iraq, pointing out that the Hussein regime used chemical weapons against its own Kurdish population and harbored Palestinian terrorists. The White House rejected that advice, claimed that the Hussein regime was liberalizing, and rebuked Congress for attempting to "micromanage" foreign policy. Between 1985 and 1990, the White House approved 771 licenses to export $1.5 billion in advanced equipment and technology to Iraq, much of it with direct military applications, and an additional $5 billion in agricultural credits.[1] Only after Iraq invaded Kuwait did the White House place it on the list of countries that support terrorism. The Reagan and Bush ad-

A triumphant General "Storming" Norman Schwartzkopf during the American-led campaign that liberated Kuwait from Iraq in 1991.

ministrations thought that it could moderate Iraq's behavior by appeasing President Hussein with technology, weapons, and trade.[2] Instead, by building up President Hussein's military Reagan and Bush strengthened a Frankenstein monster that eventually turned against them.

Would Iraq have invaded Kuwait if the White House had not built it up militarily and seemed to be indifferent to Kuwait's fate? In the half-year leading up to Iraq's invasion, Baghdad's actions revealed that the Reagan and Bush appeasement policy had failed. Intelligence sources had long known that Iraq was trying to build nuclear weapons, and estimated that Baghdad could successfully detonate one within five years.

The "crisis" between Washington and Baghdad that culminated with Iraq's conquest of Kuwait actually unfolded over seven months before the actual invasion. During this time the Bush White House either ignored or appeased Hussein's aggression. Iraq test-launched its first SCUD missile in December 1989, and in February 1990 demanded that the United States withdraw its forces from the Persian Gulf. In March 1990, U.S. intelligence revealed that Iraqi SCUDs were located near the border with Jordan and thus within range of Israel. In April 1990, Hussein threatened to "burn half of Israel" with chemical weapons if Israel launched any attack on Iraq. Throughout these months, Bush was more puzzled than worried about Hussein's actions and was quoted by one senior adviser as saying, "Gee, we are trying to be reasonable, yet this guy says and does these crazy things."[3] Yet Bush never considered any alternative to his appeasement policy. In the first half of 1990, the White House approved $500 million in agricultural credits for Iraq and asked Congress for another $500 million.

In the weeks leading up to Iraqi invasion, the White House sent Hussein a series of messages that seemed to tolerate Iraq's threat to invade Kuwait. Although some in Congress called for economic sanctions against Iraq, Bush rejected those calls. On July 28, 1990, Bush sent a personal message to Hussein saying he wanted peace in the region and better relations with Iraq. There was no mention of Iraq's threats against Kuwait, whether the United States would object to an Iraqi invasion, or what it would do if an invasion actually occurred. Bush's passivity is partly understandable: When Bush asked whether Saddam Hussein would fulfill his threat to invade Kuwait, Jordan's King Hussein I and Saudi Arabia's King Fahd replied that it was all a bluff.

Within hours of the invasion, Kuwaiti Prime Minister and Crown Prince Sheikh Saad al-Abdullah al-Sabah called the White House and pleaded for help against the Iraqi invasion. The Bush administration denied the request, concluding that Kuwait was already lost and, anyway, the United States did not have enough military forces in the Persian Gulf to defeat the invasion. The White House fo-

cused on what to do if Iraq invaded Saudi Arabia and on the effects of higher oil prices on the global economy. Bush, however, did denounce the invasion as "naked aggression" and ordered the freezing of all Iraqi and Kuwaiti assets in the United States. The U.N. Security Council voted to condemn the invasion and demanded Iraq's total and unconditional withdrawal.

For several days following the invasion, the White House was split between those who wanted to accept it as a fait accompli and a few who argued for resistance. The turning point in the White House policy occurred after Bush met with British Prime Minister Margaret Thatcher, who urged him to resist Iraq's aggression. On August 5, Bush declared that the Iraqi invasion "will not stand," implying that his administration was committed to use any means to bring about an Iraqi withdrawal.

After Bush's decision, the White House began forging the international coalition that would eventually drive Iraq from Kuwait. On August 6, the U.N. Security Council voted to impose a trade and financial embargo on Iraq and occupied Kuwait. On August 7, American forces began landing in Saudi Arabia to help deter a possible Iraqi invasion. The following day, Bush vowed to protect Saudi Arabia. On August 10, the Arab League voted to send troops to Saudi Arabia. On August 12, the U.S. Navy began blocking all Iraqi trade except some food shipments.

Hussein escalated the crisis on August 19 when he declared he would use foreign civilians interned in Iraq

as "human shields" in military and industrial sites. On August 25, the U.N. Security Council voted 13 to 0, with two abstentions, to give the United States and other nations the right to enforce its previously declared embargo. On August 29, OPEC voted to allow its members to pump all the oil they wanted to alleviate the shortage caused by the boycott of Iraqi and Kuwaiti oil. On August 30, Bush announced that he would pass the hat to his allies to help defray the costs of the Persian Gulf buildup and possible war.

But the possible costs of war mounted. As Iraqi forces in Kuwait were reinforced, the United States had to increase its own forces to give it an edge in any future fighting. On October 30, Bush approved a timetable for launching an air war against Iraq by mid-January and ground war by mid-February. Meanwhile, throughout October and November, Secretary of State Baker shuttled around the world to convince the Security Council members and Arab states to support the U.S. plan for evicting Iraq from Kuwait. Buying the support of some key countries was costly. For example, the White House agreed to forgive Egypt's $7.1 billion military debt to the United States. In late November, the Bush administration announced that new intelligence revealed that Hussein would be able to detonate a nuclear bomb within half a year.[4] The U.N. Security Council voted on November 29 to allow the use of force if Iraqi forces did not withdraw from Kuwait by January 15, 1992. Having won U.N. approval, Bush now put pressure on Congress to support possible war with Iraq. Congress finally granted approval in late December.

There were attempts to negotiate the peaceful resolution of the conflict. Between August and January, American and Iraqi diplomats met numerous times to address the Iraqi invasion and related issues, but all the meetings ended in deadlock. In the week leading up to the air war, the Soviet Union and France also failed in their independent attempts to negotiate the withdrawal of Iraqi troops.

The air campaign began on January 17, 1991. For six weeks Coalition air forces and cruise missiles systematically destroyed Iraqi forces in Kuwait and Iraq's entire logistical, communications, and command infrastructure. Each air attack was preceded by electronic countermeasures (ECMs), which either destroyed or neutralized the Iraqi radar. Coalition losses were minimal.

Despite these successes, the White House feared that the Israelis would retaliate against Iraqi missile attacks, and then the Arab states would withdraw from the Coalition. However, when asked about that possibility, the Arab leaders replied that they would tolerate any Israeli retaliation against Iraq as long as it was "proportionate." The United States sent Patriot antimissile batteries to Israel to help defend against the Iraqi SCUD attacks.

The ground war began on February 23 and lasted 100 hours. The Coalition commander, American General H. Norman Schwarzkopf, conducted a brilliantly conceived and executed offensive. Coalition forces quickly outflanked and encircled Iraqi forces in Kuwait and southern Iraq. With Coalition forces prepared to completely destroy his army, Saddam Hussein indicated that he would accede to the U.N. resolutions. The peace terms imposed on Iraq were tough. The U.N. International Atomic Energy Agency (IAEA) was allowed to systematically inspect Iraq's suspected chemical, biological, and nuclear facilities and supervise their destruction.

Bush's handling of the crisis from Iraq's invasion on August 2, 1990, to his order to end the fighting on February 26 1991, was masterly. During those seven months, Bush overcame formidable international diplomatic and domestic political challenges to forge the Coalition, which eventually decisively destroyed Iraq's army in Kuwait and liberated that country. Eventually, 37 states contributed troops to the Coalition, although American troops composed 70 percent of the total ground, air, and naval forces.

Yet American policy can be criticized before the Iraqi invasion and in Bush's order to stop fighting. The Reagan and Bush administrations helped build up the Iraqi army that the United States and its allies eventually had to destroy. The Bush administration's indecisive and ambiguous response to Iraq's buildup on Kuwait's borders and threats to invade may have given Saddam Hussein the green light. And then in mid-February 1991, with Coalition forces poised to decisively destroy the Iraqi army and march to the gates of Baghdad itself, an action that would have probably resulted in Hussein's overthrow, Bush ended the fighting. The man Bush described as "worse than Hitler" remained firmly in power into the 21st century. Meanwhile, although Bush's popularity rose to 89 percent immediately following the war, it then steadily diminished over the next year and a half until he lost the November 1992 election.

America's high-tech weapons gave a much more mixed performance than indicated by the film footage released to the mass media by the Pentagon. Although the Pentagon claimed that its Patriot missiles destroyed 70 percent of the SCUDs fired at Saudi Arabia and 40 percent against those fired at Israel, an independent MIT report concluded that the Patriots destroyed at most only one SCUD and probably none. In contrast, 85 percent of the U.S. Navy's Tomahawk cruise missiles hit their targets.

Overall, the United States accomplished some important objectives in the Persian Gulf War. Iraq's military was forced to withdraw from Kuwait and the United Nation's IAEA has demolished virtually all of Iraq's nuclear, biological, and chemical weapons and facilities. As part of his concessions to the Arabs for their participation in the Coalition, Bush pressured Israel to join a series of negotiations with Syria, Jordan, and the Palestinians to resolve their deep and bitter conflict. Saddam Hussein, however, remains firmly in power. And although Iraq's offensive military capability may have been temporarily destroyed, the military power balance in the Persian Gulf has shifted to Iran.

The war cost the region $676 billion in destruction and war-fighting costs. The figure does not include the region's environmental devastation and forgone economic opportunities. The Persian Gulf's average 7 percent economic growth rate turned into a seven percent economic contraction during the year surrounding the war. An additional $51 billion was lost in capital flight and canceled foreign investments. In one year alone Iraq may have lost at least $256 billion in oil revenues and infrastructure destruction, and in the eight years since, another $141 billion in revenues because of the embargo. Countries outside the Persian Gulf such as Egypt, Yemen, the Philippines, Bangladesh, Pakistan, and India also lost an important source of income and employment when their citizens who worked in the region were sent home.[5] Like all wars, the Persian Gulf War had its share of heroes and villains, and victors and losers at all levels and in every country directly or indirectly engaged.

When, where, and why, if ever, will another war of that magnitude again ravage part of the earth? Why do wars occur? What impact did the cold war and nuclear arms race play in promoting or containing violence? How is the nature of warfare changing into the 21st century?

Contents

Chapter 8 Why Nations Go *to* War *or* Stay *at* Peace

Key Concepts and Terms

War is the central problem of international relations.[1] For as long as humans have existed, they have been murdering each other in increasingly well-organized, large-scale, and devastating ways. The human and material destruction of war in this century alone is incalculable. Why do nations go to war or stay at peace?

Every war has its own unique set of causes, which are invariably multiple, complex, and interrelated. Wars have been fought either exclusively or in some combination to gain or defend territory; security; wealth; national, religious, cultural, racial, and/or ideological identity and values; political dynasties; colonies; independence; allies or other friendly states; power balance; power imbalance; hegemony; freedom of the seas; foreign economic interests; endangered citizens; or national honor. Wars have also been fought to weaken or destroy rivals, retaliate against the aggressive actions of others, pre-empt an imminent or inevitable attack, avenge insults or past losses, fill power vacuums before someone else does, and/or maintain alliance credibility.[2] And these are merely some of the more prominent reasons for war.

To determine the reasons for any particular war, let alone the general phenomenon, one must tap into such fields as psychology, sociology, history, economics, political science, religion, biology, demography, ecology, game theory, decision making, and philosophy—to name the more prominent. As Quincy Wright puts it, "A war, in reality, results from a total situation involving ultimately almost everything that has happened to the human race up to the time the war begins."[3]

Given the array of reasons that states war against each other, is it possible to discern any underlying patterns that lead states to war or keep them at peace? There are some. War, essentially, arises from conflict. Wars do not occur unless one or more sides in a conflict are convinced that their vital interests are threatened. States initiate war when they expect to win. Not surprisingly, most wars are fought by neighbors.[4] The wars of each historic period and geographic region have often had distinct patterns of causes. For example, throughout Europe's early modern era, the central reasons for war have changed dramatically: religion (1519–1648), dynastic rule (1648–1763), and revolution and nationalism (1776–1870).

Given the virtual universality of war, can we ever expect violent conflict between or within states to end? Many say no, maintaining that wars are perfectly natural and are simply a violent means to resolve conflict:

> War is a means for achieving an end, a weapon which can be used for good or bad purposes. Some of these purposes for which war has been used have been accepted by humanity as worthwhile ends; indeed, war performs functions which are essential in any society. It has been used to settle disputes, to uphold rights, to remedy wrongs. . . . One may say . . . that no more stupid, brutal, wasteful, or unfair method could ever have been imagined for such purposes, but this does not alter the situation.[5]

Traditionally, a state's ultimate sovereign power was the ability and right to wage war. Historian Karl von Clausewitz (1780–1831) considered war merely an extension of diplomacy by other means and rejected any limits to the violence of battle: "War is an act of force, and to the application of that force there is no limit."[6]

Yet others argue that although wars grab the headlines, most states are at peace most of the time. From the mid-19th century through today, states have signed a series of treaties limiting war's weapons and targets, and in the 20th century actually outlawed war itself. These international agreements and the international organizations such as the United Nations that seek to uphold them, have slightly reduced the number of international wars being waged around the world. Most states obey the restrictions on weapons and behavior. As the world becomes increasingly interdependent economically and politically democratic, international war will just as steadily diminish as its economic and political costs rise and benefits fall. Despite these changes, war will remain a scourge for many peoples around the world, although increasingly within rather than between states.

Even if this decline occurs, it remains to be seen whether war's increased moral and practical obsolescence will also reduce the range of reasons why states go to war. In his book *Man, the State, and War*, Kenneth Waltz points out that all theories of war find their source in the character and behavior of one of three areas: human nature, the nation-state, and the international system.[7] I will use that typology here.

War *and* Human Nature

Humans, along with many animals, are territorial. They struggle to acquire, maintain, and expand property, and are one of the few animal species that kill their own kind. But is violence innate (nature/hereditary), learned (nurtured/socialized), or some combination of both?

NATURE AND NURTURE

Many argue that human beings, and the groups to which they belong, are naturally aggressive. War, thus, is inevitable. Waltz agrees: "Our miseries are ineluctably the product of our natures. The root of all evil is man, and thus he is himself the root of the specific evil, war."[8] Or, as Albert Einstein put it in a letter to Sigmund Freud: "Man has within him a lust for hatred and destruction. . . . It is a comparatively easy task to call this into play and raise it to the level of a collective psychosis."[9]

After studying aggression in various animal species, ethologist Konrad Lorenz concluded that humans were "killer apes, one of the few species which kills its own kind."[10] Aggression, in his view, comes from and is essential to evolution. Charles Darwin theorized that life evolved from a few simple species to millions of complex species through a survival of the fittest struggle as each attempted to adapt to hostile environments. *Social Darwinism,* popularized by Herbert Spencer and others, argued that nations, like animal species, were engaged in a perpetual war of all against all in which the stronger conquered the weaker. All humanity from the simplest hunter-gatherer groups of 100,000 years ago to the complex nation-states of today, has continually struggled to survive. Progress comes from competition as the strong and more advanced vanquish the weak. Thus imperialism is natural and even moral because it allows "superior" peoples to subdue and civilize the "inferior" ones. During the 19th century and the 1930s, governments used social Darwinism to justify their imperialism. As Hitler put it, "Nature knows no political boundaries. First she puts living creatures on this globe and watches the free play of forces. She then confers the master's right on her favorite child, the strongest."[11]

Others—notably behaviorists—argue that the environment rather than inner drives shapes human behavior. Thus human aggression is learned rather than innate.[12] Some environments promote and others inhibit aggression. Wars are fought by governments, not individuals, and therefore are political cultural inventions rather than biological necessities.[13] A Hitler or a Hussein can skillfully use ideology,

Geopolitical Ambitions *in* Africa

When the Europeans carved up Africa into colonies, they deliberately split peoples sharing the same culture and grouped them with traditional enemies to play them off against one another and thus better control them. Decades after those colonies achieved independence, the legacy of multinational states haunts the continent. Nations sprawl across one or more international borders. Ambitious rulers can use the excuse of repression against people of their own ethnic background in neighboring countries to intervene there.

During the 1990s, Uganda's President Yoweri Museveni did just that. In 1994, he helped engineer a coup that brought his Tutsi allies to power in Rwanda, where most people were Hutus; the Tutsi slaughtered a million people before they consolidated their rule. In 1997, Uganda and Rwanda invaded the eastern Congo (then called Zaire), which tipped the balance in a civil war in which Laurent Kabila chased Mobuto Seke from power. (Mobuto died in exile in September 1997). Kabila soon turned

on his benefactors. Although Uganda and Rwanda withdrew their troops after Kabila's victory, he feared that their influence would increase in the rich Katanga region. Kabila turned to the Sudan to contain the ambitions of Uganda and Rwanda, a move that provoked rather than deterred Uganda and Rwanda from invading eastern Congo in 1998 and supporting the anti-Kabila Congolese Rally for Democracy. The Sudan meanwhile continues to try to undermine President Museveni by sponsoring the Lord's Resistance Army, dedicated to taking over Uganda. Kabila's forces beat the rebels literally at the doors of the capital Kinshasa. He did so in part because three other countries, Zimbabwe, Angola, and Namibia, intervened on his side to thwart the ambitions of Uganda and Rwanda.

How does the war in the Congo threaten the national interests of those countries? Angola and Namibia face a threat from the revolutionary movement Unita, which straddles their mutual border and has bases in the southwestern Congo. Zimbabwe's intervention is mostly explained by the am-

bitions of its president Robert Mugabe, who wants to enhance his status. But that provoked South Africa's indirect involvement as President Nelson Mandela pressured Zimbabwe, Namibia, and Angola to withdraw from the Congo. Why should South Africa care what happens far to the north? Mugabe and Mandela's successor Thabo Mbeki are bitter rivals who aspire to be known as southern Africa's most prominent leaders. But their feud threatens to split the Southern African Development Community (SADC), of which all the region's 14 countries are members.

Thus the ambitions of one ruler in northern central Africa set off a tragic chain reaction of violence and bloodshed that years later eventually exacerbated the rivalry of two other ambitious rulers in southern Africa. But megalomania alone does not explain that trail of gore. Ethnic rivalries, the logic of power's distribution, opportunism, and the perennial greed for more wealth, prestige, and power are among the more important reasons for that iron chain of wars gutting much of Africa.

religion, and/or nationalism to whip a population from passivity into aggression, and to channel that collective emotion into imperialism. *Behaviorism* also distinguishes between sporadic acts of violence by individuals and small groups, and war organized and conducted by states.

Humans have a need to identify with things greater than themselves. During the modern era, the nation has become the primary source of identity for many.

Jack Levy explores the relationship among human psychology, nationalism, and war, which occurs when people

> acquire an intense commitment to the power and prosperity of the state and this commitment is strengthened by national myths emphasizing the moral, physical, and political strength of the state and by an individual's feelings of powerlessness and their consequent tendency to seek their identity and fulfillment through the state, then assertive and nationalist policies are perceived as increasing state power and are at the same time psychologically satisfying for the individual and, in this way, nationalism contributes to war.[14]

Psychological and sociological theories of war, particularly the innate aggression school, have been criticized on several grounds. If humans (or human males) are innately aggressive and that aggression leads to war, why then are not men at war all or most of the time? In reality, most states and humans are at peace most of the time. Although conflict among humans is inevitable, violence inherently is not. Studies of primitive societies find as many peaceful as violent ones.[15] Humans are certainly capable of violence, but they seldom commit it and instead resolve most conflicts peacefully. Most humans use rationality to check their aggressive drives. A human drive to cooperate with others may be more important than the drive to vanquish them. The aggression of states or individuals may well be deviant rather than natural behavior.[16] Although some peoples such as the Germans and Japanese are commonly thought to be more aggressive than others, studies have failed to find a connection between the two.[17]

There is not necessarily a link between human and state aggression. Wars can occur even when the respective populations are disinterested or opposed; wars can be averted through skilled diplomacy even when the respective populations feverishly demand it.[18] Some argue that for every leader who dragged a reluctant populace to war, one may find a reluctant leader who was pushed into war by an eager populace.[19] Yet one study of 25 wars found no case "precipitated by emotional tensions, sentimentality, crowd behavior, or other irrational motivations."[20]

MISPERCEPTION AND ESCALATION

The decision to conduct a war is not taken lightly, even among the most aggressive of governments and peoples. Few states and their peoples have ever wanted to risk destruction for political objectives. Yet most states have experienced war's horrors. Why the discrepancy?

Some theorists argue that most wars happen because of mutual misperceptions about the other's intentions and power.[21] How do misperceptions occur? Misperceptions can involve a range of images, attitudes, and behaviors, including a government's angelic self-image and diabolical image of the rival government; overconfidence in one's military power and disregard for that of the other; missed signals that show the other side's willingness to compromise; and lack of understanding or empathy for the other's interests. In conflicts, communications break down or were limited from the start. Governments and their peoples project their fears, ambitions, and capabilities on their rivals. Each side interprets the other's actions in the worst way and are then countered accordingly, resulting in spiraling tensions and saber rattling. Governments misperceive each other's military capabilities and intentions. Once a decision for war is made, leaders convince themselves and their publics that they will enjoy a quick and easy victory.

Give Peace *a* Chance? An Election *in* Israel

Can an election make peace more or less likely? Israel has one of the world's most politically splintered democracies. With a proportional electoral system that rewards representatives to parties with as little as 1 percent of the vote, a spectrum of large and small parties fill the 120 seats of the Knesset, Israel's parliament. The two largest parties, Likud and Labor, are split over what to do about the Palestinians who comprise 1.7 million of Israel's 6 million people itself, and another 2 million in the occupied West Bank and Gaza strip.

Likud and its allies want to prevent the Palestinians from becoming a sovereign state and to continue building Jewish settlements on the West Bank. Ideally they would like to expel the Palestinians and annex that land to Israel. Labor and its allies are willing to trade land for peace by allowing a neutral, demilitarized Palestinian state that recognizes Israel and is economically dependent on Israel. Ashkenazi Jews, with European origins and socialist and secular sentiments, tend to vote for the Labor party and its allies. Sephardic Jews, with Middle Eastern roots and ultra-Orthodox religious and authoritarian sentiments, tend to support the Likud party. The million recent Russian Jewish immigrants are a political wild card. They tend to lean toward secular and socialist policies but are also anti-Arab, and hawks on military issues.

A vast majority of Israelis chose to give peace a chance. In the May 17, 1999, election, the Labor party's candidate for prime minister, Elihu Barak, trounced Likud party sitting prime minister Benjamin Netanyahu, winning 56 percent to 44 percent. Russian Jews tipped the balance by voting overwhelmingly for Barak. As usual, no party won a majority. Barak formed a coalition government of his Labor party, which won only 26 seats, with enough other small parties to gain a slight majority.

The Labor party returned to power after a four-year hiatus. That was challenging enough. But even more difficult will be negotiating treaties—not just with the Palestinians but also with neighboring Syria and Lebanon—to resolve the bitter conflicts that have exploded into five large-scale wars and continual terrorism to the region over the last 50 years.

---

mirror image an opposing view that describes how parties in conflict view each other's actions as malevolent and aggressive and their own actions as innocent, just, and defensive.

At the root of misperception is the human tendency to simplify information. There is only so much that any human or group of humans can comprehend. Instead of attempting to understand the world's complexities, decision makers and the public cling to and become trapped by a collection of simple prejudices and stereotypes. In a conflict, people see what they want to see and hear what they want to hear. *Mirror images* occur when each side "believes the other to be bent on aggression and conquest, to be capable of great brutality and evil-doing, to be something less than human. . . . To hold this conception of the enemy becomes the moral duty of every citizen, and those who question it are denounced. . . . The approaching war is seen as due entirely to the hostile intentions of the enemy."[22] In conflicts and particularly in a crisis, governments tend to assume the worst about each other's intentions, power, and goals. Tragically, mirror images often become self-fulfilling prophecies as even the most innocent of the rival's actions are interpreted in the worst possible way. The result is an existing gap between image and reality that widens with conflict. The more tense a situation, the more humans stereotype themselves and their opponents, thus making mutual understanding and reconciliation increasingly difficult. Governments tend to believe their own propaganda about themselves and their rivals. This tendency is particularly heightened in an age of intercontinental missiles and supersonic bombers.

Statesmen often have several audiences: their domestic constituents, their foreign rivals, and the international community. Misunderstandings can arise when governments send different messages to different audiences. Even authoritarian governments can become the prisoners of public expectations. Once a government draws a line in the sand for a domestic audience, it often feels compelled to stick to it even if it secretly wishes to be more conciliatory toward its rivals. As conflicts escalate, states get trapped in a game of "chicken" with their rival in which they charge each other, hoping the other will give way. The result is often war, as neither side wants to step aside and compromise.

Misperceptions themselves do not cause war. Real conflicts over vital issues must be present for either side to consider war as a means to resolve them. Often the different sides in a dispute understand each other's intentions and capabilities quite clearly, and yet war occurs anyway because one or both sides made a rational decision that they could succeed by using force.

War *and the* Nation-State

IDEOLOGY

People often go to war over ideas. The better organized those ideas and the more fervent their claim to be the one and only truth, the more frequently such ideologies provoke wars. Ideologies can be both secular and religious.

Some ideologies may not overtly be about God, but may inspire in their followers beliefs akin to religious zeal and structure. Communism and fascism have often been called secular religions because they promoted visions of class and national struggles that justified aggression, and brought to power charismatic leaders who championed those crusades. Communism, after all, was an ideology that promised world revolution and wars of national and class revolution. The variants of fascism in Japan, Germany, and Italy all justified aggression for the greater glory of that nation and the authoritarian state that embodied it.

At various times, most religions have provoked crusades against peoples of other faiths, and even warred against their own members who proposed alternative interpretations of sacred scriptures. Christianity has been interpreted by some of its followers to inspire wars against nonbelievers. For two centuries, from 1095 when Pope Urban II called for the first crusade against the "infidel" Muslim Arabs who had conquered the Holy Land, to 1291 when Acre, the last Catholic bastion in Palestine fell, the Catholic princes of Europe obeyed Rome's orders and launched eight major campaigns. A series of religious wars between Catholics and Protestants plunged much of Europe into bloodbaths from the revolt of the Anabaptists in 1525 until the Treaty of Westphalia in 1648. Western imperialism was usually justified in part as an attempt to bring Christianity to benighted peoples elsewhere. But other religions have provoked wars just as vicious. The Bible's Old Testament reveals how the Hebrews warred continually and sometimes committed genocide against neighboring peoples. Islam's Koran explicitly calls on its adherents to wage holy wars against infidels and assures martyrs in those struggles a prominent place in heaven.

Ideologies have at times been a major cause for some wars. But ideologies are rarely the sole cause for any war. Other forces invariably motivate a state or

When is it in a nation's interests to go to war? When is it in a nation's interest to forge peace? Here President Bill Clinton warmly embraces Israeli President Yitzhak Rabin and Palestinian leader Yassir Arafat, who shake hands over the peace treaty they have just signed. Israel has occupied the West Bank and Gaza Strip ever since it took over those lands in response to an attack by Arab armies in June 1967. The Palestinian people who live there and elsewhere have struggled for their own country. The result has been a chronic guerrilla war and Israeli attempts to plant Jewish settlements amidst the Palestinian population. But during the 1990s, moderate Israeli and Palestinian leaders negotiated a series of agreements that brought peace in return for greater Palestinian control over parts of the West Bank and Gaza Strip. Palestine may eventually become an independent country.

Reuters/Gary Hershom/Archive Photos

groups of states with one ideology to attack a state or group of states with a different ideology.

Indeed, most ideologies have not prevented its adherents from warring against each other. Ideals of communist brotherhood were not powerful enough to prevent the Soviet Union and China from fighting a border war in 1969, or China from invading Vietnam in 1979. Christian states have warred repeatedly against one another, as have Muslim, Hindu, and Buddhist states, respectively, warred against others sharing the same faith.

NATIONALISM, SEPARATISM, AND IRREDENTISM

Nationalism is a type of ideology that has increasingly been a major cause for war.[23] Virtually every one' of the over 195 sovereign states has significant minority ethnic, religious, linguistic, and/or racial, populations that either currently or potentially demand independence or merger with a similar group in a neighboring country. Nationalism can spark a war for independence within a state (*separatism*) or a war by one state to "liberate" those of the same nationality in a neighboring state (*irredentism*).

The boundaries of modern nation-states were often drawn with complete disregard for the inhabitants. Frontiers grouped different nationalities and separated similar nationalities. Africa is the most glaring example. At the Berlin Conference of 1885, the imperial powers satisfied their conflicting claims to the continent by simply drawing lines across a map of Africa. Today Somalia is the only country with no significant minority group, although national unity did not prevent it from plunging into civil war in the early 1990s.

War often happens when a government refuses to accept a minority's demands and actively attempts to suppress them. Nationalism has destroyed all the great modern empires, from the Dutch independence struggle against Spain in the late 16th century, America's against Britain in the late 18th century, and Latin America's against Spain in the early 19th century, to the over 100 nation-states that emerged from the breakup of the British, French, Dutch, American, Portuguese, and Japanese empires after 1945, to the present wave of independence struggles in the former Soviet Union, Yugoslavia, Iraq, Israel, India, and dozens of other countries.

Irredentism has also been a major cause of war. In 1938, Hitler seized Czechoslovakia's Sudetenland province to "liberate" the three million ethnic Germans living there. The North Vietnamese fought the United States and South Vietnam (1954–1975) as much to unify the country as to impose communism on the South. However, economic as well as nationalist motivations can prompt a state's irredentist claims for neighboring territory. Hitler not only rejoined the Sudeten Germans to "the fatherland," but took over two-thirds of Czechoslovakia's industrial capacity. Iraq's attempts to swallow Kuwait in August 1990 had as much to do with taking the latter's oil as joining two separate Arab populations.

The global system upholds two conflicting values—*self-determination* and stability. The world becomes increasingly unstable as more people demand autonomy or outright independence. These demands often result in war.

WARS FOR NATIONAL COHESION

Conflict is inseparable from life. When two or more groups spar over an issue, the solidarity of each is usually enhanced. Conflict among groups can be a safety valve that releases hostility caused by conflict within groups.

Sometimes a government may deliberately square off with another state just to divert the population's attention from internal problems and divisions. According to the *scapegoat theory,* war with others "is sometimes the last chance for a state ridden with inner antagonisms to overcome these antagonisms, or else break up indefinitely."[24] For example, in 1861 Secretary of State William Seward encouraged President Lincoln to pick a fight with another state to unite the country and prevent civil war. The decision by Argentina's government to invade the British Falkland Islands in 1982 may have been largely an attempt to distract the public's attention from economic stagnation and political oppression at home. One motive for President Saddam Hussein's decision to send his army into Kuwait may have been to sublimate the Sunni–Shiite and Arab–Kurdish strife within Iraq. Although victory might have helped repress these divisions, defeat only exacerbated them.

How common is this cause of war? Different studies reach different conclusions over how often "scapegoating" occurs. One study revealed that over half of all international wars between 1823 and 1937 were preceded by serious conflicts in one or more of the states.[25] Most others, however, found little correlation.[26] Resorts to war to heal internal divisions, relative to the number of countries torn by internal conflict, are minute.[27]

The cement holding healthy societies together is shared values, traditions, behavior, and ambitions, not fear of government repression or foreign attack. From a practical point of view, if a nation is already divided, a government's decision to go to war would most likely weaken its cohesion and ability to fight.

War aside, do governments use foreign conflicts to heal internal conflicts and strengthen their own legitimacy? Sometimes. It depends on how serious the domestic problems are. For example, American presidents have been known to manufacture an international crisis in an election year, particularly when the economy is ailing, to distract people from their problems and rally them around both the flag and the president.

WARS FROM NATIONAL INCOHESION: CIVIL WARS AND UNCIVIL WARS

civil war also known as internal war or large-scale violence by two or more sides within one country.

More commonly, civil wars lead to international wars. *Civil wars* occur when one group—class, religious, ethnic, regional, and so on—rebels against a brutal, corrupt, exploitive regime dominated by another group. The rebellion is usually inspired, organized, and justified by an ideology, whether it be religion, nationalism, Marxism Leninism, democracy, or some other. Rebel and government leaders struggle to win popular support ("hearts and minds") by presenting themselves as saviors and the other as vicious enemies. *Uncivil wars* are violent struggles by groups simply to rob, rape, and murder anyone in their way, and carve out a criminal empire usually funded by smuggling illegal drugs such as cocaine, heroin, or marijuana. Some criminal groups such as Peru's Shining Path and Cambodia's Khmer Rouge, use some vague ideology to justify its genocide; most simply wield terror without comment, as in Sierra Leone, Mozambique, or Liberia. Civil wars fall generally into two types, *state control wars* when rebels try to capture the government and *state formation wars* when they seek independence. Uncivil wars are *failed state wars* in which criminal groups take advantage of a government's inability to govern. Regardless of which type afflicts it, a state torn by war offers an opportunity for other ambitious states to intervene on one side to advance their interests.[28]

Civil wars can involve mostly conventional warfare, such as the U.S. Civil War. Most civil wars, however, are guerrilla struggles. Arguably the most successful guerrilla leader in history, Mao Zedong argued that victory depended on five elements: a sympathetic population, a strong military force, a tightly organized party, favorable terrain, and an ample and secure source of supply. Although guerrilla warfare can successfully defeat the government on the battlefield, a revolutionary struggle can only overthrow the government with conventional warfare. After the rebels have bled, discredited, and demoralized the government to the breaking point, they shift their strategy from a hit-and-run guerrilla war to a conventional war in which they try to crush the enemy's armies.

Civil wars are the most common armed conflicts. More than 85 percent of all wars between 1945 and 1976 were civil wars. Most of these were extremely destructive—10 of the 12 bloodiest wars of the last two hundred years were civil wars. Of those relatively few international wars since 1945, most occurred when a great power became involved in a civil war. There were 161 civil wars with over 1,000 deaths between 1816 and 1988. Civil wars occur mostly in poor countries. In 1998, there were 36 armed struggles within 31 countries (India suffered three) and no international wars. In 1999, the number of internal wars remained unchanged, but an international war broke out between Ethiopia and Eritrea.[29]

Table 8.1 Civil and Uncivil Wars, 1998

Region	Number of Countries	Number of Conflicts	Number of Countries with Conflicts	Percentage of World Conflicts
Africa	50	13	13	36%
Asia	42	13	9	36%
Europe	42	1	1	3%
The Americas	44	2	2	6%
Middle East	14	7	6	19%
World Totals	192	36	31	100%

These figures include all armed conflicts in which combat deaths exceeded 1,000.

Source: Project Ploughshares, *Armed Conflicts Report 1999.*

Civil wars can become international wars when the government and/or antigovernment forces receive outside help. Throughout the cold war, civil wars almost inevitably became international wars as Washington, Moscow, and sometimes other states lined up behind the side that seemed to best represent their interests—even if that interest involved simply bleeding the material, human, and psychological resources of the other side. For example, during the 1980s, Washington sponsored guerrilla forces against pro-Soviet regimes in Afghanistan, Ethiopia, Angola, and Nicaragua. Ideally, Washington wanted the pro-Soviet regimes toppled and the Soviet advisers and troops removed. But usually the United States was content with forcing the Soviets to commit even more resources to maintain their position. Over the years, Moscow played the same game against the United States in Vietnam, El Salvador, and the Korean peninsula, to name a few. Sometimes a power will justify intervening in another state to prevent its subversion by the other side, as Moscow did when it crushed democratic forces in East Germany (1953), Hungary (1956), Czechoslovakia (1968), and Poland (1980), and Washington did when it toppled unfriendly governments in the Dominican Republic (1965), Grenada (1983), Panama (1990), and Haiti (1994).

In the post–cold-war era, the United Nations intervened in ever more civil or uncivil wars. In the year 2000, there were peacekeeping missions in 17 of 33 countries torn apart by violence. Sometimes a peacekeeping mission, which simply tries to maintain a truce between warring sides, becomes a peace enforcement mission, which uses force to restore order, as happened unsuccessfully in Somalia in 1993 and successfully in Kosovo in 1999.

DEMOCRACY AND WAR

In 1795, Immanuel Kant argued in his essay "Perpetual Peace" that humans are naturally inclined to peace, that democracies are more peaceful than dictatorships, and that the number of wars will diminish as more countries become democratic.[30]

It is true that democratic countries have never warred against each other.[31] Why? The rise of the democratic industrial state brought a shift from a *high politics* emphasis on military security issues to a *low politics* emphasis on welfare; geo-economic interests have eclipsed geopolitical interests in importance for most democratic states. A common democratic ideology and economic interdependence prevent democratic states from going to war against each other. The implications of this phenomenon are profound. Levy states that the "absence of war between democracies comes as close as anything we have to an empirical law in international relations."[32] It follows that as more states become democratic, the possibility of war decreases accordingly, and if all states were genuine democracies, war would cease to plague humankind, thus fulfilling Kant's dream of a "perpetual peace."

Encouraging as the propensity for peace among democratic states is, Levy points out that "democratic states have been involved proportionately in as many wars as nondemocratic states."[33] For example, of the 50 wars examined between 1816 through 1865, liberal democratic states were involved in 19 and started 11.[34] Another study concluded that democracies are in fact less militaristic than authoritarian states.[35] According to Michael Doyle, the reason for continued armed conflict between democratic and authoritarian states is that "the very constitutional restraint, shared commercial interests, and international respect for individual rights that promote peace among liberal societies can exacerbate conflicts in relations between liberal and nonliberal societies."[36] However, as increasing numbers of states become democratic, we can expect to see the numbers of international wars decline.

DEVELOPMENT AND WAR

Many studies have shown a close correlation between wealth and violence—the poor tend to wage war more than the rich.[37] Of 120 armed conflicts between 1955 and 1979, all but 6 involved Third World nations.[38] Since World War II wealthy states simply have not warred against each other. Between 1945 and 1990, no war occurred between or took place within the then 24 members of the *Organization for Economic Cooperation and Development (OECD)*, the world's most developed nations. There were eight wars (defined as an armed conflict with over 1,000 battle deaths) between OECD countries and less developed countries (LDCs), and one with a communist country. Communist countries fought five wars, four of which were against other communist countries and one against an LDC. The LDCs were clearly the most war prone. In addition, to the 1 war fought against a communist country and 8 against OECD countries, the LDCs fought 19 wars against each other. In 1998, 41 percent of all countries in the bottom half of countries ranked by income had suffered wars in the previous decade, whereas wars afflicted only 15 percent of states in the top half.[39]

The lack of wars between wealthy countries represents a major change in international relations. Traditionally, the wealthier a country the more it warred against wealthy and poorer countries alike. Throughout the modern era, Europe was the world's wealthiest and most war-torn region, accounting for 65 percent of all wars in the sixteenth and seventeenth centuries, and 59 percent of all wars between 1816 and 1945, or one every 1.5 years.[40]

The wealthier a country, the more it can financially afford to go to war. Yet even more important are the greater psychological and political constraints on doing so. There are over 800 million people in the OECD. Shared values and needs account for peace between OECD countries. Most OECD states are liberal democracies, and all are increasingly interdependent. The benefits of international trade and investment far exceed any costs. Genuine peace, as opposed to a state of cold war, between these states is not simply war's absence, but the complete lack of a perception among the leaders and public in each country that war could go on between them, and thus no preparations to do so.

Arabs *versus* Iranians

A religion can divide as well as unite its followers if it inspires competing interpretations. Add to that opposing nationalities, power, and ambitions, and you have the tense standoff between Iran and the Gulf Cooperation Council, which includes Saudi Arabia, the United Arab Emirates, Kuwait, Qatar, Bahrain, and Oman. Those countries all share Islam and an oil-rich Persian Gulf region. The Council was formed as a military alliance after Iran's Shah Reza Pahlavi ordered his army to occupy the islands of Abu Musa and the Greater and Lesser Tumbs in 1971. Those islands are not only oil rich, but they also extend Iran's potential striking power over Persian Gulf shipping lanes. The other Gulf states were then too weak militarily to do more than protest Iran's island grab and sever diplomatic ties. Relations worsened with the 1979 revolution, which overthrew the Shah and transformed Iran into a fundamentalist Islamic state. Iranians are devoted to Islam's Shiite interpretation, whereas most Arabs practice Sunni Islam, a theological and political split as sharp as the Catholic and Protestant versions of Christianity and potentially as deadly. Iranian agents have tried to radicalize the Shiite minorities in those conservative Gulf states with hopes of sparking fundamentalist revolutions there.

But revolutions can age and lose the passions that once spawned them. In 1997 Iranians, exhausted by nearly two decades of harsh restrictions, an American-led embargo, and war, overwhelmingly voted for moderate Mohammad Khatami for president. But fundamentalists continue to dominate other areas of Iran's political, religious, and social life. Khatami is determined not only to liberalize Iranian life but also to bring détente to the Persian Gulf's cold war. In May 1999, he became the first Iranian leader since 1979 to visit the Arab world, being hosted in Saudi Arabia, Qatar, and Syria. Fearing that Khatami's presence would stir up their Shiite minorities, the other Gulf states protested the visit as a diplomatic Trojan horse.

Will the Persian Gulf cold war persist or melt with détente? Who will win the tug-of-war for Iranian hearts and minds, the moderates or the radicals? How will the victorious faction affect Iran's foreign relations, especially with the Gulf states? Time will tell.

The economic development and interdependence among the OECD countries was accelerated by the challenge posed by their common enemy, the Soviet Union. These countries could contain the Soviet threat by creating a grand economic and military alliance. Yet none of the OECD countries ever fought the Soviet Union.

The world's wealthiest states have no desire to war against each other because the costs would be too great. Yet that does not inhibit them from warring against poorer countries when vital interests are at stake, or poorer countries warring against each other.

ECONOMIC INTEREST GROUPS AND WAR

Self-interest shapes national interests; the more powerful the interest, the greater its ability to substitute its interest for the nation's. Some argue that *military-industrial complexes* are the most powerful interest groups in the United States, Russia, China, and other great powers. The military and the industries and politicians that benefit

military-industrial complex the economic and political relationship between industries that produce military goods, the U.S. Defense Department, and congressional representatives with military industries in their districts. Together, they have a powerful interest in maintaining high levels of defense spending regardless of what kind of foreign threats the country faces.

from and support it have a vested interest in ever more military spending and in war itself. Military-industrial complexes constantly try to justify and expand their existence. They do so by identifying real and often exaggerated or outright imagined enemies. Throughout the cold war, the military-industrial complexes of the United States and Soviet Union fought any attempts to limit arms races, military intervention overseas, or the peaceful resolution of conflicts.

The military-industrial complex theory for war has little evidence. Most wars have not been fought primarily for economic gain.[41] War has rarely conferred direct economic benefits on those who fought it. In any national economy, war benefits only a few businesses while hurting most. Thus, most businesspeople prefer peace to war. Profits instead went to those who sat on the fence and sold to both sides.

Military-industrial complexes may not be as omnipotent as their critics maintain. Other factors, such as nationalism, ideology, the power balance, and so forth are much more important in explaining the reasons why countries with large military-industrial complexes go to war.

War *and the* International System

THE POWER BALANCE, IMBALANCE, AND WAR

Many theorists maintain that wars explode not from the quirks of humans or the states in which they live but from the configurations of power in the international system itself. Few concepts of international relations are cited more frequently and interpreted more widely than "the balance of power."

balance of power term used to label various power configurations among **states.** The classic balance of power has changing alliances of half-dozen states of relatively equal military power against, and in response to, aggressive states. Some theorists argue that the balance involves the power distribution among states; others argue that it involves the power distribution among alliances.

Ernst Haas found seven distinct ways of using the term *balance of power.*[42] Three involved how power was distributed and the subsequent relations among states: (1) any distribution of power; (2) an equilibrium of power; and (3) hegemony of power. Two concentrated on the notion of an equilibrium of power having two very different impacts on international relations and war: (4) stability and peace; and (5) instability and war. The two final uses of the term claim that either (6) states will always attempt to strengthen their national security by countering the power of others and thus try to maintain an equilibrium in the international system (universal law of history), or (7) whether or not they do, they should (prescriptive).

The debate between A. F. K. Organski and Hans Morgenthau exemplifies the difficulty in achieving a consensus over just what "balance of power" means.[43] To Organski, the balance of power simply means the constantly shifting distribution of power among individual states, whereas Morgenthau maintains that the balance of power refers to shifting alliances of states rather than among individual states.

The most common use of the term asserts that international power can be distributed in several patterns or poles, each of which makes war more or less likely. *Unipolarity* occurs when one state has predominant or hegemonic military power, as the United States has since the Soviet empire's collapse in 1991.

Bipolarity involves two states or alliances with a relative military power balance between them. In the late 1940s the United States and Soviet Union clustered weaker European states around themselves either through coercion or persuasion, and from the 1950s until the late 1980s competed for allies throughout the Third World. As these two alliances solidified and Moscow exploded an atomic bomb in 1949, breaking America's atomic monopoly, the global system became characterized as bipolar.

During the 1960s, the rigid alliances of NATO and the Warsaw Pact began to loosen, prompting analysts to label the new system *bipolycentric* or *bimultipolar*.[44] The United States and Soviet Union remained the sole superpowers, but their ability to pressure their respective alliance members into compliance diminished and some states, such as China and France, asserted their independence from their blocs. Relations were forged between members of the two blocs, such as West Germany's *Ostpolitik* policy toward Eastern Europe and East Germany. Some of this *decoupling* from the alliances occurred because ICBMs lessened the superpower need for forward bases from which to attack the other, whereas the NATO members in particular increasingly questioned Washington's resolve to retaliate with nuclear weapons in response to a Soviet attack on Western Europe. Great Britain, China, and France developed their own nuclear weapons. As the European (Union) and Japan economically caught up to the United States, they increasingly followed policies that promoted their own interests even if they clashed with the Western alliance. China meanwhile challenged the Soviet Union for leadership of world communism. Under bipolycentrism, Washington and Moscow remained the sole superpowers, but other regions and countries became increasingly powerful and assertive economically and militarily.

If the United States and Russia continue to reduce their nuclear and conventional arsenals while the world becomes ever more interdependent, a genuine *multipolar* system may emerge in which half a dozen states have relatively equal military and economic power, including the United States, Japan, the European Union, China, and Russia. A neoclassical balance of power system could emerge in which states compete and combine against each other, as they did in an earlier era (1648–1792), but now for geoeconomic rather than geopolitical reasons. Or the power balance might be made of regions rather than states, with a North American economic bloc led by the United States, an expanded European Union embracing Eastern Europe and Russia, and a Japan-led East and Southeast Asian bloc.

So how does power's distribution make war more or less likely? Theorists disagree over whether a balanced or imbalanced power system is more susceptible to war. Some argue that power imbalances rather than balances make war more likely. When one state has more power than others, it is more likely to go to war because it has a greater chance of winning.[45] Other theorists argue that the more egalitarian the power distribution, the more states feel they could win a war against their rivals, and thus war is more likely: "An even distribution of political, economic, and military capabilities between contending groups of states is likely to increase the probability of war; peace is preserved best when there is an imbalance of national capabilities between disadvantaged and advantaged nations; the aggressor will come from a group of dissatisfied strong countries; and it is the weaker, rather than the stronger, power that is most likely to be the aggressor."[46]

Both arguments are partially right. A study of all wars between 1820 and 1965 found that there was no correlation between the power balance and war.[47] When power was distributed relatively equally, war was likely 50 percent of the time; and when power was unequally distributed, war was likely 46 percent of the time. There was a difference between the 19th century, during which wars were more likely when there was an imbalance of power, and the 20th century, during which a relative power balance made war more likely. Wars of rivalry are more likely when there is a power balance; wars of opportunity, when there is a power imbalance.[48]

Those who maintain that a power balance increases the chance for war differ over whether a bipolar or multipolar system is more unstable. Some argue that in a bipolar world, each side focuses its attention on the other and counters every move the other makes. The increased tension and arms races inevitably make war more likely.[49] In contrast, the proliferation of issues and actors in a multipolar system tends to defuse tensions and thus the possibility of war. Destabilizing arms races are more likely in a bipolar than in a multipolar system. Others argue just the opposite, and point out that the multipolar system of the early 20th century led to two world wars, whereas the post-1945 bipolar system has remained at peace. Multipolar systems involving three powers, they argue, are much more unstable than a bipolar system because two tend to ally against the third.[50]

Who is right? One study of all wars of the last five centuries found that wars were less likely in a multipolar system but far more bloody because they involved far more people.[51] No general wars (such as those of the Napoleonic era or the 20th century's two world wars) occurred during bipolar periods, but wars were more likely. However, of all the systems throughout history, unipolar international systems have been relatively more peaceful than other power distributions. Roman and British hegemony were known respectively as the Pax Romana and the Pax Britannica (*pax* is Latin for "peace") because other states lacked enough power to challenge the prevailing system. Will the Pax Americana that emerged from the Soviet Union's collapse in 1991 provide a similar era of peace? How long before the Pax Americana is challenged by others?

Regardless of whether the global system is predominantly multipolar or bipolar, war is more likely when that power distribution is changing. Power is more than tanks and missiles. The size and quality of the two sides' respective populations, industries, geographies, natural resources, technological levels, and, most importantly, political wills and national cohesions, all shape the power calculus. Karl Deutsch argues that whenever "there is a major change at any level—culture and values, political and social institutions, laws, or technology—the old adjustment and control mechanisms become strained and may break down. Any major psychological and cultural, or major social and political, or legal, or technological change in the world thus increases the risk of war, unless it is balanced by compensatory political, legal, cultural, and psychological adjustments."[52]

Many theorists believe that the most important shifts in regional or global power balances are technological and economic.[53] Organski and Kugler maintain that "war is caused by differences in the rates of growth among the great powers and . . . the differences in rates between the dominant nation and the challenger that permit the latter to overtake the former.[54] One side's introduction of a new weapon system can dramatically shift the power balance. For example, the English won the Hundred Years War as much with the longbow as anything else. Although larger states are more aggressive than smaller states, the distribution of military technology can supply smaller or poorer states with an ability to wage war that they formerly did not have.[55]

HEGEMONIC STABILITY, LONG CYCLES, AND WAR

hegemonic stability theory argues that international relations in the global political economy has been shaped by the rise and fall of hegemons, or those states that briefly become the most powerful in the system.

Some see international relations as shaped not by a balance of power but by a hierarchy of power. The great powers struggle for power, and eventually one emerges from a war to become a hegemon over the system, until eventually that power is vanquished by another. The concept of the rise and fall of hegemons, or *hegemonic stability theory* as it is known, is closely linked to the *long cycle theory* of history.[56] Shifts in economic and technological power and war are seen to reoccur in long cycles, generally of a century. The hegemonic wars of the modern era include

Part 4   Geopolitical Conflict and Cooperation

(1) the Italian Wars (1494–1517), from which Portugal emerged as the world power; (2) the War of Dutch Independence (1585–1609), leading to the rise of the Netherlands as a world power; (3) the Wars of Louis XIV (1689–1715), which gave way to British leadership; (4) the French Revolutionary and Napoleonic Wars (1792–1815), which renewed the world power role of Britain; and (5) the two World Wars of this century (1914–1945), marked the transition of the United States to world power."[57]

Joshua Goldstein nicely summarized the rise and fall of hegemons and other great powers: "Countries rebuilding from war incorporate a new generation of technology, eventually allowing competition with the hegemonic country. For these reasons, each period of hegemony gradually erodes. Recurring wars, on several long wave upswings, eventually culminate in a new hegemonic war, bringing another restructuring of the core and a new period of hegemony."[58]

Most studies, however, do not find a war cycle for nations.[59] Jack Levy effectively demolishes the long cycle and hegemonic stability theories.[60] Even if these long cycles ever existed, hegemonic wars are increasingly unlikely as the world becomes ever more interdependent.

ARMS RACES

In an anarchic global system, states must rely on themselves for their own security. "If you want peace, prepare for war," has been the guide for leaders throughout history. The power balance or peace-through-strength theory, however, can lead to arms races that destabilize international relations and make war more rather than less likely. Arms races occur when states become trapped in a *security dilemma*.[61] One state perceives a foreign military threat so it builds up its forces. In alleviating its own security problem, it simultaneously threatens the security of the other state, which responds by building up its own forces. The first state then reacts by further enlarging its forces, and the arms race thus spirals indefinitely. Arms races are easy to begin, very difficult to end, and often end in war.

Any participant in a given arms race may well have no hostile intent, but each becomes a prisoner of its own fear and distrust for the other and the possibly dire results of not keeping up. Each side sees only the other's offensive capabilities and not its defensive intentions. Thus the race continues. This phenomenon is known as the *prisoner's dilemma*.[62]

Arms races occur because of both international rivalries and domestic politics. Which is more important? Nazli Choucri and Robert North argue that

> The primary importance of domestic factors . . . does not preclude the reality of arms competition. Two countries whose military establishments are expanding largely for domestic reasons . . . almost certainly will become acutely aware of each other's spending. Thereafter, although spending may continue to be powerfully affected by domestic factors, deliberate military spending may be over specific military features and may be a very small portion of total military spending.[63]

Do arms races tend to end in war? Scholars exploring the question have reached different conclusions.[64] One study of great power arms races since 1815 found that most have ended in war.[65] Another study, which examined 13 arms races in the 19th and 20th centuries, found that only 5 ended in war.[66] Yet another study of arms races between 1816 and 1980 found that only 20 percent were followed by war.[67] One study found no example of an arms race being the primary cause of any war.[68]

Whom are we to believe? Arms races themselves may be difficult to define. Just because rival states annually increase their military budgets does not necessarily

prisoner's dilemma the choice faced by a participant in a conflict or arms race between self-imprisonment behind the bars of fear and distrust of another nation (in which there may well be no hostile intent) and the possibly dire consequences of reducing **deterrence.** Each side sees only the other's offensive capabilities and none of its defensive intentions. Thus the conflict or arms race continues.

mean they are engaged in an arms race. Domestic politics and military-industrial complexes may be more important in determining the amount and priorities of a nation's military budget than the international power balance. States may build up their arms yet not feel they are racing against others, and thus tensions remain low. The study which "found" that most arms races ended in war analyzed only those in which the participants increased their spending in direct response to that of their rivals. Clearly, some arms races do lead to war, whereas others are substitutes for war.

Arms races are symptoms rather than causes of war. Genuine arms races do not occur unless those countries already have deep conflicts. Arms races exacerbate existing conflicts; they do not create conflicts. Although the mere possession of weapons is not enough to start a war, the more powerful a government's military forces, the more inclined it might be to use those weapons in a conflict. A state's military power is less important than what it intends to do with those forces. States with good relations do not engage in arms races. As Hans Morgenthau put it, "Men do not fight because they have arms. They have arms because they deem it necessary to fight."[69]

Regardless of whether or not they end in war, there is nothing positive about arms races. They consume enormous amounts of human, scientific, financial, and political resources that could be more profitably invested elsewhere. If a war does occur, it will probably be more destructive than if the arms race had never preceded it. Although most people would agree that "Guns don't kill, people do," the proliferation of guns certainly increases tensions that may result in war. It also makes war more likely because in a crisis, leaders might feel more confident about militarily asserting their position.

ALLIANCES

People commonly believe that alliances, like arms races, can increase tension and make war more likely. Alliance with other states can obviously augment a nation's power, which in turn must be calculated into the overall power balance. Alliances are formed when its members anticipate the strong possibility of war.

Some consider alliances destabilizing because

> First, alliances look menacing; hence it is likely that they will cause others to scramble for allies of their own, and therein raise tensions to a new, more dangerous level. Second, alliances are entangling; they can drag members into conflicts which do not affect their vital interests; Finally, alliances are sanguineous; their very existence means that even if a nation's armies are beaten and its leaders can see that resources are inadequate to sustain further combat, it would be encouraged to continue fighting by the hope of aid from its allies. In sum, whereas some theorists and statesmen advance the proposition that alliances sustain peace, others echo Sir John Frederick Maurice's lament that "if you prepare thoroughly for war you will get it."[70]

Do allies make war more or less likely? In fact, alliances seem no more likely to cause a war than do arms races. A study of 256 international conflicts between 1815 and 1965 concluded that wars were just as common whether or not an alliance was involved, although it did find that being in an alliance made smaller powers more likely to go to war.[71] Minor powers with great power allies went to war in 42 percent of conflicts; without such allies, they went to war only 17 percent of the time. An even more comprehensive study involving the last five centuries reached the same general conclusions.[72]

One study found that alliances decreased the chance for war throughout the 19th century, increased it in the 20th century up through 1945, and decreased it thereafter.[73] Another study, which spanned 1495 to 1975, found that most alliances led to war within five years of their formation, except between 1815 and 1914, when no wars followed within five years of an alliance's formation.[74] Alliances, like increased arms, may not be a war's underlying cause but aggravate existing tensions and thus make war more likely. In both studies, the most important effect was whether or not the alliance stabilized relations.

INTERDEPENDENCE, SECURITY COMMUNITIES, AND WAR

The reasons why the world's wealthiest states do not war against each other may have less to do with their wealth than the interdependence between them. The OECD countries have created, what Karl Deutsch would call a *"security community,"*— "a group of people which has become 'integrated.' By integration we mean the attainment, within a territory, of a 'sense of community' and of institutions and practices strong enough and widespread enough to assure . . . dependable expectations of 'peaceful change' among its population. By sense of community we mean a belief . . . that common social problems must and can be resolved by processes of 'peaceful change.'"[75]

security community an alliance of countries dedicated to collective security.

That is not to say there is no conflict among or within the OECD countries. Economic disputes among the OECD are rife, yet are handled diplomatically with no thought of using military force. Violence within some OECD members is common— race riots in the United States, IRA bombings in Britain, Basque bombings in Spain, ethnic violence in Germany and France, and so on. But the governments successfully contain if not solve these conflicts, and there is little chance that they can affect international relations.

Although security communities are most common between ideological allies, they can also exist between countries that are ideological rivals. A security community evolved between the United States and Soviet Union after 1945 as the crises, saber rattling, and brinkmanship of the 1950s were eventually transformed into the détente and restraint of the 1970s and 1980s. The superpowers continued to compete across the global geopolitical chessboard, but avoided any direct confrontation after the 1962 Cuban missile crisis. They bolstered this "crisis avoidance" understanding with more than a dozen conventional and nuclear arms control treaties. With the collapse of the Soviet Union's communist regime and empire, Russia and the other newly independent countries are being slowly drawn into the interdependent global economy, a trend that will only strengthen the prevailing peace.[76]

Mutually assured destruction (MAD) was the basis of the American-Soviet security community. Robert Gilpin writes that

> it was not until after 1945 that the threat of an all-out military conflict (including the use of nuclear and thermonuclear bombs) became catastrophic so that such wars as did occur took on a more limited character. The risks of trying to take new territory through military invasion mounted while the alternative of development through rational industrial and trade policies heralded new rewards for a peaceful strategy. This shift . . . has largely escaped notice in the study of international politics.[77]

The greater the world's economic, nuclear, and environmental interdependence, the lower the chance for war. According to Rosecrance,

War and refugees are as old as international relations, indeed have plagued the world for as long as humans have occupied it. Every war has its own unique primary, secondary, and tertiary causes. But are there similar reasons for wars during different epochs? If so what are they and why do they change from one epoch to the next? Can war ever be eliminated from international relations?

AP/Wide World Photos

a new "trading world" of international relations offers the possibility of escaping such a vicious cycle [war] and finding new patterns of cooperation among nation-states . . . the benefit of trade and cooperation today greatly exceeds that of military competition and territorial aggrandizement. States, as Japan has shown, can do better through a strategy of economic development based on trade than they are likely to do through military interventions in the affairs of other states . . . the new world that is unfolding contrasts very sharply with comparable periods of major historical transition. Unlike those earlier periods, no major new military threat is likely to replace the old one anytime soon.[78]

INTERNATIONAL MORALITY AND WAR

International law outlaws war, or at least aggressive war. Although some may scoff at the effectiveness of international law in deterring war, others argue that "statesmen nearly always perceive themselves as constrained by international principles and rules that prescribe and proscribe behavior" and that these "international norms are more important than countervailing power in constraining states."[79]

Until recently, the idea of outlawing war would have puzzled most philosophers and spiritual leaders, let alone state leaders. The notion of a *just war* emerged from early Christendom, and Islam promotes the concept of "holy war" (*jihad*) in which it is not only just but also obligatory for Muslims to fight infidels. Although the debate over when going to war is justified can be traced to the ancient Greeks, it was St. Augustine (345–430) who most systematically addressed the subject. St. Augustine argued that "just wars" (*jus ad belli*) "are usually defined as those which avenge injuries, when the nation or city against which war-like action is to be directed has neglected either to punish wrongs committed by its own citizens or to restore what has been unjustly taken by it. Further that kind of war is undoubtedly just which God himself ordains."[80] In other words, murder is not committed when killing done in self-defense or God's glory. Killing is justified in this view.

Carnage off *the* Beaten Track: Eritrea *versus* Ethiopia

In February and March 1999, a fierce border war exploded between Ethiopia and Eritrea. What started it? Nationalism, territorial disputes along a 650-mile frontier, an obsession with avenging wounds festering from a previous war, and miscalculation were the worst culprits. Never since World War II has battle killed or wounded so many in so short a time.

In two days of fighting the Ethiopians may have suffered 10,000 casualties and the Eritreans twice as many. The war is mismatched, with Ethiopia's population of 65 million dwarfing Eritrea's 3.5 million people. Will Ethiopia reconquer Eritrea, which only won its independence after a bloody 30-year struggle? That is unlikely, with nearly all of Eritrea's population mobi-

lized for war, well armed, and dug in. As of July 2000 a peace settlement was being negotiated but the fundamental issue of who owns the disputed land remains unresolved. The animosities between the Ethiopians and Eritreans will probably persist indefinitely, much as Pakistanis and Indians still fight over Kashmir.

During the 16th century, three Spanish legal scholars—Francisco de Vitoria, Alberico Gentili, and Francisco Suarez—attempted to synthesize ancient and medieval writings on warfare, in part to justify the Spanish conquest of the western Hemisphere. Horrified by the slaughter of the Thirty Years War, Hugo Grotius, the Dutch legal scholar, then built on their efforts. Grotius accepted war's inevitability, but argued that there should be treaty and ethical constraints governing its conduct. He distinguished between "the justice of a war" (*jus ad bellum*) in which a government must decide whether its decision to go to war is just, and "justice in a war" (*jus in bello*) in which governments accept restraints on the tactics used in warfare. His arguments influenced the Treaty of Westphalia of 1648, which inaugurated a period of restraint in warfare that lasted until the Napoleonic era.

Today, according to Inis Claude, international relations are governed by "the *neo-just war doctrine* . . . [which] no longer seriously purports to accept the view that peace is unconditionally a higher view than justice. We have returned to the medieval view that it is permissible . . . to fight to promote justice, broadly conceived. Evil ought to be overturned, and good ought to be achieved, by force if necessary."[81] The neo-just-war doctrine includes six key components: (1) war can only be fought after all other means of resolving the issue have been exhausted, (2) only legitimate governments can decide to go to war, (3) wars should be fought for self-defense and not revenge, (4) there should be a good chance of winning, (5) the war should be fought to achieve conditions that would have been better than those which have occurred through nonresistance, and (6) war should be fought to resist aggression, not change the enemy's government or society.[82] This conception of morality helped justify U.N. intervention in Kuwait, Somalia, and Bosnia during the 1990s and will prove an essential argument for similar interventions in the future.

These principles have been codified in a range of treaties throughout the 20th century. Even self-defense is limited. Literally interpreted, the right to self-defense does not extend to launching a pre-emptive attack in response to the belligerent actions or words of another state unless fighting has already broken out. According to various International Court of Justice rulings, there are three other restrictions on self-defense. Attacks on one's nationals abroad does not justify retaliation. Self-defense does not allow reprisals against the enemy territory. Any force used in self-defense must be necessary and proportional to the armed attack.

Although one state can sell arms to or station troops in another state, it is illegal for a state to do so without that other state's permission. In the case *Nicaragua v. USA* (1986), Nicaragua sued the United States for blockading its ports and aiding rebels fighting against the government. The United States argued that its actions were justified under the principle of collective self-defense—the Nicaraguans were sending arms to rebels fighting against the neighboring state of El Salvador. The International Court of Justice ruled that collective self-defense was valid only in the event of any actual attack, which never transpired. Thus it ruled against the United States and ordered it to compensate Nicaragua for its losses. The Reagan administration dismissed the court's rulings, claiming that it did not have jurisdiction.

International law has been used to prosecute war criminals. Defendants at the Nuremberg and Tokyo war trials were charged with three types of crime:

1. *Crimes against peace:* namely, planning, preparation, initiation or waging of a war of aggression, or a war in violation of international treaties, agreements, or assurances, or participation in a common plan or conspiracy for the accomplishment of any of the foregoing.

2. *War crimes:* namely, violations of the laws or customs of war. Such violations shall include, but not be limited to, murder, ill treatment, or deportation of slave labor or any other purpose of civilian population of or in occupied territory, murder or ill treatment of prisoners of war or persons on the seas, killing of hostages, plunder of public or private property, wanton destruction of cities, towns, or villages, or devastation not justified by military necessity.

3. *Crimes against humanity:* namely, murder, extermination, enslavement, deportation, and any other inhumane acts committed against any civilian population, before or during the war, or persecutions on political, racial, or religious grounds in execution of or in connection with any crime within the jurisdiction of the tribunal, whether or not in violation of the domestic law of the country where perpetrated.

How effective has international law been in deterring war? It is difficult to say with certainty. One sign of its increasing importance is that most governments rigorously claim they are following it even as others maintain those governments are breaking it.

Conclusion

Although each war has its own unique set of causes, we can make some general observations. States are shaped by the international system of which they are a part. In a global system with no government, every state ultimately must fend for itself. At any given time in history, some countries are largely satisfied with the international status quo, whereas others wish to change it, sometimes by violent means. Wars occur because governments perceive them as being useful for resolving conflicts. "War," as Karl von Clausewitz pointed out, "is simply the continuation of politics by other means."

Yet there are signs that war is becoming an increasingly unimportant part of international relations. The cold war is over. The Soviet empire and the Warsaw Pact have disappeared. Liberal democracy has replaced communism throughout eastern Europe and tentatively in Russia. The superpowers have made significant agreements to "build down" their respective forces. As countries become more wealthy and democratic, war's costs rise and benefits plummet. Throughout the 20th century, international morality and law has evolved to the point where wars of aggression are outlawed and condemned. The national and international constraints on war are growing. Nations increasingly settle their differences peacefully. The percentage of conflicts that end in war have steadily diminished from about 15 percent from 1815 to 1945 to only 3 percent since.[83] Between 1919 and 1986, 68 of 97 international conflicts, or 70 percent, were settled peacefully, although there were 168 attempts to do so.[84]

Despite these favorable trends, it is unlikely that war will ever entirely disappear. Although international wars have diminished, civil wars continue to tear apart some states. People will continue to kill each other as long as they perceive a need to do so.

Study Questions

1. Are violence and war part of human nature?

2. What is social Darwinism, and how has it affected attitudes toward war and peace?

3. Define behaviorism. How has it affected attitudes toward war and peace?

4. How can misperceptions affect conflict? Give an example.

5. Explain how nationalism has contributed to war.

6. What is the "scapegoat" cause of war, and how common is it?

7. How can a state's political and/or economic instability lead to war?

8. Why have liberal democratic countries never warred against each other? What implications does this have for international relations as more countries become liberal democracies?

9. How is a state's level of economic development related to its propensity for war?

10. What is the military-industrial complex theory of war? How valid is that theory? (Explain.)

11. How is the power balance related to the likelihood of war?

12. What are the different ways in which the term "balance of power" can be interpreted?

13. Evaluate the "hegemonic stability" and "long cycle" theories of war.

14. Define the security dilemma and the prisoner's dilemma. How do they affect conflict, arms races, and war?

15. Do alliances make war more or less likely? Explain.

16. What are security communities? How do they affect conflict and war?

17. How has international morality changed concerning questions of war? How does international morality affect the propensity for war today?

18. How effective has international law been in regulating or preventing war?

⚕ *InfoTrac College Edition* Sources

Using the Subject Guide, enter the search terms *just war, social Darwinism,* and/or *behaviorism.* Using Keywords, enter the search term *military industrial complex.*

Bacevich, A. J. "Morality and High Technology."

Bennett, D. Scott, and Allan C. Stam III. "The Duration of Interstate Wars, 1816–1985."

Christensen, Thomas J. "Perceptions and Alliances in Europe, 1865–1940."

Collier, Paul, and Anke Hoeffler. "On Economic Causes of Civil War."

Copeland, Dale C. "Economic Interdependence and War: A Theory of Trade Expectations."

Dawson, Doyne. "The Origins of War: Biological and Anthropological Theories."

Harper, John L. "The Dream of Democratic Peace: Americans Are Not Asleep."

Hehir, Brian. " 'Just War' Applied Anew to 'Genocide', Civil War."

Lloyd, John. "Who Will Now Master the Universe?"

Mansfield, Edward D., and Jack Snyder. "Democratization and Danger of War."

Johnson, James Turner. "The Broken Tradition."

Papayoanou, Paul A. "Interdependence, Institutions, and the Balance of Power: Britain, Germany, and World War I."

Pipes, Daniel. "A New Axis: The Emerging Turkish-Israeli Entente."

Pollins, Brian M. "Global Political Order, Economic Change, and Armed Conflict: Coevolving Systems and the Use of Force."

Powell, Robert. "Uncertainty, Shifting Power, and Appeasement."

Renner, Michael. "How to Abolish War."

Seabrook, Jeremy. "What Is the 'International Community'?"

Stott, Robin, and Douglas Holdstock. "Eradicating War Is Essential to Eliminate Poverty and Improve Health."

🌐 On *the* Web

hrrp://www.foreignpolicy-infocus.org/papers/micr/index.html
Discussion of the military-industrial complex

http://hagar.up.ac.za/catts/learner/peterdl/Behav.html
Behaviorism links

http://www.constitution.org/prisdilm.htm
Prisoner's dilemma, with numerous links

Contents

Chapter 9 *The* Cold War: Origins, Strategies, Aftermath

Key Concepts and Terms

Why are these people so happy? On November 9, 1989, the East German government announced that it would demolish the Berlin Wall, the cold war's greatest symbol, which was erected in 1961 to prevent those desiring freedom to flee the communist East to the democratic West. How would your life have differed had you been born under a communist regime? Would you have made the most of its system or escaped to greater opportunities in the democratic industrial countries?

AP/Wide World Photos

For nearly 50 years, the United States and Soviet Union were locked into a *cold war* in which they used every means short of direct war between them to win their respective security and ideological interests in virtually all regions and countries around the world, and to surpass each other militarily. During that half-century the Americans and Soviets spent trillions of dollars and rubles on a conventional and nuclear arms race, fought or instigated wars in Vietnam, Afghanistan, and in scores of Third World countries in which millions perished, and in the Berlin, Cuban missile, and other crises marched to the brink of World War III, which would have most likely resulted in a nuclear holocaust that killed hundreds of millions of people in both countries and elsewhere. Then, suddenly and dramatically, the cold war ended in the early 1990s as the Soviet empire and communism collapsed.

The cold war had two finales rich in symbolism. On November 9, 1989, the *Berlin Wall* crumbled amid thousands of joyous sledgehammer blows and glasses of champagne. Over three years later, on May 6, 1992, Mikhail Gorbachev, the former Soviet president who freed the subjugated peoples of eastern Europe and the Soviet Union, gave a speech in Fulton, Missouri, where on March 21, 1946, Winston Churchill had warned that an *iron curtain* had clanged shut across Europe, dividing a liberal, democratic West from a totalitarian, aggressive communist East. Standing in the shadow of a huge bronze statue of Churchill, Gorbachev argued that the cold war had been a vast unnecessary tragedy, that Moscow and Washington had completely misunderstood each other's intentions and capabilities, and interpreted the other's actions in the worst possible way. The result was a spiraling arms race that eventually devastated both countries economically and a series of crises around the world in which the Soviet and American blocs more than once almost launched World War III and nuclear Armageddon.

Have we come full circle in the more than fifty years since Churchill's warning? Was the cold war really simply born of a tragic misperception, as Gorbachev and others maintain, or were there genuine national and ideological interests at stake that made conflict between the United States and Soviet Union inevitable?

The Cost of Victory

The Center for Defense Information, an independent research organization, estimates that the cold war's total cost for the United States in 1996 dollars was $13.1 trillion, with an average annual defense budget of $298.5 billion. Was any of that money squandered? How can analysts determine which of those programs helped and which actually hurt American national interests? Of the money that was wasted, how do you believe it should have been spent?

Was the cold war simply a long and tragic detour in the world's inevitable march toward international cooperation and the celebration of human rights? Why did the cold war occur? How was it waged? Why did it end when and as it did? What were its costs? This chapter explores these and related questions.

Why Did *the* Cold War Start?

Why did the wartime alliance between the United States and Soviet Union breakdown into nearly a half-century of cold war? Scholars have debated the question since the late 1940s and have yet to achieve a consensus. Some argue that the Soviet Union was clearly at fault.[1] After all, it was the Soviets that toppled one government after another throughout Eastern Europe and imposed communist dictatorships in their place. Others argue that actually the United States was at fault.[2] According to that view, a cold war between the Soviet Union and the West had existed ever since the Bolshevik Revolution, when British, French, American, and Japanese troops intervened in the civil war on the side of the counterrevolutionaries. Although the Western powers set aside their containment of the Soviet Union during World War II, in the late 1940s the United States resorted to anti-communism as an excuse to mobilize the American public behind the measures needed to revive the global economy.

Most scholars conclude that the cold war was inevitable and no one country was to blame.[3] With the Germans and Japanese devastated by defeat, and the British and French by victory, the United States and Soviet Union were the only genuine great powers when World War II ended in 1945. That would have been grounds enough for conflict. Historically, great powers have always competed and frequently gone to war over vital and even superfluous issues. But this great power rivalry was exacerbated by the diametrically opposed ideologies that each power espoused—the United States, liberal democracy and free markets for all; the Soviet Union, one-party rule, state control of all property and production, and global revolution. Finally, both the Kremlin and the White House locked themselves psychologically into viewing the other's actions in the worst possible way, and then took countermeasures that seemed aggressive to the other side. Great power rivalry, conflicting ideologies, and misperceptions were all essential to converting the World War II allies into cold war enemies.

THE CLASH OF IDEOLOGIES

The cold war was at root a conflict between diametrically opposed world views. Hans Morgenthau nicely summed up the role of ideology in the cold war:

> The claim to universality which inspires the moral code of one particular group is incompatible with the identical claim of another group, the world has room for only one, and the other must yield or be destroyed. Thus carrying their idols before them, the nationalistic masses of our time meet in the international arena, each group convinced that it executes the mandate of history, that it does for humanity what it seems to do for itself, and that it fulfills a sacred mission ordained by Providence, however defined.[4]

American foreign policy has been shaped by several powerful and sometimes conflicting values. From the first settlements in what became the United States, Americans have believed that their institutions and way of life were freer and presented more opportunities for individual advancement than those elsewhere, and thus were superior. Borrowing a phrase first used by Massachusetts governor John Winthrop in 1630, President Reagan predicted in 1984 that America would become a *"shining city on a hill"* for all of humanity to emulate. He summed up this belief in his 1987 State of the Union address when he said, "I have always believed that this anointed land was set apart in an uncommon way, that a divine plan placed this great continent between the oceans to be found by people from every corner of the world who had a special love of faith and freedom."

isolationists those who want to minimize their country's involvement in international political affairs.

expansionists those who want to expand their country's power and territory.

Although most Americans held this belief, they differed over how it should be applied to foreign policy. Many were *isolationists,* who agreed with President George Washington that the United States should trade with all nations while remaining aloof from foreign wars and intrigues that did not directly affect American interests. Others were *expansionists,* who argued that the United States had a moral responsibility as well as economic interests to spread its concepts of democracy to all the world's peoples.

In fact, these two visions have coexisted within American foreign policy from independence through today. The United States expanded across the continent to the Pacific and then beyond, defeating or negotiating with hundreds of Native American nations, along with Spain, Mexico, France, Great Britain, Germany, France, China, Japan, and other countries. Like the other great powers, the United States designated certain regions its sphere of influence in which others should not interfere. In 1823, President James Monroe announced what became known as the *Monroe Doctrine,* a policy in which the United States supported the independence struggles of Latin Americans against Spanish rule and thus would not tolerate any renewed European colonization in the region. America's perception of its foreign interests expanded with its industrial, territorial, and military power. In 1899 and 1900, the McKinley White House asserted that it was committed to an open door for free trade and would oppose any attempts of the other great powers to shut American merchants out of China or elsewhere. Despite the continual assertion of American power, until World War I the United States avoided any European alliances or wars. After World War I, which ended in 1918, Washington returned to political isolation until 1941.

It has only been since World War II that the United States has consistently been involved in shaping the world according to American ideals of free trade and anticommunism. During World War II, President Franklin Roosevelt clearly articulated U.S. foreign policy goals for the postwar world as based on universal economic and political freedom. To realize these goals, Washington led the creation of the United Nations and such international economic institutions as the IMF, World Bank, and later GATT, today's World Trade Organization.

However, by 1947 the Truman administration realized the Soviet Union posed a threat to America's foreign policy goals. Containing the Soviet Union became essential to successfully expanding the global political economy and achieving American ideals. Believing their country to be the personification of "good," by definition anyone fundamentally opposed to the United States and its ideals must be "evil" in some profound way. Throughout the cold war, Washington and the American public came to view the Soviet Union as an *evil empire* bent on achieving global conquest and communism.

Russia's world view has been shaped by over 1,000 years of continual invasions by foreign powers. In the 20th century alone, the Soviet Union lost over 10 million lives in World War I and the Russian civil war, and over 20 million in World War II. Not surprisingly, Russians are naturally suspicious of foreigners. To survive, Russia had to develop a highly authoritarian system to mobilize the population and continually expand against its neighbors. In addition to simply surviving the onslaughts of others, Russians saw themselves as the champions of the Christian Orthodox Church and Slavic peoples. Thus the Russians were not just survivors but a special people who championed both a great religion and millions of Slavs far beyond the state's immediate borders.

Moscow's foreign policy has thus largely involved deterring or defeating surrounding hostile states and expanding Russian territory until national security was ensured. Like Washington, Moscow identified its own *spheres of influence* that were considered vital to Russian security, such as eastern Europe, the Black Sea and access to the Mediterranean Sea, and the Far East and access to the Pacific Ocean. Empires, however, can never be truly secure, because each new conquest must be defended, thus making other states more fearful and resistant to that expansion.

Russia's geography and its deeply ingrained xenophobia and exclusiveness have set it apart from the West. Russians have traditionally felt a sense of cultural, political and economic inferiority to the West and have been torn over proper relations with it. Since Tsar Peter the Great first tried to westernize Russia in the late 1600s, Russia's elite has been split between *Westernizers* who see Western Europe (and, later, the United States) as models for political and economic development, and *slavophiles* who advocate continued Russian authoritarianism and isolation from the West while asserting leadership over all the Slavic peoples of Eastern Europe. These divisions remain as sharp as ever even after the collapse of the Soviet empire and communism.

Soviet foreign policy incorporated traditional Russian features. The Russian view that warfare was the natural characteristic of international relations was reinforced by *communism,* with its conception of class and international warfare between capitalists and socialists. Lenin's idea of a *"dictatorship of the proletariat"* and the totalitarian system created by Stalin were built on a millennium of authoritarian tzarist rule. Between the time of Lenin and Gorbachev, Moscow's foreign policy clearly rejected the West and attempted to assert direct Soviet control over eastern Europe and spread communism worldwide. Like Washington, Moscow saw the world divided into two diametrically opposed and hostile camps in which it was the champion of all socialist and progressive forces and the United States championed all imperialist and antirevolutionary forces.

George Kennan captured the essence of Soviet strategy and its relationship with traditional Russian foreign policy:

The Kremlin is under no ideological compulsion to accomplish its purposes in a hurry. Like the Church, it is dealing in ideological concepts which are of long-term validity, and it can afford to be patient. . . . [The] teachings of Lenin himself require great caution and flexibility in the pursuit of Communist purposes. Again these precepts are fortified by the lessons of Russian history: of centuries of obscure battles between nomadic forces over the stretches of a vast unfortified plain. Here caution, circumspection, flexibility, and deception are the valuable qualities. . . . Thus the Kremlin has no compunction about retreating in the face of superior forces. . . . The main thing is there should always be pressure, increasing constant pressure, toward the desired goal.[5]

THE CLASH OF MISPERCEPTIONS

Whether the cold war was inevitable or not rests on whether each side could have overcome a worsening vicious cycle of misperceptions about the other. Ideological differences did not prevent the United States and the Soviet Union from being allies in World War II. But that effort against a common enemy only briefly obscured animosities that extended back over half a century.

Washington's first attempt to contain Moscow occurred in the 1890s when it joined with Tokyo in supporting an "open door" of trade and investment opportunities in Manchuria, which Russia was attempting to colonize. President Theodore Roosevelt stereotyped the Russians as "utterly insincere and treacherous; they have no conception of the truth . . . and no regard for others."[6] A decade later President Woodrow Wilson's closest adviser, Edward House, lamented, the dilemma that he saw facing the United States on the eve of its entry into World War I: "If the Allies win, it means the domination of Russia on the continent of Europe; and if Germany wins, it means the unspeakable tyranny of militarism for generations to come."[7] Throughout the 20th century, most presidents and foreign policy makers would echo and act on Roosevelt's stereotype and House's dilemma.

Moscow, too, tended to interpret every American action in the worst way. To the Soviets, America's containment of communism began, not in 1947, but between 1918 and 1920 when Washington deployed 10,000 troops in Russia to aid the "White" noncommunist forces in the civil war against the "Red" communists. Soviets have avoided the fact that the primary reason American troops were sent there was to offset the power of a Japanese army that had already invaded Siberia, and to guard millions of tons of supplies sent to the czarist regime during World War I. Moscow has avoided educating its public that after withdrawing its troops the United States sent millions of dollars in humanitarian aid to the Soviet Union during the early 1920s to relieve that country's mass famine. Although Washington refused to open diplomatic relations with Moscow until 1933, bilateral trade continued until it surpassed the prewar level in the late 1920s.

Throughout World War II, Stalin believed that Washington and London refused to open a *second front* in northern Europe until mid-1944, and limited the supplies it sent to Moscow so that the Soviet Union and Germany would destroy each other. Although there is no evidence that this was official policy, many Americans supported that strategy, including then Senator Harry Truman, who said in June 1941, "If we see that Germany is winning we should help Russia and if Russia is winning we ought to help Germany and that way let them kill off as many as possible, although I don't want to see Hitler victorious under any circumstances."[8] Roosevelt and Churchill twice promised a second front but instead sent their forces to North Africa and Italy before finally landing in, Normandy, France in June 1944. The reason for the Mediterranean campaign involved Churchill's tragically misguided strategic concepts rather than a conscious attempt to weaken the Soviet Union. Washington sent Moscow $11 billion of lend-lease military supplies during the war, accounting for nearly 10 percent of Soviet supplies and equipment. This aid may very well have made the difference between victory and defeat on the Russian front. But the Soviets lost sight of this reality and increasingly dwelled on perceived affronts by the United States as their war dead surpassed 20 million victims and much of the country's western half was devastated.

Likewise the Americans also interpreted Soviet actions as aggressive steps in a systematic strategy to conquer the world. Was the Soviet Union inherently expansionist? Answers to this question range from depicting the Soviet Union as an evil empire bent on global conquest to a peace-loving state that solely tried to defend itself. Most analysts, however, agree that the Soviet takeover of Eastern Europe and attempts at expansion elsewhere were largely opportunistic rather than part of some grand design for global conquest. In 1945, the Soviet Red Army simply moved into the political vacuum left by Germany's defeat. The Soviet empire inherited the Russian empire's xenophobia and search for defensible borders. That expansionist mentality was primarily defensive, forged by a millennium of continual attacks by neighboring aggressors on a Russia exposed on the vast steppes. This traditional drive combined with and was often justified by the communist ideology of global revolution. Most American policymakers understandably believed Moscow's inflammatory ideological rhetoric when evaluating Soviet actions in terms of national interests.

THE CLASH OF SECURITY INTERESTS

The most important conflict between Moscow on one hand, and Washington and London on the other, however, centered on Eastern Europe's postwar fate. The August 1941 Atlantic Charter issued by Roosevelt and Churchill proclaimed that the war should be fought for democracy and free trade everywhere. Roosevelt sincerely believed in these ideals; Churchill was more willing to compromise them. In 1944, the *Bretton Woods Conference,* attended by representatives of 44 countries, agreed to create the International Monetary Fund (IMF) and International Bank for Reconstruction and Development (IRBD, World Bank) to supply the finance vital for reconstructing the global economy, and began talks that culminated with the General Agreement on Trade and Tariffs (GATT) in 1947, whose expanding membership agreed to free trade principles and policies. Washington hoped to include all Eastern Europe in the free trade system even if Moscow refused to open its own economy.

While creating the infrastructure of the global political economy, however, Roosevelt also agreed to allow Moscow a sphere of influence in Eastern Europe after the war. The alternative, Roosevelt feared, was a separate peace between Hitler and Stalin that would allow German forces to be transferred to the western front. Roosevelt envisioned a postwar world ruled by both the United Nations and the *"Four Policemen"*—the United States, Great Britain, the Soviet Union, and China, each of which would be responsible for maintaining order in their respective regions or sphere of influence. In October 1944, Churchill flew to Moscow to cut a deal with Stalin in which Soviet control over Romania and Bulgaria would be exchanged for British control over Greece.

Eastern Europe's fate was sealed by two conferences during 1945. At the February *Yalta Conference,* Roosevelt, Churchill, and Stalin formally agreed to a

Cold War Relic *or* New World Order Champion? Whither NATO?

In May 1999, representatives of NATO's 19 members gathered in Washington, D.C., to celebrate the alliance's 50th anniversary. As they raised champagne glasses and toasted one another, NATO jets were systematically bombing Yugoslavia in what would be a 78-day campaign that won the first war in NATO's history.

Although irony haunts most human acts, including the most tragic, it was especially heavy amid NATO's war against Yugoslavia. NATO existed for 50 years during the cold war's worst crises and never fired a shot in anger. According to its treaty, NATO is purely a defensive alliance. Members agree to go to war if one or more members are attacked. NATO's war against Yugoslavia for human rights violations in its own province of Kosovo is a startling departure from NATO policy. Nothing in NATO's treaty legally justifies its intervention there. Certainly NATO turned a blind eye to the brutal Soviet destruction of mass democracy movements that challenged communist and Soviet rule in East Germany in 1953, Poland and Hungary in 1956, Czechoslovakia in 1968, and Afghanistan from 1970 to 1989.

Ironically, not only did NATO not fight its first war until after the cold war ended, it has more members now than when the Soviet empire existed. France rejoined the pact in 1995, having left in 1964 when President Charles de Gaulle took his country out of the alliance in a bid for a more independent foreign policy. In 1998 former Warsaw Pact countries Poland, Hungary, and the Czech Republic joined.

So just what is NATO's purpose in a post–cold-war world? Has NATO in its zeal to justify its own existence transformed itself, as some suggest, into the Balkan/Atlantic Treaty Organization (BATO)? By the year 2000, NATO had committed 80,000 troops to the Balkans, with 30,000 in Bosnia, 40,000 in Kosovo, 7,000 in Albania, 2,000 in Macedonia, and 1,000 in Croatia. Given how unstable and war ravaged those countries are, the NATO contingents will likely be bogged down there indefinitely. Although the debate over whether NATO is a cold war relic will continue, the alliance's commitments to peace in the Balkans seem to have decided that question.

Declaration of Liberated Europe that promised free elections and trade, while informally agreeing that the East European governments be "friendly" toward Moscow. They also agreed on the division of Germany and Berlin into three temporary occupation spheres that would eventually be reunited following a peace treaty. After prolonged protests by provisional French President Charles de Gaulle, Washington and London agreed to allocate part of their spheres to create a French sphere. At the June *Potsdam Conference,* Truman, Stalin, and Churchill agreed that each power could take reparations from their respective spheres and, in addition, the Soviets could have 25 percent of the reparations from the three western zones.

However, as the Soviet Union began undermining noncommunist political parties and groups and imposing Communist party rule throughout Eastern Europe, the Roosevelt and (after April 1945) Truman administrations protested. The Soviets rigged elections in Poland, Romania, and Bulgaria to bring communist parties to power and overthrew democratic governments with military *coups d'état* in Hungary in 1947 and Czechoslovakia in 1948. Having been devastated by the German invasion, the Soviets began the systematic looting of Germany and the rest of Eastern

Europe, shipping back entire industries. Meanwhile, communist parties in Western Europe, particularly in France and Italy, acquired increased representation in local and national elections.

Washington's worries about Europe's fate soon expanded to East Asia. At the Yalta Conference, Roosevelt had elicited Stalin's promise to fight against Japan within three months of Germany's defeat. At the time, having the Soviets as an ally in Asia seemed essential to winning the war against Japan, whose armies fought to virtually the last man for tiny coral islands in the Pacific and whose government was mobilizing every old man, woman, and child in the Japanese islands themselves for suicide mass human wave attacks on the American invaders. An invasion of Japan was expected to cost at least half a million American dead atop tens of millions of dead Japanese. The successful explosion of an atomic bomb at Alamogordo, New Mexico, in June 1945 completely changed the power calculus. Japan now could be defeated without an invasion—Soviet troops were no longer needed.

But the promised Soviet attack came anyway. On August 6, the United States dropped an atomic bomb on Hiroshima. On August 8, the Soviets invaded and quickly overran Manchuria and Korea. On August 9, an atomic bomb destroyed Nagasaki. Then, on August 15, Tokyo announced it would surrender. In a matter of weeks, the Soviet Union had enormously expanded its influence throughout northeastern Asia.

Washington feared that Moscow's influence would soon engulf China as well. A civil war in China between a corrupt, oppressive Nationalist Party or *Kuomintang (KMT)* regime under Chiang Kaishek and the Chinese Communist Party (CCP) under Mao Zedong had raged since 1927, and continued throughout the war against Japan from 1937 to 1945. When Japan surrendered, the communist forces controlled one-fifth of the population and land mass, and their influence expanded daily. Roosevelt and Truman had persuaded Stalin to support Chiang's regime as the fourth "policeman" in return for Soviet-Chinese joint control over the railroads and economic infrastructure of Manchuria and northern China, which was legalized by a Treaty of Friendship and Alliance signed between Chiang and Stalin. As historian Walter LaFeber put its, "Stalin preferred a chaotic, divided China that would not threaten Russia rather than a united China under either Chiang or Mao."[9] But despite the deal with Chiang and the desire to keep China divided, after overrunning northern China, the Soviets transferred captured Japanese arms and equipment to the communists. Meanwhile, Truman sent 100,000 American troops to China and allowed Japanese troops to maintain their arms in order to support Chiang's forces against the communists. In addition, Truman sent special envoy George Marshall to help negotiate peace between the KMT and CCP. The communists gained steadily despite America's efforts.

The Middle East was another disputed region. In 1941, Great Britain and the Soviet Union occupied Iran to prevent, among other things, the shah from allying with Germany. The United States joined the occupation in 1942. Later that year the three powers signed an agreement pledging to withdraw their forces once the war had ended. By March 1946, the British and American troops had largely withdrawn. Soviet troops not only stayed in violation of the occupation agreement, but incited a revolt by the Azerbaijani people in northeastern Iran. The Truman administration severely protested the Soviet actions. In March, Moscow agreed to leave after signing a treaty with Teheran, which created a Soviet-Iranian oil company that would pump and ship oil to the Soviet Union. After the Soviet troops withdrew, the Iranian parliament rejected the treaty.

The eastern Mediterranean became another contested region. During the war, Churchill and Roosevelt had agreed to allow Soviet control of the Dardanelles, straits linking the Black Sea and the Mediterranean. After the war, Moscow demanded that Turkey agree to joint control of the straits. Washington then reversed its policy, flatly rejecting any Soviet control over the Dardanelles, and sent a U.S. fleet to the eastern Mediterranean to emphasize its position. By autumn 1946 Moscow backed off. Meanwhile, a civil war raged in Greece between communist and noncommunist factions. The British supported the noncommunist faction but had to solicit American help in the struggle. In 1946 alone, Washington sent $260 million in aid to Greece. Although Soviet contact with the Greek communists was minimal, the White House increasingly saw the communist threat to take over Greece as part of a global conspiracy directed by Moscow.

Fearing that Washington would use Moscow's dependence on American largesse and the global economy to force it to retreat from Eastern Europe, in 1946 Stalin rejected a $1 billion American loan and membership in the IMF and World Bank. Stalin also rejected an American proposal (the *Baruch Plan*) to give up its monopoly over the atomic bomb to the United Nations in return for all other countries to agree not to research or possess such weapons. Compliance would be ensured through U.N. inspections and control over the raw materials that make atomic bombs.

Although the Soviet Union continued to probe for advantages around the world, it posed no military threat. As early as November 1945, an American intelligence report argued that the Soviet military was severely stretched to fulfill existing commitments and had no significant offensive potential against Western Europe, and would be unlikely to become a threat for another 15 years.[10] Despite the growing international tension, the Soviet Union and United States continued their mass troop demobilizations. Between 1945 and 1947, the Soviet military declined from 12 million to 3 million troops and the American military from 10 million to 1.4 million troops. Although the Soviet army was twice the size of America's, it was mostly deployed to maintain the Soviet Union's Eurasian empire, and, unlike the United States, lacked an atom bomb or vast navy.

How *the* Rivals Sought *to* Contain Each Other

SELECTIVE CONTAINMENT (1947–1950)

The Soviet and British declarations of the cold war preceded America's by a year. On February 9, 1946, Stalin declared that the wartime alliance with the West was dead and that war between capitalism and communism was inevitable, and thus all Soviet people and resources had to be mobilized for that struggle. Churchill echoed those fears a month later on March 5, 1946, at Fulton, Missouri, when he warned that an "iron curtain" had descended on Europe dividing the free West from the communist East.

More than a year later, on March 12, 1947, President Truman asserted that henceforth the United States would aid "free countries which are resisting attempted subjugation by armed minorities," a policy that became known as the *Truman Doctrine*. To that end, he asked Congress for $400 million in military and economic aid to support friendly governments in Greece, Turkey, and elsewhere threatened by communism. American commitments expanded. On June 5, 1947, Secretary of State George Marshall announced that the United States would have to extend enormous aid to help reconstruct Europe's economy for the United States and global economies to revive, a program that became known as the *Marshall Plan*. Between 1947 and 1952, the United States gave Europe $17 billion and Japan $2.2 billion in economic aid, which was essential for their economic revival. Although Congress did not approve the Marshall Plan until March 1948, in July 1947 it passed the *National Security Act*, which created the *National Security Council (NSC)*, the Central Intelligence Agency (CIA), the Joint Chiefs of Staff (JCS), and the Defense Department to plan and execute America's anticommunist and anti-Soviet policies with the goal of "containing" communism.

How was the *containment* policy conceived? George Kennan, an American diplomat in Moscow during the war years, was containment's architect. In early 1946, he sent a policy paper, known as the *Long Telegram*, to Washington in which he carefully analyzed the Soviet threat. According to Kennan, Soviet expansion in Eastern Europe was simply an extension of the traditional Russian drive to secure a buffer zone of natural frontiers and compliant states. As for Western Europe, the Soviet threat was primarily ideological and political, not military. The fear was not that Soviet tanks were going to burst across the West German border, but that Soviet backed communist parties in Western Europe and elsewhere would take advantage of the pervasive postwar poverty, chaos, and uncertainty, and through both subversion and elections seize those governments. The result would be an enormous expansion of Soviet power and influence.

How could communism's spread be stopped? Communism flourishes in societies in which a small, wealthy class exploits poverty-stricken masses. If mass poverty were eliminated, communism's appeal would shrivel. *Liberal democracy*, in contrast, is best nurtured in a middle-class society. Thus Kennan urged Washington to extend massive economic and political aid to the world's most important industrial countries and regions. If the United States helped Western Europe and Japan reconstruct their economies, revive their prosperity, and expand their middle class, communism's popularity would disappear and with it the indirect Soviet threat.

Kennan warned that Washington should not try to pour money into every country ripe for revolution. Many countries lacked geoeconomic or geopolitical importance, or their revolutions were primarily nationalist struggles against colonialism. The United States, he argued, would simply throw away its money if it tried to counter the tide of history in such countries. Those communist movements, even if successful, posed no threat to American security, because those governments could only survive through integration into the global economy.

The Soviet and communist threat would prove to be a fleeting phenomenon in world history. Within several generations, the Soviet Union itself would eventually crumble as all empires do but sooner than most because of communism's internal contradictions and its inability to distribute anything other than poverty or to provide any meaningful life for those doomed to exist under its rule. Communism elsewhere would collapse because of its inability to develop those nations' economies or provide higher living standards for the people.

Kennan elaborated this analysis and coined the term *containment* in his anonymous *"Mr. X" article* in the spring 1947 issue of *Foreign Affairs*. He advocated a *selective containment* policy targeted on those regions of the world—Western Europe, Japan, and the oil-rich Middle East—that were of vital geoeconomic and thus

containment the strategy by which the United States attempted to restrict Soviet expansion through economic, political, and military means.

geopolitical importance to the United States. He advised ending American involvement in China and other poor countries where some kind of revolution was inevitable and where the United States had no real interests. In mid-1947 Kennan was made head of the State Department's policy-planning section.

Despite Kennan's selective containment strategy, America's global commitments expanded. Throughout the summer of 1947, representatives of the western hemisphere countries met in Rio de Janeiro to negotiate a collective self-defense treaty, signed on September 2, 1947, in which an attack on one would be considered an attack on them all. In Southeast Asia, Washington abandoned Roosevelt's pledge to advocate decolonization and now began to supply limited aid to the Western powers attempting to reassert their control, such as the French in Vietnam, the Dutch in Indonesia, and the British in Malaya and Burma. After granting independence to the Philippines in 1946, the United States extended considerable aid to the new government to help it suppress a communist insurgency. But America's most important efforts were in China, where it gave the KMT billions of dollars in military and economic aid, most of which was squandered by Chiang's corrupt regime.

For the first few postwar years, the public was ambiguous over the country's new role despite the White House's internationalist policies and America's vast power. Many called for a return to political if not economic isolation. It was the outbreak of the cold war with the Soviet Union that tipped the balance decisively between the isolationists and internationalists to the latter, and stimulated the global economy's revival.

How was the containment policy sold to a war-weary, traditionally isolationist public? President Harry Truman once said that the only way to stir and mobilize the American public from their isolationist lethargy was to scare the hell out of them. He did just that when he depicted the conflict with the Soviet Union in the most apocalyptic of images. Other American leaders joined that chorus of rhetoric, including George Kennan, who publicly argued in 1947 that

> Today we Americans stand as a lonely, threatened power on the field of world history. Our friends have worn themselves out and have sacrificed their substance in the common cause. Beyond them—beyond the circle of those who share our tongue and our traditions—we face a world which is at worst hostile and at best resentful. A part of that world is subjugated and bent to the service of a great political force intent on our destruction. The remainder is by nature merely jealous of our material abundance, ignorant or careless of the values of our national life, skeptical as to our mastery of our own fate and our ability to cope with the responsibilities of national greatness."[11]

The Soviets were also busy expanding their influence during this time. In 1947, Moscow announced the creation of the *Communist Information Bureau (Cominform)*, through which it would forment and coordinate communist revolution worldwide. As early as July 1947, Moscow began integrating the Soviet and eastern European economies, and in January 1949 formalized these ties by creating the *Council for Mutual Economic Assistance (COMECON)*, the Soviet equivalent of the Marshall Plan. On June 24, 1948, Moscow blocked the overland routes to the Allied sectors in Berlin in hopes that the West would eventually surrender their sectors. On June 28, the United States began the *Berlin airlift*, which lasted 324 days and delivered 13,000 tons of supplies a day to the beleaguered city. In April 1949, Moscow began lifting its blockade.

With a monopoly of atomic power, the Truman administration could always deter a Soviet attack on Western Europe by threatening to bomb Soviet cities. However, once the Soviets developed atomic power, America's atomic power would be neutralized and its deterrent value diminished. Clearly the United States had to develop conventional as well as atomic military power in order to maintain an effective deterrent against Soviet aggression. Washington encouraged the *Brussels Pact* of 1948, in which Great Britain, France, Belgium, the Netherlands, and Luxembourg agreed that an attack on one would be considered an attack on all. In 1949 the United States, Canada, Norway, Denmark, and Portugal joined the alliance, which was renamed the *North Atlantic Treaty Organization (NATO)*, with the same "one for all and all for one" commitment. Congress quickly ratified the treaty and passed the *Mutual Defense Assistance Act*, which initially supplied its allies with $1.5 billion in military aid.

Despite NATO's creation, several other events occurred in 1949 and 1950 that dramatically changed the global power balance. In September, the Soviet Union exploded its first atomic bomb. On October 1, the Chinese communists announced their victory in the civil war, and KMT troops and followers retreated to the Chinese island of Taiwan for a last stand. On January 13, 1950, the Soviet delegation to the United Nations walked out after the Security Council refused its proposal to eject the KMT Chinese delegation and seat the CCP representatives. On January 14, the Chinese invaded the U.S. consulate in Beijing. Then, in February, news leaked out that the previous month Moscow and Beijing had signed a treaty of friendship, which Washington interpreted as essentially an alliance. Elsewhere Ho Chi Minh's communist forces battled French colonial forces in Vietnam, and communist guerrillas plagued governments throughout East and Southeast Asia. Even Japan had a growing Communist party. The global power balance seemed to have shifted decisively in Moscow's favor.

GLOBAL CONTAINMENT (1950–1969)

In response to these changes, Paul Nitze, who headed the National Security Council's policy-planning section, formulated a new version of the containment policy known as *NSC-68*, and presented it to Truman in April 1950. *Global containment* rejected Kennan's selective strategy for the premise that the Soviets had a grand plan for world conquest and that Marxism-Leninism rather than geopolitics primarily drove its foreign policy. Thus, if the United States did not hold the anticommunist line everywhere, it would be challenged and eventually overrun everywhere. A loss of one country to communism would lead to a *domino effect* as neighboring countries succumbed. Emboldened by these victories, the Soviet Union would become increasingly aggressive. What, then, was the best American strategy to counter this Soviet threat? Every government anywhere besieged by a communist movement must be protected. No country was too small or remote. Military rather than economic power was the key to containing the Soviet Union and its worldwide system of revolutionary communist movements. Nitze was global containment's architect; Secretary of State Dean Acheson and adviser John Foster Dulles (later secretary of state) implemented it. Although Kennan and other selective containment advocates protested Nitze's vision as self-defeating and exaggerated, global containment's advocates seemed vindicated on June 24, 1950, when communist North Korea attacked South Korea. The United States was soon locked into a three-year war in Korea that cost 38,000 American lives.

With the Korean War's outbreak, America's containment policy would be global for the next two decades. The domino theory's logic dictated that every noncommunist country, no matter how remote or economically insignificant, must be defended against any insurgency, no matter how nationalistic it may have been. The

The Cold War Turns Hot: *The* Korean War (1950–1953)

Why did the Korean War occur, and why did the United States join the fighting? In 1945, Moscow and Washington had agreed to divide the peninsula at the 38th parallel, with Soviet troops occupying the country north of that line and American troops to the south. Both sides withdrew their troops by 1949, but only after imposing sympathetic governments on their respective halves. In the months preceding the North Korean invasion, Pyongyang's communist dictator Kim Il Sung and Seoul's noncommunist dictator Syngman Rhee both repeatedly threatened to unify the peninsula by invading the other. There were border clashes and South Korean troops succeeded in routing several thousand guerrillas plaguing parts of the country. Between January and June 1950, Washington had sent mixed messages about its commitment to South Korea. At a press conference on January 12, Secretary of State Dean Acheson seemed to leave out South Korea in a discussion of America's defense perimeter in East Asia, although he

pointedly included South Korea in other briefings throughout the next few months. Kim had traveled to Moscow in early 1950 to receive Soviet approval for the invasion, although Stalin refused to commit Soviet forces and did not know exactly when the attack would occur.

The Truman White House assumed that Moscow not only supported the invasion but also largely controlled the communist governments of China and North Korea. The North Korean attack was thus seen as part of an orchestrated communist offensive across East and Southeast Asia, and most likely a prelude to another crisis in Berlin or elsewhere in Europe. In response, Truman ordered General Douglas MacArthur in Japan to supply South Korea's armies, and, in addition, sent the U.S. 7th fleet between China and Taiwan to prevent a communist invasion, and stepped up aid to French forces in Vietnam and the Philippine government. With the Soviets continuing to boycott the United Nations, the United States was able to get the U.N. Security Council to pass two resolu-

tions on June 27, one branding the North Koreans as aggressors and demanding an immediate cease fire and withdrawal north of the 38th parallel, and the other calling on the U.N. members jointly to aid South Korea. On June 30, Truman sent American troops to bolster the defense perimeter around Pusan, the last South Korean stronghold. Although military contingents from 16 countries joined the alliance, the United States led it and contributed 50 percent of its ground, 86 percent of its naval, and 93 percent of its air forces. In August 1950, MacArthur launched a brilliant attack behind the North Korean lines at Inchon, routed the North Korean army, and in September pushed the remnants far north of the 38th parallel. MacArthur disregarded intelligence reports that Chinese troops had infiltrated North Korea and were massing to attack. On November 26, a Chinese and North Korean counterattack caught MacArthur's forces by surprise and forced them back down the peninsula, where the lines solidified and were accepted by an armistice in 1953.

assumption was that if one country in a region fell to communism, it would simultaneously weaken the resolve of noncommunist governments and strengthen communist forces in neighboring countries. Thus the fall of one domino would bring down the rest. As President Johnson put it, "If we don't stop the communists in Vietnam, they'll march into Hawaii today, and San Francisco tomorrow."[12]

Washington worked hard to globalize its containment strategy. Over the next few years following the North Korean attack, the United States negotiated and signed half a dozen bilateral and multilateral defense treaties, including ones with

Australia and New Zealand (1951), Japan (1952), and the *Southeast Asian Treaty Organization* (*SEATO;* 1954). The U.S. defense budget increased from $13.5 billion in 1950 to $50 billion in 1951 and $60 billion in 1952, and the number of troops increased during those years 50 percent to 3.5 million. In 1955, Washington rearmed West Germany and made it part of NATO in 1955. Moscow responded to West Germany's rearmament and integration within NATO by organizing its eastern European satellites into the Warsaw Pact, also known as the *Warsaw Treaty Organization* (*WTO,* not to be confused with the World Trade Organization, which uses the same initials).

In 1952, Dwight Eisenhower was elected president, partly because of his platform, which rejected the containment policy as too passive. He promised instead to *roll back* communism. Eisenhower's Secretary of State, John Foster Dulles, rejected any possibility of negotiating with the Soviets whom he considered incapable of being trusted. Despite his own tough campaign rhetoric and his ideologically minded Secretary of State, Eisenhower actually modified the global containment policies of his predecessor. He reduced the military budget to $31 billion by 1955, canceled plans for an American troop buildup in Europe to 50 divisions, reduced the American military from 1.5 million to 1 million men, and ordered an increase in America's nuclear forces, which he argued would give the United States *"more bang for the buck."*

Under this plan, Washington would respond to any Soviet invasion of western Europe with a *massive retaliation* of nuclear weapons. For the massive retaliation deterrence strategy to be the most effective, an optimum number of American troops had to be stationed in Europe. The fewer American troops in Europe, the greater the chance of a Soviet conventional victory, and thus the more certain Washington would massively retaliate with nuclear weapons. But there had to be enough American troops to act as a *trip wire* for massive retaliation. The stakes of American lives had to be enough for Washington to retaliate to avoid losing but not enough to win a conventional war. Such was one of many cold war paradoxes.

Ironically, while Washington's global containment and massive retaliation policies were being implemented, Moscow briefly became more conciliatory. Stalin died in February 1953, and his successors announced the policy of *peaceful coexistence*, in which war between the communist and capitalist worlds was not inevitable and both systems could coexist peacefully. In 1955, the Soviets signed a peace treaty with Austria that reunited that country in return for its neutrality. Between 1953 and 1956, power in the Kremlin was shared by several leaders. In 1956, Nikita Khrushchev emerged as the Soviet Union's undisputed ruler. At the 20th Communist Party Congress in February 1956, he revealed details of Stalin's genocidal policies and proclaimed that the Soviet Union would adopt more humanistic policies. In April 1956, the Kremlin announced the dissolution of Cominform.

peaceful coexistence 1956 declaration by the Soviet Union that communism and capitalism could coexist without going to war.

Despite these changes, it soon became apparent that there were limits to Soviet liberalization. In June 1956, demonstrations protesting communist rule broke out in Hungary and Poland and continued sporadically into the autumn. In Poland, Wladyslaw Gomulka, a reform communist, came to power and advocated sweeping political, economic, and social changes. When Khrushchev denounced Gomulka, the latter threatened to mobilize the Polish people against the Soviets. Khrushchev backed down. Heartened by Gomulka's victory, a mass demonstration in Hungary forced Khrushchev to allow the Stalinist Erno Gero to be replaced as president by reformist Imre Nagy and to withdraw Soviet troops from Hungary. On October 28, while this crisis was occurring, Israel launched a sneak attack on

Egyptian forces in the Sinai peninsula and by early November, in conjuncture with British and French troops, captured the Suez Canal that had been nationalized by President Gamal Abdel Nasser in July. Washington protested the invasion and threatened to cut off financial ties with the belligerents until they withdrew. Moscow used the Middle East war to reverse its own policy in Eastern Europe. In early November, Soviet troops crushed Nagy's reformist regime and imposed a puppet dictatorship ruled by Moscow. Not just Hungary and Poland but all of Eastern Europe might have been liberalized or even outright liberated had it not been for that joint attack of Israel, Great Britain, and France on Egypt.

Meanwhile, the Moscow–Beijing axis crumbled steadily throughout the 1950s. A shared communist ideology poorly veiled the great power rivalry between the two countries that had lasted several hundred years. Mao proclaimed himself Stalin's successor after the Soviet leader died in 1953 and maintained that a Chinese-style peasant-based revolution was far more relevant to the Third World than a Soviet-style industrial worker revolution. Beijing also rejected Moscow's peaceful coexistence approach toward the West and instead advocated a more confrontational policy. In 1958, Mao rejected the Soviet development model and launched his *Great Leap Forward,* in which he tried to distribute wealth and industry as widely as possible. The result was mass famine. The Soviets responded by withdrawing their technicians and aid.

Although it would be another 13 years before Washington would take advantage of the Sino-Soviet rift by playing each side against the other, some American policies were adapted to other geopolitical realities. Washington's massive retaliation policy essentially gave the United States the options of either surrender or full-scale nuclear war in response to a Soviet attack on Western Europe. In August 1957, Moscow launched the world's first intercontinental ballistic missile (ICBM), and in October beat Washington into space when it launched its *Sputnik* satellite into orbit. Although the United States soon launched its own ICBMs and satellites, America's nuclear supremacy had seemed to disappear and with it Washington's massive retaliation policy. As the Soviet nuclear arsenal grew, massive retaliation would mean the devastation of both countries—mutually assured destruction (MAD). Although massive retaliation and MAD might deter a Soviet attack, if one did occur an American administration might well run up the white flag rather than risk annihilation.

Once the Soviet Union began to acquire its own nuclear arms, they became political rather than military weapons. World opinion has solidly rallied against any use of nuclear weapons, which may have been an important factor in restraining the White House from using such weapons to defeat North Korea or North Vietnam. At most Washington twice hinted vaguely about considering them as an option during the 1950s, once to bring about a settlement with the North Koreans and Chinese during the Korean War in 1953, and another to deter China from attacking the tiny Taiwanese islands of Quemoy and Matsu in the late 1950s. And even then, there is no evidence that Washington's quiet nuclear saber rattling was an important factor in settling those conflicts. Once Moscow achieved nuclear parity, Washington never even hinted at the use of nuclear weapons in any conflict.

America's nuclear might and strategy clearly did not deter the Soviets from continuing to provoke crises. In November 1958, Khrushchev demanded that the Western powers withdraw their military forces from Berlin, make it a "free city," and negotiate with East Germany. Washington rejected those demands, and the second Berlin crisis continued until August 13, 1961, when the Soviets built a

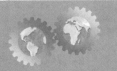

Washington and Moscow used similar tactics throughout the cold war, including spying, overthrowing unfriendly governments or repressing rebellions against unfriendly states, waging wars in Afghanistan and Vietnam, and so forth. For example, in 1965 the Johnson administration sent 25,000 troops into the Dominican Republic to help its right-wing government suppress a rebellion by supporters of elected president Juan Bosch, which the right-wingers had recently overthrown. Bosch had been the first freely elected president in 38 years and had promised sweeping reforms. Johnson ordered the invasion, arguing that it was helping defeat a communist revolution that was just using Bosch as a symbol. The Soviet Union and others condemned the American invasion as violating the U.N. Charter. In 1968, the Soviet Union launched Warsaw Pact forces into Czechoslovakia to put down a reformist socialist government under President Alexander Dubcek. Moscow justified the invasion by declaring that Dubcek was a tool of the Western imperialists and that his actions would lead to anticommunist revolutions elsewhere. Now it was Washington's turn to condemn the Soviet Union for its invasion.

The similarities between the two invasions are obvious. There were differences. The Dominican Republic soon had democratic elections and American forces were withdrawn. Czechoslovakia, however, remained under a dictatorship until 1990. In terms of their relative strategic importance, Czechoslovakia was a key member of the Warsaw Pact, the equivalent, say, to Italy or Norway for NATO. The Dominican Republic is a poor Caribbean country with no strategic importance. A communist revolution in the Soviet Union could have made it a "second Cuba" but Havana itself has never posed any military threat to the United States except for the missile crisis of 1962, and there was little likelihood that the Soviets would try to reimpose missiles in Cuba or elsewhere in the western hemisphere.

wall around the western sectors. The Berlin Wall became the cold war's most vivid symbol.

With the power balance settled in Europe between its increasingly prosperous western and harshly suppressed eastern halves, the superpowers turned their struggle toward gaining the hearts, minds, and pockets of governments throughout the often abysmally poor countries of Latin America, Africa, and Asia, collectively labeled the Third World. Regional conflicts, some of which had seethed for generations and even centuries, were globalized as the Soviets and Americans provoked arms races and coups, and manipulated politics and economies. National leaders played Washington and Moscow off against each other and were in turn manipulated by the Americans and Soviets. The Eisenhower White House sponsored coups in Iran in 1953 and Guatemala in 1954, and poured aid into the South Vietnam regime created at the Geneva Conference of 1954, in which the French granted independence to Vietnam. Vietnam was then "temporarily" divided between a communist north under Ho Chi Minh and noncommunist south under Ngo Dinh Diem until national elections were held. The Middle East has been torn by conflict ever since the United Nations created Israel in 1948. Eventually the Americans and Soviets became deeply involved in the region's wars and rivalries between the Israelis and Arabs, and among the Arab states.

The nuclear arms race became so deadly that one U.S. submarine could destroy 200 cities with each nuclear explosion 100 times more destructive than the Hiroshima bomb.

Dennis Brack/Black Star

In 1960, John Kennedy won the White House in part by claiming there was a missile gap with the Soviets that he was determined to overcome. In fact, the United States still maintained a healthy nuclear lead. The Kennedy administration, however, abandoned the massive retaliation deterrent strategy in favor of *flexible response* in which there would be a gradual, controlled escalation of warfare from the conventional level through the nuclear levels of tactical, regional, and intercontinental if Soviet forces prevailed at lower levels. This new strategy was almost tested in the October 1962 *Cuban missile crisis,* but fortunately both the White House and Kremlin made concessions that prevented a nuclear holocaust.[13]

The brush with nuclear annihilation and flexible response strategy worried most Europeans, especially French President Charles de Gaulle, who strongly protested the shift. Under massive retaliation, the United States and Soviet Union would fire over the heads of the Europeans at each other; under flexible response, they would first devastate Europe and then later, maybe each other. Even if a nuclear war never occurred, flexible response would be more expensive for Americans and western Europeans alike, because it required a massive increase in conventional forces. In 1966, President de Gaulle withdrew his country from NATO's command structure, although not from the treaty itself, in which an attack on one member was considered an attack on all.

During the 1950s and into the 1960s, the world was bipolar only militarily, never economically. The bipolar balance was based on conventional and nuclear power. Despite the occasional crisis, the bipolar world was highly predictable and stable. According to John Gaddis, "the two superpowers have so ordered their affairs that they have neither stumbled into another war nor allowed others to upset the international system in which they coexist."[14] Washington and Moscow carefully managed not only their respective systems, but their bilateral relationship. Each side escalated its conventional and nuclear power, but never used the vast arsenals to destroy the international status quo. Even Moscow's probes of Western resolve, as in Berlin twice (1948–1949, 1958–1962) and Cuba (1962) were rare, and those crises were carefully managed by both sides so they did not escalate into war. The geopolitical and ideological differences between the American and Soviet blocs were largely fought throughout the Third World where the stakes and chances of a direct clash were relatively low. Although most sides largely refrained from stirring up trouble on the other's side of the iron curtain, spheres of influence elsewhere in the world were fair game. When Washington began to aid a government, Moscow was certain to aid groups trying to overthrow that government, and vice versa.

Global containment's "logic" led America inevitably into an unwinnable war in the region of Southeast Asia known as Indochina, whose countries Vietnam, Cambodia, and Laos were all threatened by communist revolutions. Washington's anticommunist efforts there began shortly after World War II when Ho Chi Minh and his communist movement declared independence from France. The United States sent military aid to France's attempts to crush the independence movement. The communists defeated the French decisively twice in 1954, once at the battle of Dien Bien Phu, where 30,000 French troops surrendered, and then at the diplomatic table in Geneva, where Vietnam received independence and temporary division at the 17th parallel between a northern half under Ho and southern half under President Ngo Dinh Diem. Washington extended vast economic and military aid to Diem in his struggle against the communist Viet Cong insurgency. But the communists continued to gain ground despite American aid. On taking office President Kennedy increased the number of American military advisers from 500 to 16,000 by 1963. Yet the communist insurgency continued despite America's increased involvement.

President Lyndon Johnson accepted the Defense Department analysis that a major effort could destroy the Viet Cong. But to do so America's mission would have to change from advising the South Vietnamese regime to direct combat. The excuse for making that policy shift came with reports, since proven false, of an August 1964 attack by North Vietnamese gunboats on American ships operating in the Gulf of Tonkin. Johnson demanded and received a congressional resolution empowering him to take "all necessary measures to repel any armed attacks against the forces of the United States and to prevent further aggression." This was just short of a formal war declaration. Congress then gave Johnson and later the Nixon administrations essentially a blank check for fighting the war by appropriating all their military budget requests.

Johnson increased the number of American troops in South Vietnam to 550,000 and launched a massive bombing campaign across Indochina that eventually dropped 2.5 times more tonnage of explosives than in all World War II! But despite this huge military escalation, the American forces were incapable of decisively defeating the communists, who won the war for the hearts and minds of most Vietnamese and intimidated nearly all the rest.

America's vast military efforts succeeded in achieving only a battlefield stalemate, while a growing majority of the American population favored the war's end. The communists suffered a terrible military defeat but great political victory in their Tet offensive in early January 1968 as the American public saw on television Viet Cong attacking the American embassy itself. Many Americans reasoned that if the American army could not protect the American embassy, then how could it defeat the Viet Cong elsewhere? The Vietnam War seemed unwinnable.

By the late 1960s, American power was dangerously overextended around the world. The United States was bleeding its wealth, technology, industries, and personnel into distant places such as Vietnam for which no one could identify any concrete American interests. The United States protected the "free world" (which included dozens of highly authoritarian and repressive states) with a matrix of alliances, military bases, and billions in military and economic aid to anticommunist governments and movements. America's commitments were vast: "The United States had more than 1,000,000 soldiers in 30 countries, was a member of four regional defense alliances and an active participant in a fifth, had mutual defense treaties with 42 nations, was a member of 53 international organizations, and was furnishing military or economic aid to nearly 100 nations across the face of the globe."[15]

As if Vietnam were not challenging enough, all international relations were becoming ever more complicated. During the 1960s, the once tightly structured bipolar world centered around Soviet and American blocs broke up into a much more fluid multipolar ideological, military, and economic world. The nonaligned movement that emerged in the mid-1950s, followed by the breakdown in Sino-Soviet relations during the late 1950s, and France's withdrawal from NATO in 1966, were significant steps toward a multipolar world. Meanwhile, the European Community and Japan grew enormously from the 1950s through the early 1970s and caught up to the United States in per capita income and economic dynamism. By the 1968 presidential election campaign, the global containment strategy was thoroughly discredited for another decade.

DÉTENTE AND SELECTIVE CONTAINMENT (1969–1979)

Richard Nixon won that election and entered the White House in March 1969 determined to realign American power to promote its genuine national interests. In 1969, Nixon announced a return to selective containment. Henceforth the United States would not directly fight communist insurgencies but would only aid those governments willing and able to protect themselves, a policy known as the *Nixon Doctrine* or the *Guam Doctrine* (after the site of Nixon's speech). In Indochina, Nixon's Vietnamization policy slowly withdrew American troops and turned over the fighting to the South Vietnamese armies, while negotiations opened with the North Vietnamese for a peace treaty.

The White House played off the Soviets and Chinese against each other by pursuing détente or a relaxation of tensions with both. With the Soviets, Nixon entered the *Strategic Arms Limitation Talks,* which culminated in 1972 with the signing of the SALT I treaty, in which both sides agreed to limit their antiballistic missile (ABM) sites and ICBMs, and in addition, signed several trade agreements. Nixon's most dramatic policy was to establish relations with communist China. In July 1971, national security adviser Henry Kissinger flew to Beijing for talks with China's leader Mao Zedong and his second, Chou Enlai. Then in February 1972, Nixon himself flew to China to meet with those leaders. In doing so, Nixon drove deeper the wedge between the Soviets and Chinese, as each sought closer relations with the United States to counter the other. As Kissinger put it, "the hostility between China and the Soviet Union served our purposes best if we maintained closer relations with each side than they did with each other."[16]

Meanwhile, the global geoeconomic balance of power continued to shift against the United States. Global economic power had decentralized from American hegemony during the 1940s and 1950s to a balance of geoeconomic power among the United States, Japan, and the European Community during the 1960s. In 1971, America suffered its first trade deficit since 1888. The burdens of containing communism and maintaining the global economy were becoming increasingly intolerable for the United States. On August 15, 1971, Nixon announced his "New Economic Policy," which proved as important a shift from past policy as his détente with the Soviet Union and China. Nixon imposed a temporary 10 percent surcharge on existing import tariffs and revoked the dollar's convertibility into gold, thus essentially scrapping the fixed exchange rate system that had been the world economy's central girder since 1944. Although the United States continued to encourage greater European unity and Japanese growth, Nixon urged them to take responsibility for a larger share of the common burden of defending and managing the global political economy.

But the United States and other industrial democracies were helpless to prevent the Organization of Petroleum Exporting Countries (OPEC) from twice boosting oil prices during the 1970s. In November 1973, using as an excuse the Arab–Israel Yom Kippur War, OPEC quadrupled oil prices from $2.50 a barrel to $11.50 a barrel, which led to a dramatic shift in global economic power and dynamism. The industrial economies became hobbled by inflation and slow growth that persisted for a decade.

Nixon's *Vietnamization* policy ultimately failed. In February 1973, after years of grueling negotiations, Washington, Saigon, Hanoi, and the South Vietnamese communists signed a peace treaty designed to preserve the existing status quo. But after the American forces left, the communists broke the agreement, conquered South Vietnam, and reunited the country under communism in April 1975. That same year communist revolutions took over neighboring Cambodia and Laos.

Nonetheless, *détente* continued through the Ford administration (1974–1976) and most of the Carter years. In 1975, Washington, Moscow, and 33 other countries signed the *Helsinki Accord,* which accepted the existing boundaries as permanent and required signatories to respect human rights. In 1977, Washington signed a treaty with Panama in which it agreed to return the Panama Canal by the year 2000. That same year, Carter helped negotiate the Camp David peace accords between Israel and Egypt. In July 1979, Washington and Moscow signed SALT II, which imposed new limits on ICBMs. In 1979, Washington and Beijing formally established full diplomatic relations and exchanged ambassadors.

Despite these triumphs, the United States faced growing geopolitical and geoeconomic challenges. Détente did not inhibit Moscow from aiding Marxist governments or guerrilla fighters in Ethiopia, Angola, Somalia, Sudan, and Mozambique. In February 1979 America's ally, the shah of Iran, was toppled by a fundamentalist

détente a period of relaxed tensions between the United States and Soviet Union during which important nuclear and trade agreements were signed; inaugurated by President Nixon in 1969 and lasting until the Soviet invasion of Afghanistan in 1979.

Islamic revolution and the new government under the Ayatollah Khomeini was fiercely anti-American. That same month, Iranians invaded the American embassy in Teheran and held 54 diplomats prisoner for the next 444 days. In July 1979, the communist Sandinista movement overthrew the Somoza dictatorship of Nicaragua, and the new government threatened a "revolution without borders" that would replace other Central American governments with communist governments. To make matters worse, OPEC further doubled oil prices in 1979 and 1980, worsening global inflation and stagnant economic growth. The global balance of power seemed to be tipping against the United States.

GLOBAL CONTAINMENT (1979–1991)

The Soviet invasion of Afghanistan in December 1979 ended a decade of détente and began yet another decade of global containment. The Carter administration cut agricultural and technology exports to the Soviet Union, boycotted the Olympic games in Moscow, and withdrew SALT II from ratification procedures in the Senate. Carter also announced that the Persian Gulf was a region of vital American interests and that the United States would go to war if the region were invaded by an outside power, a policy known as the *Carter Doctrine*.

Promising to revive American power, Ronald Reagan beat Jimmy Carter in the 1980 presidential race. Reagan expanded the global containment strategy reestablished by Carter, intervening in Central America, southern Africa, the Middle East, and Southeast Asia. Defending the administration's policies, Secretary of State George Schultz captured the essence of global containment when he said, "Either we are willing to act on a vital issue close to our shores at a critical moment when the world is watching or we are not. Either we help Nicaraguans to gain their freedom, or we do not. In Europe, and in the Middle East, in Afghanistan, and in Cambodia, in South America, and in southern Africa, our friends and our enemies will draw their own conclusions about what we decide."[17]

Reagan Doctrine the Reagan administration's **global containment** strategy of intervening in Central America, Africa, the Middle East, and elsewhere.

The *Reagan Doctrine* embodied Reagan's belief that America had a moral obligation to support all attempts to overthrow communist governments in Third World nations. Under Reagan, the United States funded anticommunist guerrilla armies in Afghanistan, Nicaragua, Angola, Ethiopia, and Kampuchea; invaded tiny Grenada to topple a Marxist government; and nearly tripled defense spending. But rather than strengthen America, Reagan's policies weakened the country. America's relative economic decline accelerated, with the national debt tripling from $970 billion in 1981 to over $2.7 trillion in 1989, while its trade and payments deficits soared, leading to the nation's transformation from the world's banker to greatest debtor. Its economic growth hobbled along at rates lower than in preceding decades, and average real per capita income continued to fall. Japan surpassed the United States as the world's leading banking, manufacturing, and technological power. Washington seemed increasingly impotent in the face of deepening global economic, political, and environmental challenges. What had gone wrong? Essentially, the United States had failed to adapt to revolutionary changes that had been active for decades in the global political economy but by the late 1980s became known as the "new world order."

But the Soviet Union was faring even worse. Shortly after taking power in March 1985, Mikhail Gorbachev inaugurated a second period of détente in which Moscow and Washington negotiated and agreed on several key issues, including a treaty eliminating all intermediate nuclear forces from Europe. But of far greater

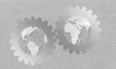

For half a century, the United States and Soviet Union battled in a cold war for global supremacy. The Soviet Union lost—its empire, economy, and military crumbled onto history's ash heap. China is now the world's leading communist country. Could China and the United States become locked into a new cold war?

With 1.2 billion people, an economy growing so fast it may reach $16 trillion by 2025, three million troops, nuclear weapons, and claims over Taiwan and the Spratly, Paracel, and Daiyutai island groups in neighboring seas, many wonder whether China will be a constructive or destruction force in international relations.

Most analysts doubt that China has imperial ambitions or the means to fulfill them. China's defense spending is modest, $8.7 billion in 1996 compared to $260 billion for the United States, and its conventional and nuclear forces antiquated. Military spending actually declined slightly when adjusted for inflation between 1984 and 1994. As for communism, that ideology is meaningless in a country where capitalism flourishes.

China's prosperity grows with its interdependence with the global political economy. Any aggression would provoke international sanctions that would cripple China's economy and discredit communist rule. Thus, as in other countries, as China's geoeconomic interests deepen, they steadily push aside and eventually swallow any potential imperialist ambitions. The pragmatists running China understand that. China already plays a largely constructive role in international relations, and most likely its national interests will dictate that it become even more responsible in the decades ahead.

But the future is never certain. The resurgence of the Communist party's anticapitalist radicals and takeover of China is unlikely but not inconceivable. American right-wing radicals, who view China as an enemy, could capture the White House and Congress; subsequent anti-Chinese policies would create the enemy they now just imagine. If Taiwan declares its independence from China, Beijing will probably use force to subdue it. That could provoke conflict with the United States, which is dedicated to the peaceful reunification of China and Taiwan. Those worst-case scenarios are unlikely but not impossible.

importance was Gorbachev's policies, which were designed to revitalize the Soviet Union and which actually destroyed it.

Why Did *the* Cold War End?

Starting with the Berlin Wall's fall in 1989, George Kennan's predictions proved correct. From 1989 through 1992, the two Germanys were reunited, Eastern Europe was liberated, the Soviet Union broke up, and communist dictatorships were overthrown almost everywhere.

For 72 years (1917–1991), the Soviet Union's system remained intact. For at least 47 years (1947–1991), the United States and the Soviet Union were locked in a cold war. Then in 1991, the communist system collapsed. Why?

There are two long-term reasons and one short-term reason. George Kennan had been right all along. America's containment policies eventually helped topple the Soviet empire and communism. Containment and communism's fatal flaws were the two long-term reasons for the cold war's end. Gorbachev was the short-term catalyst.

THE FAILURE OF COMMUNISM

The most important long-term reason was communism's inability to achieve anything other than a totalitarian system that supported repression, exploitation, and often murder or imprisonment of the people by a tiny well-organized elite that enjoyed what little wealth and privilege the system produced. At worst, as in the Soviet Union, China, and Kampuchea, to name a few, communism resulted in genocide. State ownership and planning of the entire economy failed, often tragically, to achieve sustained economic development. The massive industrialization efforts of communist states contributed little to development or wealth. Central planning failed to create dynamic, profitable industries, infrastructure, or agriculture. Instead, what happened in every communist country was a tremendous misallocation or waste of human, natural, technology, and financial resources. Soviet statistics about becoming the world's largest producers of steel, for example, were often grossly inflated and actual production often grossly misallocated. Russia actually produces less grain today than before the revolution. Virtually none of the former Soviet Union's industries are competitive with foreign industries. By emphasizing the distribution rather than the creation of income and wealth, the communists have merely succeeded in making more people poor. Although the communist systems did achieve significant gains in literacy, health care, and safety, these gains could not balance the system's economic failings. Meanwhile the democratic industrial nations forged further ahead economically.

Although communism's collapse was inevitable, the rulers remained largely blind to their system's vast inadequacies. At the 1962 Communist Party congress, Khrushchev confidently predicted that the Soviet Union would economically surpass the United States by 1970 and achieve full-fledged communism (elimination of private property and equal distribution of goods) by 1980! Khrushchev had this in mind when he arrogantly declared at the United Nations in 1962 that he would "bury the United States."

Communism's collapse was accelerated by America's containment policy. If Soviet-backed communist parties had taken power in the industrial powerhouses of western Europe and Japan, communism's demise would have been delayed immeasurably as those geoeconomically strategic regions became communist, rather than liberal democratic, showcases.

GORBACHEV'S REFORMS

The short-term reason for the democratic revolutions that swept eastern Europe and the Soviet Union was Mikhail Gorbachev. He understood that central planning had failed to achieve prosperity or equality. By the late 1980s, the Soviet Union could no longer afford to maintain its eastern European empire, its military buildup, and operate a centrally planned economy. Gorbachev chose to give up the empire and military buildup, in a desperate attempt to concentrate all resources to reform and revive the Soviet economy. In February 1986, Gorbachev denounced the *Brezhnev Doctrine,* which justified a Soviet invasion of any communist country that was threatened by a democratic revolution. Instead, Gorbachev called for radical reforms in the Soviet Union, which would be achieved by *glasnost*

A Race to the Bottom: Who Was *the* Worse Leader?

Mikhail Gorbachev and Ronald Reagan. Policies often have unintended consequences. Although both Premier Mikhail Gorbachev and President Ronald Reagan deserve credit for signing the Intermediate-Range Nuclear Forces (INF) treaty, which eliminated nuclear weapons from Europe, many of their other policies were disastrous for their respective countries.

Both Mikhail Gorbachev and Ronald Reagan fervently believed that their policies advanced their countries' national interests. Instead, their policies were largely disasters for the Soviet Union and United States.

In his mere six years as premier (1985–1991) of the Soviet Union, Gorbachev won the cold war by losing it. In trying to reform a corrupt, inefficient, backward, exploitive Marxist-Leninist system, he unleashed suppressed antagonisms and aspirations that swept away communism and the Soviet empire. Today he is a hero in the free world and a villain among die-hard communists and nationalists in Russia and elsewhere.

Like Gorbachev, Reagan (1981–1989) based his policies on false assumptions. Reagan vastly increased the defense budget in the belief that the Soviets would bankrupt themselves trying to catch up. The Soviets, however, did not try to match America's military buildup. Reagan also cut taxes for the rich (on the trickle-down theory) and overvalued the dollar in the belief that those measures would revive the economy. Instead, in a mere eight years, Reagan's policies tripled America's national debt, converted the United States from the world's largest creditor to worst debtor country, racked up the worst trade deficits in the nation's history and the lowest growth since the 1930s, and shrank even more the already shrinking incomes of the middle and lower classes.

So which leader's policies damaged his country the worst and for the longer term?

or open information and discussion, *perestroika* or institutional restructuring, and democracy. Political prisoners were released, Jews and others were allowed freely to emigrate, labor unions were given the right to bargain and strike, religions were allowed freely to worship, and the mass media was allowed to investigate and publish freely. In March 1989, Gorbachev allowed competitive elections for the national People's Congress, and many reformist communists won seats from hard-line communists. In March 1990, Gorbachev announced that the Communist party would no longer monopolize political power. In 1990, Russia held democratic elections for the first time in 1,000 years of history. The people elected representatives to the Russian parliament, which in turn elected Boris Yeltsin as president.

THE COLLAPSE OF EMPIRE

Although Gorbachev intended to reform the Soviet Union and Communist party, the political changes that he enacted proved so revolutionary that they eventually destroyed both the Soviet empire and communism. Ironically, the domino effect of revolution that American policymakers feared so much throughout the cold war occurred only in Eastern Europe. The democratic revolutions that swept Eastern Europe in 1989 and 1990 were largely the result of peaceful mass demonstrations that convinced the communists to allow free elections. Only Romania experienced a violent revolution, in which the communist dictator Ceausescu and other members of his government were executed. Elections brought democratic parties to power in Poland, East Germany, Hungary, and Czechoslovakia, and reformist communist governments to power in Romania and Bulgaria. Gorbachev's policy of allowing each eastern European country, and eventually each of the 15 Soviet republics, to choose its own system, even if it meant the end of communism, was popularly known as the *"my way" doctrine.*

The only significant resistance to the democratic revolution was in the Soviet Union itself. On August 19, 1991, the day before Soviet President Gorbachev would have signed a treaty allowing the Soviet republics to become independent, hardline communists attempted to overthrow him. For three days between August 19 and August 21, the conspirators held Gorbachev hostage at his Crimean home and attempted to besiege Russian President Yeltsin with his supporters inside the Russian parliament. Over 50,000 Russians rallied around the Russian parliament building, putting their bodies in front of the Soviet tanks and troops loyal to the communists. As increased numbers of Russian troops defected to Yeltsin, the coup leaders gave up and released Gorbachev, who returned to Moscow. The coup leaders were arrested and tried for treason.

The failed coup accelerated the destruction of communism and the Soviet empire. During the coup, Latvia and Ukraine declared their independence, and statues of Lenin were toppled in Estonia and Lithuania. On August 24, Gorbachev resigned as head of the Communist party and recommended that its central committee be disbanded. On August 29, Yeltsin and Gorbachev appeared before the Russia parliament. Over Gorbachev's protests, Yeltsin dramatically issued a decree abolishing the Communist party across Russia. On September 2, the Soviet Congress of People's Deputies approved a plan to reduce the Kremlin's authority and allow a looser federation of the Soviet republics. On September 6, the Soviet Union recognized the independence of Latvia, Lithuania, and Estonia. On October 18, Gorbachev and presidents of eight other Soviet republics agreed to join an economic union; the Ukraine joined on November 4. On December 4, 1991, Russia, the Ukraine, and Belarus declared the Soviet Union dead but agreed to form a commonwealth. Communism and the Soviet empire had all but vanished.

How did the Bush White House respond to all this? Ironically, throughout the course of these revolutionary events of August and September 1991, President George Bush's response was either passive or actually seemed to favor retaining the communist and Soviet status quo and avoided any support of Yeltsin. In September, Bush flew to Kiev to stand beside Gorbachev and actually implored the Ukrainians not to break away from the Soviet Union. Yeltsin proved of sterner stuff; he shoveled communism's remnants into the gutter of history.

Triumph *or* Travesty?: Why Chinese Communism Survives

As Soviet communism crumbled, China's "communist" rulers remained in power by following the opposite policies—they made sweeping economic reforms while maintaining tight political controls. Since 1978, Beijing has steadily reduced central planning and allowed ever more private property and production within relatively free markets. The result has been a steady rise in living standards. Ironically, China's rulers may be undermining their own legitimacy and power through these successful policies. In 1989, hundreds of students and other sympathizers occupied Tiananmen Square in Beijing and called for democracy. The government responded by massacring the protesters. China's democracy movement collapsed. But in the decades ahead, as China's middle class further widens, people will increasingly demand more political freedoms as they did in neighboring South Korea and Taiwan. Chinese communism will most likely continue as long as the country's prosperity does not falter. But in transforming China from communism to capitalism, the ruling party's name will be ironic indeed.

CONTAINMENT AND THE REAGAN MILITARY BUILDUP

During the Republican national convention in August 1992, speaker after speaker claimed that the Reagan and Bush military buildup had won the cold war. These claims were continued throughout the 1992 elections and have been echoed ever since. Did Reagan and Bush really win the cold war?

The founder of the containment policy, George Kennan, dismissed the Republican victory claims as "ridiculous" and went on to argue that "Nobody—no country, no party, no person, 'won' the cold war. It was a long and costly political rivalry, fueled on both sides by unreal and exaggerated estimates of the intentions and strength of the other party."[18] Kennan, of course, had predicted in the late 1940s that the collapse of the Soviet empire and communism was inevitable, given the historic tendency of all empires eventually to collapse and the inability of communism to satisfy even the most basic needs of the people. Containment was a bipartisan policy that was started by a democratic president and continued by Republican and Democratic presidents alike.

There is no evidence that the Reagan military buildup contributed to, let alone caused, the Soviet economy's collapse. Moscow did not significantly increase military spending to keep up with that of the Reagan administration. The Soviet economy would have collapsed regardless of American policy. Soviet Marshall Nikolai Ogarkov admitted in 1983 that the cold war had essentially ended with the West's victory. Ogarkov argued that "we will never be able to catch up . . . in modern arms until we have an economic revolution. And the question is whether we can have an economic revolution without a political revolution."[19] In other words, communism failed.

The Reagan buildup may have actually propped up rather than undermined the Soviet empire.[20] After Gorbachev took power in 1985, Kremlin hard-liners pointed to the Reagan buildup and argued that reforms were dangerous and should not be attempted. Gorbachev complains that Reagan's policies ironically prevented him from implementing his reforms sooner and more comprehensively. Reagan led the United States into an arms race against itself. By tripling America's national debt during the 1980s, the Reagan administration undermined American rather than Soviet power.

The Reagan and Bush policies reflected the flaws of the global containment strategy. As Kennan pointed out,

> the extreme militarization of American discussion and policy, as promoted by hard-line circles . . . consistently strengthened comparable hard-liners in the Soviet Union. The more America's political leaders were seen in Moscow as committed to an ultimate military rather than political resolution of Soviet-American tensions, the greater was the tendency in Moscow to tighten the controls by both party and police, and the greater the breaking effect on all liberalizing tendencies in the regime. Thus the general effect of cold war extremism was to delay rather than hasten the great change that overtook the Soviet Union at the end of the 1980s."[21]

The Post–Cold-War Relationship

Although the cold war is over, many problems remain, including the reduction of nuclear and conventional forces and political and economic development in Russia and the other former communist countries. The collapse of the Soviet empire and communism has allowed the United States and its allies an enormous peace dividend. Some of the savings have been invested in Russia and the other newly independent states to help them reconstruct their economies. Whereas the eastern European economies have managed to transform themselves from communism into managed market economies, Russia's economy continues to teeter on the brink of collapse. In 1998, President Yeltsin admitted that Russia could not meet payments on its immense debts to international financiers and Western governments. President Clinton helped engineer a $25 billion bailout of the Russian economy that combined government and IMF loans. But will the Russians invest those funds any less recklessly than previous infusions from the West?

Why has Russia failed to transform its economy? In contrast to the revolutionary impact of Gorbachev's political reforms, his economic reforms failed to revive the fossilized Soviet economy. He allowed for some limited privatization, less controls on foreign investment, and leasing of land to farmers. But all this was too little, too late. After Russia seceded from the Soviet Union, Yeltsin dismantled central planning, privatized many industries, and allowed entrepreneurs to start their own businesses. The result has been the worst excesses of capitalism, with ever worsening corruption, organized crime, unemployment, inflation, poverty for most, and vast riches for the elite.

More than any other reason, the legacy of communism explains Russia's failure to transform its economy. With communism's collapse, many former Soviet citizens are experiencing a deep ideological void. Throughout their lives, Soviets were socialized to believe in communism as a religion that contained eternal truths and Marx and Lenin as gods. Now those gods and that religion have been all but destroyed. A fierce nationalism has filled the void for many former Soviets. One of communism's worst legacies is the destruction of entrepreneurial instincts in people. The saying "The state pretends to pay us, and we pretend to work" was mostly true. Communism was synonymous with shoddy workmanship, inefficiency, absenteeism, rudeness, drunkenness, and red tape. Communism repressed and exploited people politically, economically, and socially, but it also gave them a basic material and psychological security. Although there was clearly a class system dominated by the Communist party, whose 5 percent of the population monopolized what meager wealth and privileges the system created, their consumption was not conspicuous and most people could believe they were all equally poor.

In postcommunist Russia, most people still fear taking risks, competing, and trying new things, and they deeply resent it when others are successful at enterprise. Those few who have made money have often engaged in orgies of conspicuous consumption that seems to mock the poverty and hopelessness of everyone else. Russia's nascent democratic political system is just as fragile, with rumors of military or communist coups swirling. Communism may be officially dead, but communists continue to hold or struggle for power. And the government remains as stifling as ever. No matter what their political orientation, bureaucrats continue to do what they do best—obstruct. As if all this were not bad enough, there is some fear that Russia itself could dissolve. Only about 82 percent of the 150 million inhabitants are actually Russians. Russia is a federal republic of 130 recognized nationalities and ethnic groups, with 31 autonomous republics. In 1996, after a bloody civil war, the autonomous republic of Chechnya forced Moscow to grant it independence in five years. In the spring of 2000, Russia's new president, Vladimir Putin, crushed Chechnya and reintegrated the ruins within Russia. That brutal example may cow the other nationalities for the near future—but not forever.

The United States and most other countries hope that a democratic, free-market, peaceful Russia will emerge from the ruins of the Soviet empire and communism. Whatever form Russia's political and economic systems eventually take, it is unrealistic to expect the outcome to be an American-style system. Liberalism in Russia must take root in the soil of a millennium of centralized political and economic authoritarianism.

The United States is now the world's only genuine military superpower. Although Moscow continues to maintain a vast conventional and nuclear force, it is oriented toward maintaining the cohesion of Russia itself in the face of economic depression and chaos and deep political divisions. Like the United States, Russia must significantly reduce its military establishment and invest the peace dividend in productive economic and social enterprises. Tensions and conflicts between the United States and Russia will continue.

Yet there is room for guarded optimism for Russia under its new leader. On December 31, 1999, Yeltsin resigned and Vladimir Putin, his vice-president, took power. Putin was overwhelmingly re-elected as president in the March 2000 election. Only 47 years old at the time of his election, Putin is highly intelligent, was a career KGB officer before he entered politics, and despite his actions in Chechnya is thoroughly committed to burying communism and building a prosperous democratic Russia. But even if he should fail and Russia plunges deeper into economic depression and political chaos, resulting in Putin's overthrow by a nationalist communist regime, the new government will face the same crisis as the old one and will be even less able to handle it. A highly nationalistic, antagonistic Russia will pose no threat to the United States. Moscow's policies will be focused on economically and territorially maintaining Russia itself with no power or inclination left for expansion. For very practical reasons, the cold war is over forever.

Study Questions

1. Was the cold war really born simply of a tragic misperception, as Gorbachev and others maintain, or were genuine national and ideological interests at stake that made conflict between the United States and Soviet Union inevitable?

2. Was the cold war merely a long and tragic detour in the world's inevitable march toward international cooperation and the celebration of human rights? Explain.

3. Why did the cold war occur? How was it waged? What were its major phases and crises?

4. Describe the strengths and weaknesses of the three major schools of thought regarding the cold war's origins.

5. List the conflicts in the Middle East, China, and eastern Europe during the late 1940s that helped escalate the cold war.

6. Why and how was the Korean War the cold war's turning point?

7. Describe George Kennan's analysis of the Soviet threat. What strategy did he propose to counter it? How was the strategy implemented? What were its successes and failures?

8. What was Paul Nitze's analysis of the Soviet threat? What strategy did he propose to counter it? How was the strategy implemented? What were its successes and failures?

9. Explain the difference between selective and global containment. Why did American policy alternate between them?

10. What caused the Sino-Soviet threat?

11. Why did the United States intervene in Vietnam? What were the sweeping consequences of that intervention?

12. Trace how America's nuclear strategy shifted throughout the cold war.

13. Why did the United States inaugurate détente with the Soviet Union and China in the late 1960s? What were détente's major successes? Why did it end in December 1979?

14. Describe the Nixon, Carter, and Reagan Doctrines. How did they complement and contradict each other?

15. What were Gorbachev's reforms? Why did he make them? What did he hope to accomplish? Why did they lead to the collapse of communism and the Soviet empire?

16. What were President Reagan's military and economic policies, and what effect did they have on the United States and the world?

17. Why did the cold war end when and how it did?

18. What significant problems among Russia, the former Soviet republics, eastern Europe, and the West continue into the post–cold war world?

☝ *InfoTrac College Edition* Sources

Using the Subject Guide, enter the search term *cold war.* Using Keywords, enter the search terms *Soviet Union politics and government, Soviet Union relations with the United States, Cuban missile crisis,* and/or *détente.*

Batyuk, Vladimir. "The End of the Cold War: A Russian View."

Broderick, Jim. "Berlin and Cuba Cold War Hot Spots."

Church, George J. "A Tectonic Shift: Moscow Collapsed Under the Staggering Cost of the Cold War."

Desch, Michael C. "Soldiers, States, and Structures: The End of the Cold War and Weakening U.S. Civilian Control."

D'Souza, Dinesh. "How Reagan Won the Cold War: Ronald Reagan Came to the Presidency Without Foreign-Policy Credentials, But His Victory in the Cold War Was No Lucky Accident."

Ellwood, David. "'You Too Can Be Like Us': Selling the Marshall Plan."

Fusfeld, Daniel R. "Economics and the Cold War: An Inquiry into the Relationship Between Ideology and Theory."

Goode, Stephen. "Westerners Took a While to Grasp Soviet Threat."

Hixson, Walter L. "Reassessing Kennan After the Fall of the Soviet Union: The Vindication of X?"

Holden, Robert H. "Securing Central America Against Communism: The United States and the Modernization of Surveillance in the Cold War."

Ikenberry, G. John. "The Myth of Post–Cold War Chaos."

Johnson, Robert David. "The Government Operations Committee and Foreign Policy During the Cold War."

Kovalio, Jacob. "Battling Western Imperialism: Mao, Stalin, and the United States."

"The Lessons of the Marshall Plan: The Expansion of NATO."

Lukacs, John. "The Poverty of Anti-Communism."

Naimark, Norman M. "Ten Years After: Perspectives on 1989."

Nelan, Bruce W. "Unity and Division: Fifty Years After the Marshall Plan Began, Europe Is Feeling the Pain of Political Integration."

Newman, Richard J. "A U.S. Victory, at a Cost of $5.5 Trillion: The Nuclear Arms Race Gets a Price Tag."

Nye, Joseph S., Jr. "Conflicts After the Cold War."

Orme, John. "The Unexpected Origins of Peace: Three Case Studies."

Pratt, William C. "The Farmers Union, McCarthyism, and the Demise of the Agrarian Left."

Roberts, Geoffrey. "Stalin and the Cold War: A Review Article."

Ruether, Rosemary Radford. "Cold War Teaches That What We Resist Persists."

Sarfas, Stefan. "Professional Soldiers and Politics: A Case of Central and Eastern Europe."

Sniderman, Mark S. "Monetary Policy in the Cold War Era."

Thatcher, Margaret, and Raymond L. Garthoff. "Q: Did the Reagan Doctrine Cause the Fall of the Soviet Union?"

On *the* Web

http://www.cnn.com/SPECIALS/cold.war/
CNN's Cold War Series

http://www.coldwar.org/
Cold War Museum On-Line

http://lcweb.loc.gov/exhibits/archives/intro.html
Revelations from the Russian Archives

Contents

Chapter 10 *The* Nuclear Arms Race *and* Its Control

Key Concepts and Terms

These soldiers are nuclear guinea pigs. This 1951 U.S. military test recorded both the explosion and its effects on soldiers. A nuclear bomb was first tested in June 1945. Two months later, Japan surrendered after the United States destroyed Hiroshima and Nagasaki with nuclear bombs. Nuclear war has not occurred since, even though at least nine countries have developed nuclear bombs and have at least 50,000 weapons, about 95 percent of which are held by the United States and Russia. Has nuclear deterrence prevented war among these countries, or were other forces more important? The nuclear genie is out of the bottle. Can governments ever force the genie back inside by eliminating all nuclear weapons? Should they do so if they could?

Archive Photos

Humanity is increasingly interdependent in many ways, not all positive. The world today groans under the weight of perhaps 50,000 nuclear weapons, which pack the destructive power of one million Hiroshima *atomic bombs,* or 1,600 times the "firepower released in World War II, the Korean War, and the Vietnam War that killed 44,000,000 people."[1]

One *kiloton* equals 2,200 pounds of TNT. The atomic bomb dropped on Hiroshima was equal to 20 kilotons or 44,000 tons of TNT. One *megaton* equals 2.2 million pounds of TNT. The destructive power of one B-52 or cruise missile, let alone an MX, is mind-boggling. One B-52 alone carries 25 megatons of nuclear explosives or 12.5 times the destructive power of all bombs dropped during World War II![2] A cruise missile launched from a submarine can fly 1,500 miles and explode with 13 times the destructive power of the Hiroshima bomb. *ICBMs (intercontinental ballistic missiles)* are the most destructive nuclear weapons of all. An MX ICBM launched from Nebraska can travel 8,000 miles at 15,000 miles per hour to explode with 300 times the destructive power of the Hiroshima bomb.[3]

A nuclear explosion includes three elements: initial blast, thermal or heat, and radiation. An 1-megaton bomb can destroy all brick buildings within four miles and burn human flesh up to nine miles of ground zero. A 10-megaton bomb can destroy up to nine and burn up to twenty-four miles. A 100-megaton bomb can destroy up to eighteen and burn up to seventy miles. The explosion's intense heat creates a firestorm that sucks in oxygen and hurls out vast winds that vaporize virtually everything around. A 100-megaton nuclear bomb could cause firestorms up to seventy-five miles away. The radiation fallout of a 10-megaton bomb could spread to 100,000 square miles. Human exposure to 100 to 200 *roentgens* of radiation would cause vomiting, nausea, and weakness, and almost inevitably cancer and genetic mutations. Exposure of over 200 roentgens can cause death for most people either immediately or shortly thereafter. The psychological effects would be devastating for those who escaped direct injury but understood that their society was destroyed and would never recover.[4]

Although there are nine known nuclear powers and perhaps several others, the United States and Russia have by far the most nuclear weapons. The number of *strategic nuclear weapons* (those used against each other's homeland) peaked in 1988, when the United States had 13,000 and the Soviet Union 11,000, while each had an additional 20,000 *tactical* (battlefield) *warheads*.

America's nuclear war fighting strategy is known as the *Single Integrated Operational Plan (SIOP)*. It involves strikes on Russian nuclear and conventional forces, industrial bases, and command, control, communication, and intelligence centers (*C3I*). Over 120 warheads are targeted on Moscow alone, a situation known as *overkill*. The National Security Council estimated that a full nuclear exchange would kill a minimum of 115 million Soviets and 140 million Americans.[5] Tens of millions more would die of starvation, radiation sickness, and disease as the transportation, communications, and energy systems failed, crops rotted in the fields, medical supplies ran out, refrigeration failed, and so forth.

In the worst case, a nuclear exchange of 5,000 megatons would throw so much ash into the atmosphere that most of the sun's rays would be blocked from Earth. Some predict that the result would be a *nuclear winter* in which temperatures plunged as much as 36 degrees Fahrenheit (20 degrees Celsius) in the northern hemisphere—where 90 percent of the world's population lives—wiping out crops and causing mass starvation. The radiation would also destroy Earth's protective ozone layer, without which virtually all life would become extinct.[6] A different study concluded that a 5,000-megaton nuclear exchange would "merely" create a *nuclear autumn* in which temperatures would fall 9 to 27 degrees Fahrenheit (5 to 15 degrees Celsius), although the effects on human life might well be just as catastrophic.[7]

The nuclear threat may be more insidious than an all-out nuclear war. Accidents have left at least 50 nuclear warheads and nine reactors strewn across the world's oceans. The Chernobyl meltdown rendered a huge area of the Ukraine uninhabitable and spewed radiation that drifted world wide. At least a dozen other Chernobyl-like plants may be on the verge of meltdown. Twice as much radiation as let loose by Chernobyl has been released as nuclear waste into Lake Karachay from the nearby Chelyabinsk nuclear warhead production plant, making it the most polluted spot on earth.[8] Without protective clothing, someone standing on its shores would die instantly.

nuclear winter the theoretical effect of a 5,000-megaton nuclear exchange that would cause so much ash to ascend into the atmosphere that most of the sun's rays would be blocked from the earth and temperatures would plunge as much as 36 degrees Fahrenheit (20 degrees Celsius) in the northern hemisphere where 90 percent of the world's population lives, wiping out crops and causing mass starvation. The radiation would also destroy the earth's protective **ozone** layer, without which virtually all life would become extinct.

Table 10.1 **World Nuclear Arsenals, 1997**

	Suspected Strategic Nuclear Weapons	Suspected Nonstrategic Nuclear Weapons	Suspected Total Nuclear Weapons
United States	7,300	4,700–11,700	12,000–19,000
Russia	7,500	7,000–15,500	14,500–23,000
France	482	0	482
China	290	120	410
Great Britain	100	100	200
Israel	100+	0	100+
India	60+	0	60+
Pakistan	15–25	0	15–25

Source: Center for Defense Information Report, 2000. Adapted with permission.

Between 1945 and 1998, the six nuclear powers conducted 2,050 nuclear explosions at 35 sites, an average of one every nine days. From 1945 until the 1963 *Limited Test Ban Treaty,* 424 nuclear bombs were exploded in the atmosphere, an average of 23.6 times a year. China and France refused to sign the treaty, which banned tests in the atmosphere, underwater, and in space. Between 1963 and 1991, France conducted 41 atmospheric tests and China 23, for a combined average of 2.4 times a year.[9] The fallout from every atmospheric nuclear test since 1945 has drifted around the world, and all human beings have a cocktail of radioactive elements in their bones. In all, the United States conducted 1,030 tests, the Soviets 715, France 210, Great Britain and China 45 each, India 3, and Pakistan 2.

What purpose is served by these vast nuclear forces, and all the testing, tens of thousands of scientists and engineers, trillions of dollars and forgone development opportunities they consume?

Many people argue that, paradoxically, the superpowers' vast nuclear arsenals preserve the peace. By the late 1950s, the United States and Soviet Union had each accumulated enough weapons to annihilate the other, a situation known as *mutually assured destruction (MAD)* and the essence of nuclear *deterrence.* Early in the nuclear age, Winston Churchill captured the paradoxes of deterrence: "It may be that we shall by a process of sublime irony have reached a stage where safety will be the sturdy child of terror and survival the twin brother of annihilation."[10]

Deterrence occurs when the other side does not attack because it believes it would lose far more than it would gain—nuclear deterrence involves the fear of being destroyed as a civilization. To wield deterrence, a state needs two essential elements: capability and credibility. Capability includes not just a large and survivable nuclear force, but also a C3I system that can survive a nuclear attack and a leadership with the political resolve to retaliate. A state with the military and political capability to defeat a foreign attack has only the power to win. To deter a foreign attack in the first place, it must clearly communicate its military capability and resolve to any potential enemies, and establish its credibility by not failing to use that power when its interests are threatened. Only then does it have deterrence power. Psychology is as important as hardware to deterrence.

Nations possess nuclear weapons to deter other nuclear powers from attacking them.[11] Nuclear power is effective only in how convincingly its holders can

deterrence made up of two essential elements—capability and credibility—that enable a country to make an opponent believe that if it attacks, it will lose far more than it gains.

threaten its use, and in how rationally and carefully national decision makers analyze the costs and benefits of their actions. Deterrence cannot be a bluff because it just might be called. If nuclear power is actually used, deterrence has failed.

This chapter explores the key concepts, developments, and paradoxes of the nuclear arms race and its control.

The History of the Nuclear Arms Race

MASSIVE RETALIATION

During World War II, four nations—the United States, Germany, Japan, and the Soviet Union—raced to create an atomic bomb. The United States won—a controversial victory only if the alternatives are dismissed. Code-named the *Manhattan Project,* America's $2 billion effort was the only one among the four that had the scientific, financial, and material resources necessary for the bomb's creation. On July 16, 1945, at *Alamogordo,* New Mexico, American scientists exploded the world's first atomic bomb.

President Truman received word of the successful test while he was meeting with Prime Minister Churchill and Premier Stalin at Potsdam, Germany. These Allied leaders were discussing the strategy for defeating Japan and determining the postwar world's fate. Truman realized that with the atomic bomb the war could be won quickly without the estimated loss of half a million American lives necessary to invade and defeat Japan (as well as tens of millions of Japanese who were determined to fight to the death), and the need for the Soviet armies that Stalin had promised would soon attack Japanese forces in China. Truman casually mentioned to Stalin that the United States now had an atomic bomb. The Soviet dictator was not visibly moved by the news; his spies had already passed along the word, with secrets that would be essential to the Soviet testing of a bomb four years later. The United States dropped an atomic bomb on the Japanese city of Hiroshima on August 6. Soviet forces attacked the Japanese army in China on August 8. An atomic bomb was dropped on Nagasaki on August 9. On August 15, Japan surrendered.

The nuclear age, which began with the atomic bombing of Hiroshima and Nagasaki, has passed through two phases and is entering a third. The first phase lasted from 1945 to 1957 and was characterized by American nuclear dominance, one that the United States almost gave up. Fearing the proliferation of nuclear power, in March 1946, the Truman administration asked the U.N. Security Council to approve a plan whereby all countries would surrender atomic power to the United Nations that could authorize its use. The Soviet Union vetoed the *Baruch Plan* because it included a provision that would take away an permanent Security Council member's right to veto decisions of the atomic authority and the fear that the United States would still retain knowledge of how to manufacture such bombs. Moscow then offered to give up its own nuclear program but only if Washington first surrendered its atomic weapons and technology. Truman refused.

Initially disappointed by the Soviet veto, the Truman administration soon reasoned that it did not matter if the nuclear genie was out of the bottle as long as the United States controlled it. With a monopoly over atomic power, the United States could deter any attack on its vital interests and defeat any enemies it should war against. After America's wartime alliance with the Soviet Union broke

Ripping Out Enemy Fangs: America's Cooperative Threat Reduction Program

At $475.5 million, the Cooperative Threat Reduction Program was a tiny part of the year 2000 defense budget of $289 billion and it cost only $2.7 billion from 1992 to 1999. But no program or policy did more to slash the nuclear threat overshadowing America. That program helped dismantle 1,538 nuclear warheads, 254 ICBMs, 30 SLBMs, 148 submarine cruise missiles, and 40 heavy bombers from the former Soviet Union's deadly arsenal. The program also helped convert weapons-grade plutonium for use in nuclear energy, construct storage facilities for radioactive and chemical materials, and transform factories for weapons to civilian products. Finally, the program helped pay the salaries of an army of scientists, engineers, and technicians who otherwise might have sold their expertise or even nuclear materials or weapons to the highest foreign bidder, including terrorist groups.

Although the Pentagon and the Democratic party supported the program, predictably the Republicans split between its idealists and its realists. Idealists complained that the money was used to finance nuclear arms reduction treaties, which they vehemently opposed, and propped up Russia's economy, which they would sooner see collapse; they slashed $85 million from the year 2000 budget that would have built a chemical conversion plant there. Realists argued that this was a brilliant means of at once reducing the nuclear threat and developing Russia's economy; the more militarily weak and economically strong Russia becomes, the more secure and prosperous the United States becomes. With its bankrupt economy, however, Russia and the other former Soviet republics would have been unable to pay for the conversion, thus making the horror of "loose nukes" all the more likely. In the post–cold-war era, containment involves preventing nuclear weapons, materials, and experts from seeping out of Russia and into the ranks of anti-American countries and groups. Who is right?

down into cold war in 1947, nuclear weapons became central to America's containment policy.

Although the Soviet Union exploded its first nuclear bomb in September 1949, the United States had an overwhelming superiority in the number, quality, and delivery of nuclear weapons for the next decade. Moscow had nuclear bombs but lacked the means of delivering them. Soviet bombers had only enough fuel for a one-way trip to the United States, and America's air defense system of radar and interceptors would probably have wiped out such an attack before it reached the country. In contrast, American B-36 bombers based in Great Britain, Italy, Japan, and Alaska could quickly reach most of the Soviet Union. Nuclear technology advanced steadily during this period. The first bombs were fission (atomic bomb), but they were rendered obsolete in 1952 when the United States tested its first fusion (*hydrogen bomb* or thermonuclear) bomb. The Soviets exploded their own hydrogen bomb the following year.

American nuclear strategy during this period was based on *compellence* or using the nuclear threat to force others to concede in diplomatic problems, and deterrence of a Soviet invasion of western Europe, Japan, or the Middle East. The United States played the game of *brinkmanship* in which it would go to the brink

compellence an attempt to force an individual or state to give up something valued.

of war with the Soviet Union and other adversaries in order to force them to back down. If war broke out and Moscow attacked the West, then Washington would respond with the *massive retaliation* of all its nuclear arsenal against the Soviet Union. Since slow-flying bombers were the only means of delivering the nuclear payload, the targets would be relatively accessible Soviet cities and industries, a strategy known as *countervalue*.

Although this strategy was an integral part of American policy from 1947, it became explicit following the North Korea attack on South Korea in 1950, when American Secretary of State John Foster Dulles announced that henceforth any communist attack on the West would be countered "in a manner and at a place of our own choosing." He was implying strongly that Washington would retaliate with nuclear weapons against the Soviet Union even if it was not directly involved militarily in that communist aggression. The Eisenhower administration threatened nuclear war against North Korea and China during negotiations for an armistice for the Korean War in 1953, and to compel China to back off from its threat to attack Taiwan's islands of Quemoy and Matsu in 1957.

American nuclear superiority clearly began to erode when the Soviet Union in 1957 was the first to launch an intercontinental ballistic missile (ICBM) and place its *Sputnik* satellite into orbit. Although the United States successfully launched both an ICBM and a satellite shortly thereafter, the Soviet ability to target ICMBs across America seemed to be a significant shift in the nuclear power balance. Psychologically, Americans perceived themselves to be vulnerable and in danger of losing their lead. The 1960 American presidential election was fought and won partially over the issue of a "missile gap" the United States suffered with the Soviet Union. In reality, the Soviet Union did not achieve genuine nuclear parity with the United States for another decade. The Soviets had many nuclear bombs but were unable to deliver more than a handful at that time. It was estimated that a full nuclear exchange would have resulted in as many as 50 million Soviet deaths but "only" 5 to 10 million American deaths.

FLEXIBLE RESPONSE

With nuclear parity and the development of new weapons systems, Washington shifted its nuclear war strategy from massive retaliation to *flexible response*. Henceforth, if the Warsaw Pact attacked NATO, Washington would only use nuclear weapons if the Soviets appeared on the verge of winning a conventional war. But rather than launch ICBMs against Moscow, the United States would use tactical nuclear weapons against Warsaw Pact armies in central Europe. If the Soviets responded by using their own tactical nuclear weapons, the United States would escalate to regional nuclear weapons that could hit targets in Eastern Europe and the western Soviet Union. If Moscow matched that escalation, only then would Washington launch ICBMs at targets across the Soviet Union. With the highly accurate and fast ICBMs, the United States now targeted Soviet missile silos and command and control centers rather than cities and industries, a strategy known as *counterforce*. Fearful that its brinkmanship and compellence games with the Soviet Union or another country could lead to nuclear war, Washington abandoned those strategies and concentrated on deterring a Soviet attack on the West, and striking first at each level of nuclear escalation should deterrence fail and a conventional war ensue.

The flexible response strategy had several flaws. Most basic was the question of whether the United States could control a step-by-step escalation up the *nuclear ladder*, from conventional to tactical to regional, and finally strategic levels. A counterforce strategy depends on striking first. Obviously, there is no point in targeting the other side's silos and waiting for them to fire first, because if you retaliate you will simply be destroying empty silos. If one side either explicitly or implicitly declares a first strike strategy, then both must adhere to the logic of *"use 'em or lose 'em,"* which in turn exacerbates tensions and the chance for nuclear war in a crisis. Not surprisingly, Moscow rejected Washington's flexible response strategy and maintained that it would massively retaliate against the United States itself even if Washington exploded just one nuclear device on the battlefield of central Europe.

And although there was little question that Washington would retaliate if Moscow fired nuclear weapons at the United States, there was doubt whether it would be willing "to trade Chicago for Hamburg." In other words, the flexible response strategy dictated that if Moscow dropped a nuclear bomb on Hamburg, the United States would respond by destroying a comparable Soviet city such as Minsk. This threat of American retaliation presumably would deter a Soviet nuclear attack on western Europe.

Was flexible response credible? Many Soviets and others thought Washington was bluffing in its determination to uphold its *extended deterrence* strategy for Europe, as opposed to its *basic deterrence* of protecting solely the United States. If a Soviet attack on Hamburg was followed by an American attack on Minsk, Moscow would certainly retaliate by striking an American city such as Chicago. Faced with this probability, an American president might well abandon Europe to a Soviet takeover rather than risk the nuclear devastation of the United States. After leaving the presidency, Jimmy Carter admitted that if faced with this dilemma, he would have backed down rather than escalated the nuclear war. Henry Kissinger also asserted that extended deterrence involves "strategic assurances that we can not possibly mean or if we do mean, we should not execute because if we should execute, we risk the destruction of civilization."[12] Thus nuclear deterrence can work both ways; an American attack on the Soviet Union can be deterred as well as a Soviet attack on the United States.

There are "first-strike" and "second-strike" nuclear abilities and weapons. A *first-strike capability* means a country can strike first and destroy most of the enemy's nuclear force so that it would not retaliate with its remaining forces, because it would then suffer a nuclear attack on its cities. A country has a *second-strike capability* if it can absorb an enemy first strike and then retaliate and inflict "unacceptable damage" to the enemy, which Secretary of Defense Robert McNamara defined in 1964 as the ability to destroy half of Soviet industry and a quarter of its population. As will be seen, the United States may well have a first-strike capability and most certainly has a second-strike ability. Arguably, despite its vast array of nuclear weapons, the Soviet Union had neither, nor does its successor, Russia.

Washington has a *triad* strategic force built on *first-strike weapons* such as ICBMs, which are fast and accurate but, in their fixed silos, vulnerable to an enemy attack, and *second-strike weapons* such as *air-launched cruise missiles (ALCMs)*, and *surface-to-surface ballistic missiles (SSBMs)* or *submarine-launched ballistic missiles (SLBMs)*. Nuclear bombs launched from bombers and submarines are slower and

basic deterrence nuclear deterrence that covers the United States.

first-strike capability a country's ability to strike first and destroy most of the enemy's nuclear force in silos; theoretically, the enemy would not retaliate with its remaining forces because it would then suffer nuclear attack on its cities.

One False Step *to* Armageddon!
The Cuban Missile Crisis

The 1962 Cuban missile crisis was the closest the two superpowers came to starting World War III. Without a Cuban revolution, there would have been no Cuban missile crisis. From 1956, Fidel Castro organized and led a rebellion in Cuba that eventually overthrew the corrupt Bastista regime on January 1, 1959. Although Castro had originally fought as a reformist, he soon publicly embraced communism and signed a friendship treaty with the Soviet Union in 1960. In April 1960, the United States launched an American-trained Cuban exile force against the Castro regime at the Bay of Pigs. The attack failed and its 1,500 men were killed or captured. In January 1961, Washington severed its last trade and diplomatic relations with Cuba after Castro ordered the nationalization of American property. In early 1962,

Khrushchev and Castro agreed that the Soviet Union would deploy, in Cuba, intermediate-range ballistic missiles with a 2,000-mile range. On October 14, an American satellite revealed the construction of missile silos in Cuba.

The Cuban missile crisis lasted for the next ten days, during which the Kennedy administration debated and decided on a proper response, and then negotiated with Khrushchev for an agreement that defused the crisis. In the first few days of the crisis, Kennedy's cabinet was split over those who advocated an air strike or blockade and those who favored a diplomatic approach. Kennedy finally decided on backing up his demand that Khrushchev remove the missiles, with a naval blockade (which was officially described as a quarantine, because a blockade was considered

an act of war) of Cuba and placing American forces on full alert. Khrushchev eventually agreed, in return for a public American pledge not to invade Cuba and a private pledge to remove American nuclear missiles from Turkey.

During the 10-day crisis, nuclear war seemed imminent. The Cuban missile crisis vividly presented the risks of mutually assured destruction (MAD) to Americans and Soviets alike, along with the rest of the world. Although Moscow became more than ever committed to achieving parity with the United States, both sides realized that they risked nuclear annihilation by playing the game of brinkmanship in crises. During the 1960s, Washington and Moscow avoided direct crises with each other and began a series of negotiations over nuclear arms control.

less accurate than those dropped directly, but also less vulnerable to an enemy attack. Cruise missiles are the most versatile nuclear weapons, because they can be launched by submarines, surface ships, bombers, and land-based systems. First-strike weapons are best used in a counterforce strategy against the enemy's ICBM silos and headquarters, whereas second-strike weapons are better targeted against an enemy's cities and armies. There is some overlap between second- and first-strike weapons. An ICBM in a hardened missile silo could survive an enemy strike and retaliate, whereas SLBMs are now as fast and accurate as ICBMs, and thus have first-strike capabilities without the same vulnerability.

Although by the late 1960s, there was a rough parity in the number of warheads, there was and remains an asymmetry in the superpowers' types of nuclear weapons and delivery systems. By the 1990s, about 80 percent of America's strategic nuclear weapons were in second-strike delivery systems—sea based (41 percent) and air based (40 percent), and only 19 percent in land-based ICBMs. Thus, in a nuclear war Washington could launch a first strike with its ICBMs against Russian missile silos and bomber bases while using its attack submarines and helicopters to destroy Soviet nuclear submarines. Even though some Russian nuclear forces would probably survive an American attack, Moscow would probably not retaliate, knowing that the United States would use its second-strike SLBMs and bombers against Russian cities.

Although Moscow also had a triad system, its ICBM leg is overwhelmingly the largest, with 59 percent of the total strategic warheads, while air-based account for 10 percent and sea-based 31 percent. None of the Russian triad legs is considered very sturdy. The Russian bomber command is thought to be unable to successfully penetrate American air defenses and its submarine fleet is vulnerable to American attack submarines and helicopters. Although its SS-18 ICBM is huge—ten 750-kiloton *multiple independently targetable re-entry vehicles (MIRVs)* or 600 times the explosive power of the Hiroshima bomb, with the *throw weight* or ability to launch a 200-ton, ten-story high missile or twice the throw weight, and explosive size of an American MX ICBM—it is considered far less accurate. Although an MX has a circular error probability (CEP) of 265 feet after a 6,500-mile flight, the SS-18's CEP is only 1,000 feet, which means that half of all SS-18s would probably fall within and half beyond 1,000 feet of the target and most would fail to destroy a hardened silo. Moscow reduced the vulnerability of its land-based forces during the 1980s by deploying MIRVed SS-24s and single-warhead SS-25s ICBMs, which are much smaller than SS-18s and can be mounted and launched from tractor trailers and railroad cars.

Yet Russia's nuclear forces remain much more vulnerable than Washington's. In a war, Moscow might feel compelled "to either use or lose" its entire system, particularly its most vulnerable ICBM force. However, Moscow has ruled out a first strike because it is deterred by America's vast second-strike capability. The Soviet Union claimed it would only use nuclear weapons if the United States employed its flexible response strategy of gradually moving up the nuclear ladder from tactical to regional to strategic. Once the United States exploded the first nuclear bomb, even if it were tactical, Moscow would respond with a massive retaliation or full-fledged nuclear war against the United States. Although Moscow hopes to deter an American flexible response strategy, that strategy may encourage an American massive retaliation if war breaks out in Europe.

Several technical factors further deter an ICBM first strike by either side. First, missiles flying over the Arctic would probably be thrown off course by the magnetic north pole. Second, even if the ICBMs were able to fly directly to their targets, the explosion of one bomb would throw out an immense *electromagnetic pulse (EMP)* that would knock all other incoming missiles off course and might well destroy them in flight. Building thousands of dummy silos while camouflaging the real ones can make accurate first-strike targeting nearly impossible. Electronic countermeasures can jam the sensitive guidance systems of the incoming missiles and shove them off course. Finally, both sides have already hardened their missile silos to survive an impact of 2,000 pounds of explosives per square inch.

Calculations of the nuclear balance and appropriate strategies were complicated by the development of multiple warheads or MIRVs during the 1970s, and the Reagan administration's *Strategic Defense Initiative (SDI)* or Star Wars during the 1980s. Of America's strategic nuclear force, a Minuteman III carries three MIRVs; a D-5 Trident submarine SLBM, eight MIRVs; and a MX (Peacekeeper) missile, ten MIRVs. The Russians have a similar MIRV system. MIRVs simultaneously

Strategic Defense Initiative (SDI) better known as Star Wars, President Reagan's scheme to create a anti-ICBM defense shield over the United States. Over $45 billion was invested in the scheme before the Clinton administration finally admitted it was impossible to achieve and canceled the project in 1993.

Not *in* My Backyard? *The* Distribution *of* American Nuclear Weapons

Just where does the United States keep all its nukes? Most are either in the United States or on American naval ships. But during the 1970s, the United States based over 12,000 nuclear weapons in 23 foreign countries and five overseas U.S. territories. Although most of those were based in NATO countries, thousands of other nuclear weapons were stored in Japan, Morocco, Iceland, Puerto Rico, and Cuba. Mass demonstrations against those weapons broke out in many of those countries.

How many nuclear weapons are still stored overseas and in which countries? The exact information is top secret.

weakened American and strengthened Soviet deterrence. The more Moscow MIRVed its ICBMs and SLBMs, the greater would be the chance that enough nuclear forces would survive an American first strike to retaliate against American cities. Knowing this, Washington would hesitate before launching a first strike, even at the tactical level. Thus America's vast nuclear arsenal might not deter a conventional Soviet attack on the west.

America's submarine fleet is particularly formidable. One submarine equipped with 20 MIRVed D-5 Trident SLBMs could devastate over 200 targets across Russia. The D-5 SLBM can be used as both a first- and second-strike weapon. It is as accurate as an ICBM and far less vulnerable to an enemy attack. Yet it has its drawbacks. A Trident submarine's wake, even deep underwater, can be detected by satellites and its engine noises picked up by listening devices. In wartime, communications between the commander-in-chief and the submarine fleet would be tenuous at best, which is why submarine commanders are given the discretion or *permissive action link (PAL)* to fire their SLBMs without a direct command under certain circumstances.

Although the number of nuclear warheads increased steadily until the late 1980s, their destructive power has been decreasing since the 1960s. In 1988, America's total warhead destructive power was only 25 percent of its 1960 level. Russia's destructive power has also declined, although not as dramatically. Increased accuracy has negated the need for immense payloads. Now that both American and Russian missiles can theoretically strike within 100 yards of their target, they no longer need to be equipped with enough megatons of explosives to devastate everything within 20 or so miles. Another reason is the development of conventional weapons with as much destructive power as small nuclear bombs but without the radioactive fallout, thus rendering the latter obsolete.

FROM "MAD" TO "NUT"

In 1980 Ronald Reagan won the presidency in part because of his claim that there was a nuclear "window of vulnerability" with the Soviet Union and his promise to revive American military power, which would include regaining nuclear superiority over the Soviet Union and the ability to "win" a nuclear war. Despite Reagan's claims, there was no more a *window of vulnerability* in 1980 than there was a *missile gap* in 1960. Although the Soviets had a greater number of ICBM missiles and warheads, or more *equivalent megatons (EMT)* of explosives, the advantages were more than offset by the greater accuracy or *hard-target kill (HTK)* capability of American ICBMs and its second-strike superiority in SLBMs, bombers, and cruise missiles. By placing its ICBMs in superhardened silos (theoretically impervious to a nuclear strike), America's land-based missiles were relatively protected, which helped deter a Soviet first-strike on them. And only 20 percent of America's nuclear bombs were atop land-based ICBMs, while ICBMs made up 70 percent of the total Soviet nuclear forces. The Soviets not only had no first- and perhaps no second-strike capability, but they were the ones who suffered the window of vulnerability to a first strike.

The idea of winning a nuclear war, known as the *nuclear utilization theory (NUT)*, was diametrically opposed to MAD, whose premise was that there would be only losers in a nuclear exchange. NUT advocates claimed that increasing America's ability to win a war would strengthen deterrence and thus lessen the actual chance of war. MAD advocates countered by arguing that the opposite would occur, that in a crisis the White House would be more inclined to pull the nuclear trigger than retreat from the brink. Henry Kissinger dismissed NUT by pointedly asking, "What in the name of God is strategic superiority? . . . What can you do with it?"

In 1983, President Reagan announced his goal of creating a space-based anti-missile system that he claimed would shield the United States from a Soviet attack and make "nuclear weapons impotent and obsolete." A Reagan administration television commercial promoting SDI had a little girl's voice describing a child's drawing of the world in which Soviet missiles were being exploded high in space while Americans with smiling faces survived down below.

The initial SDI scheme would have involved at least three different ballistic missile defense (BMD) layers of satellites placed between the Soviet Union and United States, and a fourth stationed on the ground in the United States. The first defense layer would be parked in space directly above the Soviet ICBM silos to destroy as many as possible in their relatively slow-moving, easily tracked "boost phase" before the MIRVs are released in space. Another layer would counter the "busing phase" where the cone releases the MIRVs along with such decoys as metal flakes and infrared aerosols to reflect laser beams. A third layer would counter the "midcourse phase" where the MIRVs disperse toward their separate targets and their speeds reach the highest levels. The ground-based fourth layer would target those remaining missiles in their "terminal phase" whereby they had re-entered the atmosphere. Each layer would fire a barrage of lasers or particle beams at the incoming ICBMs.

Reagan's scheme was attacked from several directions. SDI was seen by many experts and Moscow as the most destabilizing system yet devised. The Soviets argued that SDI would give the United States an overwhelming first-strike advantage. In a crisis Washington could launch an overwhelming first strike against Soviet ICBMs, SLBMs, bombers, and command and control centers, and then use SDI to destroy any remaining missiles that Moscow launched in retaliation. SDI could be used for offensive as well as defense purposes, destroying Soviet satellites and even radar and communications facilities on the ground. Moscow threatened to counter SDI by building thousands of more ICBMs in superhardened bunkers that could withstand an American first strike and overwhelm the SDI system. Or the Soviets could avoid the expense of building more missiles by simply putting hundreds of decoys in their existing ICBMs. The SDI satellites would be overwhelmed by having to fire at hundreds of targets, only a fraction of which were actual nuclear warheads. A final Soviet option was to deploy antisatellite (ASAT) weapons, park them in space beside SDI, and detonate them before launching a first strike. It would have cost the Soviet Union a small fraction of what it cost the United States to build SDI to neutralize or overwhelm it. The closer the United States got to deploying SDI, the more incentive the Soviets would have to strike first. Moscow also stepped up its own SDI research.

In addition to this argument, American critics pointed out that SDI would cost at least $500 billion and possibly $1 trillion, consuming scarce resources that were desperately needed for investment elsewhere in the economy. Most scientists, including the U.S. Office of Technology Assessment, argued that the technological obstacles to SDI were insurmountable; SDI would require the ability of a bullet to hit another bullet traveling as fast as 30,000 miles per hour. Furthermore, there were no means of testing it if it should become operational, and it would have to work perfectly the first time. Just how could those satellites generate enough energy to shoot a laser beam hundreds of miles through space to penetrate a hardened steel missile cone? Advocates could only sheepishly shrug and mention a few ideas such as nuclear reactors or space mirrors to use solar energy. But knowledgeable scientists dismissed those ideas as fantasies, given current technologies. It would take only 30 minutes for an ICBM fired from Siberia to run the SDI gauntlet and obliterate New York. And an operational system could be easily destroyed by Soviet ASAT weapons or overwhelmed by decoys. Even if it worked, the space shield against an ICBM attack would not protect the United States against an attack by SLBMs, cruise missiles, or bombers. In addition, SDI would violate both the 1968 Weapons in Outer Space Treaty and the 1972 Antiballistic Missile Treaty. Finally, America's allies complained that the scheme could protect the United States while they would remain vulnerable to an attack. Thus SDI would spark an endless nuclear arms race, which would deepen tensions, economically debilitate both sides, increase the chance for war, and not even protect the United States from a nuclear attack.[13]

By 1999, the "modest downpayment on the future" that Reagan had promised for SDI had cost American taxpayers over $110 billion and some of their best scientists, technicians, and laboratories, while the program remained stuck in the theoretical stage. Reagan's original $500 billion scheme for protecting population centers had been rejected as unfeasible and the goals shifted to protecting ICBM sites. In the late 1980s, SDI advocates shifted from the layered defense system to a *"brilliant pebbles"* scheme, involving thousands of small nonnuclear satellites in orbit that would ram incoming missiles. But that idea too was shelved as technologically impossible. The next version was the ground-based *Theater High Altitude Area Defense (THAAD)*, which has the more modest goal of shooting down a few rather than hundreds of incoming missiles, although it is supposed to protect the whole United States. THAAD has failed all its tests to date.

Despite the mounting bills and failures, SDI will not die. A coalition of politicians motivated by porkbarrel politics and Reaganite ideology has succeeded in resurrecting scaled-down versions. Rather than giving up when tests fail, adherents simply demand more money. In 1999 its supporters pushed through another $10.5 billion in funding for a National Missile Defense based on THAAD that would run through 2005. Not wanting his party to be smeared with the label "weak on defense" in the 2000 election, Clinton signed the bill. SDI remains the technological holy grail of American politics.

SDI was the most controversial of many weapons or delivery systems of questionable strategic and technological worth. The less vulnerable one's nuclear force, the greater its deterrent value. During the late 1970s and into the 1980s, Washington debated whether to mount MX ICBMs on tracks and move each one among as many as 20 different silos. The plan would have cost over $150 billion and a chunk of the American West as large as Connecticut in which to base it. Although many in Congress and across America's political spectrum wanted to cancel the MX program altogether as wasteful and unnecessary, the Reagan administration ruled that it would drop the mobile base scheme and would simply replace the older but highly accurate Minutemen ICBMs in their hardened silos with the newer MXs, and use the MX as a "bargaining chip" in negotiations with Moscow.

Eventually it was hoped to replace the MX with mobile *small ICBMs (SICBMs)* or Midgetmen, which would not require the mobile MX's vast and expensive tracking system. In fact, they could be placed in trucks and wheeled around the nation's interstates making it impossible for the Russians to ever know where they were. The SICBM did have some drawbacks. Each missile had only one warhead, so it was necessary to deploy 10 times as many to give the same punch as one MX. The Midgetman's small size, accuracy, explosive power, and mobility were very expensive. In the mid-1980s, whereas fifty MX missiles with 500 warheads cost about $10 billion, 500 SICBMs would have cost $50 billion or five times as much per warhead. In 1990, the Bush administration dropped the Midgetman plan as too expensive and disquieting to a public that finds the interstate highway system dangerous enough without it being used to hide ICBMs.

Controlling Nuclear Arms

NUCLEAR PROLIFERATION CONTROL

The term *vertical proliferation* refers to one country diversifying its type, and increasing its number, of nuclear weapons, such as has occurred between the United States and Soviet Union; *horizontal proliferation* refers to new countries acquiring nuclear weapons. Regardless of who owns them, the possession of nuclear weapons has clear benefits and costs. Nuclear weapons can bring a country more prestige, allies, power over others, independence, and security from attack. They can also suck up scarce resources and undermine economic development, spark one's adversaries to get or increase their own nuclear weapons, and make the owner a nuclear target in the event of war.

By 1999 there were seven official nuclear powers—the United States, which exploded its first atomic weapon in 1945; Soviet Union, in 1949; Britain, in 1952; France, in 1960; China, in 1964; India, in 1974; and Pakistan, in 1998. In 1998 Russia had 27,300 nuclear weapons, the United States 19,000, China 415, Britain 200, France 525, and India and Pakistan from 0 to 20. In addition to Russia, three other countries with nuclear weapons emerged from the Soviet Union's breakup— Ukraine with 1,650 nuclear weapons, Kazakhstan with 1,400, and Belarus with 72. On May 23, 1992, those three countries signed a treaty with Moscow and Washington in which they agreed to either destroy or surrender their nuclear weapons to Russia.

In addition to these official nuclear powers, there is evidence that Israel and South Africa have long cooperated on developing nuclear weapons, and may have tested such a weapon in 1977. Israel is said to have an arsenal of between 100 to 200 nuclear weapons, and South Africa is thought to have had 10 to 20.

Table 10.2 **Nuclear Tests, 1945–2000**

Country	
United States	1030
Soviet Union	715
France	210
Great Britain	45
China	45
India	3
Pakistan	2

Source: Arms Control Association, 2000.

In March 1993, South Africa announced that it had first started to develop nuclear weapons in 1974 and eventually deployed six, but had destroyed them in 1989. North Korea is also suspected of having one or two nuclear weapons. Other countries, such as Taiwan, Argentina, Libya, South Korea, Iran, Algeria, and Iraq, are known to have attempted to create nuclear weapons.[14]

Although it took decades for Washington and Moscow to agree to cap their own nuclear arms race, by the 1960s they had reached a firm consensus that they wanted to limit the proliferation of nuclear weapons among other states. Neither side wanted to see unstable countries led by messianic and irrational leaders armed with nuclear weapons. Even worse than the fear that someone such as Libya's Mu'ammar Gadhafi, Iraq's Saddam Hussein, or North Korea's Kim Il Sung might get his hand on the nuclear trigger was the fear that terrorist groups could acquire them.[15]

Not everyone agrees that nuclear proliferation is necessarily bad. Some argue that "the spread of nuclear weapons is something that we have worried too much about and tried to hard to stop . . . the measured spread of nuclear weapons is more to be welcomed than feared."[16] If nuclear deterrence can work for the superpowers, why not for everyone else, including the Third World—so the argument goes.

Nuclear Proliferation Treaty (NPT) 1968 signatories agreed not to produce, accept, or seek nuclear weapons from others.

Washington and Moscow sponsored and guided the negotiations for the *Nuclear Proliferation Treaty (NPT)*, which was signed in 1968. NPT signatories pledged "not to receive the transfer from any transferor whatsoever of nuclear weapons or other nuclear explosive devices directly, or indirectly; not to manufacture or otherwise acquire nuclear weapons or other nuclear explosive devices; and not to seek or receive any assistance in the manufacture of nuclear weapons or other nuclear explosive devices." The *International Atomic Energy Agency (IAEA)* is empowered to regulate the treaty by inspecting nuclear energy and other facilities to ensure they are not being used to create nuclear weapons. To date, all the known nuclear powers have signed it, and none of the 30 nonsignatories have publicly violated the treaty. By 1999, 153 countries had signed the NPT. Unfortunately, some of the holdouts include those most capable of producing nuclear weapons—Argentina, Brazil, India, Israel, Pakistan, Chile, and South Africa.

In addition to the NPT, the 1959 Antarctic Treaty, 1967 Outer Space Treaty, 1967 Treaty for the Prohibition of Nuclear Weapons in Latin America, 1971 Seabed Arms Control Treaty, and 1985 South Pacific Nuclear Weapons Treaty limited nuclear weapons in those regions. In 1975, Washington attempted to strengthen NPT by

Part 4   Geopolitical Conflict and Cooperation

Will Israel ever be truly secure from attack, whether it be from foreign invasions or terrorist bombs? By skillfully wielding the arts of war and diplomacy, Israeli has defeated, neutralized, or coopted its enemies and emerged ever more prosperous and secure. In five wars—1948, 1956, 1967, 1973, and 1982—Israel has defeated various combinations of enemies. Using an array of clandestine tactics, including assassination, Israel's secret service, the Mossad, has thwarted or damaged numerous terrorist groups and garnered essential information about the intentions and capabilities of its enemies and allies alike. Over the last two decades Israeli leaders have forged an outright alliance with Turkey, peace treaties with Egypt, Jordan, and Palestine, and unofficial relations with Saudi Arabia.

But despite all those victories, other states in the region still vow to destroy Israel, most notably Syria, Iraq, Iran, and Libya. Of those states, only Syria shares a heavily armed border with Israel. Yet all four of the hostile states, as well as Saudi Arabia, have missiles capable of exploding on Israeli territory. The Iranian rocket Shahab-3, developed with Russian and North Korean technology, has a 1,300-kilometer range. The Syrian, Libyan, and Iraqi SCUD-C, developed with North Korean technology, have a shorter range of 550 kilometers. Saudi Arabia's SCC-2, developed with Chinese technology, some of which ironically might have first come from Israel, has the longest range, at 2,800 kilometers.

How serious are these missile threats? None of those states have nuclear weapons. With at least a hundred nuclear weapons, Israel can threaten any aggressor with devastation should it consider launching a missile attack against Israel. Not only does Israel have planes capable of dropping nuclear bombs, but it has its own missile, the Jericho, developed with French technology, with a 1,500-kilometer range.

But would Israel retaliate with nuclear weapons against a conventional missile attack? How powerful a deterrent is Israel's nuclear deterrent? Paradoxically, nuclear weapons are so powerful that they are powerless. After all, nuclear weapons have only been used once, in 1945, by the United States to force Japan's surrender.

Israel did not retaliate against the one conventional missile attack it suffered. During the Persian Gulf War (1990–1991) Iraq fired a score of SCUD missiles at Israel, which killed and wounded several people. Why did not Tel Aviv hit back? Washington exerted enormous pressure on Tel Aviv not to do so, fearing that an Israeli attack on Iraq might splinter America's carefully forged coalition, which included Egypt, Saudi Arabia, and Syria, among other Arab states. Even then, Israel would have hit back with conventional rather than nuclear weapons, and most likely with bombs dropped by its air force rather than missiles.

So the regional missile race continues. Will Israel ever again be the target of a missile attack? If so, under what circumstances? What then would be the most appropriate Israeli response?

founding the Nuclear Suppliers' Group, which regulates the export of nuclear technology and materials. And in 1978 Congress followed this up by passing the Nuclear Non-Proliferation Act, which authorizes the White House to retaliate against any nuclear transfers that violate the NPT or Nuclear Suppliers' Group.

Although the NPT has clearly slowed proliferation, it has not stopped it. As Iraq's nuclear weapons program of the 1980s proved, there are ways in which states determined to develop nuclear weapons can bypass the NPT. There are over

850 nuclear power plants in more than 60 countries. Running a nuclear plant and dealing with its plutonium by-product provides some of the essential expertise and raw materials necessary to build a nuclear bomb. The rest can be obtained from illegal imports of technicians, parts, and plans from advanced nuclear powers. With the Soviet Union's breakup and with recent nuclear treaties reducing the nuclear weapons and facilities of the Commonwealth of Independent State's, it is feared that thousands of unemployed nuclear experts may sell their services abroad.

On March 12, 1993, North Korea gave the required three-month notice that it was withdrawing from the NPT. Pyongyang signed the NPT in 1985, but did not begin to allow the required inspections until May 1992, and then refused to permit the IAEA to inspect suspected nuclear weapons laboratories. North Korea's action reversed several years of reduced tensions on the Korean peninsula and in northeast Asia. If North Korea does deploy nuclear weapons, South Korea and perhaps even Japan will feel compelled to follow suit, making the region even more volatile. Washington's threats to use the U.N. Security Council to force North Korea to comply with the NPT were blocked by China's veto threat.

President Bill Clinton broke the impasse. By October 1993, the Clinton White House concluded an agreement with Pyongyang whereby North Korea promised to comply with the NPT and dismantle its nuclear weapons program in return for 50,000 metric tons of oil a year and the construction of two light-breeder nuclear reactors to be supplied by the United States, South Korea, and Japan. Although the North Koreans have largely complied with the agreement, they are suspected of secretly continuing their nuclear weapons program and having at least one or two bombs actually operational.

BETWEEN THE SUPERPOWERS

Throughout the cold war, most leaders have clearly recognized the horrors of nuclear war. As President Kennedy put it in his 1961 State of the Union address:

> Today, every inhabitant of this planet must contemplate the day when this planet may no longer be habitable. Every man, woman, and child lives under a nuclear sword of Damocles, hanging by the slenderest of threads, capable of being cut at any moment by accident or miscalculation or madness. . . . The mere existence of modern weapons—ten million times more powerful than any that the world has ever seen, and only minutes away from any target on earth—is a source of horror, and discord and distrust . . . in a spiraling arms race, a nation's security may well be shrinking even as its arms increase.

A year later Soviet Premier Nikita Khrushchev put it even more starkly and succinctly when he declared that after a nuclear war "the survivors would envy the dead."

By the 1960s, nuclear parity and MAD gave Washington and Moscow strong incentives to negotiate some limits to the nuclear arms race. The object was not to eliminate nuclear weapons but to achieve a stable nuclear balance. Ideally, nuclear deterrence would be based solely on each side enjoying a limited number of invulnerable second-strike weapons. The worst case would be if both sides had only first-strike weapons, the equivalent of each holding a revolver to the head of the other. In any crisis, the impulse would be to fire first (or risk dying).

Several treaties have affected nuclear testing. The most important was the multilateral 1963 Nuclear Test Ban Treaty, which prohibited atmospheric, underwater, and outer space but not underground testing. The bilateral 1974 Threshold Nuclear

Test Ban Treaty prohibited underground tests of bombs with explosive yields greater than 150 kilotons, while the 1976 Peaceful Nuclear Explosions Treaty outlawed explosions greater than 150 kilotons for peaceful purposes such as mining or excavation. The 1990 Underground Testing Verification Treaty specified the means for verifying compliance with the 1974 and 1976 treaties.

During the 1970s, Washington and Moscow signed two *Strategic Arms Limitation Talks (SALT)* treaties, which attempted to cap the expansion of destabilizing first-strike weapons while securing second-strike forces. Negotiations for the 1972 SALT I Treaty began in 1969. SALT I included two elements. First, the superpowers agreed to restrict any antiballistic missile systems to one protecting their respective capitals and one elsewhere. Secondly, the treaty restricted the growth in number of ICBM and SLBM launchers for five years while allowing their modernization. The Soviets were allowed to have 1,408 ICBMs and 950 SLBMs and the Americans 1,000 ICBMs and 710 SLBMs. The negotiators reasoned that the Soviet advantage in the numbers was offset by the American lead in bombers (450 United States versus 150 USSR) and greater number of MIRVed ICBMs.

The 1979 SALT II Treaty was more comprehensive. The superpowers agreed to limit the combined number of ICBM launchers, SLBM launchers, heavy bombers, and ASBMs (air-to-surface ballistic missiles with ranges over 600 kilometers) to 2,250 launchers and 1,320 MIRVs, of which no more than 820 could be land based, on each side.

Although SALT I was ratified by both sides, Carter withdrew SALT II from the ratification process begun in the U.S. Senate following the Soviet invasion of Afghanistan in December 1979. Both sides followed SALT II's tenets despite the failure to ratify it. To gain even initial Senate approval for SALT II, Carter had to promise to develop the MX ICBM, which further fueled the arms race. SALT II, however, did prevent the scheduled deployment of 8,500 additional weapons by 1985—2,500 additional ICBMs for the Soviet Union, 5,100 for the United States.

Then, through the mid-1980s, no progress was made on arms control. It was only after Mikhail Gorbachev took power in the Soviet Union in 1985 that this impasse was broken on nuclear weapons, conventional forces, and several other important issues. The 1987 *Intermediate Range Nuclear Force Treaty (INF)* was a turning point in arms control—for the first time, the superpowers were actually required to destroy certain weapons rather than just limit their expansion. The superpowers agreed to eliminate all missiles in Europe with ranges between 300 and 3,400 miles, which required the United States "to destroy 859 missiles: 429 medium range Pershing 2S and ground launched cruise missiles deployed in Europe, 260 medium range missiles not employed, and 170 Pershing 1A shorter range missiles stockpiled in the United States. The Soviet Union is required to destroy 1,752 missiles: 470 medium range SS-20 and SS-4 missiles deployed, 356 medium range missiles not deployed, 387 deployed shorter range missiles and 539 of those weapons in storage."[17] Also new were the verification procedures that allowed each side to conduct on-site inspections of the other.

The *Strategic Arms Reduction Treaty (START)* talks had begun as early as 1982. The Reagan administration called for cutting the number of warheads from 7,500 to 5,000, of which no more than half could be on ICBMs. After nine years of sporadic negotiations, the START I treaty was finally signed on July 31, 1991, in which both sides agreed to reduce their land, sea, and air-based ICBMs to 1,600 and their warheads to 6,000. Because the treaty allows both sides to increase and modernize other types of warheads, Russian missiles will be reduced overall from 10,841

Security *or* Insecurity?
Pakistan, *the* Bomb, *and* Development

Does military spending help or harm a country's development? Do nuclear weapons make a country more or less secure? As always, the answers to such questions depend on circumstances.

Take Pakistan, for example. Pakistan faces a perennial threat from its neighbor India. India's 966 million (mostly Hindu people) dwarf Pakistan's 130 million (nearly all Muslims). Those religious differences exacerbate geopolitical conflicts that have three times exploded into war between the two countries, in 1947, 1965, and 1971. How did Pakistan fare in these wars? Pakistan won independence from India in the first war, fought India to a draw in the second, but in the third lost its province of Bangladesh, which broke away and became an independent country.

Many animosities sparked those wars, the worst being the fate of Kashmir, which caps the northern end of both countries. India occupies two-thirds of Kashmir, which has a population two-thirds Muslim. Pakistan owns the rest. Both sides claim all of Kashmir. In between the three wars, small-scale fighting has periodically flared along the "line of control" splitting Kashmir between Pakistan and India, and has been continuous since 1989. In all, about 24,000 people have been killed in the last decade alone. Further complicating the geopolitical morass was a war between India and China in 1962 whereby the Chinese took the Aksai Chin region of Kashmir, which contains mostly Tibetan people. The U.N. Security Council issued a resolution as long ago as 1948 calling for a Pakistani with-

drawal and plebiscite among the people to determine their fate. If that plebiscite were held, independence rather than union with Pakistan would be the most likely result. A 1995 poll indicated that 72 percent of the population favored independence.

Given these wars and India's threat, Pakistan's government not only maintains a large conventional military but has also developed nuclear weapons and missiles. In May 1998, India tested five and Pakistan six nuclear weapons, along with missiles capable of devastating the other. India had previously tested a nuclear weapon in May 1974. The tensions eased somewhat when, in February 1999, the two countries signed the Lahore Declaration, whereby they pledged to avoid nuclear war and negotiate a solution to Kashmir.

to 8,040 and American warheads from 12,081 to 10,395. The treaty allowed for 12 types of on-site inspections of both missile sites and production facilities.

START was followed by a series of unilateral announcements in which both sides reduced their nuclear forces. In September 1991, President George Bush announced that he would cancel the 24-hour alert for long-range bombers, remove nuclear weapons from many U.S. Navy ships, halt the planned deployment of MX ICBMs on railway cars, and called for even greater bilateral cuts in nuclear weapons. President Boris Yeltsin announced in January 1992 that Russia no longer considered the United States its enemy and would no longer target American cities. Four days later, Bush responded by announcing that the United States would cease production of the B-2 bomber, the Midgetman mobile nuclear missile, advanced cruise missiles, and Trident SLBM warheads. Hours later, Yeltsin countered by calling for cuts of up to 2,500 warheads for each superpower and the reduction of strategic nuclear weapons by 2,000, and announced he would cut

Are Pakistan and India locked into a security dilemma whereby steps taken to build up one's military actually make war not only more likely but more destructive? Can spending too much or too little on the military actually provoke the attack a country wants to deter?

It is difficult and often impossible to measure just what benefits high military spending bring a country. The costs of military spending, however, are easier to calculate. Pakistan's government spends ever more on a military it cannot afford. Two-thirds of Pakistan's budget goes to the military and debt servicing. By 1998, the government's debt surpassed $20 billion. Pakistan's economy is an increasingly fraying basket case. The country runs perennial trade deficits that are paid for only by borrowing ever more money. Only one million of its citizens pay any income tax.

Pakistan's nuclear tests imposed enormous costs on the country. The direct costs of its nuclear program are not public knowledge. Although the IMF and the United States imposed economic sanctions on both countries after their tests, they hurt Pakistan worse. The Pakistani rupee plunged 25 percent in value, raising the country's import bill another $3.5 billion, and sending inflation and unemployment soaring, while remittances from Pakistanis living abroad dropped. Thus an already poverty-stricken country was rendered more so.

Pakistan and India alike are abysmally poor, ranking number 138 and 139 respectively in the U.N. Development Program's 174-country ranking of human development. With a per capita GDP of $490 in 1997, Pakistanis were slightly less poor than Indians with $390. From 1980 to 1997, Pakistan's economy grew slightly slower, at a 5.7 percent annual rate, compared to India's 5.8 percent rate. With a smaller population and economy, Pakistan must spend more on the military to keep up with India, 5.8 percent of its GNP compared to 3.3 percent for India.

What policy would better secure Pakistan from an Indian attack? Should Pakistan borrow and spend even more on the military? Or would negotiations with India to reduce their respective military budgets and resolve the Kashmir conflict actually make Pakistan more secure militarily and economically?

Russian military spending to one-seventh the previous year's budget and to halve the Russian army. At this point the momentum of arms cuts broke down as Bush refused to reduce SLBMs, in which the United States had an advantage, below one-third of the then current level and called for the elimination of ICBM MIRVs, in which the Russians were superior. But at the June 1992 Washington summit, Bush and Yeltsin agreed to reduce their combined warheads from 16,000 to 6,527 by 2003, of which they would be allowed roughly 3,250 each, and eventually eliminate all their land-based MIRVs. This agreement eliminated "the most threatening Russian missiles while allowing the United States to retain its most advanced missiles."[18] Although the United States clearly got the best deal, Russia and all humanity benefit from the elimination of the most destabilizing weapons.

Although START I was to have lasted 15 years, a START II agreement was signed in January 1993 that incorporated many of the unilateral announcements and additional bilateral agreements. Under START II, by 2003 the United States and Russia would cut their nuclear forces to 3,500 and 2,997, respectively. Moscow and Washington agreed to eliminate all MIRVed ICBMs. Each side would retain about 500 single-warhead ICBMs, while the United States would keep 1,728 SLBMs and 1,272 cruise missiles and Russia, 1,744 SLBMs and 752 cruise missiles. Although the previous nuclear treaties were balanced, START II overwhelmingly favored the United States. Russia had to eliminate the backbone of its ICBM forces, whereas the United States retained its superior SLBM and cruise missile forces. Unfortunately, right-wing hard-liners in both countries have prevented the U.S. Senate and Russian Duma from ratifying START II. In November 1998, the Defense Department tried to break the impasse by urging the Clinton White House and Republican controlled Congress to cut unilaterally America's nuclear arsenal to START II levels, in hopes of both annually saving billions of dollars on unnecessary weapons and encouraging the Russians to reciprocate. The Republican party split over the issue, with its realists supporting the Pentagon's initiative and with ideologues opposed. The unilateral cuts did not occur.

Nonetheless, the nuclear arms race appears to have been finally stopped and reversed. SALT I and II mostly affected weapons systems that had become obsolete or were simply developed as bargaining chips. INF and START, however, have actually begun to build down nuclear arsenals. Yet there are still important areas of disagreement.

The Clinton administration led negotiations that culminated with a Comprehensive Test Ban Treaty (CTBT) on September 24, 1996, which has since been ratified by over 150 countries. Of the 44 states with the current capability to build nuclear weapons, all signed the treaty except India, Pakistan, and North Korea. The treaty would not prevent any country from testing nuclear weapons if it wanted to do so. At best the treaty is a *confidence-building measure* that could possibly create an impetus for more sweeping arms reduction initiatives. But if testing stops, America's nuclear lead is cemented for a decade or so, because only the United States currently has the computer technology to test weapons without actually exploding them. Testing is essential to ensure the safety, effectiveness, and thus deterrent value of nuclear weapons. Thus could the United States continue to upgrade its nuclear force while other nuclear forces deteriorated. Indeed, computer technology has allowed the United States to forgo actually exploding nuclear weapons since 1992, thus saving hundreds of millions of dollars. Exploding bombs is actually an inefficient way to detect possible defects in the 4,000 components of a nuclear bomb. From 1958 to 1993, less than 1 percent of 830 defects discovered were revealed by test explosions.

That is not the CTB's only advantage for the United States. The treaty would be a boon for American intelligence gathering. To reinforce compliance, over 321 monitoring stations—including 170 to detect underground vibrations, 80 to sniff airborne radioactivity, 60 to reveal sounds, and 11 to sense underwater signs—would be constructed around the world. They could detect a blast of less than 1 kiloton, equal to 1,000 pounds of explosives. In contrast, the atomic bomb dropped on Hiroshima packed 15,000 kilotons of explosives. The United States would provide 25 percent of the detection system's cost.[19]

With so much to gain at such a little financial cost with no risk, it might seem that the Senate would vote overwhelmingly in favor of the CTB. In fact the Senate vote fell short of the necessary two-thirds favorable vote for ratification by 52 to 42. Once again the ideologues opposed on "principle" to any arms control beat the realists dedicated to bolstering American national security.

What Has *the* Nuclear Arms Race Taught Us?

Was the nuclear arms race necessary? Could deterrence, assuming that either side ever had any intention of attacking the other, have been purchased at a much lower cost in financial, technological, and human resources? Did the nuclear arms race make the superpowers and the world more or less secure? Was a Third World War prevented because of or despite the nuclear arms race?

COMPELLENCE AND DETERRENCE

The United States did use nuclear weapons to compel other states to change their behavior. By one authoritative account, America's nuclear strategy may have prevented at least 10 crises from escalating into war. In his book *Nuclear Blackmail and Nuclear Balance*, Richard Betts carefully examined four crises when Washington's nuclear forces either probably prevented war or protected American interests—Cuba (1962), Berlin (1948), Korea (1953), and Taiwan (1955), and were of uncertain value in the another six crises—Berlin (1958–1961), Middle East (1973), Suez (1956), Lebanon (1958), Taiwan (1958), and the Persian Gulf (1980).[20] But Washington's power to compel others diminished steadily as the Soviet Union achieved parity.

And what of nuclear deterrence? Although deterrence is supposed to prevent an attack, we can never truly know whether deterrence has actually worked. It could be that the other side never intended an attack in the first place regardless of how much or little military power its opponent held. Nuclear deterrence, like power, is more about psychology than weapons. It also involves paradoxes—Moscow and Washington safeguarded peace by preparing for nuclear annihilation, and expanded their number and type of weapons while negotiating arms control treaties.

If deterrence worked at all, it did so because both sides' forces were relatively invulnerable to an enemy first strike, and thus retained enough power to wipe out the other. The Americans and Soviets have protected their second-strike capabilities by several means. One is through sheer numbers—simply producing so many ICBMs, SLBMs, and bombers that enough would survive even the luckiest first strike to devastate the enemy. Dispersing those weapons as widely as possible increases their invulnerability, as does protecting ICBMs in hardened sites, keeping SLBMs underwater and bombers in the air, and both constantly on the move and hidden. Two other policies might strengthen one's second-strike capability at the expense of creating more tension and the chance of war between the superpowers. Antiballistic missile systems (ABM) such as SDI, although forbidden by the 1972 ABM Treaty, might further protect nuclear weapons but could be used in conjunction with that side's first strike against the enemy. Likewise, a "launch on warning" system in which American missiles automatically fire if there is an attack on the United States increases the odds that the country will survive but would devastate the other side even if the initial attack was caused by an accident or a madman.

Nuclear weapons have become useless for actually fighting wars or even preventing a war with a nonnuclear country. When the United States dropped atomic bombs on Hiroshima and Nagasaki, no one understood the grievous harm that

A Maginot Line *in* Space? *The* National Missile Defense—Fantasies, Possibilities, *and* Tradeoffs

Is a defense against ICBMs possible? If so, how much would it cost? Would it make the United States more or less secure?

From 1983 through 1999, the United States spent $110 billion on various Star Wars antinuclear missile projects including the Strategic Defense Initiative (SDI), "Brilliant Pebbles," and most recently the Theater High Altitude Area Defense (THAAD), to name the most prominent. Every scheme has failed spectacularly and expensively. Nearly all scientists predicted those failures. They argued that building a magic shield that defends the United States from a high- or low-altitude missile attack is simply not scientifically feasible, now and into the future.

Yet others argue that THAAD has actually made steady progress and could go from the lab to the field within a few years. THAAD would be the backbone of a National Missile Defense with over 400 exoatmospheric kill vehicles (EKVs) clustered in sites around the United States. The system is scheduled to be deployed in 2005. But the budgeted $10.5 billion for the National Missile Defense is a fraction of the actual estimated cost of at least $60 billion.

Moscow and other nuclear powers fear that the primary purpose of any Star Wars scheme would help the United States launch rather than defend against a first nuclear strike. If a crisis exploded into war, Washington could order a massive first strike against Russia's nuclear forces, wiping out nearly all land- and sea-based missiles. If any Russian missiles survived, Moscow would be deterred from using them, because the United States could then destroy its cities with second-strike weapons and possibly shoot down Russian missiles with its defense.

Yet few Russian analysts lose any sleep over the National Missile Defense. Like their American counterparts, they see it as a massive squandering of American wealth, something of course they applaud rather than deplore because it weakens rather than strengthens America. Even if some missile defense were possible, the Russians could neutralize or outflank it. Moscow could neutralize any American Star Wars defense by tearing up nuclear arms control treaties and building more ICBMS, filling their missile and cones with hundreds of decoys, which would divert any missiles or lasers. They could outflank Star Wars by firing low trajectory SLBMs or cruise missiles beneath any "shield." Star Wars would truly be a Maginot line (the defensive wall built by France in the 1930s for billions of dollars which the Germans simply outflanked in 1940) in space. But all of those scenarios are unlikely.

The most probable nuclear horror scenario involves a man with a heavy briefcase, or the truck driver, pilot, or boat captain with an unusual load. The target would be the heart of Washington or Wall Street or any large population area. The personnel for the National Missile Defense would at least be far from any nuclear blast. The only way to thwart nuclear terrorists is with old-fashioned spying backed with high technology.

What of the future? Should more money be spent in the hope that a National Missile Defense is just a few more years and billions of dollars away? Or, assuming that the scientists are correct that a missile defense is a fantasy, was the $110 billion spent on various Star Wars schemes a waste of taxpayers' hard-earned money? If so how should that money have been invested in a way that enhanced rather than diminished American wealth and power? Should it have gone to tax cuts for the rich, as Reaganites advocated? Or should taxes have been cut instead for the middle class and poor, as Clintonites asserted? Should it have been invested in infrastructure and industries? Should it have gone to schools and inner cities? Should it have been used to "save" Medicare and social security? Should it have been used to reduce the national debt? Should it have been split among all or none of these targets? If you were president, what would you have advocated? Which interest groups would have supported and which would have opposed your proposals? Would your proposals have succeeded or failed, given the Republican control of Congress?

radiation could do humanity. As an understanding of their vast and continual destructiveness grew, more governments and people became convinced that nuclear weapons should never be used. The nuclear standoff and international morality have deterred the other nuclear powers from using their weapons even against nonnuclear countries. The Americans in Vietnam (1964–1972), the Soviets in Afghanistan (1979–1989), the Chinese against Vietnam (1979), and the British against Argentina (1982) never considered even threatening to use, let alone use, nuclear weapons to win those wars.

Nuclear weapons may well diminish rather than enhance a nation's power. Clearly, nuclear weapons provide the bearer with prestige. Yet the scientific, financial, and psychological costs of developing and deploying nuclear weapons are enormous. Those same resources invested properly elsewhere in a state's economy could produce far larger amounts of wealth, and ultimately power. Nuclear weapons are largely very elaborate and costly ornaments. They can be brandished, but their use might well result in national suicide.

THE CHANCES OF NUCLEAR WAR

Nuclear war is the world's worst nightmare. How possible is it?

Even during the cold war's height, the chance of nuclear war was remote. The *Cuban missile crisis* was the closest the world came to a nuclear war, although the superpowers also neared the brink of war during the Berlin crises of 1948–1949 and 1959–1961. There is no evidence, however, that either power at any time considered launching a massive first strike. And because a conventional war never occurred, neither side ever employed either a massive retaliation or flexible response strategy. In any event, the second-strike capabilities of both sides would have probably deterred a first strike.

Nuclear war, however, could have been sparked by other causes. An accidental launch caused by computer error or false warning of an enemy attack, unauthorized firing by crazy people in a submarine or silo, or attack by a third country on a superpower could have caused the victim to retaliate or the attacker to launch a pre-emptive attack in anticipation of just such a retaliation. During an 18-month period between January 1979 to June 1980, America's nuclear forces received 3,703 warnings of an incoming missile attack, of which 147 were deemed serious enough to cause an alert and evaluation. There have been at least 32 accidents involving American nuclear weapons, although none detonated.[21]

The superpowers, however, have taken significant steps, known as "fail-safe" systems, to minimize these chances of war. As important as the nuclear weapons in the field, is the "command, control, communication, and intelligence" (C3I) system. Both have continually upgraded their C3I systems to avoid human and technical error, while strengthening the national command authority (NCA) or hierarchy to determine who has the power to authorize an attack if the leaders above are killed. Nuclear weapons can only be launched by two individuals simultaneously turning the keys to activate. The two-key system reduces the possibility of a crazy person making an unauthorized launch.

In addition, Washington and Moscow signed several treaties strengthening their ability to communicate in a crisis, including the 1963, 1971, and 1985 hotline agreements, which established and strengthened direct communications between the White House and Kremlin; the nuclear accidents agreement of 1971, which reduced the chance for an accident leading to nuclear war; the 1972 high seas agreement, which helped contain any accident or unauthorized firing between the American and Soviet ships or submarines from escalating; the 1973 nuclear war prevention agreement, which strengthened crisis management abilities and communication channels between them; and the 1987 Crisis Reduction Treaty establishing crisis control centers in each capital. The provisions of the 1968 nuclear nonproliferation treaty have reduced the chances for nuclear weapons getting in the hands of terrorist states or groups.

REASONS FOR THE NUCLEAR ARMS RACE

Why did the nuclear arms race last over four decades?

There were many obstacles to slowing, let alone reversing, the nuclear arms race.[22] Each side held a mirror image of the other as aggressive, deceitful, and dedicated to achieving superiority. Neither side trusted the other, nor were they willing until recently to include the verification procedures in a nuclear agreement that could have helped to build that trust.

There were good reasons for some of that distrust. Profound ideological differences and the aggressive actions and statements of both sides were the most important reasons for the arms race. Moscow's assertion that it was leading a global communist revolution, its subjection of Eastern Europe, invasions of Czechoslovakia, Hungary, and Afghanistan, and involvement in dozens of other countries were certainly aggressive by any measure and ultimately a threat to American security. Washington's assertion of a containment policy from 1947, its nuclear arms buildup, creation of NATO, military intervention in Korea, Vietnam, Grenada, and Panama, and indirect manipulation of politics in scores of other countries certainly seemed threatening to the Soviet Union.

But domestic politics were also important in fueling the nuclear arms race. As the budget, personnel, institutions, and responsibilities of each side's military-industrial complex expanded, it acquired increasing political power to demand and receive even more resources. All those involved in military policies and industries—bureaucrats, politicians, contractors, labor unions, scientists—had a vested interest in continually gaining more money and duty. Once a weapons program was begun, it proved almost impossible to kill it. Many weapons began as bargaining chips but, often for political rather than strategic reasons, soon became "vital" to national security. On average it took a decade to build a new weapons system from the first blueprints and models, through the testing, to the finished product. Canceling a project would put people out of work, and threaten the re-election of the congressional representatives and senators from those districts.

Politics often resulted in weapons systems being built even if they were obsolete or unworkable. For example, the Carter administration canceled the B-1 bomber, arguing that it was a waste of money that could be better spent elsewhere, because existing B-52s armed with cruise missiles could do the job just as effectively. The Reagan administration revived the B-1 project, which eventually cost American taxpayers $40 billion, and accelerated the B-2 Stealth bomber, which has cost about $50 billion so far. Although the first B-52s became operational in 1954 and the type is now 40 years old, it remains superior to the newer B-1 and B-2 bombers that appeared during the 1980s and 1990s. There have been eight different B-52 versions, each a large improvement over the previous. Technical problems have repeatedly grounded both the B-1 and B-2 bomber fleets. The Reagan administration claimed that it would enhance American security by completing the B-1 and B-2 bombers. Critics argue that American security was actually undermined because those bombers consumed vast amounts of scarce financial, human, political, and scientific resources that could have been much more profitably employed elsewhere. Moreover, Moscow felt compelled to counter the B-1 and B-2 with its own new weapons systems, and the nuclear arms race accelerated.

The arms talks themselves often bogged down over several issues. Verification was one of the biggest obstacles to nuclear arms control. Both sides were afraid that the other would cheat, yet resisted opening up their own military-industrial complex to a comprehensive inspection system that would minimize that chance. Even with verification agreements, the process becomes ever more difficult in an age of cruise missiles that are highly mobile, only 20 feet long, relatively inexpensive, can carry both nuclear and conventional warheads, and have a range of thousands of miles. The 1987 INF treaty was the first to allow on-site inspections, and subsequent treaties have included that provision.

Until recently, the superpowers disagreed on how to calculate the nuclear balance. Moscow insisted that British, French, and Chinese nuclear missiles be included with those of the United States in negotiating any limitations or actual reductions. Washington said that only the superpower missile forces should be negotiated. During the 1980s, they agreed to concentrate on their own forces.

Paradoxically, arms control talks seemed to quicken the arms race as each side tried to develop duplicate and sometimes triplicate weapons systems, which it then used as bargaining chips at the negotiating table. As a result, each side scrambled to build ever more advanced systems that would either match or surpass the others' systems.

BREAKING THE IMPASSES ON ARMS CONTROL

How can these walls of distrust be dismantled? Charles Osgood advocated a policy he called *"gradual and reciprocated initiatives in tension-reduction (GRITs)"* in which one side will make a concession such as not building or even scrapping a weapons system and then encourage the other side to reciprocate.[23] If this occurs, the first side makes another more significant concession, which ideally will be reciprocated by the other side. If the other side continues to build up its forces, the first side should only match and never exceed the other's increases. Thus, an arms buildup can be replaced by an arms build-down. President Gorbachev initiated such a GRIT with President Bush in 1991, and it was continued by President Yeltsin after the Soviet Union collapsed. The nuclear arms buildup has been replaced with its build-down.

Nuclear arms negotiations over relatively limited restrictions on slowing or capping increases in weapon numbers and types, let alone decreases, took years and sometimes decades. The recent limited steps of unilateral disarmament have been much more effective and faster than negotiations in producing deep, balanced, and reciprocal cuts in numbers and weapons systems. However, unilateral steps were not always reciprocated. Between August 1985 and February 1987, Gorbachev unilaterally stopped all Soviet nuclear tests and asked Reagan to reciprocate. Reagan refused, and Gorbachev eventually resumed testing.

There are several other ways in which small confidence-building measures could have been taken that would have stimulated more meaningful cuts later. Over the decades many have advocated a freeze on testing or building new weapons for a certain time period, to be resumed if the other side did not reciprocate. A more sweeping measure would be for the United States or Russia to announce that it would agree to reduce its overall military budget to one percent of GNP within five years if the other great powers would reciprocate.

Denuclearizing regions is also seen as a good way to build confidence and achieve more significant cuts or elimination elsewhere. Washington and Moscow negotiated agreements banning the introduction of nuclear weapons into Antarctica, space, and the moon. Although neither side may have ever had any reason to employ nuclear weapons in those realms, the successful negotiation of those agreements gave both sides the momentum to confront more contentious issues. Although the United States initially opposed the nuclear-free-zone treaties of Latin America in 1967 and the South Pacific in 1985, those zones did reinforce arms control efforts elsewhere.

THE VALUE OF NUCLEAR WEAPONS

As the atomic bombing of Hiroshima and Nagasaki proved, atomic bombs can win wars and save lives in the long run. If that is true, then why have not Washington, Moscow, and the other nuclear powers used nuclear weapons in their respective wars?

Over the past 50 years, the military value of nuclear weapons declined as their numbers, destructive power, and possessors increased. The Reagan administration initially embraced the nuclear utilization theory (NUT) that the United States could successfully wage and win a nuclear war, and should build up its nuclear forces and the Star Wars technology to do so. The NUTs argue that by trying to protect your population and nuclear weapons from attack, you enhance deterrence. They maintain that theoretically a nuclear war can be won quickly by targeting the other side's leadership (decapitation) and its command, control, communications, and intelligence (poking their eyes out). Thus in a crisis the NUTs would favor a "launch under attack" (LUA) to ensure the ability to retaliate, or even a "launch on warning" (LOW) of an imminent attack to pre-empt it.

However, most people (including eventually the Reagan administration) agree that nuclear war could only result in mutually assured destruction (MAD), and thus can never be won and should never be fought. Those who believe a nuclear war can be won and then prepare to do so, simply make a nuclear holocaust more likely. The risks of sparking a nuclear war far exceed any benefits. In a full nuclear exchange between the United States, over 200 million Americans and Russians would die immediately or shortly thereafter. The resulting nuclear winter, ozone layer depletion, radioactive fallout, collapse of the global and regional economies, and worldwide failure of crops would kill billions of people in the following months, until the human race itself might well become extinct. A LUA or LOW strategy exacerbates the "use 'em or lose 'em" mentality that makes nuclear war more likely. Furthermore, what if the warning of an impending attack is wrong. Instead, the MADs advocate a "launch upon impact" (LUI) strategy in which the United States would retaliate only if Russian missiles actually began exploding across the country. The MADs reason that the United States second-strike force of SLBMs, cruise missiles, and bombers would survive largely intact and thus deter the Russians from even considering a first strike.

In fact, America's nuclear war fighting plan (SIOP) contains elements of NUT and MAD. NUTs applaud the flexible response strategy, which involves fighting a nuclear war through first strikes at each nuclear level. America's nuclear forces, however, are heavily weighted in favor of second-strike weapons, which MADs favor because they are the essence of deterrence. In an all-out war, the Pentagon has targeted not only Russia's nuclear forces, but also 65 percent of its industrial power and 35 percent of its population. SIOP thus contains both counterforce and countervalue targets.

Most analysts agree that at some point acquiring more nuclear weapons no longer enhances that country's military or political power. With the ability to destroy the world 20 or so times (or "to make the rubble bounce" as Churchill put it), the military value of nuclear weapons was no doubt exceeded long ago. Although nuclear weapons can be used to compel or deter others, because they are so destructive, nuclear weapons are only valuable when they are used to threaten others. If nuclear weapons are actually used as weapons, they have failed to serve their purpose. It is much more difficult to determine when building more nuclear weapons no longer increases that country's deterrent or political power.

Eventually, the nuclear powers will reduce their weapons to a *minimum deterrence* that maintains "strategic parity." What is the minimal level of nuclear forces that would maintain deterrence yet reduce the chances for accidental war or a nuclear winter? Could minimum deterrence rest on, say, one American and one Russian nuclear submarine cruising a vast range of oceans into which the other side's ships and submarines are not allowed? As we have seen, one submarine with MIRVed SLBMs can destroy over 200 targets. Most analysts would answer no, and argue that a stable deterrence requires far more second-strike weapons, with up to 1,000 warheads.

minimum deterrence the minimal number of nuclear weapons deemed necessary to ensure deterrence.

Would the world be better off without nuclear weapons? Ideally, yes, of course. But the nuclear genie is loose, and increasing numbers of governments are able to use its powers. Whether nuclear power deters war and promotes stability or encourages war and instability depends on who controls it. Complete nuclear disarmament would involve all states agreeing not only to give up all nuclear weapons technology but also to submit to extensive inspection of their facilities and budgets. Knowledge, however, cannot be dismantled. A nuclear disarmament treaty would put hundreds of thousands of scientists and technicians out of work, many of whom might be desperate enough to sell their secrets to the highest bidder. A global fear would be that even with a disarmament treaty and inspection regime, somehow, somewhere a terrorist group or government is feverishly attempting to put together a nuclear bomb. It seems humanity must exist under the nuclear shadow for the foreseeable future.

Ultimately, there is no guarantee that deterrence, controls, or rationality will continue to work. Luck may well have been the most important factor in so far sparing the world from nuclear warfare. As long as there are nuclear weapons on earth, there is a chance that they will be used either from cold, rational choice, frenzied fear, or unforeseen accident.

Study Questions

1. Describe the effects of 1-megaton, 10-megaton, and 100-megaton nuclear explosions on a city.

2. Define nuclear winter and nuclear autumn.

3. How many nuclear weapons have been tested to date? What have been the human effects of nuclear testing?

4. What is deterrence? What role do capability and credibility play in effective deterrence?

5. Analyze the phases of America's nuclear war fighting strategy from 1945 through today.

6. Analyze the different force structures of the United States and Soviet Union. What were the strengths and weaknesses of each?

7. State the arguments for and against MAD and NUT.

8. What was the Strategic Defense Initiative and why did Reagan propose it? Why was it eventually abandoned as unworkable?

9. Describe the attempts taken to prevent nuclear proliferation. What countries other than the United States and Russia have or might have nuclear weapons? How large are those nuclear arsenals?

10. Was the nuclear arms race necessary? Could deterrence, assuming that either side ever had any intention of attacking the other, have been purchased at a much lower cost in financial, technological, and human resources? Explain.

11. Did the nuclear arms race make the superpowers and the world more or less secure? Was a Third World War prevented because of or in spite of the nuclear arms race? Explain.

12. Is nuclear war still possible? If so, under what scenarios? What are some ways to make nuclear war less possible?

13. Why did the nuclear arms race last over four decades? What are some ways in which an arms race might be halted and reserved? Did the superpowers use any of those methods?

14. What value do nuclear weapons have? Could the world ever be nuclear-free? Explain.

☝ *InfoTrac College Edition* Sources

Using the Subject Guide, enter the search terms *nuclear warfare, arms control, Cuban missile crisis,* and/or *détente.*

Albright, Madeleine K. "A Diplomatic Framework Guiding U.S. Efforts on Non-proliferation."

Feaver, Peter D. "Proliferation, Pessimism, and Emerging Nuclear Powers."

Fetter, Steve. "Correspondence: Nuclear Deterrence and the 1990 Indo-Pakistani Crisis."

Jones, Rodney W. "Pakistan's Nuclear Posture: Arms Race Instabilities in South Asia."

Manning, Robert A. "The Nuclear Age: The Next Chapter."

McNamara, Thomas. "National and International Efforts to Control Nuclear Weapons."

Medhurst, Martin J. "Atoms for Peace and Nuclear Hegemony: The Rhetorical Structure of a Cold War Campaign."

Parker, Christopher S. "New Weapons for Old Problems."

Perkovich, George. "Nuclear Proliferation."

Sagan, Scott D. "Why Do States Build Nuclear Weapons?"

Solomon, Theodros. "Disarmament: A Scientist's View."

Waller, J. Michael. "Subsidizing Russia's Nuclear Scientists."

🌐 On *the* Web

http://sun00781.dn.net/nuke/control/
Federation of American Scientists site on arms control

http://www.atomicarchive.com/Treaties/Treaty9.shtml
Information on nuclear weapons and nuclear arms control, including treaties

http://www.brook.edu/FP/PROJECTS/NUCWCOST/WEAPONS.HTM
Examines the costs of the nuclear arms race

Contents

Chapter 11 *The* Changing Nature *of* War

Key Concepts and Terms

If you want peace, prepare for war. (Si vis pacem, para bellum.)

The adversaries of the world are not in conflict because they are armed. They are armed because they are in conflict and have not yet learned peaceful ways to resolve their conflicting national interests.

RICHARD NIXON

Throughout the 5,500 years of recorded history, there have been over 14,500 wars, in which over 3.5 billion people have died. On average, wars occur in 94 of every 100 years.[1] Increasingly costly in lives and destruction, the wars of the 20th century alone killed over 100 million and destroyed trillions of dollars of property. One of every 20 dollars spent worldwide feeds the military. In an increasingly interdependent world, the fallout from a distant conventional war is not obvious or measurable, but nonetheless exists in terms of refugees, destruction, forgone socioeconomic development, further arms races and tensions, and so on.

War has traditionally been the engine of history, bearing with it the rise and fall of great powers and power constellations. As James Shotwell points out

> War . . . has been the instrument by which most of the great facts of political national history have been established and maintained. It has played a dominant role in nearly all political crises; it has been used to achieve liberty, to secure democracy, and to attempt to make it secure against the menace of its use by other hands. The map of the world today has been largely determined on the battlefield. . . . (E)ven in peace, the war system has to a large degree determined not only international relationships but the character and history of the nations themselves.[2]

Frederick the Great of Russia put it more succinctly: "Diplomacy without armaments is like music without instruments."[3]

War, many argue, is natural and inevitable. Wherever there are people, there are conflicts, and many will be prepared to assert violently their interests in those conflicts. Hans Morgenthau remarked, "Men do not fight because they have arms. They have arms because they deem it necessary to fight. Take away their arms and they will fight each other with their bare fists. . . . The elimination of certain types of weapons altogether would have a bearing upon the technology of warfare. . . . It is hard to see how it could influence the frequency of war."[4] Thus if you want peace, you must prepare for war. Others argue that if you prepare for war, you will probably get it. This chapter analyzes war's major characteristics.

Where in the world is this? This scene of bloated, butchered bodies could recently be from any number of countries— Rwanda, Kuwait, Algeria, Bosnia, Kosovo, Colombia, Ceylon, or Cambodia, to name a few. Actually it was shot on the border between Eritrea and Ethiopia, whose armies are battling over disputed territory. International wars have diminished but not ended even as globalization steadily strengthens ties among countries. Civil wars are as numerous and bloody as ever.

AP/Wide World Photos

What Is War?

Wars can occur between sovereign states (interstate), between sovereign states and a nonsovereign people struggling for independence (imperial or colonial), and between groups within a sovereign state (civil). But are all armed conflicts wars? The Correlates of War (COW) project at the University of Michigan, which has been studying war since 1963, uses the arbitrary threshold of 1,000 or more combat deaths to designate a war. By this standard there were 181 international wars between 1816 and 1988.[5] That rules out as wars the American invasions of Grenada in 1983 and Panama in 1991. Those Grenadans and Panamanians caught in the fighting might beg to differ with that scholarly definition of war. A broader definition of war obviously increases the number. Defining war as any time two or more states use armed forces violently beyond their borders, 269 wars involving 591 states broke out between 1945 and 1988, of which the great powers started one-fourth.[6] When would you say armed violence becomes a war?

During the industrial era, wars have steadily diminished as a percentage of the average number of states in the system: 1816–1848, 33 wars and 28 states; 1849–1881, 43 wars and 39 states; 1882–1914, 38 wars and 40 states; 1915–1944, 38 wars and 40 states; 1945–1988, 43 wars and 117 states. Only 20 of those 172 years were peaceful. Traditionally, aggression paid, but not as well as the initiators expected. Between 1495 and 1985, the initiators won 58.1 percent of the time, or 51.5 percent between 1495 and 1799 and 69.2 percent between 1800 and 1985. However, this upward trend was reversed in the 1980s, when only 18 percent of initiators won their wars![7] Peace through strength, however, may not be a foolproof means of security. Five of the nine wars involving great powers between 1815 and 1965 involved militarily weaker countries attacking stronger ones that were further building their military power.[8]

Part 4 Geopolitical Conflict and Cooperation

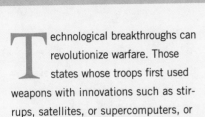

War *and* Technology

Technological breakthroughs can revolutionize warfare. Those states whose troops first used weapons with innovations such as stirrups, satellites, or supercomputers, or finished weapons such as machine guns, tanks, or airplanes, enjoyed an advantage over those that did not. Of course simply having those weapons is not enough. Strategy and tactics must be devised that best use them. Technological leads, of course, are fleeting. Inevitably others get their hands on the new weapons. At times countries create but fail to capitalize on technologies that can change the nature of warfare and the distribution of power. China, for instance, invented gunpowder, but Europeans first developed that technology into weapons so advanced that their wielders could literally rule the world.

Whom Does War Engulf?

Revolutionary technological changes in weapons, communications, and transportation have greatly expanded war's destructiveness and often geographic extent. The inventions of the railroad, rifle, airplane, tank, jet, and atomic bomb each stimulated vast changes in how wars are fought. Mass nationalism, ideologies, communications, and transportation allows governments the ability to mobilize virtually everyone for war either as a soldier, a supplier, or a supporter. Most countries have highly professional militaries that are prepared to fight on short notice.

Throughout the modern era, wars between the great powers have diminished in number but grown in the amount of troops and countries engaged, death, destruction, and the geographical area.[9] Of all great power wars between 1495 and 1980, 75 percent occurred before 1735. Before 1800 only about 3 of 1,000 people (0.3 percent) in a country directly participated in its wars. By World War I, one of seven citizens (14 percent) were direct participants in their nation's wars.[10] Only 20 percent of all countries during the past 500 years have never experienced war. Wars have become increasingly destructive. Since 1500 the world has experienced "589 wars and lost 141,901,000 lives. . . . So far, in the 90 years of this century, there have been four times as many war deaths as in the 400 years preceding."[11] Over 11 million people have died in wars since 1960, and the carnage mounts daily. About 90 percent of those who died from war in 1990 were civilians.

Since 1945 some clear and dramatic changes have arisen in where wars occur, who fights them, and how they are fought. With 29 wars between 1600 and 1945, Europe was the world's most war-prone region up through World War II; then the guns fell silent on the continent until the 1990s civil and international wars in Yugoslavia. Before 1945, the advanced industrial nations were the most belligerent both against themselves and less developed states; since then, no industrial states have fought each other, and they have fought only five wars in the Third World. John Gaddis described the lack of war between the great powers since 1945 as the "long peace."[12] There have been other periods of relatively long peace between the great powers, such as after the Congress of Vienna (1815–1848) and the Franco-Prussian War (1871–1914). But the long peace since 1945 is different in

Whither *the* Peace Dividend?

The cold war's end did bring a significant peace dividend to Americans. In constant 1995 dollars, American military spending dropped from $378 billion in 1988 to $259 billion in 1997. The less money spent on weapons, bases, and personnel, the more could be invested in new technologies, education, infrastructure, the environment, and elsewhere that increase productivity and the quality of life. America's economic expansion during the 1990s and into the 21st century is attributable partly to a lower military burden.

How much is enough for American defense? Just what quality and quantity of troops and weapons is necessary to deter or, if deterrence fails, destroy an enemy? Just who are America's political enemies as the new century dawns?

many ways. Since 1945, most international and all civil wars were fought within the Third World. The nature of war has also changed dramatically. Until 1945, 80 percent of wars were conventional international wars; since then 80 percent have been unconventional or *low-intensity wars*—guerrilla civil wars.[13]

Why have these changes occurred? For the advanced industrial nations, the costs of war far exceed the possible benefits. As economic interdependence deepens, national and international interests increasingly mesh, and war's potential destruction rises to exorbitant heights for "winners" and "losers" alike. War has become inconceivable between prosperous, democratic industrial countries. Not only have the great powers never fought since 1945, but also there have been no wars among the 48 richest countries.[14]

Why didn't the cold war turn hot? Although on several occasions the superpowers went to war's brink with each other (Berlin 1948–1949, 1961–1962; Cuba 1962), the Americans and Soviets succeeded in managing those crises. Europe was the one region where the superpowers stared eyeball to eyeball. Once Europe's two halves had been stabilized politically and economically, the superpowers largely respected the status quo. The Americans and Soviets then focused their animosities over winning the hearts, minds, and pocketbooks of the Third World, where the stakes for both were relatively low. Whether or not the mutually assured destruction (MAD) of nuclear weapons was the most important constraint on war between the superpowers is debatable.[15] Superpower military strategies emphasize deterring rather than winning wars with each other.

American Wars Since 1945

Of the two superpowers and all the great powers, no country has been more involved in armed conflicts since 1945 than the United States. Between 1946 and 1984, the United States either directly or indirectly threatened to use force 286 times, or an average of 7 times a year.[16] Another study identified 215 incidents between 1945 and 1975 in which Washington used the threat of force or proxy military forces to protect American interests.[17] Half the cases involved the movement of naval forces, and another large category includes movement of ground or air

American Wars *of the* 1980s *and* 1990s

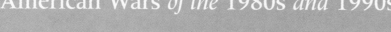

Lebanon

President Reagan ordered a marine contingent to join British and French troops in Lebanon as peacekeepers between the Israelis who had invaded the country and the PLO. After a truck bomb killed 241 Marines, Reagan withdrew the contingent. Figures on the financial cost to American taxpayers are unavailable. The deployment lasted from August 1982 to February 1984.

Grenada

President Reagan ordered an invasion of that tiny island in October 1983. The rationale was that the Marxist government was building an airport for the Soviet air force and was threatening American students. Neither claim was ever proven. The war cost American taxpayers a mere $76 million. Eighteen American troops died in the brief fighting.

Panama

President Bush ordered an invasion of Panama in 1990. The rationale was that Panama's dictator Manuel Noriega was threatening the U.S. canal, had sent soldiers to harass American soldiers, and was a major drug trafficker. The last two charges were true. The war cost American taxpayers $164 million.

Twenty-three American troops died in the fighting.

Persian Gulf

President Bush formed a coalition of 550,000 troops from 37 countries to repel Iraq from its brutal invasion of Kuwait in August 1990. The Coalition air war began on January 15, 1990, lasted six weeks, and was followed by a 100-hour ground war that routed Iraq's army and liberated Kuwait. Only about 148 Americans died in combat. The war cost $61 billion but America's allies paid for most of it.

Somalia

President Bush ordered American troops to join a U.N. peacekeeping force in 1992 to restore order in Somalia, which had fallen into anarchy. American troops joined the civil war when U.S. Rangers tried to arrest a faction's leaders. Twenty-nine American troops died and several score were wounded in that raid and other fighting. The cost to American taxpayers was $2 billion.

Haiti

President Clinton sent American troops in 1994 into Haiti to restore order after it dissolved into anarchy. After achiev-

ing their mission, the troops withdrew the following year. The cost to American taxpayers was $427 million. No Americans died in the operation.

Bosnia

President Clinton ordered American troops to join a peacekeeping mission to supervise a cease-fire in newly independent Bosnia. The yearly cost to American taxpayers is about $1.3 billion.

Kosovo

President Clinton ordered the U.S. air force to join NATO allies in pounding Yugoslavia's military and economic infrastructure in 1999 after President Milosevic ordered the Kosovar Albanians driven from Kosovo. Muslim Albanians make up 90 percent of Kosovo, which is a province of Yugoslavia dominated by Orthodox Christian Serbs. Milosevic withdrew his army from Kosovo after three months of bombardment. The cost to American taxpayers was about $2 billion, as is the yearly cost of occupying and rebuilding Kosovo.

If you were president, to which, if any of these conflicts would you have committed American troops and which, if any, would you have avoided?

---

forces. Washington's threats were not very successful—about one out of five resulted in a favorable outcome for the United States. Overall, Washington was more successful in situations where Moscow was not involved.

Although the numbers in those two studies seem immense, Washington seldom actually used force. A third study that covered the years between 1945 and 1973

What Are We Fighting *For*? . . . Next Stop Is . . . : American Military Doctrine

The Kosovo War reopened the debate over American military doctrine. When and how should American military forces be committed abroad? Former Defense Secretary Casper Weinberger formulated a policy in 1985 that American troops should only be sent into combat if the objectives were clear, overwhelming force was used, and the public solidly backed their use. But that policy, which became known as the Powell doctrine after Chief of Staff Colin Powell, presented policymakers with the stark choice of doing nothing or waging all-out war when American geopolitical interests were threatened.

Public opinion powerfully shapes American military policy. Since the United States lost its Vietnam War, the public has not tolerated American combat deaths. In 1983 President Reagan withdrew American troops from Lebanon in defeat within days after a truck bomb blew up a barracks killing 241 Marines. President Clinton withdrew American forces from Somalia weeks after a firefight left 18 American Rangers dead. Public outcries hastened both of those withdrawals. Every president faces similar constraints

when his administration debates the use of America's military.

American presidents have compared both Iraqi President Hussein and Yugoslav President Milosevic to Hitler, but failed to oust them, let alone bring them before a war crimes tribunal. Should the United States negotiate with and tolerate a "Hitler" in power?

America's overburdened economy and taxpayers have enjoyed a peace dividend since the cold war's end. Washington cut its military budget 25 percent from $378 billion in 1988 to $259 billion in 1999. Many of those savings were invested in the high-technology industries that have revived America's economic power and prosperity during the 1990s.

In 1999, politicians and ideologues masquerading as strategists and state leaders began to eat away that peace dividend. That year's military budget was $289 billion, $11 billion more than the Pentagon itself requested and a sum greater than the combined military spending of the 10 next largest countries, including Russia and China. That budget included a 4.8 percent pay raise, $91 billion for new weapons, $3.7 billion for a missile defense sys-

tem, and $3.1 billion for the next generation fighter jet, the F-22.

Was that money too little, too much, or just right to satisfy America's defense needs?

Proponents of greater defense spending claimed it was necessary to defend the United States against new threats, but could not identify such threats. Those politicians had no difficulty increasing funding for scores of bases and thousands of other expenses that the Pentagon condemned as wasteful "pork barrel" diversions that actually weakened America's defense as they diverted funds from combat training, spare parts, and logistics.

Senator John McCain, a maverick Arizona Republican and presidential aspirant, scoffed at those who demanded ever more defense spending without any concrete strategic purpose. McCain argued that the defense budget could be cut and American power increased simultaneously by carving away $20 billion or so of Pentagon fat and investing those savings in new technologies and weapon systems that cost a fraction of present systems, soldiers, and technicians. But in the end political pork defeated thoughtful strategy.

found that Washington militarily intervened only four times—Korea (1951–1953), Lebanon (1958), Dominican Republic (1965), and Vietnam (1961–1972), out of 149 situations in which American interests were threatened but its troops did not open fire.[18] The nonviolent situations include 31 cases where a communist government threatened to come to power in a country of strategic interest; 13 cases where communist countries threatened other countries; 35 threats by communist governments to strategic regions; 8 situations of conflict on the frontiers of communist states; 9 conflicts within communist states; and 53 situations where American military intervention might have propped up friendly regimes. A variety of reasons may explain the nonuse of military force in these situations. In some cases, political constraints within the United States or elsewhere may have inhibited American intervention at any level, whereas in other cases Washington may have found diplomatic, economic, and/or covert means, or the use of proxy forces more effective.

For nearly five decades, much of Washington's military planning and resources have centered on preparation for fighting a massive World-War-II–style battle in central Europe against a Warsaw Pact invasion. With the cold war over, the Pentagon and other advocates have tried to find missions to justify continued enormous military spending, forces, and facilities.[19] The shift in strategy is toward fighting *mid-intensity conflicts (MICs)* such as the Persian Gulf War against Iraq. The emphasis is on mobility, a rapid buildup, close coordination among the armed services, and the use of overwhelming force to defeat the enemy as quickly and decisively as possible while keeping American and allies losses to a minimum. Ideally, the mere presence of a large U.S. military force, periodic reassertions of American resolve to counter aggression, and memory of how easily Iraq's forces were defeated deter any challenges.

By the 1990s, the United States was the sole superpower. America's arsenal bulges with high-tech weapons such as cruise missiles so sophisticated that they hit their targets with pinpoint accuracy from so far away their crews are exposed

mid-intensity conflicts (MICs) wars on the scale of the 1990–1991 Persian Gulf War.

Table 11.1 **American Defense Spending (in billions, by 1996 dollar value)**

Year	Spending	Year	Spending	Year	Spending	Year	Spending
1945	$962.7	1961	$291.1	1977	$232.7	1993	$312.1
1946	500.6	1962	300.0	1978	233.2	1994	290.3
1947	133.7	1963	293.3	1979	237.4	1995	272.1
1948	94.7	1964	294.8	1980	246.2	1996	265.5
1949	127.8	1965	268.3	1981	260.8		
1950	133.0	1966	297.3	1982	282.0		
1951	225.7	1967	354.1	1983	303.2		
1952	408.5	1968	388.9	1984	318.1		
1953	437.0	1969	371.8	1985	343.7		
1954	402.1	1970	346.0	1986	363.7		
1955	344.5	1971	311.7	1987	371.1		
1956	320.7	1972	289.1	1988	372.8		
1957	322.4	1973	259.5	1989	376.2		
1958	317.9	1974	243.8	1990	358.7		
1959	306.7	1975	242.0	1991	316.5		
1960	289.6	1976	234.0	1992	328.6		

Source: Center for Defense Information, 2000. Adapted with permission.

Cyberwarfare: Possibly Coming Soon *from a* Terminal near You

The ever thickening worldwide computer network provides ever more benefits to its users. But those on line are also vulnerable to a new type of warfare. Cyberwarfare involves hacking into an enemy's vital defense, financial, corporate, transportation, communications, and utilities industries and firing viruses into their computers that destroy those systems. An effective cyberwarfare attack can potentially shut down an entire national economy. Bank records could disappear, wiping out business and household accounts. Electricity could burn out, leaving people in the dark with food rotting in refrigerators. The radar screens in airport control towers could darken, grounding airlines. Life

support equipment in hospitals could shut down, killing patients. The possible destruction and even death is endless. The result would be economic, social, and political chaos.

The greater a nation's computer power, the greater its vulnerability to cyberwarfare. America's computer prowess is at once an enormous source of national power and an Achilles heel. A computer genius could launch a cyberwarfare assault from any terminal in the world with little chance of being traced. Cyberwarfare will increasingly be wielded by terrorists and aggressive governments alike.

To its credit the Pentagon recognizes the importance of cyberwarfare. In 1999, it set up a cyberwarfare

center under the Air Force Space Command at Colorado Springs. The goals are to strengthen America's defenses against an attack while developing the ability to conduct cyberwarfare against an enemy. It tried to wage cyberwarfare against Yugoslavia during the 1999 war over Kosovo, apparently with limited success, because that country is not heavily dependent on computers. During that war, the Pentagon blunted cyberwarfare attacks on its computers as hackers failed to penetrate the system. But those were just the first skirmishes in a new form of warfare that will become increasingly common and sophisticated in the decades ahead.

to little or no danger. War has become a deadly video game for American servicemen and -women. The strategy involves widening the "information gap," allowing American forces to be all-seeing and all-knowing while blinding their enemies. Electromagnetic pulses and computer viruses followed up by satellite-guided missiles and bombs destroy first the enemy's command, control, communications, and intelligence system (C3I), then its supply depots and transportation lines and its troop concentrations. That power and strategy allowed America to inflict devastating defeats on enemies such as Iraq and Yugoslavia with few or no battle casualties.

The United States is sitting on cutting-edge technology that could completely revolutionize its military and warfare, enabling America to leap so far ahead of its rivals that its hegemony will be ensured for generations. The technology now exists to have an air force without pilots. Once the huge expense of manned aircraft is eliminated, the pilotless air force will cost a fraction of today's squadrons of F-16s, F-18s, and F-117s. The new-generation F-22 fighter bomber will each cost at least $100 million; an unmanned craft, $15 million. Advanced technology will revolutionize naval power as well. Aircraft carriers will become as obsolete as battleships as they are replaced by dozens of small, fast, semisubmerged, stealth "arsenal ships," packed with more firepower but staffed with 50 rather than 5,000 sailors. The cost of an aircraft carrier is over $3.5 billion; an arsenal ship $500 million. Advanced technology can even revolutionize the ground war. Satellite positioning, cell phones, laptops, and laser-guided weapons give small, elite bodies of troops unprecedented ability to know where the enemy is, and then to dash by air and ground through gaps in the lines to encircle them. Battles will be won with ever fewer combat troops, as ever leaner but more muscular Davids systematically hack apart blind, blundering Goliaths.

Thus the United States has the ability to revolutionize its military and economic power at a fraction of current personnel and costs. As the defense budget plummets, tens of billions of dollars could annually be invested much more productively elsewhere in the economy or returned to American taxpayers. American economic and military superpower could be unchallengeable for the foreseeable future. If the United States can do all this, why is it not doing so?

The answer is politics. The military revolution that could vastly strengthen U.S. national interests threatens the careers, profits, and prestige of all those in the military-industrial complex, which includes the people in and out of uniform who directly or indirectly work in the defense bureaucracy and industries, along with the politicians who represent them. They have enormous power to block any changes that adversely affect them while getting American taxpayers to fund bases, weapons, and units of often dubious strategic worth. Will the United States be like China several centuries ago, inventing technologies that rivals will revolutionize and thus convert themselves into superpowers?

Military Spending, Power, *and* Security

Military power can be a double-edged sword. Under some circumstances it may actually undermine rather than enhance a nation's security. When states become trapped in arms races that consume an ever greater amount of resources, war can become more rather than less likely, and thus render the state more rather than less vulnerable to destruction. And even when soldiers and weapons are never used, they become an enormous financial, human, economic, and technological drain on that country.

Since 1930, military spending has exceeded world population and economic growth.[20] Rosecrance dramatically reveals the ever rising costs of defense: "In constant dollar terms, tanks went from less than $50,000 per unit in 1918 to more than $2,000,000 in 1980. Fighter planes that cost less than $100,000 in 1944 rose to at least $10,000,000 per copy forty years later."[21] During the 1980s alone, the United States spent $3 trillion on defense, or $45,000 for each household. In 1989, the world's total military budget surpassed $1.035 trillion or 4.9 percent of global GNP, of which the developed countries spent $867 billion or 83 percent of the total and 4.3 percent of their respective GNP, and the less developed countries $168 billion or 17 percent of total spending, and 5 percent of their GNP![22] From one-quarter to one-third of the world's total research and development spending and 750,000 of some of the world's finest scientists and engineers goes to building better weapons.[23] Many of these were American; from 1945 through today, the United States has annually spent an average 30 percent of its total public and private research and development budget on defense, compared to 7 percent for Germany and 4 percent for Japan.[24]

America's Drug War:
Resisting Supply *and* Demand

The United States faces no threat of a foreign military invasion. Yet America's military and intelligence agencies must defend America's borders against a different kind of invasion—illegal drugs. Washington's drug war dates back several decades and is fought against smugglers from South America, the Middle East, Southeast Asia, and other regions around the world. By what means does Washington wield that war? Intelligence agencies use human and technological means to spy on drug gangs, learning when and where shipments will take place. The Air Force and satellites track suspected ships and planes heading toward the United States, which are intercepted by the police when they reach the United States. American troops work with the militaries of several Latin American

countries to locate and eradicate cocaine and marijuana fields and nab growers and smugglers.

Those policies are targeted on the supply side of smuggling. Washington's drug war budget alone was $18 billion in 1999, of which two-thirds went to interdiction and enforcement. What about the demand side? Washington spends only about $3 billion annually on treating drug addiction, even though it has a 70 percent success rate and costs $20,000 less than locking that person in jail. How would American national interests be affected if more money were shifted from intercepting supplies to reducing demand?

How does the United States fight drug smuggling from Latin America? The Joint Agency Task Force South combines intelligence, military, and police personnel and equipment to

track and intercept drugs and smugglers. Their headquarters is known as the "multilateral counternarcotics center," or CMA in the Spanish acronym, and is located at the Howard army base in Panama.

Is America winning its drug war? On the Latin American front, the United States intercepted only $1.2 billion of an estimated $30 billion worth of smuggled cocaine in 1997. Nonetheless Washington has scored some victories. Americans worked closely with Colombian officials to crush the Medellin and Cali drug organizations in that country during the mid-1990s. But like the mythical Hydra, new heads of drug smuggling pop up from every head decapitated by Washington and its allies. The war will undoubtedly drag on as long as Americans demand illegal drugs.

Many weapons are exported. Between 1960 and 1991, annual international arms sales increased from $2.4 billion to $45 billion.[25] Of the two top sellers during the 1980s, Washington supplied arms to 59 countries and Moscow to 42 countries.[26] In 1988, 116 countries, of which 84 were Third World countries, imported military weapons. During the 1980s alone, 540 warships and submarines, 3,100 combat aircraft, 20,000 cannon, 37,000 surface-to-air missiles, and 11,000 tanks and self-propelled guns changed hands.[27] About 75 percent of all weapons sales go to the Third World.[28]

The Third World annually spends twice as much on defense as it receives in foreign aid. Sixty percent of all the world's soldiers are in the Third World, and that amount doubled from 8.4 to 16.4 million between 1960 and 1988. Most of the weapons acquired by the Third World are imported. Between 1985 and 1989, the Soviet Union was the largest arms exporter to the Third World, with 43.8 percent of the total, followed by the United States with 20.2 percent, France with 11.6 percent, China with 6.3 percent, Britain with 5.3 percent, the Third World itself with

3.5 percent, West Germany with 1.8 percent, Italy with 1.6 percent, and other countries with 5.8 percent. Among the Third World, the Middle East imported 41.1 percent of these arms, followed by South Asia with 23.9 percent, the Far East with 15.9 percent, sub-Saharan Africa with 7.1 percent, South Africa with 5.5 percent, North Africa with 4.4 percent, and Central America with 2.0 percent.[29]

Increasing military budgets and arms exports occur for many reasons. Until recently cold war politics were the most important reason. Washington and Moscow filled the arsenals of their immediate allies in NATO and the Warsaw Pact, respectively, and that of scores of more ephemeral potential and actual "allies" and "friends" throughout the Third World. When one superpower began to aid a side in a regional or national conflict, the other superpower inevitably felt compelled to begin aiding the other side to maintain the power balance. To maintain the power balance against its foes, the United States still targets many of its weapons sales to friendly countries in the Middle East. The other great powers—Great Britain, France, and China—also became big arms dealers during the cold war.

Ironically, the political gains of arms sales for the sellers may be illusory. For example, Moscow sold enormous amounts of equipment and sent advisers to Egypt during the late 1950s through the early 1970s. In 1972, President Sadat ordered all the Soviet advisers to leave, and by the late 1970s was receiving most of its military imports from the United States. The superpowers and other great powers have frequently found themselves arming both sides of a conflict, which meant greater sales in the short run but a greater chance of political setbacks over the long run. During the 1980s, the Reagan and Bush administrations sold billions of dollars of military equipment to Iraq. That policy boomeranged when Iraq used its American weapons and equipment against the United States during the Persian Gulf War (1990–1991).

Although politics was the primary motive for these sales during the cold war, profit has become the most important reason since then. Weapons exports are big business and particularly an excellent source of hard currency for Russia, China, and less developed weapons manufacturers, whose governments often own those industries. Since the Soviet Union's breakup, Russia, the Ukraine, Georgia, and other former "republics" have been selling off even their most advanced and secret weapons systems for hard currency. Many of those sales have gone to aggressive

Table 11.2 Arming the Third World: Measured in Billions of Dollars

| | 1988 | | 1995 | | 1988–95 |
	Amount	Percentage	Amount	Percentage	Amount
United States	$ 5,546	11.06%	$9,537	44.08%	$54,200
USSR/Russia	24,070	48.02	2,400	11.09	81,200
France	1,351	2.70	1,600	7.39	14,200
Great Britain	4,544	9.07	4,500	20.80	35,100
China	3,684	7.35	600	2.77	14,200
Germany	860	1.72	800	3.70	5,300
Italy	368	0.74	0	0.00	1,000
Other European Countries	5,403	10.78	600	2.77	15,000
All Others	4,298	8.58	1,600	7.39	15,500

Source: Center for Defense Information, 2000. Adapted with permission.

Table 11.3 **Regional Arms Deliveries**

	Asia		Near East		Latin America		Africa	
	1988–1991	1992–1995	1988–1991	1992–1995	1988–1991	1992–1995	1988–1991	1992–1995
United States	$6,042	$6,068	$11,804	$23,937	$1,111	$857	$293	$93
USSR/Russia	26,500	4,700	16,200	2,600	5,800	300	6,200	500
France	400	900	7,300	2,400	700	300	400	300
Great Britain	800	1,900	14,200	14,900	200	200	300	100
China	1,500	2,000	7,200	1,200	0	0	400	200
Germany	700	1,700	1,000	400	700	300	0	0
Italy	200	100	200	0	200	0	200	100
Other European Countries	2,300	700	6,000	2,300	500	400	500	300
All Others	1,200	1,500	4,200	1,600	800	900	2,000	1,500
Total	39,642	19,568	68,104	49,337	10,011	3,257	10,293	3,093

Source: Center for Defense Information, 2000. Adapted with permission.

Table 11.4 Leading Third World Recipients of Arms

Country	1988–1995
Saudi Arabia	$67,100
Taiwan	14,400
Afghanistan	11,500
Egypt	10,200
Iran	10,000
Kuwait	9,500
China	6,500
Israel	6,600
United Arab Emirates	6,200
Cuba	4,900

Source: U.S. Arms Control Agency Report, 1999.

countries such as Iran, North Korea, Serbia, Syria, and others that threaten to upset regional power balances. China has been severely criticized for selling missile technology to Iran, Pakistan, and North Korea, a practice it only stopped under American pressure in 1998. A more insidious problem involves hundreds of unemployed Soviet bloc scientists getting jobs in Iraq, Iran, North Korea, and other countries that are trying to develop nuclear, chemical, and biological weapons.

The global arms trade shifted decisively with the cold war's end and collapse of the Soviet empire. The United States traded places with Russia as the world's largest arms merchant, with a 44 percent market share in 1995, while Russia plummeted to 11 percent. There are several reasons for that drop. Of $146 billion owed the former Soviet Union for weapons, 40 percent is considered uncollectible, so Russia and the others demand hard currency rather than IOUs for their hardware. U.N. arms embargoes on Libya, Iraq, Bosnia, Croatia, and Serbia cost the Soviet Union and its successors states $7 billion in lost sales in 1992 alone. Former Soviet bloc sales are further inhibited by the inferior quality of many Soviet weapons systems, and the lack of credit, spare parts, and service. Sales will likely diminish further. Although America's military industrial-complex has contracted by nearly half between 1989 and 1999, its huge economies of scale fueled by Pentagon procurements, consolidations, and applications of cutting-edge technologies have rocketed America's advanced weapons systems a generation or more beyond rivals.

Increasingly, America is in an arms race with itself. The Defense Department justifies developing new weapons systems as being needed to fight potential but usually highly unlikely enemies armed with the previous generation of American weapons.

The scramble for arms producers to sell overseas is intensifying as countries, particularly the superpowers, reduce their own military procurements. The 1990 *Conventional Armed Forces in Europe Treaty (CFE)* required signatories to sharply cut back their numbers of tanks, artillery, armored personnel carriers, and other equipment. Many of these weapons will be exported rather than destroyed. Arms producers are just as caught in the logic of scale economies as any other producer;

Peace Pays: Israel, Egypt, *and the* American Taxpayer

In 1979, the United States brokered a peace treaty between Israel and Egypt, ending 30 years of war and conflict. To convince them to sign, Washington promised to supply both sides with advance weapons and equipment. Since 1980 Israel and Egypt have received $28 billion and $19 billion, respectively, $1.8 billion and $1.3 billion in 1998 alone. Jordan signed a peace treaty with Israel in 1998 and will receive a boost in the military aid package it already receives from the United States.

Was this a good investment of taxpayer dollars? How is the United States affected by war or peace in the Middle East?

the more they sell, the lower the price of their components and lower the final price, so the more they sell, and so on. The dropping demand of the 1990s has bankrupted many producers and forced most others to consolidate.[30]

There are several other reasons for global arms sales. As engineers keep devising better ways of killing, they render obsolete existing weapons and thus create the need for their replacement. Thus arms races are fueled as much by new technology as by politics and profits. And, of course, there could not be sellers without buyers. The wealthier a country, the more arms it can afford to import. Many arms sales have gone to the Middle East, which increased its imports from 11 percent of the total arms shipped in 1967 to 26 percent in 1989.[31] It was not just the Arab–Israel, Arab–Iran, and intra-Arab rivalries that stimulated this vast influx. OPEC's quadrupling of prices in 1973 and further doubling in 1979 gave the oil-rich Middle East states the wealth to finance their military ambition, and in so doing set off an ever spiraling regional arms race.

Yet there would not be any arms exports if governments did not have real or imagined internal and international enemies that they hope to deter or defeat with more numerous and advanced weapons. Although many Third World governments import arms to counter perceived international threats, most use them against their own population, and some buy merely for the prestige that modern weapons bring, regardless of their military utility.

Arms sales and aid are closely related. States often sell their weapons at a loss or outright donate them to gain influence with the recipient, grab market share from their rivals, and thus strengthen their own military-industrial complex. In 1996 alone, the United States sold, leased, or gave arms to 160 of the world's 190 countries! In addition to equipment and weapons, the Pentagon provides training for foreign soldiers in both the United States and abroad. The Foreign Assistance Act and the Arms Export Control Act regulate American military aid. Currently only 24 countries are blacklisted from receiving American weapons, either because Washington or the United Nations has designated those countries hostile. Much of America's military aid in grants, loans, or discounted prices includes obsolete weapons in the Pentagon's arsenal. Some goods are sold for as low as 5 percent of what they cost America's taxpayers. Under the Foreign Military Financing Program, the United States has given away over $91 billion in discounted loans

Aircraft carriers with their squadrons of fighter-bombers, scores of cruise missiles, and 5,000 strong crews, escorted by a dozen other warships are the backbone of American naval power. They enable the United States to project power in every sea around the world and a thousand or more miles beyond adjacent shores. Six decades ago during World War II, aircraft carriers rendered obsolete battleships, whose various versions had ruled the waves for hundreds of years. What new technologies and strategies could eventually send aircraft carriers to the scrap yard? How can those new weapons affect international relations?

AP/ Wide World Photos

since 1951. Yet another subsidy for the American arms industry appeared in 1995 with the Defense Export Loan Guarantee, whereby the Pentagon can guarantee up to $15 billion in commercial bank loans for weapons sales. If the borrower defaults, Americans pay.

During the 1980s, the Reagan White House canceled many debts and simply donated arms. The largest debt cancellation occurred in 1990 when the Bush White House wrote off $7 billion that Egypt owed the United States in return for Cairo joining the American-led Coalition against Iraq. Such giveaways to some states encourage others to default on their loans. Since then the Pentagon wrote off an additional $10 billion in bad loans. In 1997, several dozen countries owed America's taxpayers $13.2 billion in debt payments; the Pentagon was unconcerned.

Military power is supposed to make countries more rather than less secure; it is valuable only when it actually deters or defeats real enemies. The larger and better equipped a country's military, the more likely its government might use it to resolve a conflict. Over 25 million people have died in wars in the Third World since 1945, and the international arms trade was a major contributor both to the large number of wars and deaths.[32]

The indirect costs of militarization are just as enormous. Even if arms are never used, spending ever more money on the military can actually undermine rather than enhance security. As President Eisenhower put it, the

> problem in defense spending is to figure out how far you should go without destroying from within what you are trying to defend from without. . . . Every gun that is made, every warship launched, every rocket fired signifies, in the final sense, a theft from those who hunger and are not fed, those who are cold and are not clothed. This world in arms is not spending money alone. It is spending the sweat of its laborers, the genius of its scientists, the hopes of its children.[33]

Guns *versus* Butter: Who Benefits?

For several decades the United States has been locked into a vicious cycle of low productivity, growth, investment, literacy, and student test scores and high unemployment, inflation, crime, drug abuse, poverty, and malnutrition. There is no telling how much these problems could have been alleviated if, say, the $35 billion spent on the B-1 bomber or $40 billion on the Trident II missile had been invested in infrastructure, education, or research and development, let alone if the defense budget had remained at the same level during the 1980s rather than nearly tripled.

There is enormous duplication and sometimes triplication of conventional and nuclear weapons systems that exist solely to reinforce the abstract notion of deterrence.

What level of spending and what type of military do you believe best serves American national interests?

Or as Eisenhower's chairman of the Council of Economic Advisors, Arthur Burns put it, "The real cost of the defense sector consists . . . not only of the civilian goods and services that are currently forgone on its account; it includes also an element of growth that could have been achieved through larger investment in human or business capital."[34]

Studies have shown that generally the higher a country's military budget as a percentage of GNP, the lower its manufacturing productivity growth: "Intercountry comparisons suggest that high military expenditures have curtailed productivity growth . . . heavy defense spending seems to have a particularly important impact on dampening capital formation and investment, which in turn reduces economic growth in the long run."[35] One study compared the impact on employment of $1 billion. A billion dollars worth of guided missiles created jobs for only 21,392 workers, the lowest of six different employment categories. That same amount of money would create jobs for 21,783 railroad equipment workers, 26,145 solar energy and energy conservation workers, 26,459 public utility construction workers, 27,583 housing workers, and 31,078 mass transit workers.[36] Overall, $1 billion spent on construction creates 100,070 jobs, or 1.3 times more than the 75,710 defense jobs created by those same dollars.[37] And those construction jobs are largely productive—things are built that increase a nation's efficiency and wealth. Much of the money spent on the military is nonproductive—millions of able-bodied men and women sit in barracks around the world rather than use their brains and muscle to develop their countries. Because they consume rather than produce, the impact of their spending is inflationary. In all militaries undermine rather than enhance development.

Of the two superpowers, the Soviet Union collapsed largely because of the enormous resources it had poured into the military over decades to the neglect of everything else. Although the United States did not collapse, America's economic growth, productivity, savings and investments ratio, and per capita income are among the lowest, and its infant mortality, life expectancy, low-birth-weight babies, and per-capita spending for education and health are among the highest, of the democratic industrial countries. Both the United States and Russia are trying to wean their economies from dependence on high military spending into more economically and socially productive pursuits but, like an addict kicking a tobacco addiction, the conversion is extremely painful and disruptive.

An obsession with military spending has trapped scores of Third World countries into a vicious cycle in which poverty and stagnant growth lead to political instability, which prompts governments to spend scarce resources on military equipment, which further inhibits development, causing greater instability, more military spending and so on. For every dollar the Third World spends on defense, it loses 25 cents of economic investments and 20 cents of agricultural output; thus as military spending rises, economic growth declines. By one estimate, the Third World loses 187 million human-years of income for its total annual military spending; the industrial countries lose 56 million human-years annually. There are eight times more soldiers than doctors in the Third World, and 30 times more is spent on the military than education.[38]

Global military spending peaked in the late 1980s. The end of the cold war and winding down of regional conflicts in Cambodia, Angola, Ethiopia, Afghanistan, and elsewhere has resulted in a decline in total military spending among the developing and developing countries alike.

A Purpose *for* NATO?
The War Against *the* Serbs

With the 1991 collapse of the Soviet Union, communism, and the Warsaw Pact, NATO is trying to justify its continued existence. NATO's 1991 Rome Summit issued "The Alliance's New Strategic Concept," which formed a North Atlantic Cooperation Council (NACC) to "build genuine partnership among the North Atlantic Alliance and the countries of Central and Eastern Europe." Russia and many of the former Soviet republics and eastern European countries are trying to join NATO. In 1997 Poland, the Czech Republic, and Hungary became NATO members, despite Russian protests. Meanwhile Russia's military deteriorated steadily in morale, spending, discipline, equipment, and troop numbers. Today and for the foreseeable future there is no military threat to NATO.

What, then, is NATO's purpose? Some, mostly Europeans, argue that NATO should evolve from a strictly military alliance into a broader security community that addresses economic, humanitarian, democratic, and environmental concerns. At a NATO meeting in 1998, Washington tried but failed to talk the other members into expanding the alliance's military duties worldwide. The impasse over NATO's reason for being continued. Then finally, in 1999, NATO found a war!

Just why did NATO go to war, and what were the results? On June 9, 1999, NATO won the first war in its history. After enduring 78 days of devastating bombing, Yugoslavia surrendered to NATO's demands. That brief war had important consequences that reverberated beyond just NATO and Yugoslavia. NATO's victory strengthened aspects of international law and a range of international organizations, while possibly deterring potential aggressors elsewhere. An analysis of the war provides valuable insights into the nature of contemporary international relations, especially such fields as diplomacy, the making and implementation of foreign policy, the debate over national and international interests, and why states sometimes choose to settle their conflicts with violence.

Kosovo is a province of Yugoslavia in which 90 percent of the 2.2 million population is Muslim and only 10 percent Orthodox Christian Serbs. Despite the few Serbs living there, Kosovo is crucial to Serbian culture and history. It was there in 1389 that the Turks defeated the Serbs at the Battle of Blackbirds and began a subjection of the Serbs that lasted 500 years. During that time the Serbs were supplanted in Kosovo by Albanians, with their different language, religion, and culture. Serbia, which had gained its independence in 1862 from the Ottoman empire, conquered Kosovo in 1912. In 1919 the Yugoslavian federation was formed, with Serbia as its most powerful member. For the next seven decades, Kosovo's status as a Serbian province directly ruled by Belgrade remained unchanged. But gradually the Albanian Kosovars pressured Belgrade for autonomy in running their own affairs. Those aspirations were rewarded in 1974, when Belgrade granted the province its own parliament and police.

Kosovo's autonomy lasted only 15 years. In 1987, Slobodan Milosevic was elected Yugoslavia's president. Two years later he committed the first in a series of acts that was designed to strengthen Yugoslav unity but that actually destroyed it. Fearing that Kosovar autonomy would lead to independence, Milosevic reasserted Belgrade's direct rule over Kosovo in 1989. Ironically, that became the most important reason for Yugoslavia's breakup. Fearing that Milosevic would do the same to them, the republics of Slovenia, Croatia, Bosnia-Herzegovina, and Macedonia declared their independence in 1991. Despite their loss of autonomy, the Albanians of Kosovo did not then seek their own independence.

Not until 1993 did the Kosovo Liberation Army (KLA) form and begin attacking Serbian police and soldiers. In 1998, a Serb retaliatory slaughter of Kosovar Albanian families provoked a large revolt that threatened Yugoslavia's rule. A Serbian counteroffensive that autumn forced 250,000 Kosovar Albanians to flee into the mountains, where they faced death from starvation and freezing temperatures. NATO threatened a bombing campaign unless Milosevic allowed those refugees to return to their homes and open negotiations with the KLA, which then numbered 17,000 armed men. Milosevic grudgingly agreed. In February 1999, the two sides signed an agreement at the chateau of Rambouillet near Paris. Under the Rambouillet Accord, Yugoslavia would grant Kosovo autonomy, a U.N. peacekeeping force of 30,000 troops would occupy the province, and the KLA would lay down their arms. After three years, Kosovars would vote on whether to continue autonomy or receive independence. But Milosevic no sooner signed the accord than he denounced it and made preparations for driving the Kosovar Albanians from Kosovo.

The Rambouillet Accord's collapse and Serbian threat of ethnic "cleansing" provoked another crisis with NATO. The Clinton White House sent special envoy Richard Holbrooke to pressure Milosevic into reaccepting the Rambouillet Accord or else face a bombing campaign. When they met on March 23, Milosevic angrily rejected the demand. The following day on March 24, 1999, NATO began a bombing campaign that systematically destroyed Yugoslavia's military and economic infrastructure and eventually led to Milosevic's surrender.

Was that war necessary? Why did Milosevic not back down when faced with NATO's threat as he had the previous autumn? Why did both sides march up to and then over the brink of a war that neither side wanted?

Both Milosevic and Clinton may have miscalculated the other's resolve. Milosevic seems to have believed that the United States, beset by the president's sex scandal and a right-wing dominated Congress determined to destroy Clinton, would be too distracted to go to war in a region where it had no concrete interests. And even if war broke out Milosevic may have believed he could survive. Why would he think so? He may have learned the wrong lesson from the war against and containment of Iraq—if Saddam Hussein could endure a devastating defeat in 1991 and an embargo and periodic bombings ever since, yet remain in power, could not Milosevic do the same?

The White House in turn seems to have believed a few days of bombing would force Milosevic to concede. Instead, the bombing campaign lasted several months. Why did the White House miscalculate so badly? The Clinton White House also learned a wrong lesson from previous conflicts with Milosevic. From 1992 through 1995, Yugoslavia tried to crush an independence movement by Croatians and Muslims in Bosnia-Herzegovina. That war cost over 200,000 lives and millions of refugees. In 1995 a short NATO bombing campaign seemed to work. Milosevic agreed to the Dayton Accord, granting Bosnia-Herzegovina independence under a peacekeeping force. But bombing alone did not bring the agreement. Milosevic actually welcomed the NATO bombing as a face-saving excuse to withdraw from a war he was losing. The Croatian army alone numbered over 100,000 troops and threatened to carry the fighting into Yugoslavia itself. Over 35,000 British and French troops also were on the ground and prepared to attack. Bosnia-Herzegovina was a separate nation-state within the Yugoslavian Federation, a burden rather than an asset. In stark contrast, Kosovo is not only a province of Yugoslavia but a land sacred to Serbian history and culture, to be defended at nearly all costs.

Although many believed that only an all-out war including ground troops would defeat Yugoslavia, NATO won the war militarily using air power alone. The Kosovo air campaign had two phases. The first was to establish air superiority by destroying Yugoslavia's air defense system. The second phase combined attacks on five distinct but related targets: troops and equipment at the front; the transportation network of bridges, roads, railroads, and docks; the supply network of oil refineries and pipelines, food warehouses, and munitions depots; the civilian infrastructure of electricity and water; and Milosevic's government, including his palace, television and radio stations, and defense, intelligence, and interior ministries responsible for fighting the war. Over 78 days NATO's air force flew 35,000 missions, including 12,500 bombing runs, which dropped or fired 23,000 bombs and missiles, a third of which were guided weapons. The bombing seriously degraded Yugoslavia's military, killing or wounding 10,000 or 9 percent of its 114,000 troops, destroying about 100 or 42 percent of its 240-plane air force, 203 or 25 percent of its 825 armored vehicles, 120 or 9 percent of its 1,270 tanks, and 314 or 22 percent of its 1,400 artillery pieces. The bombing also devastated Yugoslavia's economic infrastructure, inflicting an estimated $40 billion worth of damage, and killing about 1,200 civilians. It cost NATO only $4 billion to cause all that devastation.

Although the all those deadly accurate missiles and bombs eventually brought Milosevic to his knees, they failed spectacularly in one area. Despite the bombing Milosevic accelerated ethnic "cleansing"—genocide—in Kosovo. Yugoslav troops terrorized a million Kosovar Albanians to stream into foreign exile, while another 600,000 people hid in the forests within Kosovo.

That tragedy aside, with NATO prepared to bomb indefinitely, Milosevic's surrender was inevitable. The only question was, When? That timing had as much to do with diplomacy as bombing. NATO enlisted former Russian President Viktor Chernomyrdin and Finnish President Martti Ahtisaari to negotiate directly with Milosevic. The Russian and the Finn proved to be an excellent "good cop/bad cop" team. Both faithfully conveyed NATO's terms but in different ways. Chernomyrdin expressed sympathy for Yugoslavia's fate and tried to find a face-saving way for Milosevic to give up. Ahtisaari meanwhile psychologically pounded away at Milosevic to surrender now to prevent any more destruction of Yugoslavia's military and economy.

Could the war have been won sooner? Possibly. NATO made at least one mistake—the announcement that it would use bombing alone to enforce the Rambouillet Accord. By forgoing the threat of an invasion, NATO may have allowed Milosevic to stall longer. Two other unavoidable forces may also have prolonged the war. Nature was one. Bad weather limited the bombing campaign as thick, low clouds hampered NATO's ability accurately to hit the targets. Gradually the weather cleared as late winter turned to spring and then summer. As frustrating was the split with NATO over policy, highlighting the difficulties and frustrations of waging war by a committee of 19 different nations, each promoting its own interests. The Germans, Italians, and Greeks wanted to limit the bombing campaign's targets and timing, whereas the British favored a ground offensive to mop up after the bombing campaign. The Clinton White House joined with other members and took the middle course of extensive bombing alone until Milosevic conceded. NATO's open debate may have encouraged Milosevic to believe the alliance would fall apart. That belief was an illusion. Instead, Milosevic's ethnic "cleansing" unified NATO—the sight of countless, exhausted, terror-stricken refugees who had lost their homes and sometimes relatives and friends to Yugoslav brutality stiffened the will of each NATO member on the end for which they were fighting even if they disagreed over the specific means.

Although Milosevic actually gave in to NATO's demands on June 3, it took another week before all the details were worked out and the U.N. Security Council approved the agreement. During that time NATO continued bombing to maintain the pressure on Milosevic and his civilian and military advisers. On June 9, after six days of tense negotiations, Yugoslavia's military finally signed an agreement whereby it would withdraw its 40,000 troops from Kosovo within eleven days.

NATO's victory quickly exceeded that officially agreed to by Milosevic. On June 10, with China abstaining, all other 14 U.N. Security Council members including Russia voted for a resolution approving NATO's war against Yugoslavia and authorizing it to lead a U.N. peacekeeping force that would fulfill the Rambouillet Accord signed in February. Rambouillet called for an autonomous Kosovo with an elected 120-member parliament, independent judiciary, and native police and border guards. Most importantly, Kosovars would be allowed to vote for independence within three years. The Kosovars will vote overwhelmingly for independence. The only question is whether they will remain independent or join Albania. Few Serbs would remain in Kosovo to oppose them. Most of the Serbs fled with the Yugoslav army. In trying to ethnically "cleanse" Kosovo, Milosevic and the Serbs rather than the Kosovars were ultimately expelled.

Winning the war was relatively easy. Winning the peace will take years and most likely decades. Over 1.6 million refugees, two-thirds of whom fled to other countries, must be resettled in their burned and looted homes amid a devastated economy and infrastructure.

A number of international organizations will cooperate to help rebuild Kosovo. The United Nations and its various organizations will assume overall control of the reconstruction. That monumental challenge will be assisted by the 15-member European Union, which promised to give $1.5 billion in aid over three years, and the 54-member Organization for Security and Cooperation, which includes countries from both sides of the North Atlantic. The World Bank and IMF will provide low-interest loans. The Group of Seven plus Russia will solicit other donors. NATO will command the 50,000 peacekeepers from 30 countries, including 7,000 Americans and 2,500 Russians. Kosovo was divided among five occupation zones, with the United States, Great Britain, France, Italy, and Germany each commanding one. A 5-kilometer neutral zone around Kosovo completed that province's physical separation from Yugoslavia. The Security Council empowered NATO to use any means necessary to deter renewed aggression, whether from the Yugoslavs or KLA. Just maintaining those troops and workers will be enormously expensive. The 7,000 Americans will cost as much as $2 billion a year to supply.

International law also played an important role in the war. In 1993, the U.N. Security Council authorized the creation of the International War Crimes Tribunal for Yugoslavia, composed of three prosecutors and an extensive investigative and legal staff designed to uncover and issue charges against individuals accused of committing crimes during war and against humanity in Yugoslavia. In May 1999, a U.N. mission, which included representatives from 12 U.N. and private relief and human rights organizations, spent eleven days traveling 1,500 miles to investigate scores of sites in Kosovo and accumulated "indisputable evidence" of Yugoslav war crimes against humanity. On May 27, 1999, the International War Crimes Tribunal for Yugoslavia indicted Yugoslavian President Slobodan Milosevic, Serbian President Milan Milutinovic, Yugoslavian Deputy Prime Minister Nikola Sainovic, Internal Affairs Minister Vlajko Stojilkovic, and Chief of Staff General Dragoljub Ojdanic, for crimes against humanity and genocide, including deporting 740,000 Albanians from Kosovo and murdering 340 identified Albanians. Since then the tribunal's investigators amassed ever more forensic evidence from mass grave sites and destroyed villages, and thousands of witnesses.

International and national laws can affect each other. The May 27 Hague criminal indictment was preceded two days earlier by a civil lawsuit on the same charges against Milosevic, his wife, and top Yugoslav leaders in Boston's federal district court. How could an American court have jurisdiction over crimes committed in another country? The plaintiffs asserted their suit under the Alien Tort Claims Act, which allows actions against criminals who harmed American citizens or residents outside the United States. Three previous lawsuits based on the law won favorable court rulings, in 1980 against Paraguay's dictator, in 1985 against the former Philippine dictator Ferdinand Marcos, and in 1994 against Bosnian Serb leader Radovan Karadzic. The trouble is enforcing the ruling. The primary goal of the plaintiffs against Milosevic was to show The Hague how easy it was to accumulate evidence and file charges against him.

On June 2 the International Court of Justice rejected petitions by Yugoslavia that NATO's bombing was illegal and should end and that it should pay compensation for the damage it caused. A majority of the 15 permanent and 5 ad hoc judges ruled in very veiled language that the bombing was illegal because it was not sanctioned by the U.N. Security Council, but claimed that the court had no jurisdiction in the case. Yugoslavia had filed the petition on April 25 against each of the 10 NATO countries that had participated in the bombing. In doing so Yugoslavia may have made a legal mistake that weakened its case. Its petition only recognized the court's jurisdiction in the dispute after the day it filed, so that the judges would not consider any countercharges that Yugoslavia had committed genocide. The court rejected the petition on the technicality that NATO's bombing started before that date. In the three weeks it took to reach a majority decision, the judges fiercely debated the issues. Russian, Chinese, and North Korean judges predictably took Yugoslavia's side.

Are Milosevic and his four subordinates guilty as charged? Although the evidence of genocide is overwhelming, determining just who is guilty will be difficult to prove. If Milosevic did order his troops to commit genocide, he did not publicly announce it and most likely did not submit it in a written order. Furthermore, Milosevic denies issuing such orders and claims any atrocities Yugoslav troops committed were beyond his control. "Plausible deniability" is a common ploy that leaders, including American presidents, use to avoid taking blame for illegal or controversial policies.

How did the indictment affect the diplomacy attempting to end the war? The Clinton administration announced that it would negotiate with Milosevic despite the indictment. That policy had a clear precedent. In 1995, American diplomats met with Bosnian Serb leaders' envoys Radovan Karadzic and General Ratko Mladic even though they were under indictment for crimes against humanity by the International Court of Justice's tribunal for Yugoslavia.

But after Milosevic surrendered Kosovo, President Clinton was quick to call essentially for his overthrow. To the Yugoslav people, he declared, "As long as [Milosevic] remains in power, as long as your nation is ruled by a war criminal, we will provide no support for the reconstruction of Serbia. But we are ready to provide humanitarian aid now and to help to build a better future for Serbia, too, when its government represents tolerance and freedom, not repression and terror."

Will Milosevic remain in power? Will he eventually be brought before the international court on war crimes charges? Milosevic's presidential term is not scheduled to end until 2002. Although the Serbian Orthodox Church and many other groups and individuals within Yugoslavia have demanded his resignation, it remains to be seen whether he will do so. As for the indictment, if he traveled to most foreign countries he most likely would be arrested and extradited. But he is not free from arrest if he stays within Yugoslavia. A commando team could kidnap and spirit him to a trial at the International Court of Justice.

Although NATO scored a decisive victory against Milosevic, what will the future bring? Will Kosovo recover and eventually prosper? Or will it remain an international basket case, a ward of the United Nations, incapable of creating a viable economy? Beyond Kosovo, will NATO's success deter future ethnic "cleansing"? Or will it encourage other oppressed minorities elsewhere to revolt against their oppressors? Will genocide and liberation struggles be more or less likely? And has NATO finally found a reason to exist in the post–cold-war world?

Among the consequences of NATO's victory over Yugoslavia in 1999 was the reopening of a four-decade-old debate over European military power. Although NATO officially fought the war, the Americans supplied nearly all its bombers, missiles, intelligence, and supplies. The Europeans could not have possibly fought the war on their own. Once again the Americans had bailed the Europeans out of a conflict they could not resolve themselves. That continuing dependence on American power rankles and humiliates Europeans, who realize they have only themselves to blame. The European Union (EU) vowed in June 1999 to revive its own defense alliance, the moribund West European Union (WEU), conceived but never truly born in 1953.

That was easy to declare but may be economically and politically impossible to achieve. The Europeans want to shoulder a greater portion of their own security burden, something the Americans have urged for decades. But will the governments and citizens balk as the bills start to mount? To make the WEU a viable military alliance, the EU must embark on an expensive shopping spree for the latest high-technology weapons and communications equipment. Most of those sales will go to American defense firms. Currently the European Union spends 2.1 percent of its economy on defense compared to America's 3.2 percent. Under the budgetary restrictions for their monetary union, to boost defense spending the Europeans will have to sharply cut back social spending. Will the Europeans be willing to trade their social comforts for the harsh realities of preparing for and perhaps waging war?

The Europeans did take the first step toward a more assertive military policy by insisting on supplying the bulk of the occupation troops and taking four of the five sectors in Kosovo. In all, the 33,000 British, French, German, and Italian troops split among their four sectors dwarfed the 7,000 Americans in their sector. But those troops are operating under NATO, not WEU, auspices.

A harsh reality will likely set in after the initial burst of enthusiasm for reviving the WEU. Psychologically rankling as it may be, the Europeans will probably remain NATO's junior partners. Becoming militarily independent of the United States will impose economic and political burdens that nearly all Europeans are unwilling to shoulder. NATO, it seems, will prevail.

The Control of Conventional Arms and War

As globalization thickens around the world, are states becoming any more humane when they fight one another? International law increasingly restricts how and why wars are waged. But the debate over just which means of warfare are appropriate is not modern but ancient.

History records relatively limited attempts by states to negotiate arms control or more humanitarian ways of warring against each other. Treaties among ancient civilizations in China, India, and the Middle East created often elaborate restrictions against certain means of killing and tactics. For example, India's fourth-century B.C.E. Indian Book of Manu, among other things, forbade using concealed, barbed, poisoned, or fire-tipped weapons, and killing those without weapons.

Throughout the modern era, as war has become more destructive, its restrictions have increased. The earliest attempted to protect nonbelligerents. At the Concert of Europe in 1815, the delegates signed a treaty guaranteeing Switzerland's neutrality for perpetuity. In 1817, the United States and Britain signed a treaty demilitarizing the Great Lakes. In 1839, a treaty guaranteed Belgium's neutrality. In 1856, Great

Britain, France, Austria, Prussia, Russia, Sardinia, and Turkey signed the Declaration of Paris, which protected neutral shipping during war. In 1864, a dozen European states signed the Geneva Red Cross Convention protecting hospitals and medical personnel.

During the late 19th century, there was a growing consensus that states should limit the weapons and practices of war itself. During the American Civil War, the Union army issued a manual instructing officers how to deal with such aspects of war as prisoners, civilians, private property, and so on. Many European countries subsequently issued their own manuals. The first international agreement restricting war occurred with the 1868 Declaration of St. Petersburg, signed by 17 nations, which outlawed the use of certain explosives and weapons.

Many of today's restrictions on warfare derive from the 1899 and 1907 *Hague conferences,* which produced a score of treaties, including the Hague Conventions on War.

1899 Hague Convention on War

Pacific settlement of international disputes

Laws and customs of war on land

Adaptation to maritime warfare of the principles of the Geneva Convention

Prohibition on launching of projectiles and explosives from balloons

Prohibition on use of expanding bullets

Prohibition on use of gases

1904 Hague Convention on War

Exemption of hospital ships from taxation in times of war

Pacific settlement of international disputes

Limitation of employment of force for recovery of contract debts

Opening of hostilities

Laws and customs of war on land

Rights and duties of neutral powers and persons in war on land

Status of enemy merchant ships at the outbreak of hostilities

Conversion of merchant ships into warships

Laying of automatic submarine contact mines

Bombardment by naval forces in time of war

Adaptation to maritime warfare of principles of the Geneva Convention

Restrictions with respect to right of capture in naval war

Rights and duties of neutral powers in naval war

Prohibition on discharge of projectiles and explosives from balloons

A third Hague convention was scheduled for 1915, but no one showed up because most were fighting World War I. In January 1918, President Wilson announced his Fourteen Points or goals for a peace settlement for World War I, which he hoped would be "the war to end all wars." Some of Wilson's ideas were incorporated into the 1919 Versailles Peace Conference, the most important of which was the creation of a League of Nations dedicated to collective security in which members pledged to peacefully resolve conflicts and unite against aggressors. Signatories of the 1928 Kellogg-Briand Pact agreed to renounce aggressive war.

The League of Nations and the Kellogg-Briand Pact were reinforced by some significant arms control agreements during the 1920s. The 1919 St. Germain Convention, 1925 Geneva Convention, and 1929 Geneva Convention all restricted certain types of weapons, arms exports, and war practices. The Washington (1921–1922) and London (1930) naval treaties among the great naval powers imposed a strict ratio of warship tonnage among them. There were no limits, however, on the amount of firepower that those ships could deploy, and the tonnage limitations helped stimulate a technology arms race.

All these treaties were no more successful in preventing World War II than the two Hague conventions were in preventing World War I. Like President Wilson, President Roosevelt was determined to create a lasting peace. He helped found the United Nations in 1945 as a new and improved version of the League of Nations, which shared the goal of achieving collective security. Since then several important multilateral treaties have attempted to further restrict war and weapons. The 1949 Geneva Convention, 1977 Geneva Conference, and 1980 U.N. Conference systematized existing laws governing the conduct of war.

To date, the legal restrictions on war include (1) no attacking of unarmed enemies; (2) no firing on undefended localities without military significance; (3) no use of forbidden arms or munitions; (4) no improper use of immune buildings (for example, embassies) for military purposes; (5) no pillaging; (6) no killing or wounding those who have surrendered or are disabled; (7) no poisoning wells or streams; (8) no ill-treating war prisoners; (9) no assassinating and hiring assassins; (10) no compelling the inhabitants of an occupied territory to supply information about the enemy; (11) no air bombardments of civilian populations; (12) no assaults on enemy ships that have surrendered by striking their colors; and (13) no destroying civilian cultural objects or places of worship.

There have been some recent attempts to limit the proliferation of conventional weapons. Between 1973 and 1991, the *Mutual and Balanced Force Reduction (MBFR)* talks were conducted between NATO and the Warsaw Pact. During the late 1970s, Washington and Moscow conducted the *Conventional Arms Transfer Talks (CATT)*, but they were suspended in 1979 and later resumed in 1987. The *Conference on Security and Cooperation in Europe (CSCE)* has been meeting since 1973 to discuss broader security issues, including the *confidence-and-security-building measures (CSBM)*, which sought to reduce tensions by improving communications between East and West. CSCE's 35 members include all NATO, Warsaw Pact, and neutral European countries.

None of these negotiations made progress until December 1988 when Soviet President Gorbachev dramatically broke the impasse on conventional arms talks and related issues. In a speech before the U.N. General Assembly, he announced that by 1991 he would cut the Soviet military by 500,000 personnel, of which 146,330 came from Soviet forces deployed in Eastern Europe, and would withdraw large amounts of military hardware from Europe to the eastern side of the Ural mountains, which eventually totaled 15,000 tanks, 9,000 artillery pieces, and 900 aircraft. A multilateral agreement on even more significant cuts followed relatively quickly. The Conventional Armed Forces in Europe (CFE) talks started in March 1989 and were concluded in November 1990 when 23 countries signed an agreement leading to cutbacks in conventional forces. The treaty limited American and Soviet troops in Central Europe to 195,000, tanks to 20,000, other armored vehicles to 20,000, artillery to 20,000, and helicopters and aircraft to 8,500. In February 1990, amid the talks, Moscow and Washington agreed to

Table 11.5 Arms Control Treaties, 1925–1993

Treaty	Provisions	Date Signed	Number of Signatories
ABM Treaty	United States–USSR pact limits antiballistic missile sites (two each) and bars further ABM deployment	1972	2
Antarctic Treaty	Internationalizes and demilitarizes the continent	1959	39
Biological Weapons Convention	Bans the production and possession of biological weapons	1972	112
Chemical Weapons Convention	Bans the possession of chemical weapons after 2005	1993	14
Conventional Forces in Europe Treaty (CFE)	Reduces conventional forces in Europe. Nonbinding 1992 protocol covers troops	1990/1992	20/27
Environmental Modification	Bans environmental modification as a form of warfare	1977	55
Geneva Protocol	Bans use of gas or bacteriological weapons	1925	125
Intermediate-range Nuclear Forces (INF)	Eliminates all U.S. and Soviet missiles with ranges between 500 km and 5,500 km	1987	2
Latin American Nuclear Free Zone	Bans nuclear weapons in the region	1967	23
Limited Test Ban	Bans nuclear tests in the atmosphere, outer space, or under water	1963	119
Non-Proliferation Treaty (NPT)	Prohibits selling, giving, or receiving nuclear weapons, nuclear materials, or nuclear technology for weapons	1968	17
Outer Space Treaty	Internationalizes and demilitarizes space, the moon, and other celestial bodies	1967	93
Seabed Arms Control	Bans placing nuclear weapons in or under the seabed	1971	83
South Pacific Nuclear-Free Zone	Prohibits the manufacture or acquisition of nuclear weapons in the region	1985	11
Strategic Arms Limitation Talks (SALT I)	Limited the number and types of U.S. and USSR strategic weapons (expired 1977)	1972	2
Strategic Arms Limitation Talks (SALT II)	Limited the number and types of USSR and U.S. strategic weapons	1979	2
Strategic Arms Reduction Treaty (START I)	Reduces strategic nuclear forces between the United States and the USSR (Belarus, Kazakhstan, Russia, and the Ukraine)	1991/1992	2/5
Strategic Arms Reduction Treaty (START II)	Reduces U.S. and Russian strategic nuclear forces	1993	2
Threshold Test Ban	Limits U.S. and USSR underground tests to 150 kilotons	1974	2

Source: Ruth Leger Sivard, *World Military and Social Expenditures, 1991* (New York: World Priorities, 1991); Charles Kegley and Eugene Wittkopf, *World Politics: Trend and Transformation* (New York: Bedford Books, 1998).

reduce their respective forces in Europe to 195,000 each. In November 1990, the CSCE established a permanent secretariat and Conflict Prevention Center, which has tried to help manage the enormous changes caused by the collapse of communism and the Soviet empire.

Although the superpowers have made considerable progress in reducing conventional forces arrayed against each other, military power continues to expand across the Third World. Some Third World countries are either developing or acquiring "space launch vehicle" (SLV) technology that gives them the ability to hit targets thousands of miles away. In May 1989, India launched its Agni missile, which can deliver a 1-ton payload as far east as Hong Kong and far west as Teheran. Israel has its Jericho II, Argentina its Condor II, Brazil its SS-1000, and Iraq its Tammuz 1 missiles, all with ranges of 500 to nearly 1,000 miles. During the Persian Gulf War, Iraq fired scores of SCUD missiles at Israel and at Coalition forces in Saudi Arabia. In 1998, North Korea fired two Rodong missiles on a 1,500-mile trajectory over Japan and into the Pacific Ocean.

The United States and its allies have long been concerned with the proliferation of missile technology to the Third World. In 1987, the United States, Germany, Great Britain, Japan, France, Italy, Canada, and Spain negotiated the *Missile Technology Control Regime (MTCR)* in which they agreed to limit exports of ballistic missiles, their parts, or production facilities. The most successful effort to stop Third World proliferation was the cease-fire agreement imposed on Iraq following the Persian Gulf War. U.N. inspectors have searched most military and scientific facilities across Iraq to find and destroy chemical, biological, nuclear, and long-range conventional weapons. Iraq's humiliating defeat and inspection may serve as a powerful deterrent on other ambitious Third World states.

Chemical and biological warfare programs are much less expensive than nuclear programs, and thus more common. Chemical weapons were widely used during World War I, resulting in over 100,000 deaths and 1 million casualties. Both sides used chemical weapons during the Iraq–Iran War (1980–1988). Some feared that Iraq would use chemical weapons during the Persian Gulf War (1990–1991), but it refrained. As many as 20 Third World states are considered "likely" or "possible" either to develop or already possess chemical weapons, while an additional four are considered likely developers of biological weapons.[39]

There are some treaties addressing biological and chemical weapons. The 1972 Biological and Toxin Weapons Convention prohibits the development, production, and stockpiling of biological weapons, which followed up a 1925 Geneva Convention treaty banning the use but not possession of biological and chemical weapons. Although the United States, Great Britain, and Japan developed biological weapons, all have since been voluntarily destroyed. In 1990, Washington and Moscow signed the Chemical Weapons Destruction Agreement in which they pledged to stop the production and reduce their numbers of chemical weapons.

Terrorism

On February 27, 1993, a bomb exploded in one of the World Trade Center towers in New York, killing six, wounding nearly 1,000, and forcing the building's closure for over a month until it was repaired. Although many groups claimed responsibility for the bombing, investigators soon arrested and charged a fundamentalist Muslim.

Total International Attacks by Region, 1993–1998

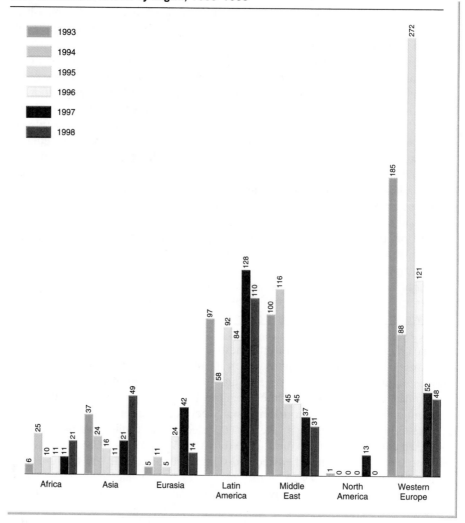

The World Trade Center bombing was a classic case of terrorism. The U.S. State Department defines *terrorism* as "the use or threatened use of violence for political purposes to create a state of fear that will aid in extorting, coercing, intimidating, or otherwise causing individuals and groups to alter their behavior." To this definition can be added the requirements that terrorism "is ruthless and does not conform to humanitarian norms, and that publicity is an essential factor in terrorist strategy."[40] Lenin put it more succinctly: "The purpose of terrorism is to inspire terror."

Terrorism thus is a group's use of violence against noncombatants in a struggle to achieve its goals. Violence against governmental institutions and personnel is not considered terrorism; violence against civilians is. For instance, it is not terror when the *Irish Republican Army (IRA)* assassinates a policeman; it is when the IRA explodes a bomb in Harrod's department store. International terrorism occurs

terrorism the use or threatened use of violence for political purposes to create a state of fear that will extort, coerce, intimidate, or otherwise cause individuals and groups to alter their behavior.

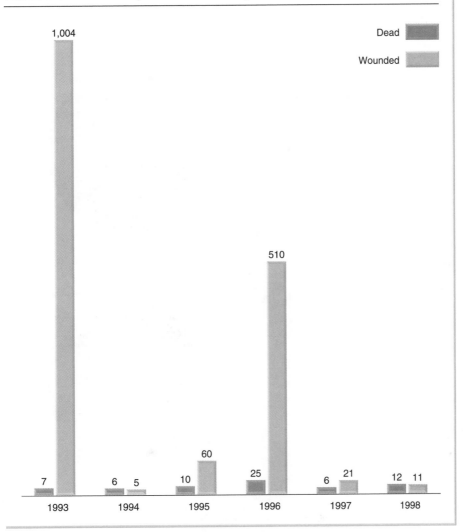

when two or more countries are the supporter, target, or refuge of a terrorist group. There is a difference in motivation, if not tactics, between criminal and political terrorists. Whereas criminals use terror to extort money or other forms of wealth from their victims, political groups use terror to change or discredit entire political systems.

Who commits terrorism? Terrorism can be one tactic of many used by a large political organization struggling for independence or revolution. Terrorism can be the sole means of a tiny, close-knit group to assert its views, whatever they may be, or even the acts of an individual. Many terrorists operate against states; others are employed by states to terrorize their own or foreign citizens. Terrorism has increasingly become a policy of some states. The United States, the Soviet

Total Anti-American Attacks, 1998

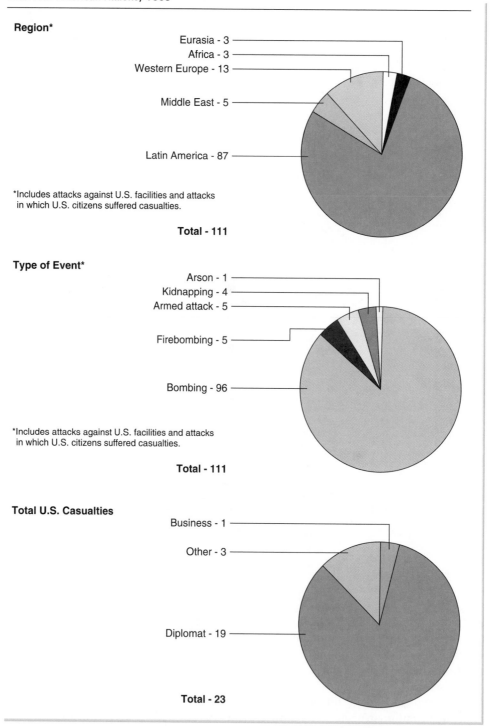

Region*

Eurasia - 3
Africa - 3
Western Europe - 13
Middle East - 5
Latin America - 87

*Includes attacks against U.S. facilities and attacks in which U.S. citizens suffered casualties.

Total - 111

Type of Event*

Arson - 1
Kidnapping - 4
Armed attack - 5
Firebombing - 5
Bombing - 96

*Includes attacks against U.S. facilities and attacks in which U.S. citizens suffered casualties.

Total - 111

Total U.S. Casualties

Business - 1
Other - 3
Diplomat - 19

Total - 23

From Terrorists *to* Politicians: *The* IRA's Long Struggle

The oldest continuous terrorist organization is the Irish Republican Army (IRA), whose efforts to liberate Ireland from British rule as the "Irish Volunteers" date to the 18th century. They organized a massive revolt against British rule in 1916, which was brutally repressed by the British Army. The struggle continued. In 1919, the Irish Volunteers renamed themselves the Irish Republican Army. In 1922, Great Britain finally granted independence to those counties that were predominantly Catholic, while retaining the six counties of Northern Ireland or Ulster, which are 60 percent Protestant, under British rule. The IRA split between those who were content with free Ireland and those who wanted to liberate all of Ireland. In Northern Ireland, the 950,000 Protestants discriminated against the 650,000 Catholics in housing and jobs.

The IRA has continued to struggle for the end of British rule over Northern Ireland since the early 20th century. Between 1971 and 1992 alone, over 3,023 people died in the fighting, of which the IRA killed over 900 security troops and suffered about 300 of their own dead. Most of the casualties were civilians. An estimated 300 to 400 IRA guerrillas have tied down over 30,000 British troops and police. The IRA subsists on about $10 million a year, and even pays its guerrillas a weekly salary of about $200.[42] Those efforts apparently paid off in 1998 when the Clinton administration brokered a peace settlement allowing home rule for Northern Ireland, and nearly all groups involved in the struggle, including the IRA, agreed to lay down their arms.

Union, Israel, Libya, Syria, Iraq, and Iran, to name a few, have all supplied, trained, and/or led groups that launched terrorist attacks against other states. Authoritarian governments frequently use terror to intimidate their own citizens into compliance.

What can terrorism accomplish? A well-publicized terrorist act causing relatively limited deaths and damage can set off a chain reaction that grievously harms the targeted country or cause. For example, the number of American tourists going to Europe halved in 1986 after terrorist attacks and American reprisals, costing Europe hundreds of millions in lost potential revenue. But to force significant change—a government's overthrow, independence, or revolution—terrorism must be one tactic of many for a well-organized group with numerous soldiers and widespread and growing popular support.

Terrorism may be more widespread than commonly perceived. It can be argued that those

> who are described as terrorists, and who reject that title for themselves, make the uncomfortable point that national armed forces, fully supported by democratic opinion, have in fact employed violence and terror on a far greater scale than what liberation movements have as yet been able to attain. The "freedom fighters" see themselves as fighting a just war. Why should they not be entitled to kill, burn, and destroy as national armies, navies and air forces do, and why should the label "terrorist" be applied to them and not to the national militaries?[41]

Islamic Terrorism: *The* Red Crescent

Islamic fundamentalism like the kind that swept Iran in 1979 seeks to reverse the tide of modernity and restore society to a pure Islamic state based solely on the Koran's teachings.[44] The Islamic world is divided into two broad sects, the Sunni and the Shiite, and there are fundamentalist adherents within each sect. Under Islam, religion and government should be synonymous. The Sunni fundamentalist Muslim Brotherhood was founded in Cairo in 1928, and soon had cells throughout the Arab world. Although the Muslim Brotherhood has failed to achieve an Islamic revolution, it continues to inspire tens of millions throughout the Arab world. Such secular governments as Egypt, Syria, and Algeria crushed and imprisoned its adherents. Yet the Muslim Brotherhood and related groups remain active and may be gaining strength.

The Sunni fundamentalists have scored some stunning coups. In 1979, a fundamentalist Muslim group took over the Holy Mosque in Mecca and demonstrated against what they called a heretical, corrupt, and hypocritical royal Saudi family. In 1981 adherents succeeded in assassinating Egyptian President Anwar Sadat. Islamic fundamentalists set off a truck bomb that killed over 241 Marines in Lebanon in 1983 and forced the Reagan administration into a humiliating retreat from the country. In March 1993, fundamentalists exploded a powerful bomb in the World Trade Tower in New York, killing six, wounding more than 1,000, and causing a billion dollars worth of damage. In December 1996 a group massacred a busload of foreign tourists at Luxor; tourism to Egypt plummeted for several years, depriving that country of a desperately needed revenue source. In August 1997, an Islamic group simultaneously blew up the American embassies in Kenya and Tanzania. However, dramatic as these actions were, none changed the target's political system or even policies.

So far Shiite fundamentalists have achieved the most lasting results. In 1979, the Ayatollah Khomeini . led a revolution that toppled the pro-American shah and imposed an Islamic regime on Iran that persists today. In 1997, after nearly two decades of civil war, the fundamentalist Taliban seized power in Afghanistan and immediately revo-lutionized that nation along funda-mentalist lines. Shadowy Islamic international organizations were behind both the Iranian and Afghanistan revolutions and are trying to foment similar changes elsewhere.

Whether a group is composed of "freedom fighters" or "terrorists" depends largely on the viewer's perspective.

International terrorism is relatively easy to commit, given the widespread availability of arms and explosives, international air travel, and mass communications. Although bombings are the most common terrorist tactic, accounting for 413 of 855 international terrorist acts in 1988, there were many others, including arson (239), armed attacks (129), kidnapping (32), assault (16), sabotage (8), barricades without hostages (5), extortion (4), non-air highjackings (3), barricades with hostages (2), skyjackings (2), thefts (1), and other means (1). Of the 185 attacks that year directed against the United States, 140 were bombings, 22 were armed attacks, 14 were arson, and 5 were kidnapping, while extortion, skyjacking, thefts, and non-air highjackings accounted for one each. Of those targeted by international terrorists, the most common was the "other" category, with 516 victims;

followed by businessmen with 256, diplomats with 96, government officials with 92, and military personnel with 50. Of those terrorist acts against Americans, the most common victims were businessmen with 96, diplomats with 42, others with 23, military personnel with 21, and government officials with 12. Although the United States suffered a disproportionate number of attacks, few countries escape terrorism's scourge. In 1990, there were 533 terrorist attacks in 73 countries.[43]

Bombing is the most popular, because it is the safest to pull off. Bombs can be planted well ahead of explosion, allowing the terrorist ample time for a getaway. They also can be strewn virtually anywhere and set off without warning. The explosion of one small bomb can thus terrorize entire populations. In 1983, in an attempt to restore order the Reagan administration sent Marines into Beirut with troops from European allies. A truck bomb blew up an American barracks, killing 241 Marines. Shortly thereafter the Reagan administration pulled out all American forces from Beirut. Kidnapping can also be effective. President Carter's inability to free the 52 American diplomats seized by Iran was the most important reason for losing his bid for re-election. In the mid-1980s, the Reagan administration violated its own pledge not to negotiate with terrorists when it traded arms to Iran to ransom American hostages held by pro-Iranian Islamic fundamentalist groups in Lebanon.

Scholars of terrorism have recently distinguished "old" and "new" versions. Old terrorism was used by groups to advance their cause, usually a nation's independence. The Palestinian Liberation Organization (PLO), African National Congress (ANC), and Irish Republican Army (IRA) are the best known of scores of liberation armies that used terrorism as one of their weapons. Of the three mentioned groups, the PLO and ANC now head governments recognized even by their former enemies, and the IRA has signed a peace treaty that, among other goals, accepts its political legitimacy. New terrorism has no end but terror itself. Nihilist hatred and an obsession with destruction drives new terrorists such as America's right-wing militia groups, adherents of which destroyed a federal building in Oklahoma City, murdering 164 people, wounding hundreds more, and inflicting over $1 billion damage, or Japan's Aum Shinrikyo or Supreme Truth cult, which released sarin gas in Tokyo's subway system, killing 12 people and sickening thousands.

Although the ends of old and new terrorism differ, their targets and methods remain the same. The more people who die, the greater the media exposure and public terror, and better chance the group will achieve its aim. Plagues will become the weapons of choice for terrorists. Biological or germ weapons are relatively easy to manufacture, transport, and release, much more so than conventional bombs. Chemical weapons such as sarin gas are more difficult to manage but can also be very deadly. Aum Shinrikyo, for example, had enough sarin gas to kill millions of people but bungled the delivery. Where did it get the weapons? The cult amassed nearly a billion dollars through various businesses and used some of that cash to buy the technology from Russia's underground arms bazaar. Cyberwarfare will also become more common. Hackers are continually burrowing "viruses" and "worms" through heavily protected computer systems. Choice targets include the Pentagon, entire cities, or the air traffic control system.

What about the ultimate nightmare—nuclear weapons in the hands of terrorists. Making nuclear bombs is too technologically and financially exorbitant for any group to undertake alone; they would mostly need to do so under a government's patronage. Stealing one, however, is much easier, especially from Russia's chaotic military system. In 1998 Russian defense minister Alexander Lebed let slip

World Enemy Number One?
The Hunt *for* Osama Bin Laden

Is Osama Bin Laden the world's most dangerous man? He is accused of being the mastermind behind the bombings of the World Trade Center in 1993, the Khobar Towers in Saudi Arabia in 1996, and, most spectacularly, the U.S. embassies in Kenya and Tanzania in 1998, which collectively killed hundreds and wounded thousands of people. Those are only the bloodiest attacks. He issued a *fatwa,* an order that any Muslim cleric can make, for all the faithful to kill any Americans anywhere at anytime. How can he and his triggermen be brought to justice? Who is that turbaned man?

Osama Bin Laden has used an inheritance worth millions of dollars to create his Al Qaeda organization dedicated to promoting fundamentalist Islam by any possible means including terrorism. What led the pampered son of a rich Saudi businessman to take

that road? After the Soviet Union invaded Afghanistan in 1979, Osama journeyed there to help the Afghans drive out the infidels. When the Soviets finally withdrew a decade later, Bin Laden was a well-known Muslim freedom fighter with a growing following. His return to Saudi Arabia deeply disillusioned him—he believed that secularism was poisoning that Islamic kingdom. Then in 1991, troops from the United States and dozens of other "infidel" nations used Saudi Arabia as a base to attack Iraq. Bin Laden vowed to drive America and its allies from the Islamic world and its 1.2 billion believers. His radicalism provoked his own country to exile him. Bin Laden took his headquarters to Sudan and there remained until his hosts kicked him out in 1996. Since then he has operated from Afghanistan, where he survived a retaliatory American cruise missile attack that

devastated his training camp. To date he remains safely ensconced there, undoubtedly plotting vengeance.

Although Bin Laden denies the charges, the evidence is overwhelming that he was behind those three bombings and a range of other planned or fulfilled terrorist attacks. The Clinton administration has used legal as well as military means to attack Al Qaeda. By mid-1999, American courts had indicted 15 of Bin Laden's terrorists, 5 of whom were already being held in the United States. Others will likely be indicted as those incarcerated inform on others and American intelligence agencies worm their way deeper into the international terrorist world. But can they penetrate far enough to nip future planned attacks in the bud, some of which might be even more devastating than those already launched?

the chilling word that as many as 100 small nuclear weapons were missing from the arsenal, their whereabouts unknown! Could one of them be ticking away near your home?

What is Washington doing to counter this real and continuing danger to the United States? The Clinton White House increased the counterterrorist budget from $5 billion to $7 billion between 1995 and 1998, and named Richard Clarke as "terrorism czar" to unite the efforts of 40 government agencies. But how can they catch the person carrying a heavy suitcase, a test tube, or a computer disc?

How specifically can terrorists be fought?[45] Because terrorists are weak, their only possible victories are political. There are several ways by which governments can contain terrorism's political victories. Governments should not overreact by imposing draconian measures that end up alienating the population and magnifying the terrorist group's importance and appeal. Nor should governments allow themselves to be paralyzed and thus appear weak and ineffectual, and even worse being intimidated into granting concessions. Governments should be particularly careful not to alienate the political moderates. Once the terrorist group captures the sympathy of political moderates, it is close to victory. Repressing moderates who are sympathetic to terrorists only drives them closer together. Isolating and retaliating against the states that sponsor terrorism can also inhibit terrorism. The most effective means are penetrating terrorist groups, either by electronic surveillance or ideally membership; learning everything possible about them; and then swooping in with overwhelming force to eliminate them in their strongholds. But terrorism will exist as long as people are so alienated from society that they believe violence is the only path toward change.

Conclusion

Throughout history, war or the threat of war has been an intricate and often dominant part of international relations. As warfare changes, so too do international relations, and new technologies drive the changes in both. New weapons—gunpowder, the tank, submarines, atomic bombs—can dramatically shift the nature of warfare, and in turn the power balance. Can those links among war, technology, and international relations ever be broken?[46]

Throughout history, people have devised more effective means of destroying lives, property, and environments. For the first several thousand years of history, bows and catapults were the most powerful delivery systems. During the 14th century in Europe, gunpowder was first used for crude muskets and cannon, and improved versions of these weapons systems shaped warfare for the next 500 years. Then, during World War I, the introduction of warplanes and dirigibles allowed the first massive air bombardments. The first missiles were developed and used by the Germans during World War II, when their V-2 rockets could deliver a one-ton bomb several hundred miles away. These first rockets were inaccurate, however, and were mostly targeted on large cities. More importantly, the United States exploded its first atomic bomb in 1945 and first nuclear bomb in 1952, and the Soviet Union and other countries soon followed with their own bombs. During the late 1940s, jet warplanes came on line, and in the late 1950s, the first intercontinental ballistic missiles (ICBMs) were deployed.

Some of the more recent developments have been just as dazzling. TV viewers during the Persian Gulf War safely witnessed the performance of a vast array of high-tech weapons, including sea-launched conventional cruise missiles that flew hundreds of miles and then precisely down the air shafts of bunkers they were programmed to hit. Conventional weapons are becoming increasingly powerful: "A bomber can drop 50 or more bombs of 500–1,000 pounds each . . . a single cluster bomb detonates into several hundred bomblets. Fuel air explosives disperse fuel into the air and then detonate the fuel cloud. Both in lethality and in area covered, so-called conventional weapons today approach small nuclear weapons in destructive power."[47] These new conventional weapons pack the destruction of nuclear weapons without the radioactive fallout and thus might make them obsolete.

How will technology affect warfare in the 21st century? That remains to be seen. Until then we can only speculate about cyberwarfare and other new technologies. One thing is certain, the dynamic relationship among technology, warfare, and international relations will continue.

Study Questions

1. Trace how the nature of warfare—its weapons, strategies, tactics, scale, and so on—has changed throughout history. What accounts for those changes?

2. Describe the major doctrines of American military strategy since 1945.

3. How has global military spending changed over time? What accounts for the increases? How has military spending been affected since the cold war's end?

4. What have been the effects of high military spending on nations' economic development?

5. Describe the relationships among military alliances, power, and security.

6. Why did NATO go to war with Serbia over Kosovo? How was the war fought? What resulted from the war?

7. What conventional arms and war restrictions have been negotiated throughout history?

8. What is the nature of terrorism? How can it be combatted?

☙ *InfoTrac College Edition* Sources

Using the Subject Guide, enter the search terms *Persian Gulf War, civil war, terrorism,* and/or *arms control.* Using Keywords, enter the search term *Palestinian Liberation Organization.*

Atlas, Ronald M. "Combatting the Threat of Biowarfare and Bioterrorism: Defending Against Biological Weapons Is Critical to Global Security."

Auster, Bruce B. "Facts, and Suspicions, About Iraq's Arsenal."

Barnett, Michael N. "Regional Security After the Gulf War."

Biddle, Stephen. "Victory Misunderstood: What the Gulf War Tells Us About the Future of Conflict."

Cohen, Eliot A. "Cascade of Arms: Managing Conventional Weapons Proliferations."

Flamm, Kenneth. "An Economic Strategy to Control Arms Proliferation."

Glaser, Charles L., and Chaim Kaufmann. "What Is the Offense-Defense Balance and Can We Measure It?"

Kaiser, Karl. "Reforming NATO."

Kaufmann, Chaim. "Possible and Impossible Solutions to Ethnic Civil Wars."

Keller, William W., and Janne E. Nolan. "The Arms Trade: Business as Usual?"

Klare, Michael. "East Asia's Arms Races."

Novotny, Patrick. "The Post–Cold War Era, the Persian Gulf War, and the Peace and Justice Movement in the 1990s."

Steinbruner, John D. "Biological Weapons: A Plague upon All Houses."

Stivachtis, Yannis. "Conventional Arms Control and European Security: Conventional Arms Control Agreements and Their Role in the Emerging European Security Architecture."

Tucker, Jonathan B. "Bioweapons from Russia: Stemming the Flow."

Vegar, Jose. "Terrorism's New Breed."
Wright, Robin. "America's Iraq Policy: How Did It Come to This?"

On *the* Web

http://www.historyoftheworld.com/soquel/gulfwar.htm
Links to Persian Gulf War sites

http://www.terrorism.com/index/shtml
Comprehensive site covering terrorism, with links to other sites

http://cisac.stanford.edu/
Arms control site from Stanford University's Institute for International Studies

I n 1998 the United States and European Union launched a trade war against each other that sputters on today. What vital industrial powerhouse creating hundreds of thousands of jobs and tens of billions in wealth was at stake that sparked the war—automobiles, computers, satellites? None of those or other vital industries was involved. Of the thousands of possible products, the war began over bananas! It then spread to another strategic industry— beef! Why?

Chiquita sales within its borders, the corporation pressured the White House and Congress to retaliate. The United States first took Chiquita's complaint to the World Trade Organization (WTO), which issued three rulings against the European Union. On April 19, 1999, the WTO authorized the United States to retaliate. Washington promptly did so by slapping tariffs on $191 million worth of European imports to the United States, the amount claimed to have been lost by America's banana exporters. The United States won an-

Part Five Geoeconomic Conflict *and* Cooperation Within *the* Industrialized World: Bananas *and* Beef: *The* United States *and the* European Union Slip *and* Gore Each Other

Politics packaged in free trade idealism explains much of it. The American-headquartered Chiquita Bananas annually contributes millions of dollars to the Republican and Democratic parties. When the European Union, to protect its own banana importers, limited

other legal victory on December 22, 1999, when the WTO ruled that America's Section 301 law, which empowers the president to retaliate against unfair traders, was legal. This was a blow against the European Union and Japan, which had jointly filed a suit against Section 301, hoping to thus weaken a key American defense.

Rather than resolve this issue, the two geoeconomic superpowers joined battle over yet another product. The United States complained that the European Union law against selling meat from livestock treated with growth hormones unfairly discriminates against American ranchers. The Americans claim there is no evidence that hormones cause cancer or other health problems; the Europeans cite studies that hormones are indeed dangerous. Here too the Americans won a legal battle, with the WTO ordering the European Union to lift its ban. Nonplussed by the legal setback, the European Union announced it would ban all American beef by June 15 unless the Americans promised not to sell hormone-laced meat.

Bananas and beef are small potatoes—at most $0.5 billion—in an annual bilateral trade of $400 billion. Although the United States suffers a worsening trade deficit with the European Union that reached $35 billion in 1998, Europe's markets are largely open to American exports and investments. Why would Washington get bogged down in a trade war with Europe over such trivial products and profits?

Special interests masquerading as national interests tend to distort trade policies. Beef and banana groups on both sides of the Atlantic paid off politicians in return for trade protection. If national rather than special interests prevailed, the Americans and Europeans would never have become

How important are bananas to the global economy? American- and European-backed corporations fought a "banana" war in the late 1990s over access to each other's banana markets.

AP/Wide World Photos

entangled into a trade war over such trivial products.

Although both the United States and European Union subsidize agriculture through a variety of means, the latter's farm welfare programs are far more costly. Over half of the European Union's $100 billion budget goes

to the Common Agricultural Policy (CAP), which props up farmers with subsidies, or payments and other protection, who otherwise would be bankrupted by international market forces. Although the European Union's trade policies are supposed to be determined by majority rule, in practice a consensus or unanimity prevails. This gives special interests enormous clout in protecting themselves from international competition.

American farmers, ranchers, and other industries demanding corporate welfare are just as powerful getting tax cuts, subsidies, and import protection from Congress and the White House. In recent years, protectionist groups have asserted their power by getting Congress to refuse to renew the White House's fast-track negotiating authority. Under fast track, the president could negotiate agreements that Congress must either approve or reject without any amendments. This prevents special interests from destroying a treaty by getting their congressional representatives to protect them with corporate welfare provisions such as protecting them from the treaty's requirements.

The trade war not only strains relations between the United States and the European Union, but also threatens the WTO's legitimacy. A WTO panel or three-judge court can rule on who is at fault but does not specify damages or just how the dispute should be settled. Those questions remain for the countries involved to resolve. The WTO has an annual budget of $80 million, only enough to finance a small staff with global duties. As if these problems were not debilitating enough, WTO was leaderless for over a year as its members stalemated over rival candidates for president. The United States, European Union, and most other countries supported Mike Moore, a former New Zealand prime minister, who promised to root out protectionism everywhere. Japan and many newly industrializing countries favored Thai deputy prime minister Supachai Panitchpakdi, who would likely have turned a blind eye to nontariff barriers in those countries. Moore led by a two-to-one margin among WTO members, but the rival's supporters were able to block a vote.

Various political disputes threaten to cripple the WTO, thus making neo-mercantilism rather than liberalism ever more prevalent in geoeconomic relations.

Why should bananas and beef be reasons for economic war? The reality is that they and other industries might have political power far beyond what little they contribute to a nation's economy. Thus special interests can spark international geoeconomic wars that, if they spread to important industries, could threaten to destroy global prosperity.

The dispute also raises important questions over sovereignty and national interests. Which among the three should prevail in world trade: (1) free trade ideals; (2) national laws protecting the environment, food safety, and labor standards; or (3) powerful corporations and industries demanding protection from foreign dumping, import barriers, and subsidies to their industries?

Contents

Chapter 12 Geoeconomic Strategies *for a* Global Economy: Regulatory, Developmental, *and* Social Capitalism

Key Concepts and Terms

For decades the United States has suffered trade and investment deficits with Japan, whose neomercantilist policies target industries and technologies for development, launch export offensives, and limit imports all to strengthen Japan's economy at the expense of its rivals. And for decades U.S. presidents have demanded that Japan truly open its markets, something Japan's government has steadfastly refused to do. Here President Bill Clinton and Prime Minister Keizo Obuchi echo the latest round of charges and denials. Who wins and who loses when one state practices liberal and another state neomercantilist policies?

AP/Wide World Photos

In the global political economy, states pursue different strategies to fulfill their different values, needs, desires, and goals. The "free world" is based on liberal political and economic values. Ideally, a liberal democratic country or *liberal democracy* has a written constitution in which all are subject to the law, sovereignty rests in the people, all people enjoy the full spectrum of human and civil rights, and a political system is created in which the people's needs and desires are served by representatives and/or referendums. As Abraham Lincoln put it, democracy is "of the people, by the people, and for the people." Economic freedom involves the ideals of *free markets,* private property, and minimal government interference.

There is inevitably a wide gap between liberal political and economic ideals and reality, and great variations in the institutions and practices of countries espousing those ideals. Although the ranks of democratic industrial countries are expanding, only about 15 percent of the world's nation-states have achieved liberal democratic cultures and institutions along with advanced economies, the 27 members of the *Organization for Economic Cooperation and Development (OECD)* or so-called rich countries' club. There are many different political systems among the industrial democratic countries, from the relatively decentralized federal systems of Switzerland, the United States, Canada, and Germany to the relatively more centralized parliamentary systems of Britain, Japan, South Korea, and Italy.

Although ever more states have realized political *liberalism,* a truly free market economy may be neither obtainable or even desirable in the real world. Most democratic industrial countries claim to have liberal economies, yet all—including the United States—have rejected pure market Darwinism, or complete absence of regulation or welfare, as disastrous for economic development and political liberty.

Expanding World Trade, 1913 to 1991
Source: World Bank 2000, Entering the 21st Century (New York: Oxford University Press, 2000), pp. 25–51.

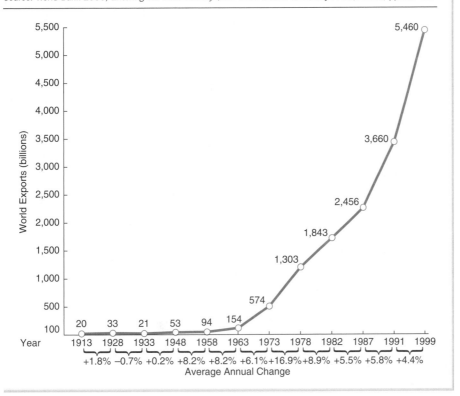

Governments vary enormously in how they manage the so-called free market. Indeed, free markets do not and never could exist in the real world. All governments intervene in the economy—the differences lie in the ways, degrees, and justifications of intervention. They do so because of market imperfections or failures that leave most people and the world in which they live worse rather than better off.

Among the free market economies there are three sharply different orientations. Of the world's economies, none have freer systems than the United States, whose government has a *regulatory market system*. In pursuing the free market ideal, the government regulates business to ensure that no domestic firms achieve *monopoly* or *oligopoly* power, and maintains minimal import barriers and export incentives. These governments generally put economic "freedom" first, even if it means continual trade and payments deficits, relatively low economic growth, and inequitable income distribution.

Then there are states such as France or Japan that have both liberal political systems and heavily state-guided market systems. These states follow a *neomercantilist* strategy in which the nation's economic security is equated with a relatively high growth rate and equitable income distribution, continual trade and payments surpluses, and diversified sources of foreign raw materials, energy, and markets. To these ends, the government targets *strategic industries* and technologies for development with export incentives, *subsidies, cartels,* protection from competitive imports, and so on.

regulatory market system minimal government interference in markets, primarily to uphold health, safety, and anti-**cartel** standards. The ideal is pursued even if it means continual trade and payments deficits, relatively low economic growth, and inequitable income distribution.

neomercantilism a government's rapid development of the economy to achieve a trade surplus with its competitors by systematically restricting imports, promoting exports, and targeting strategic industries and technologies with subsidies, cartels, and other advantages.

Finally, there are the *social market* economies, exemplified by the Scandinavian countries, in which policies emphasize the equitable distribution of existing wealth rather than the creation of new wealth. Government spending as a percentage of GNP is relatively high, the state provides citizens with *cradle-to-grave benefits,* the most important industries are often publicly owned, and markets are heavily regulated.

What must be understood is that no country falls completely into any one of these categories. Aspects of all three orientations characterize every democratic industrial country. The United States, for example, although predominantly regulatory, also has large sectors of its economy shaped by neomercantilist and social market policies. France's neomercantilist and social market policies are almost twins, and the state is gradually liberalizing some industries. The degree, types, and purposes of government management of the economy vary over time. In the 225 years since its independence, the American government has slowly expanded its duties for regulating the economy, along with neomercantilist and social market policies, almost always in response to political pressure. A state's economic orientation both reflects and shapes the culture in which it is embedded. Although cultures can change, they sometimes do so only at a glacial pace. Liberalism is as deeply embedded in American culture as neomercantilism is in Japan and France.

Although every country has a specific economic orientation and policies, this chapter concentrates on exploring the different economic orientations and policies of the advanced liberal industrial countries. It first examines the different political economic ideologies that can guide the governments of liberal democratic states, discussing their strengths and weaknesses. It then explores the range of possible industrial and trade policies that states can follow.

Political Economic Ideologies

Ideology and policy are often closely related. Ideologies are systematic, comprehensive world views that provide governments and peoples with the values, institutions, restrictions, and ideals for acting in the world. Sometimes states pursue policies that seemingly violate their values. At other times there is close accord between ideals and action. Why do countries vary in their ability or willingness to live up to their values and ideals?

LIBERAL OR REGULATORY MARKET IDEOLOGY

Notions of economic and political freedom developed together. In 1776, the United States declared its independence from England. That same year, Adam Smith's classic study of free trade, *The Wealth of Nations,* was published.[1] Smith argued that everyone benefits from free trade because competition forces all people to specialize in producing what they produce best and then trading that good for anything else they desire. The forces of supply and demand are what Smith termed the *"invisible hand"* that provides all the needs and desires of consumers and society as a whole, an idea much later called the *"magic of the marketplace."*

Markets should be free not just within, but also between states. Every nation, like every individual, has certain natural productive strengths and weaknesses known as *comparative advantage.* Smith argued that "what is prudence in the conduct of every private family can scarcely be folly in that of a great kingdom. If a foreign country can supply us with a commodity cheaper than we ourselves can make it, better buy it of them with some part of our own industry."[2] According to economist Paul Samuelson, "free trade promotes a mutually profitable division of labor, greatly enhances the potential real national product of all nations, and makes possible higher standards of living all over the globe."[3]

Like political liberals, economic liberals maintain that the less government the better. Government, according to Adam Smith, should have

> only three duties . . . first, the duty of protecting the society from the violence and invasion of other independent societies; secondly, the duty of protecting, as far as possible, every member of the society from the injustice or oppression of every other member, or the duty of establishing an exact administration of justice; and thirdly, the duty of erecting and maintaining certain public works and certain public institutions, which can never be for the interest of any individual, or small number of individuals.[4]

Liberal economic theory has been severely criticized.[5] The central criticism is that free trade is based on ideal assumptions that do not exist in the real world. *Market Darwinism,* or a survival-of-the-fittest economic world like that which existed in late 19th-century America or Britain, leads not to the utopia promised by the theorists but to an all-too-real world of the rich elite getting richer by exploiting the ever worse off and poverty-stricken masses, abysmal working conditions, price-gouging cartels, sickening and sometimes murderous air and water pollution, and the bulldozing of a nation's cultural, historical, and natural heritage. Market anarchy leads not to economic bliss but to economic tyranny. Governments sooner or later must step in and save the country from free market excesses. The more democratic the government, the greater the public's pressure on it to suppress the economic war of all against all. But states differ in how they manage their economies. Robert Kuttner points out that liberal economic theory "to most of the world . . . seems utopian and the practice hypocritical. America seems to practice a chaotic ad hoc mercantilism—weapons procurement, farm price supports, textile quotas, and various 'voluntary' restraints extracted from trading partners—while it stridently preaches free trade."[6] In reality, the trade of all states is more or less managed rather than free.

Freer trade is an advantage to a leading industrial country but can impede the growth of a country trying to catch up with more advanced nations. After studying Britain's economy, the 19th-century German political economist Friedrich List, advised Germany against free trade, arguing that "free competition between two nations which are highly civilized can only be mutually beneficial in case both of them are in a nearly equal position of industrial development, and that any nation which owing to misfortunes is behind others in industry, commerce, navigation . . . must first of all strengthen her own individual powers, in order to fit herself to enter into free competition with more advanced nations."[7] John Spanier expands the argument:

> The free market may well be a superior mechanism for allocating goods when those competing and exchanging goods are of approximately equal power. When one nation is clearly more advanced economically however, free trade benefits it more because it is able to penetrate the markets of weaker countries. The laws of the free market are not neutral. Power is the "invisible hand" determining the distribution of wealth. Among nations that are equal in economic power, economic relations may well breed interdependence, as in the EEC [European Economic Community] and relations between them and the United States. But between the economically strong and the economically weak, the inevitable result is the dependence of the latter."[8]

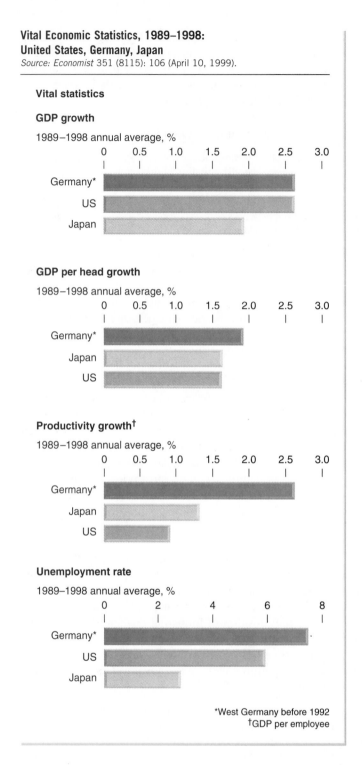

Vital Economic Statistics, 1989–1998:
United States, Germany, Japan
Source: Economist 351 (8115): 106 (April 10, 1999).

Vital statistics

GDP growth

1989–1998 annual average, %

Germany*
US
Japan

GDP per head growth

1989–1998 annual average, %

Germany*
Japan
US

Productivity growth†

1989–1998 annual average, %

Germany*
Japan
US

Unemployment rate

1989–1998 annual average, %

Germany*
US
Japan

*West Germany before 1992
†GDP per employee

As Bruce Scott and George Lodge point out, it "is not surprising that the leading advocates of free trade have been those who were strong at the time, first the United Kingdom, then the United States. . . . Free trade, like free competition, has political as well as economic content: taken literally it is a system that enhances the power of the powerful and makes it all the more difficult for the poor to catch up."[9]

Liberal Democracy, Wealth, *and* Power

Ideally a country enjoys large and rapidly growing middle and wealthy classes, and it suffers minimal and diminishing poverty. That is the essence of successful economic development.

Why are some liberal democratic countries wealthier than others? What is the dynamic among wealth, policies, and culture? Are relatively hands-on or hands-off policies more successful in creating and distributing wealth for a country? Can we generalize about whether regulatory market or liberal countries such as the United States, developmental market or neomercantilist countries such as Japan, or social market countries in Scandinavia and elsewhere provide the best economic

models? What is the relative mix of regulatory, developmental, and social policies in each democratic industrial country? How and why does that mix of policies change over time? Do some policies work better or worse during one period in a country's history than another? If so why? If not why not?

Liberals claim that economics and politics can and should be separated. But this is an impossible task in the real world, in which economics and politics are so closely meshed as to be inseparable Siamese twins. All economic conflicts are political, and all political conflicts have some economic dimension. The difficult question is determining how they influence each other. Asking

where struggles over wealth end and struggles over power begin is like asking which comes first, the chicken or the egg.

According to liberalism, all industries are of equal value—a billion dollars worth of potato chips is just as important as a billion dollars worth of computer chips, as Michael Boskin, the former chair of the Council of Economic Advisors in the Bush administration, once declared. Critics argue that equating potato and computer chips is ludicrous. The potato chip industry's technological, job, or wealth *multiplier* (or ripple) *effects* on the economy are as limited as the computer industry's multiplier effects are enormous and growing.

Liberal economists assume that the less government interference in the economy, the more and faster the development. Is this true? Completely free markets are not necessarily the best means of creating wealth and allocating resources. Perhaps no other country in the world has a more deeply entrenched free market mentality and economy than the United States. Yet America's growth, productivity rate, and middle class as a percentage of the total population have often been lower than other democratic industrial states whose governments are more active in directing the economy. Many fear that America's free trade policies are allowing the economy to be hollowed out as foreign competition undercuts American businesses while American multinational corporations transfer their operations overseas to enjoy access to markets, resources, and cheaper labor. The United States has suffered chronic trade deficits since the early 1970s.

NEOMERCANTILIST MARKET IDEOLOGY

As an ideology, *mercantilism* is much older than liberalism.[10] States have always intervened in the economy whether for generating tax receipts, promoting certain industries or classes, or realizing God's will. During the early modern era, states targeted important or strategic industries for development with subsidies, import barriers, and export incentives in order to develop the economy and protect the state. Economic and military security were closely linked. Many of the industries targeted in this *developmental market system* produced military weapons and equipment. Much of the revenue gathered by the state was used to build up the nation's military forces and either defend or expand the realm against other states.

Mercantilism, according to Jacob Viner, has four main propositions:

> (1) wealth is an absolutely essential means to power, whether for security or for aggression; (2) power is essential or valuable as a means to the acquisition or retention of wealth; (3) wealth and power are each proper ultimate ends of national policy; and (4) there is a long-run harmony between these ends, although in particular circumstances it may be necessary for a time to make economic sacrifices in the interest of military security and therefore also of long-run prosperity.[11]

Neomercantilism is the contemporary version of mercantilism; it is a developmental and national security strategy for liberal democratic countries in an interdependent world. Rather than spending scarce resources on the military sector, neomercantilist states concentrate on promoting high-technology consumer and equipment industries that most efficiently create wealth and expand the middle class.

In many ways, neomercantilism is a reaction against liberal idealism. Liberal economists construct an ideal world and then attempt to shape the real world accordingly. In contrast, neomercantilists attempt to understand the way global political economy really operates and act accordingly. Whereas liberalism's goal is free markets, neomercantilism's is the creation, distribution, and securing of wealth. Thus neomercantilists first determine which industries can create the most wealth and then map a strategy whereby those industries can be developed. In addition, neomercantilists see international trade as largely a zero-sum war in which one side's gain is another's loss. Neomercantilist governments use any means they can to tip the international trade playing field in favor of their own firms.

Free markets exist only in theory, not in the real world. All markets are distorted and often outright managed by domestic and foreign government policies. The benefits of international trade are not evenly distributed among participants. There are net winners and losers in any transaction, both over the short and the long term. For example, when foreign firms *dump* or sell their goods at a loss in a market, consumers benefit while domestic producers of those goods lose market share and profits, and are sometimes forced into bankruptcy. Over the short term, domestic consumers and foreign producers win and domestic producers lose. Over the long term, consumers lose too, because the economy suffers as wealth flows to foreign rather than domestic producers. As the nation's tax, employment, and wealth base erodes relative to voracious foreign rivals, consumers inevitably have less money with which to buy goods and services. To worsen matters, after they have driven their competitors into bankruptcy, the foreign firms usually raise prices to recoup earlier losses sustained from dumping.

There are winners and losers in international investment flows as well. Liberals claim foreign investments are mutually beneficial. The Reagan administration summed up this outlook on foreign investments in the United States in a 1983 statement: "We believe that there are only winners, no losers, and all participants gain from it."[12] Neomercantilists spurn idealism for realism and argue that it depends.[13] The country may enjoy a net gain if foreigners buy money-losing firms or real estate such as country clubs and skyscrapers. The foreign investor often must pour money, managerial expertise, and technology into the asset before it can turn a profit. After being bought out, the original owners will invest their money elsewhere, ideally in more productive domestic industries. But a country may well suffer a net long-term loss if foreign firms buy money-making high-technology firms, banks, factories, mines, or farms, which generate most of a country's wealth and thus power. Foreign investments that create a new office, factory, store, or restaurant, known as a "green field site," can also represent either a net gain or loss for the recipient country. The bottom line is whether a buyout or green field site investment brings more money, technology, skills, and dynamism into a country than it takes out over the short and long term. How would American power be affected if a foreign country's corporations bought up its computer or automobile or software industries? National security and economic vitality are inseparable.

International trade and investment battles are becoming fiercer as increasing numbers of governments understand how serious the stakes are and intervene to tip the geoeconomic power balance in their favor. Given a relatively equal power distribution and development level, neomercantilist countries usually grow faster, export more, and import less than liberal countries. The larger and more advanced the neomercantilist country's economy, the greater the adverse effects on development elsewhere. Governments that do not systematically attempt to assist the creation and distribution of wealth through rational *macroeconomic policies* according to a long-term plan increasingly find their nation's economy shaped and distorted by foreign governments that do.

Many analysts argue that America's liberal economic ideals are increasingly a disadvantage in an ever more neomercantilist world. David Blake and Robert Walters point out that the "liberal economists who dominate American economic scholarship are ill-equipped to evaluate systematically the political forces shaping, and political implications of, their prescriptions for 'rational' economic policies in an era of highly politicized global economic relations."[14] That is the key difference between economists and political economists. *Economists* start out with abstract theories into which they try—and fail—to squeeze the real world. *Political economists* analyze the vastly complex, ever changing world and then, if possible, note general patterns and concepts that help us to understand it.

The economic devastation that a neomercantilist country can inflict on a liberal country is clear. But can neomercantilism hurt those countries that practice it? Too much government protection of the economy can be as self-destructive as too little. Ideally, the state manages an economy to maximize the benefits of cooperation and competition. If neomercantilist policies are mismanaged, they can backfire and encourage a *crony capitalism* whereby corporations and industries cooperate so much that they lose their competitive edge. The East Asian economies, especially Japan, personify crony capitalism. Although those economies continue to enjoy vast trade surpluses with the relatively liberal American market, elsewhere their products slam into each others' protectionist walls. Thus during the late 1990s, the East Asian economies suffered from excess production, and low profits, growth, and innovations. That is not neomercantilism's only possible downside. If all countries practiced neomercantilism, trade would collapse to minimal levels and most people would be worse off, as happened during the trade wars of the 1930s.

SOCIAL MARKET IDEOLOGY

Liberalism and neomercantilism are concerned with the creation of wealth. Social democracy is concerned with existing wealth's equitable distribution. Markets are distrusted as arenas in which the rich and powerful feed off the poor and weak.

The freer the markets, the greater the gap between rich and poor. A powerful state must be constructed to prevent the exploitation and continued subjugation of the latter by the former.

In the late 19th century, under Chancellor Otto von Bismarck, Germany was the first country to begin establishing welfare, health, and social security institutions. Other industrial states slowly began developing their own systems. The Great Depression of the 1930s convinced the United States and a few other laggards that the state has an interest in providing a social safety net to prevent mass poverty.[15]

There are very good political as well as economic reasons for a greater state role in the economy:

> Modern governments have become increasingly sensitive to demands for a wide variety of welfare services and have taken on the responsibility for mass social and economic welfare. The improvement through state intervention of the material . . . well being of its citizens has become one of the central functions of state activity. The satisfaction of rising claims by citizens has become a major source of the state's legitimization and of a government's continuance in office.[16]

Social democracy has been criticized on several grounds. By focusing on dividing rather than expanding the economic pie, living standards stagnate over the long run. By heavily regulating and taxing markets, social democrats reduce incentives for entrepreneurs to create new wealth. Yet there are benefits, too—greater leisure time, health insurance, and social security.

Sweden has the ultimate social market system, with cradle-to-grave health, education, and welfare benefits for all citizens. These benefits have been expensive, and the price may have become exorbitant. Between 1970 and 1990, Sweden's welfare programs grew from 44 percent to 70 percent of GNP. In 1990, Swedish taxes as a percentage of GNP were 56.9 percent, compared to America's 29.9 percent. Like other democratic industrial states, Sweden has experienced an economic slowdown and rising socioeconomic problems. Unemployment rose from 1.4 percent in 1989 to 6.2 percent in 1993. Between 1992 and 1994, the annual budget deficit as a percentage of GNP rose from 5.6 percent to 11.1 percent.[17]

In 1991, a coalition of moderate and conservative parties took over the Swedish government after half a century of nearly uninterrupted social democratic rule. The reform government tried to pare back Sweden's welfare state. Payments to workers injured on the job were reduced. The age to receive partial pensions was raised from 60 to 62, and full pensions from 65 to 66. Compensation for women who choose to stay home with their children was reduced from 90 percent to

Table 12.1 **Comparative Labor Costs (1998)**

	Average Wage	State Benefits	Total	Benefit (Percentage of total)	Yearly Work Hours	Jobless Rate (July 1999)
United States	$14.34	$3.90	$18.24	27.2%	1,966	4.3%
Japan	16.52	2.85	19.37	17.3	1,889	4.9
Germany	20.94	7.34	28.28	35.1	1,574	9.1
Great Britain	13.47	2.00	15.47	14.8	1,731	5.9
France	12.36	5.61	17.97	45.4	1,656	11.1

Source: Bureau of Labor Statistics, International Labor Office, 2000.

Market *versus* State Medicine: *The* American *and* British Systems

Great Britain and the United States have starkly different medical systems. In Britain the state offers free health care to all, while allowing doctors to have private practices. The United States only covers the elderly (Medicare) and poor (Medicaid), although many recipients complain that what they get is inadequate to their needs. All other Americans have to pay for their own health care. Which health care system do you imagine is more expensive and efficient, that largely provided by the market or that largely provided by the state?

Health care is actually a field where the state is far superior to the market in nurturing a healthier population at a lower cost. In Britain everyone is insured, but health care consumes only 7 percent of GNP. Health care in the United States is the world's most expensive system, devouring 14 percent of GNP, although one of six people or 40 million Americans have no insurance. In 1997 Britain's population was actually healthier than America's, with an infant mortality rate of 6 per thousand births compared to 7 for the United States, a maternal mortality of 9 per 100,000 live births compared to 12, and an average longevity of 75 for men and 80 for women compared to 73 for men and 79 for women. The only drawback to Britain's system are slightly longer average waiting times for appointments and nonessential operations, a small inconvenience for better health. And, in the ultimate irony, British taxpayers actually paid less than Americans for their "socialized medicine," only 5.7 percent of GNP compared to 6.6 percent!

80 percent of their regular pay. The Swedish krona was devalued to boost exports. The government employed private companies to perform some tasks traditionally done by the state. In 1992, the government cut $9 billion from the budget. Those reforms worked. Between 1993 and 1998, Sweden's economy expanded by 3.8 percent, faster than America's, and its unemployment rate fell from 8.1 percent to 5.3 percent, less than the European Union's 9.4 percent rate. Yet with a per capita purchasing power parity of $19,480, Sweden ranked only 27th in the world.

Increasing numbers of countries will emulate Sweden's welfare state cutbacks in the 21st century. In every democratic industrial country the ratio between workers and retirees is shifting steadily to the latter. Simply put, people are living longer and having far fewer children than before. In Germany, for example, those 60 years or older are expected to swell to 36 percent of the total population by the year 2035! Retirees, by definition, no longer produce but simply consume. Most welfare for retirees was enacted when life expectancies were far lower and thus were designed to provide the elderly some comfort in their last few years. But today the average life in democratic industrial nations is approaching 80 years; some predict that a medical revolution will soon push that average life span to 100 years! The demands of ever more retired elderly may overwhelm the social security and health care systems.

What can prevent that? Taxes can be increased and/or benefits cut. Any reforms to defuse that demographic time bomb will ignite fierce opposition. The old will resent enjoying fewer benefits than previous generations, and the young will gripe at higher taxes—until they retire, of course. Another option is to welcome immigrants to fill jobs. If those immigrants are not assimilated into the national cultures, resentments may arise between them and the natives. Yet another possibility is to privatize social security, allowing workers to invest the savings they hand over to the state, which usually puts it in low-yield but secure government bonds. Of course, not all private investments make a profit; many lose money and some are completely lost. What should the state do if a worker wastes his or her legacy? And what about the people already drawing pensions? In the "pay as you go" system, workers pay the pensions of current retirees and will in turn be paid for after they retire by a new generation of workers. As with all socioeconomic problems, there are no easy solutions.

Political Economic Policies

Governments everywhere intervene actively in the economy to make up for myriad *market imperfections,* although they do so to greatly varying degrees and ways. Economic policy can be divided into three broad areas—macroeconomic, industrial, and trade—each of which is thoroughly integrated with the others. Macroeconomic policies are those government actions or inactions directed at affecting the entire economy. In contrast, industrial policies are focused on particular industries, regions, technologies, or firms. *Trade policies,* as the name implies, are chiefly concerned with the country's trade balance and composition of exports and imports.

MACROECONOMIC POLICIES

Governments can shape the national economy through several means: (1) fiscal or government budget policy; (2), monetary or money supply and interest rate policy; (3) tax policy; and (4) currency policy. Each of these policies is designed either to stimulate a depressed economy or to deflate an inflationary economy, a practice known as *fine tuning* business cycles. Ideally, all four macroeconomic policies are used so that they complement the government's goals. In practice, this coordination is extremely difficult to achieve; a government may follow a stimulatory fiscal policy and a deflationary monetary policy, and so on.

Fiscal policy or government budget policy is usually the most influential of the four. In every country, the government is the largest single buyer of goods and services. When governments increase spending, they stimulate the economy, and when they cut back spending they deflate it. Fiscal policy is also an important source of *industrial policies* because the budget allocates or denies money to specific industries. The British economist John Maynard Keynes popularized fiscal policy, also known as Keynesian economics.

Monetary policy primarily involves manipulating the money supply and interest rates. When an economy is depressed, a country's central bank (the Federal Reserve in the United States), can cut several different rates including the interest (discount) rate it charges banks when they borrow money from the Fed, the reserve requirements for the amount of money banks must keep in their vaults as a total of their assets, and the federal funds rate of interest on government bonds. With lower interest rates and lower reserve requirements, banks would lend more

Ninety Years of American Economic Performance
Source: Louis Achotelle, "Trickle Down: It's a Slow Growth Economy, Stupid," *New York Times,* 1 Jan. 1998.

Change in the gross domestic product of the United States each year, after inflation had been factored out.

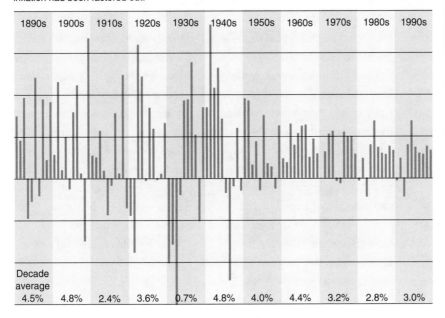

1890s	1900s	1910s	1920s	1930s	1940s	1950s	1960s	1970s	1980s	1990s

Decade average

| 4.5% | 4.8% | 2.4% | 3.6% | 0.7% | 4.8% | 4.0% | 4.4% | 3.2% | 2.8% | 3.0% |

at a lower rate to businesses, entrepreneurs, and households. Lower bond rates would encourage investors to sell their bonds and invest in stocks or elsewhere in the economy. The infusion of cash into the system stimulates the economy. When an economy becomes overheated or inflationary, central banks may raise interest rates for bank borrowing and bond along with reserve requirements to take more money and thus demand out of the economy, and thereby reduce inflation.

Raising or lowering taxes is yet another way to affect the economy. Cutting taxes puts more money in the pockets of businesses and households. If the extra money is used to buy something, it creates a demand and thus supply. If it is saved, it makes more money available to businesses or households to borrow and spend. As a result, the economy is stimulated. Raising taxes has the opposite effect. Like fiscal policy, tax policy can be an important industrial policy tool as well, because most countries' tax codes favor some industries, classes, firms, or individuals more than others. Social democratic countries have relatively progressive tax codes in which taxes are eliminated for the poor, lowered for the middle class, and are highest for the rich, known as a *trickle-up policy.* The greater income among the poor and middle class leads to greater spending and thus greater growth, a policy known as *demand-side economics.* Conservatives in the United States and elsewhere favor a regressive system of lowering taxes for the rich by cutting the capital gains tax and/or imposing a flat tax in the hopes that some of the extra wealth will be invested in businesses that create wealth and jobs, a policy known as *trickle-down* or *supply-side economics.*

trickle-down economics the idea that if a government reduces taxes or increases benefits to the rich, they will spend, invest, and/or save their additional money, thus stimulating the economy and creating more jobs and wealth; in other words, wealth from the rich will trickle down to the middle class and poor.

Does *a* Rising Economic Tide Lift All Boats *or* Swamp *the* Smaller Ones?

Economists are fond of saying, "A rising tide lifts all boats," meaning that everyone benefits from an expanding economy. Is that true?

Certainly not in the last 22 years. Although the economy expanded from 1973 to 1996, the richest 40 percent of Americans got richer and the poorest 60 percent of Americans got poorer. Four of five Americans have a thinner slice of the economic pie today than they did two decades ago. Today the wealthiest 2.7 million peo-

ple have as much after tax money as the poorest 100 million.

What explains this growing gap? Tax cuts for the rich during the 1980s partly explain the phenomenon. The Reagan administration justified cutting the top rate from 50 percent to 39 percent by promising that the economy would expand and money would trickle down to the poor. Neither promise was fulfilled. The economy actually grew more slowly in the 1980s than in the 1970s or dazzling 1990s, and the poor got poorer. That

trend may be changing. In 1998, all income groups have gotten wealthier, although the gap between rich and poor continued to widen.

Economists dismiss the importance of income distribution. Should they? Does it matter if the rich get richer and the poor poorer? What are some possible economic, social, and political consequences of a widening gap between richer rich and poorer poor? What, if anything, should be done about it?

Table 12.2 Yachts and Inner Tubes

Household Income Group	Share of Income		Average After-Tax Income		Percent Change
	1977	1999	1977	1999	
1% highest income	7.3%	12.9%	$234,700	$515,600	+119.7%
20% highest income	44.2	50.4	74,000	102,300	+38.2
20% 2nd highest	22.8	21.3	42,600	45,100	+5.9
20% middle	16.4	14.7	32,400	31,400	–3.1
20% 2nd lowest	11.5	9.7	22,100	20,000	–9.5
20% lowest income	5.7	4.2	10,000	8,800	–12.0

Figures adjusted for inflation.

Source: Congressional Budget Office, 2000.

Which tax strategy is the most effective? At best, even in the most economically advanced countries with entrepreneurial traditions, trickle-down policies simply make the rich richer while having little effect on economic growth. It fails completely in countries lacking an entrepreneurial tradition. But trickle-down policy can be disastrous. During the 1980s, the Reagan White House sharply cut taxes, most of which went to the rich. The growth rate was not only actually lower during that decade than at any time since the 1930s, but *Reaganomics,* as it was known, tripled the national debt from $970 billion to $2.9 trillion in just eight years! How did that happen? Reagan promised that the tax cuts would pay for themselves with

Women, Politics, *and* Policy

What is the dynamic among politics, policies, and women? Why do women who run for public office in some democratic industrial countries fare relatively well while most elsewhere do so poorly? What role do such forces as culture and socioeconomic level play in determining the relative success or failure of women in politics? Once in power, what impact do women have on public policy? How, of course, does all this affect international relations?

Women and Political Power in Liberal Democratic Countries
Source: Economist 350 (8103): 96 (Jan. 23, 1999).

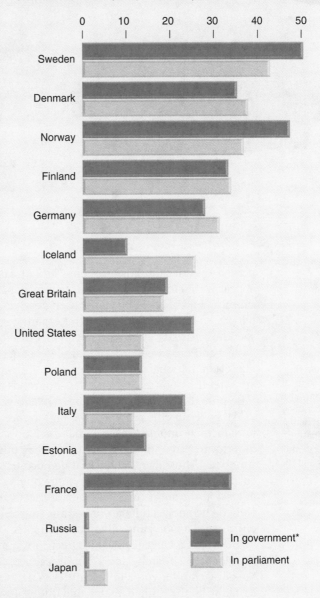

In government*
In parliament

*cabinet level, including the prime minister

Reaganomics, Clintonomics, and the Federal Budget
Source: Office of Management and Budget.

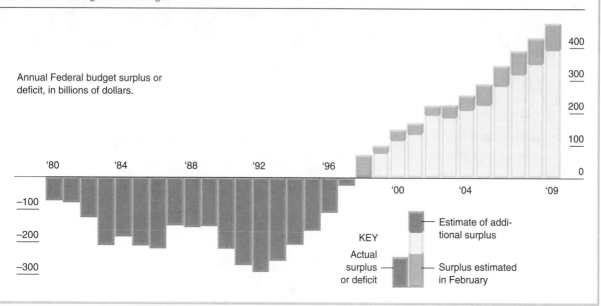

Annual Federal budget surplus or deficit, in billions of dollars.

KEY

Actual surplus or deficit

Estimate of additional surplus

Surplus estimated in February

higher revenues from the economic growth and that the budget deficit would disappear within four years. But the opposite happened. Reagan never cut spending or submitted a balanced budget to Congress, and he signed nearly every spending bill passed by Congress. Although Reagan promised to make government smaller, spending actually increased, largely because of a near tripling of the Pentagon's budget and increased farm subsidies. Revenues plunged. Hence Reaganomics' tripling of the national debt in eight years. In contrast, a *trickle-up economics* not only enriches the poor and middle class but tends to stimulate the economy and thus raise growth, incomes, and equity, while lowering unemployment.

All governments recognize the importance of *currency policy* in macroeconomics. Liberal economists believe that a nation's currency reflects national strength, or as former Treasury Secretary Don Regan put it, "A strong dollar means a strong America." Thus liberal and social democratic governments prefer an overvalued currency, which gives consumers more buying power and higher living standards, at least in the short run. Neomercantilists take the opposite view, that an undervalued currency can be an important source of national wealth and power as it encourages exports and discourages imports.

How does a currency's value affect consumer prices and national wealth? Let's say you are shopping for a family car and you find that both a Ford and a Volkswagen offer you all the features you desire. And let's say that the Ford costs $10,000 in the United States and the Volkswagen 10,000 deutsche marks in Germany. If one U.S. dollar equals one deutsche mark and the transportation and insurance costs of importing the Volkswagen are not included in the final price, then it would cost $10,000 when sold in the United States. You might well buy either car, because their quality and cost is the same. The same would be true for a German consumer, because the Ford would cost 10,000 deutsche marks.

trickle-up economics the idea that if a government reduces taxes or increases benefits to the poor, they will spend, invest, and/or save their additional money, which will stimulate the economy and thus create more jobs and wealth; in theory, this wealth will ultimately trickle up to the middle and upper classes.

Part 5   Geoeconomic Conflict and Cooperation Within the Industrialized World

But what if one dollar equals two deutsche marks? Then the American consumer has twice as much buying power for German goods, and the German consumer half as much buying power for American goods. You would definitely buy the Volkswagen, because it would be priced $5,000 in the United States. Your German counterpart would also buy the Volkswagen because the Ford's price would double to 20,000 deutsche marks. You and other American consumers would gain a tremendous savings in the short term, and Ford, other American industries, and the entire economy suffer a loss to their German counterparts. Over the long term, the American consumers' initial savings may well disappear as economic growth slows, jobs are lost or pay less, lower government revenue may be made up in higher taxes, and so on—unless, of course, you happen to be employed by or own a company that imports German products. The German consumer neither gains nor loses directly, but because Germany's economy will grow faster, its consumer will enjoy more wealth over the long term.

What determines the value of a nation's currency? Many forces do, but the most important is the relative demand and supply of that currency. Governments can manipulate a currency supply in various ways. Japan provides a good case study of how governments undervalue their currencies. After currencies began to float in 1973, the Bank of Japan bought dollars on international currency markets that increased the dollar's demand and thus its value. Meanwhile Tokyo limited the amount of Japanese trade that was denominated in yen, thus restricting the appeal to and demand for yen by international currency traders. Tokyo also encouraged Japanese firms to invest overseas while restricting foreign investments in Japan. Japanese firms invariably convert their yen into dollars when investing overseas, thus increasing international demand for dollars. Because foreign investments in Japan are limited, demand for yen is weak and the yen is thus undervalued. Whereas Tokyo pursues policies that undervalue the yen, Washington usually follows policies that overvalue the dollar. High interest rates and open financial markets attract foreign investors to the United States, which means more demand and thus a higher value for the dollar.

Direct government intervention in international currency markets is increasingly ineffective, because the amount of private trading outweighs international trading by a factor of over 30 to one. By the late 1990s, $1.5 trillion daily changed hands across international borders, an amount that surpassed the value of America's 1998 GNP $7.922 trillion in just one week! Governments can, however, affect the psychology of markets and thus the relative value of currencies. In September 1985, the *Plaza Accord* among the United States, Japan, Germany, France, and Great Britain (the Group of Five) sought to devalue the dollar by intervening in international currency markets. The amount they traded was actually quite small, but the fact that they were working together to sell dollars and buy other currencies created a bandwagon effect. Other governments and private traders dumped dollars before the price dropped, thus weakening demand for dollars and accelerating its fall. Within two years, a dollar dropped in value from 265 yen to 125 yen.

Manipulating the market value of a currency can work only in a floating system where currency values are shaped by supply and demand. In a fixed currency system a currency's value is determined by government fiat. But countries with fixed rates usually have black markets where that currency is unofficially traded. Why do black markets flourish in fixed systems? Because the fixed price usually does not reflect the economy's actual value. If the currency appears to be undervalued, traders will pay more for so-called hard currencies such as the dollar.

INDUSTRIAL POLICIES

Alexander Hamilton, America's first treasury secretary, recognized long ago that "not only the wealth but the independence and security of a country appear to be materially connected to the prosperity of manufacturers." He advocated government policies to nurture American industries, including tax cuts, infrastructure development, subsidies, and import protection.[18] Hamilton was clearly a man ahead of his time, especially in the United States, whose Congress rejected that strategy. Today Hamilton's policies would be described as neomercantilist policies designed to boost the economy's strategic manufacturing, technological, and financial sectors.

Every government either directly or indirectly picks economic winners and losers. This process is called "industrial policy" and involves any government initiatives "that will improve growth, productivity, and competitiveness," including "increasing the economy's supply potential (that is, increasing resources, and labor supply and capital stock), developing technology, fostering industrial development, and improving mobility and structural adaptation" or "a complex set of trade, financial, and fiscal policies, conducted within a political environment, with outcomes at variance from market solutions."[19] In some countries, such as France or Japan, the government creates five-year plans to develop strategic industries and technologies. In other countries, such as the United States, industrial winners and losers are determined by the relative political power balance they enjoy in Washington rather than their intrinsic value to the economy.

Like any policy, industrial policies can either succeed, fail, or have mixed results. A systematic comparison of the five leading industrial countries revealed that Japan was the only country whose industrial policies were consistently successful. Between 1967 and 1981, Japan gained market share in 13 of 20 industries targeted for development, remained the same in 3, and lost out in 4. The four losers were all chemical industries, which did fine until their "created" comparative advantage was undercut by the quadrupling of oil prices in 1973. In comparison, the four other key industrial countries—the United States, France, Germany, and Britain—stagnated or lost ground.[20]

TRADE POLICIES

There will always be a global trade equilibrium or a balance between the value of all exports and all imports. The trade surpluses of some countries must be offset by the trade deficits of all the other countries. A nation's international *trade account* includes the export and import of all material products. An international *payments account* includes the export and import value of manufactured goods, services (banking, insurance, shipping), direct foreign investments, portfolio investments (stocks, bonds, and so on), tourism, and government expenditures (foreign aid, military bases, embassies, and so on).

As we have seen, neomercantilists would argue that a state must maximize exports and minimize imports in order to boost national wealth and power, whereas liberal economists are either indifferent or would argue that a trade deficit is a sign of strength. Despite these philosophical differences, all governments manipulate trade, neomercantilist states with an overall strategic plan, liberal states largely through a political process.

Governments can use a variety of policies to affect the national trade and payments balances. Tariffs and quotas are the most obvious trade barriers. A tariff is a tax on imports that raises the prices for foreign goods and thus weakens the demand for them. *Quotas* allow only a certain amount of a product into the country. *Tariffs* are a more effective means of promoting national wealth than quotas, because they simultaneously boost government and domestic industry revenues and deplete foreign industry profits. Quotas, in contrast, do not provide any government revenues, and tend to encourage both foreign and domestic firms to raise prices at the expense of consumers.

Tariff and quotas have diminished steadily as a result of international agreements among members of the *General Agreement on Trade and Tariff (GATT)* members from the first negotiation round in the late 1940s to the eighth round in the 1990s. But as tariff and quota trade barriers declined, *nontariff barriers* have taken their place. *Voluntary export restraints (VERs)* or *orderly marketing agreements (OMAs)* are unofficial quotas that are often negotiated by governments when one country's exports capture an enormous market share in another country. About 10 percent of all global trade is currently subject to VERs and OMAs. These measures grew rapidly during the 1980s, as Japan's trade and payments surpluses soared and those of the United States and European Community plunged. Of the roughly 100 VERs or OMAs existing in the mid-1980s, the United States accounted for about half and the European Community for about one-third.[21] The poorer and weaker the country, the more easily an industrial country can force it to accept a VER. About 40 percent of all Third World exports to advanced industrial countries are restrained by nontariff barriers.[22] The *Multi-Fiber Agreement* involving 40 countries and strict quotas on textile trade is the world's largest VER. One agreement that emerged from GATT's Uruguay Round was to phase out the Multi-Fiber Agreement by the year 2002.

Red tape can also be an effective nontariff barrier. For example, in October 1982 Paris reacted to a VCR dumping campaign by Japanese consumer electronics producers by decreeing that henceforth all imports of that product had to pass through Poitiers, a small inland city in western France that (symbolically) was the site where Arab invaders were defeated in 732. The tiny customs office there simply lacked the resources to clear the hundreds of thousands of VCRs piling up. Japan's exporters filed a complaint with the European Community executive committee, which later ruled that France had violated the Brussels free trade rules. The European Community, however, later negotiated a VER with Japan, while Japanese corporations that had set up shop in Europe agreed to buy more local components. As a result of these initiatives, Europe's VCR industry was saved from sure extinction and wealth was circulated within the community that would otherwise have flowed to Japan.

There are significant pros and cons to a neomercantilist trade policy. Economists estimate that 20,000 more people are unemployed for every $1 billion of a nation's trade deficit. In 1998, the United States suffered a trade deficit of $190 billion, which meant that 3,800,000 more people were unemployed and economic growth much lower than would have been the case with a trade equilibrium. Paul Krugman has calculated the costs of a trade war between the United States, the European Community, and Japan in which 100 percent tariff barriers are raised and import levels plunge to half. Although liberals would predict a calamity, Krugman argues that the actual result would only be an average 2.5 percent decrease in income for these countries, a rate equal to a one percent increase in the

General Agreement on Trade and Tariffs (GATT) created in 1947 by 23 countries as a forum for member negotiation of the reduction of trade barriers. There have been eight GATT negotiation rounds since its founding.

A Bad Marriage? Japan in Sickness and in Health

The American and Japanese economies are interdependent. Is this economic marriage healthy for the United States? What are the costs and benefits of America's relationship with Japan?

Japan enjoys huge trade surpluses no matter whether its economy is growing or stagnating. Japan's economy annually grew 10 percent from 1950 to 1973, 4.5 percent from then until 1989, and only 1 percent thereafter. Japan won its first trade surplus in 1965 and has enjoyed huge surpluses ever since.

Why does Japan export so much and import so little? A combination of Japanese dumping, trade barriers, and a chronically undervalued yen explain that phenomena. Walls of subtle but potent trade barriers limit the volume and raise the costs for imports, thus gutting their competitive advantage. With windfall profits at home, Japan's corporate giants can afford to dump their products at a loss in foreign markets and drive their rivals into bankruptcy. Having conquered the market, the Japanese firms then raise prices to recoup earlier losses. An undervalued yen makes Japanese exports cheaper and foreign imports more expensive. That is the essence of Japanese neomercantilism.

That is bad news for all countries that bear the brunt of Japanese neomercantilism. If the economists are correct and a country losses 20,000 jobs for every billion dollars of its trade deficit, the United States suffered 1.2 million less jobs from its $60 billion trade deficit with Japan in 1998. That is an economic blow to America. But the trade deficits of poorer countries with Japan are economic disasters. Their industries are locked into vicious cycles of ever less investment, production, sales, and profit until they either go bankrupt or are bought out by their Japanese or other foreign rivals. Aggression is not just a geopolitical phenomena.

unemployment rate. The reason for this mild result is that imports would eventually be replaced with domestically produced alternatives that would contribute to that country's economic growth.[23] Yet protectionism can be expensive; by one estimate, U.S. trade barriers "were costing American consumers $80 billion a year—equal to more than $1,200 per family."[24]

The net effects of protection can either enhance or impede that nation's development. It all depends on whether or not government policies use that protection to promote strategic industries, technologies, and exports. If they do, as in Japan and *newly industrializing countries (NICs)* such as South Korea, Taiwan, and Singapore, the economy strengthens. If they do not, as in most countries, the economy stagnates as consumers suffer from higher prices and scarce resources are diverted to inefficient, declining economic sectors.

Conclusion

Political economist Charles Linblom captured well the reality of the relationship between economics and politics: "Except for the distinction between despotic and libertarian governments, the greatest difference between one government and another is the extent to which market replaces government and government replaces market."[25] Every economy thus is mixed; governments and markets interact in both the most state-controlled and laissez-faire of systems, albeit in vastly different ways and degrees. If capital is the material, financial, and human means of production, then every system is capitalist.

Most states recognize economic development as a national interest. Traditionally, this meant that a government should maximize its economic self-sufficiency and promote agriculture, mining, and other industries. In those days a trade surplus and the accumulation of gold were the primary measure of a nation's economic security. Today, the creation, distribution, and securing of national wealth in the interdependent world economy is more complex, and states differ greatly in the means by which they accomplish this.

All the theories and policies we have examined have involved a debate over the state's proper role in a nation's development. Of all these perspectives, regulatory and social market orientations provide the most extreme positions. Regulators maintain that "government is not the solution, it is the problem." Thus the state's role should be the minimal measures necessary to help markets become as free as possible. Social market adherents scoff at such notions as the "magic of the marketplace" and "the less government, the better." More, not less, government is needed to overcome entrenched poverty, inequality, and a host of other socioeconomic ills. In a truly just democratic system, the state should provide citizens with cradle-to-grave protection.

Neomercantilists reject both the regulatory and social market visions as completely unrealistic. To say that the state should do everything or nothing, they argue, is absurd. Instead, the state's role should be to maximize the creation and distribution of wealth, by whatever means possible. The means by which a state aids development will inevitably vary considerably from one country to the next, given their vastly different needs, resources, cultures, political systems, and aspirations. The means may vary just as greatly within a country as it develops and its needs, resources, and aspirations change.

America's laissez-faire traditions are the exception in a world in which states have traditionally guided economics, often heavy-handedly. Both neomercantilist and welfare state adherents argue that "classical laissez-faire liberalism may be a wasteful, experimental approach to economic problem-solving in a technocratic global economy with resource scarcity and payoffs for tightly structured teamwork."[26]

Why do states have the economic orientations they do? Among the industrial countries, there is a clear distinction in the state's role between early and late industrializers. Great Britain and the United States were *early industrializers,* and the state played a secondary role in each country's development. One reason was that in those days industrial competition between and within countries was limited, and thus there was less political pressure by industrialists on the state for protection and guidance. A liberal political and commercial culture in both countries was perhaps equally important. In relatively *late industrializers* such as Japan and Germany, the state took a much more active role in guiding development through protectionism and investing in strategic industries. The strong statist tradition of both Japan and Germany was also an important reason. More recently, the NICs of East Asia—South Korea, Taiwan, Singapore, Thailand, and Malaysia—have all pursued variations of Japan's development strategy.

Which strategy is the best means for maximizing economic development and national security? Historically each strategy has chalked up its share of successes and shortcomings. And it must be remembered that every country's policies are shaped by a mix of all three strategies, with usually one dominant.

Study Questions

1. What are the major characteristics of regulatory, developmental, and social market systems? What are their major positive and negative aspects?

2. List the major tools of macroeconomic policies.

3. List the major tools of industrial policies.

4. List the major tools of trade policies.

5. Why do states have the economic orientations they do?

6. Do some economic policies work better or worse during one period in a country's history? If so why? If not, why not?

7. Explain why some liberal democratic countries are wealthier than others.

8. What are the usual results when states allow market Darwinism or a pure free market to exist?

9. Who wins and who loses when one state practices liberal and another state neomercantilist policies? Explain.

10. Do sales of a billion dollars worth of potato chips have the same impact on the economy as sales of a billion dollars worth of computer chips? Explain.

11. If the United States, European Union, and Japan have industrial economies based on cutting-edge technology, why do conflicts over agricultural issues take up so many negotiations among them?

12. Which among the following three should prevail in world trade: (1) free trade ideals; (2) national laws protecting the environment, food safety, and labor standards; or (3) powerful corporations and industries demanding protection from foreign dumping, import barriers, and subsidies to their industries? Support your answer.

InfoTrac College Edition Sources

Using the Subject Guide, enter the search terms *Ronald Reagan, commercial policy, Organization of Petroleum Exporting Countries, monetary policy,* and/or *comparative advantage*.

"Advanced Economics: General Governmental Structural Balances [1]."
"Advanced Economics: Export Volumes, Import Volumes, and Terms of Trade."
Caballero, Ricardo J. "Sunk Investments, the Churn, and Macroeconomics."
Caballero, Ricardo J., and Mohamad L. Hammour. "The Macroeconomics of Specificity."
Cunningham, Richard O., and LaRocca, Anthony J. "Harmonization of Competition Policies in a Regional Economic Integration."
"Developing Countries: Broad Money Aggregates."
Hanson, Brian T. "What Happened to Fortress Europe? External Trade Policy Liberalization in the European Union."

Harcourt, G. C. "Political Economy, Politics and Religion: Intertwined and Indissoluble Passions."

Keating, John K. "Intermediate Monetary Targets and Macroeconomic Fluctuation."

Rosenberg, Alexander. "Economic Theory as Political Philosophy."

On *the* Web

http://www.opec.org/
The official site of OPEC

http://www.iie.com/
Website of the Institute of International Economics

http://www.occd.org/
Organization for Economic Cooperation and Development

Contents

Chapter 13 *The* Politics *of* Interdependence Among *the* Democratic Industrial Countries

Key Concepts and Terms

With modernization, all the world's countries and individuals, to varying degrees, are drawn ever more closely into an increasingly complex economic, political, technological, ethical, communications, transportation, and cultural web, a process popularly known as *globalization*.[1] The more wealthy a country or individual, the greater its interdependence with all others. Although accounting for only 20 percent of the world's population, the wealthy countries account for 80 percent of global GNP and 60 percent of its trade. About three-quarters of the advanced industrial states' trade and investments are with each other. The advanced countries are not only rich relative to the other countries, but that wealth is relatively equitably distributed so that at least 70 percent of each country's population is in the middle socioeconomic class. Interdependence is perhaps most evident in trade. An American middle-class home may include a German car with an engine that was assembled in Mexico, a Japanese stereo system with components made in Malaysia, clothing from China, Italian shoes, a shingle roof from Canadian timber, and so on. How many foreign goods can you find in your home?

Interdependence can have drawbacks. The greater the interdependence, the greater the vulnerability of nations and individuals to events taking place around the globe. A recession in the European Union or a stock market crash in the Far East can mean less demand for American goods, and thus an economic slowdown for the nation and lost jobs for many individuals. Likewise, foreign competition can bankrupt domestic firms and throw people out of work. Interdependence and economic conflict among nations increase in lockstep, as governments charge that its national firms and economy are disadvantaged by the state and corporate practices of other nations.

Yet globalization both increases and softens international conflict. The greater the interdependence between two countries and the more symmetric their development levels, economic sizes, and types of trade, investment, financial, cultural, and travel ties, the less likely that any nation would consider severing its foreign economic relations, let alone go to war, over a clash of interests. They simply need each other too much.

Hegemonic stability theory seeks to analyze relations among advanced industrial countries.[2] Adherents argue that the global economy needs a leader or *hegemon* that can manage or stabilize relations and supply the system with capital, markets, technology, and military security. Britain performed this hegemonic role in the 19th century, and the United States has done so since 1944. A hegemon is not just the world's most powerful state; it is a state dedicated to creating and developing a global free trade system. It does so first by opening its own markets to foreign goods and services and encouraging others to do the same. Hegemons can also strengthen the global economy by leading the creation of regimes, or "principles, norms, and decision-making procedures around which actor expectations converge."[3] For example, the United States led the creation of three regimes that have formed the superstructure of the global economy—the IMF, the World Bank, and GATT (or WTO) since 1994. Without hegemonic leadership, protectionist forces can deflate the global economy, leaving everyone worse off. The inability of Great Britain and unwillingness of the United States to lead the global economy during the 1920s led to economic depression and economic nationalism in the 1930s.

The same forces that allow a nation to become the global political economy's hegemon inevitably undermine that power. Great Britain in the early 20th century and the United States in the late 20th century had become exhausted from the economic and military costs of maintaining the system, and thus declined in

hegemon the number one state in the global system; the hegemon uses its power to shape international relations according to its interests and values.

relative power as other states surged ahead dynamically in manufacturing, technology, and finance. Both Britain and the United States had difficulties getting their allies to *share burdens*. A major reason for hegemon exhaustion is the problem of *free riders* or countries that enjoy the benefits of the open global system while limiting access to their own markets and contributing miserly aid or defense to help maintain the system. The United States free-rode on Britain's hegemony just as Japan has free-ridden on America's hegemony.

Henry Kissinger once wrote that the "biggest challenge to statesmen is to resolve the discordance between the international economy and the political system based on the nation-state. . . . The world needs new arrangements."[4] This chapter analyzes the geoeconomic conflict and cooperation between the advanced industrial nations in an increasingly interdependent world, and their attempts to resolve the conundrum that Kissinger identified. The chapter first recounts the major steps in the global economy's evolution, emphasizing developments from the 1930s through today. It compares the political economic orientations and strategies of the three major democratic industrial powers: the United States, the European Union, and Japan. Finally, it analyzes some of the major geoeconomic disputes among the geoeconomic superpowers.

Evolution *of the* Global Economy

The first strands of what would become a global political economy were knit in the mid-15th century when Portuguese caravels attempted to sail to the earth's far ends. From these first voyages until the mid-19th century, mercantilism and imperialism shaped global geoeconomic and geopolitical relations. During these 400 years, powerful nation-states emerged, one by one, from the political economic feudalism that had characterized Europe for the previous millennium. They derived their power from achieving a virtuous cycle of political and economic forces. The creation of professional armies, navies, and bureaucracies enabled those states to conquer and rule first outlying provinces, then adjacent territories of other princes, and finally overseas lands. But those institutions and conquests would not have been possible without the money to finance them, which was obtained from nurturing domestic industries, gathering taxes more efficiently, and economically exploiting new conquests.

Essential to the creation of wealth was the policy of *mercantilism*—maximizing the nation's exports through state-licensed monopolies and subsidies, and minimizing imports through high trade barriers. The idea was to gain a continual trade surplus and thus a steady influx of gold into the coffers of the state and domestic businesses. What did the state do with its surplus? Much was invested in a military to defend or expand the state's territory and interests, or into industries that would further increase the state's power and wealth. Overseas colonies enlarged the state's raw material and market resource base, enabling entrepreneurs to enjoy large-scale production and profits. The goal was autarchy or self-sufficiency. The result was not a unified global political economy, but one in which a half-dozen imperial systems existed alongside each other with minimal trade and frequent wars among them.

There was also sometimes a discrepancy between a state's power globally and within Europe. Some of the most powerful states in the global political economy—Spain, Portugal, and Holland—were secondary powers in Europe. Three of the most powerful states in the European system—Austria, Prussia, and Russia, along with smaller princedoms in central Europe and Italy—had no significant role in the global political economy.

This fragmented global political economy began to unite slowly during the 19th century when the world's greatest industrial and sea power, Britain, first began to use its hegemony to champion *economic liberalism*. Liberal political economic theorists such as Adam Smith, David Ricardo, and John Stuart Mill had been advocating liberalism for several generations, and their voices were joined by the new class of merchant and industrial leaders. By the 1830s, the new industrial interests had displaced the old agrarian interests in Parliament, and began dismantling Great Britain's import barriers and encouraging foreign powers to do the same. Although Britain's barriers fell rapidly, it was much more difficult to convince the other Europeans to follow suit. The other great and minor powers only slowly and partially abandoned the mercantilist policies that had enabled them to industrialize, export, and garner wealth from others.

Britain had more success in using "gunboat diplomacy" to force non-European states such as Turkey, China, Thailand, and Argentina, among others, to open their markets to British goods. More often than not, the result of this forced "free" trade was the destruction of domestic industries in those states as cheap mass-produced British textiles and other goods swamped those markets. Although nominally independent, these states became increasingly poorer and dependent on British goods and protection.

Other foreign lands suffered even worse fates. Industrial advances such as the steamship, telegraph, fast-firing rifles and cannon, and medicines that treated tropical diseases enabled most of the European powers, Japan, and the United States to conquer overseas empires. By the early 20th century, most of Africa and Asia had succumbed to Western imperialism. Despite the rapid rise of a half-dozen imperial rivals, Britain remained the world's leading global power or hegemon, supplying finance, products, technologies, and diplomacy to an increasingly interdependent global political economy. British hegemony, however, was destroyed in the trenches of World War I, and from then until World War II no nation or nations attempted to manage the global political economy and wave the free trade banner.

Although by the early 20th century, the United States was clearly the world's greatest industrial power, Washington refused to assume the role of hegemon.[5] At the Versailles peace conference ending World War I, President Wilson did attempt to create a League of Nations designed to settle international disputes, but the Senate later rejected the treaty that would have made the United States a member. Even more isolationist was Congress's 1930 *Smoot-Hawley Act*, which raised tariffs 50 percent during the Great Depression. The law was designed to help America's industries by deterring cheaper imports. But other countries also raised their tariffs and devalued their currencies, and the result was a trade war that deepened the global depression and made everyone worse off.[6]

Washington's policies toward the global economy shifted with the 1933 inauguration of the Roosevelt administration, which based its policies on the classic liberal belief that the greater the free trade and interdependence among states, the lower the likelihood of war. Writing amid the trade and military wars of the 1930s, Secretary of State Cordell Hull clearly articulated this view: "Unhampered trade dovetailed with peace; high tariffs, trade barriers, and unfair economic competition, with war . . . if we could get a freer flow of trade—freer in the sense of fewer discriminations and obstructions—so that one country would not be deadly jealous of another and the living standards of all countries might rise, thereby eliminating the economic dissatisfaction that breeds war, we might have a reasonable chance of lasting peace."[7]

Congress went along with this new approach. In 1934, it passed the *Reciprocal Trade Act,* which authorized the president to negotiate trade treaties with other countries. But the Roosevelt administration's domestic and foreign economic initiatives were no panacea—the United States remained mired in depression. America's economy was locked in a vicious economic cycle—there was not enough consumer buying power to demand more goods and not enough finance available to producers to supply more goods.

World War II was the catalyst that broke this vicious economic cycle trapping the United States and global economy. Government expenditures for the war effort stimulated production, new jobs, and wealth. The United States was converted from economic depression to rapid growth and full employment. During World War II, the United States asserted leadership over both the military effort against the Axis countries and attempts to create a liberal global political economy.

The United States could easily afford the burdens of global leadership. American wealth and power grew enormously during World War II. Even in 1938 the United States had 54 percent of the world's gold and financial reserves, compared with 11 percent each for France and Great Britain. Then from 1939 to 1945 America's GNP increased from $88.6 billion to $135 billion, and its gold reserves of $20 billion were two-thirds and its industrial output was half the world total. Fortunately, America's leaders mustered the will to match their nation's capacity to lead the world economy's revival.

Washington's most important initiative occurred in July 1944, when it invited representatives of 44 countries to meet at Bretton Woods, New Hampshire, to create a new global economy. Diplomats at the *Bretton Woods conference* signed agreements designed to end the trade barriers and competitive currency devaluations that had devastated the global political economy throughout the 1930s and contributed to the rise of fascism and imperialism in Japan, Germany, and Italy. Henceforth, there would be a *fixed currency* system in which each currency would be tied to the dollar, which in turn would be tied to gold at a value of $32 an ounce. At that time the United States owned 70 percent of the world's official gold reserves. Currency rates were allowed to fluctuate no more than one percent, plus or minus, of the parity or fixed rate. Countries that earned dollars from trade could, if they wished, redeem them with gold. This fixed gold system would eliminate the problem of competitive currency devaluations.

But the architects of the system recognized that a fixed currency system was not enough. Every advanced industrial country except the United States had been devastated by war and had to be reconstructed before world trade could revive. To assist reconstruction, the Bretton Woods participants agreed to create an *International Bank for Reconstruction and Development (IBRD,* or World Bank), which would extend low-interest loans to countries. In addition, the *International Monetary Fund (IMF)* was created to lend money to countries suffering trade deficits. The money would be invested in infrastructure and industries that would allow greater competitiveness and exports, thus eventually eliminating the trade deficit. The IMF worked like a bank. Countries could join the IMF by depositing money. Then, when that country needed money it could borrow up to 125 percent of its deposit for up to 18 months (in special cases, five years). The original membership contributions to the IMF were $8.8 billion.

Negotiations began in 1946 for the creation of an *International Trade Organization (ITO)* that would help create and maintain a global free trade system. In 1947, the Havana Charter was signed, creating the ITO. The Truman administration, however, refused to submit the treaty to the Senate for ratification, fearing that the combination of protectionists who felt that the treaty went too far, and liberals who felt it did not go far enough, made its passage unlikely.

In the ITO's place, the United States and other countries used the General Agreement on Trade and Tariffs (GATT), which had been created in 1947 by 23 countries, as a forum in which participants would negotiate tariff and other trade barrier cuts. The GATT is based on the *most favored nation (MFN)* principle, in which if one state gives an advantage to another country it must give that same advantage to all other GATT members. This multilateralism was deemed superior to the older bilateral method of conducting trade agreements.

most favored nation (MFN) clause the **GATT** principle under which a member that gives a trade advantage to another member must give the same advantage to all members.

Yet despite these new international organizations, the global political economy did not revive. Western Europe and Japan were stalled in a vicious development cycle. The war had devastated those countries economically, politically, and psychologically, and their economies remained stagnant. They were dependent on the United States for vital imports of energy, food, machinery, medicine, vehicles, and hundreds of other products to revive their economies, but had no money to pay for them. The result was a *dollar gap.* Thus the world economy remained stagnant, and by 1947 many feared it would slide into another depression, with its accompanying political chaos and perhaps even renewed aggression.

The cold war between the United States and Soviet Union proved the catalyst for overcoming the dollar gap. In 1947, the Truman administration announced its containment policy, whereby Soviet and communist advances could be checked by rebuilding Europe and Japan through massive aid, and helping any government threatened by a communist rebellion. From 1947 through 1952, Washington poured $17 billion of grants into 16 western European countries and $2.2 billion into Japan, and expended billions of dollars more by deploying its troops in those lands. Meanwhile, Washington tolerated European and Japanese protectionism, which allowed industries in those countries to resume production, exports, and the creation of wealth. With access to massive American aid and markets, Japan and the Western European countries rapidly reconstructed and developed their economies. Despite or perhaps because of the cold war, the global economy grew quickly throughout the 1950s and 1960s.

By the late 1950s, the dollar gap had become a *dollar glut.* The United States continued to send far more dollars into the global economy than it took back, thus suffering continuous balance-of-payments deficits. By 1959, the European and Japanese holdings of U.S. dollars was $19.4 billion, slightly less than the U.S. gold reserves of $19.5 billion. New gold could not be produced fast enough to keep up with the expansion of dollars. The following year, the amount of dollars in foreign hands exceeded U.S. gold reserves, a problem known as the *dollar overhang,* and this deficit deepened each year thereafter.

The result was a deepening crisis of confidence in the dollar's ability to support the global economy. If the Europeans and Japanese decided to buy American gold with their dollars, both the U.S. gold reserve and foundation for the fixed currency system would be wiped out. Starting in 1960 there were minor runs by speculators on America's gold reserves, but no government had yet challenged the system, because its collapse would hurt everyone. As long as the gold/dollar ratio remained constant and dollars could be redeemed in gold, countries were not hurt by holding dollars. In fact, most states preferred to hold dollars rather than gold because dollars earned interest and were "liquid," or easily used for transactions. And no state wanted to set off a run on America's gold reserves that would destroy the Bretton Woods system.

However, foreign states did complain that the United States could continually run deficits without taking the type of strict deflationary policies—cutting back government expenditures, devaluing the currency, and so on—that any other country would have to follow if it persistently had a payments deficit. More important for some countries was the fact that America's payments deficit was largely the result of its vast overseas military and aid commitments. By holding rather than converting American dollars into gold, those governments were financially supporting American foreign policy, including its Vietnam War, web of overseas bases, and support for a range of brutal dictators such as Somoza of Nicaragua, Thieu of South Vietnam, and Rhee of South Korea, to name a few.

French President Charles de Gaulle did not feel constrained by these restrictions and throughout the 1960s demanded U.S. gold for dollars. De Gaulle's challenge to the Bretton Woods system was part of his systematic attempt to rebuild French prestige and power while simultaneously undermining that of the United States. He condemned America's war in Vietnam, tested an atomic bomb in 1964, rapidly built up a French *force de frappe* (nuclear strike force), and withdrew France from NATO's military command in 1966, although it remained a member.

The *Group of Ten*, composed of the leading industrial nations—the United States, Great Britain, France, Germany, Japan, Italy, Canada, Sweden, Switzerland, the Netherlands, and Belgium—met throughout the 1960s to manage the dollar crisis by intervening in currency markets to maintain prices. The dollar overhang problem could have been addressed by increasing the gold's value to dollars, but this would have simultaneously devalued the dollars being held. Instead, in 1968 they created a two-tier system in which gold prices could fluctuate in a free market and would remain fixed in a government system. In 1969, the Group of Ten created *special drawing rights (SDRs)*, an artificial currency that could be used instead of the dollar to settle international accounts. Yet only $6 billion of SDRs were created that year, whereas over $100 billion in currency circulated throughout the global system.

Meanwhile, Washington tried to improve its balance of payments by trying to stimulate exports and inhibit American foreign investments. But any gains were wiped out by the tens of billions of dollars sent overseas to finance the Vietnam War. President Johnson's refusal to raise taxes to pay for both his Great Society set of welfare programs and the Vietnam War caused high inflation that further eroded America's competitiveness. Another severe problem was the dollar's increased overvaluation throughout the 1960s, thus exacerbating America's growing payments deficits and, starting in 1971, trade deficits. The dollar became overvalued as European and Japanese growth in GNP and productivity exceeded those of the United States. The fixed exchange rates were not adjusted to reflect the steadily diminishing competitiveness of America's economy, thus making it even more difficult for American producers to compete abroad or at home.

In 1971, the United States suffered its first trade deficit since 1893, running up $2 billion in merchandise and $10.6 billion in payments deficits. Meanwhile, its gold reserves shrank to $10 billion and foreign holdings of dollars rose to over $80 billion. On August 15, 1971, President Nixon dealt with these interrelated problems by announcing two international policies—henceforth the dollar would no longer be converted into gold and there would be a temporary 10 percent surcharge added to existing U.S. tariffs. In December 1971, the leading industrial nations signed the *Smithsonian Accord,* in which the dollar was devalued 10 percent against the existing price of gold, other currencies were revalued against the dollar, and currencies could now float within a 2.5 percent margin of the fixed rate.

This *new economic policy* unraveled quickly. In June 1972, Britain and Ireland broke off from the fixed rate system and allowed their currencies to float on international markets. Other countries followed suit. America's trade and payments deficits continued to mount and were unaffected by another 10 percent dollar devaluation in February 1973. By March 1973, the fixed rate system was abandoned and a *floating currency* system adopted in which currency values were set by market forces rather than government intervention.

As if these currency and payments problems were not enough, in November 1973, the Organization of Petroleum Exporting Nations (OPEC) imposed strict production quotas, and OPEC's Arab members, known as the Organization of Arab Petroleum Exporting Countries (OAPEC) temporarily refused to send oil to the United States and Netherlands for supporting Israel in the Yom Kippur War in October. The result was that global oil prices quadrupled from $2.75 a barrel to $12 a barrel over the next several months, plunging the global economy into a severe recession and imposing low growth and high inflation for another decade. In 1974, OPEC's current account surplus rose from $1 billion to $70 billion, and in 1980, after oil prices doubled again from about $18 to $34 a barrel, the surplus rose to $114 billion. These high oil prices were the underlying cause for the Third World's growing debt burden, which reached crisis proportions in the 1980s.

The United States and other leading industrial nations dealt with these new challenges through several means. Starting in 1975, the leaders of the world's most powerful industrial nations, the *Group of Seven*—the United States, Japan, Great Britain, France, Germany, Italy, and Canada—began meeting annually to coordinate broad macroeconomic policies and deal with any crises. International organizations also attempted to deal with the global slowdown. In January 1976, the IMF amended its charter to allow SDRs to replace gold as the world economy's principal reserve asset. During the Tokyo Round of GATT (1973–1979), Washington achieved some success in negotiating the reduction of nontariff as well as tariff barriers. Along with reduced tariffs, the Tokyo Round succeeded in creating a Code on Subsidies and Countervailing Duties and a Code on Government Procurement, the first comprehensive attempts to deal with some nontariff barriers. Each code included rules, surveillance, and dispute mechanisms. Yet these codes are vaguely written and relatively easily evaded.

These efforts nibbled around the problem's edges, but did not address the global economy's central problem which was the rise in oil from $2.75 to $34 a barrel between 1973 and 1980, and the corresponding stagflation (slow growth and high prices). Market rather than government action alleviated the high energy price problem. The high prices encouraged consumers to invest in energy conservation and efficiency. Meanwhile, those countries with unexploited oil reserves could now afford to invest in production. Finally OPEC members began to cheat on their quotas to garner more revenue. The result was an oil glut by the mid-1980s that brought prices down to around $20 a barrel, which in "real prices" (adjusted for inflation) were actually cheaper than before 1973.

These gains for the global economy provided little relief for the United States, which by the mid-1980s was facing an ever deepening payments and trade deficit crisis. This crisis was largely the fault of misguided American policies. The Reagan administration had hoped that by following a supply-side policy of massive tax cuts the economy would grow and the government would later recoup earlier revenue losses as larger business and household incomes generated more taxes. But the Reagan White House also increased the federal budget, largely by nearly tripling defense spending. The annual budget deficit rose from an average $50 billion during the Carter administration to an average $200 billion during the Reagan years. In 1980, the federal debt was $970 billion; in 1988, it was $2.9 trillion!

Meanwhile, the Federal Reserve raised interest rates to cut inflation and encourage both domestic and foreign investors to lend money to the U.S. government to help pay for the rising budget deficit. Foreigners invested hundreds of billions of dollars in the United States, buying government bonds, playing financial markets, taking over U.S. companies or property, and starting new subsidiaries. When they invested in the United States, the foreigners exchanged their currency for dollars. As the foreign demand rose for a stable supply of dollars, the dollar's value soared. The result for the United States was an increasingly severe trade deficit and lower American economic growth.

The global economic power balance shifted dramatically. In 1985, the United States was transformed from being the world's greatest creditor country into the worst debtor nation, as the amount of foreign money invested in the United States exceeded that of American money flowing overseas by $112 billion. By 1987, America's global trade deficit peaked at $171 billion and its deficit with Japan at $59 billion. That same year, Japan enjoyed a trade surplus of $96.5 billion and Germany one of $70 billion. Japan took over America's role as the global creditor nation, amassing $241 billion in net external credit in 1987.

The United States was trapped in a vicious economic cycle composed of high interest rates, an overvalued dollar, deep trade and payments deficits, low economic growth, low government revenues, high government deficits and long-term debt, and high interest rates. During its first five years, the Reagan administration seemed indifferent to the worsening crisis, arguing that the "magic of the marketplace" would take care of everything. Treasury Secretary Don Regan further talked up the dollar's value, claiming that "a strong dollar represents a strong America."

In 1985, President Reagan reshuffled some of his advisers, making free market purist Don Regan his Chief of Staff and economic realist Jim Baker his Treasury Secretary. Baker immediately sought to devalue the dollar. At the September 1985 secret *Plaza Accord* of the *Group of Five*—the United States, Japan, Germany, France, and Great Britain—finance minister meeting, it was agreed that there should be a joint effort to devalue the dollar to restore equilibrium to the global system. Although the other states, particularly Japan, enjoyed an enormous transfer of wealth to their own economies as a result of the Reagan administration's inept policies, they realized that the United States could not continue to run huge budget, trade, and payments deficits indefinitely. The foreign debts had to be serviced, and the larger those debts, the less money the United States had available to invest in its own economy. The result would be an America in steady decline, ultimately dragging down the rest of the global economy with it. Agreeing to intervene in global currency markets by selling dollars and buying up other leading currencies, the Group of Five succeeded in devaluing the dollar, which fell most dramatically against the Japanese yen, from about 265 yen in 1985 to 125 yen in 1987. Satisfied with the devaluation, the Group of Seven met in February 1987 at the Louvre in Paris and announced that the dollar had fallen far enough.

This realignment clearly was not enough to address the deep problems within the United States and, by extension, the global economy. Over the short term, America's trade and payments deficits continued to mount because of the J-curve effect in which the deficit increases as the cost of imported goods already ordered rises. In October 1987, rumors that Japanese investors were going to stop buying U.S. treasury bonds sent the New York Stock Market into a free fall in which it lost 15 percent of its value. In December 1987, the Group of Seven met and agreed on further measures to stabilize exchange rates and stock markets.

Since then into the 1990s, the dollar's value has remained stable while the global economy has grown steadily. Despite all of America's economic problems, the dollar remains the most important reserve currency. Although the dollar is used to pay for about 65 percent of all international trade, deutsche marks account for about 12 percent, yen eight percent, and SDRs five percent. The global economy annually expands about two to three percentage points while global trade rises even faster, about five to seven percent a year. About three-quarters of all trade and investment flows among the democratic industrial countries rather than between them and the less developed countries.

American power, meanwhile, has revived. Policies determine a nation's fate. The *Reaganomics* policies of tax cuts, increased spending, and an overvalued dollar diminished American economic power by tripling the national debt and worsening the trade and payments deficits. President Clinton's policies of cutting spending, increasing revenues, stimulating industries and technologies, and forcing open foreign markets led to a renaissance of American economic power after its nadir during the 1980s. During the 1990s, America's GNP, industries, technologies, exports, productivity, and personal income for all economic classes soared, inflation and unemployment plummeted, the budget deficit was finally eliminated in 1998, and the nation's share of global GNP expanded from 21 percent in 1993 to 24 percent in 1998!

Yet there were problems. The trade and payments deficits remained high, though lower as a percentage of GNP than a decade earlier. Clinton failed to get Congress to reapprove the president's *fast-track powers* that bring trade treaties to a direct vote in both the Senate and House without being amended by special interest groups in the committees. Despite Clinton's efforts, few other industrial and developing nations were willing to open their markets as widely as America's. Trade squabbles erupted among the industrialized countries. The WTO's conference at Seattle in November 1999 was a disaster, as delegates deadlocked over measures that could further reduce trade and investment barriers while raising environmental and labor standards, and anti-WTO riots raged outside.

Those were relatively minor setbacks. If the United States remains committed to *Clintonomics*, the economy and personal incomes will continue to expand steadily and the entire national debt will be wiped out within a decade. Stimulated by America's revived dynamism, the global economy will surge into the 21st century, bringing increasing wealth, health, and opportunities to ever more people.

The Economic Superpowers

The United States continues to lead the global economy while the dollar underwrites most international trade. There is a relative power balance among the three geoeconomic superpowers, the 15-nation European Union with 25 percent of global GNP, the United States with 24 percent, and Japan with 16 percent. Although the United States remains the world's largest economy, it continues to suffer from trade and payments deficits. In contrast, until recently Japan has a growth rate twice that of America's, runs immense trade and payments surpluses,

Clintonomics the economic policies of President Bill Clinton, which included transforming the soaring federal budget deficits of the 1980s into budget surpluses, reducing the personnel and expense of the federal government as a percentage of GNP, increasing subsidies to high technology industries, cutting taxes for the poor and lower middle class, raising taxes for the rich, and forcing other countries to reduce their trade and investment barriers, which led to the longest economic expansion in American history and reversed the steady decline in American economic power and in the incomes of middle- and lower-class Americans and the quadrupling of the national debt under Reaganomics.

Table 13.1 The Changing Face of American Corporate Power

Company	Market Capitalization (millions)	Percentage of Stock Market
1925		
AT&T	$1,318	4.82%
Standard Oil (NJ)	952	3.48
General Electric	784	2.87
U.S. Steel	691	2.53
General Motors	606	2.22
Standard Oil (CA)	589	2.15
F. W. Woolworth	549	2.01
Pennsylvania Railroad	516	2.00
New York Central Railroad	516	1.89
Southern Pacific Railroad	387	1.41
1950		
AT&T	$4,320	5.04%
General Motors	4,049	4.73
General Electric	3,782	4.41
Du Pont	2,778	3.24
Standard Oil (NJ)	1,587	1.85
Union Carbide	1,425	1.66
Standard Oil (CA)	1,317	1.54
Sears Roebuck	1,241	1.45
Texas Company	1,132	1.32
U.S. Steel	1,099	1.26

Source: Standard & Poor's DRI.

and competes fiercely with the United States in most industries and technologies. The European Union's economic bulk is clearly the largest, but its members continue to bicker over unification and lack economic dynamism and innovation compared with the United States and Japan. This section explores the different development paths that each of the three took to become an economic superpower.

THE UNITED STATES

The powers and duties of states often change over time to adapt to new political, economic, and social challenges and issues. The United States began in 1775 as a weak confederation of 13 sovereign states. That minimal state failed to deal with worsening socioeconomic problems. A political consensus arose to create a more powerful state. In 1787, the United States adopted its current constitution, which created a federal system. The power and duties of America's government have steadily risen since then to deal with new problems and public demands. Today the national government consumes nearly a quarter of GNP, and regulates directly or indirectly virtually all economic sectors.[8]

Table 13.1 *(continued)*

Company	Market Capitalization (millions)	Percentage of Stock Market
1975		
IBM	$33,289	5.06%
AT&T	28,289	4.39
Exxon	19,855	3.02
Eastman Kodak	17,148	2.61
General Motors	16,503	2.51
Sears Roebuck	10,189	1.55
Dow Chemical	8,491	1.29
General Electric	8,446	1.28
Procter & Gamble	7,341	1.12
Texaco	6,344	0.97
1999		
Microsoft	$584,692	3.93%
General Electric	496,564	3.28
Cisco Systems	341,053	2.25
Wal-Mart Stores	289,493	1.91
Exxon Mobil	286,013	1.89
Intel	274,171	1.81
Lucent Technologies	244,812	1.61
IBM	196,709	1.30
Citigroup	183,756	1.21
SBC Communications	175,260	1.16

The turning point from the government's largely passive to active role in managing the economy occurred in the early 1930s. America's stock market crash and the subsequent Great Depression discredited classical economic theory that asserted that markets should be self-regulating rather than government regulated. Unbridled speculation had created and then popped a huge speculative stock bubble. The resulting depression was deepened by President Hoover's classic liberal economic hands-off response. While the economy was sinking further into depression, Hoover actually called for federal spending cuts to balance the budget.

After Franklin Roosevelt became president in 1933, the government increasingly assumed more responsibility for managing the economy. In his first 100 days in office, Roosevelt pushed 15 bills through Congress that, by a variety of means, stimulated the economy with greater government spending and programs. This represented the first time the United States had systematically attempted to smooth out economic boom and bust cycles. During World War II, the government shifted its policy from stimulating specific economic sectors to direct management of the economy for the war and targeted strategic industries for development.

From World War II through today, the government has continued to target specific economic sectors for development with industrial policies. But instead of the rational, far-sighted policies of the war years, Washington now picks industrial winners and losers largely through a political process in which the most established industries pour money into the re-election funds of enough politicians until they are rewarded with a range of government subsidies, protection, and other advantages. The power of the agribusiness and textile lobbies have enabled them to receive vast government largesse and import protection. Other industries have been favored by being a part of the military-industrial complex. America's semiconductor, computer, aerospace, and microelectronics industries, to name some of the more prominent, were all shaped by Washington's military-industrial and technology policies.

Just as it initiated the process of industrial policies that has continued through today, the Roosevelt administration forged a consensus on the importance of international trade and prosperity for American prosperity, and the president's role in regulating it. The American Constitution grants the power of regulating trade to Congress. Since 1934, however, Congress has periodically allocated powers to the president to negotiate trade agreements. The greatest increase in presidential trade power occurred with the passage of the 1988 *Omnibus Trade Act*, which made it much easier for the president to retaliate against foreign dumping and other unfair practices that can harm America's economy. All the American presidents from Roosevelt to Clinton have recommitted the United States to the ideal if not practice of free trade. Like any country, the United States has industrial and trade policies designed to give its industries advantages over their foreign rivals. The difference is that most officials and politicians deny it and continue to champion liberal economic theory as the basis for America's economy.

America's traditional *free trade* liberalism has been criticized. Many argue that Washington's piecemeal and politically shaped industrial, technology, and trade policies are hurting the United States in an increasingly competitive, interdependent global economy. Martin and Susan Tolchin write that "none of America's major trading partners subscribe to the U.S. vision of free trade. None regard technology with the cavalier notion that ownership doesn't matter—unless they are the owners. Instead each nurtures technologies it deems vital to its economic competitiveness in the 21st century."[9]

The United States has attempted to increase its economic growth and bargaining power with other countries by forging a free trade association with its neighbors. In 1988, the United States and Canada signed a free trade agreement whereby they would eliminate tariffs and nontariff barriers toward most of each other's exports. In 1991, the United States, Mexico, and Canada began negotiations to create a *North American Free Trade Association (NAFTA)*, which that year unified 363 million consumers and $6.5 trillion in economic activities. A treaty was signed in May 1992, but most in Congress vowed to vote against it for fear that the United States would lose jobs to Mexico. During the 1992 campaign, candidate Bill Clinton supported Bush's treaty in principle but vowed to overcome its defects by negotiating labor and environmental side-agreements. In his first year as president, Clinton negotiated his promised agreements with Mexico and after a major push during the autumn to rally congressional support, succeeded in gaining NAFTA's ratification by November 20, 1993.

The United States had far more to gain from NAFTA than Mexico, whose trade and investment barriers were three or more times higher than those north of

North American Free Trade Association (NAFTA) a common market of the United States, Canada, and Mexico; the details are still being negotiated.

Too Little, Too Late?
America Blunts Japan's Steel Offensive

On June 11, 1999, six members of the U.S. International Trade Commission (ITC) ruled unanimously that punitive tariffs ranging from 18 percent to 67 percent would be imposed on imports of Japanese steel makers, with the penalties retroactive to February when the dumping reached its height. The Japanese dumping of hot-rolled carbon steel at below production costs over the previous year had severely damaged America's steel industry by destroying profits and tens of thousands of jobs. The ITC acted on a petition filed by the Commerce Department in response to bitter complaints from American steel makers of not only unfair Japanese trade tactics but dumping by Russia and Brazil as well. But Washington reached voluntary export restraint (VER) agreements with Moscow and Rio de Janeiro, so those countries evaded retaliation. Tokyo refused to negotiate. The tariffs will remain as long as five years.

Are the tariffs too little, too late? Will America's steel makers be able to recover their former dynamism, profits, and jobs, or did the Japanese dumping onslaught permanently weaken them? Will the punitive tariffs deter foreign dumping attacks on America in other industries?

---

the border. The United States has already gained from the closer ties. In 1986, the United States suffered a $5.7 billion trade deficit with Mexico. A 1987 trade agreement with Mexico nearly doubled bilateral trade and tripled American exports from $15 billion until the United States enjoyed a trade surplus of $5.4 billion and $41 billion in exports in 1992. America's trade surplus has translated into 350,000 net new jobs for the country. In 1992, 8.5 percent of total American exports went to Mexico, making that country America's third largest trade partner after Canada and Japan. The Economic Policy Institute, a Washington think tank, predicts that over the next decade NAFTA will create for the United States 325,000 new jobs in export industries and will lose 150,000 jobs in agriculture, textiles, and other labor-intensive industries. Thus, overall the United States will enjoy not only more but better paying jobs, because export-related jobs pay 17 percent more than non-export jobs.[10]

Corporations set up shop overseas for many reasons, including gaining access to restricted markets, raw materials, and technology, lower operating costs including cheap labor and weaker environmental standards, and/or access to government investment incentives. Red tape, poor infrastructure, political instability, corruption, and unskilled workers can inhibit foreign investments. American corporations that set up shop in Mexico will do so to take advantage of the $1.80-an-hour average wages there in contrast to the $14.77-an-hour average for American wages. Only 1 percent of production costs are related to environmental regulations, thus few firms would relocate to Mexico only because of its lax environmental protection. Jobs lost in the United States to Mexico would have disappeared even without NAFTA, because American corporations would have had to respond to the ever fiercer foreign competition by either investing overseas in cheap labor countries or declaring bankruptcy.

Recently the United States appeared to be moving toward even greater management of its economic development and trade relations. By the late 1980s, the notion of *fair trade* rather than *free trade* largely shaped American perceptions and policies. The 1992 election was clearly a choice between President Bush's "laissez-faire," then Governor Clinton's "plan," and Ross Perot's "bitter medicine" approaches to the economy. Clinton rejected the old dichotomy between free trade and protectionism, and said his policies would be based on a "third way" that would restore America's competitiveness. He won largely because a majority of Americans agreed that strong measures had to be taken, and a plurality thought Clinton's plan was the best of the three. As has been seen, Clintonomics largely succeeded in reviving American power, although trade and payments deficits persist. During the year 2000 elections, the presidential candidates differed on most issues but embraced the fair trade policy established by the Clinton administration.

JAPAN

No country has developed more successfully since 1945 than Japan, which surpassed the United States by most measurements during the 1980s before falling behind during the 1990s. Between 1950 and 1973, Japan's economy grew at an average annual rate of 10 percent, four times America's 2.5 percent rate; from 1974 through 1989, Japan's economy has grown at an average annual rate of 4.5 percent, more than twice America's 2.2 percent rate. Then, from 1989 through 1998, Japan's economy expanded only 1.3 percent a year, as that nation failed to revive from a collapse of its financial and real estate markets.

Overall, Japan's economy grew from 3 percent of global GNP in 1950 to peak at 18 percent in 1989, and then recede to 16 percent in 1998, while America's share shrank from 35 percent to its nadir of 21 percent in 1989 before expanding to 24 percent in 1998. Although the United States has suffered trade deficits since 1971, Japan has enjoyed trade surpluses since 1965. In 1998, Japan boasted a $107.434 billion surplus, whereas America wracked up a horrendous $261.509 billion deficit! Of Japan's $387.965 billion exports, 96 percent were manufactured goods, compared to only 65 percent of America's $682.977 billion exports during the same period. In 1985, Japan became the world's greatest net creditor country, whereas the United States plummeted, becoming the world's worst debtor. A 1992 U.S. Commerce Department report revealed that Japan was ahead in 10 of 12 technologies considered essential for an advanced economy in the 21st century, and neck-and-neck with the United States in the other two technologies.[11]

Japan has achieved this remarkable development by following rational policies designed to create, distribute, and secure wealth, and establishing the institutions to implement those policies. The Ministry of Finance (MOF) and Ministry of International Trade and Industry (MITI) shared the creation and implementation of most policies designed to systematically target and develop strategic industries and technologies within the context of five-year indicative plans. Other ministries such as those of Construction, Transportation, Posts and Telecommunications, Education, Justice, and so on have their own industries that they carefully nurture. Each industry, in turn, is organized into an industrial association and cooperates in both writing and implementing government policies through cartels, the diffusion of technology, import barriers, and export promotion.

Obtaining foreign technology has been a vital component of Japan's rise into an economic superpower. The 1949 Foreign Exchange Control Law and 1950 Foreign Investment Law gave Tokyo enormous powers to restrict foreign trade and investments. Unable to import to or invest in Japan because of government restrictions, foreign firms often simply licensed their advanced technology to their nascent Japanese rivals as the only way to make money there. Between 1950 and 1980, the Japanese spent about $10 billion buying or licensing over 30,000 foreign technologies. The total cost for the foreign companies to research and develop these technologies was anywhere from $500 billion to $1 trillion![12] Japanese firms used this technology to modernize their factories and mass-produce inexpensive products, which were then sold and often dumped at below production costs around the world to capture a large share of the market and drive their rivals out of business.

During the 1980s, as Japan caught up to the United States and Europe. Tokyo then embarked on a "leap-frog" or technology substitution strategy whereby it tried to jump far ahead of its competitors industrially and technologically. To do so, it has targeted a series of advanced technologies that have yet to be mastered, such as fifth- and sixth-generation computers, superconductors, virtual reality, and micromachines. Tokyo organizes consortia of private corporations to work together to develop these technologies and the hundreds of products they spawn. But the Japanese found that it is much tougher to create than to copy or lease technologies. They have failed to surpass the Americans and Europeans as they had hoped.

The importance of industrial policies has diminished as Japan's economy has grown more complex and powerful. Although MITI and other ministries continue to target industries and technologies for development, their ability to force recalcitrant firms to cooperate with their rivals has diminished as corporate financial power has grown. Tokyo has dismantled most of the more blatant trade and investment barriers, and its tariff rates are now lower than those of either the United States or European Community. Japan's markets, however, remain guarded by arrays of nontariff trade barriers.

As important as rational industrial, technology, and trade policies, were macroeconomic policies that maintained a high savings/investment ratio and undervalued yen. Although the household savings rate has fallen from about 34 percent of income in 1950 to 14 percent of income in 1998, the current rate is over five times higher than that of the United States. Tokyo traditionally encouraged high savings by limiting such government benefits as welfare, education, and social security, and keeping consumer prices high and credit limited. Consumers thus had to save a huge percentage of their income not only to educate their children and survive after retirement, but also, without access to credit, to pay for an automobile or home. Tokyo further limited the investment opportunities for savers by providing mostly bank or post office savings accounts that paid very low interest rates. Tokyo then channeled these vast savings—the Postal Savings Bank assets alone in 1998 were $2.1 trillion or 40 percent of all of Japan's banking assets and four times larger than the world's largest commercial bank—into cheap loans for strategic industries, which in turn invested the money into the most advanced production techniques and technologies.

Also vital to Japan's development was an undervalued yen. Originally set at 360 yen to a dollar in 1949, the yen became increasingly undervalued as Japan's economy expanded over the next 22 years. The yen remained undervalued even after Nixon forced the yen's revaluation to 308 to a dollar in December 1971, and the yen, like other currencies, began to float in 1973. Tokyo used a variety of means to maintain an undervalued yen. The Bank of Japan intervened in global currency markets to buy dollars and sell yen. The Finance Ministry continued to restrict foreign investments in Japan while allowing increased Japanese overseas investments, and similarly restricted the use of yen in trade, all in an attempt to limit demand for yen that would raise its value.

The dynamic core of Japan's economy are its six major industrial groups (*keiretsu*) whose combined economic activity accounts for 25 percent of GNP. Each keiretsu has a range of interrelated manufacturing firms in steel, petrochemicals, microelectronics, automobiles, mining and metal forging, shipbuilding, aerospace, and so on. These firms are largely financed by the keiretsu bank, trading firm, and insurance company. Each corporation within the keiretsu either wholly or partially owns scores of smaller subcontracting and distribution firms. About 70 percent of each keiretsu's stock is directly owned by other keiretsu members or affiliates. The Big Six own parts of each other. There are scores of smaller keiretsu. Washington and Brussels have complained for decades that the keiretsu discriminate against foreign firms and violate antitrust laws. But Tokyo refuses to break up such vital sources of Japan's power.

These institutions and policies were not created and implemented in a void. They would never have succeeded if the United States had not imposed revolutionary political and economic changes during its occupation of Japan (1945–1952). First, the United States pumped in $2.2 billion of humanitarian and development aid over seven years, and then contributed tens of billions of dollars more through the procurement policies of its military forces based in Japan and the region. The United States scrapped Japan's totalitarian political system and replaced it with a democratic constitution that guarantees the full spectrum of human rights. The Americans also pushed through land, labor, and industrial reforms that coopted the major reforms advocated by the socialist and communist parties, thus allowing the conservatives to establish political power, which they have held for all but nine months since 1945. In addition, the occupation authorities forced Tokyo to adhere to strict macroeconomic policies and set the yen at a rate whereby all of Japan's major industries could export successfully. The Americans created MITI and helped launch the industrial and technology policies that fueled Japan's economic development. Although America's defense burden averaged 6–7 percent of GNP, the United States allowed the Japanese to keep their defense spending at around 1 percent of GNP, which meant that the Japanese had five percentage points of GNP more to invest in far more productive consumer industries. The United States overcame the resistance of the Europeans to integrating Japan into the regional and global systems. Finally, the United States continues to keep its own markets largely wide open to Japanese goods while tolerating firmly closed Japanese trade and investment markets.

Successful development depends on the integration of traditional and modern values and institutions. Although Japan's contemporary political and economic system is superficially modern, it is built on traditional values and institutions. The Japanese have achieved a societal consensus over where and how they want their country to develop. No country has been more successful in creating, distributing, and securing the sources of wealth than Japan.

THE EUROPEAN UNION

The more economically, politically, and socially entangled states become with each other, the more inconceivable the use of force to solve differences. Federalism is a theory that recognizes the political and economic benefits of integration, and advocates uniting peoples, policies, and markets through a web of institutions.

Table 13.2 **EU Economic Power and Member Nations, 1999**

Members				
Germany	82.1	$1,779.5	$21,700	1.3%
France	59.0	1,371.4	23,300	2.3
Great Britain	59.1	1,307.8	22,100	1.5
Italy	56.7	1,235.2	21,800	1.2
Spain	39.2	679.6	17,400	3.4
Netherlands	15.8	367.4	23,200	2.9
Belgium	10.2	233.5	22,900	1.6
Sweden	8.9	192.0	21,500	2.0
Austria	8.1	185.0	22,700	1.9
Portugal	9.9	139.9	14,700	2.9
Greece	10.7	133.9	12,500	3.4
Denmark	5.4	128.9	24,100	1.1
Finland	5.2	114.2	22,100	3.7
Ireland	3.6	85.5	23,500	8.7
Luxembourg	0.4	16.6	38,700	3.1
Negotiating Membership				
Poland	38.6	$294.8	$7,600	3.8%
Czech Republic	10.3	99.2	9,600	−0.4
Hungary	10.2	80.9	7,900	3.8
Slovenia	2.0	27.9	14,200	2.0
Estonia	1.4	12.9	9,200	0.6
Cyprus	0.8	12.5	16,600	4.1
Applied for Membership				
Turkey	65.5	$427.2	$6,500	−1.7%
Romania	22.3	66.4	3,000	−2.1
Slovakia	5.4	45.5	8,400	1.6
Bulgaria	8.2	31.1	3,800	2.1
Latvia	2.4	15.7	6,700	0.6
Lithuania	3.6	14.5	4,000	−2.4
Malta	0.4	5.1	13,400	3.8

Source: Standard & Poor's DRI.

The *European Union (EU)* provides the most successful example of integration.[13] Federalists had advocated European unity throughout the early to mid-20th century, arguing that Europe's perennial problem of war could only be solved by dissolving the endlessly squabbling sovereign nations into one grand European state. This drive for European unity became increasingly powerful after World War II as Europeans feared the ultimate revival of German economic and military power. Rather than isolate Germany, the federalists proposed integrating Germany within

Europe's larger economy. With the cold war, Washington joined the integrationists, seeing an economically united Europe as the best bulwark against possible Soviet expansion.

There was perhaps no more fervent federalist than former French Foreign Minister Jean Monnet who argued,

> There will be no peace in Europe if countries build up their strength on the basis of national sovereignty.... The countries of Europe are too limited to assure their people the prosperity that modern times afford.... Larger markets are needed. Prosperity and social development are inconceivable unless the countries of Europe unite into a federation or a European entity which in turn creates a common economic union.[14]

Europe's integration has been accomplished in a series of stages. Monet advocated political and then economic union, but the opposite has occurred. In May 1950, France and West Germany announced that they were uniting their coal and steel industries to create economies of scale and alleviate tension between them. The following year in April 1951, six states—France, Italy, West Germany, the Netherlands, Belgium, and Luxembourg—signed the Paris Treaty, which created the *European Coal and Steel Community (ECSC)*. In 1957, the six states signed the Rome Treaty, which created the *European Economic Community (EEC)*, whose members pledged to gradually reduce their trade barriers toward each other and create common external tariff and nontariff barriers. They also signed a treaty in which they agreed to standardize and work jointly to develop their nuclear energy industry, an organization known as Euratom. In 1967, the EEC and Eurotom were merged into the *European Community (EC)*. The EC's membership expanded along with its economic integration: Britain, Ireland, and Denmark in 1973, Greece in 1981, Spain and Portugal in 1986, and Austria, Sweden, and Finland in 1994. In 1986, the 12 signed the Single European Act, whereby they pledged to remove all remaining trade barriers by December 31, 1992, and rename their association the European Union.

Creating a customs union was only the first step to economic union. The European Union could never be truly unified without a central bank and a common currency. The first significant step taken toward this goal occurred in December 1978 when the members created the European Monetary System (EMS), in which the currencies would be tied to each other with 2.5 percent fluctuation margins, the system would float against other currencies, and the system would be anchored by the creation of *European currency units (ECUs)*, the European equivalent of IMF SDRs. The German central bank and the deutsche mark have played a role similar to the role played by the Federal Reserve and the dollar for the global economy.

The second stage toward financial union was taken with the December 1991 Maastricht Treaty, by which the members promised to merge their national banks and currencies into one European central bank and currency by 1997 at the earliest and 1999 at the latest. Europeans were evenly divided over whether or not they supported this measure. Throughout the summer and fall of 1992, one by one, each member voted on the Maastricht Treaty, either through a parliament or a referendum. In June, Denmark voted down the treaty in a referendum, with 51 percent against. In September, in France the treaty barely passed ratification with a referendum in which 51 percent voted yes. Although 11 of the 12 EC members eventually voted for the treaty, the ratification had to be unanimous in

order for the treaty to take effect. Throughout 1993, the members renegotiated the treaty to make it universally acceptable. By autumn 1993, all the EU members had ratified the treaty, allowing financial union by 1999. On January 1, 1999, 11 of the 15 EU members joined their currencies and central banks; the other four have promised to join sometime during the first decade of the 21st century.

The European Union is governed by its *Commission* located in Brussels whose members are appointed by the member states. But the Commission receives broad directives from the decisions of the Council of government heads that meet annually to address issues. Unlike the Commission, the European Parliament located in Strasbourg, is popularly elected. The powers of its 626 members are advisory rather than legislative. The European Court of Justice serves as the union's supreme court and is located in Luxembourg. The union's bureaucracy has grown steadily in pace with its expanded responsibilities, from 1,000 in 1960 to 25,000 today. The European Union pays for its operation by receiving a portion of each member's value-added tax (VAT) or sales tax.

European Union policies largely reflect those of its member states. None of the European states has ever entirely abandoned the mercantilist outlook and policies of the early modern era. Europeans have always intervened far more in their respective economies than the Americans. The western European countries are to greatly varying degrees welfare states in which the government heavily subsidizes its citizens' health, education, income, and employment, as well as strategic industrial sectors.

Yet, unlike Japan, Brussels has no overall five-year development plans that target virtually every economic sector for government protection and nurturing. European industrial policy is actually a collection of policies for specific industries and technologies. The European Union's most important and controversial initiative is its *Common Agricultural Policy (CAP)*, which subsidizes agriculture under which the union's 12 million farmers received about $45 billion in various direct and indirect subsidies in 1998 alone, 65 percent of Brussels's $87 billion budget. As the continent's environmental problems worsen, the union has issued strict standards on water and air pollution, energy use, and waste disposal.

Brussels also supports an increasing range of industries and technologies to make Europe more competitive against its American, Japanese, and other foreign rivals. From the 1980s, Brussels has implemented high-technology policies such as the European Strategic Program for Research and Development (ESPRIT) and Research and Development in Advanced Communications Technology (RACE). Brussels has also helped raise $180 billion for the development of a unionwide high-speed train

Table 13.3 **EU Donors and Recipients**

Country	Net Contribution ecu bn	Net Contribution per Person ecu	Net Contribution per Person Rank	GDP ecu bn	GDP per Person ecu
Germany	10.0	121.6	2	1,910.3	23,225.5
Netherlands	2.4	152.9	1	334.5	21,316.6
Great Britain	2.3	38.9	4	1,248.7	21,102.9
Italy	1.3	22.6	6	1,049.0	18,209.0
Sweden	0.7	78.3	3	210.1	23,511.6
France	0.4	6.8	7	1,280.5	21,748.7
Austria	0.2	24.7	5	188.8	23,385.6
Finland	−0.1	−19.4	8	109.8	21,299.7
Denmark	−0.2	−37.8	9	149.9	28,293.7
Luxembourg	−0.8	−1,875.7	15	14.8	34,701.1
Belgium	−1.8	−176.3	11	221.0	21,649.7
Ireland	−2.3	−622.3	14	70.2	18,993.5
Portugal	−2.8	−283.2	12	89.4	9,043.1
Greece	−4.1	−387.9	13	104.6	9,895.9
Spain	−6.1	−154.9	10	492.2	12,501.6

Source: Word Bank 2000, Entering the 21st Century (New York: Oxford University Press, 2000), pp. 22–49.

Table 13.4 Neck and Neck: Airbus versus Boeing

The European Union's most successful industrial venture has been Airbus. Having received over $30 billion since its inception in the 1970s, Airbus rose steadily in global market share until it surpassed Boeing in the late 1990s both for the number of new airplanes ordered and for their value. In 1999, Airbus captured 55 percent of the large airliner market to Boeing's 45 percent share.

	1988 Orders	1998		1999		Backlog of Orders
		Orders	Value (in billions)	Orders	Value (in billions)	
Airbus	265	556	$39.0	476	$30.5	1,445
Boeing	788	648	$40.0	391	$28.3	1,512

Source: Center for Defense Information, 1999.

network known by its French initials, TGV (Train à Grande Vitesse). The union's role is to coordinate each member's contributions so that they adhere to the same construction, speed, and safety standards.

Brussels's macroeconomic policies have also been successful. It imposes strict fiscal and monetary discipline on its members whose budget deficits are not allowed to exceed 3 percent of GNP or inflation more than 1.5 percent above the average of the three lowest members' inflation rates. Since its creation in 1999, the Euro has become the most common currency after the dollar, and is now trading at nearly an equal value with the dollar.

There is no question that these integration, trade, industrial, technology, and macroeconomic policies have been successful. Between 1960 and 1986, intra –European-Community trade rose from 34.4 percent to 56.8 percent of its total trade, and its percentage of world trade rose from 24.5 percent to 38.8 percent. Europeans are far more wealthy and economically dynamic than if their respective countries had decided not to integrate. Yet despite these successes, there is a great debate among those who want to broaden the European Union by adding more members, those who want to deepen it by working toward a genuine federalism, and nationalists who want to opt out altogether.

European leaders are rethinking the concept of "subsidiarity" that appeared in the Maastricht Treaty. The concept is Europe's equivalent of American federalism, in which any powers not constitutionally given to the national government revert to state and local government. But about half of the European public and many of its leaders oppose the federal United States of Europe that subsidiarity implies. The close votes over ratification of the Maastricht Treaty reveal that many greatly fear they are giving away their national sovereignty and identity for rule by "Eurocrats" and perhaps domination by a unified Germany. Nonetheless the union continues to lumber forward into deeper and broader economic and political integration.

Conflicts *of* Interdependence

GATT AND WTO

The international organization dedicated to expanding and regulating international trade was known as the General Agreement on Trade and Tariffs (GATT) from 1947 until 1996 when it was renamed the *World Trade Organization (WTO)*. GATT largely

World Trade Organization (WTO) the successor to the **General Agreement on Trade and Tariffs (GATT);** empowered to judge trade cases and allow countries to impose sanctions on violators.

The *Price of* Beans:
Farm Welfare, Free Trade, *and* Uruguay

American and European farmers delayed the successful conclusion of GATT's Uruguay Round (1986–1992). Ironically, no industry is better protected among the democratic industrial countries than agriculture. Farmers comprise a small and diminishing percentage of population in all three economic superpowers—the United States, 2 percent; European Union, 5 percent; and Japan, 7 percent. But the political clout of farmers far exceeds their numbers. Although sparsely populated, farm districts are numerous and farmers are well organized. Over the decades the farm lobby in each of these states has been able to wring increased benefits from the system. The governments of the United States, the European Union and its members, and Japan all promote agriculture through a range of subsidies, import barriers, price supports, and infrastructure. The degree and type of protection offered, however, varies considerably among these states.

Some countries have a greater natural advantage in agriculture than others. During the Uruguay Round a coalition of 14 countries with a comparative advantage, including the United States, Canada, Australia, Argentina, and Hungary, made agriculture a key issue. Washington led the charge in addressing this issue by demanding that all countries completely dismantle their farm protection policies, and singled out the European Union for its huge subsidies.

Brussels's farm subsidies are larger than Washington's, and are the most important reason for the increasingly larger share that European farmers take in the global agricultural market. The European Union's share of the global grain market rose from 16 percent in 1982 to 21 percent in 1992, while America's share fell from 46 percent to 31 percent. During the same decade, the union's overall share of agricultural trade rose from 14 percent to 18 percent, while America's fell from 23 percent to 19 percent.[17]

Although Washington initially demanded complete elimination of farm supports, by late October 1992 its position had modified considerably. Now Washington demanded merely a 24 per-

cent reduction in the European Union's export subsidies over seven years. Brussels countered by offering an 18 percent reduction over six years or 21 percent over seven years. But Brussels asserted that it would have to be coupled to new taxes on imports of American corn gluten and the cancelation of the so-called Andriessen Understanding, under which it promised not to subsidize meat exports to Japan and other East Asian countries. In addition, Brussels asked Washington not to challenge as illegal the direct payments it now made to farmers instead of the previous price supports.

In early November the dispute narrowed to European Union subsidies for soybean and rapeseed products. Washington contended that the United States could sell another $1 billion worth of soybean products in Europe if the union rapeseed subsidies and barriers were dismantled, an action that would benefit America's 400,000 soybean farmers. Throughout October and early November, Washington made 11 proposals to resolve the issues and Brussels rejected them all. The last American proposal was for Brussels to

accomplished its mission. During its four decades, GATT's members engaged in eight extensive negotiation rounds that succeeded in gradually reducing tariffs for all its members, especially the industrialized countries, which now average 2.5 percent for Japan, 3.4 percent for the United States, and 4.3 percent for the European Union. The Tokyo (1973–1979) and Uruguay (1986–1992) rounds achieved significant results in addressing nontariff barriers, intellectual property protection, and trade in services and agriculture. GATT's membership expanded from 23 to 135.

cut its future production to 8.9 million metric tons from an estimated harvest of 13 million tons in 1992. Brussels agreed to reduce its acreage to 1986 levels, which it claims will reduce the harvest to 10 million tons. The Americans countered that under the Brussels proposal the real figure would be over 10.5 million tons. They also complained that Brussels was not offering any real concession, that it would simply take away with one hand any advantages it offered with the other. Trade Representative Carla Hills threatened to impose the punitive tariffs on $1 billion in EU exports, the amount that American producers are estimated to lose from European barriers and subsidies. Washington also repeatedly pointed to the decisions of two GATT panels (1989, 1992) ruling that European oilseed subsidies were unfair and violated GATT trade rules. Brussels argues that these decisions have no standing unless the GATT approves them. Brussels, however, has

(continued from previous page)

vetoed their approval. GATT's credibility itself was at stake in the conflict. Hills argued that the U.S. action should be seen not as retaliation, but as a legitimate procedure that upholds GATT. The U.S. position was strongly backed by other soybean exporters, including Argentina, Australia, Chile, Brazil, Uruguay, New Zealand, and Canada.

The impasse was partly the result of French politics. President Francois Mitterand faced legislative elections in spring 1993. His popularity was extremely low, and the farm sector was especially disgruntled. Any concessions would mean the loss of seats for his Socialist Party. Meanwhile Commission President Jacques Delors was said to want Mitterand's job as president, and thus took a protectionist line. Another reason for the stalemate was EU hopes that if Bill Clinton were elected president in November he might be more conciliatory.

On November 5, the Bush administration declared that it would impose 200 percent import taxes on $300 million of European imports within 30 days if no progress was made in the trade talks. The White House singled out white wine and truffles as the target for some of the sanctions, because they were luxury goods that would not hurt America's economy, rather than components or intermediate goods, and were mostly French goods, which would hurt the prime European protectionist. Washington was prepared to escalate the trade war. Trade Representative Carla Hills also released a list of $1.7 billion worth of manufactured goods that would also receive tariff hikes if the Europeans retaliated.

Each side blamed the other for the trade war. Although Brussels responded by threatening to retaliate, officials and prime ministers negotiated behind the scenes to avert a war. In late November a compromise was struck between Washington and Brussels in which there would be a 21 percent reduction in the international tonnage of subsidized grain exports. However, Brussels and France squabbled over the decision until June 8, 1993, when Paris finally agreed in return for promises of higher EU subsidies for affected French farmers. The farm dispute was just one of many reasons why the Uruguay Round lasted half a dozen years.

Members agree, among other things, to fulfill the most-favored-nation principle that any concession granted to any other member must be granted to all members.

The World Trade Organization carries on GATT's work. Like the GATT, the WTO faces sharp challenges to fulfilling its mission. Although the WTO's powers to pressure members into fulfilling their pledges are greater than GATT's, they remain inadequate. As with the GATT, members can bring disputes before WTO panels, which can issue judgments. GATT panel decisions were merely advisory; WTO's are legally binding. But WTO panel judgments are implemented by those charged with noncompliance. The WTO lacks enforcement powers. Legal loopholes that allowed various forms of trade discrimination under the GATT have not been closed by the WTO. Members can still create regional free trade associations, discriminate in favor of less developed countries, and temporarily impose higher trade barriers to offset persistent trade deficits. Like the GATT, the WTO also fails to address the more insidious and effective nontariff trade barriers such as government red tape, business cartels, import licensing, export subsidies, and undervalued currencies, which some countries, most notably Japan, use to systematically minimize the penetration of competitive imports.

Perhaps the most glaring WTO weakness is its failure to allow states victimized by predatory trade strategies of other states to retaliate. A more common predatory trade strategy is dumping whereby firms sell their products at below production cost to drive their rivals out of business, capture market share, and recoup earlier losses by raising prices to gouge consumers. The WTO does not allow states to retaliate directly against the country whose firms have engaged in dumping. Import barriers must be erected against all countries, even those which are fair traders. Faced with this dilemma in which the only way they can protect themselves is to hurt everyone, most states seek alternative means of dealing with dumping by negotiating such voluntary restraint agreements (VRAs) as voluntary export restraints (VERs) or orderly marketing agreements (OMAs) with states whose corporations have engaged in widespread dumping and captured enormous market share. These arrangements tend to reward rather than punish the predatory firms and their countries with set market shares.

The WTO has yet to convene a negotiation round to further reduce trade barriers. Of the GATT's eight rounds, none was more contentious than the Uruguay Round. From 1986 through 1993, GATT's then 108 members addressed several broad issues—safeguards such as VRAs, the settling of disputes, and such products as textiles, tropical products, agriculture, services, and intellectual protection. Washington had pushed for negotiations in the last two areas because they were increasingly important to America's economic vitality. In 1986, when the talks began, American service exports were $148.4 billion or 39.8 percent of total exports.[15] Liberal economists argued that a successful GATT round would annually increase global economic activity by $100 billion as each country specialized in producing what it produces best and imports everything else.[16]

Deadlocks over half a dozen key issues persisted into late 1993. Between June and December 15, 1993, diplomats squabbled over such issues as European farm and aerospace subsidies, American attempts to retain its legal ability to retaliate against foreign dumping and subsidies, and French subsidies to its film industry at the expense of America's film industry. Last-minute compromises allowed the Uruguay Round to be completed with a package of trade, investment, financial, intellectual protection, and technology agreements that when implemented could spur global economic growth by an estimated $280 billion annually.

Will future WTO rounds be as complex, prolonged, and contentious as the GATT's Uruguay Round? Most likely they will be even more so. States are finding more sophisticated means to capture foreign markets, protect their home markets, and promote domestic industries. All these practices violate WTO principles if not specific laws. It remains to be seen whether the WTO can expand its liberal laws and enforcement powers to counter its members' neomercantilism. These issues and others caused the November 1999 WTO conference at Seattle to break up without any agenda or timetable for another trade reduction round.

Trade Wars, Dumping, *and* Defense

States and corporations use a range of strategies to fight trade wars. One of the most devastating weapons is dumping, which occurs when corporations sell their goods at a loss in a foreign market to drive rivals into bankruptcy and then recover earlier losses by raising prices and enjoying windfall profits. The World Trade Organization (WTO) allows states to defend themselves against dumping if it can be proved that the sales are at a loss and have damaged the domestic industry. The victim can then retaliate by imposing tariffs (duties) on the predator country's imports to compensate for the wealth lost from the dumping attack.

The more open and larger a nation's markets, the more vulnerable it is to a dumping offensive. As the two largest and most open economies, the United States and the European Union continually struggle to fend off destructive dumping attacks. In 1998 alone, Washington opened 25 investi-gations into complaints by American industries, up from 16 investigations in 1997. In 1998, the European Union opened 13 dumping investiga-tions in the steel industry alone, and extended duties on magnetic discs dumped by Japan, China, and Taiwan. Overall from 1980 through 1997 the United States and European Union won 80 percent and 71 percent, re-spectively, of the dumping cases they confronted. European and American duties have averaged 29 percent and 57 percent of the dumped prod-ucts' price.

But sometimes those successes followed years of industrial losses from foreign dumping. Often the duty is imposed too late, after the domes-tic industry has been weakened or destroyed. In the 1970s, America lost its television industry because it failed to respond to a decade of sustained Japanese dumping. Still, a successful case against one dumper can deter other foreign rivals from attacking.

Table 13.5 **Dumping Offenses and Defenses: Antidumping Cases, 1997**

Main Users		Main Targets	
Australia	42	China	31
European Union	41	South Korea	16
South Africa	23	Taiwan	16
United States	15	United States	15
Argentina	15	Germany	14
South Korea	15	Japan	12
Canada	14	Indonesia	9
India	13	India	7
Brazil	11	Great Britain	6

Source: World Trade Organization, *Journal of World Trade*, 2000.

MULTINATIONAL CORPORATIONS

Multinational corporations (MNCs), which conduct business in two or more coun-tries, have been around a long time. During the late Middle Ages, firms such as the Fuggers, based in Augsburg, Germany, and the Medici in Florence, Italy, con-ducted trade, extended credit, and nurtured industries across Europe. Most of the ships that sailed to the earth's far ends during the early modern era were privately owned by corporations that received a charter from the crown to explore, con-quer, and govern distant realms. The British East India Company and the Hudson Bay Company in particular enjoyed monopoly rule over vast territories. From the

multinational corporations (MNCs) a corporation with one or more overseas enterprises.

18th through the 20th centuries, scores of other MNCs emerged to conduct business and investments around the world.[18]

Today, probably no greater force has contributed more to interdependence than MNCs. The world is girded together by tens of thousands of MNCs, whose ranks swell daily. Although most of these MNCs are from advanced industrial states, increasing numbers come from newly industrializing countries. This proliferation of MNCs was stimulated by the telecommunications, computer, and transportation revolutions since 1945 in which global communications and financial transactions take place instantaneously, huge container ships can cross the largest oceans in days, and jets can crisscross the globe in hours.

MNCs are involved in every imaginable type of business—extraction (mining, logging, oil production), agriculture, manufacturing of both finished and semifinished goods, finance (banking, investing), and services (insurance, tourism, wholesale and retail sales, advertising, management, transportation, public utilities). Some multinational corporations actually have overseas businesses in all these categories. An MNC's control over its foreign subsidiary ranges from whole to partial ownership. Many MNCs will form joint business ventures with other MNCs or local entrepreneurs to spread the investment risks. Others prefer to maintain a wholly owned subsidiary because they have total control over its operations. When an MNC buys up an existing factory, office, or business or builds a new one, it makes a "direct investment" in that country. When an MNC buys stocks, bonds, or other financial assets, it makes a "portfolio investment."

Although MNC activities have risen steadily since 1945, the amount of new annual direct foreign investments more than doubled from $192.662 billion in 1990 to $400.394 billion in 1998. The United States, European Union, and Japan accounted for about 80 percent of this total, and three-fourths of that was among themselves.[19]

Periodically, host countries have expressed concern over the influx of direct foreign investments. In the 1960s, many Europeans feared that a mounting wave of American investments was jeopardizing the European Union's political economic independence.[20] During the 1980s, the overpriced dollar and higher trade barriers attracted a huge wave of foreign investment into the United States, prompting some Americans to fear that their sovereignty was threatened. The Tolchins' book *Buying into America* and Pat Choate's *Agents of Influence* made powerful cases that this foreign investment was hindering rather than helping America's economic development.[21] The Tolchins revealed how foreign corporations succeeded in lobbying California and other states to repeal their unitary taxes, which taxed both foreign and domestic firms on their global rather than local sales to limit their ability to engage in transfer pricing (overcharging products that an MNC sends to its overseas subsidiaries in order to evade currency controls). Choate pointed out that Japan's government and businesses annually spent at least $400 million at the federal, state, and local level to influence policy in their favor, an amount greater than the sum of money spent by America's leading business federations. The business and political practices of some foreign corporations that invested in the United States were criticized, and American MNCs were blasted for exporting jobs, wealth, and tax revenue by investing overseas. Once the United States largely exported products; now it builds many of them overseas and often exports them back to the United States. Economists dismissed these criticisms as groundless, arguing that free trade and investment markets are always good, and if other countries do not reciprocate America's relative openness they are only hurting themselves. Political economists dismissed the economists'

Part 5   Geoeconomic Conflict and Cooperation Within the Industrialized World

Racism *or* Retaliation? *The* Fairchild Case

In 1987, a controversy arose when Japan's Fujitsu Corporation tried to buy the American firm Fairchild Semiconductor. Many in and out of Washington argued that the sale should be blocked because it would reinforce Japan's semiconductor industry at the expense of America's, despite the fact that Fairchild was owned by a French firm, Schlumberger. Although the Japanese cried racism, opponents of the sale countered that there was investment reciprocity between the United States and France, and France's microelectronics industry is far behind America's. In contrast, Japanese firms can invest freely in the United States and buy out virtually any American firm they desire, whereas American and other foreign firms are restricted from investing in Japan and prevented from hostile takeovers of Japanese firms. In addition, Japan's semiconductor firms had dumped their products for years in the United States and captured a huge market share, yet American and other foreign firms still faced heavy Japanese trade barriers and thus had only a minuscule market share. Although the Reagan administration did not block the sale, Fujitsu eventually dropped its bid.

dogmatism and instead tried to determine the relative merits of American investments abroad on a case-by-case basis.

Each of the superpowers has a different policy toward foreign investments. The European Union has dealt with the problem of transfer pricing and aggravated trade and payments problems by setting "domestic content" laws for some products. For example, an automobile built in Europe must contain at least 45 percent parts made within the European Union to be considered European. In 1988, Brussels allowed France to block the importation of 300,000 Japanese television sets that had been assembled in Europe but failed to meet domestic content standards.

Washington has been far less restrictive of foreign investments than Brussels. Citing free trade, the Reagan and Bush administrations blocked congressional efforts to push through domestic content laws similar to those of Brussels. However, the United States does have considerable power to limit the activities of foreign firms in the United States. The 1976 International Investment and Trade in Services Act and 1977 International Emergency Economic Powers Act enable the president to block or force the divestiture of any foreign acquisition of an American firm that is considered vital for America's national security. Presidents have rarely used these laws. Fearing that disclosure would inhibit foreign investment in the United States, the Reagan administration blocked the Bryant amendment to the 1988 Omnibus Trade Bill, which would have required foreign firms to disclose the details of their operations. Critics blasted Reagan's policies as unilateral economic disarmament.

In the 1992 presidential campaign, Governor Clinton promised to eliminate the transfer pricing of foreign corporations in the United States that allows many of them to pay no taxes at all. In 1988, foreign firms with American subsidiaries enjoyed $825.6 billion in business but paid a minuscule $5.8 billion in taxes. Through closing loopholes and investigations, Clinton hoped to raise $45 billion, of which $7 billion would go to state coffers. American firms will indirectly profit too, because they have been hurt by the foreign ability to evade taxes. The Bush administration was opposed to Clinton's plan because they claimed it would deter foreign investments in the United States.[22] Since taking office, Clinton has not yet made good on his promise.

JAPAN

Of the three economic superpowers, none restricts foreign investments more systematically than Japan. Until recently, Tokyo sharply limited the amount and type of foreign investments within Japan. The government screened all foreign investments and allowed entry only if the MNC's products did not compete with those of Japanese firms targeted by the government for development, and even then were limited to a 49 percent share of the investment, with Japanese investors holding the other 51 percent. Profits from most foreign investments could not be repatriated. The screening process did not end, and 100 percent foreign ownership was not allowed until passage of the 1980 Foreign Exchange and Foreign Trade Control Law. That same law allows the government the right to impede any foreign investments that violate "national security." Despite these legal changes, Tokyo continues to screen foreign investments, inhibits those which are competitive with Japanese industry, and has specific industry laws that empower it to impede competitive foreign investments. Foreign MNCs face numerous unofficial obstacles to investing in Japan, including government red tape designed deliberately to impede foreigners, restrictions on advertising, buying or renting land, and business cartels that will not sell to or buy from the foreigners.

There is conflicting evidence over the positive and negative effects of foreign investments. MNCs clearly affect the trade balance. For example, the automobile VER that Washington negotiated with Tokyo in 1981 was partially an attempt to encourage Japan's manufacturers to invest directly in the United States in the hope that it would help reduce Japan's growing trade surplus. Japan's auto makers did open factories in the United States during the 1980s, but those investments actually exacerbated the trade deficit because most of the components were shipped from Japan.

Most studies indicate that American foreign investments actually help America's trade and payments accounts. Were it not for American MNCs and their foreign subsidiaries, America's trade deficit would be much worse. American corporations selling to their foreign subsidiaries account for about 35 percent of all American exports.[23] Some argue that the exports from the United States would have often been lost whether or not the American MNCs invested abroad because other foreign firms simply filled the gap. If American MNCs invest abroad, they continue to hold on to those markets.

Other studies show that welcoming foreign investments can help an economy. An extensive Canadian study in 1968 concluded that "the host country typically benefits and often substantially from foreign direct investment."[24] The report did note, however, that there was a tendency for foreign MNCs to buy goods and services from their subsidiaries rather than from local businesses. The European Community Caborn Report of 1981 found "favorable impacts on productivity, growth rates and overall level of employment, on the dissemination of new products and processes and also of managerial know-how."[25] Other benefits included better payment and trade accounts, greater research and development, and technology advances. A study of foreign investments in the United States likewise found a largely positive impact.[26]

There are winners and losers in any economic transactions, but overall foreign investments between advanced industrial countries are probably a net gain for all.

Yet, although the fears of foreign investments may be exaggerated, there may be good reasons for states to regulate the type, amount, and practices of some foreign investments. Those foreign investments that do not compete directly with domestic industries or buy up real estate usually have a net positive effect on that country. But when foreigners buy out a nation's cutting-edge corporations, industries, and technologies, that nation is usually worse off.

At his first press conference on March 23, 1993, President Clinton declaredthat

> If you look at the history of America's trade relationships . . . the one that never seems to change very much is the one with Japan. That is, we're sometimes in a position of trade deficit, but we're often in a position of trade surplus with the European Community. . . . We once had huge trade deficits with Taiwan and South Korea, but they've changed now quite a bit; they move up and down. . . . But the persistence of the surplus the Japanese enjoy with the United States and with the rest of the developed world can lead one to the conclusion that the possibility of obtaining real, even access to the Japanese market is somewhat remote.

In other words, all of America's bilateral trade relations seem to be governed by market forces except trade with Japan.

Statistics support Clinton's assertion. Between 1987 and 1992, as the dollar's devaluation took effect, an American trade deficit of $24.3 billion with the European Community was converted into a trade surplus of $16.7 billion surplus! During the same period, America's trade deficit with Japan dipped slightly from $59.3 billion to $52.7 billion, despite the fact that the American dollar declined in value far more sharply against the Japanese yen than the European currencies.

In 1992, Japan enjoyed a trade surplus of $132 billion, of which $52 billion was with the United States and $31 billion with the European Community. That same year, while the total direct investments of Japanese corporations had reached $93 billion in the United States and $55 billion in the European Community, total American and European direct investments in Japan were only $9.5 billion and $3.2 billion, respectively. Both Washington, Brussels, and the various European capitals have continually condemned Japan's immense and intractable trade and investments surpluses, but to no avail.

Japan has posed a serious geoeconomic issue since its economy began to revive in the late 1940s. For four years between 1951 and 1955, the Europeans opposed Washington's attempts to sponsor Japan's membership in GATT. The Europeans argued that Tokyo would continue its neomercantilism despite its promises to abandon them to join GATT. In 1955, Washington finally succeeded in gaining Tokyo GATT membership, but most of the other members used GATT Article 35, the "safeguard clause," which allowed them to continue discriminating against Japanese imports. The EC and Japan negotiated away these barriers through the 1960s. In retaliation against Japanese neomercantilism, Europeans continued to keep out specific Japanese goods, although the type and amount varied from one country to the next. For example, Italy restricted Japanese automobiles to a 1 percent share, France to 3 percent, and Britain to 11 percent, while the other Community members had fewer or no restrictions. Brussels retaliated promptly against most Japanese products, which quickly captured large market shares through dumping. By 1992, VRAs restricted 40 percent of Japanese exports to the European Community.[27]

Washington itself clashed frequently with Tokyo over waves of Japanese dumping of various products in the United States that hurt or bankrupted many American firms.[28] The first negotiations began in 1955 over Japanese "dollar blouses," which were gaining market share from American producers. Conflicts and negotiations continued over various types of Japanese textiles throughout the 1960s, culminating with a 1969 agreement limiting Japanese imports to certain levels. In the late 1960s and into the 1970s, Japanese television and steel producers captured increased market share, and the remaining beleaguered American producers pressured the White House to intervene. The government's response to the television industry was too little, too late, and today no American television producers remain of the 24 that existed during the mid-1960s. The White House was more prompt in responding to Japanese and European steel dumping. In 1968, Washington negotiated VRAs with Japanese and European steel producers to limit their share of America's market. In 1978, the Carter administration responded to a new surge of Japanese steel dumping by imposing the "trigger price mechanism" in which any steel entering the United States below a certain average Japanese production cost would automatically trigger a dumping investigation.

During the 1980s, the Reagan administration conducted two sets of negotiations. One tried to stem the influx of Japanese imports that threatened to destroy America's automobile, semiconductor, motorcycle, and other industries. Another attempted to reduce Japanese trade barriers and gain greater market share for such American products and services as baseball bats, beef, oranges, semiconductors, portable telephones, satellites, lawyers, telecommunications equipment, and banks, to name a few.

Perhaps the most important of these conflicts was over automobiles. Washington negotiated with Tokyo a VER that restricted Japanese exports to 1.68 million from 1981 to 1984, and from 1.85 million from 1984 through the present. These restrictions may well have prevented the total collapse of America's automobile industry, but they cost consumers over $5 billion in higher sticker prices as both American and Japanese producers raised prices in the restricted markets. Each American job saved cost $160,000.[29] Between 1980 and 1985, the American automobile industry lost over $6 billion and 200,000 jobs, while Japan's share of America's market rose to 21 percent. By the late 1980s, Detroit was making a profit again but Japan's producers made even higher profits and soon got around the restrictions by building automobile plants in the United States. Between 1991 and 1992, America's Big Three lost over $6.5 billion and Japan's market share from exports and transplants rose to 30 percent.

Despite these losses, American auto makers have made enormous cost reduction and quality gains over the past decade, surpassing their Japanese rivals by many measurements. In 1981, the average American car cost $1,500 to $2,500 more to produce than the average Japanese car. Today, the cost for Ford to produce a small car is $5,415 and Chrysler $5,841, while the lowest-cost Japanese producer was Toyota at $6,216. General Motors at $7,205 was by far the highest-cost producer among both American and Japanese firms. Although American labor costs still exceeded those of Japan, Ford and Chrysler have brought their parts, materials, and other production costs far below those of their Japanese competitors. American labor costs are driven up by health and pension costs. The American producers are also penalized by the fact that they only used 62 percent of capacity in 1991 whereas the Japanese used 95 percent, a difference that cost the Americans $800 to $1,500 more per car.[30] Overall, America still suffers a nearly $45 billion automobile trade deficit with Japan despite the comparative advantage of Ford and Chrysler.

Another major trade battle of the 1980s was fought over computer chips. The Japanese are leading the microelectronics revolution, mastering such interrelated fields as semiconductors, telecommunications, fiber optics, virtual reality, and industrial ceramics. Industries are composed of "food chains" that include equipment makers, components, and finished products. Semiconductors are to the microelectronics industry what steel is to automobiles and shipbuilding.

Japan's semiconductor makers captured enormous market share during the early 1980s because of the overvalued dollar and undervalued yen, and massive dumping designed to drive their American and other foreign rivals into bankruptcy. This advantage was further strengthened by the ability of Japanese firms to raise money at 4 percent interest rates in Japan's managed financial market system, whereas American producers paid 12 percent in America's open capital markets. By being able to spend twice what the Americans were spending on research and development, the Japanese were able to offer a cheaper, better quality product.

In 1986, after years of pleading from American chipmakers, the Reagan White House agreed to negotiate a VER with Japan. An agreement was finally struck in which floor prices were set for Japanese chipmakers and United States chipmakers were promised a 20 percent market share in Japan by 1991. The White House followed up this agreement by attempting a Japanese-style industrial policy in 1987, in which the White House allocated $100 million to help create Sematech, a semiconductor research consortium in a belated attempt to emulate and catch up to the Japanese.

Although the bilateral agreement and Sematech helped save the American semiconductor industry, neither has fulfilled expectations. America's market share in Japan has risen from 8.5 percent to 17.5 percent, which represented $1 billion in additional sales. But the current share is short of Tokyo's promised 20 percent share. Likewise, Sematech has failed to achieve any major technological or product breakthroughs. Throughout the 1980s, America's global market share tumbled from 59 percent in 1980 to 39 percent in 1991 after bottoming out at 37 percent in 1988, while Japan's rose from 32 percent to 49 percent after peaking at 51 percent in 1988. In 1991, $20.9 billion worth of semiconductors were sold in Japan, $15.4 billion in the United States, $10.1 billion in Europe, and $8.2 billion elsewhere.[31] American chipmakers have retreated up-market to more sophisticated microprocessors, while the Japanese dominate the memory chip market. Many believe that the Japanese producers will eventually master microprocessors as they have memory chips.

The Reagan and Bush administration efforts to open Japan's markets had a mixed success. After years of tough and sometimes bitter negotiations, Tokyo agreed to liberalize its orange and beef markets, but remains adamantly opposed to any concessions on rice. One measure of the farm lobby's political clout is that Washington chose to spend enormous diplomatic resources on agriculture, which comprises a small percentage of total bilateral trade when so many other American industries and technologies are struggling against Japanese exports and allowed only a limited share of Japan's markets.

Although negotiations were conducted over specific products, Washington also tried to address the problem of systematic Japanese import and investment barriers. Between 1988 and 1991, Washington and Tokyo conducted the *Structural Impediments Initiative (SII)*, in which the Americans cited examples of Japanese trade barriers such as the industrial groups (keiretsu), which tend to buy from each other, distribution cartels, highly subsidized agriculture, lack of patent protection, artificially high savings rates, and so on, while the Japanese pointed out examples of American practices that inhibited economic growth such as low savings and investment, the (then) large budget deficit, crumbling infrastructure, and crime. Both sides promised to reform their respective systems. The United States fulfilled its promise under President Bill Clinton when the budget deficit was finally eliminated in 1997, but the Japanese refused to end any of their neomercantilist strategies.

Instead, Tokyo turned the tables on the United States and European Community, labeling them "protectionists" and demanding that they remove their barriers. On June 8, 1992, Tokyo released a report labeling the United States as being the most unfair trader among the advanced industrial countries.[32] The report cited Washington's tendency to impose unilateral and often protectionist decisions in bilateral trade disputes, unfairly use dumping laws to restrict imports, impose so-called voluntary export restraints on others, and widely use "Buy American" laws. Tokyo claimed that Brussels was only slightly less protectionist than the United States. Tokyo is increasingly turning to GATT and the WTO to help settle trade conflicts.

As long as the imbalances between trade practices and results exist, there will be continued bitter conflicts.

TRADE BLOCS

The global economy is increasingly defined by three trade blocs comprising European Union, North American, and Asia-Pacific countries. A 1991 World Bank study compared these blocs.[33] The North American bloc or NAFTA includes the United States, Canada, and Mexico with a $6.203.1 trillion GNP, 363.6 million population, and $17,060 per capita income. The European Union has 15 members—Germany, France, Great Britain, Italy, Spain, the Netherlands, Belgium, Denmark, Ireland, Portugal, Greece, Luxembourg, Sweden, Austria, and Finland—with a $5.517.4 trillion GNP, 342.5 million population, and $16,107 per capita income. The European Union's total GNP, population, and per capita income would be much higher if the seven-nation European Free Trade Association (EFTA), and Switzerland were included. Although there is no formal Asia Pacific trade alliance, an informal Japan-centered bloc has been evolving for several decades. The combined assets of Japan, Hong Kong, Malaysia, South Korea, Singapore, and Thailand alone amount to a $3.592.8 trillion GNP, 248.3 million population, and $14,467 per capita income. The Asia Pacific bloc would be the largest in GNP and population and much lower in per capita income if China, Taiwan, Indonesia, Brunei, and the Philippines were included.

A trade bloc's strength can be measured in several ways. One is its degree of intraregional trade as a percentage of total trade. By that measurement, the European Union's is the most cohesive of the blocs, with its 60 percent intraregional trade, compared to about a quarter each for NAFTA and Asia Pacific.[34] All the blocs clearly depend far more on other countries than on their members for their trade.

Another way to measure strength is whether or not a trade bloc is running a trade surplus with the others. By this measure the European Union is the weakest of the three. In 1991 it ran $38.390 billion and $24.406 billion trade deficits with Japan and the United States, respectively. Although the United States enjoyed a huge surplus with Europe, it also suffered a $46.863 billion deficit with Japan. The figures for the United States and Japan, of course, do not take into account the effects of other bloc members.

Yet another way of determining a bloc's strength is to measure its relative trade dependence in relation to the others. Despite its lower relative economic size if

Japanese Hegemony *over* Southeast Asia: Eclipse *of the* Rising Sun?

For several decades Japan has enjoyed economic hegemony over Southeast Asia, running huge trade surpluses, and dominating the region's trade, loans, investments, aid, and tourism. In 1998, Japan's trade surplus was 2.1 trillion yen, or $210 billion if one dollar equals 100 yen!

Although Japan continues to enjoy huge trade surpluses and account for nearly half of all trade with all the Southeast Asia countries, it has recently lost its leadership in foreign investments in that region to Britain. From 1995 to 1999, Japan withdrew $108 billion from the region and halved the value of its lending to those countries. Why did Japan do so? Its corporate giants cut back their investments and lending to service huge and growing bad debts at home and to cut their losses after the region's 1997 financial plunge. The Southeast Asia countries themselves are seeking to reform their own mercantilist economies modeled after Japan's, in part by opening their markets and seeking more diversified sources of foreign investments.

The eclipse of Japanese power in Southeast Asia is limited to investments, not trade (where it reigns supreme). Will Japan make a comeback in investments or cede the ground to Britain and other foreign investors? It would be unwise to count the Japanese out. Japanese economic behemoths have suffered brief checks and retreats before but have always come roaring back even more powerful than before.

other countries are added to the Union and Asia Pacific blocs, NAFTA will remain the most important of the three because the other two blocs depend on America's huge affluent market as a source of exports. The United States and NAFTA can use the threat of closed markets to counter any European or Asia Pacific protectionism. The Asia Pacific bloc is particularly vulnerable. Although most of the countries run trade deficits with Japan, they enjoy trade surpluses with the United States. Thus any threat of closed NAFTA markets can wring concessions from the Asia Pacific bloc. But NAFTA's potential power has never been used and thus squandered in trade conflicts with the Asia Pacific countries.

Some fear that these regional economic blocs will eventually declare an all-out trade war on each other. This fear is unfounded. Autarchy, or the severing of one's economic relations with other countries, is nearly impossible in an increasingly interdependent world. Although it is true that most of the European Union's foreign trade occurs among the 15 members, that intraunion trade does not mean that Europe's continued prosperity is any less dependent on the global system. The same can be said of America's 50 states; more than 80 percent of all trade occurs within the United States and less than 20 percent with foreign countries. Yet America's foreign trade is accounting for an increasingly important slice of the economy, up from about 10 percent in 1960.

President Clinton has skillfully played the trade bloc game to enhance American geoeconomic interests. First, he succeeded in getting NAFTA's ratification, which most members of Congress solidly opposed. In late November 1993, he won by stressing that NAFTA would lead to more and better American jobs rather than less, but also warned that if the United States did not form closer ties with Mexico, Japan might, to America's detriment. "If we turn our back on free trade with our closest neighbor," the president asked, "how credible will we be in the eyes of the

The Cost of Economic Alliance: NAFTA and American Jobs

Whatever NAFTA's merits as an economic alliance, the United States has lost jobs to Mexico and Canada since 1993. The primary reason, however, is not the reduction of trade barriers among those countries. America's market was largely open to imports from both countries before 1993. Mexico and Canada were forced to lower their much higher barriers to roughly equal those of the United States. The most important reasons for the shift in trade flows and jobs were the halving of the Mexican peso's value and lesser devaluation of the Canadian dollar since 1993, combined with the direct investment of American corporations in both countries to take advantage of cheaper labor and in Mexico weak environmental laws. Those corporations then sell part of their production back to the United States. Most of the American jobs lost to foreign investments by American firms would have disappeared anyway as globalization forces all businesses to search the world for the cheapest and most skilled labor. NAFTA advocates argue that it was better for those firms to invest in America's neighbors than elsewhere in the world.

Table 13.6 **NAFTA and American Jobs**

	United States (1993)			United States (1998)			
	Exports	Imports	Trade Balance	Exports	Imports	Trade Balance	U.S. Jobs Lost
Mexico	$36,390	$35,915	$415	$33,521	$50,035	−$16,514	−232,669
Canada	84,055	102,715	−16,660	131,875	163,114	−31,239	−207,503
Total	120,445	138,630	−16,185	201,787	249,065	−47,278	−440,172

Source: Economic Policy Institute.

Europeans or Japanese in asking them to accept lower trade barriers?" He argued that the United States could use NAFTA's geoeconomic power to pry open closed markets in Japan, the European Union, and other countries and regions, then proceeded to do just that. Fresh from his congressional victory, the president flew to Seattle for a summit meeting of the four-year-old, 15-member Asia Pacific Economic Cooperation (APEC) forum on November 19 and 20. America's trade with the Pacific basin is 50 percent greater than its trade with the Atlantic basin. But although the United States enjoys a trade surplus with Europe, it suffers a trade deficit with Asia. During the summit, Clinton pressed for and succeeded in gaining APEC's approval to convert the forum into a huge free trade association by the late 1990s. With the APEC and NAFTA victories under his belt, Clinton trained his geoeconomic guns on France, which was holding up a GATT accord. By December 15, 1993—the date the president's congressional authorization for trade negotiating powers ran out—last-minute compromises by all sides allowed the Uruguay Round to be successfully completed, which will stimulate a stalled global economy.

Clinton's deft and farsighted diplomacy on NAFTA, APEC, and GATT will characterize global geoeconomic relations into the 21st century. Although trade squabbles will continue, there will be no return to the "beggar thy neighbor" currency devaluations and high trade barriers of the 1930s. International trade and investments will continue to expand. Geoeconomic relations, however, will be increasingly managed between countries and blocs to prevent anyone from garnering too many benefits by following predatory industrial, technology, investment, and trade policies. In an increasingly interdependent global economy, most governments will become more neomercantilist as their nation's dependence on international trade steadily deepens. Trade conflicts will involve specific cases of dumping, subsidies, market share, or investments and broader negotiations over national industrial and trade policies. Yet more geoeconomic management will mean more rather than less global trade and prosperity.

Conclusion

Since 1945, the global economy has been enormously resilient, continuing to expand despite the occasional oil price hikes, recessions, trade battles, and stock market crashes. Global GNP has expanded in volume over 20 times and trade over 25 times since 1950, and both continue to increase at average annual rates of 5 and 7 percent, respectively. In 1998, over $4 trillion in goods and services were traded internationally, around 15 percent of total global GNP. The three great geoeconomic powers—the European Union, United States, and Japan—account for over two-thirds of world GNP and half of trade.

The benefits of world economic growth and trade, however, have not been evenly distributed among the participants. Some countries have grown faster than others and thus there have been huge shifts in the geoeconomic power balance. Although overall globalization undoubtedly increases prosperity, there are clearly winners and losers. Jobs, wealth, revenues, firms, and entire industries can be lost as well as gained from the international flow of trade, investments, and finance. Economists estimate that a nation loses 20,000 jobs for every billion dollars it suffers in trade deficit. So America's trade deficit of over $261.509 billion in 1998 meant that 13 million more Americans were unemployed than would have been the case if there were a trade balance. The nearly $80 billion deficit America suffered with Japan translated into 4 million net lost American jobs. Some have argued that the United States is "deindustrializing" or being "hollowed out" by the effects of American multinationals investing abroad and foreign multinational corporations and governments engaging in unfair trade and investment practices against the United States.

The United States has declined relative to the rise of Japan and the European Union. Between 1888 and 1971, the United States continuously ran trade surpluses, which showed that America's industrial base was dynamic, diversified, and globally competitive. Since 1971 the United States has continually run trade deficits, which rose steadily to $15 billion in 1981, then, because of the Reagan White House's policies, skyrocketed to $152 billion in 1987, declined to $62 billion in 1991, and then rose to $260 billion in 1998. The European Union's growth rate is comparable to that of the United States. But with 80 million more consumers than the United States and other countries waiting to join, the union's GNP is larger even while its per capita income is lower. Until its stock and real estate market bubble burst in 1990, Japan's economy grew twice as fast as America's and its GNP was poised to surpass that of the United States within a dozen years. But from 1990 to 2000, Japan's growth lagged behind America's as President Clinton's sound policies revitalized the nation's economy into its best performance since the 1960s.

The United States and European Union continue to suffer vast trade deficits with Japan and have become increasingly protectionist, restricting about 45 percent and 60 percent of manufactured imports, respectively. Meanwhile Japan, largely because of foreign pressure, has become less restrictive. During the 1980s, the Reagan and Bush administrations tried to convince Japan and the European Union "to be more like us," all the while imposing greater import restrictions. The Clinton administration was more protectionist in rhetoric as well as policy. "Fair" rather than "free" trade has been the battle cry since the 1990s. Trade battles among all three economic superpowers will become more frequent and bitter.

Despite these challenges and relative decline, the United States will continue to be the center of world trade and two vast regional systems spanning the northern Pacific and Atlantic basins. The economic power balance among the United States, the European Union, and Japan will persist.

Study Questions

1. What are the advantages and disadvantages of interdependence?

2. Describe, in order, the major stages in the evolution of the global political economy.

3. Define mercantilism, and list its strengths and weaknesses.

4. Define economic liberalism, and list its strengths and weaknesses.

5. Define neomercantilism, and list its strengths and weaknesses.

6. What steps did the United States take in the 20th century to first push the global economy into depression and then reconstruct the global economy and lead into prosperity?

7. List the institutions created in the 1940s that became the superstructure of the global economy. What are their functions?

8. How did the fixed currency system work? What pressures built on it during the 1960s? Why did President Nixon abandon the fixed system in 1971? How has the new floating currency system worked?

9. What problems did the American and global economy suffer throughout the 1970s and 1980s through today?

10. What was the 1985 Plaza Accord supposed to accomplish? How successful was it in achieving its goals?

11. Describe the advantages and disadvantages of NAFTA for its members.

12. List and explain the major characteristics and government policies shaping America's economic development.

13. Describe the major characteristics and government policies shaping Japan's economic development.

14. What have been the major characteristics and government policies shaping the European Community's development?

15. List the GATT's strengths and weaknesses. How have the GATT rounds varied in the focus of negotiations?

16. Discuss the pros and cons of allowing unrestricted foreign investment in one's country.

17. What conflicts and different policies have the three economic superpowers had over multinational corporations and foreign investments?

18. Why have Japan's economic policies and trade surpluses been so severely criticized by the European Community and the United States? What have been the major trade conflicts among these economic superpowers and how have they been managed?

19. Analyze the power balance among the three economic blocs—the EU, NAFTA, and East and Southeast Asia. Will the conflicts among the three continue to be managed, or will relations break down into trade war? Explain.

20. What was the purpose and significance of such international economic organizations as the IMF, World Bank, and GATT, and international political organizations as the United Nations? What was the American role in creating those institutions?

♀ *InfoTrac College Edition* Sources

Using the Subject Guide, enter the search terms *World Trade Organization, euro, currency, tariffs,* and/or *Group of 8.*

DiGiovanna, Sean. "Regions and the World Economy: The Coming Shape of Global Production, Competition and Political Order."

Grant, Jonathan. "Globalization and History: the Evolution of a Nineteenth-Century Atlantic World Economy."

Green, John, and Phillip L. Swagel. "The Euro Area and the World Economy."

Grigera Naon, Horacio A. "Sovereignty and Regionalism."

Lloyd, John. "If Japan Goes, We All Go."

Olsen, Gregg M. "Re-modeling Sweden: The Rise and Demise of the Compromise in a Global Economy."

Pain, Nigel. "Prospects for North America and Japan."

Pain, Nigel et al. "Prospects for Europe."

Pain, Nigel et al. "The World Economy."

Poon, Jessie, and Kavita Pandit. "The Geographic Structure of Cross-National Trade Flows and Region States."

Rouse, David. "The Challenge of Global Capitalism: The World Economy in the 21st Century."

Sachs, Jeffrey. "Interlocking Economics: Unlocking the Mysteries of Globalization."

"The World Economy."

🌐 On *the* Web

http://www.wto.org/
World Trade Organization website

http://www.g7.utoronto.ca/
Group of 8 website

http://www.freetrade.org/pubs/freetotrade/chap2.html
Policy analysis of the danger of tariffs

Hegemons can be either locomotives of development or leeches of wealth from the countries they dominate. Nearly 40 percent of Mexico's economy depends on its ties with the United States. But America's hegemony promotes rather than exploits Mexico's economy. When Mexico's economy collapsed in 1993, the United States organized a $45 billion international bailout in return for sweeping reforms, encouraged the peso to fall to stimulate exports, and then bought as many goods as possible. Within two years, Mexico's economy was not only rapidly growing but was significantly modernized. The North American Free Trade Association (NAFTA) allows Mexican goods and services easy access to America's huge market, thus enriching both countries along with the other member, Canada.

Contrast America's largely beneficial hegemony with Japan's mostly exploitive hegemony over East and Southeast Asia. In 1997, Japanese trade accounted for 45 percent of the region's trade, and Japanese direct and financial investments reached $249 billion, one-third of total foreign lending. Japanese hegemony, however, is largely predatory rather than beneficial to the region. An undervalued yen fuels Japanese exports to the region and repels East Asian exports to Japan.

When the region's economy collapsed in 1997, Japan's government and corporations exploited rather than alleviated the problem. Tokyo pushed down the yen's value so that its

Part Six Geoeconomic Conflict *and* Cooperation Between *the* First *and* Third Worlds: Locomotives *or* Leeches? Hegemony, Development, *and the* Poorest *of the* Poor

exports to the region remained strong and imports limited. Indeed, Japan's imports from the region fell 26 percent that year. Rather than pump more money into the region, Japan forced those countries to continue paying their debts. The result of Japan's actions was simultaneously to deepen the region's depression while enriching Japan's economy and corporations.

Although American liberalism and Japanese neomercantilism determine their very different policies as hegemons, sometimes Washington can pressure Tokyo into contributing to the global economy. For example, over 700 million people in forty-two countries are among the most wretchedly poor of the earth. Known as the "heavily indebted poor countries" (HIPCs), their per capita incomes range anywhere from $100 to $500, their economies are stagnant or shrinking, and most are mired in abject poverty so harsh they barely glean enough scraps of food to stay alive. As if all that were not bad enough, those countries are deeply in debt. In 1999 they owed $170 billion to a range of international lenders including the IMF, the World Bank, various regional development banks, and governments. Most of those debtors have to borrow more money just to repay the ever larger yearly interest. None are likely ever to repay the principal. Those loans they received were supposed to help them develop from poverty to prosperity. Instead, the debt burden has locked them into a vicious cycle whereby any export earnings are immediately whisked off to foreign

Puppet masters? Finance ministers of the world's richest countries coordinate plans to manage the global economy.

Reuters/John Schults/Archive Photos

banks rather than invested in the infrastructure, industries, education, farm technologies, and health care that might slowly lift them from poverty. The average HIPC ratio of export earnings to interests payments is 1 to 4. What stops them from defaulting? New debts to cover interest payments on the old debt plunge them ever deeper into the red.

What if anything should be done about that debt? The lenders' official position is that those low-interest loans must eventually be repaid. Any debt relief for some countries would encourage others to demand similar privileges. That could weaken the international banking system and perhaps threaten the global political economy. Corruption and mismanagement rather than debt is the reason

these countries cannot break poverty's shackles. Thus the lenders will offer better terms only to those countries that complete an eight-year program of IMF fiscal reforms. So far only Bolivia and Uganda have qualified.

The group Jubilee 2000, which includes such different celebrities as Pope John Paul II, the rock singer Bono, and Jesse Jackson, insists that the international bankers should forgive the entire debt. That is not just the right thing to do from a Christian perspective, they argue but it makes economic sense as well. Those countries can only escape their vicious economic cycles if they invest their earnings rather than send them abroad. The various banks have already written off nearly 90 percent of that debt anyway, so complete forgiveness would cause barely a ripple to the global financial system.

The debate was resolved in June 1999 when the Group of Seven leading industrial nations agreed to cut that debt by up to $90 billion. About $15 billion would be immediately written off and the rest eliminated in return for reforms in those countries. Although the Japanese would have lost only several billion dollars of the total, they were still reluctant to cancel that debt. But eventually Tokyo gave in to the pressure of the Americans and others in the Group of Seven Nations. Although Japan grudgingly accepted the liberal position on that issue, its neomercantilist hegemony over East Asia will probably remain unchanged and unchallenged.

Contents

Chapter 14 Political Development, Underdevelopment, *and* International Relations

Key Concepts and Terms

Why have these people formed a human snake in the desert? Are they starving refugees waiting for food? Are they unemployed hoping for work? Actually, they are waiting patiently to vote in South Africa's 1999 election, the second since 1994, when the racist apartheid system was abolished and blacks received full political rights with whites and other races. Democratic experiments in nearly all African countries have failed. What causes democracies to flourish in some countries and wither in others? Will South African democracy survive?

Modernization's most central concept is development, which is essentially how well society adapts to the challenges of a rapidly changing world while fulfilling its goals and ideals. A country develops economically when it achieves self-sustaining economic growth that brings a higher living standard and quality of life to an ever greater percentage of the population. It develops politically when its government adapts its institutions and policies to meet society's growing needs and desires.

Politics and economics are intricately related, hence the term "political economy." There is clearly a long-term dynamic relationship between economic and political development. Political philosophers since Aristotle have observed that democratic political systems are middle-class societies. Today almost all the world's wealthiest states are liberal democracies. In contrast, although there are exceptions such as India or Costa Rica, authoritarian governments rule most poor countries. Are most countries poor because they are authoritarian, or are they authoritarian because they are poor?

What is the relationship between national development and international relations? A nation's political economic development is shaped by the policies its government pursues in an increasingly interdependent world. Those policies and that development in turn can be adversely or beneficially affected by the world's international forces, whether they are international development organizations such as the IMF or World Bank, multinational corporations, arms and drug dealers, humanitarians such as the Red Cross, environmentalists such as Greenpeace, and countries eager to help or grab profits, influence, or even territory, or to take sides in religious, ethnic, or racial conflicts. A nation-state's relative degree of development is often synonymous with its relative power in the world. There is a chicken-and-egg question, Which comes first, development or power? A related question is whether national development is affected more by internal policies, natural endowment, and problems, or by foreign forces such as trade, aid, and rivalries. To put it even more simply, why are the poor poor and the rich rich? Development thus is a vital concept for understanding international relations.[1]

This chapter analyzes the prerequisites for successful political development and its relationship with economic development within the Third World. First it addresses the controversy over just what the Third World is, then discusses some major arguments of those who advance external and internal explanations for development. Then the chapter explores political instability, coups, and revolutions in some countries. A country's relative developmental successes or failures depend, to varying extents, on that country's foreign relations and dependence on the global political economy. Each section examines the relationship between a nation's political development and international relations.

What Is *the* Third World?

There are many names for the world's poorer countries: the *Third World,* "the South" (because many of them are in the southern hemisphere), "the less developed countries" (LDCs), and "developing countries." This group of countries is contrasted with the *First World,* "the North," "the more developed countries," "the developed countries," and "the industrialized countries." Those who use "First and Third World" terminology also include a *Second World* of communist countries that are industrializing. With communism's collapse in Eastern Europe and the Soviet Union, this category has fallen into disuse.

None of these categories adequately captures the range of development levels among these 150 or so countries. The terms "developed" and "developing countries" are particularly inadequate. If development is synonymous with progress, then most rich and many poor countries are "developing" as measured by achieving higher living standards and quality of life. If measurable progress is truly unending, then we cannot say any country is "developed" per se. Likewise, the terms "North" and "South" are inadequate, because many poor countries are found in the northern hemisphere and some rich countries in the southern hemisphere.

Although the terms "more" and "less" developed countries capture the relative differences in development, they lack precision in explaining exactly when a country is one or the other.

For convenience's sake, if nothing else, most people use the term Third World to designate the world's relatively poorer countries. The term *Tiers Monde* (Third World) was coined by French intellectuals in the 1950s as a means of distinguishing between the First World or American bloc and the Second World or Soviet bloc. It has since been heavily criticized, in part because it may denote third rate in social or ethnic as well as economic terms. Another problem is that it groups together too many very different countries. Although Third World countries are said to share poverty and victimization by Western *imperialism*, even these two characteristics are inadequate. Not every poor country was a former colony. Iran, Turkey, Thailand, Ethiopia, Afghanistan, Liberia, Yemen, China, and Japan were never directly colonized, and most of Latin America received its independence from Spain in the 1820s. Also, the degree of poverty varies so greatly from one country to the next that the category appears meaningless. For example, the gap in political economic development between the Third World countries such as Bangladesh and Malaysia may be as wide as that between Malaysia and the United States.

Yet another criticism is that the term implies shared political as well as economic orientations. The over 150 countries grouped in the Third World include flourishing liberal democratic states and brutal authoritarian states; free market, mixed market and centrally planned economies; and pro-Western, nonaligned, and (at least until recently) pro-Soviet governments. The Third World includes such countries as China and India, both armed with nuclear weapons and huge armies, and with 1.2 billion and 980 million people, respectively, and microstates such as Nauru with 9,000 and Vanuatu with 23,000 people. Shiva Naipaul, the noted Trinidadian novelist, complained that the "Third World is a form of bloodless universality that robs individuals and societies of their particularity. To blandly subsume, say, Ethiopia, India, and Brazil under the banner of Third Worldhood is as absurd and as denigrating as the old assertion that all Chinese look alike."[2]

Some argue that the term can have more meaning if we limit the category of Third World countries to those that have achieved relatively high degrees of economic, social, and infrastructure development and have the potential to develop into First World states.[3] Countries such as Argentina, Chile, China, South Korea,

Table 14.1 **The Global Distribution of Income**

	Population (1998)	Per Capita Consumption (1980–1997)	Per Capita Income (1980)
World	5,897 billion	3.1 percent	$ 4,890
High Income	885 million	2.1 percent	$25,510
Middle Income	1,496 billion	1.2 percent	$ 2,950
Upper Middle Income	588 million	1.5 percent	$ 4,860
Lower Middle Income	908 million	—	$ 1,710
Low Income	3,515 billion	3.9 percent	$ 520

— indicates no available information for that period.

Source: World Bank Report, 2000.

Part 6 Geoeconomic Conflict and Cooperation Between the First and Third Worlds

South Africa, Costa Rica, Saudi Arabia, Brazil, and the former socialist countries in the Soviet Union and Eastern Europe would be among those designated as Third World countries. The Fourth World would include such countries as Zambia, Malaysia, and Indonesia, which remain poor but because of their human and/or natural resources and development policies have the potential and will to develop further. The Fifth World would include those with little real potential or will to develop, such as Niger, Chad, Nigeria, and Bangladesh, to name a few. This distinction among Third, Fourth, and Fifth worlds is certainly an analytical improvement on the older model.

The World Bank designation of 130 countries is still more precise. It divides states into four broad classes. High-income countries have per capita incomes over $9,360; upper middle-income, from $3,031 to $9,359; lower middle-income, from $761 to $3,060; and lower income, below $760.

This book uses all these possible terms for differentiating among countries to familiarize students with their use.

Third *and* First World Perspectives

Four of five people in the world are poor; one of five exists in poverty so crushing that he or she is chronically malnourished and often diseased. What explains the persistence of poverty among the Third World countries? Can every country in the world develop successfully? If so, what explains the reality that some poor countries have managed to alleviate their plight, others have stalled, and still others have actually gotten worse? What can or should be done about the world's poor? Are economic winners and losers inevitable? Is the success of some actually built on the exploitation, dependence, and continued poverty of others? Is the failure to develop largely a result of internal or external forces? Will these issues become more or less prominent in the post–cold-war era? Dependency and modernization theories offer conflicting answers to these and related questions.

Dependency theory and its offshoot, *world systems theory,* assert that all countries are caught up in a vast global system in which the rich industrial or *core countries* exploit the poor *peripheral* and *semiperipheral countries.*[4] Third World countries, they claim, cannot develop because the core countries will not allow them to do so. The poor are dependent on the industrial countries for markets for goods, finance, technology, managerial expertise, and weapons. The core countries use that Third World dependence to prevent them from developing. Multinational corporations corrupt the local elite by sharing profits with them as investors and slipping them bribes as public officials. The local elite then betray their own people by adopting the values and lifestyles of Westerners. They send their money to safe havens abroad rather than invest it at home. Thus *colonialism,* in this view, has simply been replaced by a more subtle but no less effective form of exploitation called *neocolonialism.* Newly independent states are still dependent on their former masters, and other industrial countries for technology, finance, markets, and products. The plantations, mines, and factories first created by the imperial powers often remain in foreign hands, and regardless of independence continue to be economic enclaves or islands within the former colony. Little if any wealth from this production trickles down to the native population. Those countries that use much of their arable land to plant one or a few cash crops for export often end up importing most of their food. The result, say the dependency theorists, is

dependency theory argues that **Third World** countries are doomed to remain poor because they are trapped in an exploitive global economy in which rich countries collaborate with the elites of poor countries to exploit the mines, plantations, and cheap wages of the Third World countries.

neocolonialism the idea that **colonialism** has simply been replaced by a more subtle, but no less effective, form of exploitation. Newly independent states are still dependent on their former masters and other industrial countries for technology, finance, markets, and products. The plantations and mines first created by the imperial powers often remain in foreign hands and continue to be economic islands within the former colony. Little if any wealth from this production trickles down to the native population.

the *"development of underdevelopment"* in which multinational corporations (MNCs) serve the same function in administering these countries as the old colonial governments did. The multinationals form political economic alliances with the elite of the Third World country in exploiting the population.

modernization theory argues that every state can modernize in a series of stages similar to those experienced by the Western countries.

Modernization theorists argue that reality is far more complex than dependency theory allows.[5] They point to vast differences between countries within the so-called Third World and further argue that despite these differences, the Third World is developing and the First World is becoming as dependent on its markets, products, and resources as vice versa. In this view, a country's success or failure to develop depends primarily on the decisions of its government. If a government pursues policies that strengthen political institutions, attract investments, and promote trade, the country will develop. If a government mismanages the economy, it has only itself to blame. Although it is true that multinational corporations are powerful, even the poorest of Third World countries can harness them by playing them off against each other to get the best investment and trade deals from all. The less and more developed countries can use each other to mutual advantage. A 1978 U.S. State Department publication pointed out that "by the mid-1980s, the World Bank expects economic growth in the more advanced LDCs to have a significant, positive impact on the growth rates of the developed countries. The collective demand of the LDCs is already influential in sustaining the production of goods and services in the U.S. and other industrialized countries during periods of economic recession and in accelerating their recovery from recession."[6]

Despite this growing interdependence and contrary to the claims of dependency theorists, the advanced industrial countries do not gain most or even much of their wealth from the Third World. In 1987, only 21 percent of all advanced industrial country exports were with the Third World, whereas only 22 percent of their total imports were from the Third World. Likewise, about 75 percent of foreign investments are within the advanced industrial countries rather than between them and the poor countries. Joan Spero points out that in 1987, 76 percent of total American direct foreign investment was in other industrial states and only 24 percent in the Third World.[7] The share of American direct foreign investments in the First World had risen since 1961, when they accounted for 61 percent of the total, whereas 35 percent were in the Third World. Altogether, in 1987, American firms earned only 30 percent of their total profits from Third World countries, which consisted of only 2.2 percent of all U.S. business earnings, and an infinitesimal part of American GNP. The rate of return on investments was an average 20.3 percent in the developed and only 13.7 percent in the Third World countries. Clearly, the advanced industrial states rely mostly on relations with each other for the bulk of their prosperity.

Who is right? Conflicting evidence can be marshaled to support both the dependency and the modernization theories. There is no doubt that the First World generates most of its wealth within itself rather than from the Third World, and in relative terms the Third World's importance to First World development is diminishing. Still, both the First and Third Worlds need each other, although the Third World depends on the First World much more than vice versa. The global economy provides every country goods, services, technology, finance, managerial expertise, and ideas that it otherwise would not have. Those Third World countries that have grown the fastest have been the most heavily involved in world trade. Yet the rules and power distribution within the global economy may well mean a very uneven playing field between First and Third World countries.

What Hinders Successful Development?

Daily the headlines blare news of coups, mass poverty, or famine in faraway countries. Less often, one can read stories of some nations that have experienced economic growth, rising health standards, or democratic elections. Why do some states succeed and others fail to develop politically and economically? This section will examine the roles that leadership, ideology, institutions, mobilization, legitimacy, and corruption can play in a country's *political development* within a global system.[8]

LEADERSHIP

Leadership is the ability of a government to mobilize a population and promote the policies that better people's lives. Max Weber identified three types of legitimate leadership—rational or constitutional, traditional, and charismatic.[9] *Development theory* argues that rational or constitutional-style governments have the best chance of achieving *economic development.* Chiang Kaishek and Park Chunghee of Taiwan and South Korea, respectively, offer good examples of dictators of sophisticated states who spurred development. The Saud family of Saudi Arabia offers an excellent example of a traditional leadership that has tried to bring economic development to their kingdom while fairly successfully staving off modernization's social forces such as premarital sex and MTV. A traditional leader such as King Jigme Singye Wangchuk of Bhutan makes no significant contribution to his realm's development, but he does maintain order for decades until he is overthrown. In contrast, *charismatic leaders* such as Ghana's President Jerry John Rawlings, lack the

development theory argues that rational or constitutional-style governments provide the best chance for achieving **economic development.**

Table 14.2 **Quality-of-Life Indicators**

	Per 1,000 Mortality, under 5 Years		Life Expectancy at Birth, 1997		Adult Illiteracy (%), 1977	
	1980	1997	Male	Female	Male	Female
World	125	79	65	69	18	33
Low Income	151	97	62	64	22	42
Excluding China/India	178	130	55	58	30	47
Middle Income	—	42	66	72	10	16
Lower Middle	—	47	65	71	11	18
Upper Middle	—	34	67	74	9	13
Low/Middle Income	137	83	63	67	19	34
East Asia/Pacific	81	46	67	70	9	13
Europe/Central Asia	—	30	64	73	2	6
Latin America/Caribbean	—	41	66	73	12	14
Mideast/North Africa	137	62	66	68	27	50
South Asia	180	100	62	63	34	63
Sub-Saharan Africa	189	147	49	52	34	50
High Income	15	7	74	81	—	—

— indicates no available information for that year.

Source: World Bank Report, 2000.

institutions that constitutional or traditional governments have for maintaining political stability and mobilizing resources. Thus charismatic leaders have particular problems in achieving economic development.

Most independence struggles have been led by charismatic leaders who succeed by getting most of the population to identify with their successes, dynamism, and dreams. Charismatic leaders appeal to the dominant segments of the population and can provide unity when there might otherwise be factionalism. They become symbols of the state and thus rise above criticism. They also serve as role models and sources of pride and national unity for most people. The net effect is to give the new regime stability while it attempts to fulfill its promises. Often vague about the specific policies he or she will follow once in office, the charismatic leader captures people's hearts rather than their minds.

Charismatic leaders have an enormous psychological grip over most of the population. They claim—and seem—to personify the nation. Many people want to believe in a messiah who will make everything right, and charismatic leaders fulfill that need. The more fervent followers of China's Mao Zedong and Indonesia's Sukarno actually deified them. The power of charisma is nicely illustrated by Cuba's president, Fidel Castro. Why has Castro remained in power since 1959 despite the failure of his economic policies and the collapse of communism elsewhere? His magnetic charisma may be the most important reason, followed closely by brutal oppression. He still electrifies the Cuban people, when most other leaders would have been overthrown long before. By continuing to mobilize the population against a nonexistent American threat, he distracts them from protesting his own failures.

Charismatic leaders often devise their own ideologies—Maoism, Nasserism, Nkrumahism, Sukarnoism—to justify their actions and ambitions.[10] Many of these ideologies share similarities. They identify a past golden age that was destroyed by Western imperialism. The leader promises to revive the nation's past glories by forging a modern, just society built on workers and peasants. Although the population must be mobilized to devote itself to building a future ideal society, liberal democracy is deemed unsuitable for the nation's needs. Instead the charismatic leader imposes a social or guided democracy in which he listens carefully to the masses and fulfills their wishes. Likewise, the economy is guided rather than free. Although the country has cast off colonialism's shackles, the leader and people must remain vigilant against foreign powers. Western imperialism remains a threat and must be constantly thwarted.

These ideas are nicely captured by the charter of the United Arab Republic:

> This socialist solution is the only path where all elements participating in the process of production can meet, according to scientific rules, capable of supplying society with all the energies enabling it to rebuild its life on the basis of a carefully studied and comprehensive plan. Efficient socialist planning is the sole method which guarantees the use of all national resources, be they material, natural, or human, in a practical, scientific, and humane way aimed at realizing the common good of the masses, and ensuring a life of prosperity for them.[11]

revolution of rising expectations popular mass anticipation that a government will keep its promise to quickly achieve ambitious political, economic, and/or social goals.

revolution of rising frustrations popular mass frustration, which often leads to political instability when a government fails to fulfill promises to overcome problems.

Although charismatic dictators do provide their countries with a source of unity and pride, there are dangers as well. Charismatic leaders are particularly notorious for generating the *revolution of rising expectations* that soon becomes a *revolution of rising frustrations* when promises remain unfulfilled. All the power that charisma brings often goes to a leader's head and he embarks on programs that squander scarce human, natural, and material resources on wasteful monuments to himself and the country rather than investing those resources in development. When a population is loyal to a person rather than to a constitution and its institutions, the regime crumbles easily when the leader is deposed or discredited. Charismatic leaders are often loath to designate successors, and there is often a bitter power struggle when one dies or is driven into exile or the grave. And for nearly all charismatic leaders, behind the stirring words and images, brute force and often terror kept them in power and the population as intimidated as inspired.

One by one the world's charismatic dictators are being replaced by a new generation of leaders. These "technocrats" are usually trained at Western universities and are dedicated to developing modern political institutions and economic sectors. Unfortunately their efforts are usually stymied by the chaotic, corrupt, and poverty-stricken national legacy of their charismatic predecessors.

POLITICAL INSTITUTIONS AND SYSTEMS

Leaders, whether traditional, constitutional, charismatic, technocratic or some mix, must operate within some type of political system.[12] The most charismatic of leaders will accomplish nothing without a government that can impose order and implement policies. Governments rule through political, media, social, and economic institutions. Stability is essential. As Samuel Huntington put it, "The primary problem is not liberty but the creation of a legitimate public order. Men may, of course, have order without liberty, but they can not have liberty without order. Authority has to exist before it can be limited, and it is authority that is in scarce supply in those modernizing countries where government is at the mercy of alienated intellectuals, rambunctious colonels, and rioting students."[13] The more efficient and comprehensive the institutions, the more easily a government can rule and develop a population.

But institutions and order are not enough. Governments must be able to devise and implement policies that develop the economy and improve most people's lives. Until recently, communist countries have experienced stability largely because of the Communist party's ability to create a national organization that controlled every neighborhood, village, and workplace. But communism never succeeded in significantly raising people's living standards. Although most observers were surprised by the democratic revolutions in 1989 through 1991 that swept away one communist regime after another, the collapse of the communist bloc was inevitable (although Gorbachev's revolutionary policies hastened its demise) given its developmental failures.

The most important political institutions for any country are the bureaucracy, political parties, interest groups, and the police and military. The bureaucracy gathers information and revenues, and formulates and implements policies. Political parties link the government with the people; they act to mobilize the population and determine the people's needs and dissatisfactions. Interest groups lobby the political parties, bureaucrats, and politicians for privileges or redress of grievances. Finally, the police and military maintain order and collect political information (the role of the military and police in politics is discussed in the coup section). Political instability often results if one or more of these institutions or forces are corrupt, inefficient, and/or disloyal.

Ideally, a bureaucracy is an apolitical set of institutions whose role is to gather information, present policy options to the leadership, and then implement the subsequent choices. The bureaucracy is divided into ministries or departments, each of which deals with a specific area of responsibility—welfare, education, defense, industrial development, and so on. Bureaucrats or officials are highly educated and trained experts who conscientiously fulfill their respective ministry's responsibilities. They have been selected and are promoted on the basis of their skills.

Unfortunately, few national bureaucracies match this ideal. The bureaucracy is often largely a huge drain on scarce financial, human, and material resources, and impedes rather than promotes development. In many countries, particularly less developed ones, the bureaucracy is simply a jobs program for those loyal to the government. Officials lack training, education, and commitment to their ministry's mission, and are often corrupt, inefficient, and wasteful. That was characteristic of bureaucracies in all the democratic industrial countries, including the United States, before a political backlash led to reforms that transformed them into the professional organizations they are today. Reforms do not occur in isolation. Bureaucratic reform is an essential part of broader political development, which is interdependent with economic development.

Political parties mobilize segments of the population, provide a power base for elected officials, gather information on popular views and frustrations, socialize the population into certain attitudes and opinions, define issues, and criticize opposing parties. There is a wide spectrum of political parties and systems in which they operate throughout the world. Some parties have an extremely narrow scope, and only attempt to represent a particular religion, ethnic group, or class. *Catch-all parties,* as the name implies, strive to include as much of the population as possible under their banner. Many less developed countries are essentially *one-party states* that may tolerate opposition parties but dominate most reins of political, economic, and social power. In Mexico, the Party of Revolutionary Institutions (PRI) has ruled since 1929. India's Congress party ruled for decades until the 1990s, when other parties pushed it into opposition. Genuine *multiparty* or *two-party systems* in which parties change power have succeeded most prominently in many Latin American countries, South Korea, Taiwan, India, South Africa, and are emerging sporadically elsewhere.

In every political system there is a danger that political parties will lose touch with their primary purpose—serving as a conduit of needs, ideas, support, and accountability between the government and the people. Because they already dominate the system and are not accountable to the public through competitive elections, political parties in one-party systems are particularly apt to disregard the need to address society's ills. Yet there is no guarantee that a multiparty system will better address a country's problems than a one-party system. Many political parties in both multiparty and one-party systems are simply personal political machines created by politicians to win elections and maintain power.

Every social grouping, whether religious, ethnic, regional, professional, gender, sexual, generational, racial, urban, or rural, has distinct interests or needs that ideally government can better serve. Sometimes these interests are organized and systematically lobby the government for help. There are six types of interest groups: (1) *business groups,* which pressure government for more protection from competition and subsidies, less or no taxes, and often fewer or no restrictions on safety, pollution, or quality; (2) *industrial worker or farm labor groups,* which support higher wages, health, safety, and job security standards for employees; (3) *consumer groups,* which seek lower prices, and safer and better quality products; (4) *environmental groups,* which advocate restricting businesses' destruction of the natural and human environment through their pollution, logging, mining, and construction; (5) *humanitarian groups,* which advocate programs that help those who cannot help themselves; and (6) *religious groups,* which advocate policies based on their sacred texts.

Burying Apartheid's Ghost: South Africa's 1999 Elections

Democracy is now flourishing in South Africa. In June 1999, South Africa held its second election since the apartheid system by which whites deprived blacks and other minorities of their human and civil rights was demolished. In fiercely contested campaigns, 13 political parties managed to win seats in the parliament, up from 7 in the 1994 election. President Nelson Mandela's African National Congress Party (ANC) won 266 seats, up from 252 seats. The Liberal Democratic Party also emerged stronger, increasing its seats from 7 to 34. Other prominent parties lost. The Zulu-nationalist Inkatha Freedom Party's seats dropped from 43 to 34, the conservative New National Party (formerly the National Party), from 82 to 28 seats, and the communist Freedom Party from 9 to 3 seats.

At times a defeat can be a disguised victory. By falling one seat short of the two-thirds majority needed to change the constitution, the ANC leaders can resist the demands of their more radical constituents and factions that they change the constitution. Any constitutional changes would open the ANC to opposition party charges that it has become a "tyranny of the majority" subverting democracy.

Governments ideally find a balance between giving too much or too little to the interest groups that make demands on them. This is best accomplished when there is a power balance among a profusion of contending interest groups. Few if any political systems achieve this ideal. Of the six types of interest groups, business interests are the most powerful in most nonsocialist, secular countries. Business groups gain the upper hand by their greater financial and organizational resources and thus overwhelm the often vocal but poorly financed and organized demands of labor, consumer, environmental, humanitarian, and religious interests.

MOBILIZATION AND LEGITIMACY

Mobilizing the people's energies, loyalties, and efforts is essential for political stability and economic development. The population must be convinced not only to support but make sacrifices for governmental policies and national identity. Under the right circumstances, the state can mobilize virtually anyone no matter whether by appealing to their passions or reason. Governments mobilize the loyalties of people through the mass media, political parties, and local patron–client systems.

Although mass rallies and constant socialization through the mass media are important, a government's success in mobilizing its population ultimately depends on its ability to tap into local *patron–client groups*. Patrons are usually local strongmen with wealth and political power who dispense favors—jobs, loans, housing, help in forming a business, protection to businesses, entrance to college, potential spouses, advice and information, and so on—to those in the community in return for their political loyalty and a portion of their income. Local patrons in turn become the clients for national leaders and parties in which each does favors for the other. Patron–client groups tend to diminish in power as a country modernizes and its citizens find alternate ways to achieve their interests.

People are loyal to those individuals, governments, and institutions that they believe are legally, morally, and culturally legitimate. An individual, government, or institution loses its legitimacy and loyalty if it is corrupt, inefficient, or brutal, or if it grossly violates cultural norms. The ease with which the legitimacy of a political systems' leaders, institutions, and values are questioned, however, varies with a society's modernization level. Traditional peoples generally do not question the legitimacy of their culture's political, economic, and social institutions, and the actions or inaction of those who control them. They do not expect much, so they do not demand much. Although modern individuals believe they can make a difference and thus question their society's leadership and policies, by definition a modern society provides most of its members with enough benefits and opportunities so that there is no need to question the culture's basic values and institutions. Modern individuals are loyal by choice, and they choose to remain loyal because most of their material and psychological needs are met. Traditional individuals are loyal because they cannot imagine being anything else. The most intense questioning of a political system's legitimacy comes from people within countries that are in a transitional stage between tradition and modernity. In *transitional societies,* political system are often unable to satisfy most people's needs, expectations, and demands.

Like the Wizard of Oz, governments, corporations, bureaucracies, universities, and other institutions hide behind elaborate curtains and manipulate "sound and light" shows designed to instill awe and devotion in their subjects. Presidents claiming to personify the nation are housed in massive buildings, presented with trumpets and motorcades, and surrounded by the symbols of office.

In any political system, a government's greatest power is the power to persuade. The more democratic the country, the more a government must attempt to persuade a population to follow its policies. The more authoritarian a government, the greater the tendency to coerce a population into compliance with its policies. Coercive power, however, often proves ultimately self-defeating. Mass alienation deepens even if most people sullenly perform their duties. There are always at least a handful of radicals agitating for the government's overthrow. Too much economic deprivation or political brutality can swell the antigovernment forces' support and lead to civil war.

CORRUPTION

Corruption is the illegal use of public or private resources for personal gain. Every society has a different threshold for the tolerable amount and type of corruption. If officials exceed that threshold, there will be a backlash and they may end up in jail or against a wall. A society's corruption threshold varies over time and is related to the evolution from an agrarian into an advanced industrial nation. Agrarian societies and their sources of wealth are relatively simple. Corruption and the toleration threshold increases with industrialization as enormous amounts of wealth are created. Some governments are outright *kleptocracies* that seem to do little more than transfer enormous amounts of national wealth into private estates, businesses, or bank accounts. Duvalier of Haiti, Marcos of the Philippines, Somoza of Nicaragua, and Mobutu of Zaire were among the most notorious pillagers of their countries' public and private wealth. The more corrupt a country, the more scarce resources are diverted from potential investments in health, education, infrastructure, and industry that could develop the country into luxury lifestyles for the elite.

Structural corruption characterizes many countries in which everyone from the president to the lowest official requires a "gift" in return for favors. In many

structural corruption systematic and accepted corruption.

countries, there is no concept of civil service in which officials are devoted solely to national goals. Instead, one's primary loyalty is to one's kinship group. Those who attain powerful political or economic positions are expected to aid others from their clan. This is particularly a problem in nation-states with little or no national consciousness.

Rather than being civil servants, all too many bureaucrats abuse their power for private rather than national gain. Although they usually have security, salaries are low. Officials supplement their meager paychecks by demanding "tips" from the public just to perform simple functions. The size of the "bite" (*mordida*, in Spanish-speaking countries) depends on the official's rank and the supplicant's needs. A multinational corporation requesting, for example, a building permit might have to hand over thousands of dollars to top officials.

This official corruption is often reinforced by culture.[14] In many cultures, an office job is considered to have high status, whereas a business, construction, or factory job has lower status. Thus the most talented and best educated individuals may strive for a bureaucratic career that may offer little responsibility or pay but does have high status. With no responsibilities or accountability, absenteeism is rife. A survey of Turkish officials found that 76 percent of 362 surveyed preferred "maximum security/low salary."[15] Of course, it is expected that they will supplement their salaries with "tips." In 1982, a Egyptian newspaper editorial pointed out that "No sooner is an official promoted to the post of manager than he ceases to accomplish any constructive work. His primary concern is to receive the compliments indiscriminately leveled at him from every quarter, and to smile with condescending magnanimity at the servile flattery lavished at him by his former colleagues."[16]

Another problem is the refusal of many officials to take responsibility for a problem. Bureaucrats avoid any innovation or experimentation and simply follow "standard operating procedures" (SOPs) even if they do not work at all. Fearing that they will be scapegoated if anything goes wrong, many officials simply direct a public appeal to another bureau. Supplicants wander through a seemingly endless maze of officials with none willing to address their particular problem. Thus "Trial and error and free discussion might only prove that superiors are not infallible. . . . Confronted by a basic sense of insecurity, everyone must fall back on the safest course of action; everyone must adhere strictly to form, to procedure, and to ritual."[17]

Can this corruption ever be rooted out? A 1976 survey of Thai corruption mirrors the bureaucracies of many less developed countries, with 80 percent of public officials and 86 percent of citizens identifying "teamwork corruption" embedded in the system; 65 percent of public officials and 71 percent of the citizens were pessimistic about uprooting corruption.[18] The reasons given for this entrenched, structural corruption included (1) "endless desires of human beings; (2) opportunities and loopholes in laws and regulations; (3) deep-rooted habits arising out of being accustomed to resorting to corruption; (4) lack of control by superiors; (5) learning from others' experiences; (6) excessive authority; (7) economic necessities; (8) need for convenience; (9) demise of morality; and (10) patron–client relationships."[19]

In such a work environment, even the most idealistic of individuals who really wants to accomplish the ministry's responsibilities soon settles down into the bureaucracy's routine. What else can one do when all the others have their hands in the till and enrich themselves and their families while disregarding their professional responsibilities?

Corruption may not be all bad. Bribery or the "user pays" system, does generally accomplish specific tasks, while the bureaucracy provides some welfare to the extended families of the officials.[20] There is no doubt, however, that corruption is an enormous drag on a country's political and economic development.

What Causes Political Instability?

A political system is stable when the population views its basic institutions and processes as legitimate, decision makers have enough authority to make and implement national policies, and the transfer of power from one leader to the next is smooth and widely accepted. What governments tend to be more stable? In the most poverty-stricken authoritarian states, the masses of poor usually do not challenge the government because they are ignorant of alternatives or fatalistic about improving their lot, and their existences are so consumed with day-to-day survival that they lack the energy and time for anything else. Nonetheless, a military *coup d'état* may occur even if revolutions are unlikely. Most citizens in liberal democracies accept the system as legitimate because their lives are secure and comfortable and the government seems largely responsive to the demands made on it.

Societies in transition from traditionalism into modernity are the most politically, economically, and socially unstable. Political economic development has failed when armed bands take to the hills and streets. Why do states dissolve into civil war?[21]

Unrealistic goals and the means to achieve them are the most common reason for a nation's failure to develop. Even seemingly modest plans are unrealistic if a nation lacks the institutions necessary to implement them. Many countries lack enough experts with the technical and administrative knowledge necessary to fulfill even the simplest development projects. Even if the experts are in place, the country may still lack the material and technological resources with which to build a project, or the communications, marketing, or transportation infrastructure that can service it. Money is a perennial problem. Most Third World countries do not have a banking system that can gather and lend enough capital for the nation's development demands. Governments often end up importing everything needed for a project—experts, institutions, technology, finance, construction materials—and thus deepen rather than alleviate their foreign debt and dependence.

Likewise, political institutions fail if they are not rooted in the country's culture. Virtually every Latin American country has experienced swings between authoritarianism and democracy, with neither system able to achieve the socioeconomic development promised and demanded. As they won their independence from Spain in the 1820s, the newly independent Latin American countries created liberal democratic constitutions modeled on that of the United States. However, the cultures and institutions of these new countries, unlike in the United States, were rooted in authoritarianism and feudalism rather than democracy and free enterprise. The newly created democratic political systems were unable to manage the growing problems posed by independence and internal rivalries, and in one country after another military coups took over the government. In the late 19th and early 20th centuries, many of these countries reverted to democratic rule as a growing middle class clamored for representation. Democracy in Argentina, Chile, and Uruguay seemed to become particularly well rooted. Yet military coups toppled their democratic governments during the 1970s. These Latin American democracies failed for many of the same reasons Germany's democracy failed in the early 1930s: The governments were unable to deal with worsening economic

All six countries of Latin America's southern cone—Argentina, Bolivia, Brazil, Chile, Paraguay, and Uruguay—along with Guatemala converted from authoritarian to democratic rule between 1983 and 1989. When a dictatorship yields to democracy, should the newly elected leaders prosecute the crimes of their predecessors? Although the rule of law demands justice, the rule of politics might insist that the past be buried with the dead.

The former dictatorships imposed reigns of mass murder, imprisonment, torture, and looting on the people of those countries. Horrific as those crimes were, prosecuting the criminals might unleash more horrors. Blanket amnesties for former dictators and their henchmen makes political sense. Those who committed those crimes might have handed over the government but retain enormous military, economic, and social power. Zealous prosecutors might provoke a coup or civil war that destroys the nascent democracy. Yet can a government be genuinely democratic if it tolerates criminals in its midst, if it turns a blind eye to justice? How did the new democratic leaders of the seven countries handle that moral and political dilemma?

The Argentinean junta murdered at least 30,000 people and was deeply feared. Yet that regime was completely discredited by humiliating defeat in the Falklands War against Britain, and yielded power shortly thereafter. The new democratic government boldly created a truth commission that thoroughly investigated the genocide and jailed the dictators and many of the criminals in their organization.

The body count of Chile's dictatorship was over 4,000. The new government's truth commission not only chose not to name names, but also allowed former dictator General Augusto Pinochet to remain the military head and a senator for life. At most it prosecuted some low-ranking murderers.

Brazil's dictatorship was relatively benevolent by regional standards—it only murdered about 200 people from 1965 through 1985. Amnesty was extended to all associated with the old regime, and compensation was given to families of the victims.

Paraguay's General Alfredo Strossner enjoyed the longest rule of these dictators, imposing his will from 1954 to 1989. During those 35 years, his regime murdered several hundred people. As in Brazil, Paraguay's new leaders chose to shut the book on that gruesome past.

Uruguay's junta fought a civil war against an elusive guerrilla force during much of its rule from 1973 to 1985, during which it killed about 250 people. The new regime issued a blanket amnesty to the old.

Several hundred murders each are attributed to Bolivia's three most recent dictatorships, General Hugo Banzer's from 1971 to 1978, General Luis Garcia Meza's from 1978 to 1980, and Colonel Luis Arce Gomez from 1980 to 1981. Under pressure from Washington, the new government did send Meza to prison for a 30-year term and extradited Gomez to the United States, where he was charged and imprisoned for leading a drug cartel. However, Banzer remains a free man.

But the human rights abuses in all those countries combined pale beside those of Guatemala. After three decades of civil war, peace finally settled across Guatemala in 1996 when the army yielded power to democracy and the new government signed an agreement with the rebels. A truth commission found that over 200,000 people were slaughtered during the war. Ninety percent of the victims died at the hands of a succession of dictatorships, the most brutal of which were those of Romeo Lucas Garcia and Efrain Rios Montt from 1978 to 1983. But neither of these men nor any others are likely to stand trial. As in most other countries experiencing a transition from dictatorship to democracy, the Guatemalan government has put stability before justice.

How democratic are the new regimes? All have the trappings of democracy, with elections, several political parties, constitutions, and bills of rights. But Amnesty International and America's Watch note that police brutality and human rights violations occur to varying degrees in all these countries. Will democracy establish deep roots and flourish? Or will it wither and die, as has happened in those countries' past?

problems such as hyperinflation, capital flight, stagnant growth, and mass poverty, along with the subsequent political unrest.

Governments must have the means to achieve their development ends. Many countries have dissolved into chaos and civil war because the government promised more than it could provide—a revolution of rising expectations soon became a revolution of rising frustrations. A transitional society "teaches people to become consumers long before it teaches them to become producers; it teaches them to place demands upon the government long before it imbues them with the responsibilities of citizenship."[22] If only a minority of people in even the most modern societies are entrepreneurs, then the possibility of an entrepreneur class emerging from a traditional society is remote.

Violence usually occurs amid a sharp socioeconomic and widening chasm between rich and poor, cities and countryside, ethnic groups, religions, and/or regions. Economic problems are often exacerbated by a rapidly increasing population. If the population increases faster than the economy grows, then, overall, people are becoming poorer. Most of the new wealth flows into the bank accounts of those who are already rich.

Ethnic rather than class conflict seems to be the primary cause for the civil wars tearing apart some countries such as Malawi and Azerbaijan. Elsewhere, religion is seen as the stimulus for violence in Ireland, Yugoslavia, Israel, and Lebanon. Yet beneath both ethnic and religious violence, economic inequalities and sense of *relative deprivation* are invariably present. In each of these countries one ethnic or religious group is better off than the others, a condition that in some cases has lasted hundreds of years.

In many countries, a lack of political and socioeconomic mobility frustrates the rise of those who aspire to more. Economic development often creates new socioeconomic classes. Industrialization, for example, creates a class of factory workers that may make political demands that are not satisfied. The creation of new wealth, if it remains concentrated in the hands of a few, can disrupt a society. For example, the discovery of oil in Libya in the 1950s caused a small segment of the population to become very rich while the rest of society suffered from inflation and poverty. As a result, King Indrus was overthrown in 1969.

Sometimes governments are too traditional, and their policies and attitudes fail to keep up with the modernity that is sweeping the country. By resisting change rather than attempting to channel it into constructive directions, most traditional regimes are eventually swept away by modernity. New sources of wealth and classes emerge to surpass and challenge the traditional rulers. The regime may respond with a crackdown that may succeed in quelling dissenters in the short run but further undermines the government's *legitimacy* over the long run.

Likewise, sometimes a government's policies and attitudes are too modern for the population. For example, the shah's "White Revolution" attempted systematically to transform Iran from a traditional into a modern state. Increasing segments of the population rejected the shah's attempts to destroy traditional society. The shah invested in symbols of modernity—dams, steel mills, petrochemical plants—while neglecting such things as education, welfare, and small businesses. Rapid economic growth was inflationary, which made the poor poorer and increasingly disgruntled as they compared themselves to the small populations of rich and middle class and their conspicuous consumption. The result was the 1979 revolution that swept the shah from power and imposed an Islamic regime.

relative deprivation a situation in which a group or individual feels less privileged than others (and resents that).

When *and* Why Coups May Occur

In all there are at least 11 conditions that make coups likely:

1. The government's prestige sharply declines.
2. There are deep schisms among political leaders.
3. There is little chance of foreign intervention to help the government.
4. There have recently been coups in neighboring countries.
5. The nation is split by deep and growing social, economic, ethnic, religious, and/or political antagonisms.
6. There is a growing economic crisis, and worsening gap between rich and the masses of poor.
7. Government and bureaucratic corruption and inefficiency are entrenched and growing.
8. There is a rigid class structure in which military service is the only means of social mobility.
9. The military increasingly believes it is the only institution with the power, legitimacy, and ideas to reform the country.
10. Foreign business interests, diplomats, and/or military advisers encourage a coup.
11. The military has recently been defeated in war and blames the civilian government for the defeat.[24]

MILITARY COUPS

Prolonged political instability often leads to a military coup d'état in which one government is violently overthrown and a new one imposed.[23] The successful coup is well-planned, includes elite or strategically placed units, targets the leading government leaders and mass media outlets, is executed quickly and decisively, and can justify its takeover. Usually a coup involves only a small segment of the military. Most commanders and their troops stay in their barracks until they see which way the coup is going. Fighting rarely lasts long. Escalation into civil war is uncommon. Most people's lives are unaffected. Anywhere from one-third to one-half of all coups are crushed by troops loyal to the existing government. Some governments have attempted to guard against coups by creating a paramilitary or national guard to offset the regular military. Coups breed coups. Once a country has an established tradition of military intervention, it is hard to shake that pattern.

In some countries the military is the most modern institution and the only one capable of pushing through commands. Most militaries in less developed countries are primarily used to maintain internal rather than external security. Thus the military already intervenes in politics at the government's behest. Most military forces believe they personify the nation and contrast their national role with the corruption or inefficiency of politics.

The socioeconomic composition of the officer class is an important factor in coups. In many militaries there is a class division between the high-ranking officers, who have come from the traditional elite, and the lower- and middle-ranking officers, who have risen from more humble backgrounds. The lower-ranking officers are often appalled by the corruption they see in the military as well as politics and are frustrated by the lack of advancement opportunities and discrimination.

An officer's military education and experience also help determine whether or not he will participate in a coup. Some officers receive training in the United States, and most of them are socialized to support pro-American rulers and oppose anti-American rulers. The more military aid the United States gives a country, the more likely that country's military will overthrow its government. In contrast, some officers may have participated in an independence struggle during which they became fiercely anti-Western.[25]

The ability of a coup government to maintain power varies considerably. A study identified 60 countries that had experienced military governments from 1946 through 1984 and found the length of time varied from the still-in-power Taiwanese government (although technically Chiang Kaishek's takeover might be better considered an invasion from mainland China that he later "legitimized with a rigged election in 1947), to lasting only a few days for Gambia.[26] Most coup governments are sooner or later overthrown by another military faction. Some either directly hand power over to civilian leaders or call elections that result in a return to civilian rule.

There are both advantages and disadvantages to military rule.[27] The military is often development oriented and is inclined to favor policies that expand the economy. With its command system, it can make decisions relatively easily, and can back up its decisions with force. It also appears to represent the entire nation, compared to the politicians who represent special interests, so military rule can have a certain amount of legitimacy. The military coup leaders in Brazil in 1964 and Chile in 1973 hired foreign experts who helped develop those economies. Yet overall, the development record of military regimes may be no better than the records of the civilian regimes they replaced. Most military officers have no conception of how a modern economy works. With their hands in the treasury, many succumb to the same temptations of their civilian counterparts.

REFORMS

The same conditions that prompt a military coup can also stimulate a mass reform movement that "attempts to change limited aspects of a society but does not aim at drastically alternating or replacing major social, economic, or political institutions."[28] America's political development has been pulled along by a series of mass reform movements. The antislavery movement of the 1850s, the civil rights and antiwar movements of the 1960s, and the women's, environmental, gay, anti-pornography, prayer-in-public-schools, and pro- and antiabortion movements of the 1970s and 1980s were all organized mass attempts to reform through accepted political means what their adherents believed were defective parts of the existing system rather than to overthrow and transform the entire society through violence.

There is a clear connection between economic and political development. The demands for political representation expand with a country's middle class. As people achieve material security, many of them demand more intangible benefits from the state, such as human rights, a multiparty system, or a cleaner environment. Members of the middle class—businesspeople, homemakers, the retired—may join students and unions in protesting government corruption or repression. Faced with these mass protests, most governments eventually promise reforms.

During the mid-1980s, the Philippines experienced a successful democratic reform movement in which the government was forced to abide by its constitution. Under American rule (1899–1946), democracy and free markets took root in the Philippines. For nearly three decades after its independence, the Philippines grew steadily although unevenly. The rich got much richer and the middle class expanded, but more than 70 percent of the population remained mired in poverty. Then, in 1972, President Marcos declared martial law to deal with growing political and economic crises. The military successfully defeated a separatist movement among Muslims in the southern Philippines and contained a growing communist insurgency. But rather than use the power to develop the Philippines, Marcos and his cronies looted the country and worsened economic conditions. In the mid-1980s, Corazon Aquino, the wife of a former political rival of Marcos who was murdered by Marcos's henchmen, helped lead a mass democracy movement against Marcos. The United States pressured Marcos to resign and leave the country. Corazon Aquino became the president, and since 1986 the Philippines has enjoyed democratic rule.

Since "people power" helped overthrow the Marcos dictatorship in the Philippines in 1986, similar democratic movements have succeeded in South Korea, Taiwan, Bangladesh, Mongolia, and Thailand, whereas others in China and Burma have been crushed. Most of these reform movements have been stimulated by profound economic changes, often for the better, that enable many people to demand greater representation in government.

In South Korea and Taiwan, rapid growth and the emergence of a large middle class stimulated mass pressure for political reforms. Authoritarian governments in Taiwan and South Korea succeeded in rapidly developing their once poverty-stricken peoples into increasingly wealthy middle-class ones. In the late 1980s, South Korea's government experienced increasing mass pressure to democratize, and in 1987 it did so, allowing a free presidential election that year and free parliamentary elections the following year. Today South Korea has a multiparty liberal democratic political system. For similar reasons Taiwan's political system was democratized a decade later. Taiwan is rapidly evolving into a multiparty liberal democracy in which human rights are guaranteed.

REVOLUTION

Revolutions are as rare as military coups, and even mass reform movements are relatively common. A revolution can occur when coups or reform movements fail to alleviate harsh and worsening political and socioeconomic conditions. A revolutionary movement "is a social movement in which participants are organized to alter drastically or replace totally existing social, economic, or political institutions."[29] Revolutionaries "picture a vastly improved pattern of human relationships in a future realization, then impart their vision to the masses, hoping to motivate them to revolutionary action. The revolutionary describes a more perfect social situation—more freedom; more equality; more consciousness of community; more peace, justice, and human dignity; more of the transcendentals that appeal to human beings everywhere."[30] Or, as Hannah Arendt eloquently puts it, revolutionaries are fueled by a "pathos of novelty" in which "the notion that the course of history suddenly begins anew, that an entirely new story, a story never known or told before, is about to unfold."[31]

Autocracy *versus* Democracy *in* Indonesia

Few Third World countries have experienced as much political stability as Indonesia. From its independence from the Netherlands in 1948 through its 1999 election, Indonesia experienced only autocracy. Sukarno ruled until 1965 when he was forced to resign in a coup by Suharto who ruled until May 1998 when mass demonstrations and violence exploded against months of economic depression and decades of corrupt, inefficient rule. Suharto turned over power to his vice president B. J. Habibie, who calmed much of the violence by promising free elections within a year.

Indonesia's first democratic election was held in June 1999. United-Nations–trained monitors could only staff a handful of the 312,000 polling stations. Forty-eight parties, of which all but three were new, contested the election. The three most popular opposition parties, the Democratic Party of Reform, led by Sukarno's daughter Megawati Sukarnoputri, and the secular Islam parties of Abdurrahman Wahid and Amien Rais, joined in a "united front" to compete with Golkar, Suharto's official party, which he bequeathed to Habibie.

Sukarnoputri's party won the largest share of the votes, 33.7 percent, a plurality rather than majority. The election appears to have been largely fair. The long time it took to calculate the results came from inexperience rather than deliberate fraud. Was her victory also one for democracy? Many observers fear not. Sukarnoputri was noted for her opposition to the man who overthrew her father; she never expressed a deep commitment to democracy. In contrast, Habibie worked as an engineer in Germany for 20 years before he returned to enter his country's politics and is considered liberal by Indonesian standards.

But the parliamentary elections were just the first vital step toward democracy. The 500-member parliament will include 462 popularly elected seats and 38 reserved for military appointees. In November 1999, the 500 members of parliament joined with 200 appointees in a body known as the People's Consultative Assembly to vote for a president. They chose Abdurrahman Wahid to be Indonesia's first democratically elected president.

Extraordinary as this event was, democracy is about more than elections and even competitive parties. It includes the protection and promotion of civil and human rights as well. Can democracy be realized in a country with such a diverse population and such autocratic traditions? Indonesia's government faces grave challenges. With 203 million people scattered among 13,000 islands, Indonesia has the world's fourth largest and one of its most diverse populations. Independence movements are fighting against the government in three of the more distant and populous islands, East Timor, Aceh, and Irian Jaya. The challenges are great but perhaps not overwhelming. After all India, with a population nearing one billion, offers a model of successful multiparty democracy in a similarly diverse Third World population and culture. But India's success is one of the rare exceptions rather than the rule in the Third World. Indonesia's experiment with democracy continues.

Revolutions can differ greatly in their goals. Until recently, left-wing or socialist revolutions that aimed at achieving equality through a massive redistribution of wealth and state ownership of property were the most common. Yet there are conservative or right-wing revolutions as well, which aim at restoring society's traditional institutions, values, classes, hierarchy, and behaviors that modernization has lost or eroded. Iran's Islamic revolution is a classic conservative revolution that has attempted to transform the country into a strict fundamentalist theocracy. In contrast to the left- and right-wing revolutions that espouse a total-itarian system are liberal democratic revolutions that espouse political, economic, and social freedom. Liberal democratic revolutions swept away the communist regimes of eastern Europe from 1989 to 1991.

Revolutionary conditions may exist for decades before a revolutionary move-ment emerges. When revolutions do occur, we must ask why, given the history of repression, exploitation, brutality, and corruption that preceded it, did it not oc-cur earlier? Several vital conditions precede every revolution.[32]

Mass poverty itself is not enough. The most impoverished nations are often the least revolutionary. When most people are illiterate, teeter on starvation's brink, and spend virtually all waking hours scrounging for food, fuel, or shelter, they do not have the time or energy to question let alone challenge the prevailing order.

What is necessary is a widespread view that the vast gap between a few rich and many poor is unjust. This mass awareness of unjustness emerges in changing rather than stagnant societies. Revolutionary conditions proliferate in rapidly modernizing societies rather than traditional ones. Modernization promises prosperity, social mobility, and new opportunities. Increasing numbers of people must be motivated by the possibility of achieving a better life. Revolutionary conditions flourish when modernization's fruits appear to be enjoyed only by the few. There must be a vast, obvious, and growing gap between a small minority of political, social, and eco-nomic "haves" and the masses of "have nots." As Ted Gurr puts it, "the necessary precondition for violent civil conflict is deprivation, defined as the actors' percep-tions of discrepancy between their value expectations and their environment's ap-parent value capabilities."[33] Some people are enriching themselves, but conditions must be perceived as getting worse for most. Shantytowns ring wealthy neighbor-hoods, armies of unemployed wander the cities, crime rises, population growth spirals. Much of the population glimpses but fails to grasp a better life. Thus a "rev-olution of rising expectations" becomes a "revolution of rising frustrations."

But even this is not enough. Revolutions cannot happen unless society's tradi-tional values, institutions, behaviors, expectations, and leaders are largely discred-ited. The movement from countryside to city, from field to factory or schoolroom, from candle to electricity can as severely disturb as enhance an individual's life. Rapid modernization can completely disorient people, destroying old communities and beliefs while failing to provide new ones. Modernization swamps society's ex-isting institutions and leaders. Society's institutions are increasingly incapable of serving their functions, are deadlocked and impotent, and eventually collapse. Inefficiency and corruption are often closely tied. Officials abuse their positions for private gain rather than public service, and that corruption pervades the entire sys-tem rather than being confined to a few nefarious individuals. The demands for changes increase. Although a successful revolution may be centered in one partic-ular class or group, it must appeal to most classes and groups. Unions, farm coop-eratives, student organizations, churches, and other groups demand sweeping changes. The society is polarized between radically different extremes with no compromise possible. The political, social, economic, and religious elite becomes demoralized, split, and indecisive, while continuing to reject the membership of the radical elite in its ranks. Increasing numbers of the old elite defect to the radical elite. The military and police both increase their repression and are incapable of contain-ing the protests. Increasing numbers of officers, soldiers, and police either sympa-thize with or openly join the radical cause. When the old order fails to accommodate the needs and demands of the new, its legitimacy becomes thoroughly destroyed.

Despite all these preconditions, not everyone joins a revolutionary movement, let alone leads one. Most people usually avoid taking sides and just try to stay out of the line of fire. Peasants are particularly traditional, apathetic, and unwilling to challenge the status quo.

A revolution needs leaders, an ideology for change, and an organization. Increasing numbers of prominent intellectuals must not only criticize the old order but also advocate a new order. New myths must replace old myths. The masses can be won over with simple slogans, but the revolutionary leaders themselves must have an ideology or analytical framework for understanding the world, exposing the defects of the old order, and proposing revolutionary changes that will inaugurate a new ideal order.[34] Revolutions are ultimately organized and won or lost by small, cohesive, highly motivated conspiratorial elites that can mobilize masses of loyal followers willing to risk their lives for ideals, such as are epitomized by Vladimir Lenin's "dictatorship of the proletariat."

Revolutions are usually preceded by a crisis that thoroughly discredits the existing system. Defeat in war, natural disasters such as earthquakes or typhoons, invasion, the massacre of opponents, economic crises such as a depression, withdrawal of foreign aid, or a foreign embargo can all spark a mass insurrection that joins hands with existing guerrilla movements. For example, the 1917 Russian revolution would not have occurred without Russia's military defeat by the Japanese and the massacre of hundreds of protesters before the tzar's Winter Palace in 1905, and the deaths of millions and severe deprivation for virtually all in World War I.

Although revolutionary movements involve a broad coalition of groups, they are usually centered around one particular class, region, or group, or start in rural or urban areas. Marxist-Leninists based their entire philosophy and struggle on factory, mine, and other blue-collar workers known as the proletariat. Mao, in contrast, realized that the proletariat was only a tiny percentage of China's vast population. Instead, Mao based his revolution on the peasants, which comprised 85 percent of the population. Sometimes the most disaffected members of a society are its middle class. The American revolution was largely a middle-class revolution.

Revolutions are often sparked as much against foreign influences as domestic power holders. The Cuban, Vietnamese, and Chinese revolutionaries, for example, tapped deeply into the mass resentment against the respective American, French, and Japanese interference in their countries' internal affairs. Many revolutions are meshed with independence struggles. The United States simultaneously achieved independence from Britain and a democratic revolution; Ho Chi Minh, independence from France and a communist revolution; and from 1989 to 1991, Eastern European revolutionaries overthrew both communist and Russian rule.

Revolutions, in turn, often have profound international consequences. The American and French revolutions stimulated revolutionary movements elsewhere. The Latin American independence and revolutionary struggles of the 1820s were inspired by America's similar struggles 50 years earlier. The French revolutionary ideals of liberty, equality, fraternity, and nationalism spread with Napoleon's troops across Europe. Those ideals provoked revolutions in Europe throughout the early and mid-19th century. The impact of revolution is even more powerful today in an age of instant mass, global communications. People can turn on their radio or television and learn of foreign revolutionary conditions, ideals, and strategies.

A revolution's success or failure often depends on the reaction of other countries. Could America's revolution have succeeded without massive French aid? Throughout Eastern Europe and the Third World, the United States, Soviet Union, and

During the spring of 1989, thousands of students demonstrated for democracy in Beijing's Tiananmen Square. Fearing that the demonstration might undermine its rule, China's Communist party ordered it crushed on June 4, 1989. Mao Zedong and the Statue of Liberty symbolize two very different concepts of revolution and freedom. What are those differences? How have those differences affected the development of China and the United States, and international relations between them and among all the world's countries?

sometimes China backed different revolutionary or counterrevolutionary groups with arms, money, propaganda, advisers, and even troops. Revolutions are sometimes imposed by foreign forces. After 1945, the Soviet Red Army replaced the existing governments of eastern Europe with communist dictatorships. Revolutions are also at times squashed by foreign forces. The Soviet Union destroyed democratic revolutionary forces in Hungary in 1956, Czechoslovakia in 1968, and Poland in 1981. The United States successfully helped quell communist revolutionary movements in Guatemala, El Salvador, Nicaragua, and the Philippines but failed in Cuba, Vietnam, Cambodia, and Laos. In 1989, a majority of Nicaraguans voted for the liberal democrat Violeta Chamorro rather than the Marxist-Leninist Sandinista party. Would the Sandinistas have retained power without a decade of America's covert attempts to undermine their rule?

Conclusion

Over 135 countries have achieved independence since 1945. These predominantly poor countries, along with Latin America and other countries that had already gained independence, became known as the Third World, in contrast to the First World of the democratic industrial countries and Second World of the communist countries. A trickle of newly independent states in the late 1940s and 1950s, India (1947), Pakistan (1947), Burma (1948), and Indonesia (1950) became a flood after the mid-1950s as the rest of colonial Asia and Africa became sovereign states.

Imperialism planted the seeds of its own destruction. The colonial process of creating an administrative region and exploiting it inevitably raised the cultural and political consciousness of its inhabitants, a consciousness that eventually swelled into an independence movement. Ironically, the more enlightened the rule, the more the indigenous elites received the formal and political education that allowed them to lead the independence struggle. It is no coincidence that the first independence movement rose in the relatively liberally governed British India, while the relatively tightly controlled Portuguese colonies of Angola and Mozambique were among the last to achieve independence. Regardless of the colonial policies, a combination of the independence movements and growing international condemnation of colonialism inevitably convinced the imperial states to give up their holdings.

The path to independence and its aftermath were rarely peaceful. Some newly independent countries themselves experienced independence movements. Shortly after India achieved independence, a genocidal war broke out between Hindus and Muslims in which as many as 10 million people may have died. Most of the Muslim regions broke away to form Pakistan, while 50 million Muslims remained under Indian rule. The violence of the independence struggles, however, varied considerably from the relatively peaceful independence of most of France's West African colonies to the bitter warfare that preceded independence in Vietnam, Malaysia, Indonesia, Algeria, and Kenya.[35]

Few of the newly independent states were prepared for independence. One reason was that virtually all these states were not nations but multinations. Each colony's borders had been drawn to satisfy the imperial state's political and economic needs, an important part of which was to discourage national unity. Thus each colony became a crazy quilt of national fragments, many of which were linguistic, religious, cultural, or historic rivals.

The newly independent nation-states were just as divided between rulers and the ruled. The political and economic elites who had led the independence struggle were often educated in the imperial capital and acquired that colonial powers' values, manners, and even language. For example, although only 1 percent of the population speaks it, English is one of India's official languages because it provides a neutral means of communication and thus gives no single ethnic group an advantage.

As the Marxist theoretician Frantz Fanon said, "The colonized man is an envious man."[36] The rhetoric of the independence movements fueled a popular revolution of rising expectations for the political, economic, and social gains that would presumably accompany liberation. Most people were brutally disappointed. The independence leaders may have been skilled at leading an underground struggle, but few had any understanding of how to run a modern political economy. The revolution of rising expectations turned into rising frustrations when mismanagement and corruption often caused people's lives to worsen rather than get better.

Many new governments sought to legitimize their rule by creating official national creeds, such as Indonesian President Sukarno's "Five Principles" (Pantja Sila), which called for nationalism, humanitarianism, authoritarian democracy, social justice, and god; Egyptian President Nasser's "Philosophy of the Revolution," which described Egypt's role as the natural leader of the Arabs, Africa, and Islam; or Ghanaian President Nkrumah's "I Speak of Freedom," which asserted a similar role for Ghana in Africa. Some leaders of the newly independent nations, such as Nasser, Nehru, and Nkrumah, even claimed leadership over peoples beyond their respective national borders and became the heroes to millions throughout the developing world. Nkrumah declared in 1961 that "All Africans know I represent Africa and that I speak in her name. Therefore no African can have an opinion that differs from mine."[37]

The governments of many newly independent countries espoused "socialism" as their state creed, and to that end began nationalizing industries and submitting five-year development plans. Yet few of these states ever came close to achieving the complete abolition of private property and a centrally planned economy. Regarding his government's first five-year plan, Nehru admitted, "We just took what was there and called it a plan."[38] Often socialism was simply used as an excuse to create a dictatorship. Nkrumah argued that "Capitalism is too complicated a system for the newly independent states. Hence the need for a socialist society. But even a system based on social justice and a democratic constitution may need backing up, during the period following independence, by emergency measures of a totalitarian kind. Without discipline true freedom cannot survive."[39]

The potential power inherent in a nation's human and natural resources is only as good as its political system, which offers individuals and groups the opportunity to exploit and mobilize those resources. Some political systems are clearly better able to realize some aspects of a nation's potential power than others. For example, communist systems are more adept at mobilizing raw human and natural resources than other states, but have failed miserably at creating wealth. Other types of authoritarian regimes can also make relatively quick decisions and mobilize a nation's population, but have a mixed development record.

There is a chicken-or-egg relationship between political and economic development. Political instability leads to economic stagnation *and* vice versa. Countries experience riots, coups, and insurgencies for many reasons. Often the government has created a revolution of rising expectations based on unrealizable goals that eventually becomes a revolution of rising frustrations. The political leadership fails to socialize and mobilize a population behind it, and is instead perceived to be excessively corrupt, brutal, and/or inefficient. There is a widening gap between a few rich and growing numbers of poor and a shrinking middle class.

Political stability, whether rooted in an authoritarian or liberal government, does not always lead to economic development. Both authoritarian and liberal democracies alike have either successfully promoted or bungled economic development. China maintains a communist dictatorship and crushed a mass democracy movement in June 1989. Yet since China's government launched a mixed market system and land reforms in 1978, the economy has grown about 10 percent annually. During the 1980s, although some democratic countries, such as Jamaica, Costa Rica, and Venezuela, experienced stagnant growth, others, such as Botswana, Malaysia, and Thailand, experienced rapid growth. Liberal democracies can be very poor—although India's democratic political system has been evolving for over a century, that country has a per capita income of $600.

In the 1980s and into the 1990s, increasing numbers of Third World countries adopted liberal democratic political systems based on universal adult suffrage, competitive elections, and civil rights. Liberal democratic economies are largely privately owned, although the government's economic role varies starkly from South Korea's carefully state-managed markets to Hong Kong's more loosely regulated markets.

Meanwhile, political instability and violence has lessened. The ratio of successful coups to elections in the Third World has shifted remarkably, from 1974, when there were five coups and two elections, or 1980, when there were eight coups and 10 elections, to the late 1980s, when democratic revolutions broke out in Eastern Europe, East Asia, Latin America, and elsewhere. In 1989, there were three coups and 18 elections and in 1990, there was only one coup and 17 elections.[40]

Whether liberal democracy will take firm root in the Third World is questionable. Liberal democracy has the best chance of success when it promotes economic development and will probably fail if it does not. The greater a society's creation and distribution of wealth, the fewer the popular demands on government that prevent it from concentrating on policies that enhance wealth's creation and distribution. Democratic values and behavior will expand with the middle class. Yet, as we have seen, political systems fail to achieve socioeconomic development for many reasons. Misguided policies and inefficient and/or corrupt institutions can impede rather than promote economic development, and thus ultimately undermine political stability.

Study Questions

1. Define economic development and political development. What is the relationship between the two?

2. Which comes first, development or power? Explain.

3. Are most countries poor because they are authoritarian, or are they authoritarian because they are poor? Explain your answer.

4. Why are the poor poor and the rich rich?

5. List the factors essential for political development.

6. What causes a revolution of rising expectations, and why does it often lead to a revolution of rising frustrations and political instability?

7. Define and give an example of a charismatic leader. How can a charismatic leader aid and hinder development?

8. Among less developed countries, how can bureaucracies, political parties, interest groups, and patron–client groups hinder and aid development?

9. Define mobilization and legitimacy. What is the relationship between the two, and what is their significance for development?

10. What is corruption? Why is it a severe problem in many less developed countries? How does a country's relative corruption level change with development?

11. Explain why some political systems are stable and others, unstable.

12. What are military coups, and when are they most likely to occur?

13. List some countries that experienced successful reform movements. Why were they successful?

14. What are revolutions, and under what conditions are they most likely to occur? What makes for a successful revolution?

15. Discuss the reasons for and consequences of the vast decolonization process that brought over 135 countries to independence following 1945.

InfoTrac College Edition Sources

Using the Subject Guide, enter the search terms *revolution, coups d'état, economic development, one party systems,* and/or *developing countries.*

Anderson, Donald. "European Monetary Union in a Globalized World Economy: The Beginning of the End for Europe."

Boka, Eva. "From National Toleration to National Liberation (Three Initiators of Cooperation in Central Europe)."

Boswell, Nancy Zucker. "The Law, Expectation, and Reality in the Marketplace: The Problems of and Responses to Corruption."

Brademas, John, and Fritz Heimann. "Tackling International Corruption: No Longer Taboo."

Burke, Edmund, III. "Theorizing the Histories of Colonialism and Nationalism in the Arab Maghrib."

Collie, David R. "Bilateralism Is Good: Trade Blocs and Strategic Export Subsidies."

Cooper, Frederick. "'Our Strike': Equality, Anticolonial Politics and the 1947–48 Railway Strike in French West Africa."

Dare, Leo. "Political Instability and Displacement in Nigeria."

Eberstadt, Nicholas. The United Nations' 'Development Activities': What Impact on Third World Development?"

Feng, Yi. "Democracy, Political Stability, and Economic Growth."

Gyimah-Brempong, Kwabena, and Thomas L. Traynor. "Political Instability and Savings in Less Developed Countries: Evidence from Sub-Saharan Africa."

Howell, Llewellyn D. "Corruption and Crisis in the Global Economy."

Jackson, John H. "Perspectives on Regionalism in Trade Relations."

Klitgaard, Robert. "International Cooperation Against Corruption."

Leiken, Robert S. "Controlling the Global Corruption Epidemic."

Miller, Victoria. "Political Instability and Debt Maturity."

Monshipouri, Mahmood. "Human Rights and International Political Economy in Third World Nations: Multinational Corporations, Foreign Aid, and Repression."

Mukisa, Richard S. "Toward a Peaceful Resolution of Africa's Colonial Boundaries."

O'Leary, Brendan. "On the Nature of Nationalism: An Appraisal of Ernest Gellner's Writings on Nationalism."

Park, Kang H. "Income Inequality and Economic Progress: An Empirical Test of the Institutionalist Approach."

Perez, Sofia A. "Gatekeepers of Growth: the International Political Economy of Central Banking in Developing Countries."

Rothgeb, John M. "Testing Mobilization Views of the Relationship Between International Interdependence and Political Conflict in Developing Countries."

Speth, James Gustave. "The UN, the US, and Development Cooperation: Time for a Reunion."

Stopford, John. "Multinational Corporations."

Wijkman, Anders. "Does Sustainable Development Require Good Governance?"

Wold, Chris. "Multilateral Environmental Agreements and the GATT: Conflict and Resolution?"

 On *the* Web

http://www.fordham.edu/halsall/mod/modsbook34.html
Many links to primary and secondary sources on imperialism

http://www.undp.org/indexalt.html
United Nations Development Programme

http://www.fordham.edu/halsall/africa/africasbook.html
History and political development of African states

Contents

Chapter 15 Economic Development, Underdevelopment, *and* International Relations

Key Concepts and Terms

In the interdependent modern world, perhaps no national interest is more important than successful economic development.[1] What is *economic development*? It is more than simply economic growth. A country develops economically when the middle class expands and gets wealthier; poverty shrinks steadily in numbers and severity; the range of industries increases in number, sophistication, international competitiveness, and shares of foreign markets; the web of the country's communications and transportation infrastructure embraces ever more people ever more efficiently and links them with the rest of the world; the population's health, education, longevity, and leisure time improves; the number of parks, universities, and museums swells; literature, music, and the arts flourish; the air, water, and streets get cleaner; crime, homelessness, and despair diminish; careers are open to all talents; and an ever stronger economy is better able to resist recession, inflation, and unemployment. All these are types of wealth. The more economically developed a nation, the greater its potential power to wring even more wealth from its own people and the international system.

Although all nations aspire to develop, there remains a vast and widening gap between the world's wealthiest and poorest countries. Are the rich getting richer and the poor poorer? By comparing the *per capita income* (national income divided by population) and the human development index (HDI), which combines life expectancy at birth (longevity), adult literacy rate (knowledge), and per capita income, it is clear that the rich have steadily gotten richer. But the world's poorer regions vary starkly in whether they are getting richer or poorer. The Third World is increasingly split between regions that are developing and those that are actually imploding.

Table 15.1 Are the Rich Getting Richer and the Poor Poorer?

Region	Gross Domestic Product Per Capita					Human Development Index (HDI) 1997
	1975	1980	1985	1990	1997	
Developing States	$600	$685	$693	$745	$908	0.637
Least Developed	287	282	276	277	245	0.430
Sub-Saharan Africa	671	661	550	542	518	0.463
Arab States	2,327	2,914	2,252	1,842	—	0.626
East Asia	176	233	336	470	828	0.712
East Asia Without China	1,729	2,397	3,210	4,809	7,018	0.849
Southeast Asia and Pacific	481	616	673	849	1,183	0.695
South Asia	404	365	427	463	432	0.544
South Asia Without India	857	662	768	709	327	0.542
Latin America and Caribbean	1,694	1,941	1,795	1,788	2,049	0.756
Eastern Europe/Former Soviet Union (CIS)	—	—	—	2,913	1,989	0.754
Developed States	12,589	14,206	15,464	17,618	19,283	0.919
World	2,888	3,136	3,174	3,407	3,610	0.706

— indicates no available data for that year.
Source: U.N. Development Program, *Human Development Report*, 1999.

What explains these differences? Why has development soared in East Asia and Southeast Asia; plummeted in eastern Europe and the former Soviet Union (CIS), sub-Saharan Africa, the Arab states, and South Asia; and fluctuated in Latin America?

The global political economy offers many opportunities and pitfalls for governments determined to develop their country. This chapter analyzes aspects of the dynamic relationship between the global economy and national economic development, exploring national policies and international forces that can enhance or impede development. It concludes by analyzing the successful development strategies of the *newly industrializing countries (NICs)*, Taiwan and South Korea, and the relevance of those countries' experiences to other Third World countries.

The Challenges *of* Development

Clearly, no country is an island in the modern world. All are linked together in an increasingly dense web of economic, social, cultural, political, technological, and ethical ties, known as globalization, which varies considerably from one country to the next. Although every one of the more than 190 countries has its own mix of economic strengths and weaknesses rooted in culture and history, many in the so-called Third World countries share similar obstacles to and opportunities for development. Successful development ultimately rests on a government's ability to mobilize and fulfill the country's potential. To do so in an interdependent world, states must integrate foreign capital, technology, markets, and managerial skills with their country's nascent enterprises, infrastructure, and human and natural resources. This section explores those challenges.

THE COLONIAL LEGACY

Over five centuries, the Western powers and Japan colonized virtually every region on earth. It is not easy to weigh imperialism's relative costs and benefits. Colonialism's impact varied from one imperial power and colony to the next, each wielding its own administrative philosophy and style. Some colonies were administered for several centuries, others for several decades. Some were extensively developed, others largely left as they were found.

Western imperialism did grant some long-term benefits. There is a tendency for many inhabitants of countries that experienced Western imperialism to lament a lost precolonial "golden age." That golden age almost never existed. In many lands, Western rule toppled more oppressive regimes, imposed order on regions of incessant warfare, and abolished such local customs as human sacrifice and mutilation. For example, the Chinese Imperial Customs Service generated far more revenue for China under the efficient British than the previous corrupt Chinese administration. Notions of human rights, sexual equality, political representation, and constraints on government were profound if originally unintended gifts to all non-Western cultures. People today live far longer, healthier, more leisurely, and wealthier lives than they did when the first Western gunboats or troops appeared on their respective frontiers.

Many argue, however, that the costs have far outweighed the benefits. In many places, Western imperialism's short-term impact on *traditional societies* was devastating. There were an estimated 25 million people in Mexico and Central America

Basket Case Economy, Political Chaos: Nigeria's Struggle *for* Development

I s democracy possible in Africa's most populous and ethnically diverse country? Nigeria's 121 million people are splintered among 400 ethnic groups and three major nations, the Christian Ibo in the southeast, the Christian Yoruba in the southwest, and the Muslim Hausa in the north. These nations are traditional enemies that often war against each other when the central government's rule has broken down from military coups and corruption.

After decades of military rule, Olusegun Obasanjo, who is Hausa, was elected president in February 1999. That should have been cause for celebration. Instead, Yorubas looted and killed Hausas in many areas where the two nations overlapped. The military restored order with great brutality.

Political and economic development are intricately linked. As if quelling riots were not difficult enough, Obasanjo faces the herculean challenge of trying to develop a country mired in mass poverty, corruption, and violent crime. Most Nigerians barely survive on minimal food, shelter, and clothing, while a tiny elite siphons off what wealth the economy yields. Nearly all that wealth comes from oil, which accounted for 98.9 percent of export earnings in 1998. But that was only $15.2 billion in 1998, even though with a daily output of 2 million barrels Nigeria is the world's eighth largest oil producer. But because so much of Nigeria's wealth ends up in foreign bank accounts rather than the infrastructure and enterprises that could develop the economy, the country lacks enough oil refineries to supply its own needs. Nigeria actually has to import gasoline.

Can Obasanjo or anyone else nurture development and democracy in such bloody, hate-filled, and economically barren soil? Will dictatorship tempt Obasanjo or some other military faction, as it has so many others in Nigeria's history? Nigeria's political and economic development faces extremely harsh odds.

---

when Cortez arrived in 1521. Within 50 years, European diseases, for which the natives had no immunity, had reduced the population to two million! Everywhere colonialism destroyed not just native political elites but traditional culture. Western imperialism simultaneously discredited and transformed native cultures so that every culture around the world to varying extents is now a hybrid of traditional and Western values. In Latin America especially, the cross was more important than the sword in forcing these changes. Western missionaries pressured the natives to reject old gods and embrace Christianity. This conversion was frequently incomplete. Today many peoples find themselves neither fully of the old or the new faith, but somewhere in between.

Colonialism created a small, well-educated, Westernized elite, which it used to help administer and exploit the territory. Ironically, that elite usually led the independence movement and ruled the newly independent country. The same orientation that helped free their country often impedes the elite's ability to rule. The elite often remains more culturally Western than native, and thus has trouble relating to the population's attitudes and problems. Their ranks and minds often remain as closed to the population as those of the Western imperialists they overthrew.

Both the elite and the masses of people from less developed countries often feel inferiority to the more developed Western countries. Defeat, subjugation, and the imposition of second-class status by a foreign power, often combined with the failure of that country to develop following independence, has forced people to feel somehow beneath as well as behind the West. People with inferiority complexes sometimes try to compensate by being overly assertive toward or critical of those to which they feel inferior, or toward their own society. Von Laue describes among non-Western peoples a perennial

> search of roots, and certitude; inwardly split, part backward, part Western, camouflaging their imitation of the West by gestures of rejection; forever aspiring to build lofty halfway houses that bridged the disparate cultural universes, often in all-embracing designs, never admitting the fissures and cracks in their lives and opinions; and always covering up their unease with a compensating presumption of moral superiority based on the recognition that the promptings of heart and soul are superior to the dictates of reason."[3]

Leaders of Third World countries are aware of this identity crisis and its potential negative impact on development. Mohatma Gandhi was one of the first to recognize and try to overcome an increasingly entrenched Westernization within traditional culture, arguing that "if India copies England, it is my firm conviction that she will be ruined."[4] Gandhi tried to base the independence struggle on select traditional Indian concepts.

Most of the 190 nation-states existing today are the artificial creations of imperialism and most are multinational. When the Western powers carved up Africa, for example, they arbitrarily drew lines across the map and divvied up the continent among themselves without regard to the mosaic of existing nations, which were often splintered among two or more states. Thus every country in Africa today is multinational except Somalia, and in most of these countries the different nations co-exist uneasily and in many their antagonisms have deteriorated into violence and civil war. In most multinational states, the colonial language is the only lingua franca. It was deemed better to use a foreign language than to allow one of the native languages to become dominant. Nonetheless, often only a small percentage of the population speaks the foreign language, thus isolating the government all the more from its people.

Virtually every seemingly positive contribution of imperialism also has its negative side. Although the colonists improved living conditions by introducing higher standards of health care, hygiene, nutrition, and education, they set off a population explosion as the death rate fell dramatically, while the birth rate remained largely unchanged. Thus in many countries the population exceeds the territory's ecological *carrying capacity,* setting off rapid environmental degradation, crop and livestock loss, and mass starvation. Many survivors flee to the cities where they overwhelm existing job opportunities and social services.

Imperialism completely disrupted the native economy. Traditionally, most villages were self-sufficient. Land was often held communally and the people usually grew enough to survive, although droughts, monsoons, and other natural disasters sometimes led to famine. There was little trading among villages. The imperial power introduced the notions of private property by brute force. It confiscated communal village cropland and converted it into huge, privately owned plantations. In Latin America, the land was divided up into *latifundias* or huge estates owned by the conquistadors and their families. Elsewhere, huge companies acquired the land. The plantations converted land that had grown food for the local people into the mass production of such products as cotton, sisal, coconut oil, coffee, tea, hemp, tobacco, pepper, sugar, jute, and other largely nonfood crops for

A Civilizing Mission?
The Conqueror's View

Some imperial leaders were well aware of the revolutionary impact of their culture on traditional cultures. As Lord Lytton, the Viceroy of India, put it in his speech before his Legislative Council in Calcutta in 1878:

> The problem undertaken by the British rulers of India . . . is the application of the most refined principles of European society, to a vast Oriental population, in whose history, habits, and traditions they have had no previous existence. Such phrases as "religious toleration," "Liberty of the Press," "Personal freedom of the subject" . . . are here in India . . . the mysterious formulas of a foreign . . . administration . . . to the greater number of those for whose benefit it is maintained . . . there is no disguising . . . [that] we have placed, and must permanently maintain ourselves at the head of a gradual but gigantic revolution— the greatest and most momentous social, moral, . . . religious, . . . and political revolution which . . . the world has ever seen."[2]

Was Lytton right? Did that revolution succeed?

export. Thus the typical colonial economy was divided into urban (commercial and light industrial), large plantation and mining, and subsistence-level agrarian sectors. The cities, plantations, and mines were linked to the global economy with modern transportation and communication, but most peasants remained isolated and backward. Often the agrarian sector was too inefficient to produce enough food for the cities and plantations, so the colony ended up importing food. For most countries little has changed since independence, at least for the better. Most continue to rely on one or two cash crops or minerals that are subject to sometimes wide price fluctuations in international markets.

In most colonies, little if anything was done to prepare the country for independence. When the colonizers left, they often took with them most of the skills, capital, and equipment necessary to run the modern sectors. Most Third World bureaucracies were inherited from colonialism. Colonial bureaucracies had two main tasks—to extract wealth from the territory while controlling the population. Few imperial powers allowed natives to climb high in the civil service. At independence, the bureaucracy—particularly the higher echelons—was gutted by the withdrawal of the foreign specialists. For example, when the Belgians retreated from the Congo (Zaire) in 1961, they left only 20 natives with a college education and three high-ranking civil servants to run a country with 14 million people divided among over 200 tribes.[5]

What, then, is imperialism's impact on Third World development? After reminding us that the concept of development itself is Western, Von Laue maintains that the blame for development failures must be shared by all:

> Westerners must accept the blame for the hardships and tragedies in the developing countries. The anti-imperialist radicals are right. Before the Western impact, traditional societies existed in reasonable harmony within the intellectual, spiritual, and material resources at their command, in precarious balance with their environment. It was the Western impact which forced them, against their will, into a complex world beyond

their comprehension and resources, destroying in the bargain the former bonds of community. The anti-imperialists in turn should recognize the inevitability of inter-cultural contact in a shrinking world; let them also appreciate the goodwill and opportunities that came with the West. In any case, there is no chance of returning to the pre-colonial era, nor comfort in the nostalgic yearning, sometimes heard, for the good old days of colonialism. Both sides have no choice but to look forward.[6]

Postindependence Socioeconomic Stagnation

Most Third World countries, whether they achieved their independence during the 1820s, like most Latin American countries, or since 1945, like most African and Asian countries, have had limited success or have failed outright to develop economically. These countries share many characteristics.

The most obvious similarity is that in Third World countries a majority of the population is not only poor but often lives a hand-to-mouth existence in which they are malnourished, illiterate, unemployed, homeless, and wracked by health problems. Although most Third World countries are experiencing some economic growth, their populations are growing at an even faster rate. Thus overall most people are becoming poorer. Most of these people are landless peasants who must hand over what little crops they produce to wealthy landlords. Others live in overcrowded disease- and rat-infested shantytowns lacking sewage, running water, and most importantly, well-paying jobs.

Most Third World countries are locked into a vicious political and economic cycle that prevents them from developing—political instability and violence disrupts business and impedes economic development, which in turn spawns more political instability and violence. Economic growth is stimulated by the wealthy and middle classes, not the poor.[7] The poor number anywhere from 50 to 90 percent of the population, but the middle class accounts for only from 25 to 40 percent, and

Table 15.2 **Growth, Stagnation, and Trade Among the Largest Latin American Countries**

	GDP Percent Change on Previous Year			Consumer Prices Percent Increase on Previous Year		Current Account Balance as Percentage of GDP		
	1997	1998	1999	1998	1999	1997	1998	1999
Argentina	8.6%	4.8%	1.8%	1.2%	0.6%	−2.9%	−2.9%	−3.5%
Brazil	3.2	0	3.0	2.3	8.0	−4.2	−5.0	−2.2
Chile	7.1	4.8	1.0	5.0	5.0	−5.3	−7.5	−6.2
Colombia	3.1	1.5	1.5	19.4	19.0	−5.7	7.7	−5.0
Ecuador	3.4	1.0	1.5	40.0	23.0	−3.9	−10.0	−4.6
Mexico	7.0	4.3	2.3	16.6	13.3	−1.9	−1.6	−2.3
Peru	7.4	2.2	4.5	8.0	8.5	−5.2	−6.2	−5.8
Venezuela	5.1	0.5	0.5	38.0	28.0	6.9	−1.6	1.8
Overall	**5.5**	**2.3**	**0**	**8.8**	**9.4**	**−3.1**	**−4.3**	**−2.7**
						(−$58 billion)	(−$81 billion)	(−$50 billion)

Source: J.P. Morgan report, 2000.

Pitfalls *of* Liberalization:
The Fate *of* Indonesia's Textiles

Even simple labor-intensive industries such as textiles have trouble competing with the multinational corporations. For example, Indonesia once had a flourishing textile industry but opened its markets to foreign investment in the 1970s. Japanese multinational textile corporations took advantage of this opening, set up automated factories, and within a decade succeeded in wiping out Indonesia's less efficient, labor intensive businesses. As a result, hundreds of thousands of Indonesians lost their jobs, while most profits are sent back to Tokyo rather than reinvested in Indonesia. Japan developed, rather than Indonesia.

the wealthy, about 5 percent. The more poverty-stricken a country, the slimmer the chance it can achieve sustained development. Because most people are poor, their ability to buy things is extremely limited. Thus a Third World economy has a very small market confined to the middle and upper class. Market size is important because the more a business sells, the more profit it makes and the more it can reinvest to increase productivity and its competitive power.

Domestic businesses trying to compete with multinational corporations are like unarmed Davids fighting Goliaths—they have little chance of success. Entrepreneurs often lack technology, equipment, managerial skills, and access to foreign markets, which are vital to creating a prosperous business. They often must license or buy these things from multinational corporations—sometimes the very ones they are competing against. Gaining access to foreign technology, equipment, managerial skills, and markets costs money. Without access to large domestic or foreign markets, businesses cannot expand and are often squeezed out by supercompetitive multinational corporations that sell or invest in their country.

Money is in short supply in Third World countries. One result of political instability and economic stagnation is that the rich send their money to safe havens and rising stock prices overseas rather than invest it at home. To attract those savings that remain at home, states set high interest rates. But high interest rates discourage businesses and households from borrowing money to invest in improvements. States must borrow heavily from foreign sources to fulfill their development and other goals. Had capital stayed at home rather than been spirited abroad, states would have borrowed much less foreign capital. For example, without capital flight, Argentina's foreign debt would have been $1 billion instead of $50 billion, Mexico's $12 billion rather than $97 billion, and Venezuela's zero instead of $30 billion![8]

Domestic banks lack financial clout and investment skills. Thus entrepreneurs often cannot find enough money at home to finance their businesses. To start a business they must either borrow from an international bank or form a joint venture with a multinational corporation. Either way they end up sending much of their earnings overseas to pay interest on their debt or share profits from their joint venture.

Perhaps the most crippling problem that many less developed countries face is a lack of private entrepreneurial spirit. Many Third World governments attempt to make up for the lack of private business drive by building huge heavy industries from the ground up. The trouble with this strategy is that the state—its political leadership and bureaucracy—lacks the skills vital to create and manage a modern economy and industry.[9] More often than not the newly independent government used the bureaucracy as a *spoils system* to reward their political followers rather than filling those positions with lower-ranking officials who had at least some inkling of the ministry's duties. Thus most postindependent bureaucracies bear no resemblance to the ideal of an apolitical institution designed to address specific national problems. Instead, most Third World bureaucracies have simply become a source of wealth and security for its appointees and the political leadership. A particular problem with coup-prone countries is that each new regime packs the bureaucracy with its own followers and devises its own often grandiose development projects and priorities while abandoning those of the previous government.

As if this were not bad enough, the independence governments and their successors often had a set of national goals that the existing bureaucracy was ill equipped to administer. Third World governments often embarked on highly ambitious crash industrialization and welfare programs, and new ministries were created to implement these programs. *Import substitution* policies in which the government attempts to create industries from scratch are very expensive. Lacking significant indigenous financial resources, governments embarking on ambitious industrial development programs had to borrow the money from global bankers. The result was that such countries as Brazil, Mexico, Argentina, South Korea, Venezuela, and Chile, which followed import substitution, became the world's heaviest debtors. The state-created industries in particular are rarely successful and act like black holes in a nation's economy, sucking in huge amounts of financial, natural, and human resources and contributing little if anything to development. Sometimes the state-owned industries sell their products for less than the sum of their raw materials, let alone labor costs. Bela Balassa, a classical economist, argues that "the export performances of a number of developing countries were adversely affected by their own policies: the bias against exports in countries

import substitution a means of industrialization through which a government erects high trade barriers against competitive products to encourage foreign investment, and creates an overvalued currency that affords the purchase of the machinery and raw materials to make those industrial products.

Table 15.3 **Non-trade Sources of Income (in billions) for the Third World Top Ten**

Worker Remittances, 1996		Foreign Direct Investment, 1997		Portfolio Investment, 1997	
India	$9.326	China	$45.300	Brazil	$18.495
Mexico	4.224	Brazil	16.330	Mexico	16.028
Turkey	3.542	Mexico	12.101	Thailand	11.181
Eqypt	2.798	Singapore	10.000	Argentina	10.132
Lebanon	2.503	Argentina	6.327	Indonesia	10.070
Morocco	2.165	Russia	6.241	China	9.920
China	1.672	Chile	5.417	Malaysia	7.596
Jordan	1.544	Indonesia	5.300	Russia	4.975
Pakistan	1.461	Poland	5.000	Turkey	4.913
Bangladesh	1.217	Venezuela	4.893	Colombia	4.413

Source: U.N. Development Program, *Human Development Report*, 1999.

How *to* Build *a* Dynamic Industry: Brazil's Aircraft Producers

Unlike most countries that have followed them, Brazil's import substitution policies have been largely successful in developing a range of advanced industries such as automobiles, steel, aircraft, weapons, petrochemicals, and so on, which generate enormous wealth within the country that otherwise would have flowed overseas to foreign producers.

Brazil's development of an aircraft industry from nothing was a typical success story. Until the mid-1970s, Brazil imported all its light passenger planes, mostly from the United States and most of them from Piper Aircraft—408 in 1974 alone. The Brazilian government targeted light industry as a strategic industry, and created and implemented a plan for its development. First it negotiated a joint production agreement with Piper Aircraft Corporation, using the threat of buying its planes from other corporations as the means of forcing an agreement. Then it imposed a 50 percent tariff on all imported planes, including those from Piper. By 1976, Piper Aviaco produced 75 percent of all light planes purchased in Brazil and began exporting them to other Latin American and to African countries, while the U.S. export share fell from 100 percent to 1 percent![11] Today Piper Aviaco exports planes to countries all around the world.

pursuing import substitution policies led to a loss in their world shares in primary exports and forestalled the emergence of manufactured exports."[10]

Nonetheless, import substitution largely succeeded in industrializing some countries. Brazil and Mexico, for example, targeted and developed such strategic industries as automobiles, steel, and petrochemicals. They did so, however, by heavily borrowing the essential ingredients of finance, technology, managerial skills, and so on from overseas banks and corporations. Why would a foreign automobile maker want to sell manufacturing techniques rather than vehicles to Mexico or Brazil? Those countries erected trade barriers that prevented foreigners from selling directly in those markets. Instead, the foreigners set up shop behind those walls. Laws that limited how much money could be taken out of the country forced the foreigners and natives alike to reinvest at home. But inefficiencies proliferate behind trade and investment barriers. Those manufacturers enjoyed exclusive access to those large domestic markets of Brazil and Mexico. But the lack of competition kept the price of their products high and quality low. Thus they were not competitive in global markets. Most of those profits that did not go to foreign corporations or financial institutions mostly made rich Brazilians and Mexicans richer. Very little wealth and few jobs trickled down to the populace.

Brazil and Mexico are exceptions. Most Third World countries have developed little if any viable industry. Some countries, such as Nigeria and India, have tried to build huge steel or petrochemical plants but the production is often more expensive than similar American, Japanese, or German products. The result of import substitution policies, more often than not, was chaos, waste, inefficiency, disillusionment, and political instability. Aware of those pitfalls, few countries use import substitution today as a development strategy. Recognizing the failure of state-owned industries to make a profit or to be internationally competitive, many Third World countries have recently tried to privatize their industries. For example, between 1982 and 1990, Mexico sold off 875 of 1,155 existing government-owned

The Oil Giant's Fate: Who Will Rule Saudi Arabia, and Why Does It Matter?

OPEC's price leader is Saudi Arabia, which has one-fifth of the world's known oil reserves. Saudi Arabia has played a mostly moderate role in OPEC policy and Persian Gulf politics. The United States has nurtured Saudi Arabia as its key ally in the region ever since an Islamic revolution toppled the pro-American shah of Iran in 1979. Will Saudi Arabia indefinitely remain a staunch American friend and force for regional and oil price stability?

Saudi Arabia's government faces a leadership and succession problem that could become a crisis. In 1999, King Fahd was 78 years old and largely incoherent after a series of crippling strokes and other diseases. But because of a policy adopted by King Abdel Aziz before his death in 1953, Fahd's successor most likely will be a brother rather than son. To avoid possible civil war among his 44 sons from his many wives, Aziz favored a succession to the oldest brother. A 1992 law further muddies the problem of who follows by allowing a king to designate the "most upright candidate" among the sons or grandsons of Aziz. Although a grandson would possibly bring more vigorous leadership, the tradition of picking brothers will no doubt continue. Un-fortunately, as the brothers age their ability to rule declines. The current heir apparent is Fahd's 76-year-old half-brother Crown Prince Abdullah, who is commander of the national guard. He, in turn, is expected to designate his half-brother 75-year-old Prince Sultan bin Abdel Aziz, who has been defense minister since 1962.

Why does succession matter? Strong or weak leadership can mean the difference between stability and chaos. Given Saudi Arabia's geoeconomic and geopolitical importance, those concerned with the viability of the global political economy should care very much indeed who rules that kingdom.

corporations, which attracted more than $10 billion back to the country that had previously been expatriated.[12]

What wealth a Third World economy generates often comes from the sale of one or two agricultural or mineral products such as cotton, rice, iron ore, or bauxite. The companies that own these plantations or mines are often foreign, and thus once again profits flow overseas rather than remain in that country. Price levels for these products are often erratic. Gluts in international markets cause prices and profits to drop for that Third World producer. For example, the American-owned United Fruit Company owns most of the banana production in Guatemala, Costa Rica, El Salvador, and Honduras, giving it enormous political as well as economic power in those countries. In 1954, President Jacobo Arbenz Guzman of Guatemala attempted to nationalize United Fruit's unused landholdings. United Fruit complained to Washington. The Eisenhower administration used the CIA to sponsor a coup to overthrow Arbenz and install a new government that continued to allow United Fruit a free hand in Guatemala.

Although many Third World countries have rich troves of a natural resource or two, that is no development guarantee. Uganda, Burma, Peru, and Bolivia, to name a few, are rich in natural resources yet their people remain mostly poor, malnourished, and illiterate, and plagued by violence long after independence. Some oil-rich countries such as Nigeria, Indonesia, and Mexico also have huge populations to support. The only resource-rich countries that have achieved any significant development are those with large oil reserves and small populations such as

Less Is More:
Mexico, People, *and* Prosperity

What is the relationship between prosperity and population? Can a country have too many people? Mexico's experience offers some lessons.

Mexico's population quadrupled from 25 million in 1950 to 100 million in the year 2000! The result is ever more crowded cities, schools, and buses, exhausted soils, clear-cut forests, and depleted aquifers, and more poverty, crime, pollution, and despair.

But that rate is slowing as mothers have fewer children. The birth rate has plunged from 5 to 2.5 children per woman between 1965 and 2000. The "dependency ratio" has also plummeted. A hundred workers supported 100 children in 1970, 60 in 2000, and will perhaps drop to 40 in 2020; it will rise thereafter as the population ages and retired people must be supported.

Why did the fertility rate fall? Different policies led couples to behave differently. After decades of encouraging a high birth rate, Mexico's government finally concluded that fewer rather than more births were better for families and the nation. In 1974, the government established the National Population Council and its national network of clinics, to promote birth control.

A lower birth rate means more prosperity as less quantity means more quality. Rather than spread already thin paychecks to support many children, parents can give more nutrition and education to fewer children. Money might even be left over to save or invest, something that enhances not just that family but the nation's economic well-being as well.

But Mexico's birth rate has not fallen far enough. If the population rate surpasses the economic growth, most people are getting poorer. That has happened in Mexico. Every year about 1.3 million people join a workforce in an economy that generates only 900,000 new jobs. About 20 percent of those 400,000 excess workers fall into poverty. Eighty percent or about 277,000 a year head north to look for work in the United States, where jobs pay 10 times more than in Mexico. A portion of their paychecks support relatives left behind in Mexico. That is good for Mexico but bad overall for the United States as its already bloated population swells and wages decline. Thus a nation's population policies and growth affect its own economy and relations with its neighbor.

Kuwait, the United Arab Emirates, and Saudi Arabia. The governments of these countries have distributed enough of the oil revenues to satisfy most people's basic needs and forestall any pressures for political change, whether it be into a liberal democracy, Marxist, or radical Islamic state.

There is a popular image that Third World countries are rich in natural resources. In fact, almost all Third World countries must import most of their vital staples such as energy and food. When OPEC quadrupled its oil prices in 1973 and further doubled them in 1979, the poorest countries were worst hit. Without oil their economies would collapse completely, so they had to use what little money they had to pay the higher prices. Eventually, most Third World countries went deep into debt to international bankers to cover their oil bills. Less money than ever went into development projects, and those countries became poorer. Yet even resource-rich countries suffer the same fate if they fail to use profits to diversify their economy. Eventually the mines or oil wells run out, eliminating the major source of wealth.

Does a nation's relative success or failure in development boil down to culture? Theodore Von Laue argues that Third World countries cannot master Western industries and technology until they internalize Western values:

Cultures evolved in different natural settings are essentially incompatible with each other, like languages.

External manifestations like weapons, machines, written constitutions, or political values can be transferred, but not the aptitudes and social habits responsible for their successful operation. Unless these already exist in some form in the receiving country—as in Japan—their acculturation cannot be forced by the will of a leader or a decision of government. The transfer of cultural achievement demands no less than a permanent revolution of reculturation, the recreation of the original setting in a new and uncongenial environment, a feat never yet accomplished.[13]

Do you agree? What is the relative importance of culture among all those forces determining development?

Modern prosperous economies are built on advanced, complex transportation and communications systems—highways, ports, telecommunications, railroads, and computer networks. This infrastructure is often severely deficient in Third World countries. Telephones do not work; mail is not delivered; roads are narrow, unpaved, and potholed; electricity is erratic; food rots for lack of refrigeration or storage.

Equally important to development are skilled, literate workers and technicians who build, repair, and invent things. Many people lack even the most basic reading, writing, and arithmetic skills. And those who finish high school or college may not have received the technical training necessary to keep an economy running, let alone develop it. The lack of health care or family planning education ensures that most people will remain assailed by preventable diseases and that the population continues to soar, exacerbating all other development problems.

The cold war may have impeded development in several ways. Certainly the coups, guerrilla movements, and enormous military aid backed by the United States and the Soviet Union grossly distorted the target countries' development. Latin American intellectuals argue that the cold war distorted the choices available to Third World nations, particularly for those who followed Marxism-Leninism. The crumbling of communism through eastern Europe and the Soviet Union completed the discrediting of statism that had been popular among many Latin American intellectuals and governments throughout the postwar era. Mexican poet Octavio Paz asserts, "It is as though the Cold War had been a mask that blinded us to the reality of the world," an argument picked up by another Mexican writer, Carlos Fuentes, who argues that the "fact that we can see the problems in their proper perspective rather than through a mask of anti-communism or pro-communism is the beginning of the resolution of those problems on their real terms."[14] Sergio Bitar, a former minister in President Allende's socialist government of Chile, admits that communism's fall "has forced us to look much more at concrete proposals rather

Why do some countries become wealthier while others remain mired in poverty? Is there one policy path or many among those countries that are successfully developing? Poor countries need foreign finance, direct investments, managerial skills, technology, products, markets in which to sell their own goods, and sometimes aid. In their quest for development, how far should a country open itself to international economic and cultural forces? What is gained and lost when American multinational corporate and pop culture powers such as the McDonald's restaurant chain become ubiquitous in a developing country?

than theoretical ideas, to understand that we need to be more competitive and productive, and to put democracy at the center of all progressive thinking."[15]

The United States has been obsessed with destroying communist movements in Latin America through the 20th century. During the early 20th century, the United States periodically sent the Marines into Central America and the Caribbean to protect American economic assets and shore up friendly governments. Direct intervention subsided with President Franklin Roosevelt's "Good Neighbor" policy,

Turn *the* Other Cheek, *or* Overturn *the* Temple? Liberation Theology

The Catholic Church is not as monolithic as it seems. There is great debate over theology and its application to the contemporary world. No issue has more greatly divided Catholicism than liberation theology, which sees Jesus as a social revolutionary who championed the poor and condemned the rich, warning them that their salvation depended on giving away their wealth to the poor and living among them. Adherents reject the Catholic Church's hierarchy, which they accuse of abandoning the religion's essential teaching, propping up corrupt, unjust regimes, and tolerating a decadent, exploitive society. They attempt to mobilize the masses of largely illiterate poor into a peaceful revolutionary struggle against those who oppress them, including the state.

During the 1970s, three works from Latin American theologians and political philosophers captured these ideas: Argentinean José Míguez Bonino's *A Theology for Artisans for a New Humanity,* the Peruvian priest Gustavo Gutierrez's *The Writings and Lectures on Liberation Theology,* and Brazilian Friar Leonardo Boff's *Jesus Christ, Liberator.* Liberation theology has been influenced by Marxist notions of class struggle. Sandinista Culture Minister Father Ernesto Cardenal succinctly captured the essence of liberation theology: "For me the four Gospels are equally communist. I'm a Marxist who believes in God, follows Christ, and is a revolutionary for the sake of His Kingdom." In Latin America and the Philippines, most of the lower-ranking priests are considered sympathetic to liberation theology, while in some countries, such as Brazil, at least half of the bishops are also advocates.

In 1986, the Vatican and Catholic liberation theology adherents achieved a consensus. According to the Vatican's "Instruction on Christian Freedom and Liberation," it is "perfectly legitimate that those who suffer oppression on the part of the wealthy or the politically powerful should take action." After reading the four gospels, what do you believe was the central mission of Jesus?

but the United States continued to aid its regional allies to promote political and economic stability.

Castro's 1959 Cuban revolution became the catalyst for a revival of direct American intervention. Washington feared that the Cuban revolution would set off a domino effect of communist revolutions throughout the western hemisphere. From President Kennedy's Alliance for Progress in 1961 to President Reagan's Caribbean Basin Initiative, the United States has attempted to counter communism's appeal by building up Latin America's economic vitality. Meanwhile, Washington intervened covertly to topple unfriendly governments in Guatemala, Chile, the Dominican Republic, and Nicaragua, while supporting friendly governments elsewhere.

The cold war's end was no panacea for resolving Latin America's problems. After the El Salvadoran government settled with the communist rebels and the communist Sandinistas were swept from power in Nicaragua, the White House no longer felt the need to pour as much aid into the continent; American aid to Latin America dropped 27 percent from 1990 to 1991 alone and has dwindled steadily since. The region is not free of political violence and instability, most notably in Colombia. Castro's communist dictatorship aside, every Latin American government espouses liberal democracy. In Venezuela, President Hugo Chavez is steadily transforming the country from a democracy to a popular dictatorship. Yet those democracies remain fragile with shallow cultural and institutional roots. The military still sits impatiently in the wings of some Latin American countries, ready to take over if the civilian politicians blunder badly. Nonetheless, Latin America has made significant strides in economic and political development in the decade since the cold war.

African development was also distorted by the cold war as the United States, Soviet Union, and lesser powers extended tens of billions of dollars in economic and military aid to various governments and movements. African dictators became adept at playing off the foreigners against each other to obtain greater aid. The superpowers, in turn, converted civil wars in Angola, Ethiopia, and Somalia into cold war battlegrounds. Today socialism and statism are becoming as discredited in Africa as they are elsewhere. As in other Third World countries, foreign aid has dropped considerably with the cold war's end.

Yet another important obstacle to development is time. Third World countries that have achieved independence since 1945 are attempting to do in a generation or two what the United States, Britain, and France achieved over several hundred years. Unfortunately, few politicians have the patience or vision to invest in long-range development projects. Political leaders worried about the next election or coup are particularly tempted to promote policies—tax cuts, unimpeded consumer imports, high defense spending, subsidized food, fuel, or housing, or generous welfare—that pay off key interest groups but may actually impede national development. Governments without a long-term development strategy often find themselves merely reacting hastily to one worsening economic crisis after another until they are swept away by ballots or tanks.

The Newly Industrializing Countries

In stark contrast to the mixed or dismal development records of most countries, are the dazzling successes of the newly industrializing countries (NICs) such as South Korea, Taiwan, Malaysia, Singapore, Thailand, and Chile, to name the most prominent. Those countries transformed themselves from mass poverty and economic stagnation into dynamic industrial and trade powers and middle-class societies. How did they do it? This section analyzes the strategies of South Korea and Taiwan while relating general development lessons.

DEVELOPMENT PREREQUISITES AND UNIQUE FACTORS

South Korea and Taiwan are the two most successful NICs. Both were Japanese colonies. During its rule over Taiwan (1895–1945) and South Korea (1910–1945), Japan developed a certain degree of human, transportation, and communications infrastructure as well as mines, plantations, and light industry. South Korea received its independence in 1948, and Taiwan became the sanctuary for Chinese nationalist forces defeated by the Communists in mainland China in 1949.

Had it not been for American military intervention in 1950, both South Korea and Taiwan would have been overrun by victorious communist armies. In June 1950, communist North Korea invaded South Korea and quickly conquered most of the country except for a small perimeter around the port of Pusan in the southeast. President Truman chose to save both noncommunist regimes. He sent the

The Newest NIC: China

Policies shape a nation's fate. Sensible policies can nurture prosperity just as senseless policies can impose misery on a country. China provides an excellent example.

In the three decades following the 1949 Communist Revolution, radicals and pragmatists battled for control over China. The radicals usually won and asserted their policies over the country. The results were disastrous, miring the country in poverty and at times provoking famines that killed tens of millions of people.

By 1979, Deng Xiaoping's pragmatist faction had defeated the radicals and established firm control over China. He embarked on policies of privatizing the economy, encouraging free markets, entrepreneurship, exports, foreign investment, and a get-rich mentality. The results have been astonishingly successful. China's economy has annually grown 8–9 percent ever since. If the current growth rates hold, by 2025 China's economy will be $16 trillion and its people will enjoy a $10,000 per capita income, an extraordinary achievement.

U.S. 7th Fleet between mainland China and Taiwan, thus preventing a communist invasion, and got the United Nations to authorize an American-led and largely American-manned army to push the communists out of South Korea. Washington then poured billions of dollars of economic and military aid into both countries while opening wide American markets for South Korean and Taiwanese products. The United States also exerted pressure on both Seoul and Taipei to launch sweeping land reform programs. Thus Japanese colonialism and American cold war imperatives gave both Taiwan and South Korea all the essential developmental prerequisites.

AGRICULTURAL REVOLUTION

An industrial revolution must be preceded by an *agricultural revolution*, which in turn depends on successful land reform. South Korea and Taiwan both experienced massive land reform programs in which land tenancy was reduced from over 50 percent to less than 10 percent, and in the process disgruntled peasants were transformed into conservative, affluent farmers. How was this achieved? The government broke up the huge plantations and distributed the land to the peasants, along with easy access to market, cheap credit, fuel, fertilizer, and other technological inputs that were essential for the new landowners to prosper. But in both countries, land reform would never have been implemented had not the United States exerted enormous pressure on those governments to do so, and then held out the promise of providing massive financial aid and open American markets if they succeeded.

In addition to land reform, an agricultural revolution involves developing through four stages. Using the example of rice production, in the first stage farming is conducted by traditional methods of animal or human plowing, uses rainfall for water, and yields 1 metric ton per hectare. During the second stage, land is improved with irrigation, drainage, and organic fertilizer, and yields two metric

agricultural revolution a increase in farm productivity resulting from innovations such as mechanization, new crops or fertilizer, easy bank credit, improved infrastructure, and better access to markets.

tons per hectare. In the third stage, the farmer introduces improved types of seed, fertilizers, pesticides, storage, and transportation, and the harvest rises to four metric tons per hectare. In the final stage, the farmer can use the fruits of credit banks, cooperatives, laboratories, and weather services, and the crop rises to 6 tons per hectare.[16]

Few Third World countries have successfully completed an agricultural revolution. In the 1960s and 1970s, some tried a massive investment in the *green revolution*, which involved the introduction of new high-yield strains of rice, wheat, and other grains. The trouble was that many of these seeds required large infusions of fertilizer and water in order to flourish, which raised the costs. Without credit, few peasants could afford to invest in the "revolution." Most Third World farms still rely on traditional means of sowing, fertilizing, and reaping. Much of the crop rots on the way to market for lack of storage or refrigeration. Harvests steadily diminish as the topsoil erodes or degrades from poor planting techniques. The production and wealth gap between wealthy landowners and poor peasants steadily widens. In contrast, agriculture in the industrial democracies has reached the fourth development stage and heavily uses hybrid seeds, fertilizer, irrigation, herbicides, and insecticides. Thus food production in most Third World countries lags far behind that in the advanced industrial countries. South Korea and Taiwan, in contrast, have largely succeeded in reaching the fourth agricultural development stage.

green revolution the introduction of new strains of seed, fertilizer, and mechanization promoting high crop yields for farmers.

IMPORT, EXPORT, AND TECHNOLOGY SUBSTITUTION

Taiwan and South Korea, followed by the other NICs, have excelled at creating and distributing wealth largely by targeting for development a set of "strategic industries"—those that create the most wealth, the best jobs, the most advanced technology, and a range of related industries. Not all industries were developed at once. The government first targeted such labor-intensive strategic industries as textiles and consumer electronics. After acquiring expertise, technology, markets, and capital from these industries, the government then gradually added other, more sophisticated capital- and technology-intensive industries to the economy, such as steel, automobiles, ships, semiconductors, computers, and so on. These strategic industries and the entire economy are nurtured through two distinct stages. During the first stage (import substitution), the government faces the problem of creating the targeted industries, while in the second stage—*export substitution*—it must nurture those newly created industries into global champions.

Because other countries already have developed the targeted industries, the first stage is obviously the toughest. The government must attract foreign technology, equipment, and capital while preventing foreign control. To this end the state uses a combination of high trade barriers to force consumers to buy domestic products, an overvalued currency to lower the price for buying essential foreign technology, machinery, and equipment, and low investment barriers to encourage foreign corporations to establish factories in the country.

The export substitution phase begins after the new industries have become established and have saturated domestic markets. The goal now is to create even greater economies of scale by selling in global markets. To do so, the currency is devalued so that the country's products have a comparative price advantage over those from other countries. Trade barriers might be slightly reduced to force domestic industries to become more productive in order to compete. By following

China: *The* Happy Hunting Ground *for* Women?

Life is full of tradeoffs. China's one-child policy has arrested the population explosion and thus rendered the environmental crises plaguing the country less catastrophic than otherwise. But the policy has imposed on China an ever heavier social cost.

Chinese culture values boys over girls. With the pressure to have only one child, couples sometimes kill a girl baby and try for a boy with the next pregnancy. Access to ultra-sound technology, which reveals a fetus's sex, have resulted in massive abortions of females. As a result, there are now 120 male children for every 100 females. That gap will steadily widen in the coming decades as ultra-sound technology becomes more available. By the year 2020 China will have 20 million more eligible bachelors than potential brides.

This is great news for the surviving women and a disaster for the hordes of lonely, desperate men. A man will have to be very rich, handsome, and loving indeed to have even a fighting chance of catching a date, let alone a wife. But finding "Mr. Right" will be much easier for Chinese women.

Things could be worse for Chinese men. Chinese women marry more readily than their Western sisters. By age 30 only 1 percent of Chinese women are unmarried; 15 percent of Western women are still unmarried by age 40.

this two-stage strategy, the government has nurtured a range of strategic industries into global champions.

Successful industrialization depends on acquiring and adapting advanced technology. Although many countries have tried licensing foreign technology, only a few have succeeded in building that technology into viable products. A country must already have advanced laboratories and a well-educated corps of technicians in order for a technology-buying strategy to succeed. The nation must also be able to gradually wean itself from dependence on foreign technology by creating its own. Many cultures lack a tradition of experimentation and innovation necessary to develop simpler technology into more advanced technology.[17]

CULTURE AND DEVELOPMENT

Some theorists argue that development ultimately rests on a society's values, and point to a Protestant or a Confucian work ethic as being essential to Western and East Asian development, respectively. Historically, "Confucian capitalism" was an oxymoron. Although Confucianism formed a basis of Chinese, Korean, Japanese, and Vietnamese culture and society throughout their histories, it may well have impeded rather than enhanced development. As important as values is an elite consensus regarding the means and ends of development. The "Confucian capitalists" did not begin to develop from feudal into modern societies until their leaders achieved a consensus to do so. Japan and the other East Asian "miracles" only began to develop after their political and economic leaders agreed to concentrate single-mindedly on rapid economic growth.

Although modernization clearly is impossible without modern values, it can certainly exist independently of Protestantism or Confucianism. The revival of trade and the first nascent industries emerged in Catholic northern Italy long before the Protestant Reformation. Traditional Confucianism actually relegated merchants to society's lowest rung because they made money from exchanging rather than producing things.

EVALUATING DEVELOPMENT

Modernization theorists uphold South Korea and Taiwan as development models. Dependency theorists discount the development of South Korea and Taiwan by claiming that those countries were geopolitically and geoeconomically vital to Washington's containment of communism, and were thus allowed to develop as noncommunist models. To that end, Washington pumped up both countries with billions in aid and gave them access to American markets.

Dependency theorists neglect to point out that Washington also targeted dozens of other countries as vital to its containment strategies (Vietnam, Pakistan, Egypt, Panama, the Philippines, and so on), poured billions into those countries, and allowed their products preferential access to America's markets. Yet those countries failed to develop successfully. It was up to the governments of those countries to create and implement successful developmental policies. In contrast, Taiwan and South Korea made the most of American aid and open markets. They modeled their industrialization strategy on that of Japan, and targeted a series of industries for export-led development.

Clearly, the development successes of Taiwan and South Korea give ample weight to those who argue that development ultimately depends on government policies that make the best of internal human and natural resources in a global economy. It is unlikely, however, that many countries can successfully industrialize by rigidly following the strategies of South Korea and Taiwan.[18] Those countries were aided by a range of other development factors that most countries do not enjoy. South Korea and Taiwan began their export substitution phases in the early 1960s, a decade before global trade and development was damaged by OPEC's quadrupling of oil prices. World trade has slowed, and the advanced industrial nations are becoming more protectionist.

Conclusion

Third World representatives to tend blame their developmental problems on the rich industrialized nations. Reality is much more complicated. Even a Marxist once admitted that "the misery of being exploited by capitalists is nothing compared to the misery of not being exploited at all."[19] The only thing worse for a Third World nation's development than being dependent is not being dependent at all. Those countries, such as China until 1978, Burma, North Korea, and Albania, that tried self-reliance policies failed miserably in increasing their wealth.

In contrast, those countries that have grown the fastest and often the most equitably have been the most involved in international trade. No country can industrialize and modernize on its own. Successful industrialization depends not just on factories and heavy machinery, but involves the development of a complex national transportation, communications, financial, technological, market, educational, and entrepreneurial infrastructure. The components and knowledge for creating modern industry comes from those who have already achieved it.

Governments make choices. There is clearly a virtuous development cycle. Sensible policies bring economic development that builds that government's political legitimacy that in turn helps create a stable environment in which more economic development can occur. Sensible policies are determined by the constraints and opportunities offered by national history, culture, natural and human resource endowments, and socioeconomic conditions.

Although each country has its own distinct development, they can be grouped into one of five patterns: (1) states that achieved both rapid economic growth and a more equitable income distribution, such as the NICs; (2) states that achieved economic growth but maintained a relatively inequitable income distribution, such as Mexico and Brazil; (3) states that achieved a more equitable income distribution but no significant growth, such as North Korea; (4) states that have had little growth or income distribution, such as Bolivia or Peru; and (5) states whose growth and income distribution has stalled or worsened, such as much of sub-Saharan Africa.[20] Whatever development path a government chooses, it is often extremely difficult to measure just what positive or negative changes have resulted. The most obvious means is to look at economic growth rates, per capita income, purchasing power parity (purchasing power), income distribution, literacy, infant mortality, and so on. These statistics must be weighed against the government's stated goals and ideals. We can then compare the performance with that of countries with similar socioeconomic, geographic, natural and human resources and similar historical and cultural conditions—Peru and Ecuador or Kenya and Tanzania, for example. Then we can compare a nation's current economic performances with those of the past.

The trouble with this approach is that statistics can be very misleading. Even the most advanced countries with small armies of statisticians evaluating a range of socioeconomic conditions will only give a more or less accurate impression of that country's reality. The less well run a country, the more inefficient and corrupt its bureaucracy, the more questionable the socioeconomic statistics it submits to the World Bank or other international development agencies. Frankly, the books are often cooked to give as favorable a view of the country as possible. Another problem is that much of the poor population uses barter rather than money for trading, and, to avoid paying taxes, many businesses rarely report all their income. As a result, many people may be better off than official statistics indicate.

Per capita income, the income divided equally among the population, is a less accurate measure than the actual buying power of that income (*purchasing power parity, PPP*) and the human development index (HDI), which combines life expectancy at birth, the adult literacy rate, and the PPP. By this measure some seemingly very poor peoples have a relatively high quality of life.

The socioeconomic gap among people within a single Third World country is often as great as the gap between that country and the world's wealthiest countries. Virtually all Third World countries have two societies, one relatively small but modern, urban, industrial, and literate, and the other trapping most of the population in tradition, poverty, subsistence farming, and illiteracy. When a country's population grows faster than its wealth, it becomes poorer overall. Trickle-down economic theory appears to work no better in poor countries than in rich countries.

Table 15.4 Comparisons of Development and Underdevelopment Among Neighboring Countries, 1998

	Per Capita Income	Purchasing Power Parity	Human Development Index
Pakistan	$ 480	$1,560	0.508
India	430	1,700	0.545
Malaysia	3,600	6,990	0.768
Thailand	2,200	5,840	0.753
Kenya	330	1,130	0.519
Uganda	320	1,170	0.404
Jordan	1,530	3,230	0.715
Syria	1,020	3,000	0.663
Bolivia	1,000	2,820	0.652
Paraguay	1,760	3,650	0.730

A U.N. Development Program (UNDP) report showed how the concept of development is changing:

> Human development is moving to center stage in the 1990s. For too long, the question has been how much is a nation producing? Now the question must be: how are its people faring? The real objective of development is to increase people's choices. Income is one aspect of these choices—and an extremely important one—but it is not the sum-total of human existence. Health, education, a good physical environment and freedom—to name a few other components of well-being— may be just as important.[21]

The report concluded that "there seems to be a high correlation between human development and human freedom."[22] Once again political and economic development are thoroughly intertwined.

Study Questions

1. What is modernization theory? What are the strengths and weaknesses of modernization theory?
2. Define dependency theory. What are its strengths and weaknesses?
3. List the attributes of traditional, transitional, and modern societies.
4. What are the prerequisites for successful industrial development?
5. Describe Western imperialism's legacy to the Third World. How has that legacy affected those countries' economic and political development?
6. What accounts for the continuing stagnant or declining economic and political life of many Third World countries?
7. Explain the successful development of such newly industrializing countries (NICs) as South Korea, Taiwan, Singapore, and so on.
8. Why are the rich rich and the poor poor?
9. Why does capital flight occur, and what are its consequences?

$\mathcal{P}$ InfoTrac College Edition Sources

Using the Subject Guide, enter the search terms *colonies, imperialism, economic development, agricultural development,* and/or *underdevelopment.*

Allen, Linda, and Christos Pantzalis. "Valuation of the Operating Flexibility of Multinational Corporations."

Aninat, Eduardo. "Chile in the 1990s Embracing Development Opportunities."

Berger, Mark T. "Specters of Colonialism: Building Postcolonial States and Making Modern Nations in the Americas."

Greene, Jack P. "Social and Cultural Capital in Colonial British America: A Case Study."

Gurria, Jose Angel. "Mexico Recent Developments, Structural Reforms, and Future Challenges."

Ho, P. Sai-wing. "Multilateral Trade Negotiations and the Changing Prospects for Third World Development: Assessing from a Southern Perspective."

Hopkins, A. G. "Back to the Future: From National History to Imperial History."

Rajan, Rajeswari Sunder. "The Third World Academic in Other Places; or, the Postcolonial Intellectual Revisited."

On *the* Web

http://www.devdir.org/
Directory of various groups and institutions involved with economic development

http://www.nuff.ox.ac.uk/Economics/Growth/
Oxford University site with numerous resources

http://www.worldbank.org/
Official website of the World Bank

Contents

Chapter 16 *The* Politics *of* Dependence Between *the* First *and* Third Worlds

Key Concepts and Terms

About 20 percent of the world's people control 80 percent of its wealth, while the remaining 20 percent of wealth is spread among 80 percent of its population, known as the Third World. Although most people in the Third World have enough food, clothing, and shelter to survive, starvation from crop failures, war, or disease annually kills millions of people. What domestic and international forces can affect a country's level of development? How can advanced industrial countries help or hinder Third World development? What duties, if any, do wealthy countries have toward the world's poor?

Reuters/Jim Hollander/Archive Photos

One of the modern world's paradoxes is that it offers so many life-enhancing economic, social, and political opportunities, yet so much of humanity can only dream of attaining them. The 2000 World Bank report revealed a Third World that largely remained mired in poverty: "Of the 4.4 billion people in developing countries, nearly three-fifths lack basic sanitation; a third have no access to clean water; a

Table 16.1 A Dollar a Day or Less: Regional Proportions of Poverty

	1987		1993	
	Total	Percentage	Total	Percentage
East Asia and Pacific	464 million	28.8%	446 million	26.0%
Europe and Central Asia	2 million	0.6	3.5 million	3.5
Latin America and Caribbean	91 million	22.0	110 million	23.5
Middle East and North Africa	10 million	4.7	11 million	4.1
South Asia	480 million	45.4	515 million	43.1
Sub-Saharan Africa	180 million	38.5	219 million	39.1

Source: World Bank Report, 2000.

Table 16.2 The Global Distribution of Wealth

	Richest 20 Percent	Middle 60 Percent	Poorest 20 Percent
Share of World GNP	86%	13%	1%
Share of Exports	82	17	1
Shares of Direct Foreign Investment	68	31	1
Internet Users	93.3	6.5	0.2

Source: U.N. Human Development Report, 1999.

Table 16.3 Relative Growth Rates

	1980–1990	1990–1998
World	3.2%	2.4%
Low Income	6.6	7.3
Excluding China and India	4.1	3.6
Middle Income	2.6	1.9
Lower Middle Income	—	−1.3
Upper Middle Income	2.7	3.9
Low and Middle Income	3.5	3.3
East Asia and Pacific	8.0	8.1
East Europe and Central Asia	—	−4.1
Latin America and Caribbean	1.6	3.7
Middle East and North Africa	2.0	3.0
South Asia	5.7	5.7
Sub-Saharan Africa	1.8	2.2
High Income	3.1	2.1

— indicates no available information for that period.

Source: World Bank Report, 2000.

Part 6   Geoeconomic Conflict and Cooperation Between the First and Third Worlds quarter lack adequate housing; and a fifth have no access to modern health services. About 20 percent of children do not complete five years of school, and a similar percentage do not receive enough calories and protein from their diet."[1]

The advanced industrial and Third World countries are deeply *dependent* on each other, although in vastly different degrees, ways, and impacts. The world's rich and poor countries are divided by more than wealth. Although relations among advanced industrial states are characterized as *interdependent,* implying a relative power balance, there is a power imbalance between rich and poor countries in which the latter are dependent on the former.

The world's poor countries are becoming relatively poorer as the vast income gap widens between them and the wealthiest countries. In the global economy, there is a rich class of about 15 percent of the total number of countries, a middle class of about 35 percent of all countries, and a low-income class that includes more than half of all countries. The Third World holds 85 percent of the world's population but only 14 percent of its wealth. Although Third World growth rates exceed those of the democratic industrial countries, they often cannot catch up to population increases, which means that poverty increases rather than diminishes.

How do we explain the vast gulf between the world's few rich countries and its many poor countries? There are no easy answers. Most Third World countries are trapped in a vicious cycle of political and economic underdevelopment, but others have broken free of that trap and are rapidly developing. Why have a few succeeded and most others failed? Why can't all poor countries be equally successful? And what role does the global economy and relations between advanced industrial and Third World countries play in development or *underdevelopment*?

There are bitter divisions over these questions of dependence and relative development, and whether internal or external factors are more important.[2] Modernization theorists argue that a country's relative success or failure is mostly explained by internal factors such as government policies, the political economic system, national culture, and national human, natural, and technological resources. The leaders of the advanced industrial countries and organizations, such as the *International Monetary Fund (IMF),* assert that the poor mostly have only themselves to blame. Follow our successful policies and you too will succeed, they maintain.

Dependency theorists and many representatives of the world's poorer countries point the finger of blame at the wealthy. They argue that external factors such as imperialism, foreign aid, multinational corporations, and international markets make the difference. The industrial countries have used their political, economic, and military power to create a global economy in which they exploit the natural resources and cheap labor of the poor countries, and have an interest in keeping the poor poor.

This chapter analyzes the debate by examining important issues dividing the world's wealthier and poorer countries including trade discrimination, foreign aid, multinational corporations, the debt crisis, and globalization versus the *new international economic order (NIEO).*

underdevelopment the inability of a country locked in poverty with few if any viable industries to raise its standard of living or otherwise meet the needs of its population.

Should We Trade Freely *or* Fairly?

Can *free trade* be unfair? What is *fair trade*? Why do so many of the world's poorer countries complain that the wealthier countries discriminate against them? Is that charge of unfairness fair? Regardless, how have Third World countries tried to rectify this perceived injustice?

From the negotiations leading up to the never implemented Havana Charter of the International Trade Organization (ITO), the *General Agreement on Trade and Tariffs (GATT)* which was actually created in 1947 and developed through its transformation into the World Trade Organization in 1996 and since, less developed countries have sought favorable trade concessions from the advanced industrial countries. The Third World countries argue that GATT's free trade and *most favored nation (MFN)* principles actually harm rather than help their development. How can that be? If Third World countries removed their trade barriers, their few industries would be bankrupted by the much cheaper and better made products of the advanced industrial countries. The result would be economic stagnation and the development of underdevelopment rather than development as the Third World countries were forced to continue to rely on exporting commodities in which they have a natural comparative price advantage. Thus the less developed countries have requested infant industry protection, the elimination of trade barriers with the industrial countries, and stable prices for Third World commodity exports.

Many of these demands were actually incorporated in the Havana Charter, which would have created this ITO. This was the major reason why American industries lobbied against the Havana Charter, and the Truman administration decided against submitting it to the Senate for ratification. As a result, GATT became the world's trade organization even though it was intended as an interim measure that would eventually yield to the ITO. GATT was much more strictly based on *economic liberalism* than the ITO, and less developed countries have lobbied since its inception for relief from many of its tenets. Another problem with GATT was that most negotiations involved eliminating barriers to manufactured goods rather than commodities. Thus Third World countries still find that their commodity exports are inhibited by relatively much higher tariff barriers.

A continuing Third World complaint is that the commodity goods they export are losing their value relative to the consumer goods, equipment, and other finished goods that they import. The average value of primary commodities (other than oil) imported as a percentage of the value of manufactured goods exported by developed countries has declined from 130 to 70 between 1957 and 1990.[3] In other words, the industrial countries received almost twice as many primary goods for their manufactured exports in 1990 as they did in 1957, whereas Third World countries were receiving less than half the value for their commodity exports as they were 33 years before. Commodity prices have not only declined steadily in relative value over the last three decades, but fluctuate sharply over the short term as they are traded on markets by investors. Both long-term drops and short-term fluctuations in commodity prices can devastate countries that depend on one crop for most of their export earnings. About 85 percent of Cuba's export earnings come from sugar, 60 percent of Ghana's from cocoa, 50 percent of Bolivia's from tin, 60 percent of Sri Lanka's from tea, 65 percent of Honduras's from bananas, and 50 percent of Zaire's from copper, to name a few of the more highly dependent economies.

There are several reasons for the decline in the relative value of commodities. The prices for some commodities have dropped because industrial countries have found substitutes. For example, fiber optics has replaced copper wiring in telecommunications. The 20 percent drop between 1973 and 1986 in demand for copper has deeply hurt such producers as Chile. Consumers are increasingly substituting saccharin and aspartame for sugar, thus hurting sugarcane-producing countries. Nylon has replaced cotton or wool in textiles, depressing prices in cotton- and sheep-producing countries.

Meanwhile, trade unions in the industrial countries have kept wages and benefits up; trade unions either do not exist in the Third World or are ineffective. Because wages constitute an important part of a good's final price, prices of goods from industrial countries are more apt to rise than those of goods from less developed countries. Productivity gains in the First World that bring down prices are often offset by labor demands that raise costs, and thus the good's price remains relatively stable. Increased productivity in the Third World in the absence of labor unions may simply mean cheaper prices.

Many industrial countries are also major commodity producers. The United States, Canada, Australia, and New Zealand produce grains, livestock, and minerals. Because of their higher labor costs, these goods are often more high priced than those from the less developed countries. Thus these industrial countries have erected high trade barriers to protect their own less competitive commodity producers.

However, most industrial country tariffs on commodity imports are lower than those on finished goods, a phenomenon known as "cascading tariffs." These higher tariffs are often accompanied by other trade barriers, including strict labeling, health, and inspection standards. The result is to restrict Third World exports to commodities rather than allow them to expand into semifinished or manufactured goods.

GATT itself sometimes blatantly discriminated against the Third World. In 1962, GATT negotiated the Long-Term Arrangement Regarding Trade in Cotton Textiles (LTA), which allowed members to impose quotas and market share limits on

Table 16.4 **Economic Profiles: Growth Rates by Sectors**

	Agriculture		Industry		Service		Exports	
	1980–1990	1990–1998	1980–1990	1990–1998	1980–1990	1990–1998	1980–1990	1990–1998
World	2.7%	1.2%	—	2.1%	—	2.0%	5.2%	6.4%
Low Income	4.1	3.5	7.8%	11.0	8.0%	7.3	5.9	11.1
Excluding China and India	3.0	2.5	4.6	5.9	5.0	4.7	2.7	7.0
Middle Income	2.6	−0.2	2.5	1.6	2.7	2.7	6.1	7.5
Lower Middle Income	—	−2.2	—	−2.8	—	0.4	—	2.8
Upper Middle Income	2.5	1.9	2.5	4.4	2.7	4.0	7.6	11.5
Low and Middle Income	3.4	1.7	3.7	4.2	3.7	3.7	6.1	8.4
East Asia and Pacific	4.4	3.5	9.5	11.5	8.8	7.9	9.6	14.0
East Europe and Central Asia	—	−6.3	—	−5.5	—	−1.4	—	3.9
Latin America and Caribbean	2.1	2.6	1.2	3.7	1.6	3.4	5.4	9.3
Middle East and North Africa	5.5	1.7	0.6	2.2	2.1	3.6	—	—
South Asia	3.2	3.2	6.8	6.5	6.5	7.1	6.6	10.5
Sub-Saharan Africa	2.5	2.6	0.9	1.2	2.4	2.1	2.4	4.6
High Income	—	0.3	—	1.5	—	1.8	5.1	6.1

— indicates no available information for that year.
Source: World Bank Report, 2000.

cotton textile imports. The advanced industrial countries then negotiated bilateral agreements under the LTA. In 1974, under GATT auspices, the *Multi-Fiber Agreement (MFA)* was signed by industrial and less developed countries, creating a multilateral quota system for the global trade of artificial fiber and wool textiles and materials. Two decades later, the Multi-Fiber Agreement still upholds a global quota system for textiles, although it is supposed to expire by 2006. In 1990, over 60 percent of Third World yarn and fabrics and 80 percent of clothing exports were restricted under the MFA. The World Bank estimated that a free global textile market would increase textile and clothing manufacturing in the Third World by 35 percent and create $11.3 billion in additional wealth for those countries.[4]

Not only do Third World countries get less money for their commodity exports, but they also complain that when the industrial countries catch an economic cold (recession), the poor countries get pneumonia (depression). There is a direct relationship between the growth rates of industrial countries and that of developing countries.[5] The most important reason is that less buying power for consumers means less money to buy goods from the poorer countries. But the United States, Europe, and other industrialized countries tend to raise trade barriers during recessions, whereas Japan's trade barriers always shut out most competitive imports.

The Third World's political economic fate is particularly tied to the United States, which usually absorbs about 70 percent of Third World exports, and almost 90 percent of Latin America's. To protect American jobs, Washington has often temporarily limited Third World products. For example, over two decades through 1988 American barriers against agricultural imports rose from about 30 to 90 percent of the total.[6] Between 1975 and 1985, the American imposition of voluntary export restraints (VERs) on imports, many of which came from developing countries, rose from 10 to 25 percent of total imports. When the United States raises import barriers, the exports of Third World countries suffer greatly. Inevitably, almost everyone is hurt by protectionism. Recession in the Third World means less demand for American and other First World products. With 40 percent of American exports going to the developing world, the United States then loses potential economic growth.

Perhaps the most negative U.S. effect on developing countries is America's own foreign debt, which is now greater than that of the entire Third World. There is only a finite amount of global finance—the more the United States borrows, the less is available for the Third World. Commercial bankers would much prefer to lend to the still creditworthy United States than to a poor country whose existing debt is huge and has been often rescheduled. And America's huge demand for international finance raises world interest rates, which means that yet more Third World income is transferred to global bankers.

But what about the charges that the more developed countries are holding back the less developed countries by trade barriers, declining commodity prices, and other discriminatory practices. Statistics reveal that overall Third World economies are in transition from agriculture to industry and manufacturing as the advanced economies gradually shed those industries for high-technology service industries. But as always, the beneficiaries of this transition vary among the world's regions and countries, with a few gaining much and many going without.

Modernization theory adherents dispute the assertion of dependency theorists that trade harms rather than helps the world's poorer countries. What does freer trade do? The competition brings down prices, forces domestic producers to improve

Table 16.5 **Economic Profiles: By the Percentage of Value to GDP**

	Agriculture		Industry		Manufacturing		Services	
	1980	1998	1980	1998	1980	1998	1980	1998
World	7%	5%	38%	—	25%	20%	56%	61%
Low Income	31	21	38	41%	27	29	30	38
Excluding China and India	29	25	32	33	13	18	39	42
Middle Income	13	9	41	36	25	21	46	56
Lower Middle Income	—	12	—	36	—	—	—	52
Upper Middle Income	11	7	42	35	26	22	47	57
Low and Middle Income	18	12	40	37	25	23	42	51
East Asia and Pacific	24	15	42	45	31	31	33	41
Europe and Central Asia	—	11	—	34	—	—	—	55
Latin America and Caribbean	10	8	40	34	29	22	50	58
Middle East and North Africa	10	—	53	—	9	—	37	—
South Asia	36	25	24	29	16	19	43	46
Sub-Saharan Africa	18	17	39	34	16	19	43	50
High Income	3	2	37	—	25	19	59	65

— indicates no available information for that year.
Source: World Bank Report, 2000.

their productivity and quality by emulating the technological, managerial, service, financial, and accounting strategies of foreign rivals. Meanwhile, those who cannot compete start new businesses. In this way competition allocates resources more efficiently. Although short-term disruptions such as higher unemployment may occur, everyone benefits in the long term as cheaper, better quality, and more diverse and abundant goods are available, and unemployment drops and incomes rise. Thus trade liberation promotes economic development and converts poverty to wealth. Dependency theorists, however, disagree.

Globalization, Nonalignment, *and the* New International Economic Order

As early as the mid-1950s, representatives of Third World states met to discuss their common problems and to present a united front to the democratic industrial and communist blocs alike. The first nonaligned summit was held in Belgrade in 1954, and was followed up by the larger Bandung Conference of April 1955 in which representatives of 20 countries swore to remain independent and forge a political economic alternative to the cold war rivalry. Indonesian President Sukarno captured the conference's mood when he said, "We have been the un-regarded, the peoples for whom decisions were made by others whose interests were paramount, the people who lived in poverty and humiliation. Then our nations demanded, nay fought for independence, and achieved independence, and with that independence came responsibility."[7]

Third World nonalignment and solidarity has been more rhetorical than real. Few states actually watched the cold war from the sidelines. The United States and Soviet Union each had client states throughout the less developed world. Conflicts between less developed states sometimes broke down into war. India and Pakistan fought three border wars, and other wars broke out between China and India, China and Vietnam, and Iraq and Iran, to name the largest. Most wars, however, were civil rather than international as suppressed and brutalized peoples fought for independence from the dominant ethnic group. Many governments in the less developed world displayed a double standard in denouncing "imperial exploitation" while often much more brutally exploiting their own people whom they were supposed to represent. Tanzanian President Julius Nyerere, for one, bravely decried "this tendency in Africa that it does not matter if an African kills other Africans. . . . Being black is now becoming a certificate to kill fellow Africans."[8]

The *nonaligned movement* was reinforced by the emergence of regional organizations such as the League of Arab States (1948), the Organization for African Unity (1963, OAU), and the Association of Southeast Asian Nations (1967, ASEAN), along with the U.N. *Group of 77* (Third World countries) in the 1960s, which formed to promote shared political and economic goals.

Of these organizations the Group of 77, which now has 132 members, has been the most assertive. In 1963, the group issued its "Joint Declaration of the Developing Countries," which argued that "The existing principles and pattern of world trade still mainly favor the advanced parts of the world. Instead of helping the developing countries to promote the development and diversification of their economies, the present tendencies in world trade frustrate their efforts to attain more rapid growth. These trends must be reversed."[9] The group called for an international conference to address these trade and investment concerns.

In 1964, the United Nations created the *U.N. Conference on Trade and Development (UNCTAD)* and named Raul Prebisch, the father of dependency theory, as its first secretary-general. Prebisch tried to make UNCTAD an alternative to GATT, the IMF, and World Bank.[10] These efforts eventually succeeded in several ways. UNCTAD pressured GATT to address many Third World issues. In 1965, GATT issued a Part IV to its charter, calling for the elimination of trade barriers to products from less developed countries, allowing commodity price agreements, and permitting Third World countries to opt out of the reciprocity principle. The only trouble with Part IV was that adherence to it by GATT members was voluntary.

In 1968, after several years of negotiation, most of the advanced industrial countries agreed in principle to a *general system of preferences (GSP)* in which they would reduce their trade barriers to Third World products. But it was not until 1971 that GATT approved the GSP by waiving its most-favored-nation reciprocity principle. The GSP did not formally emerge until 1975 when 19 advanced industrial countries agreed to unilaterally eliminate tariffs for a decade on a range of manufactured and semifinished goods for 140 poor countries. The agreement lasted for 10 years and was renewed in 1985. In the recent GSP agreement, the United States has eliminated tariffs on $13 billion of imports from developing countries.

Although the GSP has helped promote some Third World exports, its value has been more symbolic than economic. The advanced industrial countries found ways around these concessions. Generally, they remove only barriers to Third World products that do not compete with their own. For example, the United States excludes textiles and shoes as well as import-sensitive steel, electronics, and glass from the GSP and refuses to extend it to any *OPEC (Organization of Petroleum Exporting Countries)* country or any product that captured more than a 50 percent share of America's market.

During the 1970s, the Group of 77 movement reached its peak of activism. In 1974, it proposed in the U.N. General Assembly the creation of a new international economic order (NIEO) that would run on different principles from the liberal international economic order developed by the United States (see list, below). In December 1974, the Group of 77 also got the General Assembly to pass the Charter of Economic Rights and Duties of States, including (1) sovereignty for all states, which means the right to use any wealth and resources in whatever way it wants; (2) the right to nationalize all foreign property in return for appropriate compensation; and (3) the right of states to create commodity cartels and the duty of other states to adhere to those prices and other arrangements.

U.N. Conference on Trade and Development (UNCTAD)
Demands for a New International Economic Order

1. The creation of buffer stocks to prevent fluctuations in commodity prices

2. Multilateral long-term contracts for commodity prices that guarantee prices

3. Massive debt writeoffs

4. Elimination of trade barriers in industrial countries to Third World exports

5. Liberalization and extension of GSP privileges to semifinished and finished goods

6. Increase in the Third World share of global industrial production to 25 percent by the year 2000

7. Increase in foreign aid from donors at least equal to 0.70 percent of their GNP

8. Increased technology transfers and the setup of research and development institutes within the Third World

9. Stabilization of exchange rates, movement away from the dollar as the international currency, and increased use of SDRs issued by the IMF

10. Regulation of multinational corporation investments and profits[11]

In 1976, UNCTAD inaugurated the Integrated Program for Commodities (IPC) to help control fluctuations in prices and the average price level for commodities. The IPC has attempted to negotiate such agreements for 18 commodities that comprise 75 percent of the Third World's commodity exports. Prices can be further managed by stockpiling some commodities and selling off some stock when the price rises too rapidly and buying more when the price falls. The IPC identified 10 of these buffer stocks: rubber, sugar, tea, tin, cocoa, coffee, copper, cotton and cotton yarns, hard fibers, and jute and jute products. By 1980, UNCTAD had granted the IPC a $400 million fund to finance these buffer stocks, and allocated another $350 million to help diversify Third World economies particularly dependent on sales of one or a few commodities. States join the IPC by making a financial contribution to the buffer stock finance pool.

The IPC has had limited success in achieving its ambitious goals. By the late 1990s, there were only five international commodity agreements (ICAs)—cocoa, tin, sugar, rubber, coffee, and tropical lumber. Only rubber and tropical lumber involved IPC agreements. The industrial nations were leery of the IPC and other ICAs, fearing that they would spawn OPEC-type cartels that would raise prices. These agreements are further undercut by the fact that some industrial nations such as the United States, Canada, Australia, and South Africa are also important commodity exporters. The Third World contributes only 32 percent of the world's nonoil commodity exports and 45 percent of its known nonenergy minerals.[12]

Among the advanced industrial states, the European Union has been the most accommodating to Third World demands. Since 1975, Brussels has signed four agreements (known as the Lome Conventions) with 66 developing countries. STABEX, a system instituted under Lome I, acts like an IPC or club in which states join by making a contribution to a common fund. STABEX covers 48 commodities and extends grants or loans to any member whose commodity earnings fall below a certain percentage of its exports to the European Community (Union) for three previous years.

UNCTAD was also influential in the GATT Tokyo Round of negotiations from 1973 through 1979. The GATT approved the various agreements that UNCTAD has negotiated with the industrial countries. However, GATT also passed a "graduation" clause in which countries that achieved a certain level of development would no longer be eligible for preferential treatment.

During GATT's Uruguay Round (1986–1993), the less developed countries were put on the defensive by industrial country demands that they grant intellectual property protection and reduce their trade barriers. Meanwhile, four industrial and nine Third World agricultural exporting countries, known as the Cairns-Group after the Australian city in which they first met, have joined to pressure the European Union to abandon its agricultural trade barriers and export subsidies.

Throughout the Uruguay Round, there was a clear division between the First and Third Worlds over technology. The advanced industrial nations believe that the inventors have rights to withhold or license their technology as they see fit. If intellectual property is not protected and compensated, there will be no incentive for inventors to create new technology. Computer software, for example, is easily copied, thus costing the creators lost royalties and giving them little incentive to create new software. Third World countries argue that technology should be used by all without restriction or compensation. They argue that intellectual property protection simply perpetuates the political economic supremacy of the advanced industrial countries and the subjection of the poor. Although the World Intellectual Property Organization (WIPO) was set up to address the problems of intellectual piracy, it has been unable to stem such thefts. The Uruguay Round failed to resolve the technology issue.

UNCTAD continued to be active during the 1980s and 1990s and its ranks swelled to 132 members. But its power decreased despite its growing membership. As we have seen, in the Third World, countries' interests are not identical. The range of development levels within the Third World has expanded enormously. As countries develop their interests change. Third World solidarity was always more of a slogan rather than a reality, but never more so than today. And when some Third World countries do attempt to work together on an issue, the

South *of the* Border:
Mexico's Miraculous *Maquiladoras*

Maquiladoras are perhaps the best economic idea the Mexican government has ever put into effect. *Maquiladoras* are duty-free manufacturing zones across northern Mexico where over one million workers in over 4,000 firms produced $7 billion worth of goods in 1998, a figure that will rise steadily. That is the second largest contribution to Mexico's economy after the oil industry.

Why are the *maquiladoras* so popular? The ability to import parts duty free reduces costs for manufacturers.

Cheap, skilled labor is also important: Mexican wages are one-seventh those of American workers. But even cheaper labor can be found in scores of other countries. With their factories just south of the border linked by superhighways to advanced assembly plants or stores in North America, producers have easy access to integrated low-cost production or mass markets of 271 million American and 25 million Canadian consumers. Yet another attraction are the North American Free Trade Association (NAFTA) "domestic content" rules whereby anywhere from

60 to 80 percent of a product's value made in those three countries must come from parts manufactured there.

The *maquiladoras* benefit every corporation that sets up shop there, along with NAFTA as a whole. NAFTA combines an economy that in 1999 produced $8.8 trillion worth of wealth and included 390 million people among the United States, Canada, and Mexico. Because the industries of those countries largely complement rather than compete with each other, the members have experienced more benefits than costs since they joined.

industrialized countries invariably play them off against each other through offers of aid, investments, lower trade barriers, and so on. Stockpiling, conservation, alternative products, and multiple suppliers doomed any attempt by countries to stabilize commodity prices. Finally, the collapse of communism has removed both a state development model and source of support for UNCTAD's more radical members. Faced with these realities, UNCTAD has quietly set aside its NIEO goals and focused on working with WTO on specific issues.

The Organization *of* Petroleum Exporting Countries (OPEC)

Until the early 1970s, no economic sector seemed a more blatant example of Third World dependence than oil.[13] Seven oil corporations, known as the "Seven Sisters" (the American firms Exxon, Chevron, Gulf, Mobil, and Texaco, British Petroleum, and Dutch Royal Shell), controlled virtually all the world's noncommunist oil wells, transportation, refineries, and markets. They had operated as a global cartel since the 1920s, when they first began to split markets, fix prices, drive independents out of business, and impose lucrative extraction agreements on governments. Their wealth grew even greater as oil replaced coal as the most important energy resource. In 1952, the Seven Sisters produced 90 percent of the oil outside

Table 16.6 Crude Oil Reserves and Production

	January 1, 1999, Reserves (in billion barrels)	1998 Production[a] (in million barrels per day)
Saudi Arabia	262	8.4
Iraq	113	2.1
United Arab Emirates	98	2.3
Kuwait	97	2.1
Iran	90	3.6
Venezuela	73	3.1
Russia	57	6.9
Mexico	48	3.1
Libya	30	1.4
China	24	3.2
United States	23	6.4
Nigeria	23	2.0

[a]Excludes natural gas liquids.

Source: Cambridge Energy Research Associates Report, 2000.

Table 16.7 OPEC Members and Value of Oil Exports

	Exports (billion $)		
Member State	1988	1991	1996
Saudi Arabia	$27	$52	$52
Venezuela	11	15	19
Iran	13	19	18
United Arab Emirates	10	17	15
Nigeria	9	14	15
Kuwait	9	1	15
Libya	8	12	9
Algeria	8	10	9
Indonesia	7	8	8
Qatar	2	3	1
Iraq	13	0	1
Totals	**118**	**150**	**165**

Note: Major oil exporters not in OPEC include Russia and Kazakhstan (the Soviet Union was the world's largest exporter in the late 1980s, although exports have since dropped sharply), Mexico, China, Great Britain, and Norway. Ecuador and Gabon, both minor exporters, left OPEC in 1992 and 1995, respectively. The United States, until several decades ago a major oil exporter, is now a major importer.

Source: Data adapted from United Nations, *World Economic and Social Survey, 1997* (New York: United Nations, 1997), p. 281.

North America and the communist countries, a percentage that dropped to 75 percent by 1968.[14]

The first challenge to the Seven Sisters occurred in 1953 when the Iranian government attempted to nationalize the holdings of British Petroleum's subsidiary, Anglo-Iranian Oil, which monopolized Iran's oil industry. Britain responded with an economic embargo and threats to invade Iran unless compensation was made. The United States succeeded in overthrowing Iran's government, imposing the shah, and cutting a deal with the new government whereby American oil firms would replace British Petroleum.

During the mid-1950s several Persian Gulf governments succeeded in negotiating a 50–50 split on extraction profits, resulting in a significant increase in revenue. For example, Saudi Arabia's profits rose from $0.17 to $0.80 a barrel between 1956 and 1957 when a barrel of oil cost about $1.80. In 1961, representatives of Iran, Iraq, Kuwait, Saudi Arabia, and Venezuela, the world's five leading oil producers other than the United States and the Soviet Union, met to discuss the possibility of acting jointly to offset recent price decreases pushed through by the Seven Sisters. Although they failed to arrest the price drop, they did form the Organization for Petroleum Exporting Countries (OPEC), whose ranks increased to 13 by the early 1970s. Despite these developments, the Seven Sisters continued to dominate the global oil market from oil well to gas station.

Although OPEC remained quiescent during the 1960s, the vulnerability of the industrial world to a potential oil cutoff grew steadily. In 1973, OPEC accounted for 65 percent of global oil exports, and the Middle Eastern countries represented about 75 percent of that. Middle Eastern and North African oil accounted for 75 percent of Japan's total oil imports, 60 percent of Western Europe's, and 15 percent of America's.[15]

OPEC's 1970s activism was stimulated by Colonel Mu'ammar Gadhafi, who took over Libya in a 1969 coup. In 1970, Gadhafi threatened the nationalization of foreign oil holdings if they did not grant Libya higher taxes and boost prices. The oil firms gave in to Gadhafi's demands. In December 1970, OPEC also demanded tax and price increases. In February 1971, faced with this collective demand, the oil firms signed a five-year oil price and tax increase agreement with OPEC in which oil would rise from $1.80 to $2.29 a barrel. OPEC soon called for a renegotiation of the agreement when it became clear that the dollar's devaluation in December 1971 had cut its members' revenues. The price was subsequently raised to $2.48 a barrel. In December 1972, OPEC called for an ownership share of the oil subsidiaries in its countries starting at 25 percent and eventually rising to 51 percent by 1982. The oil firms complied with these demands. Despite these agreements, the dollar's floating and devaluation in spring 1973 had diminished OPEC's revenues, and it called for even greater price increases from the oil firms.

Two days before these negotiations were to commence, the Arab states attacked Israel on October 6 in what became known as the Yom Kippur War. Although initially caught by surprise, Israel counterattacked and, with massive American military and intelligence aid, managed to defeat the Arab armies. On October 16, the Organization of Arab Petroleum Exporting Countries (OAPEC), an OPEC subgroup, increased the oil price to $5.12 a barrel, and on December 23 raised it further to $11.65, effectively quadrupling oil prices within a month. OAPEC also imposed a temporary boycott on oil sales to the United States, the Netherlands, and Portugal for helping Israel during the war.

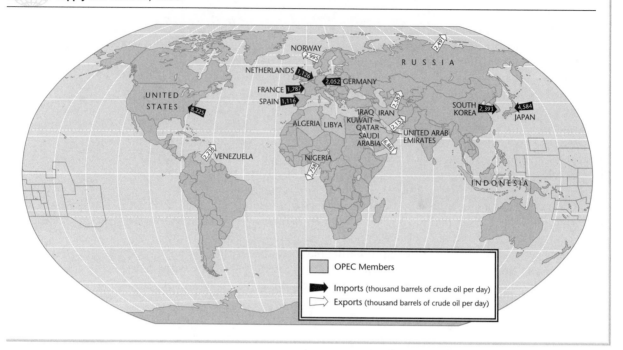

The United States responded to this crisis by attempting to organize a buyers' cartel called the International Energy Agency (IEA), which would attempt to off-set OPEC's power by its members stockpiling at least a 90-day oil supply, sharing supplies, developing alternative fuels, and acting together diplomatically. France, however, refused to join. The IEA was largely ineffective in countering OPEC.

OPEC's oil price hikes succeeded for three central reasons. First, there was no easy energy alternative to oil. Second, the Europeans and Japanese were dependent on OPEC for most of their oil needs. Third, the oil sources were dispersed so widely and could be so easily sabotaged that it would have been impossible for the United States and its allies to take them over.

OPEC maintained prices by assigning production quotas for its members. With the world's largest proven oil reserves, Saudi Arabia served as OPEC's price leader. When global oil supplies were tight, Saudi Arabia increased production and when supplies were abundant it cut back. OPEC was divided between countries such as Iran, Iraq, Venezuela, and Nigeria, which had smaller reserves, larger populations, and more ambitious development strategies and thus wanted ever higher oil prices, and more moderate countries such as Saudi Arabia, Kuwait, and the United Arab Emirates, which were content with existing increases.

Between 1974 and January 1979, prices drifted up to $14.34 a barrel, then more than doubled in 1980 to $33 a barrel. There were several reasons for this second dramatic oil increase. Throughout 1978, Iran was torn apart by a revolution in which the pro-Western shah was overthrown and the fundamentalist Ayatollah Khomeini was brought to power in January 1979. Iranian oil shipments had been cut during the last months of 1978, exacerbating existing global supply shortages. In December 1978, OPEC agreed to a 10 percent price hike, followed by another in July 1979. In December 1979, the Soviet Union invaded Afghanistan, prompting fears among some that this was the first step in the Soviet conquest of the Persian Gulf. In September 1980, Iraq attacked Iran, limiting oil shipments from both countries as each side bombed the other's oil facilities. Throughout these two years, oil prices on the "spot market" or the free market beyond OPEC's control rose higher and faster than the OPEC prices. By December 1980, OPEC's official price reached $33 a barrel, while spot market prices topped $41 a barrel.

The result of the oil price hikes between 1973 and 1980 was a startling shift in global geoeconomic power. OPEC countries received huge financial windfalls—from $15 billion in revenues in 1972, OPEC earned an additional $70 billion in 1974, an average annual $200 billion from 1975 to 1979 and, after further doubling its prices, received $300 billion in 1980! Meanwhile, American oil imports soared from $4.8 billion to $80 billion during the same period, and other industrial nations posted similar increases in their oil bills. The result was a decade of stagflation—high unemployment, interest rates, and inflation, and low economic growth. Although the less developed nations initially cheered OPEC's actions, the poorer countries were the worst hit by the grossly inflated prices.[16]

What did OPEC do with all this money? Most of the oil-rich countries could not absorb that flood of cash into their own economies and ended up investing it in Western banks, which in turn lent it out to the poorer countries to help them pay for their own oil and other imports. The Third World's debts mounted rapidly and, with their economies stalled, they had difficulty paying off the interest, let alone the principal. There was a very real danger that if the major Third World debtors, such as Mexico or Brazil, defaulted on their loans, they would bankrupt the world's major banks, which in turn would cause the entire global economy to collapse.

OPEC's success inspired developing countries to attempt to force concessions from the industrial democratic countries in other areas. The Group of 77 unsuccessfully pushed its NIEO agenda during 1974 and 1975. Also during this time, many feared that other commodity producers would follow in OPEC's footsteps by creating cartels and raising prices. These fears were unfounded. Although several commodity producers did try to form cartels, none became another OPEC. Stockpiles, diverse and abundant sources, and alternatives undermined efforts to create bauxite, copper, phosphate, banana, cocoa, tea, and natural rubber cartels.

OPEC's overwhelming triumph in raising oil prices during the 1970s turned to failure during the mid-1980s when international oil prices dropped to half their highest level. Prices collapsed for several reasons. As prices rose throughout the 1970s, non-OPEC members such as Great Britain, Norway, Mexico, Malaysia, and China began exploiting sources and discovering new ones that would have otherwise been too expensive. Between 1973 and 1983, OPEC's share of the global oil market dropped from 63 percent to 33 percent.[17] Hard pressed for additional revenues, OPEC members themselves cheated by selling more oil than allowed by their own quotas, and flooded the spot market with it. Meanwhile, almost all countries, but particularly the oil-guzzling industrial countries, embarked on conservation policies to make their energy use more efficient. They also created huge oil reserves that could supply their respective needs for up to 90 to 120 days. The combination of increased supply and decreased demand led to a global oil glut and subsequent oil price drop in 1986 from $30 to $15 a barrel. The glut continued despite the Persian Gulf War, which temporarily eliminated Kuwaiti and Iraqi oil production from global markets. By November 1992, OPEC's daily production of 25.15 million barrels was the highest since 1980, which helped push oil prices down from $21 a barrel to $19.60 a barrel. By early 1999 the price for a barrel of oil fluctuated around $15, which is actually cheaper in constant dollars (adjusted for inflation) than before 1973. Later that year OPEC succeeded in cutting back production so that prices doubled by early 2000 to $28 a barrel.

OPEC currently has 11 members—Algeria, Indonesia, Iran, Iraq, Kuwait, Libya, Nigeria, Qatar, Saudi Arabia, the United Arab Emirates, and Venezuela (Ecuador left OPEC in September 1992). These countries vary considerably in wealth, population, and territory, from states such as Kuwait and the United Arab Emirates, with small populations and lands and large per capita incomes, to countries such as Nigeria and Indonesia, with huge territories and populations but mass poverty.

OPEC's power will probably not revive during the 21st century's first decade at the very least. The oil glut will continue as supplies steadily rise while demand remains slack from extensive conservation and efficiency efforts. Although OPEC currently produces only about 45 percent of global oil exports, 65 percent of the world's proven oil reserves are within the Persian Gulf countries. Over the long term, OPEC's power, and particularly that of its Persian Gulf members, may well re-emerge as finite oil reserves eventually dwindle. OPEC's will definitely revive if the new central Asian producers join. Whether the global economy will have found and shifted to nonoil energy sources by that time remains to be seen.

Who Gives Foreign Aid?

Foreign aid remains an important if diminishing source of international development funds and expertise for most Third World countries.[18] From 1990 to 2000, foreign aid fell from almost one-third to about one-fifth of the Third World's sources of international finance as the direct foreign and portfolio investments soared. Foreign aid is from both bilateral (country to country) and multilateral (international organization to country) sources. There are several types of aid. Humanitarian aid is generally for crises such as famines and natural disasters, and includes supplies of food, medicine, and clothing. Development aid is generally targeted to specific projects, whether it be a village well or huge dam. Although military aid is not considered *official development assistance (ODA),* advocates argue that development of a nation's military forces can contribute to both political stability and economic development. Opponents argue that the opposite effect is much more common.

official development aid (ODA) the official aid that one government gives another.

BILATERAL AID

After 1945, the United States was the most important aid donor and continues to provide the most aid in volume if not as a GNP percentage. Between 1945 and 2000, the United States dispensed more than $300 billion in official development aid, and throughout the 1980s and 1990s has annually dispensed about $9 billion to the Third World. In the late 1990s, Japan surpassed the United States to become the world's largest donor.

Table 16.8 **The World's Most Generous Aid Donors**

	Total (billion $)	Percentage of GNP		NGO Aid (Percentage of GNP)		Aid to Poorest (Percentage of Total)	
		1986–1987	1996–1997	1986–1987	1996–1997	1986–1987	1996–1997
By Dollar Volume							
Japan	$9.358	0.30%	0.22%	0.00%	0.01%	27%	19%
United States	6.878	0.21	0.09	0.04	0.03	18	20
France	6.307	0.58	0.45	0.01	0.00	27	22
Germany	5.857	0.41	0.28	0.06	0.05	28	19
Great Britain	3.433	0.29	0.26	0.03	0.03	31	22
By Percentage of GNP							
Denmark	1.637	0.88	0.97	0.02	0.02	38	30
Norway	1.306	1.13	0.86	0.08	0.07	41	39
Netherlands	2.947	0.99	0.81	0.08	0.01	34	27
Sweden	1.731	0.87	0.79	0.07	0.01	39	30
Luxembourg	0.095	0.17	0.55	0.00	0.03	—	29

Note: NGO aid is the amount given by private donors based in that country.

Source: U.N. Human Development Program, *Human Development Report, 1999.*

America's aid program started out vast and generous. For a decade after 1945, Washington's aid policy concentrated on reconstruction of the industrial countries rather than on development of the world's poor countries. The United States gave $17 billion to 16 European countries and $2.2 billion to Japan between 1945 and 1952. But from the mid-1950s, for several reasons, the Third World became the recipient of massive aid. One reason was that the reconstruction of Europe and Japan was finished. Those countries had been restored to rapid economic growth and relative prosperity, and were now able to begin their own foreign aid programs. During the 1950s and into the 1960s, an increased number of colonies achieved independence and were in desperate need of economic assistance. Finally, in 1956, Soviet Premier Nikita Khrushchev announced that his country would compete with the Western powers for the loyalty of developing countries, with aid an especially important enticement.

To counter Soviet advances and deal with the development problems of a rapidly enlarging Third World, the United States and its allies significantly boosted their foreign aid programs. For two decades after the mid-1950s, global foreign aid increased steadily. After OPEC's quadrupling of oil prices in 1973, many of the wealthier Arab states also began large aid programs, although most of these targeted poorer Arab or Muslim states.

Washington clearly linked American economic and political security with that of the less developed countries, and saw its aid program as a vital means of achieving that security. A Senate committee nicely summarized the ends and means of the U.S. foreign aid program:

> A comprehensive and sustained program of American economic assistance aimed at
> helping the free underdeveloped countries to create the conditions for self-sustaining

Table 16.9 **Amount of Official Development Assistance (ODA) and Top Five Recipients (in billions of dollars)**

	1988	1997
Net ODA	$48	$50
Bilateral	37	32
Multilateral	11	18
Net ODA (1995 dollars)	61	48
Share to Poorest Recipients	28%	14%
Recipients of Greatest ODA		
Israel	$1.5	$2.2
China	2.5	2.0
Egypt	1.9	2.0
India	2.4	1.7
Bangladesh	2.2	1.0

growth [which] can, in the short run, materially reduce the danger of conflict triggered by minor powers, and can, say, in two or three decades, result in an overwhelming preponderance of societies with a successful record of solving their problems without resorting to coercion or violence. The establishment of such a preponderance of stable, effective, and democratic societies gives the best promise of a favorable settlement of the Cold War and of a peaceful, progressive world environment."[19]

By the mid-1970s, most of the advanced industrial countries, especially the United States, began to experience donor fatigue. Classical economic assumptions guided America's aid program. It was thought that a lack of money was the most important development constraint for poor countries. Thus large American grants to a country would theoretically set off a virtuous savings/investment cycle. Unfortunately, development proved far more complex than liberal economic theory allowed. In all too many poor countries, there seemed to be little development to show for all the cash. Instead, the result of most aid programs was widespread waste, corruption, and inefficiency. And for the United States, often the recipient country politically bit the hand that fed it, by refusing to go along with Washington on U.N. votes, military bases, or economic policies. For these reasons plus the global economic slowdown, from the late 1970s the amount of aid from the United States and many other industrial countries leveled off. Then, during the 1980s, OPEC aid declined in absolute and relative terms as oil prices plunged.

Few countries give aid for purely altruistic purposes. The United States, Soviet Union, and some other aid donors have often used aid to influence the recipient's policies.[20] Aid with this motivation does not always succeed in advancing the donor's national interests. For example, the massive economic and military aid that Moscow extended Egypt did not prevent President Sadat from kicking out all Soviet advisers and reducing bilateral diplomatic ties in 1972. Nor did the tens of billions of dollars the United States gave South Vietnam, along with a massive U.S. military involvement, prevent Saigon from falling to communism in 1975.

Despite such failures, America's aid program has, largely for political reasons, shifted in type and targeted countries. In 1973, 78 percent of American aid was for economic development and 22 percent for direct geopolitical purposes. By 1985, the Reagan administration nearly reversed these priorities, allocating 67 percent of American aid to Third World militaries and 33 percent to those economies.[21] American law also prohibits aid to countries that have nationalized American assets without adequate compensation.

Net ODA by Amount and Percentage of GNP
Source: World Bank 2000, Entering the 21st Century (New York: Oxford University Press 2000), pp. 270–271.

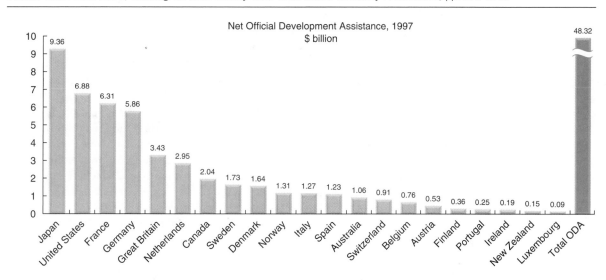

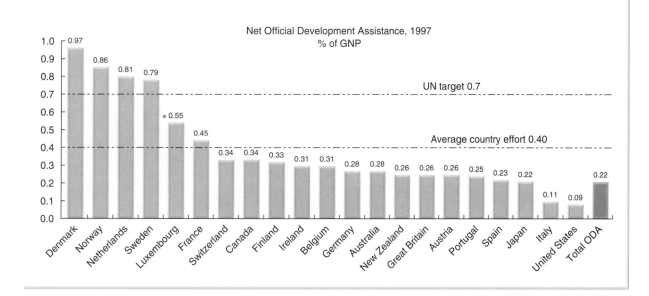

Several major aid donors have concentrated their aid on a relatively few recipients. Since the 1977 Camp David Accords signed between President Sadat and Prime Minister Begin, about 40 percent of American aid goes to Egypt and Israel. President Carter used the promise of massive aid to both countries as a lure for a peace agreement. The Reagan administration concentrated its aid even more narrowly by emphasizing "front-line" states in regional conflicts such as Turkey, Pakistan, and the Central American countries, as well as Israel and Egypt. By 1992, $5.1 billion or 36 percent of America's $13.9 billion aid budget still went to Israel and Egypt, whereas only $650 million went to Russia in 1991.

Some other donors also narrow their aid to a few targets. France gives much of its aid to itself—about 40 percent of its aid goes to four of its overseas departments and territories. About 85 percent of OPEC's aid goes to Arab or Muslim countries. Until the Soviet Union's breakup, about 80 percent of Moscow's aid went to Vietnam, Cuba, and Mongolia. Now, of course, the former Soviet republics are themselves the recipients of massive foreign aid.

Most donors tie at least some aid to the recipient's purchase of the donor country's goods and services. Japan has the most blatantly tied aid program; where Japanese export subsidies end and aid begins is impossible to say. Tokyo has underwritten its exports with "aid" since it sent abroad its first reparations during the 1950s. As Japan's economic power grew, ever more donors felt compelled to follow suit. Washington's 480 agricultural aid programs for instance, give recipients loans to buy American grain, and is thus largely a subsidy to producers.

But some countries actually donate aid with no strings attached. The three Scandinavian countries and the Netherlands are the most generous in giving aid as a percentage of their GNPs. Overall aid from the wealthy to the poor, with or without benefits to the donor, declined from $61 billion in 1986–1987 to $48 billion a decade later (the figures are adjusted for inflation).

MULTILATERAL AID

Recipients generally favor multilateral over bilateral aid. Direct donor-to-recipient bilateral aid tends to be tied and restricted. Multilateral aid is usually targeted on specific projects, but at least the recipient has slightly more discretion over how it is spent. There are a variety of multilateral aid organizations, including regional development banks, various U.N. programs, the European Union, OPEC, private philanthropic institutions, and OECD's Development Assistance Committee (DAC).

International Bank for Reconstruction and Development (IBRD) also known as the **World Bank,** the IBRD was created at the **Bretton Woods Conference** of 1944 along with the **International Monetary Fund (IMF).**

The *IBRD (International Bank for Reconstruction and Development),* or World Bank, and the IMF are the world's two most important multilateral lending agencies. Their aid programs complement each other. The World Bank funds specific development projects, and the IMF extends short-term development loans to countries suffering from international payments deficits. Both institutions are headquartered in Washington, D.C., in buildings next to each other. Although the World Bank is often criticized for investing in wasteful large-scale projects that are inappropriate for the recipient country, it is the IMF's lending policies that have received the most criticism.

In 1999, the World Bank made $22.182 billion in additional low-interest loans and had $117.228 billion in outstanding loans to recipients. The International Development Agency (IDA), the World Bank's emergency loan organization, issued $6.812 billion and had $83.666 billion in outstanding loans. About 83 percent of

Table 16.10 **International Monetary Fund (IMF) New Loans**

	1990	1999
Total Loans (in SDRs)	5,266	22,240
Africa	1,289	542
Asia	525	8,918
Europe	268	5,169
Middle East	66	157
Western Hemisphere	3,119	7,454
Repurchases and Repayments	6,399	11,091
Total Outstanding Credit	23,388	67,175

Note: The figures are in millions of special drawing rights (SDRs), a currency used only to settle international accounts and not traded openly. Its value is determined by the relative values and use in international finance of the American dollar, Japanese yen, British pound, and the Euro. In 1999 an SDR was worth $0.58.

Source: International Monetary Fund, *Annual Report on Exchange Arrangements and Exchange Restrictions* (1999).

ODA loans go to countries with a 1998 GNP per capita lower than $761. Among the ODA's largest loans in 1998 and 1999 were to alleviate Russia's financial crisis and to Honduras and Nicaragua, which were battered by Hurricane Mitch. The top five borrowers from the World Bank accounted for 62 percent of total lending.

Like the World Bank, the IMF is like an international lending club. States become members by agreeing to follow IMF policy guidelines and contributing money to the IMF pool as an assigned quota of the total based on a formula that calculates their relative wealth. The 182 members vote on policy, with their votes weighted according to their financial contributions. When members are suffering payments deficits, they can borrow up to 100 percent of their original contribution in one year and 300 percent altogether, with emergency supplements allowed during financial crises. In return for the loan the recipient must strictly follow the IMF policy prescription. In 1999, the average interest charged for an IMF loan was 4.09 percent, several percentage points below the private market rate for the best risks. Members received an average 3.82 return on their money in the IMF bank. The difference between the interest rates covered the IMF's operating costs. Nearly all countries pay back their loan on time but in 1999 seven countries were behind on payments totaling 2,299.6 SDRs. The IMF suspends borrowing rights for countries that fall behind until they have paid up.

Although the IMF was founded in 1944, it did not become an important international lender until the 1970s, when the Third World debt grew rapidly. Most Third World countries take IMF loans only as a last resort. Debtors are highly critical of the IMF prescription, which includes massive cutbacks in government spending, restrictive fiscal and monetary policies, a currency devaluation, high interest rates, and the removal of trade and investment barriers. Government cutbacks in price supports for food, fuel, and other necessities hurts the poor the most. The currency devaluation inflates prices for those with enough money to afford foreign consumer goods and industries that depend on foreign equipment and technology. Finally, removal of trade and investment barriers often leads to an influx of foreign goods and services, which bankrupt domestic businesses that cannot compete. The result is that the economy is pushed into a deep and sometimes intractable recession. IMF riots are common, in which those worst hurt rampage in the streets. Thus debtors complain bitterly that the result of following IMF policies is not economic development but economic chaos and a political crisis that often leads to a coup or even revolution.

Despite these often grim results, Third World nations accept IMF loans for one clear reason—poor nations find it almost impossible to borrow money from international banks without one. An IMF loan signals to private international bankers that the recipient is considered credit-worthy, so they may also loan money to that country. If a country defaults, no one will lend to it. Given the alternatives, the IMF seems the lesser of two evils.

Third World countries have no power to change IMF policies. Although they make up 75 percent of the IMF's membership, their relatively low contributions mean that they only account for about 35 percent of the votes. The United States alone accounts for about 20 percent of the votes, and the other leading industrial states make up another 45 percent.

EVALUATING FOREIGN AID

Since its inception, the Group of 77 has called on the wealthier nations to annually transfer at least 0.7 percent of their GNP, as well as give more grants, softer loan interest rates, and longer repayment schedules, and to eliminate tying aid to purchases of the donor's goods and services. Only the Scandinavian countries and the Netherlands have complied with those requests. The two wealthiest countries, the United States and Japan, are actually among the stingiest in terms of aid as a percentage of GNP and the terms at which it is extended.

Does foreign aid help a nation's development? Over time, aid donors and recipients have learned to use resources more effectively. During the 1970s the World Bank shifted some of its funding from the development of large industrial and infrastructure projects to basic human needs, and many other countries' aid programs followed suit.[22] Humanitarian aid has generally been the most successful in nurturing development. Although many industrial projects have failed to make money, such basic needs as health, sanitation, and education have improved or at least have not deteriorated as rapidly as would have been the case without such humanitarian aid.

Yet some studies indicate that even aid that is relatively well administered may only add 0.6 percent to 1.5 percent to a nation's annual growth.[23] Donor fatigue has afflicted virtually all those who give. For many donors, the hundreds of millions of dollars in aid they have sent abroad seems to have neither sparked genuine development nor gratitude among the recipients. Although foreign aid will remain important to many Third World countries, it is clearly no development panacea.

How Do Debt Crises Arise?

During the 1980s, the global economy seemed threatened by the Third World's inability to service its rapidly growing debt. It was feared that the default of the world's largest debtors would bankrupt overextended international banks, which in turn would drag down the global economy into a deep and intractable depression. The world's leading economic powers and bankers worked together to resolve that crisis. Then, in the late 1990s, another debt crisis threatened to topple the global economy. That crisis was also successfully managed. The global economy continues to expand.

It is said that if you owe someone a thousand dollars, you are in debt to him, but if you owe him a million dollars he is in debt to you. That notion mirrors the Third World debt problem. When a huge debtor such as Mexico or Brazil threatens to default, the global bankers have no choice but to respond. The most common means of managing a crisis is to reschedule that country's debt repayment, which usually involves reducing the country's interest rates while extending its payments out over more years. Sometimes bankers or other investors actually buy back part of the debt at a reduced rate. And finally, they have simply written off large chunks of debt for countries that have threatened to default. Throughout the debt crisis, global bankers have been like firefighters, rushing from one country to the next rescheduling one debt payment after another.

The debt crisis was caused by several interrelated problems, of which the most important was OPEC's quadrupling of oil prices in 1973 and further doubling in 1979. By the early 1980s, a barrel of oil sold for $35, more than 15 times its price a decade earlier. The result was a huge shift in wealth from poor countries to OPEC.[24] Most of the OPEC states lacked a banking system sophisticated enough to manage this ocean of money or domestic development projects vast enough in which to invest it. Instead, they deposited much of the money in Western banks. But even the sophisticated international banks had trouble finding creditworthy borrowers in a stagnant global economy and became increasingly desperate for borrowers who would pay an interest rate higher than what the banks were giving to their oil-rich depositors.

Eventually many of these petrodollars were recycled to the Third World. Although OPEC had wielded its oil weapon to hurt the industrial democracies and extract revenge for decades of exploitation by the huge oil corporations, it was the poor, struggling Third World that was damaged the worst. Money earned by Third World countries from exports was used to pay for oil imports rather than being invested in domestic industries and infrastructure. As investments fell, so did economic growth and exports. When export earnings fell short of skyrocketing oil bills, the impoverished countries borrowed increasing amounts from international bankers to pay for the difference. To worsen matters, global interest rates rose to 21 percent in the early 1980s, reflecting the greater demand for funds and

Table 16.11 **Third World Debt, 1996**

Region	Foreign Debt		Annual Debt Service	
	Billions	Percentage of GNP	Billions	Percentage of Exports
Latin America	$657	41%	$97	30%
Asia	857	28	95	8
Africa	841	69	24	15
Total debt, "South"	1,826	37	213	19

the need to keep ahead of the hyperinflation set off by soaring oil prices. Poor countries sank ever deeper in the quicksand of debt with no way out. Economic development, which seemed promising for many Third World countries during the 1960s and early 1970s, stalled and often reversed. As the Third World fell deeper into debt and recession, the hard-pressed private bankers cut back their new loans to those countries, thus exacerbating the situation. The Third World's total debt rose from about $100 billion in 1973 to $831 billion in 1982 and $1.3 trillion in 1988.

The Third World leaders themselves must bear much of the responsibility for the debt crisis. Much of the borrowed money was squandered; some ended up in Swiss bank accounts, other was poured in grandiose construction projects. Little was invested in production or infrastructure that would stimulate rather than impede national development. There were some exceptions: Modeling its development on that of Japan, for example, South Korea invested most of its loans in strategic industries such as steel, automobiles, shipbuilding, consumer electronics, and semiconductors with great success—at least during that time.

Oil prices dropped to half their former price during the mid-1980s as new non-OPEC production in the North Sea, China, Mexico, and elsewhere began, and virtually every country attempted to invest in energy-saving equipment. Although this relieved the pressure on non–oil-producing nations, now it was the turn of oil-rich but heavily populated countries such as Mexico, Venezuela, Nigeria, and Indonesia to borrow heavily to maintain the huge development projects they had embarked on during the late 1970s.

Third World debt had been soaring for almost a decade when a crisis erupted in 1982. In July, the Mexican government announced that it would suspend its interest payments to foreign lenders. Mexico's foreign debt in 1982 was $85 billion, one-tenth of the total Third World debt of $831 billion.[25] Mexico defaulted as oil prices dropped and interest rates soared.

The fear was that if Mexico were allowed to default, other huge debtors would follow. Most of this debt was owed to commercial banks and a series of defaults would devastate the global financial and trading system. In 1982, five countries alone—Brazil, Mexico, Argentina, Venezuela, and Chile—had a total of $260 billion in debt, and all of them were having trouble servicing their debts. U.S. bankers were especially vulnerable to any default, because they owned 40 percent of Latin America's total debt.

The IMF led the global bankers in managing the debt crisis. The first step was for the IMF and those banks that had lent the most to the debtor country to organize an advisory committee that would negotiate directly with that government and other smaller lending banks. The government, in turn, represented all the country's debtors. Working together, the IMF, World Bank, industrial country governments, and commercial lenders formed a lender's cartel that worked with each country on a case-by-case basis, thus preventing the emergence of a debtor's cartel.

Within two days of Mexico's announcement, Washington directly lent its southern neighbor $2 billion in credits to service its immediate payments, and pressured a group of banks to reschedule payments, saving Mexico an additional $1 billion. Then the IMF and Mexico began to negotiate a more comprehensive settlement. In November 1982, in return for $3.84 billion in IMF loans and $5 billion in commercial loans, Mexico agreed to an intensive austerity program in which it devalued its currency, reduced government spending, and cut back its subsidy programs. For the first time, the IMF made its loan conditional on the recipient negotiating a large commercial loan.

The fear that other debtors would follow suit was justified. In December 1982, Brazil asserted its own inability to meet interest payments and its intention to reschedule payments on its $91 billion debt. Other debtor countries soon defaulted. By the end of 1983, 25 countries with over $200 billion in outstanding debts had convinced their lenders to reschedule their loans. Once again, prompt action prevented these crises from destroying the global economy. By following the IMF prescription, most of these countries made progress in addressing their economic problems. Within a year, Mexico and Brazil had converted a payments deficit into a payments surplus and were thus able to continue servicing their debts.

The lender cartel's worst fear, the emergence of a debtor's cartel, almost became a reality in 1984 and 1985. In early 1984, Argentina's government threatened to reject the IMF austerity plan and defer interest payments on its debt. Argentina then proposed at the September 1984 ministerial meeting of the Latin American Economic System (SEAL) that the debtor nations devote no more than 25 percent of their export earnings to service their debts. Most members of this Cartagena Group, named after the Colombian city in which they met, rejected the proposal. Brazil and Mexico then pressured Argentina to eventually settle with the IMF. In 1985, Peru became the only Latin American country to actually limit its payments to only 10 percent of export earnings. As a result, the global bankers refused to extend new loans to Peru and thus deterred other debtors from following Lima's lead.

The means by which global bankers managed the continuing crisis shifted throughout the 1980s. At first debt rescheduling lasted only one year, so countries continued having to reschedule their debts. But in 1984, Mexico again became a trend setter by agreeing to two repayment schemes—an initial four-year program that the international lenders would extend a further 14 years if Mexico kept up with its payments. This arrangement became the model for dozens of other reschedulings.

In September 1985, U.S. Treasury Secretary Jim Baker announced a plan before the World Bank and IMF that targeted the 15 most indebted countries for comprehensive debt rescheduling. In return for the recipients agreeing to the IMF austerity program, commercial bankers would extend to them a further $20 billion and the World Bank $3 billion in credits. The Baker Plan took a while to take off, because many of the countries did not make sweeping-enough reforms and commercial bankers refused to pour more money into those credit-poor countries. Although the commercial bank and World Bank targets were reached by 1988, the IMF cut back new lending, and overall the debtor countries gave back more money to the global lenders than they received.

In all, the debt crisis was alleviated rather than eliminated. Many Third World countries remained trapped in a vicious economic cycle as they sent more money abroad in interest payments than they received in loans, aid, or export earnings. The more money governments diverted to pay interest on their debt, the less money they had to invest in export industries that could earn the country money. Unable to keep up with their interest payments, governments borrowed yet more money and sank further into debt and poverty. Economic stagnation often led to political instability—food riots, coups, communist insurgencies—that further gutted the economy. Those with money often sent it to safe overseas havens

Table 16.12 **Money In, Money Out, Money Owed (in billions of dollars)**

	Net Private Capital Flow		Foreign Direct Investment		Foreign Debt	
	1990	1997	1990	1997	1990	1997
World	—	—	$192.662	$400.394	—	—
Low Income	$14.819	$88.685	5.732	59.509	$473.398	$669.626
Excluding China and India	4.840	19.551	2.083	11.922	334.380	428.525
Middle Income	28.091	210.049	18.697	103.786	998.783	1,645.941
Low and Middle Income	42.910	298.734	24.429	163.295	1,472.181	2,315.567
East Asia and Pacific	18.720	104.257	11.135	64.284	286.061	654.551
Europe and Central Asia	7.695	49.875	1.097	22.314	221.028	390.579
Latin America and Caribbean	12.411	118.918	8.188	61.573	475.366	703.669
Middle East and North Africa	0.622	7.899	2.711	5.240	182.399	192.378
South Asia	2.174	11.110	0.464	4.662	129.899	154.946
Sub-Saharan Africa	1.288	6.674	0.834	5.222	177.428	219.445
High Income	—	—	168.233	237.099	0.601	1.034

— indicates no available information for that year.
Source: World Bank Annual Report, 2000.

rather than investing it in the local economy. Third World capital flight alone is estimated to exceed its loans.[26] Between 1982 and 1988, the net outflow from the Third World was $140 billion! The 1988 outflow of $43 billion was higher than that year's total official development aid (ODA). Third World debt peaked at $1.3 trillion in 1990, a figure about half of those countries' combined GNPs and 125 percent of the total value of their exports.

Third World debt, of course, varied considerably from one region and country to the next. Africa's foreign debt represented 232 percent of its export value and 54 percent of its GNP, while debt servicing took 26 percent of all export value.[27] In 1988, the top five debtors were Brazil with $120 billion, which serviced its debt with 26.7 percent of the value of its exports; Mexico with $107 billion and 30.1 percent; Argentina with $60 billion and 45.3 percent; Venezuela with $35 billion and 22.4 percent; and Nigeria with $31 billion and 10 percent. Of the 20 leading debtors, 12 were from Latin America. During the 1980s, per capita income declined by as much as 25 percent for Africans and 10 percent for Latin Americans, while the number of humans living in "absolutely poor" conditions rose from 650 to 730 million.[28]

The Baker Plan was unable to deal with these growing problems, and there was pressure on the global bankers, particularly the United States, to come up with a less stringent plan that would include widespread writeoffs of debt for the poorest countries. In March 1989, U.S. Treasury Secretary Nicholas Brady announced a plan in which new commercial loans would be extended, more liberal means of repayment would be allowed, and in some cases there would be limited debt writeoffs. The overall goal was to reduce the entire Third World debt burden by 20 percent over three years.

Mexico was once again used as a model. Commercial bankers were given a choice of three options of dealing with $54 billion of Mexico's total $69 billion debt. Two options involved buying back Mexico's debt for bonds that would either be valued at 35 percent less than the debt's face value or the same price with a lower interest rate. The third option involved bankers extending new four-year loans to Mexico at a level equal to 25 percent of the bank's exposure. These loans would be guaranteed by the IMF, World Bank, Japan, and Mexico. The first two options meant that bankers would actually write off part of Mexico's debt to them. The third option allowed Mexico to receive fresh finance while protecting the lenders against default. This Brady Plan or formula has since been used for dozens of other debtors.

By the early 1990s, the debt crisis had passed. The Third World debt was still about $1.2 billion in 1992, but the number of defaults had lessened considerably since the Brady Plan was adopted. A small but growing percentage of debt was retired by debt-for-equity and debt-for-nature swaps in which investors would buy debt from a Third World country in return for stock in a corporation or the government's agreement to protect an area of nature from development.

But although the crisis has passed, the debt's effects on development have been profound. Although the per capita incomes of countries without debt-servicing problems rose 60 percent between 1978 and 1991, those countries that could not keep up their payments now have per capita incomes below those of 1978![29] Foreign sources of finance are essential to Third World development, but if that money is not invested wisely it may do more harm than good.

Then, in the late 1990s, another debt crisis exploded, this time in a region lauded as a paragon of Third World development, East and Southeast Asia. That crisis's roots extended to an economic superpower, Japan, whose financial and real estate markets had collapsed in the late 1980s as a result of rampant speculation encouraged by inept government policies. The financial collapse dragged the economy down to a low, sputtering annual growth rate of around 1 percent. Japanese protectionism, always formidable, was strengthened by the government and corporate leaders, while ever more excess production was dumped overseas. This crimped East and Southeast Asian economic expansion.

The crisis, however, did not emerge until the summer of 1997 when financial, real estate, and stock markets melted down first in Thailand, then Indonesia, South Korea, Malaysia, Singapore, and the Philippines, for the same reasons that Japan's had collapsed a decade earlier. Japan's crony capitalism, the dark and not necessarily inevitable side of *neomercantilism*, was emulated by the region's other government and business elites. As in Japan, cartels, protectionism, subsidies, and dumping of exports boosted economic growth to high levels at the expense of the Americans, Europeans, and others whose economies operated more closely along free market principles. But ever more of the huge profits skimmed from the global economy were badly invested in speculative rather than productive ventures. Attracted by the high growth rates, foreign investors poured hundreds of billions of dollars into the region without carefully scrutinizing whether those ventures were viable or not. By the summer of 1997, the same herd psychology among investors that had earlier rushed into the region caught a whiff of the underlying dangers. The result was a stampede of hundreds of billions of dollars out of the region. The subsequent economic meltdown among the East and Southeast Asian countries threatened a domino effect among other vulnerable countries and regions until the entire global political economy was threatened by collapse.

The Clinton administration worked with the IMF and leading private bankers to bail out the region. Unfortunately, the IMF formula that had worked so well in alleviating the debt crisis of the 1980s exacerbated that of the 1990s. During the 1980s, the problem was reckless government spending. The IMF solution was a tight fiscal conservation under which government spending was curbed and interest rates and taxes raised. That austerity program eventually revived those economies.

But the 1990s crisis was fundamentally different. Private rather than public investors were too blame for their manic speculation and squandering of investments. The sensible solution would have been for the White House, IMF, and private bankers to offer low-interest loans in return for which those countries would open their economies to foreign trade and investment. But any hint of such a policy provoked howls of protests from the region that they would lose their economic sovereignty as foreign investors bought out those countries' bankrupted firms. The IMF formula of giving low-interest loans in exchange for government austerity worsened the depression. The private sector was already deflated. Governments should have spent more rather than less to stimulate the economies. By cutting back their budgets, the governments took even more money and jobs from the economy.

The crisis spread. In early 1998, Russia actually suspended payments. Brazil and other Latin American countries threatened to do likewise. The IMF, White House, and private bankers scraped up enough money to prevent those economies from total collapse. Led by America's robust economy of the Clinton years, the global economy continues to expand slowly despite these regional depressions. By early 1999, the East and Southeast Asian and Latin American economies had started to grow again. Japanese neomercantilism, however, continued to be a deadweight on the global economy as its corporations frenziedly dumped their exports and blocked competitive imports. Will the recovery continue or will an unexpected collapse in a key region or country again threaten the global economy? Time will tell.

Where Are Multinational Corporations Headed?

Modernization and dependency theorists differ totally on the role of foreign *multinational corporations (MNCs)* in a nation's political economic development.[30] Modernization theorists believe that foreign investments represent a net gain for the recipient and are often the key to development. Poor countries lack money, technology, managerial skills, and access to foreign markets, and MNCs can provide all those assets. Dependency theorists, in contrast, see MNCs as neocolonial powers that promise but do not deliver those assets. Once entrenched, they suck out as much wealth as possible and corrupt the political process to keep that country poor and docile.

Reality, as always, is much more complex than these theories suggest. It is impossible to generalize about foreign investments in the Third World. The relative positive and negative effects vary from one country, sector, corporation, and era to the next. For every example of a foreign investment behaving according to modernization theory, another can be found that mirrors the dependency perspective.

POTENTIAL COSTS

The operations of multinational corporations in Third World countries have been criticized on many grounds. Perhaps the most important is the sheer power of most MNCs. Of the 100 largest economic entities in the world, about half are countries and the other half corporations. Many multinationals are much wealthier than many of the countries in which they invest. They thus have enormous bargaining and corrupting power to ensure that they extract the best entry and operating terms from poor, weak foreign governments. Because MNCs offer things that poor countries desperately need, they can always play off one poor state against the others. Both before and after they have set up shop, MNCs can always threaten to go elsewhere if the government does not surrender to their demands. By competing against each other to bribe officials for investment permits and other facilities, MNCs frequently exacerbate existing corruption. Those officials involved may gain riches but by allowing MNCs often unlimited and subsidized investments, the country's development suffers and wealth flows abroad.

Although any state has the sovereign right to nationalize any businesses, foreign or domestic, international law requires that a government compensate foreign investors if it does so. If a government nationalizes a MNC's holdings without compensation, other MNCs may be afraid to invest there. Thus that country's development will suffer the loss of potential jobs, wealth, managerial expertise, market access, and technology created by those potential foreign investments. Meanwhile, the victim will lobby its home government to pressure the Third World government that has nationalized its holdings, for compensation. For example, after governments nationalized United Fruit Company land in Guatemala and ITT's investments in Chile, those corporations pressured the White House, which eventually backed coups in those countries that brought more compliant elites to power. Washington is legally armed with the 1964 Hickenlooper and 1974 Gonzalez Amendments, which respectively empower the president to sever aid and GSP privileges with any country nationalizing American investments. The U.S. Overseas Private Investment Corporation insures businesses against losses in

Table 16.13 **Potential Power: Top Corporation Worldwide Sales versus GDPs of Select Countries, (1997)**

Corporation	Sales	Country	GDP	Corporation	Sales	Country	GDP
General Motors	$164	Thailand	$154	Sumitomo	$119	Greece	$123
Ford Motor	147	Norway	153	Exxon	117	Malaysia	98
Mitsui	145	Saudi Arabia	140	Toyota	109	Israel	98
Mitsubishi	140	Poland	136	Wal-Mart	105	Colombia	96
Royal Dutch Shell	128	South Africa	129				

Note: This table compares the 1997 sales figures for top-earning MNCs with roughly similar GDPs of various First and Third World nations. Sales for Mitsubishi, for example, exactly equaled the GDP for Saudi Arabia. Figures are in billions of dollars.

Source: Forbes.

many, though not all, countries. Thus with every American foreign investment, Third World governments potentially face not only the power of that particular investor, but also its home government and other MNCs.

Even when a government imposes limits on how much profit can be repatriated, an MNC gets around the limit through transfer pricing or charging enormous amounts on the equipment and components imported to its investment from other subsidiaries. The MNC does not really pay more, because it is paying itself. It is simply a method to transfer profits out of the country and evade taxes and sometimes capital controls. As a result, the subsidiary sends home money that otherwise might have been spent on much cheaper components from indigenous businesses. By manipulating their accounts to make it look as if their subsidiaries were losing money, the MNC often ends up paying little or no taxes to the host government.

Many foreign investments are seen as enclaves in which little if any wealth trickles down to the rest of the economy; instead, the investment acts like a sponge that soaks up local capital and expatriates it. For example, American investments in Latin America between 1958 and 1968 acquired 80 percent of their finance locally from loans or earnings.[31] In this way, MNCs minimize their own exposure and maximize that of their host government and local investors so that they will do all they can in support.

The MNCs often dominate the host economy's most advanced sectors, thus controlling any significant indigenous development. Once in a country, an MNC often gobbles up, Pac-Man–style, other local businesses. Few local businesses can compete against an MNC, and many are bankrupted or bought out by the new investors. Productivity is usually much higher in the MNC than in similar local businesses. Thus unemployment rises because local firms are often much more labor intensive than the MNC. The foreign investors can offer more money and benefits, and better facilities to indigenous workers and thus often mop up a country's most talented workers. The MNCs create new socioeconomic classes that widen existing gaps between the haves and have nots. They demand foreign luxury goods that further drain wealth from the economy and disrupt the culture. Meanwhile, there are no significant technology transfers. The technology that is invested is either obsolete or so advanced that it is inappropriate for that country. The result is often a net drain on a country's wealth and the development of underdevelopment. For these reasons dependency theorists condemn MNCs.[32]

POTENTIAL BENEFITS

Despite these potential costs, most governments actively solicit investments from foreign corporations. Although Marxist dogma asserts that MNCs are neocolonialist forces that enslave poor countries, even the communist governments of China, Vietnam, North Korea, and the former Yugoslavia and Soviet Union have set aside that belief and enacted policies to attract foreign investment. Few countries would attempt to attract foreign investors if the costs exceeded the benefits.

Over time, most Third World governments have become more adept at bargaining so that they maximize the gains and minimize the costs of foreign investment. Bureaucracies are slowly being manned with experts in international law, accounting, taxes, business, and other skills necessary to negotiate head to head with MNC representatives and then carefully regulate established foreign investments. Third World power increases further after the MNC has set up shop. New regulations can now be enacted, and the MNC usually goes along because the compliance costs are lower than the disinvestment costs. Laws can be enacted that limit the amount of profits, royalties, and other income an MNC can repatriate, and the amount of goods an MNC can import. Domestic content and mandated export laws further encourage MNCs to buy components locally and export the finished products. Brazil, for example, has 99 percent local content requirements for its automobile industry. Other laws are even more restrictive. Some governments have laws whereby MNCs can only set up joint ventures in which a majority of shares are held by indigenous investors. There are sunset laws whereby an increased number of shares are turned over to indigenous investors until, after several decades, the entire operation has been nationalized. Indonesia, for example, has sunset laws of 30 years for most foreign investments. Most Latin American governments follow the Calvo Doctrine, which asserts the host country's right to determine what is adequate compensation for nationalized investments.[33]

A government's success in enforcing or even enacting these laws depends on its relative power, and that power depends on how badly MNCs want access to that nation's markets and resources. Countries such as Brazil, Indonesia, Mexico, and Nigeria, with their huge populations and rich resources obviously have much more bargaining power than small states with limited markets and resources. The bargaining power of virtually all Third World countries has grown as the global economy becomes more competitive. Governments can play off one MNC against the others, a practice that was more difficult in the 1950s and 1960s when there were fewer MNCs and most were American.

An increasingly popular means of attracting and managing foreign investments is to designate an export-processing zone (EPZ) in which firms can only produce for export. Host governments provide infrastructure and freedom to investors from tariffs on imported components. In return, the government and country enjoys a controlled laboratory in which to learn production, managerial, financial, and marketing skills.

There have been international attempts by both Third World and advanced industrial country groups to regulate MNC operations. At the first GATT round in Geneva in 1947, the United States attempted to enact provisions that would safeguard foreign investments against nationalization unless compensation was given. Representatives of Latin America and other developing countries succeeded in tabling the American proposal and instead pushed through provisions that allowed host governments to restrict MNC operations. Passage of this proposal prompted American business interests to lobby against pending Senate ratification of the Havana Charter, which would have created the International Trade Organization (ITO).

During the 1970s, there were several attempts to regulate foreign investments. The 1974 U.N. Charter of Economic Rights and Duties of States declares the sovereign right of nationalization but says only that compensation should be appropriate, thus giving governments wide latitude in determining it. That same year, the United Nations followed up its charter by creating the Center on Transnational Corporations, which collects data on international investment flows, and, in 1975, the Commission on Transnational Corporations, in which issues are debated. But neither of these two organizations has adequately addressed the question of how to

Table 16.14 **World Foreign Direct Investment Stock, 1997**

	Amount	Percentage of Total
World	$3,455.5	100.0%
Industrial Countries	2,349.4	68.0
Western Europe	1,276.5	36.9
North America	857.9	24.8
Other	215.1	6.2
Developing Countries	1,043.7	30.2
Argentina, Brazil, and Mexico	249.2	7.2
China and Hong Kong	126.2	3.7
Southeast Asia	253.1	7.3
Other Asian Countries	96.3	2.8
Africa	65.2	1.9
Other	9.4	0.3

Source: U.N. Conference on Trade and Development, *World Investment Report* (1998).

determine compensation for nationalized assets. In 1980, UNCTAD formulated a code that regulated MNC business practices, including transfer pricing and cartels. There was a wave of nationalizations during the 1970s, most in extraction investments. The practice has declined since then as host governments have acquired more skill at indirectly managing foreign investments.

In 1977, the U.S. Congress addressed a different foreign investment issue by passing the Foreign Corrupt Practices Act, which made it illegal for American firms to use bribes to obtain foreign business. Shortly thereafter, with considerable American pressure, the Organization for Economic Cooperation and Development (OECD) issued its "Guidelines on International Investment and Multinational Enterprise," but the provisions are nonbinding and vague. Except for the U.S. Foreign Corrupt Practices Act, neither the U.N. or the OECD measures are legally binding.

Some go so far as to argue that MNCs can evolve into truly global organizations that transcend national concerns. This global vision was perhaps best expressed by an IBM president in 1970 who argued that

> For business purposes the boundaries that separate one nation from another are no more real than the equator. They are merely convenient demarcations of ethnic, linguistic, and cultural entities. They do not define business requirements or consumer trends. Once management understands and accepts this world economy, its view of the marketplace—and its planning—necessarily expand. The world outside the home country is no longer viewed as a series of disconnected customers and prospects for its products, but as an extension of a single market.[34]

World Bank President A. W. Clausen goes even further, arguing that "the idea that this kind of business enterprise can be a strong force toward world peace is not so far fetched. Beyond the human values involved, the multinational firm has a direct, measurable, and potent interest in helping prevent wars and other serious

MNCs *and the* End *of* Apartheid *in* South Africa

During the 1980s, foreign investments in South Africa were heavily criticized by some who argued they strengthened the apartheid system. Leon Sullivan, a former GM board member proposed what became known as the Sullivan principles as voluntary guidelines for American firms doing business in South Africa. These rules include the desegregation of the workplace and equal treatment for black, "colored," and white South Africans. In 1986, Congress passed the Comprehensive Anti-Apartheid Act, which prevented U.S. firms from investing further in South Africa or extending loans to the government. Other countries including the European Community, Canada, and the British Commonwealth imposed similar restrictions on their firms' business with South Africa. Hundreds of foreign firms closed down their South African businesses as a result of these restrictions. The sanctions may have helped convince South Africa's government to begin to dismantle the apartheid system.

upheavals that cut off its resources, interrupt its communications, and kill its employees and customers."[35]

GETTING PERSPECTIVE ON MNCS

The issue of direct foreign MNC investments in the Third World must be put in perspective. First, as we have seen, 68 percent of MNC direct foreign investments are within the First World. Of those in the Third World, many are concentrated in a few countries. In 1998, five countries—China, Brazil, Mexico, Singapore, and Argentina—accounted for more than half of all accumulated investments in the Third World. Although mining corporations have invested wherever there are viable sources of minerals and oil, manufacturing investments tend to be limited to those countries with favorable infrastructure, markets, and policies. Thus although direct foreign investment may be a minuscule portion of Third World GNP, the investments are often a prominent portion of the recipient's GNP and are concentrated in the economy's most advanced sectors. Because they are highly capital- and technology-intensive, extractive investments tend particularly to take over that entire sector. Until the early 1970s, the Western oil corporations controlled virtually all oil in the Middle East, and huge multinationals dominated the copper industries of Zambia and Chile and the bauxite mines of Jamaica. MNCs from each of the three superpowers had their own cluster of poorer countries in which they invested. The Europeans invested heavily in eastern Europe, the Soviet Union, and Brazil; the Americans throughout Latin America, the Philippines, and Saudi Arabia; the Japanese in East and Southeast Asia.[36]

Furthermore, when most people think of MNCs they imagine the IBMs, Toyotas, and Phillips of the advanced industrial countries. In fact, many MNCs are based in Third World countries such as India, South Korea, Venezuela, and Nigeria, to name a few. In the mid-1980s, there were over 10,000 Third World MNCs, with over 90,000 foreign subsidiaries.[37] Most of these Third World MNCs, however, are much smaller than those from the advanced industrial countries. Many of these Third World MNCs invest in other poor countries.

MNCs invest overseas for many reasons—access to cheap labor, closed markets, raw material, energy resources, farm land, technology, or more lax regulations. A corporation that provides a good or service to another corporation may well set up shop overseas when its client does. The bottom line is that foreign investments should make money.

Firms are sometimes pulled overseas by the actions of governments that attempt to attract foreign investment by raising trade barriers while offering investment subsidies to foreign firms. These government subsidies can include free or cheap land, tax holidays, grants, loans, and infrastructure. MNCs can increase the amount of incentives they receive by playing off one government against the others.

Firms are sometimes pushed overseas by their own governments. For example, starting in the late 1960s Tokyo offered incentives to heavily polluting Japanese industries to move overseas, in order to "houseclean" Japan. The U.S. tax code has encouraged many American corporations to move their operations overseas by deferring paying taxes on their income until they bring it home. As a result, most MNCs simply reinvest it elsewhere overseas. American firms can also deduct any taxes paid to overseas governments from the taxes they owe the United States. President Reagan's Caribbean Initiative, starting in 1985, offered tax credits and other benefits to U.S. corporations that invested in the region. The White House encourages this migration to help develop those countries; the trouble is that it means more unemployment, lower tax receipts, and greater socioeconomic problems in the United States.

Most MNCs reflect the culture, values, and sometimes even policies of the countries in which they are headquartered. For example, although it has not always been successful, the White House has not hesitated to pressure its corporations to follow government policy when the situation demands. It has imposed an economic embargo on American sales to Cuba since 1961. In 1968, the White House forbade the sale of factory equipment from a Belgian subsidiary of an American company to Cuba even though the Belgian firm had struck the deal before it was acquired by the American firm. Although Washington tried, it failed to rally American petroleum corporations around the flag when OPEC quadrupled oil prices in 1973. The American firms instead went along with OPEC, fearing that to do otherwise might result in all their foreign assets being nationalized. In 1982, the Reagan administration ordered American firms to stop selling equipment that would be used for a gas pipeline from the Soviet Union to Europe. The result was that European firms got the business that the White House denied to American firms. And sometimes U.S. government policies follow the pressure of American MNCs. The White House helped topple the governments of Guatemala in 1954 and Chile in 1973 when the American corporations United Fruit and ITT complained that their respective investments in those countries were nationalized without adequate compensations.[38] But these dramatic examples are the exception rather than the rule, and may well disappear in the post–cold-war era.

There is conflicting evidence over an MNC's effect on the recipient's international trade and payments accounts, with some studies showing a net gain and others a net loss. Traditionally, the foreign investments of MNCs in Third World countries were twice as profitable as those in other advanced industrial countries. The balance changed during the 1980s. Now the reverse is true. Yet foreign investments, if managed properly, can be a net gain for the host country.

The relationship between MNCs and host countries varies widely from one country and time to the next. Some Third World countries are increasingly able to play off one MNC against others that want entry, and thus extract more profit from the investment. Other Third World countries remain largely impotent in the face of MNC power and must accept the dictated terms.

Which Way *for* North–South Relations *and* Development?

Third World unity reached a height during the 1960s and 1970s with the programs of U.N. Conference on Trade and Development (UNCTAD), and with OPEC's success in nationalizing oil production and quadrupling oil prices in 1973 and further doubling them in 1979. In 1974, the nonaligned movement espoused the new international economic order (NIEO), which asserted that

> the remaining vestiges of alien and colonial domination, foreign occupation, racial discrimination, apartheid and neo-colonialism in all its forms continue to be among the greatest obstacles to the full emancipation and progress of the developing countries. . . . The benefits of technological progress are not shared equitably by all members of the international community. The developing countries, which constitute 70 percent of the world's population, account for only 30 percent of the world's income. It has proven impossible to achieve an even and balanced development of the international community under the existing international economic order. The gap between the developed and the developing countries continues to widen in a system which was established at a time when most of the developing countries did not even exist . . . which perpetuates inequality.[39]

Any development successes within the Third World, however, will come from immersion within rather than isolation from the global political economy. Third World attempts to gain more trade and investment concessions from the advanced industrial countries through its UNCTAD and NIEO agenda have largely failed. There were ten UNCTAD conferences between 1962 and 1999, and at best the participants succeeded in getting NIEO issues on the agenda and articulating the concerns of most less developed nations.

Yet UNCTAD, the NIEO, and the nonaligned movement collapsed during the 1980s for several related reasons. First, there was nothing "nonaligned" about the movement. Most of the members were openly tilted to the communist states, and many of the rest were leaned toward the West. The cold war's end meant that less developed countries could no longer play off the two superpowers against each other and would henceforth have to accommodate themselves to the industrial democracies. The movement was as split economically as it was politically. There was a large and widening gap between *newly industrializing countries (NICs)* such as South Korea, Taiwan, Singapore, and Chile, which had achieved rapid and equitable economic growth, and the world's poorest countries, such as Haiti, Bangladesh, Burma, and Tanzania. More and more governments have converted to the belief that expanding market power rather than state power is the key to successful development. Meanwhile, the commodity bargaining power that the Third World enjoyed during the 1970s dissipated during the 1980s and 1990s. Increasingly the Group of 77 is willing to accommodate itself to rather than transform the global political economy.

The Group of 77 is being eclipsed by the emergence of a dozen regional free trade associations throughout the Third World. For example, in January 1992 a summit of the six members of the Association for Southeast Asian Nations (ASEAN) agreed to form a free trade association over the next 15 years. In June 1992, the presidents of Argentina, Brazil, Uruguay, and Paraguay met and agreed to create a free trade zone by 1995, a union that would combine 190 million people and $450 billion in GNP. The leaders also agreed to harmonize their tax and investment policies to bring down inflation and attract more foreign investment. In November 1992, the Caribbean Economic Community (CARICOM) agreed to reduce its common external tariff (CET) from 45 percent to 35 percent by January 1, 1993, and eventually to 20 percent in 1998.

The Third World steadily accounts for a lower percentage of global trade. From 1950 through today, the total Third World share of world exports fell from about 31 percent in 1950 to about 15 percent today, and Latin America's share fell from about 12 percent to 5 percent. These statistics may not be as bad as they seem. In Latin America's case, exports have risen steadily but not as quickly as in other areas of the world, hence a decline as a percentage of the global total. The Third World is becoming increasingly dependent on the global trade system. Between 1970 and 1998, the ratio of exports to gross domestic product within the Third World rose from 11 percent to 25 percent.[40]

However, the importance of the less developed countries to the industrial countries is diminishing. About 60 percent of the industrialized countries' trade and 68 percent of its foreign investments are with each other. To worsen matters, the industrialized countries often block competitive Third World exports, which further reduces the export earnings of Third World countries. In 1986, the advanced countries imposed nontariff barriers to 21 percent of all Third World imports and only 16 percent of imports from other industrial countries.[41] The more interdependent the global economy, the more a depression or price drop elsewhere can disrupt an already troubled society. Countries dependent on one crop or mineral for much of their earnings can be devastated when the global demand and thus price for that commodity drops precipitously. Yet some countries in the Third World have experienced considerable industrialization.

Third World trade problems were exacerbated by the debt crises of the 1980s. Third World countries diverted an increasing percentage of their export earnings and savings to servicing their respective debts, thus undercutting their economic growth and worsening the debt. The global financial system itself was at risk. The fear was that the default of two or more of the biggest debtors would destroy the global financial system and plunge the world into a deep, intractable depression, possibly setting off a chain reaction of economic collapse and communist revolutions around the world. By the late 1980s, the global debt crisis had diminished. Bankers agreed to write off a large chunk of Third World debt, oil prices were halved, and the global economy began to expand again, thus giving borrowers the export revenues with which to service their debts. Despite these improvements, throughout the 1980s into the 1990s, banks have steadily reduced the percentage of their total loans to developing countries and tended to concentrate them in rapidly growing regions such as East and Southeast Asia. The debt crisis in that region during the late 1990s was eventually resolved, but made international investors even more shy of the Third World.

Poor as well as rich countries can benefit from international trade and investments. It is a government's duty to ensure that its country maximizes the potential gains and minimizes the potential costs of international trade and investment in an increasingly interdependent global political economy. Most Third World regions and countries have geoeconomic importance, whether it be for its markets, resources, or industries, and thus will remain important to multinational corporations and the countries in which they are headquartered. Foreign aid will continue, and while its total volume may stagnate or even diminish for some countries, the content will increasingly be economic rather than military assistance.

In terms of political leverage, the global environmental crisis presents the Third World with the opportunities for extracting wealth and technology from the more advanced states that the cold war once did. At environmental conferences in Rio de Janeiro in June 1992, Kyoto in December 1997, and Buenos Aires in November 1998, the Third World countries argued that any costs associated with dealing with the greenhouse effect and ozone layer should be borne by the rich countries. The Third World would continue to industrialize, and if the rich countries were concerned about pollution then they would be forced to transfer the technology and wealth necessary to cut air and water emissions. Environmental battles between the First and Third worlds may be to the 1990s and beyond what conflicts over MNCs, nationalization, commodity prices, and so on were to earlier decades. One thing is certain: Conflict between the First and Third Worlds will continue.

Study Questions

1. How do we explain the vast gulf between the world's few rich countries and its many poor countries? Why have a few Third World countries successfully developed and most others failed? Why can't all poor countries be equally successful?

2. Describe the role that the global economy and relations between advanced industrial and Third World countries plays in development or underdevelopment.

3. List the terms used to designate the world's relatively poorer and richer countries. In what ways are these terms inadequate?

4. Can free trade be unfair? What is fair trade? Why do so many of the world's poorer countries complain that the wealthier countries unfairly discriminate against them? Is that charge of unfairness fair? Regardless, how have Third World countries tried to rectify this perceived injustice?

5. Discuss which domestic and international forces can affect a country's level of development.

6. What duties, if any, do wealthy countries have toward the world's poor? Explain.

7. Which of the NIEO demands are just, and which are unreasonable? Which have been partially or completely fulfilled, and which neglected?

8. Describe the major complaints that Third World countries have in regards to their terms of trade with the industrialized countries.

9. List the major demands of the Group of 77 for the New International Economic Order. How many of these demands have been realized?

10. What is OPEC? What were the reasons for and significance of OPEC's quadrupling of oil prices in 1973 and further doubling of prices in 1979? Why did OPEC's influence decline in the mid-1980s and after?

11. Discuss the controversies surrounding foreign aid.

12. What led to the world debt crisis? How was the crisis managed?

13. What are the potential costs and benefits for Third World countries of allowing foreign investments by MNCs?

14. Discuss the origins, aspirations, successes, and failures of the nonaligned movement.

$\mathcal{G}$ InfoTrac College Edition Sources

Using the Subject Guide, enter the search terms *foreign aid, multinational corporation, debt crisis, World Bank,* and/or *green revolution.*

Ansari, Mohammed I., and Ira N. Gang. "Liberalization Policy: 'Fits and Starts' or Gradual Change in India."

Arcaya, Ignacio. "Can Commodity-Based Associations Promote the Economic Development of Their Member States?"

Arvin, B. Mak, Saud Choudhry, and Torben Drewes. "Lingering Effect of Untied Foreign Aid on Exports."

Buchmann, Claudia. "The Debt Crisis, Structural Adjustment and Women's Education: Implications for Status and Social Development."

"Chile's Non-tariff Barriers Cause Concern with U.S. Farmers."

Chossudovsky, Michel. "Global Poverty in the Late 20th Century."

DuBoff, Richard B. "Globalization and Wages: The Down Escalator."

Dunn, Bill, and Julie Cote Rumberger. "Equity-Based Compensation Plans for Multinationals: Compensation in a Worldwide Environment."

"Economic Development and Investment in Sub-Saharan Africa."

Gallagher, Paul. "International Marketing Margins for Agricultural Products: Effects of Some Nontariff Trade Barriers."

Gawande, Kishore. "A Test of a Theory of Strategically Retaliatory Trade Barriers."

Gawande, Kishore, and Wendy L. Hansen. "Retaliation, Bargaining, and the Pursuit of 'Free and Fair' Trade."

Gort, Michael, Jeremy Greenwood, and Peter Rupert. "How Much of Economic Growth Is Fueled by Investment-Specific Technological Progress?"

Grabowski, Richard. "Market Evolution and Economic Development: The Evolution of Impersonal Markets."

Graham, Carol. "Foreign Policy Tools: Foreign Aid."

Hervey, Jack L., and William A. Straus. "Foreign Growth, the Dollar, and Regional Economies, 1970–97."

Klein, Philip A. "Rethinking American Participation in Economic Development: An Institutionalist Assessment."

"Mancur Olson on the Key to Economic Development."

Mathieson, Donald J., Anthony Richards, and Sunil Sharma. "Financial Crisis in Emerging Markets."

Niggle, Christopher J. "Equality, Democracy, Institutions, and Growth."

"The Obstacles to Development in the Balkans: Interview with Ambassador Jonathan Moore."

Pakko, Michael R. "The U.S. Trade Deficit and the 'New Economy.'"

Rahim, Lily Z. "Economic Crisis and the Prospects for Democratisation in Southeast Asia."

Skud, Timothy. "Customs Procedures as the Residual Barriers to Trade."

Tamirisa, Natalia T. "Exchange and Capital Controls as Barriers to Trade."

Therien, Jean-Philippe, and Alain Noel. "Political Parties and Foreign Aid."
"Twenty-first Century Development: Why Should We Be Optimistic?"
Yeh, Y. H. "Tariffs, Import Quotas, Voluntary Export Restraints and Immiserizing Growth."

⊕ On *the* Web

http://www.unctad.org/
UNCTAD home page

http://www.g77.org/
Group of 77 home page

http://www.usaid.gov/
U.S. Agency for International Development

States have gone to war for many reasons. When is the last time people killed each other for fresh water? Perhaps not since nomadic enemy bands converged at a desert water hole. But future wars over water may not be far off.

Globalization has steadily raised the costs and reduced the benefits of war. The world's peoples are so interdependent economically, technologically, and culturally that negotiations rather than violence are the only rational way to resolve conflicts in nearly all international

Part Seven *The* Fate *of the* Earth: Water Wars

relations among the 195 nation-states. So what is worth fighting for? In 1991, the United States allied with 37 other states to drive Iraq from oil-rich Kuwait. Could water ever be as geopolitically vital to national interests as oil? In ever more countries, it already is.

The world's amount of fresh water is naturally limited, while the planet's population will continue to soar from 6 billion today to perhaps 10 billion by 2050.[1] About 166 million people in 18 countries currently suffer severe water shortages, and that crisis will engulf another 270 million (as large as America's population) in 11 other countries in a few years. In China over 300 northern and western cities of 50,000 or more have pumped their aquifers down to

the crisis point; the water table beneath the capital Beijing has plummeted over 100 feet in the last 40 years. Bangkok, Thailand's capital, is sinking as people suck dry the aquifer below them. Thirty percent of England's rivers are one-third lower than their natural level. If the Ogallala aquifer that runs under most of America's Great Plains continues to diminish at the present rate, hundreds of thousands of people will be forced to abandon their prosperous farms, ranches, and towns within a generation. A gallon of water at an American super-

market now costs more than a gallon of gasoline. How much will it cost a decade from now? In India water already costs families 25 percent of their income, a ratio that will increase steadily. Within 25 years, over two of every three people on the planet will suffer water shortages.

Ever more water is too foul to consume. Over a billion people or one of six drinks, bathes, and cooks with water laced with chemical, human, and animal wastes, many of which cause cancer and other diseases. Thirteen percent of Israel's coastal aquifer is fouled by chemicals and seawater that seeps in to replace the fresh water pumped out. Of Poland's rivers, 75 percent are so polluted they cannot even be used for industrial purposes. As water sources dry up and their use for industry, agriculture, and humans increases, the cocktail of vile and sometimes deadly pollutants concentrates.

All that is a crisis enough for countries whose swelling populations get most of their water from their own territory. But billions of people depend on water drawn from rivers and lakes linking two or more countries and aquifers in the bedrock beneath them. For now, most of these common water sources remain abundant enough to fulfill the demands of different peoples on them. Yet in many regions of the world such as those around the Jordan, Tigris, and Euphrates rivers of the Middle East, the Nile and Niger rivers of Africa, or the Indus of South Asia, to name a few of the most contended-for, the demands for fresh water are rapidly straining the existing supply. Wars have erupted among many of those countries in the past over territorial, ethnic, and/or religious disputes. Water will most likely be another potential catalyst for war there and increasingly elsewhere in the years ahead.

Yet dwindling water supplies for ever more thirsty people, along with the demands of agriculture, industry, sanitation, and so on, are only one of a web of interrelated global environmental crises that threatens our future pros-perity. People may eventually war over water, but we may simply commit slow suicide if not enough is done to arrest the other crises such as global warming, ozone layer depletion, desertification, deforestation, species extinction, and the population explosion. Those will be the most persistently vital issues of international relations in the 21st century.

The world's population is rapidly expanding while the world's fresh water is rapidly diminishing. Will wars in the future erupt over water?

© Amit Bharagaua/Newsmakers/Liaison Agency

Contents

Chapter 17 *The* Global Environmental Crisis

Key Concepts and Terms

"We master nature by obeying her."

FRANCIS BACON

"The substance of man cannot be measured by the Gross National Product. Perhaps it cannot be measured at all, except for certain symptoms of loss."

E. M. SCHUMACHER

"What does it mean to redefine one's relationship to the sky? What will it do to our children's outlook on life if we have to teach them to be afraid to look up?"

ALBERT GORE

"No more basic threat to national security exists."

AMERICAN ASSEMBLY CONFERENCE, 1990

In 1970, the ecologist Garrett Hardin wrote *"The Tragedy of the Commons,"* in which he describes a village green where all can graze their sheep but no one is accountable for its upkeep.[1] The unregulated commons is eventually overgrazed and destroyed. As that resource's degradation is ever more apparent, the herders' impulse is to graze their livestock there as much as possible before its eventual disappearance, thus accelerating the destruction. Those who graze livestock there gain in the short run; everyone in the village loses over the long term.

The earth and the humans who inhabit it face the same "tragedy of the commons." Within 50 years, the world's current population of 6 billion will most likely reach 9 billion. Like people today, future generations will demand an ever higher living standard and quality of life. If the present global income distribution remains constant, the demand for goods, services, energy, recreation, and quality of life will expand with the population. Indeed, people's material demands are growing even faster than their numbers. Just as today, people of the future who have less will desire and demand to have as many material comforts as those who have more.

As with that once rich commons, at some point the earth will be unable to satisfy the material demands of all those people. Every *ecosystem* has a *carrying capacity* or limit on the amount of life it can sustain. The earth is one vast complex ecosystem, which is rapidly deteriorating by several interrelated and accelerating environmental catastrophes—the population explosion, the greenhouse effect, *ozone layer depletion,* deforestation, desertification, air and water pollution, species extinction, and food shortages.

These crises boil down to one central problem—a *population explosion,* too many people demanding more than the earth can provide as resources or absorb as pollution. How are the world's environmental crises locked in a vicious and seemingly irreversible cycle? Since the industrial revolution began two centuries ago, an increasing amount of gases and chemicals have thickened the atmosphere. This buildup traps more and more heat that ordinarily would dissipate into the void of space. The worsening *greenhouse effect* could cause Earth's average temperatures to rise from four to nine degrees Fahrenheit over the next 50 years. Why does this matter? That soaring heat could melt the polar icecaps and permafrost, which, scientists believe, could inundate low-lying coastal areas and warp precipitation patterns so that droughts, hurricanes, floods, and other weather extremes ravage farms and communities. As if that were not dangerous enough, a cocktail of chemicals eats away at the ozone layer in the atmosphere that screens most of the sun's ultraviolet rays from reaching Earth. As the ozone layer deteriorates, the increased ultraviolet radiation could destroy sensitive microscopic plants and animals at the food chain's base, jeopardizing all other lifeforms, including humans.

Just when will people destroy the earth's carrying capacity? Experts debate just when that will occur, but there is no doubt that scores of regions around the world have already suffered the devastation that will eventually engulf the earth. Populations have grown too fast and demanded too much from the regions in which they live, rendering that land uninhabitable. Environmental refugees fleeing those wasted lands increase demands on steadily diminishing productive lands elsewhere, thus quickening their degradation and eventual destruction. The result is an environmental *domino effect.* The number of people and the percentage of the world's population ravaged by famine, drought, floods, poverty, diseases, and malnutrition of near biblical horrors worsens. Within 50 years, billions more humans will lack even such basics as water, food, fuel, jobs, or shelter, as in Hardin's overgrazed commons, and every human will be hurt directly or indirectly from the earth's worsening degradation. Lester Brown clearly states the essence of the crisis: "the global economy is literally destroying the natural systems that support it."[2]

Although ideological extremists shrilly deny these scientific realities, more and more governments and people around the world understand that the steady increase of people and pollution may provoke a global environmental Armageddon. Over the past two decades, environmental concerns have crept up the international agenda of priorities. The first comprehensive attempt to identify and deal with the range of environmental crises was the 1972 *Stockholm Conference on the Human Environment* and the creation of the *U.N. Environmental Program (UNEP).* Unfortunately, nothing much came from this initiative as most countries concentrated on geopolitical or geoeconomic issues for the next decade. Then during the mid-1980s, environmental concerns once again became a priority. In 1985, scientists discovered a hole in the ozone layer over Antarctica; two years later delegates signed the *Montreal Protocol on Substances That Deplete the Ozone Layer,* in which they pledged eventually to eliminate chemicals that cause that destruction. In 1986, the Chernobyl nuclear plant in the Soviet Union exploded, causing a massive release of radioactivity that devastated the region and drifted over Europe. That disaster starkly reminded thoughtful people of their power to destroy or nurture the earth. In 1987, the United Nations published *Our Common Future,* which systematically analyzed the environmental threats to humankind and called on

greenhouse effect increasing amounts of heat (that ordinarily would dissipate into the universe) trapped in the atmosphere by an ever growing amount of gases and chemicals poured into the air from industrial sources. The result could be **global warming.**

all nations to work together to confront those threats. In 1988, to the surprise of many, the conservative British Prime Minister Margaret Thatcher declared herself a "green" and urged sweeping international efforts to deal with the world's worsening environmental catastrophes. In 1989, green parties won 15 percent of the vote in European Community parliamentary elections. In July 1989, the Group of Seven meeting of the leaders of the United States, Japan, Germany, France, Italy, Great Britain, and Canada announced that environmental threats to the world were as important as economic ones. By the late 1980s, more than 140 countries had national environmental agencies, up from 25 countries in 1972. In 1992, the *Earth Summit at Rio de Janeiro* brought together 7,000 delegates of 178 nations and 8,000 journalists. Two treaties were signed, one addressing the greenhouse effect and the other, *biodiversity*. The 1997 *Kyoto* and 1998 Buenos Aires accords strengthened previous international efforts to alleviate global warming. Between the Stockholm Conference and the year 2000, over 130 environmental treaties emerged to address those crises.

Are all these measures too little, too late to arrest the earth's rapid degradation? Future generations will either condemn or applaud the actions or inactions of their ancestors. This chapter explores those interrelated environmental crises and the international efforts to overcome them.

Overpopulation

All the world's environmental problems inevitably result from too many people demanding too much of the planet. In "An Essay on the Principle of Population" (1798), *Thomas Malthus* predicted that in the future the world's population would grow exponentially while its food grew arithmetically. The end would ultimately be mass famine and death.

Although he did not anticipate the scientific revolutions that would increase food production, Malthus was certainly right about population. Between the time of Jesus and that of Malthus, the world's population increased from roughly 200 million people to one billion. Until then population grew very slowly, probably no more than 0.2 percent annually. Then, during the 18th and 19th centuries, humans proliferated, encouraged by the interrelated agricultural, industrial, technological, and medical revolutions, which started in Europe and spread globally through imperialism. Advances in health, hygiene, and food production and distribution cut infant mortality and malnutrition and allowed people to live longer. Population grew at an increasingly faster rate, as much as 2 to 3 percent annually in the poorest countries. By 1900, the world's population was 1.6 billion, by 1950 2.5 billion, by 1970 3.6 billion, and by 1999 it surpassed 6 billion!

In April 1992, the U.N. Population Fund published a study predicting that the world's population would annually increase by 97 million until 2000, then drop by 90 million for 25 years, and finally diminish by 60 million until by 2050 it would reach 11.6 billion. That estimate may be very optimistic because it assumes significant decreases in the birth rate from 3.8 to 3.3 children per mother by the year 2000.

The already overburdened Third World will suffer about 97 percent of that population increase and subsequent misery. In 1950, Third World countries had twice the population of advanced industrial countries, in 1990 they had three times as many people, and by 2020 they are expected to have four and a half—nearly five—times more mouths to feed. One of those five people is from China; almost

In 1960 there were only two megacities with populations over 10 million people. By 1999, 17 megacities sprawled and polluted across swaths of the earth. By 2015 there will be at least 26 megacities. Whether a megacity or not, urban areas are already overcrowded today with nearly half the world's population. Of those three billion people, over 100 million sleep in the street or beneath makeshift shelters. Thirteen percent or 220 million people have no clean drinking water and twice that number lack toilets. Half of all garbage piles up in the streets or clogs sewers, worsening floods and breeding disease. Perhaps a billion people live in shantytowns ringing city centers. For 1.1 billion people, the never ending, ever thickening fog of air pollution permeated with carcinogens sickens and shortens lives as each inhabitant daily sucks in the equivalent of two or more packs of cigarettes. City services such as water, electricity, sewage, transportation, schools, clinics, police, sanitation, and jobs are overwhelmed and falling further behind the flood of people. Disease, crime, malnourishment, ignorance, homelessness, prostitution—all this is an enormous waste of human potential. In Bangkok, for example, pollution shaved an average of four IQ points from children, and while traffic jams annually cost the economy as much as $1 billion. China's health care costs from pollution may rise from $32 billion in 1995 to $98 billion in 2020. The miserable conditions provoke violence whose global cost in injuries and lost productivity was $500 billion each year. By the year 2025 most cities will literally explode under the crushing impact of two-thirds of humanity.[3]

Population Age Pyramids for First and Third World Countries, 1985, 2025

Source: Thomas W. Merrick, "World Population in Transition," *Population Bulletin* 11 (2).

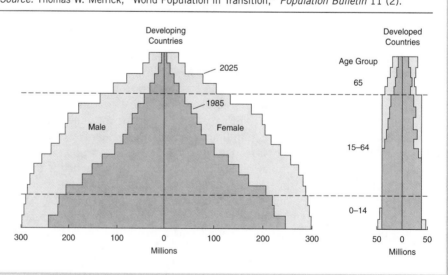

The children of the Mexican city of Torreon face a crisis. The nearby Met-Mex Peñoles factory has spewed lead and other dangerous chemicals into the air and water for decades. As a result, 92 percent of 1,518 children tested had unsafe lead levels in their brains and bodies, of which 210 children had levels so high they needed emergency medical treatment. To their credit, the factory owners agreed to create a $6.6 million trust fund to pay for the children's medical costs. But lead poisoning permanently damages peoples' minds, sharply diminishing intelligence. What gifts to humanity did that pollution destroy?

As if the chemical assault on the children was not horrible enough, Torreon faces yet another environmental crisis. The logging industry's clear-cutting of forests and the thousands of deep wells drilled to irrigate alfalfa fields and other cattle-feed crops has created a worsening water shortage for the region's million people. Deforestation destroys watersheds; denuded landscapes repel rather than absorb precipitation. Meanwhile, the wells drain aquifers faster than nature can replenish them. The Mexican government subsidizes the logging, farming, and ranching industries, and thus shares the blame for the environmental destruction. Torreon's ecological carrying capacity has been perhaps irreparably breached. If nothing is done, that region could be depopulated within a generation.

Having watched for decades as corporations eager for profits at all costs fouled their water and air, clear-cut the surrounding forests, destroyed their soil, and provoked droughts, the people in the Mexican city of Torreon now gather regularly to pray for rain. The corporations that brought environmental devastation once supplied jobs to the region. But as they exhaust the natural resources, they close their operations and take their logging, mining, smelting, and related jobs elsewhere. Torreon's experience of economic boom followed by lasting depression and environmental devastation is suffered by thousands of other cities and billions of people around the world. Who should pay for pollution? What level of pollution should be tolerated? Should property owners be free to do what they want on their land? Should they be free to pollute and destroy other peoples' lands and lives?

Hundreds of cities and thousands of communities around the world face similar environmental catastrophes. Would you want to work or raise your children in such environments? What, if anything, should be done about such chronic worsening environmental problems? Should industries be allowed to pollute for profit if they devastate a region's economy and environment over the long term? Are Torreon's crises only its own, or do they have a global impact? How do they affect international relations?

45 percent of the world's population is Asian. Although most industrialized countries will achieve zero population growth, America's population is expected to grow from 250 million to 383 million between 1990 and 2050. Some of that growth will come from the birth rate, but America's growing population will also swell from political, economic, and environmental refugees from around the world.[4]

A nation's birth rate is shaped by many factors. In traditional cultures, large families are a source of social prestige and economic security. A man is highly regarded if he fathers many children, in some cultures even with two or more mothers. Another reason is the lack of education about and access to contraception. Outside of China, only 30 percent of people in the Third World have access to scientific family planning methods. The wealthier and more educated a population, the lower its birth rate. Population increases tend to slow only after a country

Table 17.1 **A Vicious Cycle: Poverty and Fertility**

		HHD	MHD	LHD
Total Population (million)	1975	872.4	2,789.4	355.5
	1997	1,018.2	4,089.4	636.1
	2015	1,088.3	4,996.1	955.8
Annual Population Growth	1975–1997	0.7%	1.8%	2.7%
	1997–2015	0.4%	1.1%	2.3%
Urban Population of Total	1975	72.9%	29.7%	15.6%
	1997	77.9%	41.2%	27.5%
	2015	82.2%	51.6%	39.0%
People 65 years and older	1997	13.6%	5.7%	3.0%
	2015	17.1%	7.3%	3.2%
Average Number of Children per Family	1975	2.1	4.5	6.8
	1997	1.7	2.6	5.2

Note: The U.N. Development Program split 174 countries into three categories according to their relative living standards: the 45 High Human Development (HHD) countries, the 96 Medium Human Development (MHD) countries, and the 34 Low Human Development (LHD) countries.

Table 17.2 **A Top Ten List: The World's Most Populous Countries—Now and in the Future**

Year 1999		Year 2050	
Country	Population	Country	Population
1. China	1,267 million	1. India	1,529 million
2. India	998 million	2. China	1,478 million
3. United States	276 million	3. United States	349 million
4. Indonesia	209 million	4. Pakistan	345 million
5. Brazil	168 million	5. Indonesia	312 million
6. Pakistan	152 million	6. Nigeria	244 million
7. Russia	147 million	7. Brazil	244 million
8. Bangladesh	127 million	8. Bangladesh	212 million
9. Japan	127 million	9. Ethiopia	169 million
10. Nigeria	109 million	10. Congo	160 million

Source: U.N. Population Fund.

reaches a per capita income of $2,500. The world's wealthiest nations have actually experienced stagnating or declining birth rates, and those populations have increased only through immigration.[5]

Throughout the modern era, new technologies have enabled an increased percentage of the world's population to lead better lives, allowing some to argue that overpopulation was a myth. During the 1980s, the economist Julian Simon asserted that the more people on the planet the better because there would be more minds to think up new technologies to improve living standards and a larger market in which firms can sell more.[6]

Part 7   The Fate of the Earth

Population Policies

China's population control policies have been successful. Between 1960 and 1985, the birth rate plummeted from 6.0 to 2.4 children per couple, a 60 percent drop. Then, from 1988 to 1992, the average number of children born per woman dropped from 2.4 to 1.9, a level comparable to that of the advanced industrial democracies. Yet many have criticized China's policy for the pressure exerted on women to abort any additional children, as well as the unintended effect of leading to the infanticide of girl babies, which are not valued as highly as boy babies. Other governments have achieved less spectacular results with less controversial means. During the same period, Mexico's average number of children born per woman dropped from 7.2 to 3.8, or 47 percent; Brazil's, from 6.2 to 3.4, or 45 percent; Indonesia's, from 5.6 to 3.5, or 38 percent; and India's, from 6.2 to 4.3, or 31 percent.[7]

The Population Explosion, 1804–2150
Source: U.N. Population Fund, 2000 Report.

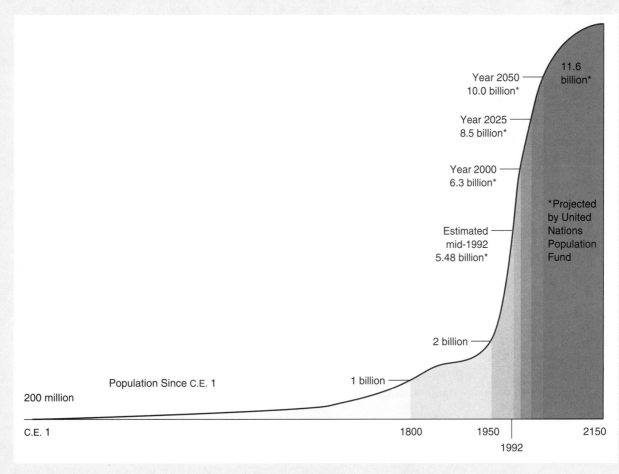

Year 2050
10.0 billion*

Year 2025
8.5 billion*

Year 2000
6.3 billion*

Estimated
mid-1992
5.48 billion*

11.6 billion*

*Projected by United Nations Population Fund

2 billion

1 billion

Population Since C.E. 1

200 million

C.E. 1   1800   1950   2150
1992

Table 17.3 **The Population Explosion by Region, 1997**

	Africa	Asia	Europe	Latin America and Caribbean	North America
Life Expectancy in Years	51	66	73	69	77
Average Number of Children per Mother	5.1	2.6	1.4	2.7	1.9
Percentage of Married Women Using Contraception	20%	60%	72%	66%	71%

Source: U.N. Population Fund.

Most analysts dismiss idealists like Simon as hopelessly naive and warn that the world's rapidly increasing population will eventually devastate the planet, bringing misery to all. They argue that a massive, systematic international effort must be undertaken simply to slow the world's population increase—family planning education and access to safe, cheap contraception must become universal. But that costs money, organization, time, and political will.

Although the *U.N. Population Fund (UNPF)* is leading an effort to encourage family planning and contraception, it has been undercut by some governments for religious or ideological reasons. In 1984 at the International Conference on Population in Mexico City, the Reagan administration announced that it would withdraw American financial and political support from international family planning programs, including the UNPF and International Planned Parenthood Federation. At the 1992 Rio de Janeiro Earth Summit, the population issue was forced off the agenda by the Bush administration, the Vatican, and Saudi Arabia. The same deadlock ruined the 1994 Cairo Population Conference.

Family planning remains a national rather than international policy, with some states trying to curb population growth while most others are either unable to or unwilling to do so. No country has taken more sweeping population control measures than China, whose government promotes one-child families as the ideal. To that end, the government gives extra benefits for 14 years to a couple that has one child, takes those benefits away with the second child, and imposes a tax on the third child. Birth control clinics and family planning information are widely disseminated. These one-child incentives are reinforced by local officials, which pressure women pregnant with a second child to have an abortion.

Tragically, natural forces such as famine and disease may succeed where governments have failed in curbing population. As the earth's arable land diminishes and population increases, food becoming scarcer and often nonexistent for many. The result is mass famine in which millions die. Disease, too, can devastate populations. For example, in some countries and regions, AIDS may accomplish what family planning has been unable to do. Those African countries worst hit by the AIDS epidemic saw their birth rates fall below zero by the year 2000.[8]

The world's birth rate has declined significantly from some combination of policy, personal choice, and nature. But it has not dropped enough to reverse the population explosion. Earth is unable to sustain all those new people born on it.

Greenhouse Effect *and* Global Warming

We take life on Earth for granted. Few understand how fragile the existence of life actually is. Only 0.03 percent of Earth's atmosphere is *carbon dioxide;* most of the rest is nitrogen. Although seemingly minuscule, that carbon dioxide is essential. If

Till Hell Freezes Over?
Icecaps, Currents, *and* Climate

Civilization developed from human ingenuity and optimum environmental conditions. The favorable environment that sustains us is rapidly dying. Global warming, thawing of the Arctic and sub-Arctic, may destroy the Gulf Stream and other currents, the oceanic "heat conveyor belts," that give Europe and the northeastern United States their temperate climate. Tropical waters are drawn north in currents as salt-laden colder waters sink. As the melting icecaps release ever more fresh water, the northern ocean's salt water steadily dilutes, stays cold at the surface, and blocks warm water from streaming north. This happened 15,000 and 12,000 years ago when natural global warming partially melted the icecaps.

Could it happen again? The Arctic icesheet has shrunk 14 percent in just the last 20 years. What will the consequences be if humans destroy the heat conveyor belt? Global warming may at once impose a deep freeze that destroys agriculture in the northeastern United States and Europe, along with hot hell for everyone on the planet.

there were no carbon dioxide in the atmosphere, Earth would be 34 degrees centigrade colder, and ice covered. Life exists on Earth because the amount of carbon dioxide in the atmosphere traps just enough heat. Other planets are not so lucky. Mars has too little carbon dioxide, so the planet is lifeless and frozen; Venus has too much—the planet's surface is so hot that lead melts.

Human beings have severely disrupted Earth's atmosphere to the point where it may eventually no longer sustain any life. On June 23, 1988, Dr. James Hansen, director of NASA's Goddard Institute for Space Studies, announced before a Senate committee that "global warming has begun."[9] The U.N. Intergovernmental Panel on Climate Change (IPCC), composed of the world's leading 2,000 climatologists, began investigating the possibility in 1988; in 1990, they announced the same conclusions—that the earth was clearly heating up and the greenhouse effect was to blame. These studies proved a theory that has been around for almost a century. In 1896, Swedish chemist Svante Arrhenius predicated a greenhouse effect and *global warming* caused by the burning of fossil fuels. Unfortunately, the next serious study did not occur until 1957, when Scripps Institution of Oceanography estimated that half of all carbon dioxide released was being trapped in the atmosphere.

The greenhouse effect can be measured by several ways. One is by examining ice cores drawn from the polar ice caps. In the mid-1980s, French and Russian scientists examined a 2000-meter core taken from Antarctica, that contained 160,000 years of accumulated ice and tiny air bubbles. By analyzing the chemical composition of each layer, they determined the amount of carbon dioxide in the atmosphere dating back 160,000 years. These results accorded perfectly with measurements taken from a Hawaiian laboratory that has been analyzing carbon dioxide in the atmosphere since 1958.

At the industrial revolution's dawn in the 1770s, carbon dioxide concentrations in the atmosphere were 280 parts per million, a rate that increased steadily to 315 parts per million by 1958. The culprits behind these changes were the industrial revolution's fuels, coal and later oil. Then, in just three decades between 1958 to 1988, the amount of carbon dioxide in the atmosphere jumped to 349 parts per

global warming the earth's heating another four degrees over the next 50 years, leading to catastrophic climatic changes.

million, the highest concentration in 160,000 years! By 1999, carbon dioxide had reached 356 parts per million, a annual rate of 1.2 parts per million. If nothing is done, the amount of greenhouse gases will double within the next century.

There is a clear connection between greenhouse gas emissions and temperature increases. In the late 19th century, scientists began making the first systematic readings of global temperatures. In the 1890s, average global temperatures were about 58.2 degrees Fahrenheit; by the 1980s, they had risen to an average of 59.4 degrees, or over one full degree. A dozen of the hottest years on record have erupted since 1980. Temperatures affect and are affected by "patterns of cloud cover, precipitation, winds, ocean currents, and glaciation."[10] Not only have average temperatures been hotter over the last decade, but global climates have been far more erratic than usual. Devastating droughts, floods, hurricanes, and wild regional swings in temperature have been severe and will worsen.

The greenhouse effect is rapidly accelerating. The result will be disaster for many, and economic and physical discomfort for all. The greenhouse effect could cause the average earth temperature to rise three to eight degrees Fahrenheit by the year 2030, which would be the warmest the earth has been for over 2 million years! Humans would definitely feel the heat. For example, it is estimated that the annual number of days in Washington, D.C., with temperatures above 90°F would rise from 36 to 87, and days above 100°F from 1 to 12. Regional climates would be severely affected with temperate regions moving north and leaving desert behind. Global precipitation rates would rise overall, but desertification would begin or hasten in many regions. Global warming will exacerbate poverty, homelessness, unemployment, inflation, malnutrition, disease, and crime while diminishing economic growth. A doubling of carbon dioxide in the atmosphere will depress growth in the industrial countries by 1.0–1.5 percent and in the Third World by 2–9 percent annually.[11] If the frozen tundra begins to melt, it will release huge amounts of methane that accelerate the greenhouse effect and make it unstoppable. Some argue that a global warming of six degrees would melt some of the polar icecaps, which in turn could cause ocean levels to rise as much as three feet. Low-lying regions around the world would be inundated with seawater. The greenhouse crisis could displace hundreds of millions of environmental refugees and their livelihoods. They would flee flooded coastal or drought-stricken areas for less affected regions, which would then be devastated as their carrying capacity was overwhelmed—an environmental domino effect!

There are four main greenhouse gases—carbon dioxide, *chlorofluorocarbons (CFCs), methane,* and *nitrous oxide,* each of which has both natural and manmade sources. The burning of fossil fuels accounts for about 45 percent of greenhouse gases. When fossil fuels such as coal, oil, wood, and natural gas are burned, the carbon combines with oxygen to make carbon dioxide. About 20 percent of the carbon dioxide emissions are caused by the destruction of the tropical forest. When those trees are cut down, they no longer absorb carbon dioxide; when they are burned, they release the stored carbon dioxide into the atmosphere. CFCs and *halons*—the same chemicals that deplete the ozone layer—also contribute to as much as 15 to 20 percent of the greenhouse effect by preventing infrared radiation from escaping into space. Methane and nitrous oxide account for the rest. About half of the carbon dioxide emissions are naturally absorbed by the world's oceans and forests through *photosynthesis.* The oceans are particularly effective at absorbing heat. The trouble is that the increased amounts of greenhouse gases spewed into the atmosphere are overwhelming nature's ability to absorb them.

The relationship between the populations and carbon dioxide emissions of the rich and poor countries has shifted over time. In 1950, there were 825 million people from rich countries, which emitted 6.3 tons of carbon dioxide per person or 90 percent of total emissions, compared to 1.5 billion from poor countries, which emitted 0.4 tons per person or 10 percent of the total. In 1985, the population of rich countries had risen to 1.170 billion, whose inhabitants emitted 13.0 tons per person or 84 percent of the total, compared to 3.680 billion from poor countries, who emitted 1.0 ton per person or 16 percent of the total. But by 2020, both the poor and the rich countries will account for half of total carbon dioxide emissions. The poor countries' population will almost double to 6.720 billion, of which 2.0 tons of carbon dioxide per person will be emitted, while the rich countries will have about 1.340 billion people and emit 10.0 tons per person.[12]

The three largest industrial countries—the United States, Japan, and Germany—had 4.7 percent, 2.3 percent, and 1.5 percent, of the world's population, respectively, and contributed 22.3 percent, 4.8 percent, and 2.9 percent, respectively, or a total of 30.1 of the world's carbon dioxide. In contrast, the three largest Third World countries, China, India, and Indonesia, had 21.0 percent, 16.0 percent, and 3.6 percent of the world's population, respectively, and contributed 10.9 percent, 3.0 percent, and 0.6 percent, respectively or 15.5 percent of the world's carbon dioxide. Yet the carbon dioxide emissions of the three poor countries will exceed that of the wealthy three by 2015 if current growth rates hold.[13]

There have been a series of international attempts to deal with the greenhouse effect. In 1979, 34 nations signed the U.N. Convention on Long-Range Transboundary Air Pollution, which dealt with atmospheric pollution. The 1987

Table 17.4 **The Enemy Is Us: The Growth in Carbon Dioxide Emissions Around the World**

	Total in Million Metric Tons		Per Capita Metric Tons	
	1980	1996	1980	1996
World	13,640.7	22,653.9	3.4	4.0
Low Income	2,126.1	5,051.8	0.9	1.5
Excluding China/India	302.0	690.9	0.4	0.6
Middle Income	2,804.5	6,871.5	3.3	4.8
Lower Middle	1,150.1	4,194.9	2.6	4.8
Upper Middle	1,654.4	2,676.6	4.0	4.7
Low/Middle Income	4,930.6	11,923.3	1.5	2.5
East Asia/Pacific	1,958.5	4,717.5	1.4	2.7
Europe/Central Asia	886.9	3,412.7	—	7.4
Latin America/Caribbean	848.5	1,209.1	2.4	2.5
Middle East/North Africa	493.6	986.9	3.0	3.9
South Asia	392.4	1,125.1	0.4	0.8
Sub-Saharan Africa	350.7	472.1	0.9	0.8
High Income	8,710.2	10,730.6	12.3	12.3

Note: — indicates no available information for that year.

Source: World Bank, 2000.

Global Average Temperatures and Greenhouse Gases, 1880–1999
Source: William K. Stevens, "If Climate Changes, It May Change Quickly," *New York Times,* Jan. 27, 1998.

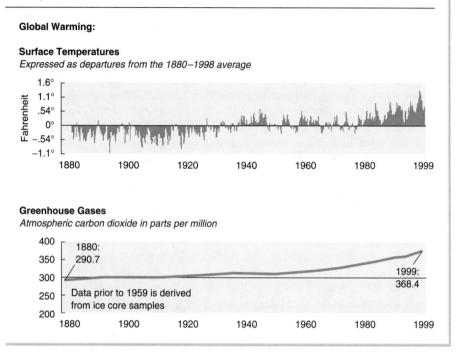

Global Warming:

Surface Temperatures
Expressed as departures from the 1880–1998 average

Greenhouse Gases
Atmospheric carbon dioxide in parts per million

Montreal Treaty on CFCs helped alleviate a percentage of the greenhouse gases. In 1987, the Intergovernmental Panel on Climate Change (IPCC) was set up to work closely with the World Meteorological Organization (WMO) and U.N. Environmental Program (UNEP) to monitor and propose policies addressing the greenhouse effect. The 1988 World Conference on Changing Atmosphere in Toronto called on nations to reduce their fossil fuel use by 20 percent by the year 2005. Although only a few nations attended the Toronto conference, it succeeded in putting the greenhouse crisis on the global agenda. In September 1989, the United Nations issued its "Climate Change: Meeting the Challenge," which included a plan for addressing the greenhouse effect. In 1990, the U.N. General Assembly resolved to negotiate and sign the Framework Convention on Climate Change or *global warming treaty* at the 1992 U.N. Conference on Environment and Development in Rio de Janeiro.

The 1992 global warming treaty called for industrial countries to reduce their greenhouse emissions and extend financial and technological aid to poor countries so they can eventually comply with the treaty. The Bush White House originally opposed the treaty, arguing that any emission reductions should be voluntary rather than mandated, along with the false claim that the United States would probably reach the targets anyway so there was no need to sign. It only agreed to sign the treaty if the timetable were removed in which each signatory agreed to reduce its greenhouse emissions to 1990 levels by the year 2000. The other countries reluctantly agreed, and the treaty was signed by over 153 countries. In April 1993, President Clinton declared that the United States would meet the original greenhouse effect treaty's goals of reducing emissions by the year 2000 below the 1990 level, and unveiled a systematic program to achieve that goal. Two new accords in the late 1990s strengthened previous initiatives. The December 1997

Kyoto and 1998 Buenos Aires accords required the advanced industrial countries to cut their emissions between 6 and 7 percent below their 1990 levels. Promises are relatively easy to make. The important question is whether the signatories will fulfill their promises.

How can these cuts be achieved? The replacement of subsidies with a high pollution tax for the fossil fuel, tax cuts and subsidies for alternative energy industries, tax cuts for conservation efforts by businesses and household, higher standards for fuel efficiency and antipollution for vehicles and other machines, which directly or indirectly produce greenhouse gases, the reversal of deforestation, and investments in mass transportation are some key policies that can begin to slow global warming. Traditionally, the creation of wealth and increased energy use marched hand-in-hand. Between the 1920s and early 1970s, energy use increased 0.9 percent for every 1.0 percent increase in GNP. OPEC's quadrupling of oil prices in 1973 and further doubling in 1979 forced most governments, businesses, and consumers to use energy more efficiently. As a result, global energy efficiency has doubled over the past two decades, which means that not only is the earth cleaner than it might have been, but more money has been available to invest elsewhere.

Further energy efficiency gains are possible. A recent study estimated that the United States would have to invest $2.7 trillion to reduce carbon dioxide 70 percent over the next 40 years. That investment, however, would generate $5 trillion in energy savings, for a net saving of $2.3 trillion. America's economy would grow faster with than without that investment.[14]

The Greenhouse Effect

Source: William Nester, *International Relations: Geopolitical and Geoeconomic Conflict and Cooperation* (New York: HarperCollins, 1995), p. 427.

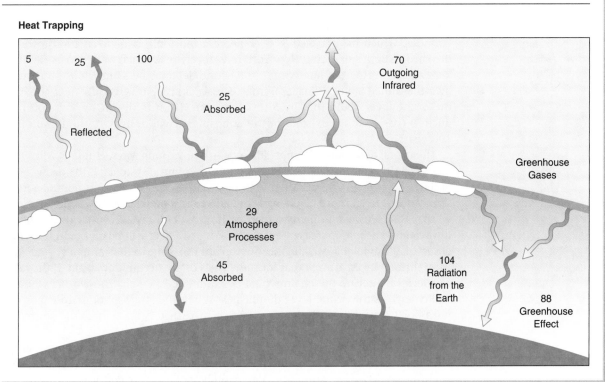

Heat Trapping

One major trouble is that with oil prices at an historic low, there is no price incentive to increase efficiency. And although the advanced industrial nations have achieved significant efficiency gains, poorer nations—many with huge populations—are rapidly industrializing.

All the international and national measures taken may be too little too late. If energy efficiency annually increases by only 1 percent, atmospheric carbon dioxide will increase from 349 parts per million in 1988 to 600 ppm in 2075. A 2 percent annual efficiency increase would hold down the concentrations to 463 ppm by 2075. Global warming and the accompanying devastation is inevitable. The only question is, How bad will it get? That depends on the extent of international efforts to curb fossil fuel pollution. So far those efforts have been mostly symbolic rather than substantive.

Ozone Layer Depletion

Until the 1980s, most people had either never heard of ozone or associated it with ground ozone pollution.[15] Human life exists, in part, because the earth is cocooned in an ozone layer that absorbs most of the harmful solar ultraviolet radiation. Sunlight causes chemical reactions that continually destroy and recreate ozone. Until recently there was a natural balance in the ozone layer.

Human-made chemicals are now destroying that balance and rapidly eating away the ozone layer. The villains are chemicals that contain chlorine and bromine, the worst of which are CFCs and halons. Each of these molecules can destroy as many as 100,000 ozone molecules. Before being banned, halons were used in fire extinguishers and CFCs were used in air conditioning, aerosol sprays, seat cushions, computer chip cleaners, and foam insulation.

The damage to the ozone layer is already severe and worsens daily. Between 1969 and 1986, the ozone layer thinned by about 4 to 6 percent in the midlatitudes, which has allowed 8 to 12 percent more ultraviolet radiation to reach the earth. The result is that New York now receives as much radiation as Caracas, Venezuela. During the late winter, the ozone depletes by as much as 40 percent over the United States, Canada, Europe, Russia, and Japan. Over the next 40 years, the ozone layer could thin by 5 to 20 percent. Even if all CFCs and halon production ceased, those existing in the atmosphere will destroy ozone for another 100 years.

The ozone depletion will affect life on earth in various ways. Humans will suffer increased skin cancer, cataracts, and depressed immune systems. If the ozone layer declines 10 percent overall, there will be a 25 percent increase in nonmelanoma skin cancers. Even more troubling is the effect on some plants. To varying degrees, all crops are sensitive to increased doses of ultraviolet rays. Crop yields will fall as ultraviolet exposure increases. Perhaps the worst effect will be on ocean life. High doses of ultraviolet rays kill the phytoplankton (one-celled animals) and krill (tiny shrimplike creatures) that form the basis of the ocean food chain. If they die, all species higher up the chain would be eliminated as well. The world's climates will change as the ozone layer diminishes. When the stratospheric ozone absorbs ultraviolet rays, heat is generated, which in turn creates winds, the source of weather patterns.

No link in the chain of interrelated environmental crises has been more effectively addressed than the ozone layer destruction. Like the greenhouse effect, some scientists predicted an ozone layer depletion before it was scientifically proven. The first warning came in 1973 when two University of Michigan professors, Richard Stolarski and Ralph Cicerone, explored the chlorine chemical effects of NASA rocket blasts on the atmosphere. The following year two professors at the University of California at Irvine, Mario Molina and Sherwood Rowland, found that, unlike most other gases, CFCs stayed in the atmosphere and destroyed it for decades.

A general scientific understanding of the CFC danger led to a public and eventually a political consensus in the United States and elsewhere. By the late 1970s, millions of Americans refused to buy aerosol spray cans and other CFC products. In 1977, the American government responded to public opinion by passing a law banning CFCs from 90 percent of aerosol sprays; Canada, Sweden, Denmark, Finland, and Norway followed suit. These countries, known as the Toronto Group, pressured other countries and international organizations to cut back their own CFC emissions. In 1980, the European Community froze production of two of the worst CFC chemicals and cut back production 30 percent from its 1976 levels.

In the 1980s, the U.N. Environmental Program (UNEP) forged an international consensus on the need to take more comprehensive measures. In 1985, the world learned of the ozone layer over Antarctica thinning by as much as 50 percent during the winter. This scientific proof was an important impetus behind the efforts of 24 countries to negotiate and sign later that year the Vienna Convention on the Protection of the Ozone Layer, which was the first international attempt to identify, if not systematically deal with, the problem. The convention called for more far-reaching measures to be undertaken by 1987. In September 1986, the Alliance for Responsible CFC Policy, a coalition of over 500 American firms and consumer groups, called for sweeping international action, and the American government helped pressure other countries. International negotiations began in December 1986 and concluded in September 1987 with the signing of the Montreal Protocol on Substances That Deplete the Ozone Layer. The 24 signatories agreed to freeze production of eight chemicals by 1989, freeze halon production by 1992, and cut CFC emissions by 50 percent by 1998–1999. In 1988, several international and NASA studies revealed that CFC emissions had doubled between 1975 and 1985 despite the national and international steps taken, making it apparent that the Montreal Protocol did not go far enough to address the problem. In March 1989, the Save the Ozone Conference called by Prime Minister Thatcher attracted 123 countries. In 1990, 93 nations signed the London Protocol, in which they agreed to end production of 97 chemicals by the year 2000. The wealthier countries created a $180 million fund to help the poorer countries convert to CFC-free technologies, and offered China and India an additional $80 million if they joined the treaty. Since 1991, they have provided an additional $1 billion to help poorer countries reach their commitment to end the use or manufacture of ozone depleting chemicals by 2010. Today 129 countries have signed the treaty.

There has been considerable progress toward reaching the London Protocol's goals. The advanced industrial countries have granted various subsidies for firms researching CFC substitutes and taxes on CFC production. As a result, corporations have created substitutes for CFCs, including some based on citrus fruits. Air conditioners and refrigerators are the largest CFC users in the United States. As much as 34 percent of CFC emissions come from leakage, 48 percent from recharging and repairs, and 18 percent from accidents, disposal, and manufacturing. CFCs in air conditioners and refrigerators are increasingly better sealed and recycled rather than released into the atmosphere. Although there are not yet any substitutes for halons, the release of that chemical could be cut by two-thirds by curbing extinguisher discharge testing.

Although virtually all governments agree on the danger of the ozone layer depletion, as usual rich and poor countries differ sharply over who should bear the costs of compliance with the treaties. About 25 percent of the world's population account for 85 percent of CFC use. The poor countries argue that either they should be allowed to use cheaper CFCs for refrigeration, air conditioning, and so on, or the rich countries should pay the tab for substitute chemicals and equipment. China, India, Brazil, Indonesia, and Iran—all with huge populations and ambitious industrialization programs—have refused to sign the various ozone treaties. The rich and poor countries remain at an impasse over the issue of transferring the CFC substitute technology. Compliance of the signatories will not end the use of ozone-depleting chemicals. The black market for CFCs is yearly as much as 30,000 tons. Overall, by the year 2000 the production and use of ozone-destroying chemicals had dropped 85 percent from its height in the 1970s. Meanwhile, chemicals are steadily eating away the ozone shield that protects us; in 1999, the European Space Agency reported that the ozone layer over Europe had shrunk to one-third its natural level.

Nonetheless, the ozone layer treaties are an outstanding example of the international identification of a problem and efforts to overcome it, even before scientific evidence established beyond a doubt the reality of the ozone crisis. Public opinion and interest groups, responding to widely publicized scientific studies, proved a decisive factor in pressuring the governments of the United States and Europe to act. National efforts led to international efforts, which became increasingly comprehensive in addressing the problem. The earlier agreements gave industry the time and incentive to develop substitutes before an outright ban took place. Signatories can retaliate against any countries that refuse to abide by the treaty. The success of the ozone layer treaty can stimulate success in dealing with other international issues.

Regional Pollution

Not all air and water pollution contribute to the ozone and greenhouse crises, yet all do inflict on nations vast economic costs in worse health, lost productivity, forgone opportunities, and blighted urban and rural regions. The World Health Organization (WTO) reported in 1999 that over 1 billion people or one-sixth of humanity live in air considered unfit to breathe. In the United States alone, over 150 million, or about two-thirds of the population, live in areas whose air the Environmental Protection Agency (EPA) deems so unhealthy that it annually inflicts on Americans 120,000 deaths and $40 billion in health care and lost productivity! In Athens the number of deaths rises sixfold on heavy pollution days. In Hungary, one of seventeen deaths is attributable to air pollution. In Bombay, breathing the air equals smoking ten cigarettes a day. In Mexico City, the pollution exceeds world health standards 300 days a year, and seven of ten newborn babies have lead levels that indicate brain damage.[16]

In high enough doses, air-borne chemicals can impair the body and mind, and the food on which we subsist. Sulfur dioxide can cause or worsen coughs, colds, asthma, bronchitis, and emphysema. Particulate matter can carry toxic metals into one's lungs. Ozone, formed when sunlight causes hydrocarbons and nitrogen oxide chemicals to react, can damage lungs. Nitrogen dioxide can cause lung problems, including bronchitis, pneumonia, and influenza. Carbon monoxide interferes with the blood's ability to absorb oxygen, which ultimately can cause death. Lead harms

Environmental Legacies *of* the Former "Workers' Paradise"

Few regions of the world suffer worse pollution problems than eastern Europe and the former Soviet Union, which together account for 25 percent of the carbon dioxide and 17 percent of the CFC emissions that cause the greenhouse and ozone depletion effects.[17] The region's centrally planned economies were grossly energy inefficient and indifferent to even basic environmental concerns.

They relied for much of their energy on high-sulfur brown coal or lignite. The result is that much of eastern Europe and the former Soviet Union has become an environmental wasteland littered with toxic chemical and nuclear dumps and beset by acid rain and by noxious air and water pollution.

The region lacks the money, expertise, organization, and political will to confront its environmental catastro-phe. All the countries are deeply in debt to international bankers and organizations. Governments hesitate to shut down even the worst polluting factories because there is no alternate employment for the tens of thousands of workers. It is estimated that the cleanup costs for East Germany alone will range from $249 billion to $308 billion. Little progress has been made.

---

the brain, kidneys, circulatory, reproductive, and nervous systems. The damage to crops can also be severe. For each percentage point increase in ultraviolet rays, soybean yields are reduced by the same amount. Ground-level ozone alone is estimated to reduce America's corn, wheat, soybean, and peanut yields by 5 percent. Cutting ozone pollution in half would annually increase crop yields by $5 billion.

Air and water pollution in the United States, the European Community, and Japan has lessened considerably because of sweeping laws passed in those countries during the 1970s and 1980s. For example, America's 1970 and 1990 Clean Air acts have had a significant effect on pollution. Between 1970 and 1987, the United States cut sulfur dioxide emissions by 28 percent and particulates 62 percent.

Environmentalism and business can complement rather than conflict with each other. Those countries that master green technologies the fastest will become the most prosperous and powerful. The annual global market for environmentally sound products is already $200 billion and will increase steadily. In the United States alone, environmental protection is a huge and ever growing industry that generates $98 billion annually and employs three million. New technologies such as scrubbers, clean-burning coal, nitrous oxide controls, energy conservation, and catalytic converters, to name a few, have cut pollution and increased productivity. Alternative fuels such as ethanol, methanol, natural gas, and hydrogen cause much less pollution than coal and oil. Likewise, mass transportation, bicycles, and walking reduce pollution.

There are many steps that governments can take to reduce pollution. Taxing emissions forces producers to pay pollution's full costs, thus providing an incentive for businesses to invest in equipment and production techniques that minimize pollution. Emission trading also diminishes the problem. Industries are assigned a pollution level. If they exceed it, they can buy "pollution rights" from firms that have reduced pollution below that level.

Recycling can dramatically reduce the fossil fuels emissions that are the greenhouse effect's major cause. For example, steel produced from scrap cuts air pollution

Environmentalism *and* Profits:
The 3M Model

Many economic theorists believe that environmental regulations hurt the economy. In the real world, the opposite is true. Environmentalism pays in greater productivity, health, profits, and lower taxes and insurance premiums. For example, the 3M Corporation's systematic waste reduction and recycling program has saved the company over $300 million over 15 years. That same program has saved America's tax and insurance payers enormous amounts because it prevents the generation of 100,000 tons of air pollution, 275,000 tons of solid wastes and sludge and 1.5 billion gallons of wastewater annually.[18]

by 85 percent, water pollution 76 percent, and eliminates mining wastes completely; recycled paper cuts air and water pollution 74 percent and 35 percent, respectively, and eliminates clear-cutting forests. Energy savings are also great: recycled aluminum costs only 5 percent of that produced from bauxite ore; steel from scrap only 35 percent that of steel from iron ore; recycled glass 65 percent that of glass from natural materials; newsprint from recycled paper 40 to 75 percent that from wood pulp.[19]

Other measures can help reduce pollution. Public opinion can have a powerful effect on polluters, and most firms do all they can to cover up their pollution. "Right to know" laws would require businesses to release data on their pollution, giving citizens an opportunity to boycott or protest those firms until they clean up their mess.

Although it has already taken some important steps, the United States could do much more to clean up its carbon dioxide and other pollution. Washington has lagged well behind its competitors in implementing policies that encourage the technological and product breakthroughs essential to remaining economically competitive and environmentally sound. America's government spending programs remain largely shaped by politics rather than an understanding of the economic and environmental challenges the country faces. In 1992, while Washington spent $540 million in subsidizing environmental technology, it gave $35 billion worth of direct and indirect subsidies to farmers. American gasoline prices are three to four times cheaper than those of other advanced industrial countries. A 50-cent federal tax on gasoline and other carbon emissions in the United States would at once force people to use mass transportation, increase efficiency, and reduce America's trade deficit and national debt, along with its dependence on foreign oil sources. Some of these carbon taxes could be invested in solar, wind, geothermal, and hydroelectric energy sources that do not contribute to the greenhouse effect.

Significant international measures were taken to deal with various forms of pollution even before the 1992 global warming treaty. In 1979, the Geneva Convention on Long-Range Transboundary Air Pollution was signed by 10 industrial countries in which they agreed to cut back air pollution. In 1984, 21 governments signed the Helsinki Protocol, in which they pledged to reduce sulfur emissions by 30 percent, which was followed up by the 1988 Sofia Convention whereby signatories agreed to a further 30 percent cut in sulfur emissions and a reduction in nitrogen oxides.

Gasping *for* Fresh Air:
South Asia's Poisonous Blanket

With increasingly advanced technologies, scientists are discovering ever more about the global environment. Most of what they uncover is very bad news for humanity. In May 1999, it was revealed that an area of stifling pollution as large as the United States blankets southern Asia and the northern Indian Ocean every winter.

The pollution comes from smokestacks and exhaust pipes not only from South Asia but from as far away as China and Southeast Asia. Winds push that thickening tide of dangerous chemicals south in winter and back north in summer. That chemical cloud already rises 10,000 feet into the air, compared to a stable cloud of 2,000 feet over Europe. The effects of that poisonous blanket on humans, animals, crops, soils, water, and foliage are disastrous and getting worse.

Identifying a problem is the first step in solving it, if those affected have the will and means to do so. So far no governments in the region have bothered to discuss, let alone act on, the poisonous cloud that engulfs them.

Regional international agreements have complemented the more global treaties. Europeans have cooperated extensively to deal with regional environmental issues. The European Community has attempted to create environmental standards to which all members must adhere. The European Community's 1988 Directive on the Limitation of Emissions of Certain Pollutants created a country-by-country plan for pollution reduction in which the richest countries were required to reduce their emissions between 60 and 70 percent by 2003, while the poorer countries such as Portugal, Greece, and Ireland were temporarily allowed to increase emissions. Other regional agreements involved a set of EC members or the EC and other countries. The 1976 Bonn Convention for the Protection of the Rhine Against Pollution by Chlorides, the 1974 Helsinki Convention for the Protection of the Baltic, 1974 Paris Convention for the Protection of the North Sea, and 1976 Barcelona Convention for the Protection of the Mediterranean addressed important pollution issues.

Although the United States, Canada, and Mexico have enacted important environmental legislation, there has been little coordination among them. Regional environmental concerns were not addressed until the 1993 North American Free Trade Association (NAFTA).

And although some countries and regions have made considerable progress in reducing some forms of pollution, it remains a severe problem virtually everywhere and imposes enormous losses in wealth, productivity, health, and life quality.

Deforestation

Only 20 percent of the world's surface is land. Temperate and tropical forests together cover two-fifths—13 and 7 percent, respectively—of that land.[20] The world's forests are essential for protecting and enhancing human life. Temperate and tropical forests act as the earth's lungs, annually absorbing vast amounts of carbon dioxide that would otherwise drift up into the atmosphere and contribute

Environmentalism *and* Wealth: *The* Kalimantan Case

A study on the huge tropical island of Kalimantan in Indonesia reveals the literal bankruptcy of clear-cutting the forests and then using the denuded land for crops. At best farming annually yielded $2 a hectare. In startling contrast, those who extracted the forest fruits, latex, medicines, and other products earned $70 a hectare! Atop that, hunters and fishermen enjoyed $1 and $16 dollars more per hectare each year. Recreation and tourism brought in an additional $12. Watershed protection and soil erosion prevention saved Indonesia an additional $10 and $2–28, respectively, along with $14 for fisheries protection and $2 for flood protection a hectare. The grand tally—farming $2 versus at least $129 for a range of economic activities!

So why would any government be so stupid as to allow clear-cutting and farming when it could reap genuine development and enormous wealth by nurturing rather than destroying the forests? The answer is simple—greed. Logging corporations bribe officials not only to give them free land but even to build roads into the forests. That is true not just in Third World countries but nearly anywhere there are forests—including the United States.

to the greenhouse effect. Forests are more than trees; they are vast, complex, and fragile ecosystems of which tree species are only some of thousands of shrubs, flowers, mosses, and animals. Once destroyed, temperate forests are difficult to regrow, and tropical forests are lost forever.

The survival of humanity and the tropical forests are intricately linked. There are anywhere between 3 million and 30 million animal and plant species on earth, most of these in tropical forests. In one 10-acre stretch of Borneo rain forest, researchers found over 700 tree species! Tropical forests are treasure stores of medicines and other products. One of four drugs currently sold is derived from tropical forests. Over 70 percent of the 3,000 plants currently known to fight cancer are tropical. In the Amazon basin, Indians use over 1,300 plants for medicinal purposes. Gathering the fruits and plants of tropical forests creates much more wealth for many more people than does clear-cutting it and converting it to pasture or single-crop farms. One study in Peru found that the net annual value of harvesting forest fruits and latex was 13 times greater than clear-cutting. Finally, tropical forest reserves can bring in tourists and thus income.

The world's forests are rapidly diminishing. One-third of the world's forests have already been destroyed, and every year 20–25 million more hectares, an area the size of Belgium, are lost to chainsaws, bulldozers, and arson. By 2020, at their current rate of destruction, between 80 percent and 95 percent of all tropical forests will have disappeared, and by 2050 all will have been destroyed!

Deforestation adversely affects both the global and regional climates as it

deforestation the rapid destruction of the world's forests by clear-cutting for logging, grazing, and other reasons; alters climates and destroys millions of potentially useful plant and animal species. Because forests are the world's lungs, absorbing carbon dioxide and turning it into oxygen, deforestation accelerates the **greenhouse effect**. Particularly in the tropics, deforestation destroys millions of species that can be used as medicines or foods for humanity.

reduces transpiration of water vapor into the atmosphere, changes the albedo (reflectivity) of the earth's surface, removes an important 'sink' for air pollutants, and, through burning, contributes to the greenhouse effect by releasing of carbon dioxide and other greenhouse gases into the atmosphere. At the same time, the essential

Will We Be Next? Biocide

The U.N.'s Global Biodiversity Assessment estimates that as many as 5 million of the estimated 20 million species on earth could become extinct by the year 2025. Anywhere from 15 to 50,000 species die off annually, a daily rate of 50 to 150, most in tropical forests. Even if humans destroyed only 2 percent of all species over the next 25 years, that rate would be 1,000 times the natural rate. There has not been such a mass species extinction since the dinosaurs died off 65 million years ago. Destroying millions of species whose benefits to humankind remain unknown has been compared to "eating our seed corn." Many indigenous peoples are dying with their forests, and with them the medicinal secrets of thousands of plants and animals. And after wiping out most of the earth's natural resources, will we end up destroying ourselves as a species?

services provided by intact forest ecosystems—such as watershed protection, flood control, the storage of carbon in plant tissues, or the breakdown of pollutants—are being degraded or destroyed."[21]

Deforestation's most serious consequence involves the greenhouse effect. The cutting down and often outright burning of forests accounts for about one-third of all carbon dioxide emissions. In 1987, 11 countries—Brazil, Indonesia, Colombia, Ivory Coast, Thailand, Laos, Nigeria, Vietnam, Philippines, Burma, and India—were responsible for 82 percent of the net carbon release from deforestation.

About 95 percent of all tropical forest soils are infertile and extremely fragile. Most of the vegetation's nutrients come from their own ability to take nitrogen from the atmosphere. Thus clear-cutting rapidly erodes the land, making it unsuitable for agriculture or even livestock within a few years. It also silts streams and rivers, which destroys fishing industries. For example, clear-cutting the South Fork of the Salmon River in Idaho earned logging corporations $14 million but cost the fishing industry $100 million. Finally, clear-cutting destroys a region's tourist industry—few tourists want to visit stump-filled and degraded landscapes.

Forests are being destroyed for several reasons. Perhaps the most important is that clear-cutting a forest is a quick and easy source of money for those involved. The huge logging corporations make most of the money; host governments skim off surprisingly little revenue—often far less than the money they invested in the infrastructure and administration to destroy the forests. The U.S. government, for example, is notorious for selling permits to clear-cut national forests for a fraction of what logging firms would pay for access to private lands. Debt-burdened Third World countries are particularly apt to clear-cut forests for short-term gains even if it means future economic and environmental devastation for that region. As forests diminish, the value of their wood rises, and thus also the incentive to clear-cut them even faster.

Huge livestock corporations clear-cut or burn forest and convert it to pastureland. Most of the beef production goes not to hungry people in that country but to hamburger chains in the advanced industrial countries. For example, although beef production in Central America increased threefold between 1955 and 1980, beef consumption in the region actually fell. But most of those ranches would be bankrupt if they did not receive huge government subsidies. Another reason for deforestation is the maldistribution of farm lands. In Latin America, for example, 7 percent of the population owns 93 percent of the land while 70 percent of the population has little or none. Thus many peasants drift into the tropical forests to slash and burn a patch for farming. The problem with both ranching and subsistence farming is that tropical soils are very fragile and easily washed away within a few years, forcing the rancher or peasant to move on and destroy yet another swath of forest.

The bottom line of deforestation, as with all other environmental problems, is overpopulation. The populations of countries such as India, Brazil, Nigeria, and Indonesia have more than doubled over the past 30 years, and the resulting increased demand for goods, services, jobs, and land devours tropical forests. Many governments actually subsidize the migration of the poor to the forests to relieve the pressure on existing cities and farmlands. Indonesia, for example, spends $10,000 for each family it relocates in the tropical forests.

About 2 billion of the world's population use wood as their primary energy source. In Africa alone, 76 percent of all energy comes from wood. Virtually everywhere, people are stripping wood from the land faster than it can be replenished. Once the local wood supply is depleted, people use dried human and animal dung for fuel rather than for fertilizer, and in so doing degrade existing farmland. Eventually the land is exhausted and the people migrate elsewhere where they repeat the same vicious cycle of land degradation. Simply building roads into tropical forests not only encourages developers to move in but destroys vast amounts of trees.

The Japanese have been particularly notorious for clear-cutting the world's tropical forests and account for one-third of world timber imports. Japanese are very wasteful of the tropical woods they import. A 1989 World Wildlife Fund study singled out Japan as the world's most voracious user of tropical woods.[22] Japan uses nonrenewable but cheaper tropical woods largely for plywood and chopsticks, even though it could use renewable but more expensive temperate woods for the same purposes. Much of the imported wood is wasted. For example, every year Japanese throw away 20 billion wooden chopsticks, which if stacked up would make a mountain as high as Mt. Fuji.

Although deforestation leads to apparent economic gains for loggers, ranchers, subsistence farmers, and foreign consumers, the nation's real assets just as steadily diminish—by as much as 4 to 6 percent annually for major tropical timber-exporting countries. Special interests benefit from deforestation in the short run; everyone suffers enormous direct and indirect costs over the long run.

A number of national measures can be taken to slow the destruction of the world's forests, particularly the priceless tropical forests. Land reform is an essential step. Peasants migrate to tropical forests and systematically destroy them because they lack land and basic needs elsewhere. Land must be redistributed from the huge plantations, which often leave vast amounts fallow, to the poor landless peasants. Land distribution, however, will not work unless it is accompanied by the extension of credit, technology, fertilizer, and education to the new peasant proprietors so that they can productively work their land. Allowing indigenous people the right to the land they have lived on for millennia would protect both them and the forests. Over the long term, family planning and free universal access to contraceptives can alleviate some of the population pressure on forests.

W hich country is the most forested? Brazil? The United States? Indonesia? Canada? Actually, Russia has the world's largest forests. And surprisingly, although environmental catastrophes ravage large swaths of Russia, the forests are among the world's least threatened with destruction. That is good for Russia and the world. Russian forests are a vital "sink" that absorbs carbon dioxide and converts it into oxygen. Indeed, Russia's forests yearly store 500 million tons of carbon dioxide. This slightly offsets the release of 1.6 billion tons of carbon dioxide annually spewed into the atmosphere by the destruction of tropical forests.

Why have Russia's forests escaped destruction? Most of those forests are in climates alien to agriculture, the source of most destruction in tropical forests. Soviet planning, which caused widespread economic and environmental destruction elsewhere, actually protected the forests. The state owns the nation's forests and carefully regulates how much is logged. Logging is forbidden on permafrost, which when stripped of the forest melts and forms swamps where trees cannot regenerate. Russia's government has continued those policies.

Other forces protect the forests. The remoteness of most of that forest inhibits their destruction. Eighty percent of the forests lie east of the Ural mountains, but the state located most pulp and paper mills west of them. Although the state subsidized the logging industry, that money disappeared when communism fell. In 1997, logging took only 88.5 million cubic meters, one-quarter the production in 1988. By using American technology and techniques, Russian loggers now retrieve nearly all the trees cut, whereas before they left nearly half to rot. That doubling of productivity means only half as many trees must be cut for the same yield in logs.

Will logging in Russia's forest remain sustainable or become destructive? As forests elsewhere are destroyed and the world's soaring population demands ever more wood and paper products, the pressures on Russia's forests will grow. Prices for forest products will rise as the supply falls. If Russia's economy fails to diversify, Moscow will be tempted to tap into that easy source of cash by removing logging restrictions. All that is likely but not inevitable. But to prevent that destruction the world's nations will have to agree on sweeping conservation, population control, and antipollution measures—a highly unlikely prospect, given the power of economic and ideological groups opposed to all that.

International debt relief including more debt-for-nature swaps that can protect forest tracts will reduce the pressures on poor governments to clear-cut other forests to help service their debts. Fourteen countries account for about half of the Third World's foreign debt and two-thirds of tropical deforestation. Targeting these countries for debt reduction, combined with sustained development and conservation policies, could remove the incentive for clear-cutting forests for short-term gains.

Economic policy in most countries is divided among a range of ministries and agencies whose interests and actions often conflict. The result is enormous mismanagement, misallocation of resources, slower economic growth, and worsening environmental problems. To be effective, development and land use planning must be coordinated under an umbrella of goals and means, which incorporate notions of sustained development for all rather than short-term special interest payoffs or market "solutions."

Environmental impact studies should precede any development schemes that will destroy forests. Short-term gains for a few must always be weighed against the long-term losses, not just for a specific nation but for all humanity. An important step in this direction would be to change the system of computing national wealth so that it includes the depreciation of national natural assets. If clear-cutting forests were counted as a net economic loss rather than gain, governments would do more to preserve rather than destroy them. Unfortunately, it is difficult to compute the value of a forest in alleviating the greenhouse effect, watershed protection, biodiversity, and so on.

New forestry techniques seek to manage existing forests rather than convert them to tree farms or wasteland. Clear-cutting is abolished. Instead, small clumps of trees are cut selectively, leaving most of the forest intact. Trees are cut down only at the rate at which they are replanted, a practice known as *sustained yield*. In the tropics, only 0.1 percent of all the forests can be logged at sustained yield. Tropical forestry involves managing the sustained yield of logging and the gathering of medicinal plants, rubber, fruits, nuts, and selective tree cutting.

sustained yield the practice of replanting trees at the rate they are cut down.

In the United States, as in most timber-producing countries, the government subsidizes the logging industry. If loggers had to pay market costs for the trees they destroyed on public lands, the U.S. Treasury would gain and the higher prices for wood products would decrease demand and stimulate greater conservation and use of substitutes. Although more logs were harvested during the 1980s, the number of people employed by the timber industry fell steadily. Meanwhile, one of four logs was exported, and most went to Japan. If the United States and Canada forbade the export of raw logs, the foreign demand for wood products would cause employment to rise in both countries as refined wood products were made at home rather than overseas.

International efforts to address deforestation have been limited. In 1985, the U.N. Food and Agricultural Organization (FAO) submitted the Tropical Forestry Action Plan (TFAP) to offer assistance to governments to preserve their tropical forests. In 1987, 48 national governments set up the International Tropical Timber Organization (ITTO) to encourage sustainable timber harvests.

The most sweeping measure addressing deforestation was the Bush White House proposal at the 1992 Earth Summit, which called for a ban on the cutting of tropical forests and pledged $150 million to aid forestry programs. The tropical forest countries protested the proposal, arguing that they had just as much right to log their forests as oil-producing countries had to pump oil. They also asked where the income forgone from logging would come from and suggested that the advanced industrial nations could pay them not to log if they were so concerned about the issue. Finally, they demanded that the proposed treaty cover temperate as well as tropical forests. The Bush administration did not effectively counter these charges, and the proposal lost its remaining credibility when aerial photos were circulated showing the devastation of America's forests from clear-cutting. The treaty was rejected, and a nonbinding statement simply recommended that countries assess their deforestation and attempt to arrest it. At home the Bush administration did nothing to prevent the destruction of America's national old-growth forests.

Although the tropical forest treaty was rejected at the Earth Summit, a Biodiversity Treaty was signed by 153 countries in which they agreed to preserve plant and animal species by creating and implementing their own management plans. The wealthier countries pledged to help the poorer countries accomplish their biodiversity preservation plans. The Bush administration refused to sign, arguing that the treaty was too vague in detailing how foreign aid would be used and that it would not agree to transferring technology to the Third World without compensation.

Desertification

We in the First World take water and food for granted. We think nothing of turning on the tap and filling our glass, taking long, hot showers, or washing our cars. We also think nothing of going to huge supermarkets that offer tens of thousands of cheaply priced products. These activities may someday be luxuries if the world's population continues to increase, freshwater sources just as steadily dry up, and once productive land is transformed to desert.

Only 20 percent of the earth's surface is land. More than two-thirds of the land's surface is already desert or mountain. Since 1945, over 3 billion acres of land, an area the size of India and China combined, or 11 percent of the world's arable land, has lost all or most of its productivity.[23] Every year, roughly 15 million acres of productive land, an area the size of West Virginia, becomes desert; an additional 50 million acres becomes too degraded to support grazing or crops. As Marlise Simons puts it, "an estimated 24 billion tons of topsoil washes or blows off the land annually—roughly the amount of Australia's wheat land. Each year, the world's farmers must try to feed 88 million more people with 24 billion fewer tons of topsoil."[24] A 1993 U.N. study revealed that *desertification* threatens about 8 billion acres on which 1.5 billion of the world's 6 billion people currently live a largely subsistence existence by raising crops and livestock. When their soils blow away, water holes run dry, and trees are hacked down to stumps, where will all those people go and how will they live? By the year 2030, if current erosion rates continue, the world may have to feed two or three times more people with 960 billion fewer tons of topsoil (more than twice the amount on U.S. farmlands) and total cropland will have fallen by one-third.[25]

Until recently, global food production kept up with the number of new mouths to feed. The global food problem involved distribution rather than production. When droughts and famines occurred around the world, foreign nations that cared tried to redistribute food to the afflicted.[26] However, during the late 1980s and into the 1990s, the world's population began to surpass the amount of food available to feed it.

Global per capita grain consumption fell 2 percent between 1986 and 1990. In 1988, America's grain production fell for the first time in history. Desertification of Africa's Sahel has caused a 28 percent drop in that region's grain production since the 1960s. The result is mass famine and death. Over 100 million Africans are thought to be malnourished. As global food supplies dwindle, prices rise, adding yet another source of debt to many struggling Third World countries.

Soil is one of our most precious natural resources. Trees, brushes, and grasses hold soil in place and absorb water. An inch of soil may take anywhere from 200 to 1,000 years to form. An exposed inch or more of soil can be swept away in one violent storm. In increasing numbers of regions, land is overcultivated, deforested, overgrazed, and/or overirrigated. Overuse erodes the soil; continued overuse converts once productive land to desert. In America's corn and wheat regions, the yield falls by three to six bushels per acre or as much as 6 percent for every inch of topsoil lost. Soil nutrients are further depleted in poor countries that have suffered deforestation. Without wood, the only fuel hundreds of millions of people around the world have to burn is human and animal waste, which would normally be used to fertilize fields. Erosion not only diminishes a land's crop or grazing productivity. When soil has been stripped away to bedrock, water runs off quickly rather than percolating down through the earth to replenish aquifers. The run off collects in huge floods downstream. Between 1960 and 1984, India's flood-prone regions almost tripled from 47 million to 124 million acres.

Fresh water comes from one ultimate source—the sky—which feeds streams, lakes, rivers, fields, reservoirs, and underground aquifers. Fresh water is disappearing for many interrelated reasons. The demand for water increases with a population's numbers and affluence and at some point inevitably overwhelms that region's existing surface and underground supplies.

Most devastated regions can never be restored. The soil has been washed and blown away or become salinated. Surface and underground waters have dried or become polluted. Those people who remain eke out meager existences. There are no financial, technological, or political resources to limit, let alone reverse, the land's steady degradation.

Deforestation and desertification change regional climates. Vegetation and rainfall decrease and increase together, a process known as evapotranspiration. Abundant vegetation absorbs moisture and then releases it back into the air, which causes clouds and more precipitation. As vegetation is destroyed, less water is absorbed and thus less released back into the atmosphere. A related phenomenon is albedo, in which more solar radiation is reflected back into the atmosphere as vegetation decreases, which in turn causes dryer air to sink and rainfall to decline further.

Perhaps nowhere has desertification been more tragic than in the African Sahel, a vast belt of savanna lands south of the Sahara desert. Over the past several decades, the human population has steadily exceeded the Sahel's carrying capacity. The land's grasses have been overgrazed, its trees chopped down for fuel, its soil blown or washed away, and its water drunk dry. The result has been the steady advance of the Sahara desert south and the equally steady march of environmental refugees to lands and cities beyond. Those lands in turn deteriorate as the population swells under the weight of a high birth rate and millions of refugees. This environmental domino effect will become increasingly severe as the population increases and available lands diminish. A fraction of Africa's soil loss represents a gain for others. Winds carry African soils all the way across the Atlantic Ocean to South America and the Caribbean.[27] Most soil, however, ends up in rivers and oceans.

The Sahel is only one of at least several dozen once verdant regions around the world that are becoming desert. The Nile River valley, the north China plains, the Indian subcontinent, the Jordan River valley, and Central Asia are the most prominent regions experiencing rapid desertification. Conflicts over remaining water sources will increase steadily and could be a major cause of future wars.

Egypt is another country highly vulnerable to desertification. In 1999, almost 61 million people were crammed along the tiny ribbon of vegetation and concrete bordering the Nile River, and the population is increasing by one million every nine months. Further up the Nile, Sudan, Kenya, and Ethiopia have embarked on development projects that could divert considerable water from Egyptian homes,

Whither Israel?
Water *and* National Security

Since its creation in 1948, Israel has fought five wars with surrounding Arab states, which, until recently, vowed to destroy that Jewish state. The Arab–Israeli stand-off is further complicated by the reliance of Israel, Lebanon, Jordan, and Syria on the Jordan River. Israel currently takes 95 percent of the Jordan River's waters. Israel's population has increased sixfold since independence. Although Israeli farmers have mastered drip agriculture, which maximizes water efficiency, the increased demand of farmers, factories, and households is rapidly outstripping all available surface and aquifer water sources. Seawater has seeped into and polluted some aquifers as they are drawn down, compounding the shortages. By 2000, Israel's water supply fell as low as 30 percent below demand. Meanwhile, neighboring states are growing just as rapidly in population and will clamor for a greater share of the Jordan River and other regional water sources for themselves. The result could be wars for water.[28]

farms, and factories downstream. To supply households, the Egyptian government may have to cut back water to cotton and sugarcane farmers, which would worsen Egypt's trade deficit and ability to service its $44 billion foreign debt.

Desertification is afflicting the Indian subcontinent. The once vast forest that protected the watersheds of the Ganges, Indus, and Brahmaputra river systems has been decimated, leading to enormous flooding downstream during the monsoon season and droughts at other times. As the populations of India, Pakistan, and Bangladesh rise steadily, the tropical forests are clear-cut, surface and aquifer water sources are polluted or dry up, and once fertile soils erode into barren desert.

China's 1.2 billion people account for one-fifth of the world's total population but have access to only 8 percent of the world's fresh water. Today, in northern China, over 300 cities suffer varying degrees of water shortages, which will worsen as surface and aquifer sources dry up or become fouled. Between 1950 and 1992, the water table below Beijing annually dropped 3 to 6 feet, for a total drop of 16 feet to 160, feet below the surface; meanwhile, Beijing's two reservoirs have frequently dried.

For several decades, the former Soviet Central Asian republics served as the Soviet Union's fruit, vegetable, cotton, and rice basket. But massive irrigation and industrialization projects have converted once rich grasslands and huge freshwater lakes into desert. The Aral Sea region has been the most devastated. The diversion of water from the Aral caused it to rapidly recede and salinate, thus destroying a once rich fishery and ruining much of the surrounding farmland.

The first serious international attempt to identify the desertification crisis and propose possible solutions was a 1977 U.N. conference in Nairobi, which produced the Plan of Action to Combat Desertification. Although the plan presented 28 recommendations, the United Nations and those countries most in need lacked the funds, organization, and political will to implement them. The International Fund for Agricultural Development (IFAD) has set up hundreds of pilot programs to teach peasants more efficient farming methods that conserve rather than exhaust the soil and their own livelihoods, but its efforts remain limited and underfunded. The U.N. Environmental Program estimated that it would take at least $4.5 billion annually for two decades to arrest desertification. That may be an optimistic assessment.

Governments can take many relatively simple measures to conserve water and soil. Contour and terraced plowing, combined with leaving strips of vegetation along and within the plowed lands, can reduce erosion and increase water infiltration into the crops and aquifers. Replanting trees and other vegetation and spreading mulch can slow the erosion of existing soils and begin the centuries-long process of soil creation. Leguminous trees are particularly good at absorbing nitrogen in the air and fertilizing the soil. The most important target for replanting should be the watersheds, where most surface water originates.

Huge water subsidies to farmers are a major reason for the overuse of water and subsequent desertification. If farmers had to pay market rates for water, they would try to conserve it as much as possible. But when they pay water rates as little as 10 percent what households pay, they are encouraged to waste as much of it as possible.

Globally, the amount of irrigated lands increased from 232 million acres in 1950 to 615 million in 1980, a rate faster than population growth. Since then, however, the amount of new irrigated lands has fallen behind population growth. Irrigated lands are generally three times more productive than rain-fed land. Yet this higher productivity can be costly. Improper irrigation techniques can both deplete underground water tables and waterlog and salinate soils. Ironically, while irrigation drains aquifers, the water table may actually rise directly under the irrigated lands. The result is sometimes a waterlogged soil in which crops rot from the roots up, a phenomenon known as a "wet desert." Drip irrigation is much more water conserving than simply flooding a field. Long hoses are stretched along each crop row, and a hole drips water at the root of each plant. The only problem is that it is initially much more expensive.

The *green revolution* of the 1960s was supposed to be the solution to predictions of growing food shortages and famine. New strains of high-yield seeds would dramatically increase farm productivity. The trouble was that these seeds required huge amounts of water and fertilizer to flourish. This was particularly costly for Third World countries, which had to import the fertilizer or divert even more water to farming from other needs. Between 1950 and 1990, world use of artificial fertilizer increased from 14 million to 145 million tons. Without fertilizer, world crop yields would plummet by 40 percent. National debts and degraded lands increased along with crop yields. A second "green revolution" would be based on new strains of seeds that can survive in poor soil with little water and can repel insects and disease.

Yet in the long term these measures will only slow rather than halt desertification. As in all other environmental crises, desertification occurs when a human population exceeds a region's carrying capacity. As long as populations steadily increase, desertification will continue to engulf one region after another around the world, letting loose floods of environmental refugees that soon overwhelm yet another region's carrying capacity. If the world is currently failing to feed all its six billion people, how can it ever feed another three billion by 2050? Thomas Malthus might be right after all.

Aquaculture: Panacea *or* Pandora's Box?

Aquaculture is often touted as the solution to the world's rapidly diminishing fish species. Fish farms for species such as salmon and shrimp have captured 20 percent of the fish food market. The number doubled between 1990 and 1996 to 26 million tons and is expected to rise to 39 million tons by 2010.

What possible objections could be made? Unfortunately, it takes fish to make fish. It seems that fish are cannibals and thrive by munching on their fellow species. About five pounds of fish must be caught and ground into meal for every pound in weight of a farmed fish. Most of those farmed fish are species that humans shun. Fish farms produce pollution, with as much as 300 to 1,000 kilograms of solid waste for each ton of fish harvested. All that fish poop can act as fertilizer for algae blooms that suck the oxygen from the water, killing all other sea life within it. Finally, the farms produce genetically identical fish. Farmed fish mate with wild fish and gradually homogenize the genetic makeup for that species. Why does that matter? There is strength in genetic diversity and weakness in uniformity. If that genetic code proves vulnerable to a disease, the entire species could be wiped out.

The Dying Oceans

Anyone who has ever stood on a beach and gazed out to sea or flown or sailed over it cannot help but feel awe at the ocean's immensity and beauty.[29] Tragically, even the oceans are not indestructible. The scouring of the ocean depths for fish and the drainage of pollution into those waters worsens as the world's population increases.

Fish are a vital food source. About 25 percent of the world's population or over 1.5 billion people rely on fish as their major source of animal protein. Some species are important for more than being part of food chains. For example, oysters filter pollution. The oyster population of Chesapeake Bay was once so abundant that it could clean the entire bay in three days; today it takes the remaining oysters one year.

Between 1950 and 1987, the world fish catch quadrupled from 21 million tons to 84.5 million tons, and is fast approaching the maximum sustainable yield of 100 million tons. Some species have already been devastated by overfishing, which of course puts more pressure on surviving species. Of the world's 280 commercial fish species, only 25 are lightly or moderately exploited while 42 have already been overexploited or depleted. In 1990, the world fish catch declined for the first time in two decades.

The world's fish species are not only rapidly diminishing because of demand, but also because of ecologically destructive fishing methods. Drift net fishing by over 700 Japanese, South Korean, and Taiwanese ships have ravaged many fish species. Drift nets, which are up to 40 miles long, act as huge vacuums that sweep up and kill everything in their way. In 1988, the salmon harvest off Alaska's coast dropped to 12 million from the usual 40 million fish, a population crash attributed to drift net fishing.

Ninjas *versus* Sea Turtles

The hawksbill sea turtle is prized for the combs, handles, and other luxury products that can be carved from its beautiful shell. The harvesting of hawksbill sea turtles is especially gruesome. The fishermen net the turtles as they swim along the ocean surface, drag them on board, rip off the shell, and then toss the dying, bleeding turtle back into the sea. The turtle may linger for hours or even days in agony before they expire or are eaten by a shark attracted by the blood.

It was over the fate of the hawksbill sea turtles that the United States finally got tough. On March 20, 1991, Washington threatened Tokyo with a cutoff on $53 million in imports because Japan continued hunting the endangered and internationally protected hawksbill turtle. Trade of products made from the hawksbill turtle has been illegal since 1975 when more than 100 countries signed the Convention on International Trade in Endangered Species. After weeks of negotiations, Tokyo angrily agreed to stop hunting hawksbill sea turtles. Did the Japanese fulfill their promise? According to environmental groups, the Japanese still profit from that bloody harvest of shells.

Pollution also destroys fish populations or makes them unfit to eat. Human waste released into water can increase nitrogen levels and the algae that feed on nitrogen. When algae blooms, it sucks the oxygen and thus fish life out of the surrounding waters. Many seas and lakes have "died" at least partly from nitrogen algae blooms, such as the Adriatic and Baltic Seas, Lake Erie, and various coastal zones along the United States. The immediate economic losses are in lost fishing and tourist revenue; the long-term losses involve increased fishing pressure on other regions, which may lead to the depletion of those sources.

Other pollutants are also harmful. Heavy metals are released in the oceans by mining, industry, ship discharges, incineration, pesticide runoffs, and other pollution sources. The ocean food chain rests on the tiny zooplankton and phytoplankton that live in the 1/100th-inch-thick microlayer of the ocean's surface. Heavy metals and chemicals such as mercury, lead, copper, PCBs, DTT, cadmium, and zinc concentrate in the microlayer at rates 10 to 10,000 times greater than elsewhere in the ocean. These heavy metals enter the ocean food chain and ultimately human beings, with harmful effects on each link. They have devastated some local animals such as seals in the North and Baltic Seas and beluga whales in the St. Lawrence Seaway, and made it advisable for humans not to eat tuna, swordfish, and other deep-sea fishes more than once a week. Sometimes these chemicals directly harm humans. Between 1953 and 1968, 649 people died from eating mercury-contaminated fish from Minamata Bay in Japan. Every year, about 21 million barrels of oil enter the sea from land runoff and 600,000 barrels are accidentally spilled into the ocean. These oil spills devastate local sea life. Plastic bags can kill animals such as turtles and seals that mistake them for jelly fish. Over 30,000 fur seals die annually from ingesting plastic bags.

Coral reefs, sea grass ranges, and mangroves are the nurseries for much ocean life and have been called the tropical forests of the oceans. Coral reefs alone are home to over one million species and 2,000 kinds of fish. Hundreds of millions of people are directly employed harvesting these species and many more people supplement their diets with seafood from the reefs. Pollution has destroyed hundreds of reefs, grasslands, and mangroves around the world. It is estimated that 100,000 jobs and $80 million in income disappears annually from reef destruction alone, while millions more suffer malnutrition.

The worst threat to the world's oceans is the ozone depletion. The amount of ultraviolet rays striking the earth will increase between 5 to 20 percent over the next half-century. Ultraviolet radiation slows photosynthesis and inhibits phytoplankton growth and mutates its genes. The 15 percent ozone depletion over Antarctica resulted in a 15–20 percent decrease in surface phytoplankton. As the ozone thins over the earth, the phytoplankton will correspondingly die off, which will in turn devastate the entire ocean food chain. This phytoplankton die-off will also exacerbate the greenhouse effect. Until now the oceans have slowed the greenhouse effect by absorbing about 45 percent of the carbon dioxide produced, with phytoplankton the major absorbent. There is no guarantee that phytoplankton ranks could eventually be filled by radiation-resistant species.

Several international agreements have helped to manage ocean fish and natural resources. More than 90 percent of all fish can be found within a couple hundred miles from shore. During the 1970s, increasing numbers of countries declared *exclusive economic zones (EEZs)* of 200 miles from their coastline. Those states then attempted to regulate fishing within their EEZs. That is a nearly impossible task for countries with tiny navies. Even the United States with its huge coast guard and navy cannot prevent poaching within its oceans.

exclusive economic zones (EEZs) the zones by which a government can claim exclusive economic exploitation rights up to 200 miles from that nation's coastline.

The assertion of EEZs was legally codified with the 1982 Law of the Sea Treaty. To date over 70 countries have declared EEZs. The Law of the Sea Treaty calls the oceans beyond the EEZs the "common heritage" of humankind and includes tenets that regulate and distribute the profits of ocean mining, as well as address navigation rights and pollution control. The Reagan and Bush administrations refused to sign the treaty and discouraged others from signing. The Clinton administration did sign the treaty and submitted it to the Senate where right-wing Republicans bottled it up in the Foreign Relations committee, preventing its ratification. The treaty needs about 20 more ratifications before it comes into force.

Another important treaty was the 1972 London Dumping Convention, which bans the dumping of hazardous radioactive, chemical, and heavy metal wastes into the oceans. Since then the treaty has been amended to ban the incineration of trash at sea by 1994 and the discharge of plastic bags and oil by ships.

Even when international treaties are ratified, countries can simply ignore them. For example, in 1982, the International Whaling Commission declared a global moratorium on whaling beginning in 1986. Japan, Norway, and Iceland continued to defy the moratorium, pointing to a loophole that allows each country annually to kill up to 2,000 whales for "scientific" purposes. In 1974 and 1988, the United States threatened to use a 1967 law that allows it to retaliate against nations that hunt endangered species. The whalers ignored the threat and kept whaling. Washington never enforced its own law.

In May 1992, 10 countries—the United States, France, Mexico, Costa Rica, Nicaragua, Panama, Spain, Japan, Venezuela, and Vanuatu—which account for virtually all tuna fishing in the Pacific Ocean, signed a treaty protecting dolphins. This recent agreement follows a 1986 agreement in which dolphin deaths dropped 80 percent up through 1992. It is hoped the present agreement will further reduce dolphin deaths from the current 25,000 level to around 5,000. The

Japan has continued to use drift net fishing despite concerted international demands that it desist. Japanese fishermen account for about half of the Pacific Ocean tuna catch, and Tokyo refused to sign any multilateral treaty restricting its catch or fishing techniques. In September 1989, Japan announced that it would cut its number of fishing boats in the Pacific Ocean using drift nets by two-thirds to 26, the same number that fished there in 1986 before the number shot up to over 60 in 1988. Tokyo's action followed years of international criticism, two months after 15 countries called on Japan to stop its drift net fishing, and pressure by groups in the United States on the government to invoke a 1987 law that would cut imports from countries that used drift nets. Tokyo all along insisted there was no scientific proof that drift nets were as destructive as claimed.

In November 1989, both the United Nations and the annual meeting of the International Fisheries Conference called for a moratorium on the use of drift nets by 1992, citing scientific studies that proved their use annually killed over 80,000 marine mammals such as whales, dolphins, and seals, and a million sea birds.[30] Salmon fisheries were devastated by drift net fishing. In contrast to the huge nets used by the Japanese, American, and Canadian fishermen are limited by law to nets no bigger than 900 feet. American fishermen suffered a huge drop in their salmon catch from 17,000 tons in the early 1980s to 2,500 in 1989. To date Japan still uses drift nets as the ocean's species and foreign fishermen dwindle.

public outcry and boycott of fish from countries that killed dolphins was the most important reason for the treaty.

As with all other environmental catastrophes, the international community has only begun to address the calamity of the world's dying oceans. Some agreements have been negotiated and signed on certain issues. Compliance is scant. What is needed is a comprehensive effort to revive the dying oceans.

Conclusion

A statement concluding the 1990 American Assembly Conference on Preserving the Global Environment captured the threat the environmental crises pose to us all:

> Three indivisibly linked global environmental trends together constitute an increasingly grave challenge to the habitability of the earth. They are human population growth; tropical deforestation and the rapid loss of biological diversity; and global atmospheric change, including stratospheric ozone loss and greenhouse warming. These trends threaten nations' economic potential, therefore their internal political security, their citizens' health (because of increased ultraviolet radiation), and, in the case of global warming, possibly their very existence. No more basic threat to national security exists. Thus, together with economic interdependence, global environmental threats are shifting traditional national security concerns to a focus on collective global security. . . .

The certainty that all nations share a common destiny demands that they work to-gether as partners.[31]

The statement goes on to argue that government agreements are not enough to address these issues—billions of people and millions of businesses around the world must shift their values and behavior from an environmental destruction to reconstruction and preservation.

International cooperation is imperative. Yet although important international steps have already been taken to address some problems, they are dwarfed by the world's interrelated environmental crises. Between the first environmental conference at Stockholm in 1972 and the Earth Summit at Rio de Janeiro in 1992, the world lost 500 million acres of trees, an area one-third the size of the United States, and 500 million tons of topsoil, which would equal the arable land of India and France combined.[32]

Can the world achieve sustainable development in which living standards and quality of life for an increased percentage of the world's population continues to improve while the environment's degradation is halted and ideally reversed? Or will the world's population and development pressures continue to degrade the global environment until living standards and quality of life decay steadily for ever more members of future generations?

The cost of simply slowing the vicious cycle of global environmental crises will be exorbitant. Nations will have to find the political will to devote as much money and effort to cleaning up the earth as they have in destroying it. By one estimate, the advanced industrial and Third World countries will have to annually expend $125 billion and $500 billion, respectively.[33] The largest international environmental program is the $1.3 billion annual budget of the Global Environmental Facility, which is jointly run by the UNEP, World Bank, and U.N. Development Program.

Political inertia remains the biggest obstacle to dealing with these problems. It is much easier to do nothing than to undertake the vast financial and administrative effort needed to address those crises. This "tyranny of the immediate" causes politicians to serve entrenched interest groups rather than the general welfare of present and future generations. Governments, businesses, and people fiddle today, while generations to come will literally burn.

Another problem is how economic growth and environmental destruction are measured. Perceptions precede policy. To act on an issue, one must first perceive it. Our perceptions are shaped by existing methods of analyzing phenomena. Many point out that many of those methods distort our understanding of the real world. Environmentalists argue that economists treat pollution as a free indulgence for business without weighing pollution's often far greater costs for society and eventually the world as a whole. Measurements of a nation's economic size do not account for such losses as clear-cut forests, polluted streams, and eroded soils. Forests, for example, are valued for their "stumpage" or the amount of cut logs and not for their value in protecting watersheds, promoting tourism, filtering pollution, producing medicines, fruits, nuts, fish, game, and biodiversity. The difficulty is in assigning values to these forgone, environmentally sound economic opportunities.

Most countries outright subsidize environmental exploitation and degradation. The United States leases at below market rates or outright gives away its public water, minerals, trees, and grazing land to farmers, loggers, miners, and ranchers, a policy known as *corporate welfare*. If these businesses had to pay the full costs of exploiting these resources, including their depreciation, they would carefully nurture rather than waste these assets. The exploitation of natural resources should reflect its true cost.

Yet there has been some progress. Ever more people understand that development and environmentalism are inseparable, that one nurtures the other. Such practices as reducing waste, conserving forests, recycling, increasing energy efficiency, promoting mass transportation, and so on, actually increase economic growth, diversity, jobs, health, wealth, and national security. Likewise, environmental degradation—pollution, deforestation, desertification, the greenhouse effect, and so on—hurt the economy and national security.

What more can be done? Some have proposed a WTO-style multilateral organization that would confront systematically, rather than piecemeal, the range of global environmental issues. U.N. Secretary-General Boutros Boutros-Ghali opened the 1992 Earth Summit by calling for all nations to embark on the development of "new collective security" in which money now spent on the military would be diverted to addressing the world's environmental crises. Every government must realize that national security ultimately depends on global environmental security, and then act accordingly. Institutions, money, understanding, laws, and enforcement—all are vital to addressing the world's environmental crises. And all are in short supply.

Study Questions

1. What is the "tragedy of the commons?" How does it serve as a metaphor for the fate of the earth?

2. What accounts for the world's population explosion? Describe its most likely consequences. What measures have been taken to slow population growth? Are these enough?

3. Describe the evidence that a "greenhouse effect" is taking place? What will be its most likely consequences? What efforts have been made to slow the greenhouse effect? Are these enough?

4. What accounts for ozone layer depletion? Describe its most likely consequences. What efforts have been made to slow the ozone depletion? Are these enough?

5. List the various forms of pollution and describe how each affects the quality of life and economic development. What efforts have been made internationally and in the United States to slow air and water pollution? Are these enough? Explain your answer.

6. What accounts for deforestation? Describe deforestation's most likely consequences. What efforts have been made to slow deforestation? Are these enough? Explain.

7. What accounts for desertification? Which regions have been the worst hit? Which others are being rapidly turned into desert? Describe desertification's most likely consequence. What efforts have been made to slow desertification? Are these enough? Why or why not?

8. What accounts for the world's dying oceans? What will be the most likely effect if oceans continue to deteriorate? What efforts have been made to slow the deterioration of the oceans? Are these enough? Explain.

9. Describe how all the world's environmental problems are interrelated. Are you relatively optimistic or pessimistic about humanity's ability to overcome these problems? Why?

10. Who should pay for pollution? What level of pollution should be tolerated? Should property owners be free to do as they want on their land? Should they be allowed to pollute and destroy other people's property and lives? Explain your answers.

InfoTrac College Edition Sources

Using the Subject Guide, enter the search terms *global warming, deforestation, desertification, population policy,* and/or *green revolution.*

Agardy, Tundi. "Creating Havens for Marine Life."

Birkland, Thomas A. "In the Wake of the Exxon *Valdez:* How Environmental Disasters Influence Policy."

Brown, Lester R. "Tough Choices: Facing the Challenge of Food Scarcity."

Buell, John. "Global Warning."

Christopher, Warren. "American Diplomacy and the Global Environmental Challenges of the 21st Century."

"Emerging Issues in Environmental Policy."

Ferrante, Francesco. "Induced Technical Change, Adjustment Costs and Environmental Policy Modelling."

Fredriksson, Per G. "The Political Economy of Trade Liberalization and Environmental Policy."

Hildyard, Nicholas. "Too Many for What? The Social Generation of Food 'Scarcity' and 'Overpopulation.'"

Matthew, Richard A. "The Greening of U.S. Foreign Policy."

McArthur, Loren, and Marc Breslow. "Polluters and Politics."

Penz, Peter. "Environmental Victims and State Sovereignty: A Normative Analysis."

Rabe, Barry G. "Federalism and Entrepreneurship: Explaining American and Canadian Innovation in Pollution Prevention and Regulatory Integration."

Raloff, Janet. "Climate Treaty Talks Mark Some Progress."

Soderholm, Patrik. "Pollution Charges in a Transition Economy: The Case of Russia."

On *the* Web

http://www.worldwatch.org/
The Worldwatch Institute

http://www.cnic.org/
National Council for Science and the Environment

http://www.earthtimes.org/
Earthtimes focuses on the global environment and related issues

Contents

Chapter 18 Globalization *and the* 21st Century: Perils *and* Prospects

Key Concepts and Terms

What is *globalization?* Essentially, it is a complete reordering of international priorities, strategies, and values as all states are drawn ever more tightly in the interdependent global economic, technological, communications, cultural, and ethical web. Geoeconomic conflicts over trade, investments, economic strategies, and the global environmental meltdown have become the most important items on the international agenda. Geopolitical conflicts in the Middle East, Yugoslavia, and elsewhere continue to make the headlines, but with the cold war's end few of these conflicts merit the attention they once did. The bipolar world in which most countries associated with one of the two superpowers has split into a geopolitical world dominated by American hegemony and a multipolar geoeconomic world fought over by the United States, European Union, and Japan. Cooperation increasingly characterizes how states handle ever more geopolitical and geoeconomic conflicts. The world is converging politically and economically. Increasing numbers of states are being transformed from authoritarianism to liberal democracy, while slowly or dramatically liberalizing their economies.

What is popularly known as globalization is really just the latest stage in the development of the global political economy forged by Western imperialism and mercantilism over five centuries ago. During that time international relations were thoroughly entangled by geoeconomics and geopolitics. War and threats of war provoked the most vigorous bouts of diplomacy and shifts in international power, but issues of trade, investment, and an array of other geoeconomic issues were always important and became increasingly so. War today is unthinkable for nearly all conflicts among nearly all states. But that reality is the natural outcome of 500 years of deepening and broadening global interdependence.

Even the idea of globalization is not new. Two centuries ago, in 1795, *Immanuel Kant* predicted in his "Essay on Perpetual Peace" that the global political economy would eventually evolve into a system in which conflicts are resolved by peaceful cooperation rather than war.[1] Kant foresaw three developments that would lead to a *perpetual peace:* (1) the conversion of authoritarian states into liberal democracies (republicanism); (2) the evolution of international law and organization into an authoritative system that binds all sovereign states (federalism); and (3) economic development and interdependence (hospitality).

Kant's vision is fast becoming a reality as geoeconomic conflict replaces geopolitics as the dominant force in international relations. Instead of a world whose relations are characterized by violence and anarchy, there is instead an increasingly orderly world in which the nature and effectiveness of power varies according to what the issue is, how other issues and priorities are related to it, and how skillfully the participants bargain.

State goals remain the same: States strive for strategic and economic security. But the means to achieve those ends have greatly changed. Richard Rosecrance neatly summarizes the differences between a geopolitical and geoeconomic outlook:

> In a power world states act as coherent units, force is a usable instrument of policy and there is a hierarchy of international issues dominated by questions of military security. Interdependence refers to a world in which states can no longer fully regulate policy, there are multiple channels of access between societies, no hierarchy of issues, and force is generally unusable. The difference between these two systems concerns the means that are used to advance state interests.[2]

This chapter discusses the changes and continuities in the global political economy and international relations now and into the 21st century.

Geopolitical Conflict *and* Cooperation

THE COLD WAR AND AFTERMATH

In many ways, the 20th century's central struggle has been between two diametrically opposed internationalist visions: *Wilsonianism* and *Leninism*. The ideals enthusiastically espoused by President Woodrow Wilson included political, economic, and national freedom, and international cooperation to resolve conflicts. Vladimir Lenin advocated a contrasting vision characterized by class struggle, revolution and war, and totalitarian state power, which is believed would lead to a classless utopia. That struggle symbolically ended with the Berlin Wall's destruction on November 9, 1989.

Complicating this ideological struggle for the hearts, minds, and pocketbooks of the world's peoples, was the military superpower of the United States and Soviet Union, which championed Wilsonianism and Leninism, respectively. The world entered a new era, the nuclear era, in July 1945 with the explosion of an atomic bomb in New Mexico. By 1949, the Soviet Union too had obtained an atomic bomb, and the nuclear race to acquire ever more and numerous destructive weapons has continued until recently. The nuclear arms race eventually led to the stockpiling of tens of thousands of nuclear weapons, overshadowing all humanity with a potential nuclear holocaust.

The cold war ended with the collapse of communism, the Soviet empire, and Red Army by December 1991. Washington and Moscow are dismantling their vast hoards of nuclear weapons under the INF, START I, and START II treaties. In their 1992 "Camp David Declaration on New Relations," President George Bush and President Boris Yeltsin declared that "Russia and the United States do not regard each other as potential adversaries."

The cold war was not a war in the traditional sense. During the almost five decades in which they were mortal enemies, the United States and Soviet Union never directly fought each other. Deterrence, not conquest, was cold war's essence. When the Soviet empire and communism crumbled, no American troops swept triumphantly into Moscow and the other former Soviet capitals. Instead, Russia and the other former communist states are being revolutionized by international corporate and financial leaders.

New Conceptions *of* War, Peace, *and* National Security

The cold war's end and globalization's relentless pace rendered military means irrelevant for resolving nearly all international conflicts. Although power is still the currency of international relations, the nature of the conflicts and the means by which states assert their interests is rapidly changing. *National security* traditionally meant freedom from the threat of foreign attack. Today and into the future, an ever smaller fraction of international conflicts will be over territory and ideology.

Globalization, however, does not necessarily mean any lessening in the number or intensity of wars occurring around the world. Nearly all these wars will be internal rather than international, with peoples tearing apart the often highly artificial nation-states imposed on them in decades past. Long-suffering minorities—or in the case of Kosovars, majorities—will revolt against the dominant nationality.

national security those measures necessary to protect a nation's vital geoeconomic and geopolitical interests.

Edward Luttwak is among those who sees profound changes in the nature of international conflict in the post–cold-war era:

> Except in those unfortunate parts of the world where armed confrontations or civil strife persist for purely regional or internal reasons, the waning of the Cold War is steadily reducing the importance of military power in world affairs. . . . Everyone, it appears, now agrees that the methods of commerce are displacing military methods—with disposable capital in lieu of firepower, civilian innovation in lieu of military-technical advancement, and market penetration in lieu of garrisons and bases.[3]

Why are wars such as Iraq's invasion of Kuwait and the subsequent international coalition against Iraq increasingly anachronistic? In an interdependent world, states can much more cheaply acquire through trade, diplomacy, and other means the security, wealth, and prestige that they formerly won through the use of force. The world's greatest military powers, the United States and Russia, are rapidly demobilizing their once vast conventional and nuclear forces, and other states are reducing their own bloated military budgets. Without the cold war, militant states can no longer play off the two superpowers against each other to receive huge amounts of economic and military aid.

Certainly the world does appear to be moving into a new and unprecedented age of cooperation. By the hour the first bombs dropped on January 16, 1991, President Bush had rallied 40 nations to his alliance to liberate Kuwait from Iraq. In a richly symbolic sequence, the president first sought U.N. approval for an economic blockade and possible military attack on Iraq before asking Congress for a similar green light. Also telling was the White House's need to pass the hat to its allies to help pay for the war. The United States is no longer the economic superpower it was at the cold war's beginning when it could single-handedly contribute $17 billion to western Europe and $2 billion to Japan to stimulate their reconstruction and prosperity, a combined figure that in today's dollars would be over $225 billion.

For those international and civil wars that do occur, the United Nations has taken the lead in mitigating the violence and finding solutions. The United Nations is conducting more peace keeping missions than ever—16 ongoing missions in the year 2000, Only budget constraints prevent more missions. In 1999, the United Nations authorized NATO to stop Yugoslavia from the "*ethnic cleansing*" of the Albanians who made up 90 percent of the population of its Kosovo province. NATO defeated Yugoslavia with bombs alone. That dazzling success might encourage dictators to think twice before they engage in ethnic "cleansing" elsewhere, although whether or not they go through with it depends on how far they are from the reach of NATO and CNN. There are clearly financial, political, economic, and military limits to international police forces either directly deployed or deputized by the United Nations. The rest of the world stood aside and watched as Russia fought wars in 1997 and 1999–2000 with separatists in its province of Chechnya. Unlike Yugoslavia, Russia is a nuclear power with an arsenal as deadly as America's. Military power will remain a potent force in international relations for the foreseeable future.

THE TRIUMPH OF LIBERAL DEMOCRACY

One place war will not intrude is in relations among liberal democratic countries. Since 1815, liberal democracies have never fought each other. Thus the more countries that achieve liberal democracy, the less chance for war. Mixing Hegel's notion that history moves by the clash of ideas with Kant's notion of perpetual peace, Francis Fukuyama writes, "the triumph of the West, of the Western idea, is evident . . . in the total exhaustion of viable systematic alternatives to Western liberalism."[4] According to Fukuyama, liberal democracy has emerged triumphant from 7,000 years of a dialectical struggle between different ideologies. History is ending in a Hegelian sense and bringing with it an unprecedented and unending era of peace among humanity.

Any victory celebration over liberal democracy's triumph is premature. Although liberal democracy is solidly rooted in North America, Europe, and Japan, and versions have spread to more than 60 percent of the world's states, authoritarian regimes control the other 40 percent of countries. Nonetheless, the liberal democratic tide does seem irreversible. What explains the democratic revolution? Is democracy for everyone?

Certainly there is a link between economic prosperity and political freedom. When people have one, most inevitably desire the other. Although most cultures do not have democratic values of political equality and liberty, democracy has become a universal good. Virtually every regime, even the most despotic, claims to be democratic in some ways. And as Fukuyama and others have pointed out, there is no universal alternative to democracy.

So has the nature of international relations and power changed fundamentally in an increasingly interdependent world? Will the collapse of communism and the Soviet empire prove to be the "end of history" as all states sooner or later adopt liberal democracy and relatively open economies? Or could the world descend once more into the maelstrom of global geopolitical conflicts? Will new ideologies arise to divide nations against each other, and provoke them to war over real and perceived differences?

SOVEREIGNTY AT BAY: INTERDEPENDENCE, INTEGRATION, AND DISINTEGRATION

Many analysts join Fukuyama in the belief that the global system is undergoing changes as profound as those following the 1648 Treaty of Westphalia, which inaugurated the modern nation-state system. With the cold war's end, the United Nations has embarked on an unprecedented series of peacekeeping ventures. Meanwhile, the world becomes ever more tightly knit economically, politically, environmentally, and socially. Regional political economic communities such as the European Union (EU) and North American Free Trade Association (NAFTA) broaden their membership and relations. Like war, is the nation-state rendered increasingly obsolete as globalization transforms the world?

National sovereignty is eroding steadily as the world becomes more interdependent. Even the most authoritarian governments are barely able to stem the influx of goods, services, investments, immigrants, drugs, pop culture, pollution, disease, money, and so on, and the outflow of technology, skilled workers and scientists, money, and secrets. International law, morality, and opinion are increasingly important constraints on state behavior. Mass communications have put every government, even the most oppressive, in media fishbowls, in which their gaffes and crimes are inevitably exposed to the world. Whether the world intervenes or not is another matter. It all depends on the power and interests of the states capable of doing so.

The nation-state is being pulled in two directions—globalization and nationalism. Even as most states are being drawn ever closer either with formal links—as is the European Union, or with interdependence, many are falling apart.[5] Within a century there may well be twice as many states as today. Nation-states will be at once more numerous and less sovereign than they are today.

What role will the United Nations, other international organizations, and international law play in globalization? Most states already obey international law most of the time, nearly all states are members of the United Nations, and most states enjoy membership in dozens of international organizations. Will this growing matrix of international organizations and law eventually develop into a world federation in which states abandon their sovereignty and accept the decisions of a global government? How interdependent can we truly become? Can diverse peoples ever truly understand and empathize with one another?

These questions can only be answered with time. One thing is certain, the nature of international relations and the world is rapidly changing.

Dilemmas *of* Development

Globalization is not painless. Jobs are lost as well as created. Venerated traditions erode, disappear, or transform. Those hooked in the web fear computer viruses and invasions of privacy. Ever more people and prosperity are destroying the environment. Although enjoying unprecedented affluence and comfort, many people living in modern industrial countries at times feel overwhelmed and imprisoned by vast economic, political, and social institutions and forces beyond their control. At times, it is not clear whether development exists for the sake of humanity, or humanity for the sake of development.[6]

The Faust story best illustrates this modern dilemma. Living on the threshold of the industrial revolution, *Faust* is a "Renaissance Man:" a doctor, philosopher, scientist, and professor. But as the story opens he is locked in his room and experiencing a midlife crisis. Something profound seems missing from his life. Empty at the core, he contemplates suicide. Church bells, which remind him of his lost, beautiful childhood, save him as he recognizes that something magical exists beyond the sterile world of his study. Marshall Berman summarizes Faust's transformation:

> In his first phase, he lived alone and dreamed. In his second period, he intertwined his life with the life of another person, and learned to love. Now, in his last incarnation, he connects his personal drives with the economic, political, and social forces that drive the world; he learns to build and to destroy. He expands the horizon of his being from private to public life, from intimacy to activism, from communion to organization. He pits all his powers against nature and society; he strives to change not only his own life but everyone else's as well. Now he finds a way to act effectively against the feudal and patriarchal world: to construct a radically new social environment that will empty the old world out or break it down.[7]

To accomplish his dreams, he makes a pact with the devil Mephistopheles and his supernatural powers. Their talents complement each other—Faust the visionary and organizer, Mephistopheles the cynical, selfish, and unscrupulous implementer.

The same spirit to destroy and create has driven all the great developers, whether their projects have been successful or not. Stalin and Mao dreamed of achieving a communist utopia. To achieve their visions, they had tens of millions of people murdered, imprisoned, or worked and starved to death. But state ownership and management of production and lives proved to be an abject failure. Roosevelt's Manhattan project to create an atomic bomb, Kennedy's Apollo project to put a man on the moon, and Reagan's Strategic Defense Initiative to create an anti-nuclear shield over the United States all were animated by their respective visions to transform the world.

Nothing illustrates the Faustian dilemma of modern humanity greater than nuclear power. Alvin Weinberg, the director of the Oak Ridge Laboratory, captured this dilemma: "We nuclear people have made a Faustian bargain with society. On the one hand, we offer—in the catalytic nuclear burner—an inexhaustible source of energy. . . . But the price we demand of society for this magical energy source is both a vigilance and a longevity of social institutions that we are quite unaccustomed to."[8] The world could still end with a nuclear holocaust.

What Will Become *of the* Earth?

If things eventually get worse rather than better, environmental rather than nuclear devastation will be the most likely cause. In an increasingly interdependent world, national security and *world security* become increasingly indistinguishable, especially in environmental issues. The world's gravest challenge involves slowing and ideally halting the earth's ecological destruction. Although humanity remains shadowed by the threat of nuclear holocaust, another Chernobyl rather than Hiroshima disaster is more likely. Over the past few decades ever more individuals and governments became aware of the calamitous nature of the greenhouse effect, ozone layer depletion, overpopulation, desertification, deforestation, and biocide. Yet awareness is only the first step. States and individuals must not only act on that awareness but they must act decisively. But decisive action seems beyond the power of humanity and the states in which they live.

Like Immanuel Kant, *Thomas Malthus* made predictions two centuries ago that reverberate today. But Malthus was as pessimistic as Kant was optimistic about the fate of humanity. He believed that the world's population will eventually exceed its ability to feed itself. Ultimately, Malthus may be right about the earth's inability to sustain a continuing swelling population that may well soar beyond 9 billion people over the next half century.

All human activities have an environmental impact, some relatively benign and others destructive. Every ecosystem has a particular *carrying capacity* or threshold beyond which too many humans or animals living there will destroy it. As the greenhouse effect, ozone depletion, deforestation, desertification, and other environmental calamities reveal, the world's population has already exceeded the earth's carrying capacity. Can we any longer speak of national interests in an age of worsening environmental crises that engulf us all?

For decades, grassroots environmental organizations in the United States, Europe, and elsewhere have struggled to make environmental problems a global priority. The cold war's end has finally brought environmental issues to the center of the world's political stages. The 1992 Rio de Janeiro Earth Summit, attended by representatives of 178 countries, created a nearly unanimous global consensus on the environmental crises and how to address them. The heart of the conference was the signing of two treaties that pledged to achieve significant reduction in

carrying capacity the amount of related life an ecosystem can bear. If too many species exceed the carrying capacity, it will degrade and possibly destroy that ecosystem. The world is one vast ecosystem whose carrying capacity is being overwhelmed as the population soars past six billion and pollution causes the greenhouse effect, ozone depletion, desertification, deforestation, biocide, and other catastrophes.

greenhouse pollution and to protect biodiversity. President George Bush played the spoiler in both treaties, refusing to ratify the biodiversity treaty and ensuring that there were no timetables or incentives for compliance with the global warming treaty. Under a new president, Bill Clinton, the United States did sign two new global warming treaties, at Kyoto in December 1997 and Buenos Aires in November 1998, both of which did provide strict timetables. But in the face of strong right-wing ideological opposition, President Clinton did not submit those treaties to the Senate for ratification.

The United States has not been the only country dragging its feet on environmental issues. At the Rio de Janeiro conference, the representatives signed the nonbinding "Agenda 21," an 800-page set of analysis and proposals. The trouble was not in creating a consensus on what was wrong and how to fix it, but acquiring the political will to act on that understanding. The estimated cost of enacting the agenda was $125 billion a year, three times the size of the world's combined foreign aid budgets and equal to 1 percent of the advanced industrial countries' GNPs.

Few governments are willing to make the short-term sacrifices vital for the planet's long-term survival. The world's poorer countries argue that environmental treaties place an unfair financial burden on them, and that the wealthier nations should pay for the antipollution technology and related costs that the poorer countries are required to adopt. While most governments continue to fiddle over environmental threats, the earth burns, at times literally.

Will the meager environmental measures states have taken prove to be too little too late? Can the earth sustain the ever more billions of people making demands on it? Will the increased competition for scarce resources unravel the recent gains in international cooperation?

Conclusion

Modernization's relentless pace accelerated during the 20th century. For the previous four hundred years, the global political economy had expanded through the stimulus of European imperialism, trade, and industrialization. Then, during the 20th century, a range of new ideological, technological, military, political, economic, and social forces arose that threatened to tear the global political economy apart or drastically alter its power structure. If the 19th century (1815 to 1914) was the "age of optimism," the 20th century (1914–1999) was an "age of anxiety" if not downright pessimism as one world war was followed, after a decade of relative prosperity, by global depression and an even more devastating world war, and then by a cold war and nuclear arms race that threatened to destroy all humankind.

Yet enormous positive achievements flowed from the late 20th century: an expanding interdependent global economy in which an increasing percentage of humankind lived prosperous stable lives; the breakup of the Western and Soviet empires, resulting in the emergence of over 135 new countries; the toppling of one authoritarian regime after another around the world to be replaced by liberal democracies; and the development of new technologies and medicines that prolong and enhance our lives.

On October 12, 1992, the 500th anniversary of Columbus's journey to the western hemisphere, NASA pointed huge radio interceptors toward the Milky Way in hopes of picking up an intergalactic message from a distant civilization. From the first humans through today, people have wondered whether there was another presence in the universe. Now we have the means to find out. Someday intergalactic relations may become as important as international relations today.

Meanwhile, the world's inhabitants must find better ways of dealing with deepening environmental crises, along with such perennial problems as war, economic conflict, disease, immigration, drugs, exploitation, and poverty, to name some of the more prominent. International relations occur in a system that is still largely characterized by "few restraints on the behavior of individual actors; mutual suspicion and competition; the need to provide for one's own security; self-interest as a guide to policy; the duty to protect one's citizens; the pain associated with miscalculation; the reluctance to depend on others; and difficulties pertaining to the judgement of what is morally proper in an international context."[9] Henry Kissinger captured the essence of these problems when he declared that we "are stranded between old conceptions of political conduct and a wholly new conception, between the inadequacy of the nation-state and the emerging imperative of global community."[10] The new century we have just entered could be an age of unprecedented international cooperation and peaceful management of most problems. Or it could be the opposite.

Despite the deepening interdependence among all peoples, can we ever truly know another? Cultures, just like individuals, are unique and endless complexes of values, perceptions, and behavior that we can never truly understand. Theodore Von Laue argues that there are "no cultural universals providing a common language for transcultural understanding; like poetry, cultures are not translatable. We have no choice but to interpret the others by our own lights."[11] And therein lies most of the trouble.

Study Questions

1. What is globalization? What are the major international issues and challenges in the 21st century?

2. What is the "Faustian" dilemma of development?

3. Define Wilsonianism and Leninism. How did the conflict between them shape international relations?

4. What was Immanuel Kant's vision for the world? Is it being realized? Explain.

☝ InfoTrac College Edition Sources

Using the Subject Guide, enter the search terms *cold war, ethnic cleansing, Francis Fukuyama,* and/or *international economic relations.* Using Keywords, enter the search term *New World Order.*

Atkinson, Glen. "The Political Economy of Liberalization and Regulation: Trade Policy for the New Era."

Billoud, Guy D. "Implications for International Business of European Economic and Monetary Unification."

"EMU and the World Economy."

Hedley, R. Alan. "Technological Diffusion or Cultural Imperialism? Measuring the Information Revolution."

"Is the World Economy Headed into Receivership?"

James, Harold. "Is Liberalization Reversible?"

"Questioning Globalization."

Roberts, Michael. "Scandinavia in the European World-Economy, ca. 1570–1625: Some Local Evidence of Economic Integration."

Wang, Zhen Kun. "Integrating Transition Economies into the Global Economy."

Wheeler, Mark. "Is the World Economy More Integrated Today Than a Century Ago?"

On *the* Web

http://www.nato.int/
NATO website

http://www.constitution.org/kant/perpeace.htm
Kant's entire "Essay on Perpetual Peace"

http://www.mason.gmu.edu/~ffukuyam/index.html
The home page of Francis Fukuyama

Notes

PART ONE

1. In this scenario and in Chapter 1, we refer to many terms that will be discussed in depth in later chapters. We define here only those terms necessary to make a start. If you're curious in the meantime, please see the Glossary.

Chapter 1

1. For an excellent overview, see Robert Jackson and Georg Sorenson, *Introduction to International Relations* (New York: Oxford University Press, 1999).

2. Thucydides, *The Peloponnesian War* (London: Penguin, 1979); Niccolò Machiavelli, *The Prince*, 1513 (New York: Oxford University Press, 1984); Thomas Hobbes, *Leviathan*, 1651 (Oxford, England: Blackwell, 1946); Hans Morgenthau, *Power Among Nations: The Struggle for Power and Peace*, 6th ed. (New York: Knopf, 1985).

3. Kenneth Waltz, *Theory of International Politics* (New York: McGraw-Hill, 1979); Thomas Schelling, *The Strategy of Conflict* (Cambridge, MA: Harvard University Press, 1980).

4. Robert Keohane and Joseph Nye, *Power and Interdependence: World Politics in Transition* (Boston: Little, Brown, 1977); Richard Rosecrance, *The Rise of the Trading State: Commerce and Conquest in the Modern World* (New York: Basic Books, 1986); Ernst Haas, *The Obsolescence of Regional Integration Theory* (Berkeley: Institute of International Studies, 1975); Hedley Bull, *The Anarchical Society: A Study of Order in International Relations* (London: Macmillan, 1995).

5. Jacob Cooke, ed., *The Reports of Alexander Hamilton* (New York: Harper & Row, 1964); Friedrich List, *The National System of Political Economy* (New York: Kelly, 1966); Chalmers Johnson, *MITI and the Japanese Miracle: The Growth of Industrial Policy* (Stanford, CA: Stanford University Press, 1982); William Nester, *Japanese Industrial Targeting: The Neomercantilist Path to Economic Superpower* (New York: St. Martin's Press, 1991); William Nester, *American Power, the New World Order, and the Japanese Challenge* (London: Macmillan, 1993); William Nester, *Power Across the Pacific: A Diplomatic History of American Relations with Japan* (New York: New York University Press, 1996).

6. Adam Smith, *The Wealth of Nations*, 1776 (New York: Modern Library, 1937); David Ricardo, *The Principles of Political Economy and Taxation*, 1817 (London: Dent, 1973); Gertrude Himmelfarb, ed., *Essays on Politics and Culture: John Stuart Mill* (New York: Anchor, 1963); Milton Friedman, *Capitalism and Freedom* (Chicago: University of Chicago, 1962).

7. Vladimir I. Lenin, *Imperialism: The Highest Stage of Capitalism* (New York: International Publishers, 1939); Immanuel Wallerstein, *The Modern World System* (New York: Academic Press, 1974); Fernando Enrique Cardoso, *Dependency and Development in Latin America* (Berkeley: University of California Press, 1980); Andre Gunter Frank, *Crisis in the World Economy* (London: Heinemann, 1980).

8. Charles Kindleberger, *The World in Depression, 1929–1939* (Berkeley: University of California Press, 1973); Robert Gilpin, *War and Change in World Politics* (Cambridge, England: Cambridge University Press, 1981); Susan Strange, *States and Markets: An Introduction to International Political Economy* (London: Pinter, 1988); Robert Keohane, *After Hegemony: Cooperation and Discord in the World Political Economy* (Princeton, NJ: Princeton University Press, 1984); Stephen Krasner, *International Regimes* (Ithaca, NY: Cornell University Press, 1983).

9. David Easton, *A Framework for Political Analysis* (Englewood Cliffs, NJ: Prentice Hall, 1965); Morton Kaplan, *System and Process in International Relations* (New York: Wiley, 1965).

10. Richard Cox with Timothy J. Sinclair, *Approaches to World Order* (Cambridge, England: Cambridge University Press, 1996); Andrew Linklater, *Beyond Realism and Marxism: Critical Theory and International Relations* (Basingstoke, England: Macmillan, 1990); Jean François Lyotard, *The Postmodern Condition: A Report on Knowledge* (Manchester, England: Manchester University Press, 1984); John A. Vasquez, *Classics of International Relations* (Upper Saddle River, NJ: Prentice Hall, 1996); J. G. Ruggie, *Constructing the World Polity: Essays on International Institutionalization* (London: Routledge, 1998); Andrew Wendt, "Constructing International Politics," *International Security* 20(1):71–81.

Chapter 2

1. For a brilliant discussion of modernity that has inspired much of the following discussion, see Marshall Berman, *All That Is Solid Melts into Air: The Experience of Modernity* (New York: Simon & Schuster, 1982); For an excellent analysis of the premodern features of non-Western states, see Janet Abu-Lughod, *Before European Hegemony* (New York: Oxford University Press, 1989).
2. Henry David Thoreau, *"Walden" and "Civil Disobedience,"* 1854 and 1849 (New York: Norton, 1966).
3. See Robert Tucker, ed., *The Marx-Engels Reader,* 2nd ed., (New York: Norton, 1978), pp. 475–476; W. G. Runciman, ed. *Max Weber: Selections in Translation* (New York: Cambridge University Press, 1978).
4. Sigmund Freud, *Civilization and Its Discontents,* 1930 (New York: Norton, 1962).
5. Franz Kafka, *The Trial,* 1925 (New York: Vintage Books, 1974); *The Castle,* 1926 (Avon, CT: Limited Editions, 1975).
6. T. S. Eliot, *The Waste Land,* 1922 (New York: Chelsea House, 1986); Herbert Marcuse, *One-Dimensional Man* (Boston: Beacon Press, 1964).
7. Michel Foucault, *Politics, Philosophy, Culture* (New York: Routledge, 1988).
8. Alvin Toffler, *Future Shock* (New York: Bantam Books, 1971).
9. See Friedrich Nietzsche, *Thus Spake Zarathustra: A Book for All and None,* 1883–1892 (New York: Penguin Books, 1978).
10. Tucker, pp. 475–476.
11. Quoted in Berman, p. 37.
12. For an excellent analysis of this question, see Paul Kennedy, *The Rise and Fall of the Great Powers* (New York: Random House, 1987).
13. Thomas Aquinas, *"Summa Theologica,"* 1266–73 in A. E. Moore, ed., *Early Economic Thought* (Cambridge, MA: Harvard University Press, 1924), p. 54.
14. *Cambridge Economic History of Europe,* vol. 2 (Cambridge, England: Cambridge University Press, 1952), p. 134.
15. Robert Heilbroner, *The Making of Economic Society* (Englewood Cliffs, NJ: Prentice Hall, 1987), p. 45.
16. Kirkpatrick Sale, *The Conquest of Paradise* (New York: Knopf, 1990), p. 41.
17. Kennedy, p. 27.
18. Theodore Von Laue, *The World Revolution of Westernization* (New York: Oxford University Press, 1987), p. 38.
19. See Skinner and Wilson, *Essays on Adam Smith* (Oxford, England: Clarendon Press, 1975).
20. Albert Bergesen and Ronald Schoenberg, "Long Waves of Colonial Expansion and Contraction" in Albert Bergesen, ed., *Studies of the Modern World System* (New York: Academic Press, 1980), p. 231–277.
21. Heilbroner, p. 77.
22. Quoted in Tucker, pp. 473–475.
23. See Phyllis Deane, *The First Industrial Revolution* (Cambridge, England: Cambridge University Press, 1965); David Landes, *Prometheus Unbound* (Cambridge: Cambridge University Press, 1969); Nathan Rosenberg and L. E. Birdzell Jr., *How the West Grew Rich* (New York: Basic Books, 1986).
24. Heilbroner, p. 78.
25. Kennedy, p. 151.
26. Arthur Louis Dunham, *The Industrial Revolution in France, 1815–1848* (New York: Exposition Press, 1955), p. 432; Kennedy, p. 149.
27. For an excellent account, see Alfred D. Chandler, *The Visible Hand: The Managerial Revolution in American Business* (Cambridge, MA: Harvard University Press, 1977).
28. Heilbroner, p. 105.
29. Ibid., p. 113.
30. Ibid., p. 115.
31. Adolf A. Berle and Gardiner C. Means, *The Modern Corporation and Private Property* (New York: Macmillan, 1948), p. 46.
32. Quoted in Richard Hofstadter, *The Age of Reform* (New York: Knopf, 1955), p. 231.
33. Adam Smith, *The Wealth of Nations,* 1776 (New York: Modern Library, 1937), p. 460.
34. Ibid., p. 734.
35. Benjamin Disraeli, *Selected Papers of the Late Right Honorable the Earl of Beaconsfield,* ed. T. E. Kebbel (London: 1889, vol. 2), p. 534.
36. Benjamin Cohen, *The Question of Imperialism* (New York: Basic Books, 1973).
37. Kennedy, p. 150.
38. Ibid., pp. 148–149.
39. Ibid., p. 153.
40. Karl Pearson, *National Life from the Standpoint of Science* (London: 1901), p. 21.
41. Quoted in Von Laue, p. 42.
42. For an excellent discussion of the relationship between economic, political, and social development, see Barrington Moore, *The Social Origins of Dictatorship and Democracy* (Boston: Beacon Press, 1966).
43. Heilbroner, p. 168.
44. Kennedy, p. 330.
45. Quoted in George L. Mosse, *Masses and Man* (New York: Howard Fertig, 1980), p. 101.
46. Von Laue, p. 109.

47. Quoted in Franz Schurmann and Orville Schell, eds., *The China Reader: Republican China* (New York: Vintage Books, 1967), p. 184.
48. Immanuel Geiss, *The Pan-African Movement* (London: Macmillan, 1974), pp. 229–230.
49. Ibid., p. 230.
50. Quoted in Arthur Mann, *The One and the Many* (Chicago: University of Chicago Press, 1979), p. 69.

PART TWO

Chapter 3

1. Walter Connor, "Nation-Building or Nation-Destroying," *World Politics* 24(1972): 319–355. Also in Fred Sondemann et al., eds., *The Theory and Practice of International Relations* (Englewood Cliffs, NJ: Prentice Hall, 1979).
2. John Clements, *Clements' Encyclopedia of World Governments,* vol. 7 (Dallas: Political Research, Inc., 1986); see such earlier similar studies as that by Walter Connor.
3. Ted Gurr and James R. Scarritt, "Minorities at Risk: A Global Survey," *Human Rights Quarterly* 11(1989): 375–405; see also Ted Gurr, "Ethnic Warfare and the Changing Priorities of Global Security," *Mediterranean Quarterly* 1(1990):81–98.
4. Theodore Von Laue, *The Revolution of Westernization* (New York: Oxford University Press, 1987), p. 375.
5. See Leon A. Festinger, *A Theory of Cognitive Dissonance* (Stanford, CA: Stanford University Press, 1957); Robert A. Wickland and Jack W. Brehm, *Perspectives on Cognitive Dissonance* (Hillsdale, NJ: Lawrence Erlbaum Associates, 1976), and Eddie Harmon-Jones and Judson Mills, eds. *Cognitive Dissonance: Progress on a Pivotal Theory in Social Psychology* (Washington, DC: American Psychological Association, 1999).
6. Lyman Sargent, *Contemporary Political Ideologies* (Pacific Grove, CA: Brooks/Cole, 1990), pp. 10–11.
7. John Stoessinger, *The Might of Nations* (New York: Random House, 1989), p. 10.
8. Hedley Bull, *Anarchical Society* (London: Macmillan, 1977), p. 8. See also Charles Tilly, *The Formation of Nation-States in Western Europe* (Princeton, NJ: Princeton University Press, 1975); William H. McNeil, *The Pursuit of Power* (Chicago: University of Chicago Press, 1982); Hedley Bull and Adam Watson, eds., *The Expansion of International Society* (Oxford, England: Clarendon Press, 1984); Alan James, *Sovereign Statehood* (London: Allen & Unwin, 1986); Michael Mann, *States, War, and Capitalism* (Oxford, England: Basil Blackwell, 1988); Yale Ferguson and Richard Mansbach, *The State, Conceptual Chaos, and the Future of International Relations* (Boulder, CO: Lynne Rienner, 1989); Charles Tilly, *Coercion, Capital, and European States, A.D. 990–1990* (Oxford, England: Blackwell, 1990); Charles Gochman and Alan Ned Sabrosky, eds., *Prisoners of War? Nation-States in the Modern Era* (Lexington, MA: Heath, 1990).

8. For an interesting discussion, see George Sabine, *A History of Political Theory* (Hinsdale, IL: Dryden Press, 1973), chapter 21.

Chapter 4

1. Hans Morgenthau, *Politics Among Nations: The Struggle for Power and Peace,* 5th ed. (New York: Knopf, 1973), p. 28.
2. Harold Laswell, *Politics: Who Gets What, When, and How* (New York: Smith, 1936, 1950).
3. Morgenthau, p. 9.
4. Robert Dahl, "The Concept of Power," *Behavioral Science* 2 (1957): 202.
5. Kenneth Waltz, "America's European Policy Viewed in Global Perspective," in Wolfram F. Hanrieder, ed. *The United States and Western Europe,* (Cambridge, MA: Winthrop, 1974), pp. 13–14.
6. Karl Deutsch, *Analysis of International Relations* (Englewood Cliffs, NJ: Prentice Hall, 1968), pp. 21–39.
7. C. W. Maynes, "Logic, Bribes, and Threats," *Foreign Affairs* 60 (1985): 111–129.
8. John M. Rothgeb Jr., *Defining Power: Influence and Force in the Contemporary International System* (New York: St. Martin's, 1993), p. 141.
9. Robert Art and Kenneth Waltz, "Technology, Strategy, and the Use of Force," in Robert Art and Kenneth Waltz, eds., *The Use of Force: International Politics and Foreign Policy* (Boston: Little, Brown, 1971), p. 6.
10. Among others, see R. J. Rummel, "Indicators of Cross-National and International Patterns," *American Political Science Review* 63 (1969): 127–147. James Lee Ray and J. David Singer, "Measuring the Concentration of Power in the International System," *Sociological Methods and Research* (May 1973), pp. 403–436; Ray Cline, *World Power Trends and U.S. Foreign Policy for the 1980s* (Boulder, CO: Westview Press, 1980); Jacek Kugler and Richard Arbetman, "Choosing Among Measures of Power: A Review of the Empirical Record," and Richard Merritt and Dina Zinnes, "Alternative Indexes of National Power," in Richard Stoll and Michael Ward, eds., *Power in World Politics* (Boulder, CO: Rienner, 1989); David Baldwin, *Paradoxes of Power* (New York: Blackwell, 1991); Michael Sullivan, *Power in Contemporary International Politics* (Columbia: University of South Carolina Press, 1990); Ken Booth, ed., *New Thinking About Strategy and International Security* (London: Unwin Hyman Academic, 1991).
11. James Lee Ray, *Global Politics* (Boston: Houghton Mifflin, 1990).
12. Jack Sawyer, "Dimensions of Nations: Size, Wealth, and Politics," *American Journal of Sociology* 73 (1967): 145–172.
13. Wolfram Hanrieder, ed. *Comparative Foreign Policy: Theoretical Essays* (New York: McKay, 1971), p. 1280.
14. Halford Mackinder, *Democratic Ideals and Reality* (New York: Holt, 1919), p. 150.

15. Alfred T. Mahan, *The Influence of Seapower upon History, 1660–1783* (Boston: Little, Brown, 1965), p. 29.

16. Nicholas Spykman, *America's Strategy in World Politics* (New York: Harcourt Brace, 1942), p. 472.

17. Steven Rosen, "War Power and the Willingness to Suffer," in Bruce Russet, ed., *Peace, War, and Numbers* (Beverly Hills, CA: Sage, 1972).

18. J. F. C. Fuller, *Tanks in the Great War, 1914–1918* (London: Murray, 1920), p. 320.

19. Paul Smith, *On Political Warfare* (Washington, DC: National Defense University Press, 1988).

20. Theodore Von Laue, *The Revolution of Westernization* (New York: Oxford University Press, 1987), p. 376.

21. Quoted in ibid., p. 338.

22. Paul Kennedy, *The Rise and Fall of the Great Powers* (New York: Random House, 1987), p. 439.

23. Quoted in Geoffrey Parker, *Europe in Crisis, 1559–1659* (London: Macmillan, 1979), p. 238.

24. Kennedy, p. 53.

25. Thomas G. Paterson, J. Garry Clifford, and Kenneth J. Hagan, *American Foreign Policy: A History,* vol. 2 (Lexington, MA: Heath, 1983), p. 245.

26. Kennedy, p. 55.

27. Ibid., p. 49–55.

28. Ibid., p. 440.

29. U.S. Arms Control and Disarmament Agency, *World Military Expenditures and Arms Transfers 1989* (Washington, DC: U.S. Government Printing Office, 1990), p. 3; (United Nations Development Programme, 1997).

30. Cynthia Cannizzo, "The Costs of Combat: Death, Duration, Defeat," in J. David Singer, ed., *The Correlates of War II: Testing Some Realpolitik Models* (New York: Free Press, 1980).

31. Zeev Moaz, "Resolve, Capabilities, and Interstate Disputes," in A. F. K. Organski and Jacek Kugler, eds., *The War Ledger* (Chicago: University of Chicago Press, 1980).

32. Andrew Mack, "Why Big Nations Lose Small Wars: The Politics of Asymmetrical Conflict," *World Politics* 27 (1975): 197.

33. Joseph Nye, *Understanding International Conflicts: An Introduction to Theory and History* (New York: Addison Wesley, 1999), p. 55.

34. For a discussion of the balance of power in history, see Quincy Wright, *A Study of International Relations* (New York: Appleton, 1955); see also Claude Inis, *Power and International Relations* (New York: Random House, 1962).

35. For a good critique, see Ernst Haas, "The Balance of Power: Prescription, Concept, or Propaganda?" *World Politics* 5 (1953): 442–477.

36. See A. F. K. Organski, *World Politics* (New York: Knopf, 1968), p. 294; Morgenthau, p. 213.

37. Organski, p. 294.

38. Ray, p. 538.

39. David Rapkin, William Thompson, and Jon Christopherson, "Bipolarity and Bipolarization in the Cold War Era: Conceptualization, Measurement, and Validation," *Journal of Conflict Resolution* 23 (1979): 261–296.

40. William Riker, *The Theory of Political Coalitions* (New Haven, CT: Yale University Press, 1962), pp. 32–33; See also Stephen Watt, *The Origin of Alliances* (Ithaca, NY: Cornell University Press, 1987).

41. Randolph Silverson and Michael Tennefoss, "Power, Alliances, and the Escalation of National Conflict, 1815–1965," *American Political Science Review* 78 (December 1984): 1063.

42. Bruce Bueno de Mesquita, *The War Trap* (New Haven, CT: Yale University Press, 1981).

43. Quoted in Robert Tucker and David Hendrickson, "Thomas Jefferson and American Foreign Policy," *Foreign Affairs* 69, no. 2 (Spring 1990): 138.

44. Ibid., 147.

45. George Kennan, *The Fateful Alliance: France, Russia, and the Coming of the First World War* (New York: Pantheon, 1984), p. 238.

46. See Richard Starr, "The Warsaw Pact Organization," in Francis Beer, ed., *Alliances* (New York: Holt, Rinehart, and Winston, 1970).

47. Bruce Russett and Harvey Starr, *World Politics: The Menu for Choice* (New York: Freeman, 1992), p. 89.

48. Niccolò Machiavelli, *The Prince and "The Discourses"* (New York: Modern Library, 1950), p. 310; some of the following discussion and statistics were culled from William Nester, *American Power, The New World Order, and the Japanese Challenge* (New York: St. Martin's Press, 1993), and William Nester, *European Power and the Japanese Challenge* (New York: New York University Press, 1993).

49. Richard Rosecrance, *The Rise of the Trading State: Commerce and Conquest in the Modern World* (New York: Basic Books, 1986), p. 13. See also Aaron Friedberg, "The Changing Relationship Between Economics and National Security," *Political Science Quarterly* 106 (1991): 265–276; Ethan Kapstein, *The Political Economy of National Security: A Global Perspective* (New York: McGraw-Hill, 1992); Clyde Prestowitz, Ronald Morse, and Alan Tonelson, eds., *Powernomics: Economics and Strategy After the Cold War* (Lanham, MD: Madison Books, 1991).

50. Rosecrance, p. 310.

51. Robert Isaak, *International Political Economy: Managing World Economic Change* (Englewood Cliffs, NJ: Prentice Hall, 1991), pp. 30–31.

52. Chalmers Johnson, John Zysman, and Laura Tyson, *Politics and Productivity: The Real Story of Why Japan Works* (Cambridge, MA: Ballinger, 1989), pp. 43–50.

53. See my books *American Power, The New World Order, and the Japanese Challenge* (New York: St. Martin's Press, 1993); *Japanese Industrial Targeting: The Neomercantilist Path to Economic Superpower* (New York: St. Martin's, 1992); *Japan and the Third World: Patterns, Power, Prospects* (New York: St. Martin's, 1992); *The Foundation of Japanese Power: Continuities, Changes,*

Challenges (Armonk, NY: Sharpe, 1991); *Japan's Growing Power over East Asia and the World Economy: Ends and Means* (New York: St. Martin's, 1991); *European Power and the Japanese Challenge* (New York: New York University Press, 1993).

54. Unless otherwise indicated, all statistics have been culled from *Entering the 21st Century: World Development Report, 1999/2000* (New York: Oxford University Press, 1999); *Human Development Report 1999* (New York: Oxford University Press, 1999); and John Allen, *Student Atlas of World Politics* (Boston: Duskin/McGraw-Hill, 2000).

55. Spyros Makridakis, "Competition and Competition," in Spyros Makridakis et al., eds., *Single Market Europe* (San Francisco: Jossey-Bass, 1991), pp. 47, 50.

56. Robert Reich, "The Quiet Path to Technological Pre-eminence," *Scientific American* 48 (October 1989), p.43.

57. Robert Gilpin, *France in the Age of the Scientific State* (Princeton, NJ: Princeton University Press, 1968), p. 25.

58. Klaus Knorr, *The Power of Nations, The Political Economy of International Relations* (New York: Basic Books, 1975), p. 3.

59. Ibid., pp. 4–5.

60. Nye, p. 99.

61. Gary Clyde Hufbauer et al. *Economic Sanctions Reconsidered: History and Current Policy* (Washington, DC: Institute for International Economics, 1990).

62. Shintaro Ishihara and Akio Morita, *The Japan That Can Say "No,"* trans. Frank K. Baldwin (New York: Simon & Schuster, 1991), p. 18.

63. Charles Ferguson, "America's High Tech Decline," *Foreign Policy* (Spring 1989): 123, 125, 129.

64. Prestowitz, pp. 11, 27.

65. Pat Choate, *Agents of Influence: How Japan's Lobbyists in the United States Manipulate America's Political and Economic System* (New York: Knopf, 1990).

66. Morgenthau, p. 9.

Chapter 5

1. For some excellent recent overviews of foreign policy making and implementation, see Margaret Hermann and Charles Hermann, "Who Makes Foreign Policy Decisions and How: An Empirical Inquiry," *International Studies Quarterly* 33 (1989): 316–388; Roger Hillsman, *The Politics of Policy Making in Defense and Foreign Affairs: Conceptual Models and Bureaucratic Politics* (Englewood Cliffs, NJ: Prentice Hall, 1990); Irving Janis, *Crucial Decisions: Leadership in Policymaking and Crisis Management* (New York: Free Press, 1989); Lloyd Jensen, *Explaining Foreign Policy* (Englewood Cliffs, NJ: Prentice Hall, 1982); Bahgat Korany, *How Foreign Policy Decisions Are Made in the Third World* (Boulder, CO: Westview Press, 1986); Jonathan Roberts, *Decision-Making During International Crises* (New York: St. Martin's Press, 1988).

2. Paul Kennedy, *Rise and Fall of the Great Powers* (New York: Random House, 1988).

3. Raymond Aron, *Peace and War: A Theory of International Relations* (New York: Doubleday, 1966), pp. 91–92.

4. See Wolfram Hanrieder, ed., *Comparative Foreign Policy: Theoretical Essays* (New York: McKay, 1971); R. J. Rummel, *The Dimensions of Nations* (Beverly Hills, CA: Sage, 1972); James Rosenau, ed., *Comparing Foreign Policies: Theories, Findings, and Methods* (Beverly Hills, CA: Sage, 1974); Robert Wendzel, *International Relations: A Policy-Maker Focus* (New York: Wiley, 1980); James Caporaso et al., "The Comparative Study of Foreign Policy," *International Studies Notes* 13.2 (1987): 32–46.

5. The classic realist study is Hans Morgenthau, *Politics Among Nations: The Struggle for Power and Peace, 6th ed.* (New York: Knopf, 1985).

6. Henry Kissinger, *The White House Years* (Boston: Little, Brown, 1979), p. 37.

7. Ted Sorensen, *Decision-Making in the White House* (New York: Columbia University Press, 1963), pp. 19–20.

8. George Kennan, *American Diplomacy, 1900–1950* (Chicago: University of Chicago Press, 1951), pp. 65–66.

9. Quoted in Carlton Hayes, *The Historical Evolution of Modern Nationalism* (New York: Macmillan, 1950), p. 40.

10. Quoted in Winston Churchill, *The Gathering Storm* (Boston: Houghton Mifflin, 1948), p. 315.

11. Cordell Hull, *The Memoirs of Cordell Hull* (New York: Macmillan, 1948), pp. 1314–1315.

12. Graham Allison, *Essence of Decision* (Boston: Little, Brown, 1971); for a recent analysis of the crisis, see James G. Blight and David A. Welch, *On the Brink: Americans and Soviets Re-Examine the Cuban Missile Crisis* (New York: Hill & Wang, 1989).

13. Among the more prominent works on the relationship between psychology, policymaking, and politics, see Ole Hosti, "The Belief System and National Image: A Case Study," *Journal of Conflict Resolution* 6 (1962): 244–252; Alexander George and Juliette George, *Woodrow Wilson and Colonel House: A Personality Study* (New York: Day, 1956); Margaret Hermann, "Explaining Foreign Policy Behavior Using the Personality Characteristics of Policy Leaders," *International Studies Quarterly* 24.1 (1980):7–46; Joseph DeRivera, *The Psychological Dimension of Foreign Policy* (Columbus, OH: Merrill, 1968); Robert Jervis, *Perception and Misperception in World Politics* (Princeton, NJ: Princeton University Press, 1976); Pamela J. Conover and Stanley Feldman, "How People Organize the Political World: A Schematic Model," *American Journal of Political Science* 28 (1984): 95–126; Jon Hurwitz and Mark Peffley, "Public Images of the Soviet Union: The Impact of Foreign Policy Attitudes," *Journal of Politics* 52 (1990): 3–28; James Kuklinski, Robert Luskin, and John Bolland, "Where Is the Schema? Going Beyond the 'S' Word in Political Psychology," *American Political Science Review* 85 (1991): 1341–1355.

14. Kenneth Boulding, "National Images and International Systems," *Journal of Conflict Resolution* 3 (1959): 120–131.
15. Alexander George, "The Operational Code," *International Studies Quarterly* 13.2 (1969).
16. Ole Hosti, "The 'Operational Code' Approach to the Study of Political Leaders: John Foster Dulles' Philosophical and Instrumental Beliefs," *Canadian Journal of Political Science* 3.1 (1970): 123–157.
17. Doris Kearns, *Lyndon Johnson and the American Dream* (New York: Harper & Row, 1976), p. 264.
18. Charles Kegley and Eugene Wittkopf, *World Politics: Trend and Transformation* (New York: St. Martin's Press, 1992), p. 17.
19. Kissinger, p. 1202.
20. Irving Janis, *Groupthink: Psychological Studies of Policy Decisions and Fiascoes* (Boston: Houghton Mifflin, 1982).
21. See Allison's examples and Morton Halperin, *Bureaucratic Politics and Foreign Policy* (Washington, DC: Brookings Institute, 1974).
22. Morton Halperin, "Why Bureaucracies Play Games," *Foreign Policy* 2 (1971): 83.
23. Glenn Hastedt, "Controlling Intelligence: Values and Perspectives of Administration," paper presented at the International Studies Association, Washington, DC, April 1987; James Risen, "CIA Counters Critics of Its Cold War Work," *New York Times* November 21, 1999.
24. Pat Choate, *Agents of Influence* (New York: Basic Books, 1991).
25. Thomas Risse-Kappen, "Public Opinion, Domestic Structure, and Security Policy in Liberal Democracies: France, Japan, West Germany, and the United States," paper presented at the International Studies Association, Washington, DC, April 1990.
26. Kenneth Waltz, "Realist Thought and Neorealist Theory," in Robert Rothstein, ed., *The Evolution of Theory in International Relations* (Columbia: University of South Carolina Press, 1991), pp. 21–38.
27. John Ruggie, "Continuity and Transformation in the World Polity: Toward a Neorealist Synthesis," *World Politics* 35(1983):261–285.
28. Kenneth Waltz, *Theory of International Politics* (Reading, MA: Addison-Wesley, 1979), p. 110.
29. Charles McClelland and Gary Hoggard, "Conflict Patterns in the Interaction Among States," in James Rosenau, ed. *International Politics and Foreign Policy*, rev. ed. (New York: Free Press, 1969), pp. 711–724; See also Arnold Wolfers, "The Pole of Power and the Pole of Indifference," in James Rosenau, ed., *International Politics and Foreign Policy* (New York: Free Press, 1961); R. J. Rummel, "Dimensions of Conflict Within and Between States," *General Systems Yearbook*, 8 (1963):1–50; R. J. Rummel, Stephen Salmore, and Donald Munton, "An Empirically Based Typology of Foreign Policy Behavior," in James Rosenau, ed., *Comparing Foreign Policies: Theories, Findings, and Methods* (Beverly Hills, CA: Sage, 1974).
30. Michael Brecher, Jonathan Wilkenfeld, and Sheila Maser, *Crises in the Twentieth Century, Vol. 1: Handbook of International Crises* (London: Pergamon Press, 1988).
31. Kissinger, p. 627.
32. The term *satisfice* was popularized by Herbert Simon, *Models of Man* (New York: Wiley, 1957), p. 89.
33. See Marc Trachtenberg, "The Meaning of Mobilization in 1914," *International Security* 15.3 (1990–1991) and Jack Levy, "Preferences, Constraints, and Choices in July 1914," *International Security* 16.1 (1991).
34. Henry Kissinger, *Years of Upheaval* (Boston: Little, Brown, 1982), p. 167.
35. Quoted in Arthur Schlesinger, *A Thousand Days: John F. Kennedy in the White House* (Greenwich, CT: Fawcett, 1967), p. 395.
36. Kenneth Waltz, *Theory of International Politics*, p. 17.

PART THREE

Chapter 6

1. For some recent excellent studies of international law, see Antonio Cassese, *International Law in a Divided World* (New York: Oxford University Press, 1989); David Forsythe, *The Politics of International Law: U.S. Foreign Policy Reconsidered* (Boulder, CO: Rienner, 1990); Werner Levi, *Contemporary International Law: A Concise Introduction* (Boulder, CO: Westview Press, 1990); Daniel Patrick Moynihan, *On the Law of Nations* (Cambridge, MA: Harvard University Press, 1990).
2. Quoted in Gerhard Von Glahn, *Law Among Nations* (New York: Macmillan, 1992), p. 32.
3. For an excellent overview of the neorealist perspective, see Eugene V. Rostow, *Law, Power, and the Pursuit of Peace* (Lincoln: University of Nebraska Press, 1968).
4. Irving Janis, *Crucial Decisions: Leadership in Policymaking and Crisis Management* (New York: Free Press, 1989), p. 11.
5. Quoted in Janis, p. 36.
6. 1969 I.C.J. Reports 4, 43.
7. Quoted in Michael Akehurst, *A Modern Introduction to International Law* (London: Allen & Unwin, 1987), p. 32.
8. Quoted in Janis, p. 38.
9. 6 F.R.D. 69, 110 (1946).
10. 1979 I.C.J. Reports 7, 19.
11. Quoted in Janis, p. 51.
12. Akehurst, p. 8.
13. Quoted in Janis, p. 93.
14. LeRoy Bennett, *International Organizations: Principles and Issues* (Englewood Cliffs, NJ: Prentice Hall, 1988), pp. 173–177.
15. Akehurst, p. 91.
16. John Rouke, *International Politics* (Guilford, CT: Dushkin, 1991), p. 27.

17. Jimmy Carter, "December 6, 1978 Speech," *Department of State Bulletin* (January 1979), p. 2.
18. Cyrus Vance, "The Human Rights Imperative," *Foreign Policy* 63 (1986): 11.
19. George Shultz, "Morality and Realism in American Foreign Policy," *Department of State Bulletin* (December 1985), p. 247.
20. See Christopher Joyner, "The Reality and Relevance of International Law," in Charles W. Kegley and Eugene R. Wittkopf, eds., *The Global Agenda* (New York: McGraw-Hill, 1992), pp. 202–215.

Chapter 7

1. Some of the best recent books on international organizations include Leroy A. Bennett, *International Organizations: Principles and Issues,* 5th ed. (Englewood Cliffs, NJ: Prentice Hall, 1991); Inis Claude, *States and the Global System: Politics, Law, and Organization* (New York: St. Martin's Press, 1988); Ernst Haas, *When Knowledge Is Power: Three Models of Change in International Organization* (New York: Council on Foreign Relations, 1990); Terry Nardin and David R. Matel, eds., *Traditions of International Ethics* (Cambridge, England: Cambridge University Press, 1992); Paul Taylor and A. J. R. Grooms, eds., *International Institutions at Work* (New York: St. Martin's Press, 1988).
2. David Mitrany, *A Working Peace* (Chicago: Quadrangle, 1966), p. 11.
3. See the *Yearbook of International Organizations* (Brussels: Union of International Organizations, 1990).
4. Theodore Couloumbis and James Wolfe, *Introduction to International Relations: Power and Justice* (Englewood Cliffs, NJ: Prentice Hall, 1990), p. 271.
5. Irving Janis, *Crucial Decisions: Leadership in Policymaking and Crisis Management* (New York: Free Press, 1989), p. 142.
6. Mitrany, p. 11.
7. See Francis W. Hinsley, *Power and the Pursuit of Peace: Theory and Practice in the History of Relations Between States* (Cambridge, England: Cambridge University Press, 1963).
8. Sally Morphet, "The Significance and Relevance of the Security Council and its Resolutions and Vetoes," paper presented to the International Studies Association, London, March 1989.
9. Miguel Marin-Bosch, "How Nations Vote in the General Assembly of the United Nations," *International Organization* 41 (1987): 713–718.
10. Quoted in the *New York Times* October 25, 1990.
11. Walter Jones, *The Logic of International Relations* (New York: HarperCollins, 1991), p. 569.
12. Ernst Haas, *Why We Still Need the United Nations: The Collective Management of International Conflict, 1945–1984* (Berkeley, CA: Institute of International Studies, 1986), p. 17.
13. John Rouke, *International Politics on the World Stage* (Boston: McGraw-Hill, 1999), p. 444.
14. For an excellent evaluation of collective security, see Inis Claude, *Swords into Plowshares: The Problems and Progress of International Organizations* (New York: Random House, 1984).
15. Haas, *When Knowledge Is Power,* p. 17.

PART FOUR

1. Elaine Sciolino and Michael Wines, "Bush's Greatest Glory Fades as Questions on Iraq Persist," *New York Times,* June 27, 1992.
2. Elaine Sciolino, "Bush Ordered Iraqis Plied with Aid," *New York Times,* May 28, 1992.
3. Sciolino and Wines.
4. Thomas Friedman and Patrick Tyler, "From the First, U.S. Resolves to Fight," *New York Times,* March 3, 1991.
5. For an account analyzing the effectiveness of America's high-tech weapons, see Eric Schmitt, "Missile's War Record Revised," *New York Times,* April 7, 1991. For an account analyzing the war's economic costs to the region and beyond, see Youssef Ibrahim, "Gulf War Is Said to Have Cost the Region $676 Billion in 1990–91," *New York Times,* April 22, 1993.

Chapter 8

1. Some material and ideas from this chapter were taken from William Nester, *American Power, The New World Order, and the Japanese Challenge* (New York: St. Martin's, 1993). For some recent prominent works on war and peace, see Robert Gilpin, *War and Change in World Politics* (Cambridge, England: Cambridge University Press, 1981); Michael Howard, *"The Causes of War" and Other Essays* (Cambridge, MA: Harvard University Press, 1983); Robert J. Art and Kenneth Waltz, eds., *The Use of Force: International Politics and Foreign Policy* (Lanham, MD: University Press of America, 1983); Melvin Small and J. David Singer, eds., *International War* (Homewood, IL: Dorsey Press, 1985); John Stoessinger, *Why Nations Go to War* (New York: St. Martin's, 1985).
2. James E. Dougherty and Robert L. Pfaltzgraff, *Contending Theories of International Relations* (New York: Harper & Row, 1990), p. 337.
3. Quincy Wright, *A Study of War,* vol. 1 (Chicago: University of Chicago Press, 1942), p. 17.
4. Lewis F. Richardson, *Statistics of Deadly Quarrels* (Pittsburgh: Boxwood Press, 1960).
5. Clyde Eagleton, *International Government* (New York: Ronald Press, 1948), p. 393.
6. Karl von Clausewitz, *On War,* 1833 (New York: Random House, 1943), p. 5.
7. Kenneth Waltz, *Man, the State, and War* (New York: Columbia University Press, 1959).
8. Ibid. p. 3.
9. Sigmund Freud, *The Standard Edition of the Complete Psychological Works of Sigmund Freud,* ed. James Strachey, vol. 22 (London: Hogarth, 1964), p. 199.

10. Konrad Lorenz, *On Aggression* (New York: Harcourt Brace Jovanovich, 1966); see also Robert Ardrey, *The Territorial Imperative* (New York: Atheneum, 1966).

11. Adolf Hitler, *Mein Kampf* (Boston: Houghton Mifflin, 1943), p. 134.

12. B. F. Skinner, *Beyond Freedom and Dignity* (New York: Knopf, 1971).

13. Margaret Mead, "War Is Only an Invention," in Leon Bramson and George W. Goethals, eds., *War Studies from Psychological, Sociology, Anthropology* (New York: Basic Books, 1968), pp. 269–274.

14. Jack Levy, "The Causes of War: A Review of Theories and Evidence," in Philip Tetlock et al., eds., *Behavior, Society, and Nuclear War* (New York: Oxford University Press, 1989), p. 271.

15. Clyde Kluckhohn, *Mirror for Man: A Survey of Human Behavior and Social Attitudes* (Greenwich, CT: Fawcett World Library, 1960).

16. For a study indicating that chemical imbalances may be responsible for aggressive behavior, see Douglas Masden, "A Biochemical Property Relative to Human Power Seeking," *American Political Science Review* 79 (June 1985), pp. 448–457.

17. R. T. Green and G. Santori, "A Cross Cultural Study of Hostility and Aggression," *Journal of Peace Research* 1 (1969).

18. Otto Klineberg, *The Human Dimension in International Relations* (New York: Holt, Rinehart, and Winston, 1964); Albert Somit, "Humans, Chimps, and Bonobos: The Biological Basis of Aggression, War, and Peacemaking," *Journal of Conflict Resolution* 34 (1990): 553–583.

19. See Margaret G. Hermann and Thomas W. Milburn, *A Psychological Examination of Political Leaders* (New York: Free Press, 1977).

20. Theodore Abel, "The Element of Decision in the Pattern of War," *American Sociological Review* 6 (1941): 855.

21. For an in-depth analysis of the role of misperception and war, see John Stoessinger, *Why Nations Go to War* (New York: St. Martin's Press, 1985); see also Jack S. Levy, "Misperception and the Causes of War," *World Politics* (October 1983); Herbert Kelman, ed., *International Political Behavior* (New York: Holt, Rinehart, and Winston, 1965); Herman Kahn, *On Escalation* (New York: Praeger, 1965).

22. Arthur Gladstone, "The Conception of the Enemy," *Journal of Conflict Resolution* 3 (1959): 132.

23. R. Paul Shaw and Yuma Wong, "Ethnic Mobilization and the Seeds of Warfare: An Evolutionary Perspective," *International Studies Quarterly* (March 1987), pp. 5–32.

24. Georg Simmel, *Conflict and the Web of Group-Affiliations* (New York: Free Press, 1964), p. 93.

25. Geoffrey Blainey, *The Causes of War* (New York: Free Press, 1988), pp. 71–86.

26. Randolph Rummel, "Dimensions of Conflict Behavior Within and Between Nations," *General Systems: Yearbook of the Society for the Advancement of General Systems*

Theory, vol. 8 (1963); Raymond Tanter, "International War and Domestic Turmoil: Some Contemporary Evidence," in Hugh Davis Graham and Ted Robert Gurr, eds., *Violence in America: Historical and Comparative Perspectives, A Report to the National Commission on the Causes and Prevention of Violence June 1969* (New York: New American Library, 1969).

27. Jonathan Wilkenfeld, "Domestic and Foreign Conflict Behavior of Nations," *Journal of Peace Research* 1 (1968): 55–59.

28. See Crane Brinton, *The Anatomy of Revolution* (New York: Vintage, 1965; Ted Gurr, *Why Men Rebel* (Princeton, NJ: Princeton University Press, 1970); Donald M. Snow, *Uncivil Wars: International Security and the New Internal Conflicts* (Boulder, CO: Lynne Rienner, 1996).

29. Gurr, p. 14; Singer, pp. 66–72; Project Ploughshares, *Armed Conflicts Report 1999*, http://www.ploughshares.ca/content/ACR/ACR99.html, p. 4. See also Loren Thompson, ed., *Low Intensity Conflict: The Pattern of Warfare in the Modern World* (Lexington, MA: Heath, 1989); Richard Little, *Intervention: External Involvement in Civil Wars* (Totowa, NJ: Rowman and Littlefield, 1975); Peter Calvert, *Revolution and International Politics* (New York: St. Martin's Press, 1984); Joseph Whelan and Michael Dixon, *The Soviet Union in the Third World: Threat to World Peace* (New York: Pergamon-Brassey's, 1986).

30. Michael Doyle, "Kant, Liberal Legacies, and Foreign Affairs," *Philosophy and Foreign Affairs* 12 (1987): 227–231.

31. Zeev Maoz and Nasrin Abdolali, "Regime Types and International Conflict, 1816–1976," *Journal of Conflict Resolution* 33 (1989): 35.

32. Jack Levy, "Domestic Politics and War," *Journal of Interdisciplinary History* 18.1 (1988): 661–662.

33. Melvin Small and J. David Singer, "The War-Proneness of Democratic Regimes, 1816–1965," *Jerusalem Journal of International Relations* 1 (1976): 50–69. See also Steve Chan and Erich Weede, "Mirror, Mirror on the Wall . . . Are the Freer Countries More Pacific?" *Journal of Conflict Resolution* 28 (1984); William Domke, *War and the Changing Global System* (New Haven, CT: Yale University Press, 1988).

34. R. J. Rummel, "Libertarianism and International Violence," *Journal of Conflict Resolution* 27 (1983): 27–71; R. J. Rummel, "A Test of Libertarian Propositions on Violence," *Journal of Conflict Resolution* 29 (1985): 419–455.

35. Levy, "Domestic Politics and War," p. 661.

36. Michael Doyle, "Kant, Liberal Legacies, and Foreign Affairs," *Philosophy and Public Affairs* 12.2 (1987): 325.

37. The classic study was Quincy Wright, *A Study of War* (Chicago: University of Chicago Press, 1942).

38. Ruth Sivard, *World Military and Social Expenditures 1979* (Leesburg, VA: World Priorities, 1979), p. 3.

39. Melvin Small and J. David Singer, *Resort to Arms: International and Civil Wars, 1816–1990* (Beverly Hills,

Notes

CA: Sage, 1991); Project Ploughshares, *Armed Forces Report 1999*, http://www.ploughshares.ca/content/ACR/ACR99.html, pp. 5–6.

40. Wright, Small and Singer, p. 58.

41. Lewis Richardson, *Statistics of Deadly Quarrels* (Pittsburgh: Boxwood, 1960).

42. Ernst Haas, "The Balance of Power: Prescription, Concept, and Propaganda," *World Politics* 5 (1953): 442–477.

43. A. F. K. Organski, *World Politics* (New York: Knopf, 1968); Hans Morgenthau, *Politics Among Nations* (New York: Knopf, 1967).

44. See Richard Rosecrance, "Bipolarity, Multipolarity, and the Future," *Journal of Conflict Resolution* 10 (1966): 314–327.

45. See Michael Wallace, *War and Rank Among Nations* (Lexington, MA: Heath, 1973); Edward L. Morse, *Modernization and the Transformation of International Relations* (New York: The Free Press, 1976); A. F. K. Organski and Jacek Kugler, *The War Ledger* (Chicago: University of Chicago Press, 1980); Jack Levy, "Declining Power and the Preventive Motive for War," *World Politics* (October 1987), pp. 82–107.

46. Organski and Kugler, p. 61.

47. J. David Singer, Stuart Bremer, and John Stuckey, "Capability Distribution, Uncertainty, and Major Power War," in Bruce Russet, ed., *Peace, War, and Numbers* (Beverly Hills, CA: Sage, 1972). For other attempts to measure the frequency of war, see Melvin Small and J. David Singer, *Resort to Arms: International and Civil Wars, 1816–1980* (Beverly Hills, CA: Sage, 1982) and Richard J. Stoll, "Bloc Concentration and Dispute Escalation Among the Major Powers, 1830–1965," *Social Science Quarterly* 65 (1984): 48–59.

48. John A. Vasquez, "Capability, Types of War and Peace," *Western Political Quarterly* 39 (1986).

49. Karl Deutsch and J. David Singer, "Multipolar Power Systems and International Stability," in James Rosenau, ed., *International Politics and Foreign Policy* (New York: Free Press, 1969). See also Kenneth Waltz, "International Structure, National Force, and the Balance of World Power," in James Rosenau, ed., *International Politics and Foreign Policy* (New York: Free Press, 1969).

50. Waltz, "International Structure."

51. Jack Levy, "The Polarity of the System and International Stability: An Empirical Analysis," in Alan Sabrowsky, ed., *Polarity and War: The Changing Structure of International Conflict* (Boulder, CO: Westview Press, 1985) 59; see also Jack Levy, *War in the Modern Great Power System 1495–1975* (Lexington: University of Kentucky Press, 1983); Alan Ned Sabrosky, ed., *Polarity and War: The Changing Structure of International Relations* (Boulder, CO: Westview Press, 1985); Michael Haas, "International Subsystems: Stability and Polarity," *American Political Science Review* 64 (1970); Bruce Bueno de Mesquita, "Systematic Polarization and the Occurrence of War," *Journal of Conflict Resolution* 22 (1978); William Thompson, "Cycles, Capabilities, and

War: An Ecumenical View," in William Thompson, ed., *World System Analysis: Competing Perspectives* (Beverly Hills, CA: Sage, 1983).

52. Karl Deutsch, "Quincy Wright's Contribution to the Study of War: A Preface to the Second Addition," *Journal of Conflict Resolution* 14 (1970): 474–475.

53. Organski and Kugler.

54. See J. F. C. Fuller, *Armament and History: A Study of the Influence of Armament on History from the Dawn of Classical Warfare to the Second World War* (London: Eyre & Spottiswoode, 1945); William F. Ogburn, ed., *Technology and International Relations* (Chicago: University of Chicago Press, 1949); John U. Nef, *War and Human Progress* (Cambridge, MA: Harvard University Press, 1950); Bernard Brodie and Fawn Brodie, *From the Cross Bow to the H-Bomb* (New York: Dell, 1962).

56. Charles Gochman and Zeev Maoz, "Militarized Interstate Disputes, 1816–1976: Procedures, Patterns, and Insights," *Journal of Conflict Resolution* 28 (1984): 585–616.

57. Some leading explorations of hegemonic stability theory include George Modelski, *Exploring Long Cycles* (Boulder, CO: Lynne Rienner, 1987); William Thompson, *On Global War: Historical-Structural Approaches to World Politics* (Columbia: University of South Carolina Press, 1988); David Rapkin, ed., *World Leadership and Hegemony* (Boulder, CO: Lynne Rienner, 1990). For theories of wars occurring in generations, in which peace lasts only so long as the memory of the last war's horrors remain vivid and a new leadership seeks to glorify itself through success in war, see Frank Denton and Warren Philips, "Some Patterns in the History of Violence," *Journal of Conflict Resolution* 1.2 (1968). See also Oswald Spengler, *The Decline of the West* (New York: Knopf, 1926); J. E. Moval, "The Distribution of Wars in Time," *Journal " of the Royal Statistical Society* 112 (1949): 446–458.

58. Jack Levy, "Long Cycles, Hegemonic Transitions, and the Long Peace," in Charles Kegley, ed., *The Long Postwar Peace* (New York: HarperCollins, 1991), pp. 154–155.

59. Joshua Goldstein, *Long Cycles: Prosperity and War in the Modern Age* (New Haven, CT: Yale University Press, 1988), pp. 436–437.

60. Jack S. Levy and T. Clifton Morgan, "The War-Weariness Hypothesis: An Empirical Test," *American Journal of Political Science* (February 1986), pp. 26–49.

61. Ibid.

62. The term *security dilemma* was introduced in John Herz, *Political Realism and Political Idealism* (Chicago: University of Chicago Press, 1951); the term *spiral model,* in Robert Jervis, *Perception and Misperception in World Politics* (Princeton, NJ: Princeton University Press, 1976).

63. The psychology of the prisoner's dilemma is explored through game theory. See Thomas Schelling, *The Strategy of Conflict* (Cambridge, MA: Harvard University

Press, 1960); Muzafer Sherif et al., *Intergroup Conflict and Cooperation: The Robber's Cave Experiment* (Norman: University of Oklahoma Press, 1961); Robert Jervis, "Cooperation Under the Security Dilemma," *World Politics* 30.2 (1978): 167–214.

64. Nazli Choucri and Robert North, *Nations in Conflict* (San Francisco: W. H. Freeman, 1975), p. 218; See also Bruce Russett, "International Interactions and Processes: The Internal versus External Debate Revisited," in Ada Finifter, ed., *Political Science: The State of the Discipline* (Washington, DC: American Political Science Association, 1983).

65. Lewis Richardson, *Arms and Insecurity* (Pittsburgh: Boxwood, 1960); Samuel Huntington, "Arms Races: Prerequisites and Results," in Robert J. Art and Kenneth Waltz, eds., *The Use of Force* (Boston: Little, Brown, 1971), pp. 365–401; Bruce Bueno de Mesquita, *The War Trap* (New Haven, CT: Yale University Press, 1981); Stephen Majeski, "Expectations and Arms Races," *American Journal of Political Science* (May 1985), pp. 217–245; Paul Diehl, "Arms Races and Escalation: A Closer Look," *Journal of Peace Research* 20.3 (1983): 205–212; Paul Diehl, "Arms Races to War: Testing Some Empirical Linkages," *Sociological Quarterly* 26.3 (1985): 331–349; Paul Diehl, "Armaments Without War," *Journal of Peace Research* 22.3 (1985): 249–259.

66. Michael Wallace, "Arms Races and Escalation: Some New Evidence," *Journal of Conflict Resolution* 23.1 (1979): 3–16; see also Diehl, "Arms Races."

67. Samuel Huntington, "Arms Races: Prerequisites and Results," in Robert Art and Kenneth Waltz, eds., *The Use of Force* (Boston: Little, Brown, 1971), p. 367.

68. Paul Diehl, "Arms Races," p. 342.

69. David Ziegler, *War, Peace, and International Politics* (Boston: Little, Brown, 1987), p. 206.

70. Hans Morgenthau, *Politics Among Nations: The Struggle for Power and Peace*, 4th ed. (New York: Knopf, 1967), p. 392.

71. Charles Kegley and Gregory Raymond, "Alliances and the Preservation of the Postwar Peace," in Charles Kegley, ed., *The Long Postwar Peace* (New York: HarperCollins, 1991), p. 275.

72. Randolph Siverson and Michael Tennefoss, "Power, Alliance, and the Escalation of International Conflict, 1815–1965," *American Political Science Review* 78 (1984): 1062.

73. Jack Levy, "Alliance Formation and War Behavior," *Journal of Conflict Resolution* 25 (1981): 581.

74. J. David Singer and Melvin Small, "Alliance Aggregation and the Onset of War, 1815–1945," in J. David Singer, ed., *Quantitative International Politics* (New York: Free Press, 1968), pp. 247–286.

75. Levy, "Alliance Formation."

76. Karl Deutsch et al., *Political Community and the North Atlantic Area* (Princeton, NJ: Princeton University Press, 1957), p. 5.

77. See Jack Levy, "The Causes of War."

78. Gilpin; see also John Mueller, *Retreat from Doomsday: The Obsolescence of Major Power War* (New York: Basic Books, 1989).

79. Richard Rosecrance, *The Rise of the Trading State: Commerce and Conquest in the Modern World* (New York: Basic Books, 1986), p. 160.

80. Terrence Hopkins and Immanuel Wallerstein, *World Systems Analysis: Theory and Methodology* (Beverly Hills, CA: Sage, 1982), p. 28.

81. Quoted in Irving Janis, *Crucial Decisions: Leadership in Policymaking and Crisis Management* (New York: Free Press, 1989), p. 130.

82. Inis Claude, *States and the Global System: Politics, Law, and Organization* (New York: St. Martin's Press, 1988), p. 132.

83. See Louis Henkin, "The Use of Force: Law and U.S. Policy," in Stanley Hoffman et al. (eds.) *Right v. Might: International Law and the Use of Force* (New York: Council on Foreign Relations, 1991), pp. 37–69.

84. J. David Singer, "Peace in the Global System: Displacement, Interregnum, or Transformation?" in Charles Kegley, ed., *The Long Postwar Peace* (New York: HarperCollins, 1991), p. 57.

85. Kalevi J. Holsti, *International Politics: A Framework for Analysis* (Englewood Cliffs, NJ: Prentice Hall, 1988), p. 420.

Chapter 9

1. Adam Ulam, *The Rivals: America and Russia Since World War II* (New York: Viking Press, 1971); John Spanier, *American Foreign Policy Since World War II* (Washington, DC: Congressional Quarterly Press, 1992); Desmond Donnelly, *Struggle for the World: The Cold War, 1917–1965* (New York: St. Martin's Press, 1965).

2. Gabriel Kolko, *The Politics of War: The World and United States Foreign Policy* (New York: Random House, 1968); Daniel Yergin, *Shattered Peace: The Origins of the Cold War and National Security State* (Boston: Houghton Mifflin, 1977); Gar Alperovitz, *Atomic Diplomacy: Hiroshima and Potsdam* (Boulder, CO: Plato Press, 1994); Walter LaFeber, *America, Russia, and the Cold War, 1945–1990* (New York: McGraw Hill, 1991).

3. Vojtech Mastny, *Russia's Road to the Cold War* (New York: Columbia University Press, 1978); William Taubman, *Stalin's American Policy* (New York: Norton, 1982); John Gaddis, *Strategies of Containment* (New York: Oxford University Press, 1982). For perhaps the best single volume on the cold war, see LaFeber. Much of the information and many of the quotations in this section come from LaFeber.

4. Hans Morgenthau, *Politics Among Nations* (New York: Knopf, 1967), p. 249.

5. George Kennan, *American Diplomacy 1900–1950* (Chicago: University of Chicago Press, 1951), p. 118.

6. Quoted in William Harbaugh, *Power and Responsibility: The Life and Times of Theodore Roosevelt* (New York: Farrar, Straus and Cudahy, 1961), p. 277.

7. Quoted in Arthur Link, *Wilson: The Struggle for Neutrality, 1914–1915* (Princeton, NJ: Princeton University Press, 1960), p. 48.

8. *New York Times*, June 24, 1941, p. 7.

9. LaFeber, *America, Russia, and the Cold War*, p. 31.

10. See Matthew Evangelista, "Stalin's Postwar Army Reappraised," *International Security* 7 (Winter 1982–1983): 121–122.

11. George Kennan, *Memoirs, 1925–1950* (Boston: Little, Brown, 1967), p. 35.

12. Quoted in LaFeber, *America, Russia, and the Cold War*, p. 73.

13. The best account of the Cuban missile crisis is James Blight and David Welch, *On the Brink: Americans and Soviets Reexamine the Cuban Missile Crisis* (New York: Hill and Wang, 1989).

14. John Gaddis, "Great Illusions, the Long Peace, and the Future of the International System," in Charles Kegley, ed. *The Long Postwar Peace* (New York: Harper-Collins, 1991), p. 34.

15. Quoted in Gaddis, *Strategies of Containment*, p. 179.

17. George Shultz, "Nicaragua: Will Democracy Prevail?" *Current Policy*, no. 97 (February 27, 1986).

18. George Kennan, "The G.O.P. Won the Cold War? Ridiculous," *New York Times*, August 21, 1992.

19. Quoted in Leslie Gelb, "GOP Can't Take All Credit for Winning the Cold War," *New York Times*, August 21, 1992.

20. Fred Chernoff, "Ending the Cold War: The Soviet Retreat and the U.S. Military Buildup," *International Affairs* 67, no. 1 (1991): 111–126; Strobe Talbot, "Rethinking the Red Menace," *Time*, January 1, 1990, 66–72.

21. Kennan, "The G.O.P."

Chapter 10

1. Ruth Leger Sivard, *World Military and Social Expenditures* (Washington, DC: World Priorities, 1991), p. 16.

2. John Spanier, *Games Nations Play* (New York: Holt, Rinehart, and Winston, 1984), p. 157.

3. Sivard, p. 13.

4. See Spanier, pp. 157–159.

5. Harold Brown, *Thinking About National Security: Defense and Foreign Policy in a Dangerous World* (Boulder, CO: Westview Press, 1983), p. 5.

6. See U.S. Congress, *The Effects of Nuclear War* (Washington, DC: U.S. Government Printing Office, 1979); Arthur Katz, *Life After Nuclear War* (Cambridge, MA: Ballinger, 1982); Carl Sagan, "Nuclear War and Climatic Catastrophe: Some Policy Implications," *Foreign Affairs* (Winter 1983–1984) pp. 256–292.

7. Stanley Thompson and Stephen Schneider, "Nuclear Winter Reappraised," *Foreign Affairs* 64 (1986): 981–1005.

8. *New York Times*, August 16, 1990, p. A3.

9. *The Defense Monitor* 21.3 (1992): 3.

10. James Simpson, *Simpson's Contemporary Quotations* (Boston: Houghton Mifflin, 1988), p. 2. For an interesting argument that nuclear deterrence has not been the reason for peace between the superpowers, see John Vasquez, "The Deterrence Myth: Nuclear Weapons and the Prevention of Nuclear War," in Charles Kegley, *The Long Postwar Peace* (New York: HarperCollins, 1991), pp. 205–223.

11. For the leading recent studies, see Robert Jervis, Richard Lebow, and Janice Gross, *Psychology and Deterrence* (Baltimore: Johns Hopkins University Press, 1985); Graham Allison, Albert Carnesale, and Joseph Nye, *Hawks, Doves, and Owls: An Agenda for Avoiding Nuclear War* (New York: Norton, 1985); Richard Betts, *Nuclear Blackmail and the Nuclear Balance* (Washington, DC: Brookings Institute, 1987); Richard Smoke, *National Security and the Nuclear Dilemma: An Introduction to the American Experience* (New York: Random House, 1987); Regina Karp, ed., *Security with Nuclear Weapons? Different Perceptions of National Security* (New York: Oxford University Press, 1991); Charles Kegley and Eugene Wittkopf, eds., *The Nuclear Reader: Strategy, Weapons, War* (New York: St. Martin's Press, 1991); and David Tarr, *Nuclear Deterrence and International Security: Alternative Nuclear Regimes* (New York: Longman, 1991).

12. Henry Kissinger, *The White House Years* (Boston: Little, Brown, 1979), p. 238.

13. See James Schlesinger, "Rhetoric and Fantasies in the Star Wars Debate," *International Security* 10.1 (1985): 3–12; Harold Brown, "Is SDI Technically Feasible?" *Foreign Affairs* 64.3: 435–454; Philip Boffey et al., *Claiming the Heavens: The New York Times Complete Guide to the Star Wars Debate* (New York: New York Times Books, 1988); Sanford Lakoff and Herbert York, *A Shield in Space: Technology, Politics, and the Strategic Defense Initiative* (Berkeley: University of California Press, 1989).

14. Eric Schmitt, "Despite Euphoria on Arms Control, Deterrence Remains a Potent Force," *New York Times*, July 30, 1991; David Sanger, "West Knew of North Korean Nuclear Development," *New York Times*, March 13, 1993. See also Stephen Meyer, *Nuclear Proliferation: Models of Behavior, Choice and Decision* (Chicago: University of Chicago Press, 1984); Leonard Spector, *Nuclear Ambitions: The Spread of Nuclear Weapons 1989–90* (Boulder, CO: Westview Press, 1990);

15. See Alva Myrdal, *The Game of Disarmament: How the United States and Russia Run the Arms Race* (New York: Pantheon, 1976).

16. Kenneth Waltz, "The Spread of Nuclear Weapons: More May be Better," *Adelphi Papers* No. 171 (London: International Institute of Strategic Studies, 1982), pp. 29–30.

17. Marshall Shulman, "The Superpowers: Dance of the Dinosaurs," *Foreign Affairs* 66.3 (1987–1988): 512.

18. Thomas Friedman, "Reducing the Russian Arms Threat," *New York Times*, June 17, 1999, A7.

19. Eric Schmitt, "50's Riddle Return in Treaty Debates," William Broad, "Undetected Indian Blasts, Cited as

Monitoring Failures, May Themselves Have Failed," *New York Times,* October 10, 1999.

20. Richard Betts, *Nuclear Blackmail and Nuclear Balance* (Washington, DC: Brookings Institute, 1987); Peter Maas, "Get Ready, Here Comes the Exoatmospheric Kill Vehicle: Star Wars Missile Defense: The Sequel," *New York Times Magazine,* September 26, 1999.

21. Arthur Cox, *Russian Roulette: The Superpower Game* (New York: Times Books, 1982).

22. See Robert Alexrood, *The Evolution of Cooperation* (New York: Basic Books, 1984); S. Plous, "Perceptual Illusions and Military Realities: The Nuclear Arms Race," *Journal of Conflict Resolution* 29.3 (1985): 363–388; Joshua Goldstein and John Freeman, *Three-Way Street: Strategic Reciprocity in World Politics* (Chicago: University of Chicago Press, 1990).

23. See Charles Osgood, *An Alternative to War or Surrender* (Urbana: University of Illinois Press, 1963).

Chapter 11

1. Francis Beer, *Peace Against War: The Ecology of International Violence* (San Francisco: Freeman, 1988).

2. James Shotwell, *War as an Instrument of National Policy* (New York: Harcourt, 1929), p. 15.

3. Quoted in Geoffrey Blainey, *The Causes of War* (New York: Free Press, 1973), p. 108.

4. Hans Morgenthau, *Politics Among Nations* (New York: Knopf, 1967), p. 392.

5. Charles Kegley and Eugene Wittkopf, *World Politics: Trend and Transformation* (New York: St. Martin's, 1993), pp. 437–438.

6. Herbert Tillema, *International Armed Conflict Since 1945: A Bibliographic Handbook of Wars and Military Interventions* (Boulder, CO: Westview Press, 1991).

7. Ruth Leger Sivard, *World Military and Social Expenditures* 11 (1991): 20.

8. J. David Singer and Melvin Small, "Foreign Policy Indicators: Predictors of War in History," *Policy Sciences* 5 (1974): 271–296.

9. Jack Levy, "Historical Trends in Great Power War, 1495–1975," *International Studies Quarterly* 25 (1982): 298; Jack S. Levy and T. Clifton Morgan, "The Frequency and Seriousness of War: An Inverse Relationship?" *Journal of Conflict Resolution* 28 (1984): 731–749.

10. John Rouke, *International Politics on the World Stage* (Guilford, CT: Dushkin, 1991), p. 264.

11. Sivard, p. 20.

12. John Gaddis, *The Long Peace: Inquiries into the History of the Cold War* (New York: Oxford University Press, 1987).

13. Bruce Russett and Richard Starr, *World Politics: A Menu for Choice* (New York: Freeman, 1990), p. 171.

14. John Mueller, *Retreat from Doomsday: The Obsolescence of Major War* (New York: Basic Books, 1989), p. 5.

15. For an outstanding collection of arguments, see Charles Kegley, ed., *The Long Postwar Peace: Contending*

Explanations and Projections (New York: HarperCollins, 1991).

16. Philip Zelikow, "The United States and the Use of Force: A Historical Summary," in George K. Osburn et al., eds., *Democracy, Strategy, and Vietnam* (Lexington, MA: Lexington Book, 1987), pp. 31–84. For studies of evaluating the United States's use of force, see Alexander George, David Hall, and William Simons, *The Limits of Coercive Diplomacy* (Boston: Little, Brown, 1971); Barry Blechman and Stephen Kaplan, "U.S. Military Forces as a Political Instrument," *Political Science Quarterly* 94: 193–210.

17. Barry Blechman and Stephen Kaplan, *Force Without War: U.S. Armed Forces as a Political Instrument* (Washington, DC: The Brookings Institute, 1978), chapter 4.

18. Herbert K. Tillema, *Appeal to Force: American Military Intervention in the Era of Containment* (New York: Crowell, 1973), chapter 5.

19. See Graham Allison and Gregory F. Treverton, eds., *Rethinking America's Security: Beyond Cold War to the New World Order* (New York: Norton, 1992); Murray Weidenbaum, *Small Wars, Big Defense: Paying for the Military after the Cold War* (New York: Oxford University Press, 1992).

20. Daniel Papp, "Soviet Unconventional Conflict Policies and Strategies in the Third World," *Conflict Quarterly* 8.4 (1988): 50–55.

21. Richard Rosecrance, *The Rise of the Trading State: Commerce and Conquest in the Modern World* (New York: Basic Books, 1986), p. 157.

22. U.S. Arms Control and Disarmament Agency, *World Military Expenditures and Arms Transfers 1990* (Washington, DC: U.S. Government Printing Office, 1992).

23. Mark Thee, "Military Technology, Arms Control, and Human Development," *Bulletin of Peace Proposals* 18: 1–11; See also Lester Kurtz, *The Nuclear Cage: A Sociology of the Arms Race* (Englewood Cliffs, NJ: Prentice Hall, 1988).

24. John M. Rothgeb Jr., *Defining Power: Influence and Force in the Contemporary International System* (New York: St. Martin's, 1993), p. 155.

25. Steven Pearlstein, "A Wholesale Change in the Arms Bazaar," *Washington Post National Weekly Edition* (April 15–21, 1991) 8.

26. Michael Klare, "Wars in the 1990's: Growing Firepower in the Third World," *Bulletin of the Atomic Scientists* 46 (1990): 12.

27. Michael Klare, "Who's Arming Who? The Arms Trade in the 1990's," *Technology Review* 93 (1990): 44.

28. "Defense Roundup," *The Defense Monitor* 20.4 (1991): 6.

29. *SIPRI Yearbook: World Armaments and Disarmament* (New York: Oxford University Press, 1990).

30. See Andrew Pierre, *The Global Politics of Arms Sales* (Princeton, NJ: University of Princeton Press, 1982).

31. ADCA (1992): 9.

32. Sivard, p. 23.

33. Dwight Eisenhower, speech before the American Society for Newspaper Editors, April 16, 1953.

34. Arthur Burns, "The Defense Sector and the American Economy," in Seymour Melman, ed., *The War Economy of the United States* (New York: St. Martin's, 1971), p. 115.

35. Steve Chan, "The Impact of Defense Spending on Economic Performance," *Orbis* 29 (1985): 407–412. See also Paul Craig and John Jungerman, *Nuclear Arms Race: Technology and Society* (New York: McGraw-Hill, 1986).

36. David Gold et al., *Misguided Expenditure, An Analysis of the Proposed MX Missile System* (New York: Council on Economic Priorities, 1981).

37. John Rouke, *International Politics on the World Stage* (Guilford, CT: Dushkin, 1991), p. 500.

38. Michael Klare, "The Arms Trade: Changing Patterns in the 1980's," *Third World Quarterly* 9 (1987): 1279–1280; Sivard, p. 11.

39. Steve Fetter, "Ballistic Missiles and Weapons of Mass Destruction: What Is the Threat? What Should Be Done?" *International Security* 16 (1991): 15, 16.

40. Walter Laqueur, "Reflections on Terrorism," *Foreign Affairs* 65 (1986): 87.

41. Conor Cruise O'Brien, "Liberty and Terrorism," *International Security* 2 (1977): 557.

42. James Clarity, "For All the Bombs, the IRA Is No Closer to Its Goals," *New York Times* December 13, 1992.

43. U.S. Department of State, *Patterns of Global Terrorism, 1990* (Washington, DC: U.S. Department of State, 1991), p. 37.

44. See John Esposito, ed., *Voices of Resurgent Islam* (New York: Oxford University Press, 1983); Malise Ruthven, *Islam in the World* (New York: Oxford University Press, 1984); Cheryl Benard and Zalmay Khalilzad, *"The Government of God": Iran's Islamic Republic* (Irvington, NY: Columbia University Press, 1984); David Menashri, *Iranian Revolution and the Muslim World* (Boulder, CO: Westview Press, 1991).

45. Uri Ra'anan et al., eds., *Hydra of Carnage: The International Linkages of Terrorism and Other Low-Intensity Operations* (Lexington, MA: Lexington Books, 1985); Charles Kegley, ed., *International Terrorism: Characteristics, Causes, Controls* (New York: St. Martin's Press, 1990).

46. For some recent perspectives, see Geoffrey Blainey, *The Causes of War* (New York: Free Press, 1988); Patrick Brogan, *The Fighting Never Stopped: A Comprehensive Guide to World Conflict Since 1945* (New York: Vintage Books, 1990); Betty Gilad, *The Psychological Dimensions of War* (Newbury Park, CA: Sage, 1990); Stuart Bremer and Barry Hughes, *Disarmament and Development: A Design for the Future* (Englewood Cliffs, NJ: Prentice Hall, 1990); Randolph Siverson and Harvey Starr, *The Diffusion of War* (Ann Arbor: University of Michigan, 1991).

47. Sivard, p. 13.

PART FIVE

Chapter 12

1. For the classic liberal economic works, see Adam Smith, *An Inquiry into the Nature and Causes of the Wealth of Nations,* 1776, ed. Edwin Cannan (New York: Modern Library, 1937); James Mill, *Elements of Political Economy,* 2nd rev. ed. (London: Henry G. Bohn, 1844); John Stuart Mill, *Principles of Political Economy,* 7th ed., 1871, ed. J. W. Ashley (London: Longmans, Green, 1909). More recent prominent free trade theorists include Milton Friedman, Robert Eisner, Herbert Stein, Robert Barro, Robert McKinnon, Robert Mundell, Jude Wanniski, and Jagdish Bhagwati.

2. Quoted in Peter Kenen, *The International Economy* (Englewood Cliffs, NJ: Prentice Hall, 1985), p. 6.

3. Paul Samuelson, *Economics,* 11th ed. (New York: McGraw Hill, 1980), p. 651.

4. Smith, p. 314.

5. For critiques of liberalism, see such leading economic realist theorists as Kenneth Waltz, *Man, the State, and War: A Theoretical Analysis* (New York: Columbia University Press, 1954); Edward Hallett Carr, *The Twenty Years' Crisis, 1919–1939: An Introduction to the Study of International Relations* (New York: St. Martin's Press, 1962); Charles Kindleberger, *Power and Money: The Economics of International Politics and the Politics of International Economics* (New York: Basic Books, 1970); David Calleo and Benjamin M. Rowland, *America and the World Political Economy* (Bloomington: Indiana University Press, 1973); Klaus Knorr, *Power and Wealth: The Political Economy of International Power* (New York: Basic Books, 1973); Peter Katzenstein, *Between Power and Plenty* (Madison: University of Wisconsin, 1978); Robert Gilpin, *War and Change in World Politics* (Cambridge, England: Cambridge University Press, 1981); Robert Gilpin, *The Political Economy of International Relations* (Princeton: Princeton University Press, 1987); William Nester, *American Power, the New World Order, and the Japanese Challenge* (New York: St. Martin's Press, 1993).

6. Robert Kuttner, *End of Laissez-Faire* (New York: Knopf, 1991), p. 141.

7. Friedrich List, quoted in John Spanier, *Games Nations Play: Analyzing International Politics* (New York: Holt, Rinehart, and Winston, 1984), p. 354.

8. Spanier, p. 355.

9. Bruce Scott and George Lodge, *U.S. Competitiveness in the World Economy* (Cambridge, MA: Harvard School of Business Press, 1987), p. 94.

10. For some classic works on mercantilism, see Eli F. Hecksher, *Mercantilism,* 2 vols., trans. Mendel Shapiro (London: Allen & Unwin, 1936); Jacob Viner, "Power versus Plenty as Objectives of Foreign Policy in the Seventeenth and Eighteenth Centuries," *World Politics* 1 (1948): 1–29. For some more recent works, see Helmut

Schoek, ed., *Central Planning and Mercantilism* (Princeton, NJ: D. Van Nostrand, 1964); R. J. Barry Jones, *Conflict and Control in the World Economy: Contemporary Economic Realism and New Mercantilism* (Atlantic Highlands, NJ: Humanities Press, 1986); Gilpin, *Political Economy*.

11. Viner, p. 286.

12. Quoted in Kuttner, p. 173.

13. Martin Tolchin and Susan Tolchin, *Selling Our Security: The Erosion of America's Assets* (New York: Knopf, 1992).

14. David H. Blake and Robert S. Walters, *The Politics of Global Economic Relations* (Englewood Cliffs, NJ: Prentice Hall, 1987), p. 67. For an interesting discussion of different theoretical perspectives on American foreign and economic policymaking and policies, see chapter 8.

15. See Charles Kindleberger, *The World in Depression, 1929–1939* (Berkeley: University of California Press, 1988).

16. Wolfram Hanrieder, "Dissolving International Politics: Reflections on the Nation-State," *American Political Science Review* 72.4 (1978): 1278.

17. Richard Stevenson, "Swedes Facing Rigors of Welfare Cuts," *New York Times*, March 14, 1993; "Nordic Countries Survey," *Economist* January 23, 1999.

18. Quoted in Eugene V. Rostow, ed., *Is Law Dead?* (New York: Simon & Schuster, 1971), p. 189. For the classic American argument for a rational national industrial policy, see Alexander Hamilton, "Report on the Subject of Manufactures," in Arthur Harrison Cole, ed., *Industrial and Commercial Correspondence of Alexander Hamilton Anticipating His Report on Manufactures* (New York: Kelley, 1968).

19. Hugh Patrick and Larry Meissner, eds., *Japan's High Technology Industries: Lessons and Limitations of Industrial Policy* (Seattle: University of Washington Press, 1986), p. xiii; Chalmers Johnson, ed., *The Industrial Policy Debate* (San Francisco: ICS Press, 1984), p. 3.

20. Scott and Lodge, pp. 80–95.

21. Clemens Boonekamp, "Voluntary Export Restraints," *Finance and Development* 23 (1987): 3.

22. *World Development Report, 1991*, pp. 104–105.

23. Paul Krugman, *The Age of Diminished Expectations* (Cambridge, MA: MIT Press, 1990), p. 105. See also Michael Mastanduno, David Lake, and G. John Ikenberry, "Toward a Realist Theory of State Action," *International Studies Quarterly* 33 (1989): 457–475; Michael Mastanduno, "Do Relative Gains Matter? America's Response to Japanese Industrial Policy," *International Security* 16 (1991): 73–113; Duncan Snidal, "International Cooperation Among Relative Gains Maximizers," *International Studies Quarterly* 35 (1991): 387–402.

24. James Bovard, "Fair Trade Is Unfair," *Newsweek* December 9, 1991, p. 13.

25. Charles Linblom, *Politics and Markets: The World's Political-Economic Systems* (New York: Basic Books, 1977), p. ix.

26. Robert Isaak, *International Political Economy: Managing World Economic Change* (Englewood Cliffs, NJ: Prentice Hall, 1991), p. 15.

Chapter 13

1. For the classic work on complex interdependence, see Robert O. Keohane and Joseph S. Nye, *Power and Interdependence: World Politics in Transition,* 2nd ed. (Glenview, IL: Scott, Foresman/Little, Brown, 1989).

2. The founder of this perspective was Charles Kindleberger, *The World in Depression, 1929–1939* (Berkeley: University of California Press, 1973). See also Robert Keohane, *After Hegemony: Cooperation and Discord in the World Political System* (Princeton, NJ: Princeton University Press, 1984).

3. Stephen Krasner, "Structural Causes and Regime Consequences: Regimes as Intervening Variables," *International Organization* 36 (1982): 185.

4. Henry Kissinger, *Washington Post,* November 24, 1984.

5. For excellent accounts of American leadership of the global political economy, see Kindleberger; David P. Calleo and Benjamin Rowland, *America and the World Political Economy* (Bloomington: Indiana University Press, 1973); and Joan Spero, *The Politics of International Economic Relations* (New York: St. Martin's Press, 1990).

6. For an excellent argument that the Smoot-Hawley Act simply exacerbated an existing global depression, see Susan Strange, "Protectionism and World Politics," in Kendall Stiles and Tsuneo Akaha, eds., *International Political Economy* (New York: HarperCollins, 1991), pp. 133–156.

7. Quoted in Richard N. Gardner, *Sterling-Dollar Diplomacy in Current Perspectives: The Origins and Prospects of Our International Economic Order,* expanded ed. (New York: Columbia University Press, 1980), p. 9.

8. William Nester, *A Short History of American Industrial Policies* (New York: St. Martin's Press, 1998); William Nester, *American Industrial Policy: Free or Managed Markets?* (New York: St. Martin's Press, 1997); William Nester, *The War for America's Natural Resources* (New York: St. Martin's Press, 1997).

9. Martin Tolchin and Susan Tolchin, *Selling Our Security: The Erosion of America's Assets* (New York: Knopf, 1992), p. 132.

10. Keith Bradsher, "An Ideological Divide," *New York Times* October 7, 1992.

11. See Selig Harrison and Clyde Prestowitz, "Pacific Agenda: Defense or Economics?" *Foreign Policy* 79 (1990): 56–57. Among the more prominent studies of Japan's development, see Ira Magaziner and Thomas Hout, *Japanese Industrial Policy* (Berkeley: Institute of International Studies, University of California, 1980); John Zysman, *Governments, Markets, and Growth* (Ithaca, NY: Cornell University Press, 1983); Ed Lincoln, *Japan's Industrial Policies* (Washington, DC:

Japan Economic Institute of America, 1984); William Nester, *The Foundations of Japanese Power: Continuities, Changes, Challenges* (Armonk, NY: M. E. Sharpe, 1990); and William Nester, *Japanese Industrial Targeting: The Neomercantilist Path to Economic Superpower* (New York: St. Martin's Press, 1991).

12. See Chalmers Johnson, John Zysman, and Laura Tyson, *Politics and Productivity: The Real Story of Why Japan's Economy Works,* (Cambridge, MA: Ballinger, 1989), chapter 1.

13. See Ernst Haas, *The Uniting of Europe* (Stanford, CA: Stanford University Press, 1957). For recent studies, see Edward Nevin, *The Economics of Europe* (London: Macmillan, 1990); William Nester, *The European Community and the Japanese Challenge* (London: Macmillan, 1993).

14. Quoted in Willem Molle, *The Economics of European Integration* (Aldershot, England: Dartmouth, 1990), p. 476; Unless otherwise indicated, all trade statistics come from the International Monetary Fund, *Direction of Trade,* various issues, Washington, D.C.

15. United Nations, *International Financial Statistics Yearbook,* (1987), p. 701.

16. *New York Times,* October 21, 1992.

17. *New York Times,* July 8, 1992.

18. For example, see Mira Wilkins, *The Emergence of Multinational Enterprise: American Business Abroad from the Colonial Era to 1914* (Cambridge, MA: Harvard University Press, 1970).

19. World Bank, *Entering the 21st Century: World Development Report 1999/2000* (New York: Oxford University Press, 2000).

20. See Jean-Jacques Servan-Schreiber, *The American Challenge* (New York: Athenaeum, 1968);

21. Martin Tolchin and Susan Tolchin, *Buying into America: How Foreign Money Is Changing the Face of Our Nation* (New York: Times Books, 1988); Pat Choate, *Agents of Influence* (New York: Knopf, 1990).

22. John Cushman, "Clinton Seeks Taxes on Hidden Profits," *New York Times* October 23, 1992.

23. David H. Blake and Robert S. Walters, *The Politics of Global Economic Relations* (Englewood Cliffs, NJ: Prentice Hall, 1987), 118–119.

24. Task Force on the Structure of Canadian Industry, *Foreign Ownership and the Structure of Canadian Industry* (Ottawa: Privy Council Office, 1968), p. 37.

25. European Communities, *Report on Enterprises and Governments in Economic Activity,* Document 1-169/81, May 15, 1981, p. 5.

26. Richard Cooper, *The Economics of Interdependence: Economic Policy in the Atlantic Community* (New York: McGraw-Hill, 1968).

27. William Nester, *European Power and the Japanese Challenge* (New York: New York University Press, 1993).

28. William Nester, *American Power, the New World Order, and the Japanese Challenge* (New York: St. Martin's Press, 1993); William Nester, *Power Across the Pacific:*

A Diplomatic History of American Relations with Japan (New York: New York University Press, 1996).

29. Robert Crandall, "Import Quotas and the Automobile Industry: The Costs of Protection," *The Brookings Review* (Summer 1984), p. 16.

30. *New York Times,* June 18, 1992.

31. *New York Times,* April 9, 1992.

32. *New York Times,* June 8, 1992.

33. *World Bank Atlas, 1991* (Washington, DC: World Bank, 1992), pp. 6–9.

34. United Nations, *World Economic Survey, 1991* (New York: United Nations, 1991), p. 6.

PART SIX

Chapter 14

1. See Max Weber, *The Theory of Social and Economic Organization* (New York: Oxford University Press, 1947); W. Chai and C. Clark, *Political Stability and Economic Growth: Case Studies of Hong Kong, Singapore, and the R.O.C.* (Lanham, MD: University Press of America for the University of Virginia Press, 1987); C. L. Taylor, "Indicators of Political Development," *Journal of Developing Studies* 8.3 (1975); P. W. Preston, *Making Sense of Development* (London: Routledge and Kegan Paul, 1987); Myron Weiner and Samuel P. Huntington, *Understanding Political Development* (Boston: Little, Brown, 1987); Stephen Chilton, *Defining Political Development* (Boulder, CO: Lynne Reinner, 1988).

2. Quoted by Charles Lane, "Let's Abolish the Third World," *Newsweek,* April 27, 1992, p. 43.

3. World Bank, *World Development Report, 1991* (New York: Oxford University Press, 1991).

4. For two classic dependency studies focusing on Latin America, see Raul Prebisch, *The Economic Development of Latin America and Its Principal Problems* (New York: United Nations, 1950); Andre Gunter Frank, *Capitalism and Underdevelopment in Latin America* (New York: Monthly Review Press, 1969).

5. For a sweeping exploration of this perspective, see Jagdish Bhagwati, *Essays in Development Economics.* Vol. 1, *Wealth and Poverty,* and Vol. 2, *Dependence and Interdependence* (Cambridge, MA: MIT Press, 1985).

6. U.S. Department of State, press report (August 1978).

7. Joan Spero, *The Politics of International Economic Relations* (New York: St. Martin's, 1991), p. 152.

8. Monte Palmer, *Political Development: Dilemmas and Challenges* (Itasca, IL: Peacock, 1997), p. 20.

9. Max Weber, *The Theory of Social and Economic Organization* (New York: Free Press, 1947).

10. See Palmer, pp. 180–181.

11. United Arab Republic, *Draft of the Charter* (Cairo: Information Department, 1962), p. 45.

12. See Gregor McLenna, David Held, and Stuart Hall, *Idea of the Modern State* (London: Open University Press, 1984).

13. Samuel Huntington, *Political Order in Changing Societies* (New Haven, CT: Yale University Press, 1968), p. 78.
14. For the relationship between culture and development, see Ralph Braibanti and Joseph J. Spengler, eds., *Tradition, Values, and Socio-Economic Development* (Durham, NC: Duke University, 1961).
15. A. T. J. Mathews, "Emergent Turkish Administrators," in Jerry Hopper and Richard Levin, eds., *The Turkish Administrator: A Cultural Survey* (Ankara: U.S. AID, 1967), p. 229.
16. Quoted in Palmer, p. 271.
17. Lucian Pye, *Politics, Personality, and Nation-Building* (New Haven, CT: Yale University Press, 1962).
18. Jon S. T. Quah, "Bureaucratic Corruption in the ASEAN Countries: A Comparative Analysis of Their Anti-Corruption Strategies," *Journal of Southeast Asian Studies* 13 (1982): 164.
19. Ibid., p. 164.
20. See, for example, Michael Johnston, "The Political Consequences of Corruption: A Reassessment," *Comparative Politics* (July 1986).
21. For a succinct and comprehensive explanation, see Harry Eckstein, "On the Etiology of Internal Wars," *History and Theory* 4 (1965).
22. Palmer, p. 136.
23. See Eric Norlinger, *Soldiers in Politics* (Englewood Cliffs, NJ: Prentice Hall, 1977), p. 20; Robert Wesson, ed., *New Military Politics in Latin America* (New York: Praeger, 1982); William Foltz and Henry S. Bienen, eds., *Arms and the African: Military Influences on Africa's International Relations* (New Haven, CT: Yale University Press, 1985); Miles D. Wolpin, *Militarization, Internal Repression, and Social Welfare in the Third World* (New York: St. Martin's Press, 1986).
24. Robert Clark, *Power and Policy in the Third World* (New York: Wiley, 1982), p. 111.
25. E. N. Muller and M. A. Seligson, "Inequality and Insurgency," *American Political Science Review* 81.2 (1987); E. N. Muller, "Dependent Economic Development, Aid, and Dependence on the United States and Democratic Breakdown in the Third World," *International Studies Quarterly* 29.4 (1985): 21–39.
26. Talikder Maniruzzaman, *Military Withdrawal from Politics: A Comparative Study* (Cambridge, MA: Ballinger, 1987), pp. 221–222.
27. See Nicole Ball, "Military Expenditure and Socio-Economic Development," *International Social Science Journal* 95.1 (1983); Bruce Arlinghaus, *Military Development in Africa: The Political and Economic Risks of Arms Transfers* (Boulder, CO: Westview Press, 1984); Steve Chan, "The Impact of Defense Spending on Economic Performance: A Survey of Evidence and Problems," *Orbis* 29.2 (1985); Basudeb Biswas and Rati Ram, "Military Expenditures and Economic Growth in Less Developed Countries," *Economic Development and Cultural Change* 34.2 (1986); Saadet Deger, "Economic Development and Defense Expenditure," *Economic Development and Cultural Change* 35.1 (1986).
28. James DeFonzo, *Revolutions and Revolutionary Movements* (Boulder, CO: Westview Press, 1991), p. 8.
29. Ibid., p. 8.
30. James Dougherty and Robert Pfaltzgraff, *Contending Theories of International Relations* (New York: Harper & Row, 1990), p. 321.
31. Hannah Arendt, *On Revolution* (New York: Viking, 1965), p. 3.
32. See Crane Brinton, *Anatomy of Revolution* (New York: Norton, 1938).
33. Ted Gurr, "Psychological Factors in Civil Violence," *World Politics* 20 (1968): 252–253.
34. Bruce Mazlish, *The Revolutionary Ascetic: Evolution of a Revolutionary Type* (New York: Basic Books, 1976).
35. Rollo May, *Power and Innocence: A Search for the Sources of Violence* (New York: Norton, 1972).
36. Frantz Fanon, *The Wretched of the Earth* (New York: 1963), p. 32.
37. Paul Johnson, *Modern Times: The World from the Twenties to the Eighties* (New York, 1985), p. 513.
38. Hiranyappa Venkatasubbiah, *Indian Economy Since Independence* (Bombay: Institute of Pacific Relations, 1958), p. 287.
39. George McTurnan Kahin, *The Asian-African Conference, Bandung, Indonesia* (Ithaca, NY: Cornell University Press, 1956), p. 42.
40. Rosemarie Philips and Stuart K. Tucker, *U.S. Foreign Policy and Developing Countries, Discourse and Data 1991* (Washington, DC: Overseas Development Council, 1991), p. 16.

Chapter 15

1. The literature on economic development is vast. Some of the leading works are Gove Hambidge, ed., *Dynamics of Development* (New York: Praeger, 1964); Albert O. Hirschman, *The Strategy of Economic Development* (New Haven, CT: Yale University Press, 1958); Gerald Meier, *Leading Issues in Development Economics* (New York: Oxford University Press, 1964); Theodore Morgan, George W. Betz, and N. K. Choudhry, eds., *Readings on Economic Development* (Belmont, CA: Wadsworth, 1963); Ian Livingston, ed., *Approaches to Development Studies* (Brookfield, VT: Gower, 1982); Kenneth Nobe and Rajan Sampath, eds., *Issues in Third World Development* (Boulder, CO: Westview Press, 1984); Andrew Webster, *Introduction to the Sociology of Development* (London: Macmillan, 1984); Charles K. Wilber, ed., *The Political Economy of Development and Underdevelopment* (New York: Random House, 1984); and J. P. Cole, *Development and Underdevelopment* (New York: Methuen, 1987). For two excellent recent analyses of development, see Jan Black, *Development in Theory and Practice* (Boulder, CO: Westview, 1991); and Leslie Sklair, *Sociology of the Global System* (Baltimore, MD: Johns Hopkins University Press, 1991).

2. Betty Balfour, ed., *The History of Lord Lytton's Indian Administration, 1876–1880* (London, 1899), pp. 510–512.

3. Theodore Von Laue, *The World Revolution of Westernization* (New York: Oxford University, 1987), p. 31.

4. W. Theodore de Bary, ed., *Sources of Indian Civilization* (New York: 1958), p. 803.

5. Tamar Golan, *Educating the Bureaucracy in a New Polity* (New York: Teachers College Press, 1968), p. 223.

6. Von Laue, pp. 315–316.

7. See Dale L. Johnson, ed., *Middle Classes in Dependent Countries* (Beverly Hills, CA: Sage, 1984); and Allan Findlay and Anne Findlay, *Population and Development in the Third World* (New York: Methuen, 1987).

8. "Has Capital Flight Made Us a Debtor of Latin America," *Business Week,* April 21, 1986; Donald R. Lessard and John Williamson, *Capital Flight: The Problem and Policy Responses,* Policy Analysis in International Economics, no. 23 (Washington, DC: Institute for International Economics).

9. For the leading literature on the relationship between bureaucracy and development, see Joseph La Palombara, ed., *Bureaucracy and Political Development* (Princeton, NJ: Princeton University Press, 1963); A. L. Adu, *The Civil Service in the New African States* (New York: Praeger, 1965); Ralph Braibanti, ed., *Asian Bureaucratic Systems Emergent from the British Imperial Tradition* (Durham, NC: Duke University Press, 1966); Ferrel Heady, *Public Administration: A Comparative Perspective* (New York: Marcel Dekker, 1984); Jamil E. Jreisat and Zaki R. Ghosheh, *Administration and Development in the Arab World: An Annotated Bibliography* (New York: Garland, 1986); Oskar Gans, ed., *Appropriate Techniques for Development Planning* (Ft. Lauderdale, FL: Breitenbach, 1986); B. Bola-Ntotele, "Introduction to a Study of the Efficiency of Administrative Systems in Sub-Saharan Africa," *International Review of Administrative Sciences* 52.2 (1986); Daniel Landau, "Government and Economic Growth in the Less Developed Countries: An Empirical Study for 1960–1980," *Economic Development and Cultural Change* 35.1 (1986); Dean Forbes, *The Socialist Third World: Urban Development and Territorial Planning* (New York: Blackwell, 1987); Jerald Hage and Kurt Finsterbusch, *Organizational Change as a Development Strategy: Models and Tactics for Improving Third World Organizations* (Boulder, CO: Lynne Rienner, 1987); Gregory J. Kasza, "Bureaucratic Politics in Radical Military Regimes," *American Political Science Review* 81.3 (1987); Monte Palmer et al., "Bureaucratic Rigidity and Economic Development in the Middle East: A Study of Egypt, Saudi Arabia and the Sudan," *International Review of Administrative Sciences* 53.2 (1987).

10. Bela Belassa, "The 'New Protectionism' and the International Economy," *Journal of World Trade Laws* 12.5 (1975): 15.

11. Robert Walters and David Blake, *The Politics of International Economic Relations* (Englewood Cliffs, NJ: Prentice Hall, 1991), p. 162.

12. Bruce Russet and Harvey Star, *World Politics: The Menu for Choice* (New York: Freeman, 1989), p. 435.

13. Theodore Von Laue, *The World Revolution of Westernization: The Twentieth Century in Perspective* (New York: Oxford University Press, 1987), p. 314,

14. Tim Golden, "Sweeping Political Changes Leave Latin Poor Still Poor," *New York Times,* May 30, 1992.

15. Ibid.

16. W. David Hopper, "The Development of Agriculture in Developing Countries," *Scientific American* 235.3: 197–205.

17. Carl Dahlman, *Local Development and Exports of Technology: The Comparative Advantage of Argentina, Brazil, India, the Republic of Korea, and Mexico* (Washington, DC: World Bank, 1984).

18. Robin Broad and John Cavanagh, "No More NICs," *Foreign Policy* 72 (1988): 81–103.

19. Joan Robinson, *The Modern World System,* 2 vols. (New York: Academic Press, 1974), p. 1980.

20. Palmer et al., p. 326.

21. U.N. Development Program, *Human Development Report, 1991:* 13.

22. Ibid., p. 37.

Chapter 16

1. World Bank, *Entering the 21st Century: World Development Report, 1999/2000* (New York: Oxford University Press, 1999), p. 26.

2. For some excellent recent studies, see Richard Feinberg and Delia Boylan, *Modular Multilateralism: North–South Economic Relations in the 1990s* (Washington, DC: Overseas Development Council, 1991); Ivan Head, *On a Hinge of History: The Mutual Vulnerability of South and North* (Toronto: University of Toronto Press, 1991); G. K. Helleiner, *The New Global Economy and the Developing Countries* (Brookfield, VT: Edward Elgar, 1990); and Edward Weisband, ed., *Poverty Amidst Plenty* (Boulder, CO: Westview Press, 1989). The same question haunts the issues of personal development, and the relative prosperity of different ethnic, religious, and racial groups in the United States and elsewhere. Does one's material status depend more on individual or cultural endowments, or does the answer lie elsewhere? Is it nature or nurture?

3. International Monetary Fund, *World Economic Outlook* 1991.

4. World Bank, *World Development Report, 1991,* p. 35.

5. See William Cline, *Systemic Risk and Policy Response* (Washington, DC: Institute for International Economics, 1984).

6. Morris Miller, *Resolving the Global Debt Crisis* (New York: U.N. Development Program, Policy Division, 1989), p. 33.

7. Kwame Nkrumah, *The Autobiography of Kwame Nkrumah* (New York: Nelson, 1957), p. x.

8. Dale Johnson, ed., *Middle Classes in Dependent Countries* (Beverly Hills, CA: Sage, 1984), p. 537.

9. U.N. General Assembly, 18th Session, Official Records: Eighteenth Session, Supplement No. 7 (A 5507), p. 24.

10. See Raul Prebisch, *Towards a New Trade Policy for Development,* report by the Secretary-General of the U.N. conference on Trade and Development (New York: United Nations, 1964).

11. David H. Blake and Robert S. Walters, *The Politics of Global and Economic Relations,* 4th ed. (Englewood Cliffs, NJ: Prentice Hall, 1992), p. 194.

12. Dennis Pirages, *The New Context for International Relations: Global Ecopolitics* (North Scituate, MA: Duxbury Press, 1978), p. 170.

13. For the definitive study of oil, see Daniel Yergin, *The Prize: The Epic Quest for Oil, Money, and Power* (New York: Simon & Schuster, 1991).

14. Mira Wilkins, *The Maturing of Multinational Enterprise: American Business Abroad from 1914 to 1970* (Cambridge, MA: Harvard University Press, 1974), pp. 386–387.

15. Joan Spero, *The Politics of International Economic Relations* (New York: St. Martin's, 1990), p. 265.

16. Daniel Papp, *Contemporary International Relations* (New York: Macmillan, 1988), p. 380.

17. Spero, p. 277.

18. For two somewhat different views, see John Lewis and Valeriana Kallab, eds., *Development Strategies Reconsidered* (New Brunswick, NJ: Transaction Books, 1986); Peter Bauer, *Equality, the Third World, and Economic Illusion* (Cambridge, MA: Harvard University Press, 1981).

19. Spero, p. 161.

20. Joan M. Nelson, *Aid, Influence, and Foreign Policy* (New York: Macmillan, 1968).

21. Organization for Economic Cooperation and Development, *Development Cooperation: 1987 Review* (Paris: OECD, 1987), p. 327; for an excellent critique of Reagan administration aid policies, see John Sewell and Christine Contee, "U.S. Foreign Aid in the 1980's: Reordering Priorities," in Kendall Stiles and Tsuneo Akaha, eds., *International Political Economy* (New York: HarperCollins, 1991), pp. 308–347.

22. See Richard Feinberg and Valeriana Kallab, eds., *Between Two Worlds: The World Bank's Next Decade* (New Brunswick, NJ: Transaction Books, 1986).

23. Robert Cassen, *Does Aid Work? Report to an Intergovernmental Task Force* (Oxford: Clarendon Press, 1986), pp. 24–25.

24. Miller, p. 50.

25. World Bank, *World Debt Tables* (1988).

26. Miller, p. 42.

27. Ibid., 24.

28. Ibid., 52.

29. Charles Kegley and Eugene Wittkopf, *World Politics: Trend and Transformation* (New York: St. Martin's Press, 1992), p. 293.

30. For arguments in favor of MNCs, see Raymond Vernon, *Restrictive Business Practices* (New York: United Nations, 1972); Herbert May, *The Contributions of U.S. Private Investment to Latin America's Growth* (New York: The Council for Latin America, 1970); John Dunning, "Multinational Enterprises and Nation States," in Ashok Kapoor and Phillip D. Grub, eds., *The Multinational Enterprise in Transition* (Princeton, NJ: Darwin Press, 1974). For arguments opposing MNCs, see Richard J. Barnet and Ronald E. Muller, *Global Reach: The Rise of Multinational Corporations* (New York: Simon & Schuster, 1974), and the dependency theorists. (See Chapter 14, note 4.)

31. Ronald Muller, "Poverty Is the Product," *Foreign Affairs* 13 (1973–1974): 85–90; see also Sidney Robbins and Robert Stobaugh, *Money in the Multinational Enterprise: A Study of Financial Policy* (New York: Basic Books, 1972), pp. 63–71.

32. Oswaldo Sunkel, "Big Business and 'Dependencia'" *Foreign Affairs* 50 (1972): 523; see also Volker Bornschier and Christopher Chase-Dunn, *Transnational Corporations and Underdevelopment* (New York: Praeger, 1985).

33. Paul Sigmund, *Multinationals in Latin America: The Politics of Nationalization* (Madison: University of Wisconsin Press, 1980).

34. Barnet and Muller, pp. 14–15.

35. A. W. Clausen, "The Internationalized Corporation: An Executive's View," *The Annals* (The American Academy of Political and Social Science) 403 (1972): 21.

36. "Foreign Investment and the Triad," *The Economist* August 24, 1991.

37. Blake and Walters, p. 94.

38. See Raymond Vernon, *Sovereignty at Bay* (New York: Basic Books, 1971) and Barnet and Muller.

39. United Nations, *United Nations Yearbook, 1974* (New York: United Nations, 1974), p. 324.

40. World Bank, *Entering the 21st Century.*

41. U.N. Development Program, *World Development Report, 1991,* p. 105.

PART SEVEN

1. Information was drawn from World Bank, *Entering the 21st Century: World Development Report, 1999/2000* (New York: Oxford University Press, 1999), pp. 1, 28–29; Turning Point Project, "The Next World War Will Be About Water," *New York Times,* December 6, 1999.

Chapter 17

1. Garrett Hardin, "The Tragedy of the Commons," *Science* 162 (1970): 1243–1248.

2. Lester Brown, ed., *The World Watch Reader on Global Environmental Issues* (New York: Norton, 1991), p. 13.

3. For these and other population statistics, see World Bank, *Entering the 21st Century: World Development Report, 1999/2000* (New York: Oxford University Press, 1999), pp. 46, 139–155, 214.

4. For a thoughtful analysis, see Nathan Keyfitz, "Population Growth Can Prevent the Development That

Would Slow Population Growth," in Jessica Tuchman Mathews, ed., *Preserving the Global Environment: The Challenge of Shared Leadership* (New York: Norton, 1992).

5. Paul Lewis, "Curb on Population Growth Needed Urgently, UN Says," *New York Times*, April 30, 1992.

6. Julian Simon, *Population Matters: People, Resources, Environment, and Immigration* (New Brunswick, NJ: Transaction Books, 1990).

7. Jodi Jacobson, "China's Baby Budget," in Brown; Nicholas Kristoff, "China's Crackdown on Births: A Stunning and Harsh Success," *New York Times*, April 25, 1993.

8. Jane Perlez, "Briton Sees AIDS Halting African Population Rise," *New York Times*, June 22, 1992, p. 7A.

9. Quoted in Christopher Flavin, "The Heat Is On," in Brown. Unless otherwise indicated, all statistics come from Flavin or George Rahjens, "Energy and Climate Change," in Mathews pp. 154–186.

10. Rahjens, p. 157.

11. World Bank, p. 87.

12. Peter Passell, "Economists Start to Fret Again About Population," *New York Times*, December 18, 1990, p. 1-C.

13. Sylvia Nasar, "Cooling the Globe Would Be Nice . . ." *New York Times*, May 31, 1992, p. 6.

14. William Stevens, "New Studies Predict Profits in Heading Off Warming," *New York Times*, March 17, 1992, p. 1C.

15. Unless otherwise indicated, all statistics come from Richard Benedick, "Protecting the Ozone Layer: New Directions in Diplomacy," in Mathews 112–153, and Cynthia Shea, "Mending the Earth's Shield," in Brown.

16. Unless otherwise indicated, all statistics come from Hilary French, "You Are What You Breathe," in Brown.

17. Statistics on this region have been taken from Hilary French, "Eastern Europe's Clean Break with the Past," in Brown.

18. Brown 20; Brown et al. in Brown, pp. 308–309.

19. French, "Eastern Europe's Clean Break," p. 20.

20. Unless otherwise indicated, all statistics in this section come from Alan Durning, "Cradles of Life," and John Ryan, "Sustainable Forestry," in Brown or Kenton Miller et al., "Deforestation and Species Loss," in Mathews, pp. 78–111.

21. Miller et al., pp. 79–80.

22. "Hard Luck for Hardwoods," *Economist* (April 1989), p. 63.

23. Twig Mowatt, "Soil Degradation Study," *New York Times*, March 31, 1992. Unless otherwise indicated, all statistics come from Sandra Postel, "Restoring Degraded Land," in Brown, p. 25.

24. Marlise Simons, "Winds Sweep African Soil to Feed Lands Far Away," *New York Times*, October 29, 1992, pp. 1, 15; Brown 148.

25. Lester Brown, "Feeding Six Billion," in Brown, 148.

26. David Pitt, "Nations Mobilize to Limit Deserts," *New York Times*, December 10, 1993; Brown et al., in Brown, p. 311.

27. Simons, pp. 1, 15.

28. Sandra Postel, "Emerging Water Scarcities," in Brown.

29. For an excellent account of the causes and effects of ocean pollution, see Nicholas Lassen, "The Ocean Blues," in Brown. Unless otherwise indicated, the statistics from this section come from Lassen's chapter.

30. Timothy Egan, "New Evidence of Ecological Damage Brings a Call to Ban Drift-Net Fishing," *New York Times*, November 14, 1989, p. 24A.

31. Quoted in Mathews pp. 325–326.

32. Philip Elmer-Dewitt, "Rich vs. Poor," *Time*, June 1, 1992, p. 42.

33. Ibid., p. 43.

Chapter 18

1. Taken from George Modelski, "Is World Politics Evolutionary Learning?" *International Organization* 44.1 (1990): 2–24; Immanuel Kant, "Perpetual Peace," in Peter Gay, ed., *The Enlightenment* (New York: Simon & Schuster, 1974), pp. 790–792. Almost two hundred years ago, Immanuel Kant distinguished between the warlike tendencies of democratic and authoritarian countries, arguing that democratic nations, tied together by trade and a respect for international law, would be unlikely to go to war. In his 1795 essay entitled "Perpetual Peace," Kant asserts that "if the consent of citizens is required in order to decide that war should be declared . . . , nothing is more natural than they would be very cautious in commencing such a poor game, decreeing for themselves the calamities of war. . . . In a constitution which is not republican, and under which the subjects are not citizens, a declaration of war is the easiest thing in the world to decide on." For a fuller discussion of the changes and continuities of international relations from which some of the following material and ideas have been taken, see William Nester, *American Power, the New World Order, and the Japanese Challenge* (New York: St. Martin's, 1993).

2. Richard Rosecrance, *The Rise of the Trading State: Commerce and Conquest in the Modern World* (New York: Basic Books, 1986), p. 62.

3. Edward Luttwak, "From Geopolitics to Geoeconomics," *National Interest* 20 (1990): 17.

4. Francis Fukuyama, "The End of History?" *The National Interest* no. 16 (Summer 1989): 3. See also Francis Fukuyama, *The End of History and the Last Man* (New York: Free Press, 1992).

5. See Daniel Patrick Moynihan, *Pandemonium: Ethnicity in International Politics* (New York: Oxford University Press, 1993). See also Zbigniew Brzezinski, *Out of Control: Global Turmoil on the Eve of the Twenty-First*

Century (New York: Scribner's, 1993); Al Gore, *Earth in the Balance: Ecology and the Human Spirit* (New York: Houghton Mifflin, 1992).

6. For a brilliant discussion of these and related questions, see Marshall Berman, *All That Is Solid Melts into Air: The Experience of Modernity* (New York: Simon & Schuster, 1982).

7. Ibid., p. 61.

8. Quoted in ibid., p. 84.

9. John Rothgeb, *Defining Power: Influence and Force in the Contemporary International System* (London: St. Martin's, 1993), p. 65.

10. Henry Kissinger, *The White House Years* (Boston: Little, Brown, 1975), p. 12. Some recent books and articles that have addressed the changes and continuities in international relations into the 1990's and beyond include Michael Brecher and Patrick James, *Crisis and Change in World Politics* (Boulder, CO: Westview Press, 1986); Ernst-Otto Czempiel and James Rosenau, eds., *Global Changes and Theoretical Challenges: Approaches to World Politics for the 1990s* (Lexington, MA: Lexington Books, 1989); Charles F. Doran, *Systems in Crisis: New Imperatives of High Politics at Century's End* (Cambridge, England: Cambridge University Press, 1991); Robert Jervis, "The Future of World Politics: Will It Resemble the Past?" *International Security* 16 (1991–1992): 39–73. Charles Kegley and Eugene Wittkopf, eds. *The Global Agenda: Issues and Perspectives* (New York: McGraw-Hill, 1992); James Rosenau, *Turbulence in World Politics: A Theory of Change and Continuity* (Princeton, NJ: Princeton University Press, 1990); Tad Szulc, *Then and Now: How the World Has Changed Since World War II* (New York: Morrow, 1990); and Paul Kennedy, *Preparing for the 21st Century* (New York: Random House, 1993).

11. Theodore Von Laue, *The World Revolution of Westernization* (New York: Oxford University Press, 1987), p. 376.

Glossary

KEY CONCEPTS AND TERMS

agricultural revolution: an increase in farm productivity resulting from innovations such as mechanization, new crops or fertilizer, easy bank credit, improved infrastructure, and better access to markets.

Alamogordo: the New Mexico site of the world's first nuclear explosion on July 16, 1945.

ALCMs: air-launched cruise missiles. Also see **second-strike weapons.**

anarchy: the absence of government.

Arab League: An IGO of 23 states with predominantly Arabic-speaking populations that attempt to forge common policies on issues affecting their common interests.

arbitration: the intercession of an interested third party in an international conflict; the third party listens to both sides and makes a binding decision through a court convened over that particular issue.

aspiration gap: a gap between what an individual or group receives and what it desires.

Atlantic Charter: An eight point declaration of principles signed by President Franklin D. Roosevelt and Prime Minister Winston Churchill at Argentia, Newfoundland, on December 13, 1941. Those principles included collective security, national self-determination, freedom of the seas, free trade, no territorial expansion, and economic cooperation.

atomic bomb: a violent weapon whose destructive power results from a fission process of splitting atoms.

authoritarianism: a political system under which the government does not permit genuine political representation or civil and human rights but does not hold total power (see **totalitarianism**).

balance of power: term used to label various power configurations among **states.** The classic balance of power has changing alliances of half-dozen states of relatively equal military power against, and in response to, aggressive states. Some theorists argue that the balance involves the power distribution among states; others argue that it involves the power distribution among alliances.

Baruch Plan: proposal presented to the United Nations by the Truman administration in March 1946, under which the United States would turn over its nuclear weapons, raw materials, and technology to a U.N. agency that would then inspect all countries to ensure that they did not try to build nuclear weapons. The Soviets vetoed the proposal.

basic deterrence: nuclear deterrence that covers the United States.

behaviorism: the psychological theory that humans are shaped by their environment rather than by inner drives; thus human aggression is learned rather than innate.

Berlin airlift: the American airlift of food and supplies into West Berlin between June 1948 and April 1949, the period when the Soviets blockaded the land routes to West Germany.

Berlin Wall: the wall built by the Soviets in August 1961 to surround West Berlin and prevent people from fleeing East Germany. When it was finally demolished in November 1989, its fall symbolized the end of the **cold war.**

billiard ball model: an abstract model of the so-called realist school, which believes that international relations consists of states colliding with one another in predictable trajectories. Like other "realist" models, the billiard ball model substitutes fantasy for the complexities, contradictions, and ambiguities of the real world.

biodiversity: the vast and interrelated web of living animals and plants.

bipolar world: a world in which two major blocs of countries oppose each other.

bipolarity: power dominance by two states in the system.

bipolycentric: the division of geopolitical power between two countries while other countries or regions hold considerable economic and military power. Also known as bimultipolarity.

Bretton Woods Conference: held in 1944 at the Bretton Woods resort in New Hampshire. Representatives from 44 countries signed treaties creating the **International Monetary Fund (IMF)** and **International Bank for Reconstruction and Development (IBRD** or **World Bank)** which were designed to reconstruct those countries devastated by war, revive their economies and trade, and fix all currencies to the dollar and gold.

Brezhnev Doctrine: the Soviet policy, announced under the Brezhnev administration, that justified Soviet intervention in any communist country that was threatened by a noncommunist revolution or coup.

brilliant pebbles: the scheme to scatter throughout space thousands of small anti-ICBM satellites that would ram incoming **ICBMs.**

brinkmanship: the cold war game of "**chicken**" that the superpowers played, in which they would escalate a crisis to the brink of war and then back off.

Brussels Pact: an alliance of Britain, France, Belgium, the Netherlands, and Luxembourg to deter a Soviet attack and revive German power.

burden sharing: the attempts by the United States to get its allies and trade partners to share the burdens of high military expenses and open markets.

carbon dioxide: a greenhouse gas increased by the burning of fossil fuels, with severe consequences to the environment.

carrying capacity: the amount of related life an ecosystem can bear. If too many species exceed the carrying capacity, it will degrade and possibly destroy that ecosystem. The world is one vast ecosystem whose carrying capacity is being overwhelmed as the population soars past six billion and pollution causes the greenhouse effect, ozone depletion, desertification, deforestation, biocide, and other catastrophes.

cartel: a group of producers that band together to split markets, maintain prices, and collude rather than compete.

Carter Doctrine: the assertion in 1979 by the Carter administration that the Persian Gulf was a vital American interest that the United States would defend should the Gulf be invaded.

catch-all party: a political party that offers promises and policies to attract groups from as many places as possible on the political, economic, and social spectrum.

charismatic leader: one who has the power to inspire mass followings through magnetic personalities, ideologies, and promises.

charter: the United Nations' constitution.

"chicken": a power game in which participants in a crisis increase the pressure and stakes until the other side gives way. Sometimes the participants carefully manage the crisis so that it is resolved short of war. At other times they mismanage the crisis and those countries go to war.

chlorofluorocarbons (CFCs): contribute to both the **greenhouse** and **ozone depletion** effects.

civil war: also known as internal war or large-scale violence by two or more sides within one country.

civilization: complex societies that have most or all of the following: the mastery of agriculture; domestication of animals; complex, hierarchic political, social, economic, and religious institutions; the use of metals, the wheel, and writing systems; clearly defined territories; and trade with other peoples.

Clintonomics: the economic policies of President Bill Clinton, which included transforming the soaring federal budget deficits of the 1980s into budget surpluses, reducing the personnel and expense of the federal government as a percentage of GNP, increasing subsidies to high technology industries, cutting taxes for the poor and lower middle class, raising taxes for the rich, and forcing other countries to reduce their trade and investment barriers, which led to the longest economic expansion in American history and reversed the steady decline in American economic power and in the incomes of middle- and lower-class Americans and the quadrupling of the national debt under Reaganomics.

cobweb model: a liberal model of international relations in which states are increasingly entangled in interdependence.

cognitive dissonance: the tension or discomfort that occurs when people encounter information that conflicts with a belief system.

cold war: a period of intense animosity and confrontation between the United States and Soviet Union during which both countries competed for allies and **spheres of influence** around the world. The cold war was fueled by the conflicting ideological and geopolitical goals of the two **superpowers** and by a mutual misunderstanding of intentions.

collective security: the means by which a community of nations attempts to maintain the peace through negotiation or the threat of **sanctions** against international aggressors.

colonialism: the means by which one country rules another.

comity: a legal principle in which one state allows the intrusion of another state's laws into its territory.

Commission: the governing body of the **European Union.**

common agricultural policy (CAP): the European Union's agricultural support policy.

communism: a political philosophy that sees all history as characterized by class struggle, the culmination of which will be a proletarian or workers' revolution that creates a society based on the common and egalitarian ownership of property.

Communist Information Bureau (Cominform): a Moscow-based headquarters to direct communist movements around the world. Replaced the older Comintern.

comparative advantage: the national or created advantage that a nation can achieve in producing certain goods and selling them at home and abroad for the lowest competitive or comparative prices.

compellence: an attempt to force an individual or state to give up something valued.

Concert of Europe: see **Congress of Vienna.**

conciliation: occurs in an international conflict when an interested third party gives advice to both sides while refraining from offering a resolution.

condominium: the joint ownership of a territory by two or more states.

Conference on Security and Cooperation in Europe (CSCE): an organization of **nation-state** representatives meeting since 1973 to improve communications and reduce tensions between eastern and western Europe.

confidence-building measures: such things as better communications, mutual inspections, and freezes on weapons development initiated to reduce tensions and to make nuclear reduction treaties more likely and nuclear war less likely.

Congress of Vienna (1815): the peace conference that attempted to undo the territorial and political changes that transformed Europe during the Napoleonic era. Following the Congress, Europe's Great Powers—Britain, Prussia, Russia, Austria, and later France—formed the **Concert of Europe,** a collective security organization committed to mobilizing troops against any forces that threatened Europe's peace. The Concert was largely successful in maintaining peace among the great powers and squashing most revolutionary and independence movements that challenged the political status quo.

constitutive theory: argues that **states** can be legitimate only if they receive international recognition.

containment: the strategy by which the United States attempted to restrict Soviet expansion through economic, political, and military means.

Conventional Armed Forces in Europe Treaty (CFE): signed in 1990 between the **North Atlantic Treaty Organization** (NATO) and the **Warsaw Pact;** both sides agreed to huge cuts in their respective conventional forces.

Conventional Arms Transfer Talk (CATT): a series of talks designed to reach agreement on the transfer of weapons to other countries.

Coordinating Committee on Export Controls (COCOM): founded in 1948 and including nearly all the democratic industrial countries, COCOM was organized to impede the export of high technology to communist countries.

core countries: the world's advanced industrial countries whose wealth, according to **dependency theory,** is based on exploiting the **peripheral** and **semiperipheral** countries.

corporate welfare: the subsidies, tax cuts, infrastructure, import barriers, and export promotions that governments give to corporations.

corpus juris gentium: the body of international law among nations.

corruption: the illegal use of public or private resources for personal gain.

Council for Mutual Economic Assistance (COMECON): the Soviet equivalent of the **Marshall Plan** and the means of integrating the Soviet and Eastern European economies.

counterforce: the targeting of nuclear weapons at other nuclear weapons.

countervalue: the targeting of nuclear weapons at cities.

coup d'état: the violent overthrow of one government to replace it with a new one; also referred to as a coup.

Court of Arbitration: established by the International Chamber of Commerce in 1922; since then, the court has heard over 5,000 cases.

Covenant: the **League of Nations'** constitution.

cradle-to-grave benefits: the system of benefits in social market countries that provide welfare to their populations from birth to death.

crisis: any unanticipated situation in which one's vital interests are threatened and there is little time in which to decide what to do.

crisis decision making: the attempt to formulate a response in a limited time to a threat of violence when vital interests are at stake. The time constraints and the high stakes limit those involved in the decision making to a small group of advisers around the leader.

crisis management: the attempts by both sides in a serious dispute to manage events so that the crisis does not escalate into an unwanted war.

critical theory: a school of Marxism whose adherents believe that all perspectives are subjective and that we can never be objective.

crony capitalism: the system devised and epitomized by Japan and emulated by many other states whereby government and business collude, keeping out foreign competitors, gouging consumers at home, and **dumping** exports and investments overseas.

cruise missiles: the most versatile nuclear weapons, because they can be launched by submarines, surface ships, air bombers, and land-based systems.

Cuban missile crisis: occurred in October 1962, when the Soviet Union tried to place nuclear missiles in Cuba and the United States demanded their removal. At first the Soviets refused and agreed only after the United States imposed a naval blockade of Cuba and secretly promised to withdraw its own missiles from Turkey and not to invade Cuba.

culture: any group's distinct collective means of interpreting and interacting with the world and each other within a given environment. More specifically, culture is a group's integrated and distinct system of values, ethics, behavior patterns, history, and language, which are in turn reflected in that group's social, economic, and political institutions.

currency policy: a government's attempts to raise or lower the value of its currency either by buying or selling its currencies, raising or lowering interest rates, and/or raising or lowering restrictions on currency trading—all in an attempt to affect the supply and demand for that currency.

C3I: "Command, Control, Communications, and Intelligence"—the means by which governments prepare for and fight wars.

declarative theory: argues that **recognition** has no legal effect; states either exist or they do not, and recognition simply acknowledges that fact.

deconstructivism: the postmodern theory that all thoughts and perspectives are subjective and consequently we can never know objective truth.

decoupling: the fear that the defense relationship between the United States and Western Europe could break apart because of political isolationism.

defense: an action taken to protect oneself against an opponent's act to compel cooperation when the opponent ignores or fails to understand one's deterrent efforts.

deforestation: the rapid destruction of the world's forests by clear-cutting for logging, grazing, and other reasons; alters climates and destroys millions of potentially useful plant and animal species. Because forests are the world's lungs, absorbing carbon dioxide and turning it into oxygen, deforestation accelerates the **greenhouse effect.** Particularly in the tropics, deforestation destroys millions of species that can be used as medicines or foods for humanity.

demand-side economics: policies that attempt to enrich consumers with a stronger dollar, lower taxes, and/or lower interest rates, which in turn stimulate production by consumer demands for more goods and services.

democracy: in Abraham Lincoln's words, a system of government "of the people, by the people, and for the people." The foundations of democratic government are the free election of leaders and the possession of human and civil rights.

dependence: the relationship between countries of different economic power in which the weaker depends on the stronger.

dependency theory: argues that **Third World** countries are doomed to remain poor because they are trapped in an exploitive global economy in which rich countries collaborate with the elites of poor countries to exploit the mines, plantations, and cheap wages of the Third World countries.

desertification: the transformation into desert of many lands that once had abundant soil, plants, and water as the demands of humans proved overwhelming to those ecosystems.

détente: a period of relaxed tensions between the United States and Soviet Union during which important nuclear and trade agreements were signed; inaugurated by President Nixon in 1969 and lasting until the Soviet invasion of Afghanistan in 1979.

deterrence: made up of two essential elements—capability and credibility—that enable a country to make an opponent believe that if it attacks, it will lose far more than it gains.

development of underdevelopment: according to **dependency theory,** occurs when foreign investors develop only small sectors of a Third World country and link them with the global economy so that wealth is siphoned out of the country and it remains poor.

development theory: argues that rational or constitutional-style governments provide the best chance for achieving **economic development.**

developmental market system: systematic government intervention to promote key industries through subsidies, import protection, and export promotion in order to achieve high levels of economic growth and a relatively egalitarian income distribution.

dictatorship of the proletariat: the **Marxist-Leninist** concept that justifies a Communist party dictatorship after the revolution and during the transition to pure communism.

dollar gap: the inability of foreign countries to pay for the American goods they wanted in the 1940s and early 1950s. The United States tried to bridge the gap through foreign aid.

dollar glut: occurred in the early 1960s when the number of dollars in the global economy exceeded the value of gold held by the United States; prompted fears that dollar holders would try to redeem their dollars for gold and thus bankrupt the United States and the fixed currency system. The dollar glut was also known as the **dollar overhang.**

domino effect: the belief that a successful communist revolution in one country would lead to similar successful revolutions in neighboring countries, thus knocking over noncommunist governments like a row of dominoes. The belief was used to justify American intervention in scores of Third World countries. More recently, the term has been used to mean the economic collapse of interdependent countries.

Dumbarton Oaks Conference: the first conference at which representatives began negotiating the organization of the United Nations.

dumping: selling below price. Can be a particularly effective **neomercantilist** strategy in which an industry dumps its products in foreign markets in order to drive competitors out of business. After taking over the market, the industry then raises prices to recoup earlier loses. But sometimes a government will attempt to protect its industry against a foreign **dumping** attack.

early industrializer: Great Britain in the late 18th century and the United States in the mid-19th century were the first countries to mass industrialize.

eclectic school: the attempt to bridge the gap between naturalists and positivists by maintaining that while **states** did indeed have natural rights and duties, they were only obliged to fulfill them if those laws were codified.

economic development: self-sustaining economic growth that brings a higher living standard and quality of life to an ever-greater percentage of the population.

economic liberalism: an economic theory under which government plays a minimal role in the economy, and the laws of supply and demand shape production and consumption. Individuals produce and trade what they can best produce and trade. Prosperity springs from all being free to fulfill their respective self-interests. Trade should be free not just within but *between* states, allowing each to specialize in those products it is best suited to produce and then to trade those products for foreign products.

economic sanctions: the severing of economic ties by a state or group of states with another state or group of states to force them to concede on an issue.

economist: someone who devises and believes in two-dimensional theories, models, graphs, and equations that purport to explain economics. If economists are theorists, **political economists** examine the real world and are thus empiricists.

ecosystem: a natural area whose plants, animals, and physical environment are closely interdependent.

electromagnetic pulse (EMP): released by a nuclear explosion; burns out electrical equipment over a huge area.

empiricism: the study of the real world.

Enlightenment (the Age of): the name for a period of European philosophy (1648–1789) that emphasized the concepts of representative government and political freedom.

equivalent megatons: the relative number of nuclear megatons each side holds.

ethnic cleansing: a euphemism for the process by which one ethnic group tries to murder or drive away another ethnic group from a territory.

ethnic group: a distinct national **culture** within a larger **nation.**

European Coal and Steel Community (ECSC): the agreement by members to integrate their coal and steel industries; created by the 1951 Paris Treaty signed by France, West Germany, Italy, Belgium, the Netherlands, and Luxembourg.

European Community (EC): created from the **European Economic Community (EEC)** in 1967, and now called the European Union.

European currency unit (ECU): the currency for the **European Community;** one ECU equals about $1.25.

European Economic Community (EEC): an agreement signed by France, West Germany, Italy, Belgium, the Netherlands, and Luxembourg to create a customs union; designed under the 1957 Rome Treaty and succeeded in 1967 by the **European Community (EC).**

European Union (EU): created from the **European Community (EC)** on November 1, 1993, from the Maastricht Treaty of 1991. Fifteen states were members in 2000: France, West Germany, Italy, Belgium, the Netherlands, Luxembourg, Great Britain, Denmark, Ireland, Spain, Greece, Portugal, Austria, Finland, and Sweden.

evil empire: a term popularized by President Reagan and used to describe the Soviet Union.

exchange rate comparison method: the relative difference between a nation's **gross national product**

(GNP) and its **per capita income** measured by converting each nation's production into dollars.

exclusive economic zones (EEZs): the zones by which a government can claim exclusive economic exploitation rights up to 200 miles from that nation's coastline.

expansionists: those who want to expand their country's power and territory.

export substitution: the government's reduction of trade barriers protecting its new industries and devaluation of its currency in order to allow its industries to become competitive in global markets; occurs after an **import substitution** phase.

extended deterrence: America's nuclear deterrence extended to Western Europe.

failed state: a war waged by criminal groups when a state is no longer capable of governing the territory or people supposedly under its sway. See **uncivil war.**

fair trade: the idea that trade should be based on reciprocity or mutual benefit to both partners; would include a trade balance.

fascism: an ideology that proclaims a **nation** superior to all others and promotes the devotion of all individuals to the state. Individuals achieve their identity and meaning, and fulfill national culture by serving the state and basking in its glories. Conquest and empire are considered to be the state's most sublime achievements. Sometimes known as state socialism. During the 1930s and through the end of World War II, Japan, Germany, and Italy had fascist governments.

fast-track powers: powers granted to the president by Congress to bring trade agreements to a direct vote in Congress without adding any amendments or reservations.

Faust: a brilliant man who sells his soul to the devil Mephistopheles in return for supreme powers that he uses to transform the world economically. The result, tragically, is destruction and chaos; instead of making the world better, Faust makes it worse. The Faust legend is treated by several authors, most notably Goethe.

feudalism: a system that organizes people into rigid political, social, and economic classes in which land ownership and power reside with a small elite.

fine tuning: the attempt by a government to adjust its policies so that the economy maintains steady rates of growth, unemployment, inflation, and other measures.

first-strike capability: a country's ability to strike first and destroy most of the enemy's nuclear force in silos; theoretically, the enemy would not retaliate with its remaining forces because it would then suffer nuclear attack on its cities.

first-strike weapons: include **ICBMs,** which are highly accurate, fast, and provide little warning time; in their fixed silos, however, ICBMs are vulnerable to enemy attack. First-strike weapons are best used in a counterforce strategy against the enemy's ICBM silos and headquarters.

first world: a category that includes all democratic industrial countries, such as the United States, Great Britain, and France.

fiscal policy: economic goals set by a government's budget. When the budget is increased, the economy is stimulated, and when the budget is reduced, the economy is deflated. The budget is also an important source of subsidies for industrial policies.

fixed currency: a system in which a currency's exchange rate is fixed or officially unchanging.

flexible response: an escalating strategy of U.S. response to a Soviet Union attack on Western Europe; rather than an immediate **massive retaliation,** the United States would try to prevail at the conventional military level, and then, if the Soviets appeared to be winning, prevail through a controlled escalation at the tactical, regional, and, if necessary, the **ICBM** level.

floating currency: a system in which a currency's exchange rates fluctuate from market forces of supply and demand.

foreign policy: a broad set of national goals and strategies that guide the formulation of specific policies affecting specific issues. A nation's foreign policy includes the specific goals that leaders pursue in the global system, the values that shape those goals, and the means by which those goals are achieved.

Four Policemen: Roosevelt's conception of the United States, Great Britain, the Soviet Union, and China acting as "policemen" and maintaining order in their respective **spheres of influence** in the postwar era.

Fourteen Points: the ideals articulated by President Woodrow Wilson on January 8, 1918, for which the United States was fighting World War I. The most important points were the creation of a League of Nations that would attempt to settle disputes peacefully; self-determination for all peoples, the end of secret negotiations and treaties, freedom of the seas, free trade, and arms reduction.

free market: the interaction between producers and consumers without any government interference such as taxation, subsidies, health or safety regulation. Free markets are an ideal rather than a reality.

free rider: a country that enjoys international economic and military benefits but contributes little to the system in the way of open markets, foreign aid, and/or higher defense spending. Japan has been most frequently criticized by other states as being a free rider.

free trade: free markets between states. Free trade is an ideal rather than a reality.

functionalism: argues that international organizations breed related organizations in related fields. Over time, different international organizations merge to form stronger and more comprehensive ones. Organizations binding nations economically or socially eventually bind them politically as people increasingly transfer their loyalties from the **nation-state** to the international state.

game theory: abstractions used by some social scientists to explain human and state behavior.

General Agreement on Trade and Tariffs (GATT): created in 1947 by 23 countries as a forum for member negotiation of the reduction of trade barriers. There have been eight GATT negotiation rounds since its founding.

general system of preferences (GSP): a system by which the industrialized countries will reduce trade barriers to Third World products.

geoeconomics: those issues that can be negotiated by any means short of violence. Disputes over trade, intellectual property, economic development, multinational corporations, industrial policy, and the environment are several important geoeconomic issues.

geopolitics: those disputes over territory, beliefs, behaviors, or some other issue over which opponents might consider using violence to resolve the conflict. Territorial expansion, human rights, arms races, drug smuggling, refugees, and ideological strife are a few prominent geopolitical conflicts. Geopolitical conflicts almost invariably have some **geoeconomic** basis.

glasnost: Gorbachev's policy of encouraging open information and debate in the Soviet Union.

global containment: a concept articulated by Paul Nitze in his National Security Council 68 (**NSC-68**) report issued in early 1950. Nitze argued that the United States was engaged in a global struggle with the Soviet Union in which one side's gain was the other's loss. The United States had to mobilize using every means possible, including military power, to defeat any Soviet advance. With the Korean War's outbreak in June 1950, the United States followed a global containment strategy.

global political economy: see **international political economy.**

global warming: the earth's heating another four degrees over the next 50 years, leading to catastrophic climatic changes.

global warming treaty (1992): signed by over 170 nations at the **Rio de Janeiro Earth Summit** to address the **greenhouse effect.** Although the Bush administration refused to sign, the Clinton administration signed the treaty in 1993.

globalization: the ever more complex interdependence embracing all nations and individuals in the world.

good offices: occurs in an international conflict when an interested third party provides a neutral location for the disputants but refrains from moderating the actual negotiations—as when the United States hosted the Middle East Peace negotiations in 1992.

Gradual and Reciprocated Initiatives in Tension-reduction (GRIT): ways to halt and reverse an arms race by making limited concessions and waiting for the other side to reciprocate.

Great Leap Forward: Mao Zedong's strategy in 1958 to industrialize China by requiring each town to build its own factories. The result was mass famine, economic depression, and Mao's temporary eclipse from power.

great powers: Russia, Britain, France, China, and Israel—those that have nuclear and conventional forces but limited power to fight overseas.

green revolution: the introduction of new strains of seed, fertilizer, and mechanization promoting high crop yields for farmers.

greenhouse effect: increasing amounts of heat (that ordinarily would dissipate into the universe) trapped in the atmosphere by an ever growing amount of gases and chemicals poured into the air from industrial sources. The result could be **global warming.**

gross domestic product (GDP): total value of a nation's annual production of goods and services, excluding imports and exports.

gross national product (GNP): total value of a nation's annual production of goods and services, including imports and exports.

Group of Five: the United States, Japan, Germany, France, and Great Britain, whose representatives meet occasionally to deal with a specific and pressing economic crisis.

Group of Seven: the United States, Japan, Germany, France, Great Britain, Italy, and Canada, whose leaders meet annually to discuss global problems.

Group of 77: founded in 1963 by Third World countries to lobby the industrialized countries for better trade, investment, and aid terms. Although its numbers have increased over the decades, it has not been successful in achieving its aims.

Group of Ten: the eleven (not ten) leading industrial nations—the United States, Great Britain, France, Germany, Japan, Italy, Canada, Sweden, Switzerland, the Netherlands, and Belgium—which meet to discuss monetary and economic matters.

groupthink: the pressure on individuals in a policymaking unit to be team players and not rock the boat with options or information that counter the prevailing assessment. Those who dissent are often left out of the policy loop by the other policymakers.

gunboat diplomacy: the ability of the great powers to use relatively small army and navy forces to wring concessions from, or take over, other countries.

Hague Conferences (1899, 1907): meetings held by 26 nations represented at the 1899 conference and 44 at the 1907 conference to negotiate and pass dozens of treaties regulating warfare, including the Hague Conventions on War.

halons: ozone-depleting compounds formerly used in fire extinguishers.

hard-target kill (HTK): the capability of one side's nuclear weapons to penetrate and destroy the hardened silos of the other.

hegemon: the number one state in the global system; the hegemon uses its power to shape international relations according to its interests and values.

hegemonic stability theory: argues that international relations in the global political economy has been shaped by the rise and fall of hegemons, or those states that briefly become the most powerful in the system.

Helsinki Accord: signed by the United States, the Soviet Union, and 33 other countries; accepted the postwar boundaries as permanent and guaranteed human rights in all signatory countries.

high politics: the traditional emphasis on **geopolitical** issues in international relations.

Hobbesian struggle: a state of nature in which there is a "war of all against all" and only the strongest survive. Named after the political philosopher Thomas Hobbes.

horizontal proliferation: the acquiring of nuclear weapons by new countries.

humanism: a philosophy that celebrates humans and their reasoning, creativity, and potential.

hydrogen bomb: created by a fusion process smashing atoms together; sometimes known as a thermonuclear bomb.

ICBMs: intercontinental ballistic missiles. Also see **second-strike weapons.**

ideology: a system of beliefs, behaviors, and institutions that can span national boundaries.

immunity: being beyond the law's jurisdiction. Sovereign states and their diplomats generally have immunity from the **jurisdiction** of national laws.

imperial overstretch: occurs, according to Paul Kennedy, when a nation's military ambitions and commitments exceed its economic ability to support those ambitions and commitments. A **nation-state** fails to reinvest enough human and material resources in the creation of wealth, the state's economy eventually breaks down under the defense burden, and its economic position in the world is overtaken by others.

imperialism: the conquest of one people by another.

import substitution: a means of industrialization through which a government erects high trade barriers against competitive products to encourage foreign investment, and creates an overvalued currency that affords the purchase of the machinery and raw materials to make those industrial products.

industrial policy: a policy that targets specific firms, industries, technologies, or economic sectors for development with such devices as tax reductions, subsidies, protection from imports, cartels, and/or export promotion.

industrial revolution: marked the shift from small-scale, handmade craft production to large-scale, assembly-line, factory production using inanimate energy sources such as coal and, later, oil and electricity.

intangible power: less easily measured or *soft* sources of power such as leadership, national cohesion, and political will. Intangible power sources often decide the winner in a conflict between forces with relatively evenly matched tangible power.

intelligence: the means by which one state gathers and analyzes information vital to understanding the capabilities and intentions of other states.

interdependence: the drawing together in varying degrees of all the world's countries and individuals into an ever more complex economic, political, technological, ethical, communication, transportation, and cultural, global political economic web.

interest groups: sometimes known as lobbying groups or lobbies, any group of people that shares and seeks to promote a common interest by organizing and pressuring those in government for favorable policies.

Intermediate Range Nuclear Force Treaty (INF, 1986): the first treaty to actually eliminate some nuclear weapons, in this case, regional nuclear missiles.

intermestic policies: those policies that involve both foreign and domestic issues.

International Atomic Energy Agency (IAEA): regulates the **Nuclear Proliferation Treaty (NPT)** through the power to inspect the signatories' facilities.

International Bank for Reconstruction and Development (IBRD): also known as the **World Bank,** the IBRD was created at the **Bretton Woods Conference** of 1944, along with the **International Monetary Fund (IMF).**

International Court of Justice (ICJ): formally established by the United Nations on April 18, 1946; in form, function, and location, the ICJ is largely the continuation of the **Permanent Court of International Justice (PCIJ).** Located at The Hague (*de facto* capital of the Netherlands), the ICJ hears and rules on cases. The court has 15 judges, five of which are elected every three years to hold office for nine years. The Security Council and General Assembly elect the judges. International organizations, including the U.N. Security Council, General Assembly, and any other institution, can ask the court for advisory opinions. Every signatory to the U.N. Charter agrees to comply with ICJ decisions. Between 1946 and 1988, the ICJ heard only 55 cases, rendered judgments on 30, and handed down 19 advisory opinions. The ICJ or a party to a dispute can call on the U.N. Security Council to act against recalcitrant states. The Security Council votes on the measures necessary to implement an ICJ decision.

international intergovernmental organizations (IGOs): international organizations of government members.

International Monetary Fund (IMF): a international bank to which member countries contribute money that is then lent to a member experiencing trade deficits. The member invests the money in its economy to strengthen it and balance trade.

international political economy (IPE): the global economy shaped by political, military, environmental, and other international forces.

international relations: the relations among sovereign states.

International Trade Organization (ITO): created by the Havana Charter signed in 1946 but because the United States did not ratify the treaty, the ITO was stillborn.

internationalism: an individual's primary identification with humanity as a whole rather than the nation into which he or she was born.

invisible hand: the idea that the forces of supply and demand in **free markets** will supply the needs of society and its members. The phrase was popularized by Adam Smith in his classic work, *The Wealth of Nations* (1776).

Irish Republican Army: a group of Irish Catholics that employs terrorism to force Britain out of Northern Ireland.

iron curtain: a phrase coined by Churchill at a speech in Fulton, Missouri, in March 1946, to describe the Soviet control over eastern Europe; helped mobilize the American public for the cold war.

iron triangle: coalitions of bureaucrats, representatives, and interest groups that work closely together to promote their collective interests on specific issues.

irredentism: occurs when a **nation** is scattered among two or more states, and there is an attempt to unify that nation into its own **state.**

isolationists: those who want to minimize their country's involvement in international political affairs.

jurisdiction: the right and power of a legal body to take responsibility for applying the law against an alleged crime.

just war: the idea that some wars are justified under certain conditions. See **neo-just war.**

Kant, Immanuel: In his 1795 "Essay on Perpetual Peace," Immanuel Kant predicted that the **global political economy** would eventually evolve into a system that resolves conflicts by peaceful cooperation rather than war. Kant foresaw three developments that would lead to a perpetual peace: (1) the conversion of authoritarian states into liberal democracies (republicanism); (2) the evolution of international law and organization into an authoritative system binding all sovereign states (federalism); and (3) economic development and interdependence (hospitality). Kant's vision is fast becoming a reality. **Geoeconomic** conflict is replacing **geopolitics** as the dominant force in international relations.

Keiretsu: Japanese industrial groups centered around a bank, trading firm, and insurance company that supply much of the financing; include a wide range of manufacturing, service, and other firms.

Kellogg-Briand Pact (1928): an agreement signed by the great powers condemning aggressive war as illegal.

kiloton: One kiloton equals 2,200 pounds of TNT. The atomic bomb dropped on Hiroshima was equal to 20 kilotons or 44,000 tons of TNT.

kleptocracy: a government whose major purpose is to loot the public treasury and economy.

Kuomintang (KMT): under Chiang Kaishek, the Chinese Nationalist Party that battled the Chinese Communist Party (CCP) in a 20-year civil war.

Kyoto accord: an international treaty signed at Kyoto, Japan, in 1998 stipulating that the industrial countries should cut their greenhouse emissions below their 1990 levels by the year 2005.

late industrializer: countries such as Germany and Japan that became industrialized in the 20th century.

League of Nations (1920–1945): charter established by the Treaty of Versailles at the peace conference in 1919;

organized the following year into an assembly that included representatives of all members and met for about one month once a year; a 10-member council in which the four great powers were permanently represented while the other seats rotated, and which met four times annually; and a secretariat that administered the organization. Decisions passed in both the Council and Assembly only with unanimous approval. Forty-five countries were members at the first session in 1920; at the league's peak it had 59 members. The league's headquarters were in Geneva. The United States was not a member.

legal person: a person, organization, and/or state that has legal rights or duties.

legitimacy: the popular acceptance of the authority of an individual, institution, group, or system.

Leninism: named after Vladimir Ilyich Lenin, who led the 1917 Russian communist revolution; Lenin advocated class struggle, revolution, and war, and totalitarian state power. Leninism ended with the destruction of the **Berlin Wall** in November 1989.

liberal democracy: a system of government based on universal adult suffrage, free elections, human and civil rights, and representative government.

liberal theory: See **liberalism.**

liberalism: a political philosophy that emphasizes the importance of human and civil rights and duties and of representative government.

Limited Test Ban Treaty (1963): signatories agreed not to test nuclear weapons in the atmosphere or underwater. China and France did not sign the treaty until recently.

long cycle theory: argues that wars occur in cycles related to shifts in economic power and dynamism.

Long Telegram: the name for the policy paper George Kennan sent to Washington from Moscow in 1946 analyzing the Soviet threat.

low politics: the term traditionally used to designate **geoeconomic** issues.

low-intensity warfare: guerrilla wars.

macroeconomic policies: those policies with primarily national effects that can also have positive or negative effects on certain firms, industries, or sectors.

Malthus, Thomas: predicted in his "Essay on the Principle of Population" (1798) that the world's population would grow exponentially while its food grew arithmetically. The ultimate result would be mass famine and death.

Manhattan Project: the code name for the American effort to build an atomic bomb during World War II.

market Darwinism: the survival-of-the-fittest, might-makes-right anarchy that results when there are no economic regulations.

market imperfections: such practices as cartels, dumping, false advertising, government regulations, consumer ignorance of unsafe products, and so on, that deviate from **free market** ideals.

Marshall Plan: the U.S. extension of billions of dollars in aid to Europe to reconstruct its economies and stabilize its politics to prevent the rise of communism; announced by Secretary of State George Marshall in June 1947.

Marxism: the philosophy named after Karl Marx, who believed that class struggle and the exploitation of the many by the few could only be resolved by a revolution of the workers, or proletariat, which would usher in a communist utopia of perfect equality and justice.

massive retaliation: the strategy of threatening a massive nuclear strike against the Soviet Union should it invade Western Europe.

mediation: a third-party proposal of nonbinding solutions to the participants in an international conflict—as in the Camp David negotiations of 1977 when President Carter mediated between Egyptian President Sadat and Israeli Prime Minister Begin.

megaton: the equivalent of 2.2 million pounds of TNT. One B-52 alone carries 25 megatons of nuclear explosives, or 12.5 times the destructive power of all bombs dropped during World War II.

mercantilism: the policy by which governments created wealth and strengthened security by maximizing the nation's exports through state-licensed monopolies and subsidies, and minimizing imports through high trade barriers. The idea was to gain a continual trade surplus and thus a steady influx of gold into the coffers of the state and domestic businesses. Overseas colonies enlarged the state's raw materials and market resource base, and enabled entrepreneurs to enjoy large-scale production and profits. The goal was autarchy or self-sufficiency within a large empire.

methane: a **greenhouse** gas with both manmade and natural sources.

middle-ranking power: a state with large conventional military forces in a regional context, but lacking the power to project it outside the region.

mid-intensity conflicts (MICs): wars on the scale of the 1990–1991 Persian Gulf War.

military-industrial complex: the economic and political relationship between industries that produce military goods, the U.S. Defense Department, and congressional representatives with military industries in their districts. Together, they have a powerful interest in maintaining high levels of defense spending regardless of what kind of foreign threats the country faces.

minimum deterrence: the minimal number of nuclear weapons deemed necessary to ensure deterrence.

mirror image: an opposing view that describes how parties in conflict view each other's actions as malevolent and aggressive and their own actions as innocent, just, and defensive.

missile gap: Kennedy's mistaken 1960 election campaign claim (which helped get him elected) that the Soviets then surpassed the United States in nuclear weapons.

missile technology control regime (MTCR): treaty signed by the United States, Germany, Great Britain, Japan, France, Italy, Canada, and Spain to control the transfer of missile technology to third parties.

mobilization: mass emotional support for certain policies, ideas, or actions created by a government, group, or leader.

modern societies: those that are predominantly urban, industrial, literate, rational, and mobile. Although often containing extremes of wealth and poverty, modern societies are generally middle class-societies whose inhabitants enjoy not only high **per capita income** and consumption but also a good quality of life ideally involving considerable leisure time, health, self-fulfillment, living space, and a clean, comfortable environment.

modernization: an umbrella term for a series of interrelated and endless intellectual, political, economic, technological, religious, sociological, and psychological changes based on the idea that human reason rather than a transcendent god is the master of humanity's fate, and that individuals should freely pursue their material, emotional, and spiritual needs.

modernization theory: argues that every state can modernize in a series of stages similar to those experienced by the Western countries.

monetary policy: the policy of raising or lowering interest rates that the government or central bank charges commercial banks to borrow money. When the central bank raises interest rates, the economy slows; when the central bank lowers rates, the economy is stimulated. In the United States, the central bank is the Federal Reserve.

monopoly: the domination and control of a particular market or industry by a single firm.

Monroe Doctrine: President James Monroe's policy opposing European expansion in the western hemisphere (1823).

Montreal Protocol on Substances That Deplete the Ozone Layer (1987): signatories to this and a subsequent London protocol agreed to eliminate all **CFCs** and **halons** by the year 2000.

more bang for the buck: the Eisenhower policy relying on nuclear weapons rather than large numbers of American ground troops for Europe's defense.

most favored nation (MFN) clause: the **GATT** principle under which a member that gives a trade advantage to another member must give the same advantage to all members.

"Mr. X" Article: the anonymous article George Kennan published in the journal *Foreign Affairs* in which he elaborated his conception of the Soviet threat and how the United States could counter it.

Multi-Fiber Agreement: signed in 1974 by industrial and less developed countries; created a multilateral quota system for the global trade of artificial fiber and wool textiles and materials. More than two decades later, the Multi-Fiber Agreement still upholds a global quota system for textiles.

multinational corporation (MNC): a corporation with one or more overseas enterprises.

multinationalism: two or more distinct nations, each with a large population, existing within one **nation-state.**

multiparty system: a political system in which three or more competitive political parties have large national followings.

multiple independently targetable reentry vehicle (MIRV): a missile armed with two or more warheads that can be launched toward different targets.

multiplier effect: a pervasive and spreading influence such as the effect of an important industry on the economy. Also called "ripple effect."

multipolar world: the distribution of power in the world among three or more great or superpowers.

multipolarity: the division of power among three or more states in the international system.

Mutual and Balanced Force Reduction (MBFR): a series of negotiations between **NATO** and the **Warsaw Pact;** resulted in significant cuts in conventional forces.

Mutual Defense Assistance Act: passed by Congress in 1949; supplied military aid to **NATO** and other American allies.

mutually assured destruction (MAD): the likelihood that a full nuclear exchange between Russia and the United States would destroy both countries. Thus both sides have been more cautious in nearing the brink of war with each other.

"my way" doctrine: the Gorbachev reversal of the **Brezhnev Doctrine.** Henceforth Moscow would allow the East European countries, and eventually the Soviet republics, to decide freely which political system they preferred.

nation: primarily a population with a common culture, language, history, traditions, ideals, and sense of common destiny.

nation building: the process by which a government attempts to build and develop the economy, political system, and common identity of a nation-state.

national interests: both the broad goals that all states share—political independence, economic growth, cultural preservation, and peace—and the distinct goals each state pursues on specific issues.

national security: those measures necessary to protect a nation's vital geoeconomic and geopolitical interests.

National Security Act: passed by Congress in July 1947; created the **National Security Council,** the Central Intelligence Agency, and the Defense Department.

National Security Council (NSC): a group of foreign policy advisers to the president; includes a national security adviser and the heads of the CIA, Defense Department, and State Department.

nationalism: a feeling of intense emotional identity with one's nation.

nation-state: a sovereign state or system of government over a clearly defined territory whose legitimacy is recognized by other nation-states.

naturalist school: argues that some laws are natural to all human beings despite their various cultures. Human reason can break free of any culture's values and customs to discover the underlying natural laws.

neocolonialism: the idea that **colonialism** has simply been replaced by a more subtle, but no less effective, form of exploitation. Newly independent states are still dependent on their former masters and other industrial countries for technology, finance, markets, and products. The plantations and mines first created by the imperial powers often remain in foreign hands and continue to be economic islands within the former colony. Little if any wealth from this production trickles down to the native population.

neofunctionalism: the attempt to overcome criticism of **functionalist theory** by recognizing that conflicts between a nation's sovereign instincts and international needs could limit or derail the development of international organizations; nevertheless, overall, international organizations would proliferate in functions, power, and interconnectedness.

neo-just war doctrine: the contemporary perspective on a **just war;** includes six key components: (1) war can only be fought after all other means of resolving the issue have been exhausted; (2) only legitimate governments can decide to go to war; (3) wars should be fought for self-defense and not revenge; (4) there should be a good chance of winning; (5) the war should be fought to achieve conditions that would be better than those that occurred through nonresistance; and (6) war should be fought to resist aggression, not to change the enemy's government or society.

Neoliberalism: a revision of liberalism that takes into account the complexity and ambiguity of human behavior.

neomercantilism: a government's rapid development of the economy to achieve a trade surplus with its competitors by systematically restricting imports, promoting exports, and targeting strategic industries and technologies with subsidies, cartels, and other advantages.

neorealist school or **neorealist theory:** argues that power and policy shape the rules or laws of the international system. International law changes and develops as the power distribution shifts and issues proliferate in an increasingly interdependent global economy. Just as the most powerful states make the system's laws to protect and promote their own—rather than international—interests, they use the same criteria when choosing to obey or disregard international law.

new economic policy: announcement by President Nixon, August 1971, that the United States would abandon the gold standard and devalue the dollar in an attempt to reverse America's growing trade deficit and economic problems.

new international economic order (NIEO): espoused by the nonaligned movement and based on the idea of new trade, investment, and aid relations between the **First** and **Third Worlds** in order for the latter to accrue more benefit.

new world order: President George Bush's term for an increasingly orderly world in which the nature and effectiveness of power varies according to what the issue is, how other issues and priorities are related to

it, and how skillfully the participants bargain—as opposed to a world whose relations are characterized by violence and anarchy. As the **cold war** ended and the world becomes increasingly bound by a web of economic, nuclear, moral, and environmental relations, international conflicts are over economic and human welfare—rather than territory and ideology—and are managed by international organizations and international law.

newly industrializing countries (NICs): countries such as South Korea, Taiwan, and Singapore, which have succeeded in industrializing and achieving high economic growth and relatively egalitarian income distribution.

ngo swarm: the strategy whereby **nongovernmental organizations (NGOs)** affected by decisions being made by an **international intergovernmental organization (IGO)** or private corporation will stage demonstrations, submit petitions, and circulate information to pressure that IGO to decide in the NGOs' favor.

nitrous oxide: a **greenhouse** gas.

Nixon Doctrine: policy announced by President Richard Nixon in 1969 under which the United States would refrain from direct involvement in Third World wars, but would provide supplies to noncommunist governments faced with communist insurgencies.

nonaligned movement: founded at conferences in Belgrade in 1954 and the larger Bandung Conference of April 1955 by a group of **Third World** countries dedicated to remaining independent and forging a political economic alternative to the **cold war** rivalry.

nongovernmental organizations (NGOs): international organizations of members that are not governments.

non-tariff barriers (NTBs): every means except tariffs that a state will use to block imports. Such means might include quotas, **cartels,** red tape, and discriminatory regulations. Japan's **neomercantilism** uses non-tariff barriers.

North American Free Trade Association (NAFTA): a common market of the United States, Canada, and Mexico; the details are still being negotiated.

North Atlantic Treaty Organization (NATO): the 1949 alliance of the United States, Canada, and most western European states to deter a Soviet attack.

NSC-68: *National Security Council report 68,* largely written by Paul Nitze and advocating a global, military-oriented **containment** strategy against the Soviet Union.

nuclear autumn: the theoretical effect of a 5,000-megaton nuclear exchange that would cause temperatures to fall 9 to 27 degrees Fahrenheit (5 to 15 degrees Celsius); the effect on human life might be just as catastrophic as a **nuclear winter.**

nuclear ladder: includes tactical, regional, and intercontinental forces.

Nuclear Proliferation Treaty (NPT) 1968: signatories agreed not to produce, accept, or seek nuclear weapons from others.

nuclear utilization theory (NUT): the belief that a nuclear war can be won; the opposite of **MAD.**

nuclear winter: the theoretical effect of a 5,000-megaton nuclear exchange that would cause so much ash to ascend into the atmosphere that most of the sun's rays would be blocked from the earth and temperatures would plunge as much as 36 degrees Fahrenheit (20 degrees Celsius) in the northern hemisphere where 90 percent of the world's population lives, wiping out crops and causing mass starvation. The radiation would also destroy the earth's protective **ozone** layer, without which virtually all life would become extinct.

official development aid (ODA): the official aid that one government gives another.

oligopoly: dominance by a few firms of a particular market or industry.

Omnibus Trade Act (1988): strengthened the president's power to retaliate against countries that engaged in predatory trade.

one-party state: a state dominated by one political party while other parties, if they are allowed to exist, have small followings.

open door policy: articulated in a series of notes (1899 and 1900) by Secretary of State John Hays urging the European powers not to carve up and colonize China—but can be taken more generally as an American commitment to **free trade.**

operational code: a system of general beliefs about fundamental issues of history and central questions of politics; offers a means to evaluate information and problems, and make choices about them.

orderly marketing agreements (OMAs): agreements between a country whose firms are **dumping** goods and a country whose markets are being deluged with underpriced imports designed to limit those imports by destroying domestic industries.

Organization for African Unity (OAU): an organization of all African states designed to deal collectively with issues affecting that continent.

Organization for Economic Cooperation and Development (OECD): the organization of the world's leading industrial countries.

Organization of American States (OAS): founded in 1947, its members include virtually all countries in North and South America.

Organization of Petroleum-Exporting Countries (OPEC): a **cartel** of oil-producing countries that attempts to keep oil prices high by assigning each member production quotas to limit supply. In 1973, OPEC succeeded in quadrupling global oil prices and further doubling them in 1979, then declined in influence throughout the 1980s into the 1990s.

Ostpolitik: West Germany's **détente** policy toward Eastern Europe and the Soviet Union in the late 1960s and throughout the 1970s.

overkill: the existence of nuclear weapons that have a destructive power exceeding that needed to destroy the enemy.

ozone layer depletion: the deterioration (caused by a variety of industrial chemicals) of the ozone layer that screens the earth from most of the sun's harmful ultraviolet rays. As the ozone layer deteriorates, the increased ultraviolet radiation will destroy plants and microscopic animals on up the food chain, ultimately threatening human food sources.

Pacta sunt servanda: the universal understanding that treaties are legally binding.

patron–client groups: associations between patrons, usually local strongmen with wealth and political power who dispense favors—jobs, loans, housing, help in forming a business, protection to businesses, entrance to college, potential spouses, advice and information—and clients in the community who return political loyalty and a portion of their income. Local patrons in turn become the clients for national leaders and parties in which each does favors for the other.

payments account: the amount of all official inflows and outflows of money through a country.

Peace of Westphalia (1648): the first attempt by European states to negotiate restrictions on warfare and reasons to go to war. The peace conference became known as the First European Congress. It ended the Thirty Years War and recognized the **sovereignty** of existing countries.

peaceful coexistence: 1956 declaration by the Soviet Union that communism and capitalism could coexist without going to war.

peacekeeping: occurs when an international military force helps maintain a peace between two or more belligerents.

peacemaking: occurs when an international military force imposes peace by fighting one or more belligerents.

people's liberation wars: a mass popular uprising in a country against a foreign power that has colonized that country.

per capita income: the amount each citizen would have if wealth of a nation were evenly divided; determined by dividing the population into the **gross national product (GNP).**

perestroika: the Gorbachev policy of restructuring the Soviet system to make it more efficient and responsive to the people's needs.

peripheral countries: the world's poor, agrarian countries that are, according to **dependency theory,** exploited and kept poor by **multinational corporations** from wealthy countries.

Permanent Court of Arbitration (PCA): established by treaty in 1899 and set up to hear and decide on grievances between states and other states, organizations, over private parties. Between then and 1914, the PCA settled over 120 conflicts. The court, however, had no power to require disputants either to appear or to comply with its decisions. Rarely used since 1914, the court has decided only 10 cases through today.

Permanent Court of International Justice (PCIJ): established on February 15, 1922, by the League of Nations. Between 1921 and 1945, the court issued 31 judgments, 25 substantive orders, and 27 advisory opinions, about three or four decisions annually. Succeeded by the **International Court of Justice (ICJ).**

permissive action link (PAL): discretionary decision-making powers given to submarine commanders to fire their weapons in the event communications are lost during a nuclear war.

perpetual peace: Immanuel Kant's conception that if all the world's nations embraced trade, liberal democracy, and collective security, then peace would be perpetual.

photosynthesis: the means by which the world's green plants absorb the **greenhouse** gas **carbon dioxide** and convert it to oxygen.

Plaza Accord: the September 1985 agreement among the Group of Five countries— the United States, Japan, Germany, France, and Great Britain—to intervene in currency markets to sell dollars and buy other currencies in order to lower the highly overvalued dollar's value, which was disrupting the global trade system.

policy: a specific course of action that those in authority decide to follow on a specific issue.

policy cluster: a loose association of groups such as bureaucrats, interest groups, and politicians operating as the **iron triangle,** along with prominent journalists and academics, public opinion, and foreign interest groups who also share an interest in the policy.

policymaking: the means by which policies are decided and acted on.

political development: the expansion and change in a government's institutions and policies to meet society's growing needs and desires.

political economists: analysts who examine political forces, events, etc., to discover general patterns or concepts shaping international economic relations rather than starting with a **theory** and applying it, as **economists** do.

politics: conflict and the ways in which participants assert their respective interests in that conflict. Politics exists wherever the interests of two or more people or groups clash.

population explosion: the anticipated growth, within 50 years, of the world's current population of 5.4 billion to more than double, at 11.5 billion. As the earth rapidly reaches a crisis point when it can no longer sustain the material demands, conditions for most people will worsen and populations may well die from mass starvation.

positivism: argues that the origins of law are human rather than divine or natural and involve consent and self-interest. Also called the **positivist school.**

Potsdam Conference (July 1945): summit among Stalin (Soviet Union), Truman (United States), and Churchill (Great Britain) at which they decided reparations from Germany following World War II.

power: the ability of an individual or group to get others to do things that they otherwise would not do, or, refrain from doing things they intended to do.

prestige: having something few people have but want. Prestige involves both symbols and concrete accomplishments; it is both a sign and source of power; it is a reputation for success, for doing things most others cannot do.

primogeniture: an eldest son's right of inheritance to all of his father's land, which usually forces the other children to seek employment elsewhere.

prisoner's dilemma: the choice faced by a participant in a conflict or arms race between self-imprisonment behind the bars of fear and distrust of another nation (in which there may well be no hostile intent) and the possibly dire consequences of reducing **deterrence.** Each side sees only the other's offensive capabilities and none of its defensive intentions. Thus the conflict or arms race continues.

propaganda: the means by which one side influences the perceptions of others by presenting only one side of an issue; also known as public relations.

purchasing power parity (PPP): a statistical method of measuring a nation's **GNP** and **per capita income** by computing how much a basket of products—including clothing, food, housing, transportation, and so on—costs a consumer in his or her own currency.

Reagan Doctrine: the Reagan administration's **global containment** strategy of intervening in Central America, Africa, the Middle East, and elsewhere.

Reaganomics: President Ronald Reagan's policies of increasing government spending, cutting taxes mostly for the rich, cutting environmental regulations, expanding corporate welfare, and over-inflating the dollar, which led within eight years to a tripling of America's national debt, the conversion of the United States from the world's greatest creditor to the worst debtor nation, worsening incomes (adjusted for inflation) for the middle class and poor, and the highest trade and accounts deficits as a **gross national product (GNP)** percentage in American history.

realism: See **realist theory.**

realist theory: argues that humans making foreign policy are essentially "rational" in the sense that they will choose what is best for their state, that states are largely monolithic actors in the world system, and that international relations are largely shaped by the responses of rational leaders to the actions of other states rather than by domestic politics or the state's ideology.

rebus sic stantibus: "fundamental change in circumstance," the principle that allows states to suspend or terminate a treaty.

Reciprocal Trade Act (1934): empowered the president to negotiate trade treaties with other countries and reduce trade barriers.

recognition: the right of every sovereign state to accept—recognize—or deny the sovereignty of another state.

Reformation: an attempt to reform the Catholic Church in Europe and the occasion for a century of religious and political upheaval. Started in 1517 when Martin Luther nailed his 95 Theses to the door of Wittenburg Cathedral and condemned a corrupt papacy for usury and selling indulgences. Other religious revolutionaries (1517–1648) emerged to found the different sects of what became known as Protestantism, named for the various "protests" against Catholicism. The Protestants' central message was that individuals could reach God directly by their own faith rather than through "good works" sold to them by a corrupt church.

regulatory market system: minimal government interference in markets, primarily to uphold health, safety, and anti**cartel** standards. The ideal is pursued even if it means continual trade and payments deficits, relatively low economic growth, and inequitable income distribution.

relative deprivation: a situation in which a group or individual feels less privileged than others (and resents that).

Renaissance: a rebirth of learning around new ideas in philosophy, the arts, and technology. The Renaissance's central pillar rested on the shift from a God-centered universe, in which individuals devoted themselves to fulfilling their class roles, to a human-centered universe, in which individuals were largely free to fulfill their creative and economic potentials. Man, most importantly the rational mind, became the measure of all things. The *uomo universale* was skilled in all the fine arts, philosophy, etiquette, languages, history, science, and music. The Renaissance saw not just a toleration but a celebration of new ideas and ways of seeing the world.

reservation: a qualification limiting a state's ratification of a treaty; the limitation, a written reservation, declares the state not bound by a single or various aspects of that treaty.

revisionist state: a state that seeks to change its current place in the international system, often through military means.

revolution: the attempt to alter drastically, or replace totally, existing social, economic, or political institutions; sometimes occurs when coups or mass reform movements fail to alleviate harsh and worsening political and socioeconomic conditions.

revolution of rising expectations: popular mass anticipation that a government will keep its promise to quickly achieve ambitious political, economic, and/or social goals.

revolution of rising frustrations: popular mass frustration, which often leads to political instability when a government fails to fulfill promises to overcome problems.

Rio de Janeiro Earth Summit (1992): gathering by representatives of 178 countries to sign several treaties dealing with global environmental crises.

roentgens: units of radiation; a human's exposure to 200 roentgens would probably cause a quick death.

roll back: Eisenhower's 1952 election campaign pledge to abandon the **containment** strategy as too passive and instead follow a strategy of "rolling back" communist advances.

satisfice: to make a decision that seems to make the most sense at the time rather than examine alternative views of the situation.

scapegoat theory: the idea that some wars are provoked by governments to distract and unify a population divided by animosities.

second front: the call by Stalin during World War II for the United States and Britain to invade France and take the pressure off the Soviets fighting German troops in the east.

Second World: a category that includes all the industrialized communist countries.

second-strike capability: the ability of a country to absorb an enemy's first strike, retaliate, and inflict "unacceptable damage" on the enemy; defined by Secretary of Defense Robert McNamara in 1964 as the ability to destroy half of Soviet industry and a quarter of its population.

second-strike weapons: those weapons that can either drop nuclear bombs directly or fire from a distance: air-launched cruise missiles (**ALCMs**), surface-to-surface ballistic missiles (**SSBMs**) or submarine-launched ballistic missiles (**SLBMs**). Nuclear bombs launched from bombers and submarines are slower and less accurate than those dropped directly, but also less vulnerable to an enemy attack. Second-strike weapons are better targeted against an enemy's cities and armies. There is some overlap between second and first strike weapons. An **ICBM** in a hardened missile silo could survive an enemy strike and retaliate, whereas SLBMs are now as fast and accurate as ICBMs, and thus have some first-strike capabilities.

secretariat: the permanent governing body of an **international intergovernmental organization (IGO).**

secretary-general: the head of the **United Nations'** secretariat.

security community: an alliance of countries dedicated to collective security.

Security Council: the 15-nation council within the United Nations that has the power to commit that organization to peacekeeping and peacemaking mis-sions, among other momentous decisions. Five of the members—the United States, Russia, Great Britain, China, and France have veto power over these decisions.

security dilemma: a situation in which the military buildup that one state undertakes to feel more secure makes other states feel more insecure so they in turn build up their own forces. The original state then feels threatened so it further builds its force to deter a perceived foreign threat. Other states do the same, and the result is an arms race that may lead to a war that all sides would have preferred to avoid.

selective containment: the doctrine that the Soviet threat was primarily ideological and political rather than military. George Kennan, an American diplomat, was containment's architect. He urged Washington to extend massive economic and political aid to the world's most important industrial countries and regions.

self-determination: the idea that every nation that aspires to independence should be allowed to organize itself into a sovereign state.

semi-peripheral countries: those countries, according to **dependency theory,** in which limited low-wage factories are set up to provide products to the industries of the **core countries.**

shining city on a hill: the image of the United States as a beacon of hope, freedom, and prosperity to oppressed peoples elsewhere, used by President Reagan in a 1974 speech and originated in 1630 by Massachusetts governor John Winthrop..

SICBMs: small intercontinental ballistic missiles, also known as midgetmen.

Single Integrated Operational Plan (SIOP): America's nuclear war fighting strategy.

slavophiles: those Russians who advocate continued authoritarianism and isolation from the West while asserting leadership over all the Slavic peoples of East Europe.

SLBMs: submarine-launched ballistic missiles. Also see **second-strike weapons.**

small power: countries with militaries that maintain internal order but offer a minimum deterrent to foreign invasion.

Smithsonian Accord (1971): the leading industrial countries agreed to devalue their currencies by 10 percent against the dollar.

Smoot-Hawley Act (1930): raised tariffs more than 50 percent; because other countries also raised trade barriers, Smoot-Hawley helped globalize America's depression.

social Darwinism: argues that nations, like animal species, are engaged in a perpetual war for survival, from the simplest hunter-gatherer groups of a 100,000 years ago to the complex **nation-states** of today. Progress comes from competition as the strong and more advanced vanquish the weak. Thus **imperialism** is natural and even moral because it allows superior peoples to subdue and civilize the inferior ones.

social market: a governmental system that emphasizes an equitable distribution of existing wealth rather than the creation of new wealth. Government spending as a percentage of **GNP** is relatively high, the state provides citizens with **cradle-to-grave benefits,** the most important industries are often publicly owned, and the government heavily regulates markets.

socialization: the means by which an individual is indoctrinated into the values and behaviors of a **culture.**

sources of international law: the **International Court of Justice** bases its decisions on three primary sources of international law (treaties, customs, and general principles) and two secondary sources (judicial opinions, and legal theorists).

Southeast Asian Treaty Organization (SEATO): founded in 1954 by the United States, Australia, Britain, and several countries in Southeast Asia to deter communist advances.

sovereignty: authority and self-rule in an independent political system, as in a sovereign **nation-state.** During the early modern era, many political philosophers argued that sovereignty, or the locus of supreme power, should rest in monarchs. During the middle and late modern eras, many political philosophers maintained that sovereignty should lie in all of a state's citizens.

special drawing rights (SDRs): artificial currency that can be used instead of dollars to settle international accounts with the **International Bank for Reconstruction and Development (IBRD)** or World Bank; created in 1969 by the **Group of Ten** advanced industrial countries.

sphere of influence: a region in which a **great power** declares that it will not tolerate any outside interference while reserving for itself the right to intervene.

spoils system: the choice of government personnel for their political importance rather than expertise.

Sputnik: the Soviet satellite, launched in 1957, that inaugurated the **ICBM** race between the Soviet Union and United States.

SSBMs: surface-to-surface ballistic missiles. Also see **second-strike weapons.**

standard operating procedures (SOPs): pre-existing plans designed to deal with anticipated problems.

state: a system of government over a clearly defined territory; sometimes used interchangeably with **nation** or **nation-state.**

state control war: a **civil war** that results when rebels try to overthrow a government.

state formation war: a **civil war** that results when a state or colony seeks independence from another state.

status quo state: a state that is satisfied with its place in the international system and seeks no significant changes.

Stockholm Conference on the Human Environment (1972): the first international conference to systematically address the global environmental crises.

Strategic Arms Limitation Talks (SALT I and II): treaties signed by the United States and Soviet Union, SALT I in 1972 and SALT II in 1979, both of which imposed caps on the numbers of certain types of nuclear weapons.

Strategic Arms Reduction Treaties (START I and II): treaties signed in 1991 and 1993, respectively, that led to significant cuts in **ICBMs** and other nuclear weapons.

Strategic Defense Initiative (SDI): better known as Star Wars, President Reagan's scheme to create a anti-ICBM defense shield over the United States. Over $45 billion was invested in the scheme before the Clinton administration finally admitted it was impossible to achieve and canceled the project in 1993.

strategic industry: an industry that supplies many other industries, produces large amounts of wealth, and provides well-paying jobs for large amounts of people relative to other industries in the economy.

strategic nuclear weapons: used against military bases, nuclear weapons, or cities far behind the immediate battleground.

structural corruption: systematic and accepted corruption.

Structural Impediments Initiative (SII): negotiations designed to remove trade barriers between the United States and Japan.

subculture: a group existing within a larger dominant culture and sharing similar values, behaviors, and institutions.

subject of the law: a person, organization, and/or state that has legal rights and duties.

subsidy: a government handout to business; can be in the form of direct grant, tax reduction, low-interest loan, and so on.

superpower: in the contemporary world, a **nation-state** with the ability to project nuclear and conventional military force virtually anywhere in the world. Today, the United States is the only military superpower. Russia has nuclear power but not the conventional power to project anywhere.

supply-side economics: raising or lowering taxes, which will either slow down or stimulate the economy respectively.

supranational culture: is a culture that extends beyond national boundaries to embrace two or more nations—such as "Western culture" or "Far Eastern culture"—that share some basic values, ethics, institutions, and history, if not language.

sustained yield: the practice of replanting trees at the rate they are cut down.

tactical warheads: nuclear weapons used on the battlefield.

tangible power: assets or resources that are relatively easy to quantify, such as relative GNP, military force, or technology.

tariffs: taxes on imports.

Terra nullius: unoccupied territory that can be claimed by anyone.

terrorism: the use or threatened use of violence for political purposes to create a state of fear that will extort, coerce, intimidate, or otherwise cause individuals and groups to alter their behavior.

Theater High Altitude Area Defense (THAAD): a ground-based scheme to shoot down incoming **intercontinental ballistic missiles (ICBMs).**

theory: a set of assumptions and analytical methods about how the world works. A good theory is clear, concise, coherent, unbiased, deep, broad in its application, and predictive.

Third World: a category that includes the world's poor and primarily agricultural countries.

throw weight: the weight of explosives that a missile can carry to its target.

totalitarianism: a system of government under which the state has total control of politics, economics, and society. Totalitarianism is made technically possible on a national scale through modern mass communications and transportation, which allow mass mobilization, surveillance and repression.

trade account: the total value of a country's imported and exported merchandise.

trade policy: a course of action aimed at affecting a nation's trade balance through export/import promotion or constraints.

trade war: conflict between two or more states that limit their markets to each other's products in order to hurt foreign producers while protecting and promoting their own producers.

traditional society: predominantly rural, agricultural, illiterate, superstitious, and immobile; most people lead hand-to-mouth, subsistence existences. Traditional societies are built on small, simply organized, and often isolated villages. Exchange in traditional economies is through barter.

traditionalism: a humanist theory that emphasizes the complexity of human relations.

"Tragedy of the Commons, The": a parable by Garrett Hardin about what happens when everyone enjoys a resource but no one is responsible for its upkeep. As the resource diminishes, people rush to use more before it's all used up, thus accelerating its loss. The result is the resource's devastation and everyone is worse off.

transitional society: a society in flux, somewhere on the spectrum between being predominantly traditional and predominantly modern.

Treaty of Versailles: signed on June 28, 1919, by the participants in World War I and ending that conflict. The settlement imposed a harsh peace on Germany by requiring payments of huge reparations to its former enemies. It also created the **League of Nations.**

triad: the U.S. nuclear force structure built on the three legs of **ICBMs, SLBMs,** and supersonic nuclear bombers.

trickle-down economics: the idea that if a government reduces taxes or increases benefits to the rich, they will spend, invest, and/or save their additional money, thus stimulating the economy and creating more jobs and wealth; in other words, wealth from the rich will trickle down to the middle class and poor.

trickle-up economics: the idea that if a government reduces taxes or increases benefits to the poor, they will spend, invest, and/or save their additional money, which will stimulate the economy and thus create more jobs and wealth; in theory, this wealth will ultimately trickle up to the middle and upper classes.

trip wire: the token, necessary number of American troops stationed in western Europe to justify massive retaliation against the Soviet Union.

Truman Doctrine: the announcement by President Truman in March 1947 that the United States would aid "free countries who are resisting attempted subjugation by armed minorities." The Truman Doctrine was essentially the declaration that the United States was committed to a **containment policy** against the Soviet Union.

two-party system: a political system in which there are only two competitive parties with large national followings.

ubi societas ibi jus: "Where there is society, there is law"; the notion that laws must bind every community, including sovereign states.

uncivil war: an internal war of anarchy that results in crimes against humanity.

underdevelopment: the inability of a country locked in poverty with few if any viable industries to raise its standard of living or otherwise meet the needs of its population.

unipolarity: the dominant power of one state in the international system.

United Nations (1945–present): established by treaty in San Francisco on June 26, 1945, and dedicated to peace, human rights, international law, prosperity, and collective security. Over 190 countries are now U.N. members. Each member casts one vote in nonbinding resolutions in the General Assembly. Binding decisions are made by a nine-vote majority in the 15-member Security Council, of which five members—the United States, Russia, China, France, and Britain—are permanent and have veto power, and the remaining ten are elected every two years. The Secretariat, headed by the secretary-general, administers the United Nations. The **International Court of Justice** is also a U.N. institution, along with dozens of other organizations.

U.N. Conference on Trade and Development (UNCTAD): a series of conferences in which **First** and **Third World** representatives negotiated better terms of trade, investment, and aid for the latter based on the **NIEO** program.

U.N. Environmental Program (UNEP): the U.N. agency most focused on environmental issues.

U.N. Population Fund (UNPF): furnishes information and helps fund family planning programs in **Third World** countries.

Use 'em' or lose 'em: the tendency in a crisis to fire your first-strike weapons before the other side has a chance to fire theirs.

vertical proliferation: increasing the number and diversifying the types of nuclear weapons required by a country.

Vietnamization: the Nixon strategy of turning over the fighting of the Vietnam War to the South Vietnamese while slowly withdrawing American troops and negotiating a peace settlement with North Vietnam.

Warsaw Treaty Organization (WTO) (Warsaw Pact): an alliance between the Soviet Union and its East European bloc countries; created by Moscow in response to the admission of West Germany to **NATO.** Not to be confused with the **World Trade Organization,** also uses the initials WTO.

Westernizers: Russians who see Western Europe and the United States as models for political and economic development.

Wilsonianism: a doctrine espousing political, economic, and national freedom, and international cooperation to resolve conflicts; named after President Woodrow Wilson and articulated most succinctly in his Fourteen Points speech delivered to Congress in January 1918.

window of vulnerability: the claim by Reagan in his 1980 presidential campaign that the Soviet Union had a nuclear advantage. Although the claim may have contributed to his victory, like the 1960 **missile gap,** no such window of vulnerability existed.

World Bank: See **International Bank for Reconstruction and Development (IBRD).**

world systems theory: an extension of **dependency theory** that emphasizes the **international political economy's** evolution throughout the modern era and the rise and fall of the **core, periphery,** and **semi-peripheral countries.**

World Trade Organization (WTO): the successor to the **General Agreement on Trade and Tariffs (GATT);** empowered to judge trade cases and allow countries to impose sanctions on violators.

Yalta Conference (February 1945): summit meeting of Stalin, Roosevelt, and Churchill at which it was agreed that postwar Germany would be temporarily divided and the Soviets could maintain order in Eastern Europe if they allowed free elections.

Photo Credits

Index

Chechens, 9, 251
Chernobyl, 256
Chiang Kai-shek, 50–51, 134, 231, 234, 235, 395, 406
Chile, 7, 96, 142–44, 403, 406, 423, 432, 473
China, xvi, 8, 9, 22, 28, 39, 41, 43, 49, 50–51, 52, 53, 56–59, 63, 67, 68, 70, 73, 84, 86, 91, 95, 96, 97, 101, 109, 110, 112, 121, 131, 134, 139, 150, 156, 157, 163, 172, 176, 177, 211, 213, 226, 229, 231, 234, 235, 236, 237, 238, 243, 246, 248, 257, 258, 267, 268, 392, 407, 411, 419, 434, 435, 436, 470, 480, 485–86, 487–88
Chinese Communist Party (CCP), 50, 58, 70, 231, 234, 235, 246
Choate, Pat, 113, 132
Christianity, 24, 65, 71, 205. 211, 218, 420, 421
Churchill, Winston, 87, 117, 126, 128, 224, 228, 229, 330, 232
Civil (Internal) War, 208–09
Civilization, 22
Clauswitz, Karl von, 200, 220
Clinton, Bill, 11, 106, 121, 140, 206, 266, 274, 290, 301–07, 325, 357, 360, 375, 381, 494, 525
CNN, 4, 521
Cobweb Model, 12
Colbert, Jean Baptiste, 33
Cold War, xv, xviii, 5, 8–9, 15, 91, 99, 119, 121–22, 224–51, 520
Columbus, Christopher, 25, 525
Columbai, 423
Communism, xv, 43, 46–47, 48, 49, 76, 91, 94, 105, 119, 162, 205, 208, 210, 226–28, 235, 245–51, 429
Comprehensive Test Ban Treaty, 57, 58
Concert of Europe, 171
Confucianism, 23, 435–36
Congress (U.S.), 56, 57, 171, 172, 195–98, 232–33, 472
Congress of Berlin, 39
Congress of Vienna, 32, 171, 287
Constructivist Theory, 14
Containment Policy, 8, 224–51
Cook Islands, 72
Coolidge, Calvin, 53
Coordinating Committee for Export Controls (COCOM), 112
Costa Rica, 156
Council for Mutual Economic Assistance (COMECOM), 234
Counterinsurgency, xviii
Cox, Robert, 14
Crimean War, 99, 171
Critical Theory, 14
Croatia, 78, 90, 230
Crony Capitalism, 467

Crusades, 25, 205
Cuba, 8, 66, 84, 96, 157, 239, 241, 275, 444
Cuban Missile Crisis, 126–27, 131, 139, 217, 240, 262
Culture, 62–63
Cyprus, 365
Czech, 33
Czech Republic, 84, 301, 365
Czechoslovakia, 43, 51, 77, 126, 128, 157, 209, 239

Dahl, Robert, 81
Dante Alighieri, 170
De Gaulle, Charles, 230, 240–41, 354
Deconstructivist Theory, 14
Deforestation, xvi, 4, 7, 10, 501–07
Democracy (Liberal Democracy), 8, 65, 66, 71, 209–10, 326, 521–22
Democratic Party, 57, 322
Denmark, 84, 235, 365
Dependence, xvii, 10, 14
Dependence Theory, 13, 15, 393–94
Descartes, René, 32
Desertification, xvi, 3, 7, 10, 507–10
Deterrence, 9
Development, xix, 4, 7, 210–11, 390–414, 418–38, 441–77, 523–24
Dickens, Charles, 37
Diem, Ngo Dihn, 241
Disney, Walt, 21
Disraeli, Benjamin, 38–39
Dominican Republic, 239, 431
Drugs (illegal), xvi, 6, 294
Dubchek, Alexander, 239
Dubois, W. E. B., 50
Dulles, John Foster, 128, 237, 260
Dumping, 6, 361, 373

Earth Summit. See Rio de Janeiro Earth Summit
East Asia (Far East), 345, 380–84, 418, 433–36, 442, 445, 447
East Germany, 224, 238, 248
East Timor, 70, 408
Easton, David, 14
Economic Development, xix, 8
Ecuador, 423
Egypt, 4, 39, 77, 84, 96, 122, 124, 135, 196, 197, 238, 298, 458, 508
Einstein, Albert, 201
Eisenhower, Dwight, 131, 237, 239, 299
El Salvador, 209, 220
Eliott, T. S., 21
Empiricism, 14
Enlightenment, 31–33
Equatorial Guinea, 66
Erasmus, Desiderius, 32
Eritrea, 219
Estonia, 43, 65, 71, 75, 76, 157, 339, 365

Ethiopia, 51, 172, 209, 219, 244, 508
Europe, 19, 22–33, 38, 45, 64, 83, 87, 124, 205, 209
  Eastern Europe, 64, 91, 132, 233, 418, 499
  Western Europe, 91, 100, 233, 342, 353–53, 418
European Coal and Steal Community (ECSC), 366
European Community (EC), xvi, 7, 169, 362, 364–69
European Court of Justice, 159, 161
European Union (EC), xvi, xvii, xviii, 6, 7, 10, 75, 76, 104, 106, 107–11, 124, 135, 161, 169, 213, 322–24, 335, 349, 358, 364–69, 376–80, 380–83, 519, 522–23

Falkland (Malvina) Islands, 97, 138, 207
Faon, Frantz, 413
Fascism, 6, 21, 43, 46, 48–49, 68
Faust, 21, 523
Federal Reserve, 356
Feudalism, 23–24
Fiji, 74
Finland, 43, 172, 365, 368
First World, xvii
Flexible Response, 240–41, 250–64
Florence, 25
Ford, Gerald, 243
Ford, Henry, 36
Foucault, Michel, 21
France, 24, 29, 31, 32, 33, 35, 36, 39, 42–43, 45, 50, 51, 52, 53, 67, 72, 76, 84, 90, 93, 95, 96, 98–99, 100, 106–11, 124, 126, 135, 139, 171, 174, 177, 196, 207, 215, 217, 225, 226, 234, 235, 238, 241, 257, 267, 327, 328, 336, 342, 352, 354, 355, 364–69
French Revolution, 31, 32–33, 98–99, 125, 215, 410
Franco-Prussian War, 42, 43, 99, 171, 287
Frank, Andre Gunter, 14
Free Trade, 7, 8, 33–34, 328–31, 358–60, 423, 443–47
Freedom House, 8, 65
Friedman, Milton, 13
Freud, Sigmund, 21
Fuentes, Carlos, 429
Fukuyama, Francis, 521–23
Functionalist Theory, 169

Gadhafi, Muammar, 126, 135, 147, 453
Gambia, 135, 406
Game Theory, 12
Gandi, Mahatma, 421
Gates, Robert, 130

Southeast Asia, 27, 53, 88, 119, 135, 172, 213, 234, 241

Southeast Asian Treaty Organization (SEATO), 237

Sovereignty, xvii, 5, 12, 30–31, 68–70, 73, 142, 151, 153, 155–56, 522–23

Soviet Union, xv, 8, 9, 13, 47–49, 50, 51, 52, 53, 70, 75, 83, 84, 91, 92, 96, 97, 100, 101, 103, 112, 113, 119, 122, 124, 125, 128, 129–30, 131, 134, 177, 196–97, 207, 209, 212–13, 214, 224–51, 255–81, 410, 412, 470, 499

Spain, 5, 24, 28, 29, 31, 32, 39, 41, 67, 72, 84, 86, 87, 88, 94, 95, 142–44, 217, 365, 368

Spanish-American War, 150

Special Drawing Rights, 354

Species Destruction. *See* biocide

Spencer, Herbert, 41, 201

Spinoza, Baruch, 32

Spykman, Nicholas, 87

Sri Lanka (Ceylon), 9, 61, 444

Stalin, Joseph, 47, 48, 76, 92, 113, 128, 134. 229, 230, 231, 237, 258

Stimson, Henry, 156

Stockholm Conference, 484, 485

Strange, Susan, 14

Strategic Arms Limitation Talks I & II (SALT), 242–43, 244, 270–71

Strategic Arms Reduction Talks, 271–75

Strategic Defense Initiative (SDI, Star Wars), 265–67, 276

Strong, Josiah, 41

Suarez, Francisco, 147, 219

Sudan, 7, 40, 84, 135, 232, 243, 508

Suez Canal, 238

Suharto, 70, 408

Sukarno, 396, 408, 447

Sully, Maximilien Bethune, Duke of, 33

Sun Yat-sen, 50

Sweden, 39, 93, 333–36, 354, 365, 368

Swift, Gustavus, 36

Switzerland, 71, 72, 93, 159, 354

Syria, 24, 61, 77, 84, 124, 197, 204

Taiwan, 8, 41, 70, 84, 96, 121, 235, 275, 345, 380, 395, 407, 432–36

Tajikistan, 65, 75

Tamil, 9

Tanzania, 188

Terrorism, xvi, xviii, 73, 194–95, 311–19

Thailand (Siam), 22, 43, 345, 432

Thatcher, Margaret, 196

Third (Less Developed, Developing) World, xvii, 4, 11, 13, 98, 164, 186, 210–11, 238, 391–414, 426–38, 441–77

Thirty Years War, 30–31, 68, 146, 219

Thoreau, Henry David, 20

Thucycides, 11, 98

Tibet, 9, 63

Tito, Bronz, 113

Toffler, Alvin, 21

Togo, 135

Totalitarianism, 8, 43, 46–47, 90

Trade, 24–25, 103–13, 121, 322–24, 326–46, 347–84, 443–47

Trade War, 6, 10

Traditionalism, 14

Treaty of Brest-Livosk, 47

Treaty of London, 44

Treaty of Utrecht, 170

Treaty of Versailles, 43, 45

Treaty of Washington, 44

Treaty (Peace) of Westphalia, 30–31, 68, 146, 170, 205, 219

Trotsky, Leon, 47

Truman, Harry, 130–31, 228, 231, 232–33, 234, 236, 258

Tull, Jethro, 35

Turkey, 39, 43, 61, 84, 124, 365

Turkmenistan, 65, 75

Tydings-McDuffy Act, 50

Uganda, 135, 202, 427

Ukraine, 65, 76, 248, 256

Underdevelopment, xix, 13

United Arab Emirates, 211, 456

United Arab Republic, 396

United Nations (UN), xv, xix, 5, 8, 53, 69, 70, 72, 74, 92, 142–44, 147, 149, 153, 155, 157, 161–62, 169, 173–86, 196–98, 232, 471, 485, 523

United Nations Charter, 8, 53, 92, 142–44, 161–62, 165, 173

United Nations Conference on Trade and Development (UNCTAD), 447–51, 475–76

United States, xv, xvi, xviii, 4, 6, 7, 8, 9–11, 13, 14, 32, 33, 36–38, 39, 41, 43, 44–46, 51–53, 56–59, 67, 69, 70, 72, 76, 81–82, 83, 84, 84–85, 86, 88, 90, 91, 92, 93, 94, 95, 96, 97, 98, 99, 100, 101, 102, 103, 104, 105–06, 106–11, 111, 112–13, 117, 118, 119–23, 124, 128, 131–32, 139, 140, 147, 150, 155, 159, 163, 172, 174, 183, 184, 194–98, 207, 209, 211, 212–13, 214, 217, 220, 224–51, 255–81, 288–93, 294–320, 322–24, 327, 328, 329–31, 334, 335, 336–41, 342, 343–44, 345, 349–50, 351–57, 358–62, 362–64, 374, 375, 376–80, 380–84, 386–88, 402, 410–13, 430, 451–52, 456–62, 474, 480, 519, 521

Uruguay, 403

Uzbekistan, 65, 75

Vance, Cyrus, 129, 164

Vanderbilt, Cornelius, 36

Vanuatu, 72, 392

Vattel, Emerich von, 148

Vasquez, John, 14

Venezuela, 423, 431–32, 452

Venice, 26, 28, 88–89

Versailles Peace (Treaty) Conference, 43, 45, 67, 99, 128, 157, 171, 172

Victorio, Francisco de, 147, 219

Vietnam, 8, 22, 50, 58, 77, 84, 96, 209, 235, 236

Vietnam War, 89, 94, 96, 97, 100, 117, 119, 128, 129, 139, 207, 241–42, 242–44, 354

Voltaire, Francois Marie Arouet, 32

Wallerstein, Immanuel, 14

Waltz, Kenneth, 12, 14, 81, 136–37, 140, 201

War, xv, xviii, 5, 6, 7, 8, 9, 11, 12, 13, 31, 32, 39, 41, 42, 61–62, 81–85, 85–87, 87–93, 93–95, 95–98, 98–100, 100–01, 101–03, 194–98, 200–22, 285–320

War of Liberation (Independence), 32

War of the Spanish Succession, 171

Warsaw Pact, xviii, 9, 182, 213, 237, 239

Washington, George, 51

Waterloo, Battle of, 171

Watt, James, 35

Weber, Max, 20–21, 395

Weldt, Alexander, 14

Welfare State, 37

Wilhem II, 99

Wilson, Woodrow, 12, 36, 43, 49, 50, 67, 128, 171, 172, 351, 520

World Bank (International Bank for Reconstruction and Development, xv, xviii, 8, 53, 57, 147, 229, 349, 352, 460–62, 464–68

World Systems Theory, 13

World Trade Organization (WTO), xvi, xviii, 3, 6, 8, 169, 190, 227, 322–34, 369–72, 386–88

World War I, 8, 42–43, 45, 46, 48–49, 139, 171, 351

World War II, 8, 14, 19, 51–53, 67, 83, 89, 134, 173, 209, 225, 226–27, 258, 352, 360

Yalta Conference, 229–30, 231

Yeltsin, Boris, 76, 248–49, 250, 520

Yeman, 198, 392

Yom Kippur War, 355, 453

Yuan Shi-kai, 50

Yugoslavia, 7, 43, 70, 90, 113, 133, 153, 157, 182, 207, 230, 301–07, 521

Zaire (Congo), 86, 181, 188, 202

Zambia, 188, 393, 473

Zhu, Rongji, 59

Zimbabwe, 188